THE SUPREME COURT JUSTICES
A Biographical Dictionary

EDITED BY Melvin I. Urofsky

Garland Publishing Inc.
NEW YORK & LONDON 1994

Library of Congress Cataloging-in-Publication Data

The Supreme Court justices : a biographical dictionary / edited by
Melvin I. Urofsky.
    p.   cm. — (Garland reference library of the humanities ;
vol. 1851)
  Includes bibliographical references and index.
  ISBN 0-8153-1176-1 (alk. paper)
  1. Judges—United States—Biography—Dictionaries. 2. United
States. Supreme Court—Officials and employees—Biography—
Dictionaries. I. Urofsky, Melvin I. II. Series.
KF8744.S859 1994
347.73'2634'03—dc20
[B]
[347.307353403]
[B]
                                       94-10028
                                         CIP

Printed on acid-free, 250-year-life paper
Manufactured in the United States of America

CONTENTS

INTRODUCTION

In the two centuries of governance under the Constitution, 105 men and two women have sat as justices on the nation's highest tribunal, the Supreme Court of the United States. Each of them has brought some unique insights or talents to that position; some, like John Marshall or Louis Brandeis, have left an indelible mark on American constitutional development. Others, like John Blair or Samuel Blatchford, are names known, albeit vaguely, only to legal historians.

What the justices bring with them to the bench determines how effective they will be, not only in terms of jurisprudence, but also in terms of how they function within the collegium of the Court. Some have utilized great political skills to put across certain views or to advance what they saw as the best interests of the Court and the country. Others have brought formidable intelligence and learning which they creatively wove into the legal and constitutional fabric of our nation's heritage.

The men and women appointed to the Court all had non-judicial careers before they donned the black robe, and those experiences surely affected their behavior as judges. But the contributors to this volume were asked to concentrate on the *judicial* tenure of their subjects, and to interpret those careers and evaluate their importance. They were asked to deal with the pre-Court years only insofar as those experiences had a major impact on jurisprudence. The Civil War experiences of Oliver Wendell Holmes, the reform efforts of Louis Brandeis, and the political offices held by Earl Warren could not be ignored in efforts to assess their years on the Court. But the primary charge to the contributors was to write an *interpretive* essay on these men and women as justices.

What makes a "great" justice is a theme that runs through many of these articles, and that is no surprise; it is a question that historians and legal scholars have debated for decades. Certainly, a man like Felix Frankfurter appeared to have all the qualifications necessary to become a great member of the Court—high intelligence, extensive knowledge of the bench and its workings, practical experience in government, and a well-developed philosophy of law and judging. Frankfurter, in fact, exerted significant influence on the Court for the more than two decades that he served, and in a 1970 poll was ranked among the twelve "great" judges to have served on the high court. A similar poll today would surely not yield that result, as Frankfurter's major opinions and ideas are now all but ignored.

Frankfurter's contemporary, Hugo Black, on the other hand, gave little evidence of greatness at the time of his appointment, and many people dismissed his nomination as a shabby political payoff. During his first few terms on the bench, Black made more than his share of mistakes, seeming to confirm the worst predictions of his critics about his qualifications. Yet Black grew into the job, and is today ranked as one of the half-dozen most influential justices to have sat on the Court in the twentieth century.

Not all important contributions to the nation's constitutional development have been made by the "great" justices. Often, important decisions are handed down by obscure members of the Court, who deserve to be remembered for their contributions. The history of the Court is only partially a history of decisions and doctrines; it is above all a history of the men and women who have shaped those doctrines. The articles in this book focus on that aspect of their lives.

I want to thank my colleagues, the men and women who allowed me to cajole them into adding one more task to their already busy schedules, and then doing everything I asked—writing creatively and clearly (always), staying within their word limits, and turning in the pieces on time (almost always).

In addition, a number of people at Garland Publishing worked on this book, and their efforts have made the collected work a far better volume than it would otherwise have been. I want to thank editors Helga McCue and Eunice Petrini, copyeditors Carl Buehler and Carl Sesar; and for the artwork and design, Patti Hefner, Jason Goldfarb, and Dora Kubek. Above all, I want to thank Leo Balk, who originally agreed to the idea, and who has since become a friend as well as a colleague.

BIBLIOGRAPHY

For those wishing to find further information on the justices, see Leon Friedman and Fred L. Israel, eds., *The Justices of the United States Supreme Court, 1789–1978* (5 vols., 1969–80), and the fascinating compilation by Roger Jacobs, *Memorials of the Justices of the Supreme Court of the United States* (5 vols., 1981). Short sketches, as well as a host of information about the Court, can be found in Kermit Hall, ed., *The Oxford Companion to the Supreme Court of the United States* (1992). G. Edward White, *The American Judicial Tradition* (rev. ed., 1989), has interpretive essays on the more important justices, as well as a useful bibliography. A general history of American constitutional and legal development is Melvin I. Urofsky, *A March of Liberty* (1987). Recent works may be found by consulting the *Index to Legal Periodicals,* as well as one of several computerized finding aids.

CONTRIBUTORS

Henry J. Abraham is James Hart professor of government and foreign affairs at the University of Virginia, where he has taught since 1972. The author of numerous books and articles, his *Freedom and the Court* (6th ed., 1994), *The Judicial Process* (6th ed., 1993), and *Justices and Presidents* (3rd ed., 1992) have become classics in the field. He holds many honors and fellowships, including Fulbright lectureships at the Universities of Aarhus and Copenhagen in Denmark.

Richard M. Abrams teaches comparative industrial economics and recent American history at the University of California at Berkeley, where he has been a member of the history department since 1961. He has held Fulbrights at London and Moscow, and also lectured at Peking on American history. A self-described "intellectual dilettante," Abrams has written in a number of fields. His books include *Conservatism in a Progressive Era* (1962) and *The Burdens of Progress* (1978). His many articles include several on members of the Supreme Court.

Judith A. Baer teaches in the political science department at Texas A&M University. A specialist in public law, she is the author of *The Chains of Protection* (1978), *Equality under the Constitution* (1983), and *Women in American Law* (1991). She is now working on a book on feminist jurisprudence.

Michael R. Belknap is professor of law at California Western Law School and an adjunct professor of American history at the University of California, San Diego. He is the author of, among many books, *Cold War Political Justice: The Smith Act, the Communist Party and American Civil Liberties* (1977), and *Federal Law and Southern Order: Racial Violence and Constitutional Conflict in the Post-Brown South* (1987), and is the editor of *American Political Trials* (rev. ed., 1993).

Gayle Binion is professor of political science and chair of the Law & Society program at University of California at Santa Barbara. Her research focuses on the intersection of socio-legal equality across lines of gender, race and class and the role of the judiciary in defining and protecting civil rights and liberties. Her articles have appeared in a wide variety of law and social science journals. She wrote her Ph.D. dissertation on the role of Potter Stewart on the U.S. Supreme Court.

David J. Bodenhamer is professor of history and director of the POLIS Research Center at Indiana University-Purdue University at Indianapolis. In addition to more than thirty articles, chapters in books, and papers on legal and constitutional history, he is the author or editor of *Ambivalent Legacy: A Legal History of the South*, with James W. Ely, Jr. (1984), *The Pursuit of Justice: Crime and Law in Antebellum Indiana* (1986), *Fair Trial: Rights of the Accused in American History* (1992), and *The Bill of Rights in Modern America: After 200 Years*, with James W. Ely, Jr. (1993).

William Bosch, S.J., holds a doctorate in American intellectual history from the University of North Carolina at Chapel Hill. He is the author of *Judgement on Nuremberg: American Attitudes toward the Major Nazi War Crime Trials* (1970), and teaches the history of American law at Le Moyne College in Syracuse, New York.

Craig M. Bradley is currently professor of law at Indiana University. He clerked for then-associate Justice Rehnquist in the October 1975 term of the Supreme Court; he has also served as an assistant United States attorney in Washington, D.C., and as a senior trial attorney in the Public Integrity Section of the United States Department of Justice.

Daniel L. Breen is a member of the Georgia bar practicing in Athens; he received a B.A. in history from the University of Wisconsin, and a J.D. from the University of Georgia. He is currently completing a master's thesis at the University of

Georgia on Gilded Age judicial philosophy as expressed in cases involving the statute of frauds.

William R. Casto is professor of law at the Texas Tech University School of Law. His primary areas of interest are foreign policy, legal philosophy, and the federal courts in the early republic.

Stephen Cresswell is associate professor of history at West Virginia Wesleyan College, where he is chair of the Department of History and Government. Professor Cresswell is the author of *Mormons and Cowboys, Moonshiners and Klansmen: Federal Law Enforcement in the South and West, 1870–1893*. He is currently studying Mississippi's history as a one-party state.

Barry Cushman is a graduate of Amherst College and the University of Virginia Law School. He teaches at the St. Louis University law school.

David J. Danelski, a lawyer and political scientist, practiced law in Seattle, Washington, before entering a teaching career. He is presently the Mary Lou and George Boone centennial professor at Stanford University and director of Stanford in Washington. He has been a Guggenheim fellow, a Japan Foundation fellow, a Fulbright-Hays lecturer in Japan, and a fellow at the Center for Advanced Study in the Behavioral Sciences. He is the author of *A Supreme Court Justice is Appointed* (1964), and the coeditor, with Joseph S. Tulchin, of *The Autobiographical Notes of Charles Evans Hughes* (1973).

Sue Davis teaches political science at the University of Delaware, and is the author of *Justice Rehnquist and the Constitution* (1989), as well as articles about the chief justice. In addition, she has examined the opinions and voting behavior of women judges on the United States Courts of Appeals, and has just finished a textbook on American political thought.

Donald O. Dewey is professor of history at California State University, Los Angeles, where he has also been dean of natural and social sciences since 1970. Before going to California, he was

associate editor of *The Papers of James Madison*. He is author or editor of *Marshall Versus Jefferson: The Political Background of Marbury v. Madison* (1970); *Union and Liberty: Documents in American Constitutionalism* (1969); and *Becoming Informed Citizens* (1988).

Norman Dorsen is Stokes professor of law at the New York University School of Law, where he has taught since 1961. He served as law clerk to Chief Judge Calvert Magruder of the Court of Appeals for the First Circuit and to Supreme Court Justice John Marshall Harlan. He is the author or editor of many articles and books, including *Frontiers of Civil Liberties* (1968), *The Rights of Americans* (1971), *Our Endangered Rights* (1984), and *The Evolving Constitution* (1987). While general counsel to the American Civil Liberties Union, Dorsen participated in dozens of Supreme Court cases, arguing, among others, those that won for juveniles the right to due process, upheld constitutional rights of nonmarital children, and advanced abortion rights. He was president of the American Civil Liberties Union from 1976 to 1991.

James W. Ely, Jr. is professor of law and history at Vanderbilt University. He is the author or editor of nine books, including *An Uncertain Tradition: Constitutionalism and the History of the South* with Kermit L. Hall (1989), *The Guardian of Every Other Right: A Constitutional History of Property Rights* (1992), and *The Bill of Rights in Modern America: After 200 Years*, with David J. Bodenhamer (1993). He has also written numerous scholarly articles and papers on legal and constitutional history.

Daniel A. Farber is associate dean for faculty and Henry J. Fletcher professor of law, University of Minnesota. He served as clerk to Justice John Paul Stevens in the October 1976 term of the Supreme Court. He is the author of *A History of the American Constitution*, with Suzanna Sherry (1988); *Law and Public Choice: A Critical Introduction*, with Philip Frickey (1991); and *Cases and Materials on Constitutional Law Themes for the Constitution's Third Century*, with William Eskridge and Philip Frickey (1993).

Paul Finkelman is a member of the history department at Virginia Polytechnic Institute and State University. He is the author of *An Imperfect Union: Slavery, Federalism, and Comity* (1981), *The Law of Freedom and Bondage* (1985), *Toward a Usable Past*, with Stephen Gottlieb (1990), *American Legal History*, with Kermit Hall and William M. Wiecek (1991), and more than fifty scholarly articles. His book, *Slavery in the Courtroom* (1984), won the Joseph L. Andrews Award from the American Association of Law Libraries.

Michael J. Gerhardt is a professor of law and lecturer in government at the the College of William and Mary, and has written extensively about constitutional law. He is the co-author of *Constitutional Theory: Arguments and Perspectives* (1993) and the author of the forthcoming book, *The Impeachment Process: A Constitutional and Historical Analysis.*

Dorothy J. Glancy is professor of law at Santa Clara University. A graduate of Wellesley College and the Harvard Law School, she has written about Justice William O. Douglas, privacy, property, administrative law, environmental law, and historic preservation. She was counsel to the United States Senate Judiciary Subcommittee on Constitutional Rights and was an assistant general counsel in the United States Department of Agriculture.

Robert M. Goldman is an historian and chairman of the department of history-political science at Virginia Union University in Richmond, Virginia.

Joan I. Greco, after graduating from Harvard Law School, clerked with future Supreme Court Justice Ruth Bader Ginsburg on the Court of Appeals for the District of Columbia, and then for Justice Sandra Day O'Connor on the Supreme Court. In addition to teaching at Brooklyn Law School, she has written and produced numerous programs for national public television, including the series, "That Delicate Balance II: Our Bill of Rights."

Michael Grossberg is professor of history and law at Case Western Reserve University and editor of *Law and History Review*. He has written extensively on the social history of American law, including *Governing the Hearth: Law and the Family in Nineteenth-Century America* (1985).

Kermit L. Hall is dean of the Henry Kendall College of Arts and Sciences and professor of history and law at the University of Tulsa. He has written widely on the history of American law, including *The Magic Mirror: Law in American History* (1989), and is the editor of *The Oxford Companion to the Supreme Court of the United States* (1992). Dean Hall has been a Fulbright scholar in Finland, and the chairperson of the Bill of Rights Education Collaborative.

Richard F. Hamm is assistant professor of history and public policy at the State University of New York at Albany. He holds a Ph.D. in history from the University of Virginia and is interested in late nineteenth- and early twentieth-century public law.

Susan N. Herman is professor of law at Brooklyn Law School, where she teaches constitutional law, criminal law and procedure, and seminars in law and literature and historic criminal trials. She writes and lectures extensively on constitutional criminal law, with an emphasis on the Supreme Court. She is a member of the national board of directors and the executive committee of the American Civil Liberties Union, and frequently gives lectures about the Supreme Court for the Federal Judicial Center.

Scott Horton is a partner with Patterson, Belknap, Webb & Tyler in New York, and in his spare time writes about nineteenth-century legal history.

Timothy S. Huebner, a member of the history department at the University of Miami, Coral Gables, specializes in the constitutional and legal history of the American South. He is the author of articles in several journals, as well as a contributor to *The Oxford Companion to the*

Supreme Court of the United States (1992), and *The Encyclopedia of Religion and Law* (1993).

Joseph Gordon Hylton is assistant professor of law at the Chicago-Kent College of Law in Chicago. He holds a law degree from the University of Virginia and a doctorate in American civilization from Harvard.

Peter Irons is professor of political science and director of the Earl Warren Bill of Rights Project at the University of California, San Diego. His books include *The New Deal Lawyers* (1982); *Justice at War* (1983); *Justice Delayed* (1989); and *May It Please the Court* (1993). He is completing a book on Justices William Brennan and William Rehnquist. He is an active civil liberties lawyer, and represented Fred Korematsu and Gordon Hirabayashi in the reopening of their wartime internment cases.

Herbert A. Johnson is a legal historian who currently is Hollings professor of constitutional law at the University of South Carolina. He served as an editor of John Marshall's papers from 1967 to 1977, and as president of the American Society for Legal History from 1974 through 1975. He is the coauthor of the second volume in the Holmes Devise *History of the Supreme Court of the United States* (1981).

John W. Johnson is professor of history and head of the department at the University of Northern Iowa. Among his books are *Historic U.S. Court Cases, 1690–1990* (1992), *The Dimensions of Non-Legal Evidence in the American Judicial Process* (1990), *Insuring Against Disaster: The Nuclear Industry on Trial* (1986), and *American Legal Culture, 1908–1940* (1981).

John Paul Jones teaches administrative law, constitutional law, and admiralty at the University of Richmond School of Law. He served as a judicial clerk for the Honorable David Schwartz of the United States Court of Claims, and has been a visiting scholar at the United States Central Intelligence Agency. Professor Jones has written on comparative constitutional law, state administrative law, maritime workers' injury compensation, and judicial administration. In 1992–93, he

advised the commission drafting Albania's new constitution.

Jonathan Kahn is assistant professor of history and political studies at Bard College. He holds degrees in history from Cornell University and in law from the Boalt Hall School of Law at the University of California at Berkeley.

Paul Kens is professor of political science at Southwest Texas State University. He is the author of *Judicial Power and Reform Politics: The Anatomy of Lochner v. New York* (1990).

Jonathan Lurie is professor of history and adjunct professor of law at Rutgers University, Newark, New Jersey, where he has been since 1969. His books include *The Chicago Board of Trade, 1875–1905* (1979), *Law and the Nation, 1860–1912* (1983), and the first volume of *Arming Military Justice: The Origins of the United States Court of Military Appeals, 1775–1950* (1992).

Thomas C. Mackey is an assistant professor with the history department and law school of the University of Louisville. He was a Samuel I. Gotlieb postdoctoral fellow of American legal history at New York University School of Law, and has taught at Michigan State University, University of Nebraska-Lincoln, and Kansas State University.

Maeva Marcus is director of the Documentary History Project at the Supreme Court of the United States and editor of *The Documentary History of the Supreme Court of the United States, 1789–1800* (four volumes to date). A visiting professor of law at the Georgetown University Law Center from 1983 to 1987, she is the author of *Truman and the Steel Seizure Case: The Limits of Presidential Power* (1977), and numerous articles published in law reviews and historical works in the United States and abroad.

Elizabeth Brand Monroe, a member of the history faculty at Indiana University–Indianapolis, specializes in American legal and constitutional history. She is the author of *The Wheeling Bridge Case: Its Significance in American Law and Technology* (1992). Her interests include the interaction of nineteenth-century law, economy, and technology.

A. E. Keir Nash is professor of political science at the University of California at Santa Barbara. He is the author of numerous articles on environmental law and policy and in the area of nineteenth-century American legal history, especially the legal history of slavery.

William E. Nelson has taught at the New York University Law School since 1979. In the October 1970 term he clerked for Justice Byron White. Among his publications are *The Americanization of the Common Law* (1982), *The Roots of American Bureaucracy, 1830–1900* (1982), and *The Fourteenth Amendment: From Political Principle to Judicial Doctrine* (1988), which received the American Historical Association's Littleton-Griswold Prize for the best book on the history of American law and society.

Jenni Parrish is director of the Legal Information Center and professor of law at the University of California Hastings College of the Law. She has taught and written in the areas of American legal history, legal research, and law librarianship.

Michael E. Parrish is currently professor of history at the University of California, San Diego. His books include *Securities Regulation and the New Deal* (1970), *Felix Frankfurter and His Times: The Reform Years* (1982), and *Anxious Decades* (1992).

Richard Polenberg is Goldwin Smith professor of American history at Cornell University where he has taught since 1966. He is the author of *Reorganizing Roosevelt's Government, 1936–1939* (1966); *War and Society: The United States, 1941–1945* (1972); *One Nation Divisible: Class, Race, and Ethnicity in the United States since 1938* (1980); and *Fighting Faiths: The Abrams Case, the Supreme Court, and Free Speech* (1987), which received the American Bar Association's Silver Gavel Award.

Robert C. Post is professor of law at the school of law (Boalt Hall) at the University of California at Berkeley. He is the editor of *Law and the Order of Culture* (1991), and is presently working on volume 10 of the Oliver Wendell Holmes Devise History of the Supreme Court, which will cover the Taft years.

H. Jefferson Powell is a deputy assistant attorney general in the Office of Legal Counsel of the U.S. Department of Justice and a professor of law (on leave) at Duke University. He was formerly special counsel to the attorney general of North Carolina. His publications include two books, *Languages of Power* (1991) and *The Moral Tradition of American Constitutionalism* (1993). Powell's primary research interests are in constitutional history and law.

Linda C. A. Przybyszewski is an assistant professor in the department of history at the University of Cincinnati.

Eric W. Rise teaches constitutional and legal history and criminal procedure in the department of sociology and criminal justice at the University of Delaware. He is the coauthor, with Kermit Hall, of *From Local Courts to National Tribunals: The Federal District Courts of Florida, 1821–1990* (1991). His research interests include the legal history of the South, the history of the criminal justice system, and the history of the federal courts.

Daniel B. Rodriguez teaches at the Boalt Hall School of Law, University of California at Berkeley. He has been a John M. Olin fellow in law and economics at the University of Virginia School of Law, a visiting professor at the Free University of Amsterdam, the Netherlands, and a lecturer at Kobe University in Japan. He has published articles on a variety of constitutional and legal questions.

Margaret M. Russell teaches at the Santa Clara University School of Law in Santa Clara, California. From 1984 to 1985, she served as law clerk to the Honorable James E. Doyle of the United States district court of the western district of Wisconsin. She is also active in civil rights and civil liberties work, and is presently a national vice-president of the American Civil

Liberties Union and an affiliate vice-chairperson of the American Civil Liberties Union of Northern California.

Herman Schwartz is professor of law at the Washington College of Law of American University. Professor Schwartz has worked for human rights both in the United States and abroad for more than three decades. He founded the American Civil Liberties Union prisoners' rights program and the US/Israel Civil Liberties Law program, and served as the ACLU expert on electronic surveillance. He has litigated scores of civil liberties cases throughout the United States and filed briefs on human rights cases abroad involving President Vaclav Havel of Czechoslovakia and others. His writings include (ed.) *The Burger Years: Rights and Wrongs in the Supreme Court, 1969–1986* (1987), and *Packing the Courts: The Conservative Campaign to Rewrite the Constitution* (1988).

Philip J. Schwarz of the department of history and geography at Virginia Commonwealth University is the author of *Twice Condemned: Slaves and the Criminal Laws of Virginia, 1705–1865* (1988).

Rebecca Shepherd Shoemaker is professor of history at Indiana State Universlty, Terre Haute, where she specializes in American constitutional history. She has published articles on the early development of the federal judiciary and on the twentieth-century development of civil liberties law. She is currently at work on a history of the Indiana Civil Liberties Union.

Rodney A. Smolla is Arthur B. Hanson professor of law and director of the Institute of Bill of Rights Law at the College of William and Mary, Marshall-Wythe School of Law. He writes and lectures extensively on constitutional law issues. His books include *Suing the Press: Libel, the Media & Power* (1986), *Jerry Falwell v. Larry Flint: The First Amendment on Trial* (1988), and *Free Speech in an Open Society* (1992).

Robert Stanley has taught at the University of Texas at Arlington, the University of New Hampshire, and Brown University, and is cur-

rently associate professor of political science at California State University, Chico. He is the author of *Dimensions of Law in Service of Order: Origins of the Federal Income Tax, 1861–1913* (1993).

Philippa Strum teaches political science at Brooklyn College and the Graduate Center of City University of New York. Among her books and articles on American government, constitutional law, and women and politics are *Presidential Power and American Democracy* (1972), *The Supreme Court and Political Questions* (1974), *Louis D. Brandeis: Justice for the People* (1984), and *Brandeis: Beyond Progressivism* (1993). She is a former vice-president and current member of the executive committee and of the board of directors of the American Civil Liberties Union.

Thad W. Tate, an historian who works particularly on the colonial Chesapeake, is Forrest G. Murden professor of humanities emeritus at the College of William and Mary and emeritus director of the Institute of Early American History and Culture and of the Commonwealth Center for the Study of American Culture. His books include *The Negro in Eighteenth-Century Williamsburg* (1972), and, with Warren Billings and John Selby, *Colonial Virginia: A History* (1986).

James A. Thomson has studied and practiced law in the United States and Australia, where he is currently a barrister of the supreme courts of Western Australia and Victoria, as well as the High Court of Australia. He teaches law part-time at the Western Australia and Murdoch University law schools, and in his spare time writes articles on federal and constitutional law that have appeared in law reviews in the United States and Australia. Thomson has also been admitted to the New York Supreme Court bar.

Mark Tushnet is professor of law and associate dean (research and scholarship) at the Georgetown University Law Center. He clerked for Justice Thurgood Marshall before beginning to teach law. He is the coauthor of two casebooks and has written five books, as well as numerous articles, on constitutional law and history. His

The NAACP's Legal Strategy against Segregated Education, 1925–1950 (1987) won the AHA's Littleton-Griswold Award. From 1975 to 1985, he was secretary of the Conference on Critical Legal Studies.

Sandra F. VanBurkleo is a member of the history department at Wayne State University in Detroit, where she teaches American constitutional and legal history, with an emphasis on colonial and early national topics. In 1989, she received a Littleton-Griswold Award in American legal history from the American Historical Association, as well as the "Best Article Award" from *Journal of the Early Republic.*

Stephen J. Wermiel is an associate professor of law at Georgia State University College of Law in Atlanta, where he teaches constitutional law, First Amendment, and education law. A former Supreme Court correspondent for the *Wall Street Journal* from 1979 to 1991, he was selected by Justice William J. Brennan, Jr., to be his biographer in 1986.

Natalie Wexler is a lawyer and historian who is currently an associate editor of *The Documentary History of the Supreme Court, 1789–1800.*

G. Edward White is University Professor and John B. Minor Professor of Law and History at the University of Virginia, where he has taught since 1972. He was law clerk to the late Chief Justice Earl Warren. He is the author of many articles and books, including *The American Judicial Tradition* (1976, 2d ed. 1988); *Patterns of American Legal Thought* (1978); *Tort Law In America: An Intellectual History* (1980); *Earl Warren: A Public Life* (1982); *The Marshall Court and Cultural Change* (1988); and *Justice Oliver Wendell Holmes: Law and the Inner Self* (1993). Professor White has been a Guggenheim fellow and twice a fellow of the National Endowment for the Humanities.

Lou Falkner Williams is affiliated with the history department at Kansas State University where she teaches constitutional history, African-American history, and history of the South. She is particularly interested in the constitutional issues of the Reconstruction era and is currently completing a book on the South Carolina Ku Klux Klan trials of 1871–72.

Victoria Saker Woeste holds a doctorate in jurisprudence and social policy from the University of California at Berkeley. She is currently visiting assistant professor of American studies at Amherst College. Her principal research interests concern regulation, farmers' organizations, and the legal culture of agricultural cooperation in the twentieth century.

Michael Allan Wolf is professor of law and history at the University of Richmond, where he teaches and writes in the areas of land-use planning, American legal history, environmental law, and property.

HENRY BALDWIN

BORN 14 January 1780, New Haven,
    Connecticut

NOMINATED to the Court 5 January 1830
    by Andrew Jackson

TOOK seat 1 February 1830

DIED 21 April 1844 in Philadelphia,
    Pennsylvania

Henry Baldwin was raised in rural Connecticut but returned to New Haven to attend Yale College, from which he graduated in 1797. He moved to Philadelphia to study law in the office of Alexander J. Dallas, a prominent lawyer, and was admitted to the Philadelphia bar. In 1799, he headed west and settled in the bustling town of Pittsburgh. He joined the local bar in 1801 and started a firm with two other young, ambitious lawyers. Baldwin and his partners soon held prominent places in western Pennsylvania legal and political circles, for a time owning a Republican paper, *The Tree of Liberty*.

In 1816, Baldwin won a seat in the United States House of Representatives and was reelected twice. Representing the manufacturing interests of Pittsburgh, and himself an iron and textile manufacturer, Baldwin favored a protective tariff and courted southern support by opposing conditional admission of Missouri to statehood. He also staunchly defended General Andrew Jackson's prosecution of the war against the Florida Seminoles.

Although Baldwin resigned from the House in 1822 due to illness, he maintained his support of Jackson and corresponded with Jackson adherents about the general's political chances in Pennsylvania. In the 1828 presidential election Baldwin ardently campaigned for Old Hickory. The Jackson victory did not bring an immediate reward to Baldwin, whose candidacy for various federal appointments was opposed by Vicepresident John C. Calhoun. But in late 1829, when Justice Bushrod Washington died, Jackson named Baldwin to the high court.

In his early years, Baldwin was noted as an amiable, pleasant, and moderate man; Joseph Story initially found the appointment of this Democrat "quite satisfactory." But Baldwin became more contentious with the years, apparently suffering a breakdown in 1832 which prevented his attendance at the 1833 term of the Court. This absence relieved his brethren of what had become an unpredictable, argumentative presence. By 1833, Story was complaining to a federal district judge that Baldwin's "distaste for the Supreme Court and especially for [Chief Justice Marshall] is so familiarly known to us that it excites no surprise."

By the mid-1830s, however, Baldwin had mellowed to the extent that his work on the third circuit had produced a volume of well-respected decisions and had raised the prestige of that circuit. He also managed to mend his relationship with the chief justice and was a frequent visitor during Marshall's last illness. According to Story, Baldwin held no one in higher "reverence or respect."

While Baldwin's initial dissatisfaction with service on the Court might be attributed to its Federalist flavor, Democratic appointments of the 1830s should have assuaged his sense of political isolation. But Baldwin's relationship with the new justices was far from harmonious. In addition, he provoked constant arguments with Court Reporter Richard Peters over the presentation of his numerous dissents. In an age when consensus (or at least the appearance of it) was the hallmark of Supreme Court decisions, Baldwin was a misfit.

Baldwin's activity on the bench falls into two major periods: a series of dissents and concurrences in 1831–32, and a second series of concurrences in 1837. In the 1831 term, the new justice dissented seven times—probably a record for a junior justice. In *Ex parte Crane* (1831), Baldwin criticized the majority decision to issue a writ of mandamus as an unwarranted and dangerous extension of federal jurisdiction. His intemperate language no doubt antagonized Marshall, who had written the opinion, as well as other members of the majority.

In *United States v. Arredondo* (1831), Baldwin's majority opinion placed the burden of proof in public land claims on the government and annoyed President Jackson in the process. The Arredondo claim dated to a vague Spanish land grant in Florida. According to Baldwin, courts must protect even ill-defined land titles predating American possession to assure security of land ownership. The Jackson administration had vigorously opposed the Arredondo claim and now found its recent appointee to the bench issuing a stern lecture on the duties of the government.

In *Cherokee Nation v. Georgia* (1831), and *Worcester v. Georgia* (1832), Baldwin's usual unpredictable attitude appeared more consistent than the majority's. In the first case, Marshall's decision held that the Cherokee had no standing to bring suit under the Court's original jurisdiction since the Cherokee were a "domestic, dependent nation." While Baldwin did not reiterate Marshall's expression of sympathy with the Cherokee's plight, his concurrence with the chief justice's opinion appeared to place him squarely in the Marshall camp. In the subsequent case, Baldwin dissented from the majority view (again written by Marshall) that the Cherokee were a special foreign nation and the Georgia act which violated this status was unconstitutional. According to Baldwin, the Cherokee were not a "nation" and "treaties" with them were merely agreements. Over the course of the two cases, Baldwin's consistency of outlook in the face of the majority's apparent reversal managed to irritate the other members of the Court.

The most remarkable product of Baldwin's tenure was *A General View of the Origin and Nature of the Constitution . . . Together with Opinions in the Cases decided at January Term, 1837,* which he wrote and published in pamphlet form. Baldwin had concurred with the majority in these cases of the judicial "revolution," particularly *Charles River Bridge v. Warren Bridge, New York v. Miln,* and *Briscoe v. Bank of Kentucky,* but had subsequently decided that the Court had not paid sufficient attention to constitutional precepts. To Baldwin, liberal and narrow interpreters of the Constitution continued to err in their judgments, and the 1837 cases were proof of his contention; correct interpretation lay somewhere between these extremes and had been most consistently delivered by "the late venerated Chief Justice" and, of course, Baldwin himself. Since Marshall could no longer speak, Baldwin proceeded to explain the "few and simple" principles which would provide "an easy solution" to all questions regarding the Constitution. In the process, Baldwin again disrupted the appearance of a harmonious and dignified Court. The last seven years of his tenure witnessed recurrent mental instability and very little productive activity.

—ELIZABETH BRAND MONROE

BIBLIOGRAPHY

Baldwin's judicial career has excited little research. The most extensive treatment is Frank Otto Gatell's essay in Leon Friedman and Fred L. Israel (eds.) 1 *The Justices of the United States Supreme Court, 1789–1969* 571 (1969) (hereafter cited as Friedman and Israel, *Justices).* G. Edward White addresses Baldwin's early judicial career in *The Marshall Court and Cultural Change, 1815–1835,* volumes 3–4 of the Holmes Devise *History of the Supreme Court* (1988), and Carl Swisher discusses Baldwin's later career in *The Taney Period, 1836–1864* (1974), volume 5 of the series.

PHILIP PENDLETON BARBOUR

BORN 25 March 1783, Orange County,
    Virginia
NOMINATED to the Court 28 December 1835
    by Andrew Jackson
TOOK seat March 1836
DIED 25 February 1841 in Washington, D.C.

Although he served less than five years on
the Supreme Court, Philip Pendleton Barbour
played a more important role in American constitutional history than is generally acknowledged. Prior to his appointment to the Court,
Barbour had contributed significantly to the development of a reinvigorated states' rights interpretation of the Constitution that would grow
increasingly important between the time of his
death in 1841 and the outbreak of the Civil War
two decades later.

The son of Thomas Barbour, a neighbor and
an early political sponsor of James Madison who
broke with Madison over the issue of Virginia's
ratification of the Constitution, Barbour briefly
studied law under St. George Tucker at the College of William and Mary. He began his legal
career in Kentucky in 1801, but returned to his
native Orange County the following year.

He was elected to the Virginia House of
Delegates in 1812, and then to Congress in 1814.
During his tenure in the House of Representatives (1814–25, 1827–30), Barbour was a leader
of the conservative faction of the Republican
party. Between 1821 and 1823 he served as
Speaker of the House of Representatives. In
1825, he declined an invitation to join the University of Virginia faculty as its first professor
of law, but stepped down from Congress to accept a position on the Virginia general court.

In 1827, he returned to Congress where he
remained until 1830 when President Andrew
Jackson appointed him United States district judge
for the eastern district of Virginia. In this capacity, he also served as a member of the fifth circuit court of the United States with his longtime
political opponent, Chief Justice John Marshall.
Barbour also served as president of both the Vir-

ginia Constitutional Convention of 1829–30 and
the 1831 Philadelphia Free Trade Convention.

In Congress, Barbour had opposed the Bo-
nus Bill of 1817, federally funded internal improvements, restrictions on the ability of Missouri to enter the Union as a slave state, the
second Bank of the United States, and the protective tariff, and while he opposed the efforts
of the South Carolina nullifiers, he accepted the
premise that a state had the right to withdraw
from the union as a last resort.

In addition to being a principle exponent for
the states' rights cause, he also played an important role in developing its central constitutional
arguments. He was, for example, the first major
political figure to argue that the protective tariff
was not just unfair, but also unconstitutional. In
this capacity, he helped define the basic tenets
of states' rights constitutionalism that would later
be endorsed by Supreme Court justices John
Catron, Peter Daniel, John Campbell, and, to a
limited extent, by Chief Justice Roger Taney.
Barbour had been critical of the Marshall Court
in the late 1810s, and in his capacity as counsel
for the state of Virginia he argued unsuccessfully
that the Supreme Court lacked jurisdiction in the
landmark case, *Cohens v. Virginia* (1821). As a
congressman, he had also sought (unsuccessfully) to require the concurrence of five of the
seven justices of the Court in any case involving a constitutional question.

The possibility of Barbour's appointment to
the Supreme Court had been rumored since his
appointment to the lower federal bench in 1830.
In February of 1831, John Quincy Adams predicted that if John Marshall were to retire "some
shallow-pated wild-cat like Philip P. Barbour fit
for nothing but to tear the Union to rags and
tatters, would be appointed in his place."
Barbour's chances for appointment improved
considerably in 1832 when he withdrew his support for a movement on the part of disgruntled
southerners to place his name on the Democratic
ticket as the vice-presidential candidate in place
of Jackson's own choice, Martin Van Buren. By
withdrawing when he did, he not only earned the

gratitude of Jackson, but allowed the president to offer Barbour's appointment as a concession to his southern critics.

The resignation of Gabriel Duvall of Maryland in 1835 and the death of John Marshall later that year created two openings on the Court. Although he had been initially rebuffed in his effort to replace Duvall with Roger Taney, Jackson ultimately submitted the names of Taney and Barbour to the Senate. After much controversy, both were approved on March 15, 1836. Two efforts to delay the vote on Barbour's nomination failed by votes of twenty-five to twenty and twenty-six to sixteen, and he was subsequently confirmed by a vote of thirty to eleven.

During his first term on the Court, he was part of the majority in a trio of cases—*Briscoe v. Bank of Kentucky* (1837), *Proprietors of the Charles River Bridge v. Warren* (1837), and *New York v. Miln* (1837)—that repudiated the nationalistic jurisprudence that had been associated with the Marshall Court. Barbour authored the majority opinion in *Miln*, using it as an opportunity to argue for a narrow definition of the federal commerce power and an expansive definition for the state police power, which he characterized as "unqualified and exclusive."

Otherwise, Barbour's four years on the Supreme Court were characterized by a near unanimity of opinion. During his tenure, the Court heard 155 cases, all but thirty of which were decided without a dissenting vote. Barbour sided most frequently with his fellow southerners John Catron (97.8 percent of the time) and Chief Justice Taney (97.4 percent), and least frequently with Justices Henry Baldwin (89.6 percent) and Joseph Story (94.1 percent).

Although he only dissented on two occasions, there is evidence that had he lived, Barbour's states' rights principles would have eventually put him at odds with his more nationalistic colleagues. While only Story dissented from his *Miln* opinion, Smith, Thompson and Henry Baldwin refused to endorse its particulars at the time, and subsequent evidence showed that neither John McLean or James Wayne accepted his comments on the limits of the federal commerce power. Furthermore, in cases in which the Court was called on to interpret the scope of federal authority, Barbour consistently advocated a narrow construction of all delegations of authority to the national government. This was apparent in his dissents in *Kendall v. United States* (1838) and *Pollard's Heirs v. Kibbe* (1840). In cases like *Holmes v. Jennison* (1840) that involved questions of implied restrictions upon state sovereignty, Barbour opposed such limitations. Had he lived, Barbour almost surely would have been as strident a defender of the states' rights position as his successor, fellow Virginian Peter Daniel.

Barbour was apparently well respected by his colleagues, including Joseph Story, who eulogized him as "a very conscientious, upright, and laborious judge, whom we all respected for his talents and virtues, and his high sense of duty."

—JOSEPH GORDON HYLTON

BIBLIOGRAPHY

There is unfortunately no biography of Barbour. The best sources for information concerning his career are Charles D. Lowery's biography of his brother, *James Barbour: A Jeffersonian Republican* (1984) and Carl B. Swisher's *The Taney Period, 1836–64*, volume 5 of *The Oliver Wendell Holmes Devise History of the Supreme Court of the United States* (1974).

HUGO LAFAYETTE BLACK

BORN 27 February 1886, Harlan, Alabama

NOMINATED to the Court 12 August 1937
by Franklin D. Roosevelt

TOOK seat 19 August 1937; retired
17 September 1971

DIED 25 September 1971 in Bethesda,
Maryland

Few Supreme Court justices have achieved the exalted status of Hugo Black, who is widely viewed as one of the Court's most influential justices and perhaps its most committed textualist. Yet much of what the public knows about Justice Black consists of the more colorful aspects of his character and judicial performance.

His contemporaries believed, for example, that President Franklin Roosevelt selected Black as his first Supreme Court appointment in 1937 because of the latter's ardent support in the Senate for the New Deal and the president's Court-packing plan. Justice Black's reputation for trying to read the Constitution as literally as possible is memorialized through his practice of carrying a copy of the Constitution in his pocket for ready reference and his persistently unique reading of the First Amendment as absolutely prohibiting any governmental interference with the freedom of speech and press. He is also widely remembered for his capacity for hard work, as reflected in his lifelong habits of reading extensively on his own and researching thoroughly any subject of personal or professional interest to him. Moreover, conservatives and liberals alike have admired Justice Black, with the former commending his steadfast commitment to judicial restraint and opposition to substantive due process, and the latter praising his efforts to secure the constitutional foundations of the New Deal and the incorporation of most of the Bill of Rights. Yet, many people still speculate about whether Justice Black should even have been confirmed in light of his membership, while a young lawyer, in the Ku Klux Klan.

These glimpses into Hugo Black's life and judicial career do not fully reflect the skills he brought to the Court, his judicial philosophy, and his influence on the development of American constitutional law. Justice Black is a seminal figure in constitutional history, but for more complex reasons than his popular image suggests.

Hugo Black came to the Court far better prepared and with more settled views on constitutional interpretation than is commonly thought. After graduating at the top of his University of Alabama Law School class in spite of having concurrently taken a full liberal arts curriculum, he moved his fledgling law practice from Ashland to Birmingham in 1907. Within his first five years in practice in Birmingham, he served part-time for a year and a half as a municipal court judge and full-time for three years as Jefferson County prosecuting attorney. In these latter two positions, he learned about police misconduct and the need for efficient but equal justice. Perhaps in his most famous case as a prosecutor, he investigated and prosecuted several area police officers for abusing and forcing confessions from black defendants. These personal experiences helped to guide him later as a senator to declare that he would not vote to confirm a former prosecutor as a federal judge if he felt that the latter had abused fair criminal procedures, and as a Supreme Court justice to recognize criminal defendants' constitutional rights.

His private practice included a substantial number of personal injury cases. This work enabled him to sharpen his talents as an eloquent, passionate advocate in countless jury trials and in more than 100 cases in the Alabama appellate courts. His oratorical skills helped him to get elected in 1927 to the United States Senate, where he developed an understanding of the relationship between the federal political process and the Supreme Court. On the floor of the Senate and in committees, he often passionately and eloquently defended New Deal legislation and criticized the activist Court. His skills as an orator were also quite evident in his first public act as an associate justice, when, immediately after his confirmation, he gave a brief but dramatic radio address to verify newspaper reports that he was once a member of the Ku Klux Klan, but to add that he had resigned many years before, and would comment no further.

Significantly, Black's second term as a senator coincided with the election of President Franklin Roosevelt. Black quickly caught President Roosevelt's attention as a committed New Deal liberal who had sponsored a statute that later became the Fair Labor Standards Act of 1938, supported antitrust and other commercial or economic regulations, and oversaw Senate investigations that exposed the abuses of the private shipping operators, major commercial airlines, and large utility holding companies. In numerous committee hearings and floor debates, Black espoused the beliefs that the Congress had the authority under the Commerce Clause to pass appropriate legislation to deal with any problem that directly or indirectly affected the national economy, and that the federal courts lacked any constitutional authority to interfere with such enactments.

In his unequivocal support for the president's Court-packing plan, he confirmed the power of Congress to change the number of members of the Supreme Court, and declared that, "neither the people who wrote nor the people who approved the Constitution ever contemplated that the Supreme Court should become all powerful." Foreshadowing the philosophy he would later espouse on the Supreme Court, Black suggested that the five conservative justices who dominated the Court made it necessary for the president to take extreme action: "The time has arrived when those who favor fitting laws to modern needs in order to correct and cure social and industrial injustice must face their problems squarely and fairly. Everybody knows that Supreme Court decisions by a bare majority have for years been thrown as impassable barriers in the way of the solemn and well-matured legislative plans supported by the people."

Once on the Court, Black quickly synthesized his views on constitutional interpretation into a coherent judicial philosophy. He declared a jurisprudence of certainty, with clear, precise standards that would limit judicial discretion, protect individual rights, and give government

room to address a significant range of social problems. He saw the Constitution as a set of commands designed to prevent the recurrence of certain historic evils. Once he had determined the scope of a constitutional mandate through its literal language or its framers' intent when its text was unclear, he rigorously applied it, regardless of the consequences or conflicting precedent.

Justice Black gave one of the fullest expressions of his approach to judicial decision making in the inaugural James Madison lecture at New York University Law School in 1960. He denounced the practice of other justices, such as Felix Frankfurter and John Marshall Harlan, to engage in judicial balancing, which "regard[ed] the prohibitions of the Constitution, even its most unequivocal commands, as mere admonitions which Congress need not always observe." Rather, Black recognized that "the whole history and background of our Constitution and Bill of Rights [belie] the assumption or conclusion that our ultimate constitutional freedoms are no more than our English ancestors had when they came to this new land to get new freedoms." He believed that the framers had resolved all of the necessary balancing of constitutional liberties in 1791: "Where conflicting values exist in the field of individual liberties protected by the Constitution, that document settles the conflict."

Despite its clarity, Black's methodology, as well as many of the results it produced, rarely commanded a majority of the Court. For example, he repeatedly argued that the Constitution meant exactly what it said in the First Amendment's command that government could never abridge freedom of speech and press. In his Madison lecture, he explained that "the phrase 'Congress shall make no law' is composed of plain words, easily understood. The language [is] absolute. Of course the decision to provide a constitutional safeguard for [freedom of speech and of the press] involves a balancing of conflicting interests, [which] the Framers [performed] when they wrote [the First Amendment.] Courts have neither the right nor the power to [make] a different evaluation." Nevertheless, a majority of the Court consistently favored a balancing approach over Black's absolutist reading of the First Amendment. Even in

Hugo Lafayette Black
Photograph by Harris and Ewing.
Collection of the Supreme Court of the United States.

the last opinion he ever wrote in *New York Times Co. v. United States* (the Pentagon Papers case) (1971), only William O. Douglas joined Black's reiteration of his view that, even when national security might be at stake, "the history and language of the First Amendment support the view that the press must be left to publish news, whatever the source, without censorship, injunctions, or prior restraints."

Ironically, Black's unique methodology led him to consistently take a far more hospitable stance toward the government in Fourth Amendment cases. He almost always gave the government wide latitude in determining the "reasonableness" of its searches, even those without a warrant. For example, in a heated dissent in *Berger v. New York* (1967), he rejected the majority's invalidation of a conviction based on electronic eavesdropping. Seemingly oblivious to the dangers of wiretapping, he argued that there was nothing in the Fourth Amendment's history to suggest that its framers intended to prohibit governmental use of technological innovations to investigate crimes and to enforce the law.

In spite of the rarity with which a majority of the Court fully endorsed his methodology, but partly as a consequence of his strong reasoning and persistent advocacy during his long tenure on the Court, Hugo Black left his mark on constitutional law in two significant ways. First, he wrote a number of influential opinions that helped to keep critical debates open long enough to allow other justices to change their thinking or to take a position similar to his own but for different reasons. Second, he cast a number of critical votes that helped to shape several areas of constitutional law.

Through his opinions, Black exerted influence in such diverse fields as freedom of speech, incorporation, criminal procedure, and reapportionment. For example, his constant assertion that the First Amendment did not permit the government to regulate obscenity helped to lead the Warren Court eventually to define obscenity in a way that made its regulation more difficult. Similarly, his persistent criticism of the government's investigations of and prosecutions for so-called anti-American activities in the 1950s ultimately helped to guide the Warren

Court to overturn a number of convictions in the McCarthy era based on "subversive activities."

Black also exerted considerable influence in keeping the debate on incorporation open and facilitating the Court's movement to make most of the Bill of Rights applicable to the states. He sought to reconcile the history and seemingly broad language of the Fourteenth Amendment with the basic need for judicial restraint in our constitutional scheme. His solution was to propose total incorporation, i.e., to define the term "liberty" in the Fourteenth Amendment's due process clause as including no more or less than the guarantees specified in the first eight amendments.

He first expressed his views on total incorporation in his dissent in *Adamson v. California* (1947). Joined by Justice Douglas, he laid down the formulation that guided him for the rest of his judicial career: "My study of the historical events that culminated in the Fourteenth Amendment [persuades] me that one of the chief objects that the provisions of the Amendment's first section, separately, and as a whole, were intended to accomplish was to make the Bill of Rights applicable to the States. [I] fear to see the consequences of the Court's practices of substituting its own conceptions of decency and fundamental justice for the language of the Bill of Rights as its point of departure in interpreting and enforcing that Bill of Rights. [To] hold that this Court can determine what, if any, provisions of the Bill of Rights will be enforced, and if so to what degree, is to frustrate the great design of a written Constitution." Black sought to restrict judicial discretion by urging the Court to define the term "liberty" in terms of another part of the constitutional text in which the original framers had explicitly defined the basic components of liberty as consisting of the specific guarantees set forth in the first eight amendments.

For the next twenty years, Black called on his fellow justices in numerous cases to apply the first eight amendments to the states. During that period, he often came into conflict with Felix Frankfurter, who rejected total incorporation and argued vigorously instead that the Fourteenth Amendment applied certain guarantees to the states as a matter of fundamental fairness. While the Court never endorsed total incorporation, it inexorably moved away from the Frankfurter position it had initially adopted in *Wolf v. Colorado* (1949) in the direction of incorporating most of the Bill of Rights. For example, in *Mapp v. Ohio* (1961), Justice Black concurred with the majority's declaration that the states must uphold the guarantees of the Fourth Amendment as incorporated through the Fourteenth Amendment. With this announcement, the Court overruled *Wolf*, which had applied the established constitutional theory that the Fourteenth Amendment's due process clause contained all the authority necessary to strike down state conduct that was fundamentally unfair.

By the time Black retired from the Court in 1971, the incorporation debate had ended. His persistent advocacy had facilitated the Court's move to incorporate all of the Bill of Rights, with the exceptions of the Second and Third Amendments, the Fifth Amendment's requirement of grand jury indictment, and the Seventh Amendment.

His success in the incorporation debate helped to set the stage for the nationalization and reformation of state criminal procedures. In contrast to his narrow reading of the Fourth Amendment, he read the Fifth and Sixth Amendments expansively. Drawing on his experiences as a police court judge and county prosecutor, he constantly tried to lead the Court to strictly enforce the Constitution's provisions defining the conditions of trial by jury and availability of counsel and prohibiting coerced confessions, compulsory self-incrimination, and double jeopardy. Indeed, one of the first Court opinions he wrote, *Johnson v. Zerbst* (1938), held that in a federal prosecution counsel must be appointed to represent a defendant who cannot afford to hire an attorney. He also wrote the Court's unanimous opinion in *Chambers v. Florida* (1940), which held that the confessions obtained by Florida authorities to condemn four black defendants to death were clearly coerced and, therefore, a violation of the Fourteenth Amendment due process clause. In language to which he and other justices often turned in subsequent criminal procedure cases, he explained that "Under our constitutional system courts stand against any winds that blow as havens or refuge for those who

might otherwise suffer because they are helpless, weak, outnumbered, or because they are nonconforming victims of prejudice and public excitement. Due process of law, preserved for all by our Constitution, commands that no such practice as that disclosed [in this case] shall send any accused to his death. No higher duty, no more solemn responsibility, rests upon this Court, than that of translating into living law and maintaining this constitutional shield deliberately planned and inscribed for the benefit of every human being to our Constitution—of whatever race, creed, or persuasion."

But when the Court refused to make assistance of counsel mandatory in state felony trials in *Betts v. Brady* (1942), he vigorously dissented. Even though he had not yet fully developed his incorporation theory, and the Court had not yet agreed to apply the Sixth Amendment to the states, Black argued in *Betts* that a state's failure to provide counsel for defendants in state felony trials clearly violated the majority's own "[standard] that due process of law is denied if a trial is conducted in such a manner that it is 'shocking to the universal sense of justice' or 'offensive to the common and fundamental ideas of fairness and right'." Eventually, Justice Black's persistence paid off in his opinion for a unanimous Court in *Gideon v. Wainwright* (1963), which overruled *Betts*. He declared that "The right of one charged with crime to counsel may not be deemed fundamental and essential to fair trials in some countries, but it is in ours. From the very beginning, our state and national constitutions and laws have laid great emphasis on procedural and substantive safeguards designed to assure fair trials before impartial tribunals in which every defendant stands equal before the law. This noble ideal cannot be realized if the poor man charged with a crime has to face his accusers without a lawyer to assist him."

Justice Black also helped to shape the Court's establishment clause doctrine. He wrote the Court's opinion in *Everson v. Board of Education* (1947), which was the first case to declare that the clause applied to the states. While the *Everson* Court ultimately concluded that the state's payment of the bus fares of all pupils, including those in parochial schools, served a secular purpose, and therefore did not violate the establishment clause, Black expressly agreed with Thomas Jefferson that the clause was intended to erect "a wall of separation between Church and State" and noted that government cannot "contribute tax-raised funds to the support of an institution which teaches the tenets and faith of any church." In *McCollum v. Board of Education* (1948), the Court, in yet another Black opinion, held unconstitutional a released time program in which religious instruction took place in public school. Fourteen years later, Justice Black wrote perhaps his most controversial opinion on the separation of church and state in *Engel v. Vitale* (1962), which held that a state-sponsored "non-denominational prayer" was "wholly inconsistent" with the establishment clause. In his view, that clause prohibited any laws that "establish an official religion whether [they] operate directly to coerce non-observing individuals or not." He explained that "Religion is too personal, too sacred, too holy, to permit its 'unhallowed perversion' by a civil magistrate."

Moreover, Black helped to lead the Warren Court to strike down enactments permitting disproportionate legislative representation at the state and federal levels. Indeed, he supported the equal protection claim in every reapportionment case that came before the Court during his tenure. He argued that Article I conferred on qualified voters the rights to vote and to have their votes counted on an equal basis in congressional elections. Yet, over his dissent, the Court declared in *Colegrove v. Green* (1946) that such matters were "political questions" whose merits the Court could not reach. Justice Frankfurter explained that the political business of reapportionment was for the politicians. By entering the "political thicket," Frankfurter warned, the Court risked political reprisals that could ultimately undercut its institutional authority. Black's dissent denounced the Court's preoccupation with political considerations rather than its paramount responsibility of determining whether legislative reapportionment violated the Constitution. He explained that both Article I and the equal protection clause required that congressional district lines be drawn "to give approximately equal

weight to each vote cast." Eventually, four other justices adopted Black's views on the justiciability of apportionment in *Baker v. Carr* (1962). Within a year, Black delivered the Court's opinion in *Wesberry v. Sanders* (1963), which formally overturned *Colegrove*. He explained that "[t]he right to vote is too important in our society to be stripped of judicial protection by such an interpretation."

Justice Black made a second significant impact on constitutional law, not through his opinions, but rather his votes in a number of pivotal cases. In this way, he influenced the Court's approaches to the commerce power, criminal procedure, school desegregation, reapportionment, and freedom of religion.

For example, Black consistently supported the Court's abandonment of its substantive due process review of economic regulations and the rise of a more deferential judicial reading of the commerce clause. Within his first five years on the Court, he joined unanimous decisions rejecting a substantive due process challenge to the provisions of the Fair Labor Standards Act in *United States v. Darby* (1941) and sustaining, in *Olsen v. Nebraska* (1941), a state statute fixing the maximum fee that an employment agency could collect from employees. In explaining the Court's unanimous decision upholding a state right-to-work law that prohibited closed shops in *Lincoln Federal Union v. Northwestern Iron & Metal Co.* (1949), Black declared that the Court had abandoned substantive due process in economic cases and returned "to the earlier constitutional principle that states have power to legislate against what are found to be injurious practices in their internal commercial and business affairs, so long as their laws do not run afoul of some specific federal constitutional prohibition." In fact, during Justice Black's thirty-four-year tenure, the Court never struck down a federal law for violating the commerce clause. For his part, Black consistently voted in the 1960s to uphold the constitutionality of congressional enactments premised on the commerce clause and the fifth section of the Fourteenth Amendment for the purpose of remedying racial discrimination in private accommodations and voting practices.

In addition, Justice Black consistently joined the Court's opinions aimed at ending segregation in the United States. For example, when *Brown v. Board of Education* (1954) was first argued and the Court under Chief Justice Vinson was first considering whether to overrule *Plessy v. Ferguson* (1896), Black was one of only four justices who voted to overturn *Plessy* and to order the end of segregation in public schools. When *Brown* was reargued after Vinson's death and the appointment of Earl Warren, Black was one of the first to join the new chief justice's subsequently unanimous opinion in *Brown*.

In *Griffin v. County School Board* (1964), Black strengthened *Brown* by writing the Court's opinion holding illegal the action of a county school board which had closed its public schools to resist integration and thereby contributed to the support of private segregated schools. He explained that "[t]he time for mere 'deliberate speed' has run out, and that phrase can no longer justify denying these Prince Edward County school children their constitutional rights to an education equal to that afforded by the public schools in the other parts of Virginia." Thus, he clarified that the trial court could, if necessary, close all the schools of the state of Virginia if the public schools were not reopened in the affected county. Justice Black also joined another important, unanimous school desegregation decision in *Green v. County School Board* (1968), which struck down a "freedom of choice" plan that failed to satisfy a district's obligation to develop a scheme to end its segregated school system immediately.

Besides delivering some important criminal procedure opinions, Black also cast critical votes in several others. For example, he was one of the five justices who formed the slim majorities in two seminal criminal procedure cases. He cast a pivotal fifth vote in *Escobedo v. Illinois* (1964), which invalidated a conviction based on statements obtained from a criminal defendant who had been interrogated by the police, but not granted any of his requests to consult his counsel or to have his counsel present. He was also one of the five justices who formed the majority in *Miranda v. Arizona* (1966), which established one of the Warren Court's most lasting but controversial principles—that a criminal defendant's Fifth Amendment right against self-incrimination and Sixth Amendment right to assistance of counsel require the police to observe or comply with certain procedural safeguards for any individual who has been "taken into custody or otherwise deprived of his freedom by the authorities in any significant way and is subjected to questioning."

Ironically, for all of the influence Hugo Black wielded, his failures often proved as notable as his successes on the Court. First, he strongly opposed but failed to prevent the Court's recognizing a constitutionally protected right of privacy. In his 1965 dissent in *Griswold v. Connecticut* (1965), he harshly criticized the majority's striking down a Connecticut law prohibiting the sale of contraceptives to married couples on the basis of a right of privacy implicitly protected by the "penumbras" of the Bill of Rights, the liberty component of the Fourteenth Amendment due process clause, or the Ninth Amendment. He argued that the original framers had already made a decision in the Bill of Rights as to which aspects of a person's privacy to give constitutional protection and which aspects to leave to the majoritarian process for protection or regulation. He viewed the Court's recognition of any implied fundamental right (such as a general marital right of privacy), other than those applied to the states by virtue of total incorporation, as the revival of substantive due process. Thus, he argued that the "[u]se of any such broad, unbounded judicial authority would make of the Court's members a day-to-day constitutional convention." Two years later, in his dissent in *Berger v. New York* (1967), he similarly lamented that a right of privacy was nothing more than a "vague judge-made goal" and "like a chameleon, has a different color for every turning."

A second notable failure occurred in cases involving equal protection/fundamental rights, which were interests found by the Warren Court to be of such importance that distinctions made on the basis of their exercise required compelling justifications. Black maintained that the Fourteenth Amendment equal protection clause had been designed primarily to end racial discrimination, and insisted that the Court should apply no more than a rational basis test to review any equal protection claim other than those involving racial discrimination. Hence, he dissented to the Court's uses of strict scrutiny under the equal protection clause to strike down laws that made it more difficult for people to exercise their right to travel in *Shapiro v. Thompson* (1969) and to exercise their right to vote in *Harper v. Virginia State Board of Elections* (1966) and *Kramer v. Union Free School District* (1969).

Yet Black also failed to oppose uniformly the Warren Court's equal protection/fundamental rights decisions. Despite his qualms about expanding the equal protection clause to strike laws down on the basis of something other than racial discrimination, his recognition of the needs for equal justice and fair criminal procedures led him to write the plurality opinion in *Griffin v. Illinois* (1956), in which the Court held that a state must furnish an indigent criminal defendant with a free trial transcript if such a transcript is necessary "for adequate and effective appellate review" of his conviction. Black explained that "[Our] constitutional guarantees of due process and equal protection both call for procedures in criminal trials which allow no invidious discriminations between persons and different groups of persons. [In] criminal trials a State can no more discriminate on account of poverty than on account of religion, race, or color. Plainly the ability to pay costs in advance bears no rational relationship to a defendant's guilt or innocence and could not be used as an excuse to deprive a defendant of a fair trial. [It] is true that a State is not required by the Federal Constitution to provide appellate courts or a right to appellate review at all. [But] that is not to say that a State that does grant appellate review can do so in a way that discriminates against some convicted defendants on account of their poverty." Similarly, he joined *Douglas v. California* (1963), in which the Court struck down a state law requiring state appellate courts, on the request of an indigent criminal defendant for counsel on appeal, to make "an independent investigation of the record" and "to appoint counsel [only] if in their opinion it would be helpful to the defendant or the court." Nevertheless, when the

Burger Court in *Boddie v. Connecticut* (1971) struck down a state law that required individuals to pay court fees and costs of about sixty dollars in order to sue for divorce, Justice Black dissented on the ground that neither the due process nor the equal protection clause permitted "judges [to] hold laws constitutional or not on the basis of a judge's sense of fairness."

Another failure involved Black's misapplication of an equal protection standard he initially had helped to define. In his controversial majority opinion in *Korematsu v. United States* (1944), he made the first reference in the Court's history to race as a suspect classification, which, he explained, must be subjected to the "most rigid scrutiny." Under this standard, he then upheld, over the heated dissents of Justices Murphy, Jackson, Roberts, and Rutledge, the constitutionality of the internment of Japanese Americans during World War II. Even though historians have subsequently established that the military in fact had no reliable evidence to substantiate its claims that Japanese Americans on the West Coast posed a threat to the national security of the United States, Black never expressed any regret over the *Korematsu* decision. Rather, as criticism of *Korematsu* mounted in subsequent years, he boldly defended it: "There's a difference between peace and war. You can't fight a war with the courts in control." He even added that all people of Japanese ancestry "look alike to a person not a Jap. [Had] they attacked our shores you'd have a large number fighting with the Japanese troops. And a lot of innocent Japanese-Americans would have been shot in the panic. Under these circumstances I saw nothing wrong in moving them away from the danger area."

A fifth, and particularly significant, failure involved Black's inability during his last decade or so on the Court to build coalitions, maintain consistency in his votes and opinions, and exhibit the tolerance he had demonstrated in the previous twenty-five years. It is hard to determine whether these changes in the style and substance of his constitutional decision making were attributable to his failing health, a changing world, or some combination of the two. In the 1960s, while new issues confronted the Court, Justice Black fought old age, particularly cataracts which interfered with his practice of researching his opinions thoroughly. During this period, his opinions grew shorter and often contained an unprecedented note of anger and exasperation. He also became more curt with his colleagues and his law clerks.

For example, despite his support for *Brown* and opposition to racial discrimination and the abridgement of freedom of speech, Black resisted extending the Constitution's protection to civil rights protesters' demonstrations on private property. Even though he had earlier written the majority opinion in *Marsh v. Alabama* (1946), in which the Court applied the First Amendment to a privately owned company town, Black later dissented in another case on the ground that the trespass convictions of civil rights demonstrators attempting to coerce a private restaurant to serve them should have been sustained. He contended that "none of our prior cases has held that a person's right to freedom of expression carries with it a right to force a private property owner to furnish his property as a platform to criticize the property owner's use of that property." He argued that a property owner, governmental or private, was under no obligation to provide a forum for speech; if owners could not control their property, Black feared, the result would be mob violence. In his view, the rule of law should take precedence over encouraging public discourse and protest. Focusing on maintaining "tranquility and order" in cases like *Gregory v. Chicago* (1969), Black criticized protestors who "think they have been mistreated or [have] actually been mistreated," and their supporters who "do no service [to] their cause, or their country." These statements contrast sharply with his prior respect for dissenters, toleration of the unorthodox, and receptivity to new ideas.

Black also failed during his last decade on the Court to persuade a majority of justices to accept fully his distinction between freedom of speech and expressive conduct. He argued that the First Amendment's guarantee of freedom of speech did not include expressive conduct. Yet, he failed to persuade the Court to accept his arguments that such activities as flag burning or wearing a jacket with a profane epithet about the draft were not insulated by the First Amendment from criminal sanction. Indeed, he joined Justice Blackmun's dissent in *Cohen v. California* (1971), characterizing the latter as conduct and not freedom of speech in the same year he reexpressed his commitment to protecting freedom of the press in the Pentagon Papers case. Black defended the former position as necessary line-drawing, but it does not comfortably coexist with his position in other cases to grant First Amendment protection to some expressive conduct, such as movies.

Black also assumed an ambivalent posture with respect to First Amendment protection for picketing. In *Giboney v. Empire Storage and Ice Company* (1949), he wrote that legislatures could regulate picketing, but in *Barenblatt v. United States* (1959) he noted that they could not abridge "views peacefully expressed in a place where the speaker had a right to be." Yet, in *Cox v. Louisiana* (1965), he wrote that "[p]icketing, though it may be utilized to communicate ideas, is not speech, and therefore is not of itself protected by the First Amendment." This position contrasts with his statement in *Feiner v. New York* (1951), in which he had labeled the Court's decision sanctioning police action to silence a speaker as "a long step toward totalitarian authority."

Lastly, Black never succeeded in persuading any other justices to join his views on *stare decisis*. He often argued that any erroneously reasoned precedent should be overruled, but throughout his tenure his colleagues refused to endorse his standard, which they believed would have introduced greater instability into constitutional adjudication.

By the time Hugo Black left the Court in 1971, more had changed than just his health, tone, and substantive views on many constitutional issues. He had succeeded in moving from being perceived at the time of his appointment as a Roosevelt loyalist to being regarded as a fiercely independent justice. Part of the explanation for this change in perception may be the fact that many of the issues presented to the Court during his tenure were unforeseen at the time of his appointment.

Moreover, social and political conditions have changed to such an extent that today, the justice who comes closest to carrying on the legacy of Hugo Black, a New Deal liberal, is

Antonin Scalia, an ardent conservative. Justice Scalia seems to share Black's widespread deference to majoritarian decisions (particularly on noneconomic matters), strict adherence to the literal or plain reading of the Constitution, and preferences to overrule wrongly decided cases and to adopt bright-line tests. Scalia has gone even further than Black as a textualist to include expressive conduct within the ambit of First Amendment protection and to argue that the Sixth Amendment confrontation clause must be read literally to mean that every criminal defendant has a right to confront his or her accusers face-to-face in the courtroom.

Of course, Black's legacy goes further than the areas in which he and Justice Scalia might have concurred. Besides having helped to secure the incorporation of most of the Bill of Rights and the foundations of the New Deal, to enliven legal and judicial debates over substantive due process and equal protection fundamental rights, and to shape First Amendment and criminal procedure principles that persist, Hugo Black exhibited an independence, integrity, and consistency against which all subsequent justices have measured themselves. Ironically, no one would have been more disappointed than Justice Black that even he could not always meet his own high standards.

—MICHAEL J. GERHARDT

BIBLIOGRAPHY

There is a small body of Hugo Black papers in the Library of Congress. Black expressed his own constitutional views not only in his opinions, but also in *A Constitutional Faith* (1968), and in the famous Madison lecture, "The Bill of Rights," 35 *New York Univ. Law Review* (1960). Both personal and professional insights can be found in Hugo L. Black, Jr., *My Father: A Remembrance* (1975).

There is a great deal of secondary literature on Black the man and the justice. See especially William Leuchtenburg, "A Klansman Joins the Court: The Appointment of Hugo Lafayette Black," 41 *Univ. of Chicago Law Review* 1 (1973); Charles Reich, "Mr. Justice Black and the Living Constitution," 76 *Harvard Law Review* 673 (1963); and the profiles by John P. Frank in Friedman and Israel, 3 *Justices* 2321, and by G. Edward White in Chapter 14 of his *The American Judicial Tradition: Profiles of Leading American Judges* (exp. ed., 1988).

For fuller biographies, see John P. Frank, *Mr. Justice Black: The Man and His Opinions* (1949); Gerald T. Dunne, *Hugo Black and the Judicial Revolution* (1977); and James J. Magee, *Mr. Justice Black: Absolutist on the Court* (1980). A unique dual biography is James F. Simon, *The Antagonists: Hugo Black, Felix Frankfurter, and Civil Liberties in Modern America* (1989).

Harry Andrew Blackmun

Born 12 November 1908, Nashville, Illinois

Nominated to the Court 14 April 1970
    by Richard M. Nixon

Took seat 9 June 1970; retired

"I suppose I'll carry Roe to my grave," Blackmun told a reporter, referring to the famous case in which he enunciated the constitutional right to abortion, *Roe v. Wade* (1973). He received thousands of letters in the following years: "Think of any name; I've been called it in these letters." Conversely, he was lauded by women's groups as a hero. It was an odd position for someone who, when nominated for the Court, was called a "strict constructionist" by conservative Senator Strom Thurmond, and who had said, "I'd like to regard myself as being a member of the center of the Court." But *Roe* signaled a major change of emphasis in Blackmun's opinions, from a deference to governmental institutions to marked empathy for those disadvantaged by society.

Blackmun was nominated by President Nixon after the Senate rejected two other nominees whom Nixon had counted on to be "tough on criminals" and supportive of governmental policies. Blackmun's decisions for the eighth circuit court of appeals fit that description. His modesty, innate decency, and intelligence nonetheless impressed dubious senators, and he was confirmed unanimously within a month.

Born in Illinois, Blackmun grew up in St. Paul, Minnesota, where his father opened a grocery and hardware store. Blackmun was educated in St. Paul and went to Harvard University on a scholarship presented by the Harvard Club of Minnesota. He supplemented it by working as a janitor, milkman, paper grader, and handball court painter. He would take his memories of poverty to the Court with him, telling an interviewer, "Maybe I'm oversensitive, but these are very personal cases. We're dealing with *people*—the life, liberty and property of *people*. And because I grew up in poor surroundings, I know there's another world out there that we

sometimes forget." He majored in mathematics, graduated summa cum laude (1929) and Phi Beta Kappa, and went on to receive his law degree at Harvard (1932). His impressive record earned him a clerkship with the Eighth Circuit Court of Appeals (1932–33).

A year later, Blackmun joined a Minneapolis firm, and by 1949, had risen from associate to junior partner and then general partner, specializing in estates, taxation, and general civil litigation. He also taught an occasional course at the St. Paul College of Law and the University of Minnesota Law School.

Blackmun had wavered between medicine and law after graduating from college. In 1950, delighted at the opportunity "to have a foot in both camps," he became resident counsel for the Mayo Clinic in Rochester, Minnesota. The job ended in 1959, when President Dwight Eisenhower appointed him to the appeals court for which he had clerked.

Blackmun wrote more than 200 signed opinions while on the Eighth Circuit court. He tended to defer to the federal and state legislatures and to the Supreme Court; to decide disputes between the government and individuals in favor of the government, particularly in criminal justice cases; and to uphold civil rights. He personally opposed capital punishment, for example, but ruled on the basis of what he considered the state's right to impose it (*Maxwell v. Bishop,* 1968). Believing that prior Supreme Court decisions gave a white homeowner the right to refuse to sell to a black would-be purchaser, he suggested that the Court alter its doctrine—which it subsequently did in *Jones v. Alfred H. Mayer Co.* (1967, 1968). He upheld the convictions of religious protesters against the Vietnamese War who demonstrated on a military reservation (*Holdrige v. United States,* 1960) and the suspension of college students also protesting the war, chiding them for not acting more maturely (*Esteban v. Central Missouri State,* 1965). He saw no violation of double jeopardy when a person was subjected to two successive trials for the robbery of two victims playing in one card game (*Ashe v. Swenson*, 1968), and almost invariably turned down appeals based on Fourth or Fifth Amendment grounds (e.g., *Cox v. United States*, 1967; *Jarrett v. United States*, 1970). He wrote opinions forbidding the perpetuation of de facto segregated schools (*Kemp v. Beasley*, 1970), ordering the rehiring of black faculty members after an all-black school was closed pursuant to a desegregation order (*Smith v. Board of Education*, 1966), and striking down racial discrimination on juries (*Bailey v. Henslee*, 1961). His fellow judges remembered him as "the most studious member of the court," "deliberate, courageous and moderate."

Blackmun continued to defer to governmental bodies and precedent in his early years on the Supreme Court. In his first opinion, a dissent from a *per curiam* decision overturning a Minnesota obscenity conviction (*Hoyt v. Minnesota*, 1970), he protested against treating state courts as "so obviously misguided" that they could be summarily reversed. The first opinion he wrote for the Court also upheld state action (*Wyman v. James*, 1971). Accepting New York's argument that home visits by caseworkers did not abridge a welfare recipient's right against unreasonable searches, he noted that seventeen additional states believed that the visits were "rehabilitative" and in the best interests of the child. Agreeing in another case that the death penalty was constitutional, he declared, "I yield to no one in the depth of my distaste, antipathy, and, indeed, abhorrence, for the death penalty," but added, "We should not allow our personal preferences as to the wisdom of legislative and congressional action, or our distaste for such action, to guide our judicial decisions such as these" (*Furman v. Georgia*, 1972).

Gradually, he adjusted to the wide-ranging implications of many of the cases handled by the Supreme Court and the exciting and sobering realization that each case affected not merely one plaintiff or defendant, but the entire country. He suggested in interviews that he was also affected by the change of justices and the Court's concomitant shift to the right, viewing his obligation as maintaining the Court's center. Whatever the explanation, his opinions became more reflective of his views and more empathetic to

individuals. He had no less respect for institutions, but insisted that they be held accountable, particularly by the Court. He began using the phrases "real life" and "real world," resembling an equity judge in his reliance on balancing tests to decide most cases, trying to ascertain where fairness and justice lay.

His sense of the "real world" was apparent in *Roe v. Wade* (1973) which, with its companion case *Doe v. Bolton*, struck down a Texas abortion law that permitted abortion only to save the life of the mother and a Georgia statute requiring that a doctor's decision to abort be approved by two additional physicians and a hospital committee. Drawing on the right of privacy implied by the Fourteenth Amendment and the Court's decisions in *Griswold v. Connecticut* (1965) and *Eisenstadt v. Baird* (1972), Blackmun suggested a legal rule based on the medically-recognized stages of pregnancy: no state health interest, and therefore no permissible interference by the state, during the first trimester, during which medicine had made abortions at least as safe as childbirth and any decision about abortion was to be made by the woman and her physician; a state interest in protecting the woman's health during the second trimester, when regulations concerning the qualifications of persons performing abortions and the facilities in which abortions were performed were legitimate; state power to prohibit abortions during the third trimester (except those necessary for the woman's life or health), when the fetus had reached "viability" and could live outside the womb. Blackmun read the constitutional reference to "person" as applying postnatally and declined to be drawn into a theological argument about whether personhood began before birth.

Justices White and Rehnquist, dissenting, questioned the Court's favoring "the convenience of the pregnant mother" over the fetus. In fact, the person Blackmun focused on was the physician, not the pregnant woman. In *United States v. Vuitch* (1971), involving a statute prohibiting physicians from performing any abortion not necessary to save the woman's life, the Court had found no constitutional right to abortion. Justice Douglas criticized the relevant statute as overly vague, giving neither the physician

Harry Andrew Blackmun
Collection of the Supreme Court of the United States.

nor a possible jury guidelines for deciding whether an abortion was necessary. During oral argument in *Roe*, Blackmun followed Douglas's *Vuitch* approach and emphasized physician's rights. The justices' conference reportedly centered on that issue, and Blackmun, after two weeks' intensive research in the Mayo Clinic library, wrote a decision that ensured women's access to abortion, but couched largely in language protective of the physicians' right to exercise professional judgment. It was only in subsequent cases that Blackmun's opinions centered on a woman's right to reproductive privacy rather than physicians' professionalism.

In the years following *Roe*, Blackmun wrote the opinion of the Court or concurred whenever the Court extended the right to abortion by striking down, e.g., spousal or parental consent requirements and waiting periods, and dissented from decisions limiting the right (*Planned Parenthood v. Danforth*, 1976; *Bellotti v. Baird*, 1979; *H.L. v. Metheson*, 1981; *Akron v. Akron*, 1983; *Planned Parenthood v. Ashcroft*, 1983). When the Court legitimized bans on government funding of abortions (*Beal v. Doe*, 1977; *Maher v. Roe*, 1977; *Harris v. McRae*, 1980), Blackmun dissented, going beyond his earlier medical concerns to condemn the hardships wrought on indigent women thereby deprived of their rights. In a First Amendment case with major implications for abortion rights, he dissented from the Court's finding of no constitutional violation in the federal government's making health care facilities' receipt of federal funds for family planning contingent on their avoiding any mention of abortion (*Rust v. Sullivan*, 1991).

In 1989, the Court upheld Missouri's prohibition on the performance of abortions by public employees or in public facilities unless they were to save the life of the mother, and legitimated the state's requirement that women seeking an abortion be counseled about alternatives, declaring that "the rigid Roe framework is hardly consistent with the notion of a Constitution cast in general terms" (*Webster v. Reproductive Health Services*, 1989). Blackmun accused the majority of "turn[ing] a stone face" to the right of reproductive freedom. "I fear for the future," he lamented. "I fear for the liberty and equality

of . . . millions of women." The majority had not overturned Roe, but "the signs are evident and very ominous, and a chill wind blows." It blew even colder in *Planned Parenthood v. Casey* (1992), in which a three-justice plurality reiterated the right enunciated in *Roe*. In permitting limitations on the right to abortion such as consent and "information" requirements, however, the Court substituted for the *Roe* trimester formula a state power to regulate abortions, at any stage of pregnancy, as long as the regulations did not place an "undue burden" on the right. A separate four-justice bloc would have overturned Roe. That left only the plurality and two others justices, including Blackmun, adhering to the shreds of *Roe*. "The distance is but a single vote," Blackmun warned in dissent. "I am 83 years old. I cannot remain on this Court forever."

After *Roe*, Blackmun evinced increasing concern both for "'the right to be let alone'" and women's rights. As the right to bodily privacy that he had emphasized began to influence lower court decisions (see, e.g., *In re Quinlan*, 1976; *Belchertown v. Saikewicz*, 1977), Blackmun attempted to extend it. Dissenting from the Court's endorsement of a Georgia sodomy statute and its implicit condemnation of homosexuality, Blackmun argued, "in a Nation as diverse as ours . . . there may be many 'right' ways of conducting . . . relationships" (*Bowers v. Hardwick*, 1986). He came to view *Roe* as a women's rights case, telling a colloquium that he believed the abortion decisions "broke some of the statutorily imposed fetters on women's freedom traceable in our country to Victorian times." He wrote decisions striking down a state law ending parental obligation for support payments sooner for female than for male children (*Stanton v. Stanton*, 1975), and a federal statute providing aid to families with dependent children only where the mother rather than the father was unemployed (*Califano v. Westcott*, 1979).

His dissent in *Ford Motor Company v. Equal Employment Opportunity Commission* (1982) reflected his disquiet at society's treatment of women, particularly poor women. The EEOC had sued Ford under Title VII of the 1964 Civil Rights Act for refusing to hire specific women at one of its warehouses that had never employed any woman, and the trial court had awarded the women back pay. Justice O'Connor wrote for the Court that because Ford had offered to hire the women when the suit was filed and they had turned down the job, Ford's back pay liability had halted. Blackmun, dissenting, drew from the "real-life concerns of the parties." Rejected by Ford, the women had gone to work for General Motors and had accumulated seniority by the time Ford offered them jobs without it. Had they moved to Ford, Blackmun noted, they would have faced lesser benefits, "lower wages, less eligibility for promotion and transfer, and greater vulnerability to layoffs than persons hired after they were unlawfully refused employment." He quoted from one employee's trial testimony: "I was just wanting that job so bad because you can't, a woman, when you've got three children, I needed the money, and I was wanting the job so bad. I worked so hard. . . . It broke my heart because I knew I had worked so hard." That, said Blackmun, showed how much job security meant and how irrationally the Court had decided.

Blackmun gradually emerged as protective of the rights of those he considered disadvantaged—not only women, but racial minorities, consumers, aliens, and the elderly. He described the Court as "the resort of . . . 'discrete and insular minorit[ies]," and argued that justice required viewing the world from the perspectives of different people. He wrote opinions validating statutory employment preferences for Native Americans in the Bureau of Indian Affairs (*Morton v. Mancari*, 1974) and school desegregation (*Columbus v. Penick*, 1979; *Dayton v. Brinkman*, 1979; *Washington v. Seattle*, 1982), and voted consistently to uphold affirmative action plans. Reacting to a series of 1989 Court decisions that increased the difficulty of proving or acting on discrimination against racial minorities and women, Blackmun wondered "whether the majority still believes that discrimination . . . is a problem in our society, or even remembers that it ever was" (*Ward's Cove v. Atonio*, 1989).

Blackmun played a central role in bringing aliens under the protection of the Fourteenth Amendment. Writing for the Court that states could not condition welfare payments to aliens on a durational residency requirement, he de-

clared that classifications based on alienage are suspect and subject to strict scrutiny (*Graham v. Richardson*, 1971). Aliens needed the protection accorded to a "discrete and insular minority" because communities could exclude them from the political process. States, therefore, could not prohibit aliens from employment in the civil service (*Sugarman v. Dougall*, 1973) or the public schools (*Ambach v. Norwick*, 1979), although they could be barred from the state police (*Foley v. Connelie*, 1978). While he agreed with the Court in *San Antonio v. Rodriguez* (1973) that there was no constitutional right to education, Blackmun argued ten years later that it was such a basic right that a state could not exclude the children of illegal aliens from public schools (*Plyler v. Doe*, 1982). He dissented when the Court upheld an Immigration and Naturalization Service decision denying asylum to a Guatemalan whom a guerrilla organization had attempted to coerce into joining its army (*INS v. Elias-Zacarias*, 1992); when it decided that the government could kidnap a Mexican citizen and bring him to the United States for trial (*United States v. Alvarez-Machain*, 1992); when it held that the INS could detain children, pending deportation proceedings, even when an unrelated adult was willing to house them (*Reno v. Flores*, 1993). When eight justices held in 1993 that neither international nor domestic law prohibited the United States from intercepting Haitian refugees at sea and returning them to Haiti, Blackmun entered an impassioned dissent. He lambasted the "land of refugees and guardian of freedom" for forcing the refugees "back to detention, abuse, and death," and castigated the Court for "strain[ing] to sanction that conduct" (*Sale v. Haitian Centers Council*, 1993).

He remained deferential to criminal justice officials, voting to limit the exclusionary rule (*United States v. Janis*, 1976), seeing no cause of action for a plaintiff whose home had been entered illegally by federal agents and who had been subjected to unreasonable force and a strip search (*Bivens v. Six Unknown Federal Narcotics Agents*, 1971), and holding that there is no due process requirement of juries in juvenile delinquency proceedings (*McKeiver v. Pennsylvania*, 1971). He dissented when the Court upheld use of evidence gathered by a warrantless overflight of a suspect's home by a police helicopter, but did so on the limited ground that the frequency of police overflights for non-search purposes, and therefore the extent to which a reasonable expectation of privacy against such flights existed, had not been established (*Florida v. Riley*, 1989).

His pragmatic, case-by-case approach emphasized facts. Thus he rarely disagreed with criminal justice verdicts. Blackmun, in dissenting from the punishing of an escaped prisoner who presented evidence of continued brutality by guards, declared that the prisoner had fled to "extricate" himself from "hell," and emphasized the "beatings, fires, lack of essential medical care, and sexual atttacks" suffered by prisoners (*U.S. v. Bailey*, 1980). He was unenthusiastic about overturning convictions on procedural grounds, urging instead that greater use be made of Section 1983 of Title 42 of the United States Code, which criminalizes deprivation of civil rights. Disagreeing with a decision that denied injunctive relief for Philadelphia citizens alleging police brutality (*Rizzo v. Goode*, 1976), for example, he argued that the police behavior constituted a pervasive pattern under Section 1983. He also advocated use of Section 1983 to challenge illegal searches (*Allen v. McCurry*, 1980), to act against ineffective public defenders (*Polk v. Dodson*, 1981), and to punish police officers committing perjury (*Briscoe v. LaHue*, 1983).

His factual approach resulted in the gradual alteration of his view of the death penalty's constitutionality. Statistical evidence persuaded him to vote against Georgia's capital sentencing process as radically discriminatory (*McCleskey v. Kemp*, 1987). While he agreed that a mentally retarded person found competent to stand trial could be executed (*Penry v. Lynaugh*, 1989), he dissented from the Court's holding that subjecting minors to execution did not constitute cruel and unusual punishment (*Stanford v. Kentucky*, 1989). Eventually he concluded that the death penalty as applied on the basis of *Furman v. Georgia* (1972) violated the Eighth Amendment, because twenty years' experience had demonstrated that attempts made after Furman to satisfy the "constitutional goal of eliminating arbitrariness and discrimination" in sentencing a convicted criminal to death "can never be

achieved without compromising an equally essential component of fundamental fairness—individualized sentencing" (*Callins v. Collins*, 1994). In an emotional dissent from a denial of certiorari sought by a defendant sentenced to death, Blackmun added that capital punishment was used disproportionately in cases involving members of racial minorities, thereby violating the Equal Protection clause as well, and declared, "From this day forward, I no longer shall tinker with the machinery of death."

The American Society of Law and Medicine gave Blackmun its first Presidents' Award for outstanding contributions to law and medicine (1987), mentioning, among other cases, *Barefoot v. Estelle* (1983). There, explaining that the American Psychiatric Association had declared that subsequent dangerousness was not predictable, he voted against the imposition of capital punishment on the basis of a prediction of future dangerousness by psychiatrists who had not even examined the defendant. With Blackmun goading it, the Court continued to overturn the careless use of psychiatry in capital trials (*Ake v. Oklahoma*, 1985; *Ford v. Wainwright*, 1986). Blackmun also argued, unsuccessfully, that the equal protection clause mandated heightened scrutiny in examining state action that discriminated against the mentally retarded (*Cleburne v. Cleburne*, 1985). He held that someone declared incompetent to stand trial could be placed only in a facility that offered appropriate treatment or training (*Jackson v. Indiana*, 1972). The Court later backed away from this standard, however (see, e.g., *Jones v. United States*, 1983); Blackmun was in dissent.

While placing a high value on speech, Blackmun considered it as subject to a balancing test as any other part of the Constitution. He dissented in *New York Times Co. v. United States* (1971) because the right of the press had not been weighed against possible national security interests. He voted against giving First Amendment protection both to what he labeled the "absurd and immature antic" of a young protester who walked into a courtroom wearing a jacket with the words "Fuck the Draft" (*Cohen v. California*, 1971) and to another young man who "harm[ed] the physical integrity of the flag by wearing it affixed to the seat of his pants" (*Smith v. Goguen*, 1974). While he concurred with the Court in remanding for trial the allegations of students that a school board's decision to remove from their libraries books it labeled "anti-American, anti-Christian, anti-Semitic, and just plain filthy" violated their First Amendment rights, Blackmun emphasized that the case involved "two competing principles of constitutional stature," one being speech and the other, the "properly inculcative purpose" of public education to "'promote civic virtues'" (*Island Trees v. Pico*, 1982). There was no absolute student right to receive ideas, but "certain forms of state discrimination between ideas are improper" and state discrimination against ideas because of their political content was particularly impermissible. For that reason, he joined the Court in striking down a flag desecration statute (*Texas v. Johnson*, 1989). He dissented on First Amendment grounds when the Court said a public indecency statute could be applied to nude dancing in a commercial establishment, because the state had not proved a sufficient interest to balance the right of expression (*Barnes v. Glen Theatre*, 1991). Although he disagreed with the Court's approach in the "hate speech" case of *R.A.V. v. St. Paul* (1992), he concurred in overturning the statute as overly broad.

Blackmun made a major contribution to the law of commercial speech by treating it as subject to the same balancing test. His first commercial speech opinion for the Court overturned the convictions of a Virginia newspaper's director and managing editor, who published a New York City organization's advertisements for low-cost abortions in accredited facilities (*Bigelow v. Virginia*, 1975). The Court had held in *Valentine v. Chrestensen* (1942) that the First Amendment did not apply to commercial speech. In the incremental manner most likely to secure agreement among the justices, Blackmun narrowed the holding in Chrestensen instead of overruling it, saying that the state limitations on the distribution of handbills at issue in Chrestensen were a "reasonable regulation." But the reasonableness of regulation of commercial speech depended on the nature of the speech involved, Blackmun continued, suggesting that the Court adopt a test balancing the right of the speaker against that of the state. As there was nothing fraudulent about

the speech in *Bigelow*, it was unreasonable for the state to punish it.

The following year, in *Virginia Pharmacy Board v. Virginia Citizens Consumer Council, Inc.*, Blackmun overturned a statute prohibiting pharmacists from advertising the prices of prescription drugs. In finding for the consumers who had brought the case, the district court had adopted Blackmun's suggested balancing test and declared that the First Amendment interest in free flow of price information outweighed any state interest. Blackmun's opinion for the Court illuminated both his attitude toward the role of speech in a democratic society and his awareness of those less favored by it. Calling advertising "dissemination of information," he asserted that such information was necessary to enlightened public decision making. The area of democratic decision making was up to the individual: "the particular consumer's interest in the free flow of commercial information . . . may be as keen, if not keener by far, than his interest in the day's most urgent political debate." Financial decisions also might be linked to political choices: "the free flow of commercial information is indispensable . . . to the proper allocation of resources in a free enterprise system . . . [and] to the formation of intelligent opinions as to how that system ought to be regulated or altered." The only interest of the state was the limited one of maintaining professionalism; anything else was "highly paternalistic." Blackmun, unlike the state, assumed "that this information is not in itself harmful, that people will perceive their own best interests only if they are well enough informed, and that the best means to that end is to open the channels of communication rather than to close them." Describing the elderly as the group least physically fit to comparison shop and equally likely to have only "diminished resources," Blackmun added that "those whom the suppression of prescription drug price information hits the hardest are the poor, the sick, and particularly the aged. . . . They are the least able to learn . . . where their scarce dollars are best spent. . . . Information as to who is charging what . . . could mean the alleviation of physical pain or the enjoyment of basic necessities."

Striking down a ban on advertising by lawyers in *Bates v. State Bar* (1977), Blackmun again questioned the state's view of the public as "not sophisticated enough to realize the limitations of advertising." "We view as dubious any justification that is based on the benefits of public ignorance," he wrote, adding that the ban "likely has served to burden access to legal services, particularly for the not-quite-poor and the unknowledgeable." There was, however, a difference between commercial and noncommercial speech. Blackmun recognized the validity of state regulation aimed at commercial speech that did not "serve individual and societal interests in assuring informed and reliable decision-making." Specifically, this meant the state could ban commercial speech that was basically false, deceptive or misleading; proposed illegal activities; established time, place, and manner limitations; or depended on coercive in-person solicitation.

Three years later, the Court edged away from its protection of commercial speech by holding it entitled to no more than an intermediate level of constitutional protection and developing a four-part test by which to judge the legitimacy of governmental regulation (*Central Hudson v. Public Service Commission*, 1980). Blackmun concurred only because the Court overturned the restriction on the speech at issue. He applauded when the Court refused to allow Cincinnati to ban freestanding newsracks that held "commercial handbills" while permitting such newsracks for newspapers (*City of Cincinnati v. Discovery Network*, 1993). The Court held that the differentiation between newspapers and commercial speech was neither neutral nor a reasonable way to reach Cincinnati's stated goals of reducing litter and street obstructions and that it "seriously underestimate[d] the value of commercial speech," suggesting that Cincinnati had misread earlier Court decisions. Blackmun, concerned about the listener rather than the speaker, added that the commercial speech here was listings of homes for sale and of adult education courses, which was information of major value to individuals.

In another First Amendment area, Blackmun's position on church and state reflected an adherence to "Madison's view that both religion and government function best if each remains independent." School districts should not lend instructional materials and equipment to private schools because of the difficulty of distinguishing the sectarian and secular functions (*Wolman v. Walter*, 1977); parochial schools should not be reimbursed for state-mandated testing and reporting services that are "an essential part of the sectarian schools' activities" (*Committee for Public Education v. Regan*, 1980). In a somewhat confusing sequence of cases, he criticized the Court's decision to treat Christmas symbols as neutral holiday decorations as a denial of the symbols' religious meaning (*Lynch v. Donnelly*, 1984) but argued that while a crèche on public property was unconstitutional, a menorah combined with a Christmas tree and a sign saluting liberty was not (*Allegheny v. ACLU*, 1989). He considered the Court wrong to endorse the air force's refusal to allow an Orthodox Jew to wear a yarmulke on duty (*Goldman v. Weinberger*, 1986). In 1987, he expressed concern that the wall between church and state "has been crumbling a little of late . . . particularly at the Supreme Court level." He repeated his concern when the Court validated a state's hiring a translator for a deaf student in a parochial school, arguing both that the Court should have decided the case on statutory rather than constitutional grounds, and that the translator inevitably was propagating religious doctrine (*Zobrest v. Catalina Foothills School District*, 1993).

Blackmun described his approach to judging when he told a law school audience in 1988 that "The Court moves first in one direction and then it shifts to another as it probes new facts, new legislation, and new theories and the issues that emerge from them." His own change of position enabled the Court to shift precisely in that manner in cases concerning federalism.

In 1968, before Blackmun joined the Court, the justices handed down a decision consistent with the post-1936 practice of upholding federal regulatory statutes based on Congressional power over interstate commerce (*Maryland v. Wirtz*). It permitted the federal government to extend the Fair Labor Standards Act (FLSA) to public hospitals, nursing homes, and educational institutions, and, by doing so, to impose federal maximum hour and overtime pay standards on those institutions. In 1976, however, with

Blackmun in the majority, a 5–4 Court reversed Wirtz in *National League of Cities v. Usery*.

Amendments to FLSA had extended federal wage and hour regulations to almost all employees of state and local governments. In striking them down, Justice Rehnquist said that Congress could not tell the states how to make "essential decisions" about "integral governmental functions." "Integral" was not defined, but was described as including functions "essential to [the] separate and independent existence of the states" and "within the area of traditional operations of state and local governments." Blackmun's unhappy concurrence reflected his fear that the decision might have a negative impact on environmental protection, traditionally within the less than zealous jurisdiction of the states. Focusing on "balancing," however, he concluded that the *Usery* doctrine struck the appropriate balance between federal regulatory power and state autonomy.

In 1982, Blackmun joined and wrote for the four *Usery* dissenters in upholding a part of President Jimmy Carter's energy program that limited the autonomy of state utility regulatory commissions (*Federal Energy Regulatory Commission v. Mississippi*). Blackmun asserted that here the federal government was merely utilizing its commerce clause power to preempt conflicting state regulations when in fact it could have preempted the entire field of energy policy. Justice O'Connor, in a dissent Blackmun called "rather loud," attacked the result as inconsistent with *Usery*, "antithetical to the values of federalism, and inconsistent with our constitutional history." Blackmun, unmoved, voted again with the *Usery* dissenters in a case extending the congressional commerce power to regulation of the mandatory retirement ages of state employees, a step designed to avoid discrimination against the elderly (*EEOC v. Wyoming*, 1983). Finally, in *San Antonio v. Garcia* (1985), the Court effectively overruled *Usery*, with Blackmun writing for the five-justice majority.

Garcia involved federal power to set guidelines under FLSA for overtime wages paid by a metropolitan transit authority. Explaining his vote, Blackmun said, "In the years that intervened between the two cases . . . I had become convinced that the 'traditional governmental function' test was unworkable. A little reflection demonstrated that mass transportation was not such a function. Indeed, nearly all transportation systems originally were privately owned." "We find it difficult, if not impossible," he continued, "to identify an organizing principle that places each of the cases in the first group on one side of a line and each of the cases in the second group on the other side." Lower courts attempting "to draw guidance from this model [*Usery*] have proved it both impracticable and doctrinally barren," issuing contradictory holdings. What was shown by *Usery* and *Garcia*, Blackmun later commented, was "how the Court veers from one side to the other or, if one will, takes two steps ahead and one back or one step ahead and two back, depending on the point of view. If the issues were to arise again today, even with facts identical to those of *Garcia*, would the result be the same with the Court as presently constituted?" In other words, the Constitution was not a static entity, the justices were fallible people limited by their own viewpoints but trying to learn from experience and societal needs, and the Court's doctrines inevitably would change again. He announced himself "mildly surprised," and presumably pleased, when *Garcia* was explicitly reaffirmed in *South Carolina v. Baker* (1988).

Implicit in Blackmun's view of the Court is the "constant development of the concepts of Justice" and the continual learning process undergone by the justices. "The Court," he has noted, "is a very special place from which to observe, for one has a view there of what is happening in the courtrooms of America. One sees what people are litigating about. . . . One gets a sense of their desires and of their frustrations, of their hopes and of their great disappointments, of their profound personal concerns, and of what they regard as important and as crucial."

This view of the "real world" appears to have affected Blackmun's evolution as a justice. He has told interviewers that his ideas have not changed. If his fervor for individual rights as against governmental institutions was as great when he joined the Court as in later years, however, that was not apparent either in the way he voted or in his language. In *United States v. Kras* (1973), upholding the constitutionality of bankruptcy filing fees for indigents, he commented that the filing fee—for someone without resources—was "less than the price of a movie and little more than the cost of a pack or two of cigarettes." It is difficult not to see the difference between that language and the empathy he displayed in *Ford v. EEOC* (1982), or *Webster v. Reproductive Health Services* (1989) as reflecting the view from the Court's special window on society. His own description of the alteration of his thinking between *Usery* and *Garcia* suggests the openness to the "real world"—whether of social realities or the gradually unfolding impact of Supreme Court doctrine on lower court decisions—that he has urged on his colleagues and that logically would result in growth and change in any justice's ideas, because the real world is not static.

A justice who is doctrinaire is unlikely to find cases difficult to resolve. Blackmun, however, does. "I probably agonize over cases more than I should," he told an interviewer. He also has referred to the justices as being "locked in combat" over the outcome of cases, "struggling for the fifth vote." Whether it was the need to secure a majority that was responsible for the difference between *Roe*, with its emphasis on physicians' rights, and *Webster*, with its understanding of the agonizing decisions faced by an unhappily pregnant woman, is unclear; the decisive factor could as easily have been the concern that Blackmun has articulated about maintaining a strong center as the Court's makeup has changed, or what he has referred to as the "educational process" that takes place on the Court. Whatever the reason, the difference expressed in his opinions during his first years on the Court and in those that followed is notable.

The one thing that did not change was the need to maintain integrity. "I hope you will always be yourself," he told the Mayo Medical School's 1980 graduating class, defining "yourself" as "human, a little sentimental, possessed of a sense of humor and a sense of humility, not possessed of a pride of authorship or accomplishment." The lack of pride was important. Blackmun may have been thinking of *Roe* when he added, "The Bench

... is no place to grow rich, and it certainly is no place to become popular."

Blackmun announced his retirement on April 6, 1994.

—PHILIPPA STRUM

BIBLIOGRAPHY

Blackmun's most important article, "Section 1983 and Federal Protection of Individual Rights—Will the Statute Remain Alive or Fade Away?" is in 60 *New York University Law Review* (1985). The Harvard Law Review collection in the Harvard Law School Library contains a transcript of Blackmun's "Remarks" at the Franco-American Colloquium on Human Rights (1979). Many of his speeches, reflecting his views of the Court, the problems facing society, and specific areas of the law, have been published in law reviews. Among them are "The First Amendment and Its Religion Clauses," 14 *Nova Law Review* (1989); "Thoughts About Ethics," 24 *Emory Law Journal* (1974); "Some Goals for Legal Education," 1 *Ohio Northern Law Review* (1974); and "Movement and Countermovement," 38 *Drake Law Review* (1989).

A number of journals have published editions containing collections of articles about various facets of Blackmun's work on the Court, particularly in the areas of commercial speech, federalism, aliens, the taxing power, reproductive freedom, and medicine. Two of the more significant are 8 *Hamline Law Review* (1985), and 13 *American Journal of Law & Medicine* (1987). Stephen L. Wasby, "Justice Harry A. Blackmun in the Burger Court," 11 *Hamline Law Review* (1981) is a good if somewhat dated overview of Blackmun's opinions, as is Michael Pollett, "Harry A. Blackmun," in the supplemental volume of Friedman and Israel 6 *Justices* (1978). Burt Neuborne, "Blackmun: Intellectual Openness Elicits Needed Respect for the Judicial Process," *National Law Journal* (18 Feb. 1980), and Norman Dorsen, "A Change in Judicial Philosophy?" *National Law Journal* (18 Feb. 1985), reflect the debate about whether Blackmun's ideas have altered during his years on the Court.

JOHN BLAIR, JR.

BORN 1732, probably Williamsburg, Virginia

NOMINATED to the Court 24 September 1789 by George Washington

TOOK seat 2 February 1790; resigned 25 October 1795

DIED 31 August 1800 in Williamsburg, Virginia

When John Blair, Jr., joined the Supreme Court at the time of its creation by the Judiciary Act of 1789, he brought with him extensive experience on the courts of his native state. Blair, who studied at the Middle Temple in the mid-1750s, entered practice before the general court of the colony of Virginia and also became a legislator. Active in the Revolutionary movement, he was a member of the Virginia convention of May 1776, serving on the committee that framed a new state constitution and declaration of rights. With the establishment of a system of state courts, he sat between 1777 and 1789 at one time or another on the general court, the high court of chancery, and the supreme court of appeals. He also became a Virginia delegate to the federal Constitutional Convention of 1787—one of three, including George Washington and James Madison, who approved the final document—and a Federalist delegate to the Virginia ratifying convention of 1788.

Blair's Virginia experience had already associated him with an early precedent for judicial review. In *Commonwealth v. Caton* (1782) the Virginia court of appeals claimed the right to declare an act of the legislature void if it contradicted the Constitution. In the case under consideration, which concerned the legality of a pardon granted by the lower house of the legislature to convicted Loyalists in alleged violation of the Virginia Treason Act of 1776, the justices concluded, however, that the law was valid and had been violated by the legislators themselves. Blair's opinion avoided a forceful affirmation of the court's right to decide constitutionality that other justices advanced, although he did not explicitly deny it. Rather, in upholding the legal-ity of the statute, he "waved the question" of constitutionality. He was also a signer of a "Remonstrance" by the judges of the court of appeals in 1788 protesting new legislation that added significantly to their duties, including riding circuit. The justices called the law a violation of the independence of the judiciary guaranteed by the state constitution. That experience must have influenced him, as he joined his fellow Supreme Court justices in attempting to alleviate the heavy burden of their service on the federal circuit courts.

Blair was hardly among the more outspoken justices of the Court, being more likely to base his opinions on a close reading of the laws or the Constitution than on sweeping principle. Yet he seems generally to have sided with the early efforts of the Court to establish its independence and the right of judicial review. On April 10, 1792, while sitting on the circuit for the Philadelphia district, he joined in a letter to President Washington protesting the terms of the Pension Act of 1792 requiring circuit judges to certify veterans' pension claims to the secretary of war, who could in turn overrule them. The justices objected to the non-judicial character of the duty and also to the power of an officer of the executive branch to override a judge. Whereas some circuit judges agreed to review the claims as commissioners rather than judges, Blair and his colleagues refused to consider the claim of William Hayburn, who thereupon appealed to Congress. In *Hayburn's Case* (1792), Attorney General Edmund Randolph then sought from the Supreme Court a mandamus commanding the circuit court to proceed on Hayburn's petition. The Supreme Court divided three to three on the motion, with Blair voting in support of Randolph. Although a subsequent revision of the Pension Act ended the necessity of deciding the case, the judges thus gave an early demonstration of their refusal to enforce legislation they regarded as unconstitutional.

The most significant case to come before the Court during Blair's tenure was unquestionably *Chisholm v. Georgia* (1793), in which the

John Blair, Jr.
Artwork by Albert Rosenthal.
Collection of the Supreme Court of the United States.

justices ruled by a vote of 4–1 on a debt claim by the executors of an estate of a citizen of South Carolina against the state of Georgia that a state could be sued in the federal courts by a citizen of another state. The core issue was whether the Constitution extended federal judicial power to suits in all cases, or only if the state was the plaintiff, but ultimately, the issue was that of state sovereignty. The justices wrote their opinions *seriatim*, and while Blair voted with the majority, he avoided the broad claims to the force of popular sovereignty advanced by two of his colleagues and rested his decision on a close reading of the language in Article III, Section 2 of the Constitution. The bold decision stirred strong political opposition and was overturned by the adoption of the Eleventh Amendment, the first instance of such a reversal.

Blair also sat near the end of his service on the Court on *Penhallow v. Doane's Administrators* (1795), a suit for damages that tested the right of the federal courts to assume jurisdiction over the objection of the state of New Hampshire in a case that had originally been decided on appeal in the defunct court of appeals under the Articles of Confederation. In ruling against New Hampshire, the Court again advanced its strongly nationalist views, and Blair again agreed, while remaining far less explicit than his colleague, William Patterson.

Blair's health was by now declining—he had complained on one occasion of "a rattling distracting noise in my head"—and he soon retired to his home in Williamsburg, where he lived until his death.

—THAD W. TATE

BIBLIOGRAPHY

For Blair's court decisions, Julius Goebel, Jr., *History of the Supreme Court of the United States, Antecedents and Beginnings to 1801* (1971), is the fullest account. Frederick Horner, *The History of the Blair, Banister, and Braxton Families Before and After the Revolution* (1898), reprints several personal letters of Blair, some of them documenting the onset of the illness that led to his retirement.

SAMUEL M. BLATCHFORD

BORN 9 March 1820, New York City
NOMINATED to the Court 13 March 1882
    by Chester A. Arthur
TOOK seat 3 April 1882
DIED 7 July 1893 in Newport, Rhode Island

Born into a wealthy New York family with strong connections to the state's financial community, Samuel Blatchford entered Columbia College at age thirteen, graduated in 1837, and gained admission to the bar in 1842. As a lawyer, Blatchford achieved a reputation as a specialist in admiralty law and, after 1852, as a reporter of federal court decisions. His tireless efforts in compiling federal case law, combined with his loyalty to the Republican party, earned Blatchford a place on the federal bench after the Civil War. He served first as a judge of the southern district of New York (1867–1872), and later as a judge on the court of appeals for the second circuit (1872–1882). With fifteen years of federal judicial experience, the moderate and noncontroversial Blatchford was a logical choice for the Supreme Court vacancy created by the resignation of Ward Hunt. The Senate approved his nomination on a voice vote.

Although the author of more than his share of opinions, Blatchford received little attention for most of his work on the Court. In the early part of his tenure, many of his decisions involved admiralty, patents, bankruptcy, and copyrights—not the stuff of landmark cases. Nevertheless, his achievements were notable, particularly in admiralty and patent law. In *Ex parte Boyer* (1884), for example, Blatchford extended the admiralty jurisdiction to canals. Meanwhile, his decisions in *Dobson v. Hartford Carpet Co.* (1884), and *Dobson v. Dornan* (1886), both of which involved patents for carpet design granted to Dobson, established rules for the infringement of design. After the second *Dobson* case, Congress passed legislation in this area, adopting many of the principles laid down by Blatchford.

As a member of the Court during the 1880s, Blatchford also took part in a number of cases involving the civil rights of African Americans and Chinese immigrants. Both groups were the subject of important federal legislation during the late nineteenth century, and Blatchford's record on such matters—like that of the Court's—was a mixed one. On the one hand, in the *Civil Rights Cases* (1883), Blatchford voted with the eight-person majority in striking down the Civil Rights Act of 1875 as an unconstitutional attempt to outlaw discrimination in privately-owned public accommodations. Moreover, in a case involving a group of Chinese aliens, *Baldwin v. Franks* (1887), Blatchford was part of a seven-justice majority that refused to interpret a treaty between the United States and China so as to protect foreign nationals from violence.

On the other hand, Blatchford supported black voting rights when, as part of a unanimous Court in *Ex parte Yarbrough* (1884), he voted to uphold Congressional measures penalizing those who conspired to prevent African Americans from exercising the franchise. Blatchford similarly stood for the protection of civil rights in *Yick Wo v. Hopkins* (1886), where he joined the rest of the justices in applying the Fourteenth Amendment's equal protection clause to a group of Chinese laundry owners, and in *United States v. Jung Ah Lung* (1888), where he wrote the majority opinion granting the release of an illegally detained Chinese immigrant.

Like his stands on civil rights issues, Blatchford's opinions in cases involving the Bill of Rights were also uneven. In *Auffmordt v. Hedden* (1890) he refused to extend the Seventh Amendment's guarantee of trial by jury to decisions of customs appraisers regarding the value of imports, and in *O'Neil v. Vermont* (1892), he held that the Eighth Amendment's ban on cruel and unusual punishment did not apply to the states.

Nevertheless, his most notable opinion regarding the Bill of Rights, *Counselman v. Hitchcock* (1892), granted extensive protection to individuals under the Fifth Amendment's self-incrimination proviso. Counselman, a grain commission dealer called to testify concerning violations of the Interstate Commerce Act, had refused to answer questions involving illegal rates he may have received for grain shipments. Although an act of Congress provided that no testimony by an individual could be used against that person in such a proceeding, Counselman thought the statute an insufficient protection against self-incrimination and refused to testify. After lower federal courts held him in contempt, Counselman appealed to the Supreme Court. Writing for the Court, Blatchford accepted Counselman's claim and broadly construed the self-incrimination clause. Rejecting the opposition's argument that the Fifth Amendment applied only to cases in which the witness himself was on trial—and thus, not to Counselman's case—Blatchford held that the amendment extended to all criminal proceedings. Moreover, he also believed that the congressional self-incrimination statute offered inadequate protection of Counselman's rights. "It is quite clear that legislation cannot abridge a constitutional privilege," Blatchford wrote, "and that it cannot replace or supply one, at least unless it is so broad as to have the same extent in scope and effect." In *Counselman*, Blatchford stood for an expansive interpretation of individual rights under the Fifth Amendment.

More significant than Blatchford's interpretation of the Bill of Rights, however, was his view of economic liberty. After the Reconstruction period, state and federal courts throughout the nation gradually began to interpret the due process clause of the Fourteenth Amendment as a guarantee of certain fundamental rights, often associated with an individual's use and pursuit of property. "Substantive due process," as it came to be called, became the means by which courts struck down regulatory measures designed to adjust the operation of the marketplace in the public interest. Blatchford's opinion in *Chicago, Milwaukee & St. Paul Railway Company v. Minnesota* (1890) was the first instance in which the Supreme Court used the due process clause to invalidate a state railroad regulation.

The case involved the Minnesota legislature's establishment of a commission charged with setting equal and reasonable rates for railroad transportation within the state. Under the

law, rates established by the commission were "final and conclusive," and not subject to judicial inquiry. The Chicago, Milwaukee & St. Paul Railway Company's refusal to comply with the commission's rates launched a dispute over the Minnesota law's constitutionality that ended up in the Supreme Court. Attorneys for the railway contended that the regulation of rates violated fundamental rights, including the right to obtain the benefits from the use of one's property. Counsel for Minnesota, on the other hand, emphasized a line of precedents, including the Supreme Court's decision in *Munn v. Illinois* (1877), that sustained state legislatures' power to establish reasonable rates for transportation.

Writing for a 6–3 majority, Blatchford concluded that the Minnesota statute, because it offered no check on the commission's rate-setting authority, conflicted with the Constitution. "Although the railroad company is forbidden to establish rates that are not equal and reasonable," he wrote, "there is no power in the courts to stay the hands of the commission, if it chooses to establish rates that are unequal and unreasonable." Lacking provisions for judicial investigation into the reasonableness of rates, the statute creating the commission stripped railway companies of their property without due process of law. "[The law] deprives the company of its right to a judicial investigation, by due process of law . . . ," Blatchford wrote, "and substitutes . . . the action of a railroad commission which, in view of the powers conceded to it by the state court, cannot be regarded as clothed with judicial functions." The question of reasonableness, Blatchford believed, was a judicial one, and, by granting the authority to establish rates to a commission without judicial investigation, the Minnesota statute failed to pass constitutional muster.

To contemporary observers, Blatchford's opinion in *Chicago, Milwaukee & St. Paul* seemed to overrule *Munn v. Illinois*, where the Court had upheld an Illinois law regulating rates for grain elevators, and appeared to signal the Court's willingness to protect property from interference by state legislatures. However, just two years after he held that the due process clause could be used against state regulation, the enigmatic Blatchford, in *Budd v. New York* (1892), steered the Court back toward an acceptance of regulatory measures. The New York statute at issue in *Budd*, like the law in *Munn*, provided for maximum rates for grain elevators. Although counsel urged that the New York legislature's establishment of reasonable rates violated the principles enunciated in *Chicago, Milwaukee & St. Paul*, Blatchford held otherwise. Following the *Munn* precedent, he concluded that the New York law did not constitute a violation of due process. Blatchford explained the apparent contradiction between his opinions in *Chicago, Milwaukee & St. Paul* and *Budd* by making a factual distinction between the two cases: in *Budd* the legislature itself determined reasonable rates, whereas in *Chicago, Milwaukee & St. Paul* a legislatively created commission had done so. "What was said in the opinion in [*Chicago, Milwaukee & St. Paul*] as to the question of the reasonableness of the rate of charge being one for judicial investigation," he concluded, "had no reference to a case where the rates are prescribed directly by the legislature."

Blatchford's murky explanation of his behavior in *Budd* and his generally incongruous record should not detract from the contributions he made as a member of the Court. Among the most steady and dependable of justices, Blatchford wrote 430 majority opinions in a mere eleven years on the Court. He wrote only two dissents, a fact that earned him a reputation as a consensus-builder. Overall, Blatchford served admirably in a particularly crucial period of the Court's history, when the justices were only beginning to come to grips with the massive social changes wrought by the nation's transition to industrial capitalism. Blatchford did not live long enough to witness the Court's continuing struggle to adapt the Constitution to modern American society.

—TIMOTHY S. HUEBNER

BIBLIOGRAPHY

There is no biography of Blatchford, only brief sketches of his life in scattered reference volumes. The best such sketch is by Arnold Paul in Friedman and Israel, 2 *Justices* 1401. The most useful discussion of Blatchford's most famous opinion is James W. Ely, Jr., "The Railroad Question Revisited: *Chicago, Milwaukee & St. Paul Railway v. Minnesota* and Constitutional Limits on State Regulations," 12 *Great Plains Quarterly* 121 (1992).

Joseph Bradley
Photograph by Matthew Brady.
Collection of the Supreme Court of the United States.

JOSEPH BRADLEY

BORN 14 March 1813, Berne, New York

NOMINATED to the Court 7 February 1870
    by Ulysses S. Grant; confirmed 21

TOOK seat March 1870

DIED 22 January 1892 in Washington, D.C.

The oldest of twelve children, Joseph Bradley was enrolled at Rutgers College in 1833 through the intervention of a former teacher. He graduated in three years, and was later described by one scholar as "a desperately serious young man." Shortly after graduation, he undertook to study law—largely with himself as the instructor. Bradley appears to have been rigorous in his preparation. One entry in his notes cites five different sources: one in Latin, two in French, and two in English. Admitted to the New Jersey Bar in 1839, for the next thirty years Bradley centered his life and legal career around Newark, New Jersey. By the Civil War era, he had become a prominent attorney, well-known among the leaders of Newark's business and legal community.

In 1862, Bradley agreed to run for Congress as a conservative Republican. He lost, but given some of his later opinions as a Supreme Court justice, his position on racial integration as a candidate is of interest. Like many Republicans, including Lincoln, Bradley had no difficulty supporting the end of slavery while at the same time foreseeing little change in racial attitudes toward blacks. It was perfectly consistent to be pro-Union, anti-slavery, and anti-black—all at the same time. Candidate Bradley's views would be echoed by Justice Bradley's decision in the *Civil Rights Cases* twenty-one years later. A strong supporter of Ulysses Grant in the 1868 presidential election—indeed, he was a presidential elector pledged to Grant—Bradley was nominated to the Supreme Court in 1870, and served on that bench for almost twenty-two years.

Although this essay focuses on Bradley's judicial career, brief attention should be given to the most controversial non-judicial episode during his tenure on the Court—his role as a member of the electoral commission in the disputed 1876 presidential election. With Congress deadlocked over the counting of the electoral votes, the solution appeared to be a fifteen-member commission to consist of five members apiece from the House, the Senate, and the Supreme Court. With fourteen commissioners divided equally between the two parties, it was widely assumed that Bradley would cast the deciding vote, and indeed he did. Bradley voted with his fellow Republicans on every question before them, giving Rutherford Hayes sufficient votes to become president.

Possibly because Bradley's views on racial relations were virtually identical with those of the southern Democrats (all the Democratic senators who voted on his confirmation had supported him), these party members may have assumed that he would vote with them. Instead, he did what every other member of the commission did: voted along usual party lines. In so doing, however, he may have switched his vote after two old friends, both Republicans and strong supporters of his judicial selection, allegedly visited him the evening before the important vote was to be taken. Whatever actually happened will probably never be known, but in the face of Democratic denunciation, Bradley maintained a blend of olympian aloofness, self-righteousness, and self-pity; his dignity, if not his integrity, remained substantially intact.

Bradley's generation fought the Civil War, his party framed the Fourteenth Amendment, and his Court formulated the new enactment's first judicial interpretation. It took the form of a major decision handed down in 1873. The *Slaughterhouse Cases* involved a group of New Orleans butchers challenging a state statute that confined all New Orleans butchering to a specific area, and mandated further that it be done on the premises of a particular meat-packing corporation. Disgruntled if not destitute, the butchers invoked the Fourteenth Amendment, claiming that the statute denied them their right to pursue a lawful calling and thus deprived them of their liberty and property in contravention of the new provision. Speaking for a bare majority, Justice Samuel Miller rejected this contention, insisting that the butchers had to seek relief from either state court or state legislature; the Fourteenth Amendment had been intended to deal with the ex-slave, not the general population. It did not, in other words, apply to their case.

Bradley strongly disagreed. The statute restricting butchering to the premises of a favored company was "onerous, unreasonable, arbitrary, and unjust." The butchers were indeed deprived of their liberty as well as property, without due process of law. "Their right of choice is a portion of their liberty; their occupation is their property." Moreover, although ex-slaves may have been the primary cause of the Amendment, "its language [was] general, embracing all citizens, and ... was purposely so expressed." Bradley reiterated these views in two later decisions, *Bartemeyer v. Iowa* (1873), and *Butchers' Union Slaughter-House et al. v. Crescent City Live-Stock Landing and Slaughter-House Co.* (1884). In spite of his repeated emphasis on the Fourteenth Amendment's scope, however, he seems to have been somewhat selective in the callings to which he attached the amendment's protection.

In the case of *Bradwell v. Illinois* (1872), Bradley's Court considered the efforts of a woman, Myra Bradwell, to gain admittance to the Illinois Bar so that she could practice law. She argued, not unreasonably, that the Fourteenth Amendment prevented Illinois from abridging her "privileges and immunities," one of which was surely her right to practice her chosen calling. The Court, Bradley included, disagreed. Since Bradley had vigorously emphasized the contrary in the *Slaughterhouse Cases*, the question of his inconsistency arises. If a group of butchers had a constitutionally protected right to practice their profession, why did not a woman qualified to practice law have a similar privilege?

In a concurring opinion, Bradley conceded no inconsistency whatsoever. Law had to reflect nature, and in the "nature of things it is not every citizen of every age, sex, and condition that is qualified for every calling and position." One

needed to consider "the peculiar characteristics, destiny, and mission of woman." After all, he intoned, the chief purpose of woman was "to fulfill the noble and benign offices of wife and mother. This is the law of the creator, and the rules of civil society must be adapted to the general constitution of things, and cannot be based upon exceptional cases." Perhaps the best assessment of Bradley's concurrence in *Bradwell* came from a writer in the Boston *Daily Advertiser*, who observed that "Judge Bradley's opinion seemed to cause no little amusement upon the bench and on the Bar."

In terms of civil rights, Bradley appears to have placed certain categories of rights higher than others. Indeed, perhaps he can be accused of suffering from a hardening of the categories, as well. In 1872, he dissented from the decision in *Blyew v. United States*, a case involving a brutal murder of an elderly, blind black woman whose death had been witnessed by several of her relatives. Kentucky law, however, forbade a black to testify at the trial of a white defendant. Federal authorities sought, therefore, to move the case into federal court. In an opinion that seems less than persuasive, Justice William Strong blocked the transfer, arguing that the federal law applied only to persons "affected by the cause," and this limitation did not include witnesses. Bradley dissented, and denounced Strong's reasoning. The result of the decision for potential witnesses "is to brand them with a badge of slavery ... to expose them to wanton insults and fiendish assaults ... to leave their lives, their families, and their property unprotected by law."

Passage of the 1875 Civil Rights Act only three years later inspired a very different response from Bradley. The new statute mandated integration in certain public establishments such as restaurants and theaters. The right to expect the law to protect one's ability to testify as a witness was very different and far more important, according to Bradley, than a desire on the part of blacks to sit next to whites while dining or at a theater. The former was a vital component of one's privileges as a citizen, the other merely a matter of social preference. In his copybook, Bradley wrote of the new law that "surely Congress cannot guarantee to the colored people admission to every place of gathering and amusement. To deprive white people of the right of choosing their own company would be to introduce another kind of slavery." Blacks were entitled to "freedom and all legal and essential privileges. . . . [But] the antipathy of race cannot be crushed and annihilated by legal enactment."

Given these views, one should not be surprised to read Bradley's opinion for the Court in the *Civil Rights Cases* (1883), in which he merely reiterated sentiments he had long held. The Fourteenth Amendment, he insisted, applied only to state action; private discrimination seemed perfectly appropriate to him. Here, Justice Bradley echoed in 1883 what congressional candidate Bradley had asserted in 1862. Moreover, every member of the Court who had participated in *Slaughterhouse* ten years before agreed with him.

Conceding that *Bradwell* and the *Civil Rights Cases* are certainly no tribute to Bradley as a civil libertarian, one of his later decisions is of much greater positive significance. In the landmark case of *Boyd v. United States* (1886), Bradley explored the scope of the Fourth Amendment and its relationship to self-incrimination. He rejected the argument "that the seizure of a man's private books and papers to be used in evidence against him is substantially different from compelling him to be a witness against himself." Anticipating later constitutional doctrine, he claimed that "a compulsory production of the private books and papers of the owner . . . compel[s] him to be a witness against himself, within the meaning of the Fifth Amendment . . . and is the equivalent of a search and seizure—within the meaning of the Fourth Amendment." Moreover, the scope and motive for the search was irrelevant.

If Bradley seemed bound to his times in matters of race and gender, he demonstrated flexibility and creativity in the areas of railroad regulation and interpretation of the commerce clause. Although he had been a very successful railroad lawyer representing the Camden and Amboy Railroad, widely regarded as one of the most notorious contributors to "political pressure and bribery," as a judge, his independent attitude toward these common carriers was noteworthy. Bradley strongly supported the Court's refusal to use the Fourteenth Amendment to block state regulation of private corporations—such as railroads or grain elevators—in the public interest. The economic clout of railroad corporations, he insisted, should not permit them to "abdicate their essential duties."

Writing a private note to Chief Justice Morrison Waite concerning the forthcoming decision in *Munn v. Illinois* (1876), one that went against the proprietor of a grain elevator objecting to state regulation, Bradley denounced the railroads in language that seems unusually harsh. Perhaps he had in mind his long experience as director and counsel for the Camden and Amboy. Bradley persuaded his chief to hold that when such a corporation "becomes a matter of public consequence so as to affect the whole public and to become a common charge, it is subject to legislative regulation and control." He insisted that there are "in this country no more absolute monopolies of public service than [the railroads] are. The public stands on no equality with them. . . . They have every thing in their own hands. . . . They impose a common charge of greater value to themselves and burden to the public than any other which exists in the present age."

When interpreting the scope of the commerce clause, Bradley demonstrated impressive sensitivity toward the need of an effective federalism. He explored with skill and insight the controversial boundaries between federal regulation of interstate commerce and the state taxing power, frequently upholding the former at the expense of the latter. In *Robbins v. Shelby County Taxing District* (1887), for example, he stated for the Court that "the United States are but one country, and are and must be subject to one system of regulations, and not to a multitude of systems. . . . It seems to be forgotten that the people of this country are citizens of the United States, as well as of the individual states, and that they have some rights under the Constitution and laws of the former independent of the latter, and free from any interference or restraint from them."

Of Grant's four appointments, Bradley was undoubtedly the strongest in intellect and learning. Familiar with the American, English, and Continental legal systems, he brought added insights to his decisions through practical experience in the business world, as well as a familiarity with other fields, including mathematics, philosophy, and natural sciences. Thus Bradley was equally at home when expounding on the appropriate, if not invariably complex, methods for calculating the earnings of a railroad, or discussing the intricacies of patent litigation. He reveled in tracking legal doctrines back through a variety of sources, and sometimes his decisions became vehicles for extended research. In an 1890 opinion, for example, Bradley traced an obscure legal doctrine back to the Pandects of Justinian and cited Latin, French, and Spanish sources, including a footnote in French!

In company with other tough-minded and able judges such as Samuel Miller or Stephen Field, Bradley more than held his own. Miller recalled of Bradley that "if there is a principle on which a case can be decided that no one else has thought of, it has for that reason a charm for him." Nevertheless, Miller believed that given "some allowance for eccentricity, he is a useful and valuable man on the bench." A Rutgers classmate noted that as with "most men who resemble him in the possession of logical power and habit, he had little or no deference for the mere opinion of others." Bradley, he added, had a compulsion "not only to be, but to know."

Bradley, wrote one contemporary, "was amusingly petulant—naturally eccentric; and he had stimulated eccentricity by its indulgence throughout his life." In 1890, an observer described Justice Bradley as "a little dried-up anatomy of a man. . . . His skin hangs in wrinkles and all of his fat has long since gone to figures and judicial decisions. He is seventy-seven years old, but there is a fair chance for his lasting at least twenty-three years longer. There is not much of him to die, and when his soul is disembodied it will not be much freer than it is now."

How can one assess his twenty-two years as a Supreme Court justice? Each generation determines for itself judicial greatness, but there is no doubt that Bradley had superb legal qualifications and was an outstanding technician of the law. Self-taught, he brought to his decisions a seasoned practicality in business affairs. Indeed, his greatest opinions in terms of influence appear to have been in the field of commercial regulation. Further, his writings indicate that Bradley passionately believed both in progress and the perfectibility of man.

Yet Bradley could not translate his broad faith in this perfectibility of man into sound judicial doctrine that went beyond gender and race. In other fields of the law that later generations have considered more important than interstate commerce, he seems to have been unable to transcend the limits of his own time. The truly great judge is somehow able to do that, by "nudging" the future rule of law into some sort of shape that goes beyond the current role of law—through decisions which have retained validity, vitality, and significance for our own time, holdings that continue to influence American constitutionalism.

Bradley, according to Leon Friedman, "had little of the skepticism and tolerance of a Holmes, and came to a conclusion about a law or legal rule because it was the *right* law or rule under the circumstances, and not because imperfect men should be allowed to bungle their way freely within broad limits of government." More than one hundred years have passed since Bradley's death. Yet, the assessment of his life and career offered by the *Washington Post* in 1892 remains valid and accurate. He was "a man of profound and varied learning, legal acumen, and moral rectitude." Beyond this, deponent sayeth not.

—JONATHAN LURIE

BIBLIOGRAPHY

Bradley's papers are housed in the New Jersey Historical Society. While there are some court-related materials among them, the entire collection appears to have been "edited" by his son before donation to the society. There is no extant scholarly biographical study of Bradley, but Charles Fairman contributed three articles which, when taken together, may make such a biography unnecessary. See "Mr. Justice Bradley's Appointment to the Supreme Court and the Legal Tender Cases," parts 1 and 2, 54 *Harvard Law Review* 977, 1128 (1941); "The Education of a Justice: Justice Bradley and Some of His Colleagues," 1 *Stanford Law Review* 217 (1949); and "What Makes a Great Justice? Mr. Justice Bradley and the Supreme Court, 1870–1892," 30 *Boston University Law Review* 46 (1950). See also Leon Friedman, "Joseph Bradley," in Friedman and Israel, 2 *Justices* 1181. An attempt to integrate much of the existing scholarship on Bradley may be seen in Jonathan Lurie, "Mr. Justice Bradley: A Reassessment," 16 *Seton Hall Law Review* 343 (1986).

Louis Dembitz Brandeis
Photograph by Harris and Ewing.
Collection of the Supreme Court of the United States.

Louis Dembitz Brandeis

Born 13 November 1856, Louisville,
   Kentucky

Nominated to the Court 28 January 1916
   by Woodrow Wilson

Took seat 5 June 1916; retired 13 February
   1939

Died 5 October 1941 in Washington, D.C.

When Louis Brandeis was nominated to the Supreme Court in 1916, his wife wrote to his brother, "I tell Louis, if he is going to retire, he is certainly doing it with a burst of fireworks." Although Brandeis would become the first Jew to sit on the Court, the fireworks resulted less from his religion than from the political philosophy and the approach to law for which he had already become famous. Both the philosophy and the approach were considered unacceptably radical by influential elements of the business and legal communities. From their point of view, Brandeis's opponents were correct: when Brandeis took his seat on the Court after a fierce and bitter confirmation process, he quickly demonstrated that his ideology and jurisprudence would illuminate his decisions as a justice. In doing so, they also permanently altered American constitutional jurisprudence.

Brandeis graduated at the top of his class (1877) at Harvard Law School, where Christopher Columbus Langdell had introduced the case method and taught that law was a dynamic entity based on social realities. When Brandeis went on to practice law in Boston, he insisted on understanding not only his clients' immediate problems but the economic and, occasionally, the political context in which they arose. He did so, he told a young associate, because "knowledge of the decided cases and of the rules of logic cannot alone make a great lawyer. . . . The controlling force is the deep knowledge of human necessities. . . . The duty of a lawyer today is not that of a solver of legal conundrums: he is indeed a counsellor at law." He noted in a memorandum on "The Practice of The Law" that a lawyer was "far more likely to impress clients by knowledge of facts than by knowledge of law."

By 1916, Brandeis had impressed enough clients to support a highly lucrative law firm. He had also made an impact on a variety of leaders in public life and on the public itself. The media referred to him as the "People's Attorney" because of his involvement in movements for social justice: legalization of unions, women's suffrage, maximum hours and minimum wage legislation, and use of natural resources for the public rather than the private good. He had fought with some success against the trusts that controlled much of America's economy. His investigation of the insurance industry resulted in his invention of savings bank life insurance. He earned a reputation for integrity by engaging in most of his battles without pay, and through his continual criticism of government and corporate corruption. He campaigned vigorously for Woodrow Wilson in the 1912 presidential election; in fact, Arthur Link, Wilson's chief biographer, has attributed Wilson's New Freedom platform to Brandeis's economic thought. Such pre-Court battles both reflected and shaped Brandeis's political ideas, which in turn underlay his judicial opinions. As Paul Freund, one of his law clerks, commented, "It is hardly likely that anyone came to the Supreme Court with a more closely articulated set of convictions than those which Brandeis held."

The opinions he wrote as a justice were logical extensions of Brandeis's ideas about the nature of the democratic state and the role of the individual within it. In the ideal society, government enabled individuals to reach their full potential as self-fulfilled members of a just community, and individuals willingly assumed their civic responsibilities. Development of human potential required that each individual have access to ideas, a concept given concrete form in the legal doctrine of freedom of speech and press. Human development also depended on the leisure to learn about potential public policies and associate with others for discussion of public matters, and in the opportunity to participate in the processes through which the policies were determined. A democratic state responsive to the electorate was one in which neither economic nor political institutions were large enough to make individual beliefs irrelevant or to stultify experimentation. To Brandeis, federalism was more than a historically useful system that had enabled thirteen colonies to unite as a nation; it was a productive mechanism for experimentation with new governmental policies. He insisted on each citizen's civic responsibility and was adamant about education, which continued in one way or another throughout life, as a precondition for a democratic electorate.

Brandeis's sociological jurisprudence followed logically from his democratic philosophy. Law represented the will of the people, which in turn reflected their perception of society's needs. As the needs changed, so should the laws; this included the Constitution, which judges had an obligation to read according to current societal necessities. Societal needs could be ascertained only by examining facts, either in legislative hearings or by evaluating data accumulated during societal experimentation. He scorned the late nineteenth- and early twentieth-century attorneys who made themselves servants of corporations, telling the Harvard Ethical Society in 1905 that his vision of the ideal lawyer was drawn from the early United States, when "nearly every great lawyer was . . . a statesman; and nearly every statesman, great or small, was a lawyer," holding "a position of independence, between the wealthy and the people, prepared to curb the excesses of either." The role of lawyers in a democratic polity was to defend legislative social experiments by providing judges with sufficient factual material for a determination that the experiments constituted reasonable responses to societal problems.

Brandeis had done precisely that in the innovative and almost immediately famous "Brandeis brief" he and his sister-in-law, Josephine Goldmark, prepared for the 1908 case of *Muller v. Oregon*. Faced with a challenge to an Oregon statute limiting the maximum number of hours women could work for pay, Brandeis and Goldmark presented the Supreme Court with two pages of traditional legal argumentation and more than 100 pages of factual data demonstrating the deleterious effect of overly long hours on women's health and the well-being of their families. After winning the case, Brandeis and Goldmark went on to use similar and equally successful arguments to defend other statutes establishing maximum hours and minimum wages for women. Brandeis realized that although it would negate his gender-based argument in *Muller*, the same approach should be taken toward hours and wage legislation for men, and he therefore helped secure publication of Goldmark's careful collections of data supporting that argument. In 1916, they labored for six months on a brief defending an Oregon law setting maximum hours for men, a case that was turned over to Felix Frankfurter when Brandeis was appointed to the Supreme Court (*Bunting v. Oregon*, 1917).

Brandeis is perhaps best known for his judicial opinions in the areas of social experimentation, the size of economic and political institutions, and civil liberties, but his reputation also lies in part on his advocacy of limited judicial intervention in policy making. He did not ignore the judicial proprieties in pursuit of his goals for the country. Judicial restraint was a key element of his sociological jurisprudence. It was as undemocratic and unwise for judges to make social policy as it was for them to jump into cases when matters were not ripe for decision. When Arizona sued to prevent the construction of Boulder Dam and the possible diversion of water to California, for example, Brandeis pointed out that construction of the dam had not yet begun and so there was no need for the Court to decide whether waters that might never be taken from Arizona could legitimately be diverted (*Arizona v. California*, 1931). If a party based its case on a right new to American law, as happened when the Associated Press claimed that it had a property right in its dispatches, Brandeis, in dissent, objected to the Court's usurpation of the legislative function by creating and legitimizing a largely undefined right (*International News Service v. Associated Press*, 1918). Similarly, he dissented from the Court's declaration that stock dividends were a category of untaxable property; that was up to a legislature to decide (*Eisner v. Macomber*, 1920).

His most explicit statement about the limits of judicial review came in *Ashwander v. TVA* (1936), where the power of the Tennessee Valley Authority to construct the Wheeler Dam was challenged by a stockholder's suit. Although Brandeis concurred in the Court's holding that the project was constitutionally valid, he stated that he would not have reached the constitutional issue because the plaintiffs had no real standing to sue. He drew on earlier Court decisions to list the restrictive guidelines he believed the Court ought to follow in dealing with constitutional questions: declining to hear "a friendly, non-adversary, proceeding," a case where the complainant has suffered no real injury, or one in which a complainant challenged a statute from which he had benefited; making no decision on constitutional grounds if others were available; and issuing rules of constitutional law that were as narrow as possible.

As a lawyer, he had fulminated against the courts' interpretation of the Fourteenth Amendment's due process clause to promulgate what he considered judge-made doctrines such as liberty of contract in order to strike down social policy enacted by state legislatures. As a judge, he maintained his insistence on judicial restraint, even when he disagreed with the legislative experiment at issue. In 1932, the Court struck down an Oklahoma law forbidding any new ice company to open without first acquiring a certificate of public convenience and necessity from the state (*New State Ice Co. v. Liebmann*). The rationale was that licensing would minimize the higher consumer costs caused by wasteful duplication of plants and delivery service. Justice Sutherland, however, speaking for the Court, said that the ice business was not "affected with a public interest" and that all the Oklahoma statute did was create the possibility of monopoly.

Brandeis had fought against monopoly and the suppression of competition as a lawyer. He nonetheless dissented from the Court's decision in the Oklahoma case and wrote fourteen heavily footnoted pages to show that social conditions in Oklahoma might well have led the legislature to believe that excessive competition had added to the impact of the Depression on unemploy-

ment and low prices. He indicated that he disliked the law, asserting that most people "realize that failure to distribute widely the profits of industry has been a prime cause of our present plight." But his own view, or that of "most" people, was irrelevant to him as a justice; Oklahoma's experiment was rational, and the Court ought to permit it to continue.

Felix Frankfurter commented that Brandeis believed that the Constitution "provided for the future partly by not forecasting it and partly by the generality of its language." The Constitution, in Brandeis's eyes, was designed to be flexible. It was as amenable to legislative experimentation as to judicial imagination, and Brandeis frequently reminded his colleagues of John Marshall's statement in *McCulloch v. Maryland* (1819) that "We must never forget that it is a constitution we are expounding." He wrote in *New State Ice*: "There must be power in the States and the Nation to remould, through experimentation, our economic practices and institutions to meet changing social and economic needs. To stay experimentation in things social and economic is a grave responsibility [which might be] fraught with serious consequences to the nation." He noted his belief that federalism enabled states to serve as laboratories for social change, and urged the Court not to hinder federalism by "erect[ing] our prejudices into legal principles." "If we would guide by the light of reason," he declared, "we must let our minds be bold."

One of Brandeis's bêtes noires was the Court's 1842 decision in *Swift v. Tyson* that federal courts were not bound by state common law, but could follow their own doctrines. Brandeis had joined fellow justice Oliver Wendell Holmes's campaign to overrule the decision, which enabled businesses to circumvent local law by litigating in federal rather than state courts. *Swift* violated Brandeis's belief in federalism, accountability of economic power, and state experimentation with controlling economic institutions. At the successful conclusion of a lengthy campaign, Brandeis was able to write the Court's opinion in *Erie Railroad Company v. Tompkins* (1938), negating *Swift* by declaring that whenever a state's laws were at issue, federal courts hearing cases in the state would be bound by the decisional rules of the state's highest court. On the same day, he wrote for the Court in *Hinderliter v. LaPlata Water Co.* (1938), a case concerning an interstate compact, that when cases involved only federal issues and state decisional rules would be inappropriate, decisions were to be made under federal common law. He thus protected federal supremacy while retaining an emphasis on federalism and state power for experimentation.

These themes, linked closely to his distaste for bigness, ran through many of his opinions. His first dissent, in *New York Central Railroad v. Winfield* (1917), rejected the Court's declaration that the Federal Employers Liability Act filled the field of compensation for injuries to interstate railroad employees. Brandeis refused to read the act as reflecting congressional intent to preclude state protection for workers, because "it is the state which is both primarily and ultimately concerned with the care of the injured. . . . Upon the state falls the financial burden of dependency, if provision be not otherwise made. . . . Upon the state also rests, under our dual system of government, the duty owed to the individual, to avert misery and promote happiness so far as possible." Clearly, he perceived the state as a positive institution that could increase individual happiness by alleviating economic injustices.

In *Winfield,* he signaled the way he would approach cases, discussing "world experience in dealing with industrial accidents" and relying on facts to bolster his argument that it was reasonable to believe that further compensation was necessary. When the Court overturned a state statute prohibiting employment agencies from charging workers for whom they found jobs, Brandeis dissented again, writing at length about the abusive practices of employment agencies that were the target of the legislation and reiterating his contention that courts lacked authority to strike down social legislation unless examination of the facts demonstrated that it was unreasonable (*Adams v. Tanner,* 1917).

Brandeis quickly realized that many attorneys appearing before the Court failed to prepare the kind of fact-laden argument he had used in *Muller.* Undaunted, he decided that if attorneys did not perform that function, the justices would have to do it for themselves. In 1924, examining the constitutionality of a Nebraska consumer-protection law that set weight standards, including maximum weight limits, for commercially sold loaves of bread, the Court's majority held that the law took bakers' and dealers' property without due process of law (*Jay Burns Baking Co. v. Bryan*). Brandeis disagreed and chastised his brethren for not examining the relevant facts. The justices, he said somewhat ingenuously, had "merely to acquaint ourselves with the art of breadmaking and the usages of the trade; with the devices by which buyers of bread are imposed upon and honest bakers or dealers are subjected by their dishonest fellows to unfair competition; with the problems which have confronted public officials charged with the enforcement of the laws prohibiting short weights, and with their experience in administering those laws." Brandeis fulfilled this "mere" task by presenting the Court with fifteen pages of information about the baking industry, most of it in lengthy and forbidding footnotes.

Brandeis's penchant for upholding state experimentation continued throughout his years on the Court. In 1933, the Court overturned a Florida law that, seeking to discourage chain stores, imposed heavier license fees on stores that were part of multicounty chains than on independent shops. The Court declared that Florida's classification of stores lacked a rational basis (*Liggett v. Lee*). Brandeis disagreed and wrote a long essay on the evils of economic bigness, and particularly of the corporations he believed had grown so large that they were a menace to American democracy. They were able to dominate states and citizens, he warned the Court: "the lives of tens or hundreds of thousands of employees and the property of tens or hundreds of thousands of investors are subjected, through the corporate mechanism, to the control of a few men." The United States was in the grip of "the rule of a plutocracy." Five of the twelve plaintiff corporations in the case had assets of more than $90 million each; among them, they controlled more than 19,718 stores throughout the country. Florida might well have believed that this "concentration of wealth and of power and ... absentee ownership" was "thwarting American ideals," making equality of opportunity impossible, "converting independent tradesmen into clerks; and that it is sapping the resources, the vigor and the hope of the smaller cities and towns."

Brandeis had declared war on concentrated power, warning that unbridled bigness ultimately would prove a false panacea for the country's economic ills. The theme resounded throughout many of his 528 judicial opinions. He was equally certain that concentrated governmental power was undemocratic, however worthy particular government policies might be. He saw federalism as similar to separation of powers: both arrangements were aspects of the Constitution's solution to the problem of governmental size. Just as jurisdictional rules helped keep the Court within the boundaries prescribed by the Constitution and prevented it from intervening in problems that were too complicated or remote for any nine justices to solve, so part of the Court's function was to maintain the margins of separation between the federal executive and Congress, and between the federal government and the states.

He therefore dissented when the Court held that a president could fire a civil servant unilaterally in spite of a statute requiring Senate advice and consent before such a removal. Answering the argument that it was more efficient for the chief executive to act unilaterally against civil servants he found unacceptable, Brandeis declared that "the doctrine of the separation of powers was adopted by the Convention of 1787 not to promote efficiency but to preclude the exercise of arbitrary power" (*Myers v. United States,* 1927). "The purpose," he continued, "was not to avoid friction, but, by means of the inevitable friction incident to the distribution of the governmental powers among three departments, to save the people from autocracy."

He held to this principle even when it meant infuriating President Franklin Roosevelt, most of whose New Deal programs Brandeis endorsed. Brandeis was not willing to permit the emergency of the Depression to be used as an excuse for concentration of power within the executive branch. This became clear when the Court pondered the constitutionality of the National Industrial Recovery Act of 1933, which Roosevelt considered a cornerstone of his recovery plan for the country. The NRA exempted industries from antitrust laws if they adopted codes providing for specific wages, hours, conditions of employment, and prices. The act provided no guidelines for the codes, however, giving the president total power to approve or disapprove them.

During oral argument in two 1935 cases resulting from the prosecution of oil company officials for ignoring the code Roosevelt had promulgated (*Panama Refining Co. v. Ryan* and *Amazon Petroleum Corporation v. Ryan*), one company's attorney asserted that his client had not known the law existed and that the only copy he knew of was in the "hip pocket of a government agent sent down to Texas from Washington." Brandeis turned to the government's lawyer and demanded, "Who promulgates these orders and codes that have the force of law?" The lawyer replied that as they were promulgated by the president, "I assume they are on record at the State Department." This was insufficient. "Is there any official or general publication of these executive orders?" Brandeis pressed further. "Not that I know of," came the answer, with the lawyer finally admitting lamely that "I think it would be difficult, but it is possible to get certified copies of the executive orders and codes from the NRA." Brandeis joined seven of his colleagues in striking down this use of the NRA.

He went further a few months later and voted to nullify the entire NRA, agreeing with Chief Justice Hughes's opinion for the Court that the massive delegation of power to the president was unconstitutional in all situations (*Schechter v. United States,* 1935). Among the other decisions handed down the same day was *Humphrey's Executor v. United States,* in which the Court effectively and unanimously overturned its ruling in *Myers,* vindicating Brandeis by holding that the president could not remove members of independent regulatory commissions. Brandeis announced a third opinion, again for a unanimous Court, holding unconstitutional the Frazier-Lemke Act of 1933, which had permitted farmers to defer mortgage payments. Brandeis and the Court declared that the statute, which authorized bankruptcy courts to take title to the property from the banks that held the mortgages, violated the Fifth Amendment's property clause (*Louisville v. Radford*). The reason for Brandeis's distaste for a law that seemed on its face to protect farmers became apparent when he noted that under the act, the definition of farmer included "persons who are merely capitalist absentees." "Capitalist absentees" was Brandeis's language for owners of land or stock whose concentrations of money gave them excessive power, and here they were being protected by the federal government.

"This is the end of this business of centralization," Brandeis told Roosevelt advisor Thomas G. Corcoran. "I want you to go back and tell the President that we're not going to let this government centralize everything." Brandeis approved of Roosevelt and used occasions such as his well-known weekly teas to tell New Dealers of his enthusiasm for the economic policies he hoped Roosevelt would propose, many of which the president in fact adopted. But bigness in government could be every bit as oppressive as bigness in business, and Brandeis would have no part of it.

Brandeis's opinions differed from those of his colleagues because he included in them the social realities leading to the legislation that came before the Court. This reflected both his belief that factual information had to underlie all constitutional adjudication and his desire to use judicial opinions as educational devices. It was as important for citizens to understand the reasons behind the law as it for was for them to know what the law was. His clerks were expected to help him make his opinions not only "persuasive" but "instructive." They were sent regularly to find additional relevant statistics in the Library of Congress, even after an opinion had been written, and they frequently discovered that in his endless rewriting Brandeis had made as many as sixty changes in a draft of ten pages and had revised an opinion for the twentieth or thirtieth time. He tried to make clear not only who was suing whom, but why.

While the decisions written by colleagues such as Justices Pitney, Taft, or Sutherland hold little information about the nature of the struggle between labor and management, for example, Brandeis's opinions reflected and explained the struggle. When the workers at the Duplex newspaper printing press manufacturer were enjoined from striking and calling on workers in similar plants to refuse to work on Duplex machines, he made sure that anyone reading the resultant case knew that there were only four such companies in the United States, and that the other three were unionized and had instituted minimum wages and maximum hours. Duplex had refused to recognize the union. This led two of the other manufacturers to threaten to break their agreements with the union, jeopardizing its existence. The laborers were neither irrational nor greedy, Brandeis told his readers: "May not all with a common interest join in refusing to expend their labor upon articles whose very production constitutes an attack upon their standard of living and the institution which they are convinced supports it?" (*Duplex Printing Co. v. Deering*, 1921).

Similarly, Brandeis explained at length why he dissented when the Court overturned an Arizona law forbidding its courts to issue injunctions against strikes and picketing (*Truax v. Corrigan*, 1921). Chief Justice Taft wrote about the equal protection and due process clauses of the Fourteenth Amendment; Brandeis, although touching on the relevant constitutional provisions, described the factual situation. Cooks and waiters at the English Kitchen on Main Street in Bisbee, Arizona, struck and encouraged a boycott of the restaurant by picketing and distributing leaflets. Brandeis could find nothing irrational in a state's decision to permit disgruntled workers to tell their story to the public and to refuse courts the power to stop them from doing so. The law admittedly was a societal experiment, he declared, and wrote fourteen pages showing that England, the British dominions, the federal government, and other states had similar experiments: that was sufficient to demonstrate that the statute could not be brushed aside as either arbitrary or unreasonable.

Brandeis was as impassioned and influential in the area of civil liberties as he was in the economic sphere. His seminal contribution to the development of free speech jurisprudence has sometimes been underrated by scholars who have given Oliver Wendell Holmes credit for the "clear and present danger" doctrine. While Holmes first formulated the doctrine, writing in *Schenck v. United States* (1919) that the federal government could punish only speech that presented a clear and present danger, he did not define clear, present, or danger; he suggested no criteria for doing so; and he stated that the doctrine was similar in peacetime and wartime. Brandeis subsequently elaborated on the doctrine, altering it substantially.

Brandeis considered free speech crucial to individual development and a necessity for the educated citizens demanded by a democratic state. Speech, privacy, education, and democracy all were elements of the ideal political system. Democracy meant majority rule with full protection for the rights of individuals. Sociological jurisprudence, which in other spheres mandated judicial deference to the will of the majority, required that the judiciary play a central role in preventing government from interfering with individual rights. An educated electorate had to be able to engage in free and open discussion if law was to reflect felt necessities, experimentation was to occur, and socially responsive policies were to be developed.

Although Brandeis silently concurred in Holmes's opinion in *Schenck*, his subsequent rethinking became apparent in three dissents he wrote in 1920. In *Schaefer v. United States*, an appeal from a conviction under the 1917 Espionage Act for printing misleading articles about the American war effort, he declared that the constitutional right of free speech was the same in wartime as it was during peace. In fact, Brandeis continued, it was precisely in time of war that free speech was most necessary, for it was then that "an intolerant majority" was most likely to be "swayed by passion or by fear."

His dissent from the Court's upholding of a second Espionage Act conviction, this one for distribution of socialist leaflets that allegedly had interfered with the operation of the war effort and had caused insubordination, reiterated his belief that the speech doctrine was identical in war and peace and that "the fundamental right of free

men to strive for better conditions through new legislation and new institutions will not be preserved, if efforts to secure it by argument to fellow citizens may be construed as criminal incitement to disobey the existing law" (*Pierce v. United States*, 1920).

His third dissent came in a case challenging Minnesota's statute prohibiting any interference with the military enlistment effort, as applied to a speaker who had criticized the war and the draft during a public meeting. Describing the law as one that criminalized the teaching of pacifism, Brandeis condemned it for violating the rights of speech, privacy, and religion. In addition, he argued strenuously that if the Court used the Fourteenth Amendment's due process clause to strike down states' economic legislation, as it regularly did, surely the Court should apply the clause to state legislation that limited something as important as speech (*Gilbert v. Minnesota*, 1920).

His dissent in Gilbert laid the foundation for a major alteration of American law and for a reassessment of political values. In 1925, adopting Brandeis's argument, the Court declared that freedom of speech and press were "among the fundamental rights and 'liberties'" protected by the due process clause (*Gitlow v. New York*). This, and subsequent cases in which the Court held one or another of the Bill of Rights' liberties to be "incorporated" into the due process clause, are responsible for the assumption, now part of American law and polity, that the Bill of Rights is a barrier to state, as well as federal, violation of individual liberties.

Brandeis's most eloquent contribution to free speech jurisprudence came in *Whitney v. California* (1927). Attacking a California statute outlawing political parties that advocated the use of illegal force, Brandeis aligned himself with the Founding Fathers who, he asserted, "believed that the final end of the State was to make men free to develop their faculties." This could be done only if "deliberate forces" prevailed over those that were "arbitrary"; if citizens were not only free to speak their thoughts, but encouraged to exercise their responsibility to do so; and if the nation understood "that the fitting remedy for evil counsels is good ones." Recognizing that by the time he wrote, the American government had become more active than it had been during its early years and that citizens now had reason to be concerned about how to keep the government within acceptable boundaries, he argued that "fear of serious injury" was insufficient justification for punishing speech, and suggested a different standard:

> There must be reasonable ground to believe that the danger apprehended is imminent. There must be reasonable ground to believe that the evil to be prevented is a serious one . . . even advocacy of violence, however reprehensible morally, is not a justification for denying free speech where the advocacy falls short of incitement and there is nothing to indicate that the advocacy would be immediately acted on. . . . In order to support a finding of clear and present danger it must be shown either that immediate serious violence was to be expected or was advocated, or that the past conduct furnished reason to believe that such advocacy was then contemplated.

Brandeis transformed Holmes's "clear and present danger" by defining "present" as meaning that "the incidence of the evil apprehended is so imminent that it may befall before there is opportunity for full discussion. If there be time to expose through discussion the falsehood and fallacies, to avert the evil by the processes of education, the remedy to be applied is more speech, not enforced silence." Brandeis also rejected Holmes's assumption that the government could act against speech presenting a danger of any evil the government had the right to prevent. The evil of "some violence or . . . destruction of property" was not enough; the evil had to be "the probability of serious injury to the State." If, as Brandeis suggested, it was unconstitutional to prevent or punish speech unless all reasonable people would agree that it represented a serious and imminent danger of probable injury to the state itself, the government's power to interfere with speech was minimal.

Brandeis had as great an impact on privacy jurisprudence, although it came in equal measure from his pre-Court career and the eventual in-

fluence of his dissents from the bench. In 1890, the *Harvard Law Review* had published "The Right to Privacy" by Brandeis and his law partner, Samuel D. Warren, Jr. When Brandeis was nominated to the Court, Dean Roscoe Pound of Harvard Law School told the Senate that the article had added a chapter to American law. Combining a formulation of law as a changing entity with the concept of privacy, the article argued that new inventions with the potential for violations of privacy had to be brought under law in the name of protecting the individual's "right to be let alone."

Brandeis and Warren were reacting to invasions of privacy by the press. By the time Brandeis joined the Court, government had access to the kind of still newer technology that the article had warned about and had become big enough to represent a serious privacy threat. Brandeis now became concerned not only about the enhanced possibilities of government intrusion and their impact on the right of privacy, so central to the individual's development, but about the nature of a government that might resort to invasions of privacy. He therefore dissented when the Court upheld a conviction, under the Harrison Anti-Narcotic Act, obtained after the government induced two state prisoners to offer an attorney money for drugs and record their conversations with him.

As Holmes wrote for the Court in sustaining the conviction in *Casey v. United States* (1928), there was no doubt that the law had been broken. Brandeis agreed, but declared that the conviction should be overturned because the government had instigated the crime and, absent government action, there would have been no evidence for the government to record. "[The government] may not provoke or create a crime and then punish the criminal, its creature," he argued. He explained that he was less concerned about Casey than about the government, and voted as he did "not because some right of Casey's has been denied, but in order to protect the Government. To protect it from illegal conduct of its officers. To protect the purity of its courts."

Similarly, Brandeis objected to a conviction under the National Prohibition Act, obtained as a result of evidence gathered during five months of government wiretapping. The Court held in *Olmstead v. United States* (1928) that wiretapping did not constitute the kind of physical trespass or seizure prohibited by the Fourth Amendment's search and seizure clause. Incredulous, Brandeis asked, "Can it be that the Constitution affords no protection against such invasions of individual security?" and answered by recalling the Founding Fathers' concern about writs of assistance and general warrants. Wiretapping was even more insidious than those devices because it was more intrusive. Brandeis urged the Court to adopt a socially responsive interpretation of the Constitution, including the search and seizure clause. "Rights of . . . the liberty of the individual must be remolded from time to time," he had written in *Truax v. Corrigan* (1921), "to meet the changing needs of society." That referred to the specific manifestations of the rights, not the rights themselves, which were unchanging, and which Brandeis found at the core of the Constitution: "The makers of our Constitution undertook . . . to protect Americans in their beliefs, their thoughts, their emotions, and their sensations. They conferred, as against the Government, the right to be let alone—the most comprehensive of rights and the right most valued by civilized men."

Privacy and speech were connected in their centrality to the free flow of ideas and to individual growth. It was insufficient to claim, as the Court did, that the government had violated an individual right in the name of the greater good, because the greater good actually was being hurt by a well-intentioned but misguided government: "Experience should teach us to be most on our guard to protect liberty when the Government's purposes are beneficent. . . . The greatest dangers to liberty lurk in insidious encroachment by men of zeal, well-meaning but without understanding." The government, by acting illegally, was encouraging disdain for law. Brandeis had warned in his dissent in *Burdeau v. McDowell* (1921) that "At the foundation of our civil liberty lies the principle which denies to government officials an exceptional position before the law and which subjects them to the same rules of conduct that are commands to the citizen. . . .

Respect for law will not be advanced by resort, in its enforcement, to means which shock the common man's sense of decency and fair play." He added in *Olmstead*, "Our Government is the potent, the omnipresent teacher. For good or for ill, it teaches the whole people by its example. Crime is contagious. If the Government becomes a lawbreaker, it breeds contempt for law: it invites every man to become a law unto himself; it invites anarchy." And he warned: "To declare that in the administration of the criminal law the end justifies the means—to declare that the Government may commit crimes in order to secure the conviction of a private criminal—would bring terrible retribution. Against that pernicious doctrine this Court should resolutely set its face."

American constitutional law today is fact-oriented largely because of the Brandeis brief and the fact-based sociological jurisprudence embodied in almost all of Brandeis's judicial opinions. Joining a Court whose members were born in the nineteenth century, he helped wrench its collective face toward the twentieth century, constantly reminding the justices and the larger legal and political communities of changing societal realities. His fervent sense of democracy and the need of the political system for free, involved, and fulfilled citizens resounds through the words he wrote while on the bench. His conception of judicial opinions as mini-lessons has been adopted, possibly to occasional excess, by subsequent justices. His innovative reaching out to the academic branch of the legal profession through citation of law review articles has now become routine in Court opinions. His insistence that both economic and political institutions had to be accountable to the people was adopted in part by the New Deal and subsequent administrations. His perception of the law as a dynamic, changing entity, and his delineation of the right of privacy have become embedded in American jurisprudence. Federal and state court decisions are replete with references to his opinions, particularly in the fields of speech and privacy. Dean Acheson, another of Brandeis's former clerks, told the mourners at the justice's funeral that "his faith in the human mind and in the will and capacity of people to understand and grasp the truth never wavered or tired." Such was his legacy to the Supreme Court and to the American people.

—PHILIPPA STRUM

BIBLIOGRAPHY

The largest collections of Brandeis's Court papers, including the Brandeis papers and the Frankfurter papers, are in the Harvard Law School Library. Court-related items can be found in the Frankfurter papers at the Library of Congress and in the major Brandeis archives at the University of Louisville. Brandeis's letters, including many from the Court years, are in the well-annotated *Letters of Louis D. Brandeis*, eds. Melvin I. Urofsky and David W. Levy (5 volumes, 1971–1978), and *"Half Brother, Half Son": The Letters of Louis D. Brandeis to Felix Frankfurter* (1991). Two useful compilations of his Court drafts and opinions are Alexander M. Bickel, ed., *The Unpublished Opinions of Mr. Justice Brandeis* (1957), and Alfred Lief, ed., *The Social and Economic Views of Mr. Justice Brandeis* (1930).

Among the major biographies of Brandeis are Alpheus Thomas Mason, *Brandeis: A Free Man's Life* (1946), and Philippa Strum, *Louis D. Brandeis: Justice for the People* (1984). Alden Todd, *Justice on Trial* (1964) is a thorough account of the fight over the Brandeis nomination. Other volumes containing information about the Court years are Alpheus Thomas Mason, *Brandeis: Lawyer and Judge in the Modern State* (1933), Felix Frankfurter, ed., *Mr. Justice Brandeis* (1932), Samuel J. Konefsky, *The Legacy of Holmes and Brandeis* (1956), and Philippa Strum, *Brandeis: Beyond Progressivism* (1993). A major and extremely insightful article on Brandeis's First Amendment jurisprudence is Vincent Blasi, "The First Amendment and the Ideal of Civil Courage: The Brandeis Opinion in Whitney v. California," 29 *William and Mary Law Review* (Summer 1988); see also Pnina Lahav, "Holmes and Brandeis: Libertarian and Republican Justifications for Free Speech," 4 *Journal of Law and Politics* (1988).

Additional sources on Brandeis's Court years and his earlier life are listed in two comprehensive volumes: Roy M. Mersky, *Louis Dembitz Brandeis, 1856–1941, A Bibliography* (1958), which contains works published by 1957, and Gene Teitelbaum, *Justice Louis D. Brandeis: A Bibliography of Writings and Other Materials on the Justice* (1988).

WILLIAM JOSEPH BRENNAN, JR.

BORN 25 April 1906, Newark, New Jersey

NOMINATED to the Court 29 September 1956 by Dwight D. Eisenhower

TOOK seat 16 October 1956; retired 20 July 1990

There are few justices in history who played more of a leadership role in helping to shape the direction of the Court than William J. Brennan, Jr.

Yet for much of his thirty-four-year tenure, this role was largely unknown to the public, as Brennan labored in the shadows of Chief Justice Earl Warren and Justices Hugo L. Black, William O. Douglas, Felix Frankfurter, and John M. Harlan. It was really only in the final decade of Brennan's service that there was widespread public recognition of the full dimension of his role as the architect of much of the revolution in constitutional law that took place in the 1960s and 1970s. Although his role and influence on the Court were complex and varied, Justice Brennan's message was relatively simple and unwavering: the role of law in society, and of judges in giving meaning to that role, is to protect the essential human dignity of every individual. The Constitution must be interpreted toward that end, he believed, and governments must be accountable toward that end. Court procedures and rules must also be drawn to further that goal.

While the constitutional landmarks to this philosophy span three decades, the erection of new monuments grew sparse in the late 1970s and 1980s, replaced by frequent dissenting opinions. Still, only a few of the monuments were toppled as the changing membership of the Court caused the pendulum to swing in the direction of a more restrained view of the Constitution and a narrower approach to the role of judges.

When he arrived at the Supreme Court, Justice Brennan was virtually unknown outside New Jersey, although within his home state he had achieved prominence in the legal community. A 1931 graduate of Harvard Law School, he joined one of New Jersey's leading law firms and soon became a specialist on the side of

management in the fledgling field of labor law. His credibility was based, at least in part, on the memory of his late father's popularity as a union leader whose reputation helped him to win election as Newark's commissioner of public safety.

In fifteen years of private practice before and after World War II, Brennan demonstrated his considerable skills as an advocate and trial lawyer, as a legal tactician and draftsman, and as a conciliator who could get along with all parties in a dispute. These qualities would prove invaluable in his Supreme Court tenure.

After World War II, Brennan became active with a group of young lawyers who were pressing reform of the state judicial system. In 1947, New Jersey adopted a new constitution, including restructured courts, and Brennan could not resist the temptation to help put the new plan into effect. He was appointed to the new superior court bench in 1949 by a Republican governor, although Brennan was a Democrat. The young reformer's more senior mentor was Arthur Vanderbilt, a nationally prominent legal figure for whom Brennan quickly became a trusted lieutenant and for whom Brennan led statewide efforts to eliminate congestion and long delays in the courts.

This interest in court reform was not simply a matter of efficiency for Brennan; it was directly connected to his view of the need for fairness and compassion in the law. Efficient court procedures, he observed in 1956, lead to "attainment of the ideal of dispositions according to right and justice."

Brennan was quickly promoted to the superior court's appellate division, and in 1952 to the New Jersey supreme court, where Vanderbilt was chief justice. Brennan cemented his relationship as Vanderbilt's right-hand man, no small achievement, since Brennan frustrated Vanderbilt by disagreeing with him on a number of important court decisions. When Brennan was appointed to the United States Supreme Court in 1956, Vanderbilt let it be known that he had planned to recommend that Brennan be his successor as New Jersey chief justice.

Brennan's record on the New Jersey supreme court has long been the subject of debate. The popular view is that he was a moderate who turned liberal once on the federal bench, much to the surprise and disappointment of President Eisenhower. (Eisenhower expressed his disagreement with Brennan in a number of conversations with friends and acquaintances, although there is no evidence that he ever said the words often attributed to him with reference to Brennan and Chief Justice Earl Warren: "My two worst mistakes are both sitting on the Supreme Court.") However, Brennan's friends in New Jersey at the time, and other local legal observers knew that he was unmistakably liberal, and his record of decisions affirms that view.

Although the state court had little occasion to deal with federal constitutional questions, Brennan touched on a number of issues that later became hallmarks of his decisions on the U.S. Supreme Court. He took a broad view of the privilege against self-incrimination in *In Re Pillo* (1952), finding the privilege in New Jersey to be based on common law tradition, rather than the Fifth Amendment. He took a strong position against prior restraint of free expression in *Adams Theatre Co. v. Keenan* (1953). In his most famous state court dissent, in *State v. Tune* (1953), he excoriated the majority for refusing to allow an accused murderer to inspect his own confession. He expressed strong support for the guarantee against double jeopardy in *State v. Midgeley* (1954).

Brennan came to the attention of Attorney General Herbert Brownell in May 1956, when he addressed a Justice Department conference on court delays. When Justice Sherman Minton announced plans to retire a few months later, President Eisenhower said he wanted to look for a Democrat, to appear more bipartisan for the impending presidential election, and a Catholic, since there had not been one on the Court for too long. Brennan fit the bill and was supported by Vanderbilt and by Brownell's conclusion, after reading all of Brennan's New Jersey opinions, that Brennan was a moderate. Justice Brennan took his seat on October 16, 1956, one week into the Court term, as a recess appointment chosen while the Senate was not in session.

It was not until March 19, 1957, that he was confirmed by the Senate, over the lone negative vote of Joseph McCarthy, the Wisconsin Republican, who opposed Brennan because of two speeches Brennan gave in 1954 criticizing congressional investigations that threaten the rights of individuals. Those speeches mark one of the earliest records of Brennan's concern with law and human dignity. "We cannot and must not doubt our strength to conserve, without the sacrifice of any, all of the guarantees of justice and fair play and simple human dignity which have made our land what it is," Brennan said in a speech to the Irish Charitable Society in Boston. Ours, he said, is "a system of government based upon the dignity and inviolability of the individual soul."

Although William Brennan did not come to the Supreme Court with a fully developed constitutional philosophy, it did not take him very long to arrive at the view that the Constitution must be interpreted for the time, not based on some fixed, permanent original understanding of its authors. "What due process under the 14th Amendment meant to the wisdom of other days cannot be its measure to the vision of our time," he said in the 1961 James Madison lecture at New York University Law School.

In the twilight of his tenure, Brennan became closely identified with this approach in a national debate over constitutional interpretation, spawned in part by the bicentennial of the Constitution, in part by the failed Supreme Court nomination of conservative Judge Robert H. Bork, and in part by the vigorous attack of aides to President Ronald Reagan. Justice Brennan's most sweeping discussion of constitutional interpretation came in a 1986 speech at Georgetown University Law School in which he boldly criticized those who advocate that determining the "original intent" of the framers is the only proper way to read the Constitution:

> In its most doctrinaire incarnation, this view demands that Justices discern exactly what the Framers thought about the question under consideration and simply follow that intention in resolving the case before them. It is a view that feigns self-effacing

William Joseph Brennan, Jr.
Photograph by Ken Heinen.
Collection of the Supreme Court of the United States.

deference to the specific judgments of those who forged our original social compact. But in truth it is little more than arrogance cloaked as humility. It is arrogant to pretend that from our vantage we can gauge accurately the intent of the Framers on application of principle to specific, contemporary questions. . . .

We current Justices read the Constitution in the only way that we can: as Twentieth Century Americans. We look to the history of the time of framing and to the intervening history of interpretation. But the ultimate question must be, what do the words of the text mean in our time. For the genius of the Constitution rests not in any static meaning it might have had in a world that is dead and gone, but in the adaptability of its great principles to cope with current problems and current needs.

This focus on adapting the Constitution to the needs of the day was only one facet of Brennan's judicial philosophy. Another principal tenet of his jurisprudence was that the law must be compassionate, preserving the essential dignity of individuals. "Law is again coming alive as a living process responsive to changing human needs," he said in a 1964 speech. "The shift is to justice and away from fine-spun technicalities and abstract rules." This approach was apparent in a multitude of Brennan decisions, cutting across different areas of the law, from the rights of the accused to government treatment of welfare recipients and illegal alien children.

One example of this approach in criminal cases provided continuity between Brennan's New Jersey tenure and his service on the United States Supreme Court. Building on the theme of his dissent in *State v. Tune* (1953), Brennan, in his first term in Washington, authored *Jencks v. United States* (1957), establishing the right of defendants in federal criminal prosecutions to inspect documents themselves upon which the government is relying rather than leaving it to the trial judge to decide which documents are relevant for the defense.

No one better captured this aspect of Brennan's philosophy than Chief Justice Warren in a 1966 *Harvard Law Review* tribute:

He administers the Constitution as a sacred trust, and interprets the Bill of Rights as the heart and life blood of that great charter of freedom. His belief in the dignity of human beings—all human beings—is unbounded. He also believes that without such dignity men cannot be free. These beliefs are apparent in the warp and woof of all his opinions.

Perhaps no case better illustrates these facets of Justice Brennan's constitutional view than *Goldberg v. Kelly* (1970), in which he wrote for the majority that the Fourteenth Amendment guarantee of "due process" applies to the termination of welfare benefits and requires notice and a hearing before benefits are discontinued. "Termination of aid pending resolution of a controversy over eligibility may deprive an eligible recipient of the very means by which to live while he waits," he wrote.

This approach was always subject to the criticism, as expressed by Justice Hugo Black's dissent in *Goldberg*, that the Court was making political judgments, acting like a legislature rather than a group of judges. However, this criticism rarely fazed Brennan, who believed unfailingly in the need for the judiciary to be the final arbiter of what is constitutionally fair and necessary.

Yet another feature of Brennan's approach was a belief that it was not simply the substance of rights that had to be protected. The procedures employed by governments to regulate modern society must be fair and must not unduly interfere with the exercise of individual rights. This focus on the unfairness of procedures—burden of proof, vagueness of laws, statutes that were too broad—was a new concept in constitutional law, particularly in the realm of First Amendment protection for freedom of speech and freedom of religious beliefs.

One example of this approach was the majority opinion in *Speiser v. Randall* (1958), striking down a California law that denied a tax exemption to individuals who refused to swear an oath that they did not advocate overthrow of the United States. The law was unconstitutional, Brennan wrote, not based on whether California could require such an oath to qualify for a tax break, but because California in effect required taxpayers to show that they had not engaged in prohibited speech. This procedure, although arguably within California's authority, posed too great a danger of self-censorship by individuals who wanted to avoid difficulty in demonstrating their eligibility for the tax break. Thus, it was the process that was deficient, not the substantive right itself. This willingness to examine the practical effects of otherwise legitimate exercises of government power also set Justice Brennan apart.

No discussion of William Brennan is complete without an examination of the way he approached the job, not so much the constitutional philosophy, but his outlook on day-to-day details. No doubt each justice aspires to influence his colleagues and to alter the course of constitutional law, but none has had a more single-minded focus than Justice Brennan on the importance of seeking a majority. It has become almost a cliché, but the story is nevertheless true that Justice Brennan would ask his new law clerks to identify the most important principle of constitutional law and then, holding up the five fingers of one hand, exclaim with glee, "You can't do anything around here without five votes." His success was aided by an almost encyclopedic memory of the Court's work during his tenure. Another story, also perhaps a cliché, but no less true, is of how, in the middle of discussing a case, Brennan would say that he had written on the particular subject in the past. Invariably, he would swivel to the bookcase of *U.S. Reports* behind his desk, pluck the correct volume from the shelves and open to the proper page.

From his earliest days on the bench, Brennan displayed an extraordinary ability to take a position and then work with his colleagues to shape and modify it until a majority was secured. He was never too set in his views to consider a colleague's request for adjustments, especially when the approach came from a justice who represented the potential fifth vote.

The means to this end were numerous. Sometimes he would gain support through his characterization of the issue. In *Goldberg v. Kelly*, he described the issue for decision as a "narrow one," although that was hardly the case. At other times, he would dispatch his law clerks to find out from their counterparts what other justices were thinking or what it would take to secure their votes. Once so engaged, there was no greater conciliator in the annals of the Court. His effervescent personality and unfailing warmth became a legend among Court employees, and particularly among his colleagues.

This approach to the job fit nicely with his approach to constitutional solutions. Brennan rejected the rigid absolutes of Hugo L. Black and William O. Douglas, who believed that the First Amendment prohibited any regulation of free speech. Brennan preferred a jurisprudence of balancing and tests that evolved into a vast body of very practical constitutional doctrine, but a body to which adjustments and variations were easily made to accommodate changed situations and to which new tests could be added to accommodate the views of other justices.

In *Plyler v. Doe* (1982), Brennan wrote for the Court that under the Fourteenth Amendment guarantee of "equal protection of the laws," the children of illegal aliens could not be singled out for denial of free, public education by the state of Texas. Brennan spent months negotiating with Lewis Powell, who was concerned about the children, but who wanted to avoid a sweeping constitutional pronouncement about education or the status of illegal aliens. In the end, Brennan was forced to lower the level of constitutional scrutiny to which the Texas law was subjected, so that an "important" government objective would suffice to justify the law, instead of the more rigorous "compelling" interest. This meant that illegal aliens and their children would not receive the same high degree of protection from discrimination that applies to racial minorities or to legal aliens. However, this change still meant that the Texas law was invalid, with Powell's crucial fifth vote providing the majority, and Brennan's opinion still made it difficult for governments to discriminate against illegal aliens.

The recognition that he was a talented lawyer and craftsman was part of the basis for the extraordinary bond of trust that developed quickly between Brennan and Chief Justice Earl Warren. It is no coincidence that Warren turned to Brennan, his colleague for only two years at the time, to draft the Court's opinion, signed by all nine justices, in *Cooper v. Aaron* (1958), the Little Rock, Arkansas, school desegregation case that affirmed the obligation of state officials to heed the dictates of the Supreme Court. Brennan quickly demonstrated an ability to write a narrow, unflamboyant, workmanlike opinion.

Indeed, Brennan's demonstrated legal craftsmanship, his ability to anticipate the other justices, and his personal warmth and charm made him a valuable ally of Warren throughout the period that is known as the Warren Court, and the two men met regularly to discuss cases and map strategy. A few commentators have even suggested that the period ought to be described as the "Brennan Court," because the strategies and constitutional doctrines were his more than the chief justice's. Brennan, however, scoffed at such suggestions, always revering the name and memory of Earl Warren and coining the term "superchief" to refer to him.

The aspects of American constitutional law in which change was affected by William Brennan are far too numerous to cover them all, but a handful stand out on the legal landscape. There are also a few places in which his legacy has been diluted or even erased by subsequent actions of the Supreme Court.

When Brennan arrived at the Supreme Court in 1956, the Bill of Rights was still largely a shield against abuse of individual liberties by the federal government. A debate had raged for nearly a decade between Hugo Black and Felix Frankfurter over whether the adoption of the Fourteenth Amendment in 1868, with its guarantee of "liberty" protected by "due process," meant that the Bill of Rights was also intended to curb the authority of the states. Black argued for wholesale application of the entire Bill of Rights, and Frankfurter argued that the Fourteenth Amendment had brought about no such result. By 1956, the First Amendment guarantees of freedom of speech and religion were the principal guarantees that had been incorporated into the Fourteenth Amendment, and they were still not vigorously enforced. Although it was Black's advocacy that created the climate for incorporation, it was Brennan, in consultation

with Warren, who set about the practical task of selecting those amendments that should logically apply to the states because they were among the "principles of a free government," and of choosing cases in which to achieve that goal. Brennan outlined his motivation in the 1961 Madison lecture:

> The need for vigilance to prevent government from whittling away the rights of the individual was never greater. . . .
>
> Far too many cases come from the states to the Supreme Court presenting dismal pictures of official lawlessness . . . Judicial self-restraint which defers too much to the sovereign powers of the states and reserves judicial intervention for only the most revolting cases will not serve to enhance Madison's priceless gift of "the great rights of mankind secured under this Constitution."

While his approach rejected Black's advocacy of wholesale incorporation of all of the first eight amendments, Brennan helped guide the application of most provisions of the Bill of Rights to limit state authority. Only the Second and Third Amendments, the Fifth Amendment grand jury provision, and the Seventh Amendment remain unincorporated. For Brennan's part, he directly contributed *Malloy v. Hogan* (1964), which held that the Fifth Amendment privilege against self-incrimination applied in state criminal courts, not just federal. It is not surprising that this piece of incorporation is included among Brennan's works, since he had expressed strong views about the privilege against self-incrimination on the New Jersey Supreme Court in *In Re Pillo* (1952).

Among his most visible and lasting achievements are those in the field of the First Amendment, where the law's broad tolerance for controversial and offensive speech is due in some significant degree to his opinions. Consistent with his criticism of prior restraint in New Jersey in *Adams Theatre Co. v. Keenan* (1953), he took a strong stand against prior restraint on speech or publication in *New York Times Co. v. United States* (1971), which thwarted the government's efforts to halt publication of the Pentagon Papers.

In *New York Times Co. v. Sullivan* (1964), Brennan's opinion gave new protection to freedom of expression, ruling that the First Amendment limits the authority of states to punish libelous speech about the conduct of public officials. A public official may recover only when a defamatory statement has been made with "actual malice—that is, with knowledge that it was false or reckless disregard of whether it was false or not." This approach was later expanded to cover speech about public figures, as well.

The decision revolutionized the field of libel law, but it also included one of the strongest statements of purpose for the First Amendment, memorializing "a profound national commitment to the principle that debate on public issues should be uninhibited, robust, and wide-open, and that it may well include vehement, caustic, and sometimes unpleasantly sharp attacks on government and public officials." His commitment to this view never wavered, and extended in *Texas v. Johnson* (1989) and in *United States v. Eichman* (1990) to striking down state and federal laws, respectively, that prohibited burning of the American flag as a protest because of the disrespect it conveys. "If there is a bedrock principle underlying the First Amendment," he wrote in the Texas case, "it is that the government may not prohibit the expression of an idea simply because society finds the idea itself offensive or disagreeable."

There are still other areas in which Brennan's vision of free expression took the Court to places that had not previously been thought to involve the First Amendment. In a number of these, his emphasis on the practical effect of government actions, as in the *Speiser* case, was most pronounced. In *NAACP v. Button* (1963), he invalidated a Virginia law and those of a number of other states that prohibited organizations like the NAACP from becoming involved in cases in which they had no direct interest. The effect of such laws was to thwart the NAACP's litigation strategy, which relied heavily on reaching out to the community to find and assist clients in school desegregation cases and other racial bias disputes. Brennan rejected the defense that such laws were a valid regula-

tion of solicitation and held that, regardless of the label attached by the state, the laws violated the NAACP's freedom of expression and association.

In two other cases, *Elrod v. Burns* (1976), and *Rutan v. Republican Party of Illinois* (1990), Brennan established that the First Amendment protects nonpolitical public employees from being hired and fired, or promoted and transferred on the basis of their loyalty to a political party, a practice generally described as patronage.

The religion clauses represent another First Amendment sphere on which Brennan left his mark, functioning as one of the Court's most zealous advocates of strict separation between church and state. This is ironic since there was concern during his confirmation hearing in 1957 about whether, as a Catholic, he could repress his allegiance to the Pope in the interests of fealty to the Constitution. Justice Brennan left no doubt as to his answer in a long concurring opinion outlining his own strong belief in separation in *Abington School District v. Schempp* (1963), in which the Court struck down a state law that required Bible reading in public school classrooms. He continued to play an important role in cases invalidating government aid to religious schools in the 1970s, but his adherence to strict separation pushed him into the dissenter's camp in the 1980s as the Court opened windows in the wall of separation.

In the other religion clause, guaranteeing the "free exercise" of religion, Brennan's pathbreaking decision in *Sherbert v. Verner* (1963) is now in eclipse. Brennan there held that South Carolina's denial of unemployment benefits to a worker who was fired for refusing to work on her sabbath day violated her freedom of religious worship. His decision required states and employers to take reasonable steps to accommodate workers' free exercise rights. That principle was largely undisputed until the decision in *Employment Division v. Smith* (1990), in which Justice Antonin Scalia ruled in the case of prohibited religious use of peyote in Oregon that the First Amendment does not require states to make exceptions to generally applicable laws simply to accommodate religious freedom.

Equality and the elimination of societal discrimination are also fields on which Justice Brennan left an indelible mark.

Cooper v. Aaron was only his first encounter with the school desegregation issue. In *Green v. New Kent County School Board* (1968), he spoke for the Court, expressing frustration with the slow pace of school desegregation and insisting that recalcitrant school officials find a solution that "promises realistically to work now." A few years later, in *Keyes v. Denver School District* (1973), the first northern desegregation case, Brennan held that once a violation is shown in one part of a system, the school board bears the burden of showing that the rest of the system is not unconstitutionally segregated as well.

Brennan also led the court in a number of major decisions—controversial and widely criticized by conservatives—upholding the constitutionality or statutory validity of affirmative action plans in the face of challenges that such programs discriminate against those who are not advantaged by them. Among these were: *Steelworkers v. Weber* (1978), upholding private employers' voluntary affirmative action under Title VII of the 1964 Civil Rights Act, which prohibits employment discrimination; *Johnson v. Transportation Agency* (1987), upholding a public employer's voluntary affirmative action plan for women under Title VII; *United States v. Paradise* (1987), upholding a promotion preference for black state troopers in Alabama, under the equal protection clause of the Fourteenth Amendment and finding that the plan was justified to correct past discrimination; and *Metro Broadcasting v. FCC* (1990), upholding, under the Fifth Amendment equal protection component, a broadcast licensing preference for minority-owned businesses to promote diversity in programming.

Until Brennan tackled the issue in the early 1970s, gender discrimination was largely unrecognized as a violation of the equal protection clause. But in a line of cases beginning with *Frontiero v. Richardson* (1973), and leading up to *Craig v. Boren* (1976), he succeeded in elevating constitutional recognition of sex discrimination, although not to as high a plane as he had hoped. In *Frontiero*, the Court struck down a federal law that made it easier for spouses of male military personnel than for spouses of female service personnel to receive increased benefits. Brennan argued that such gender-based discrimination should be viewed as every bit as "suspect" as racial bias and should be subjected to the equal protection clause's most rigorous scrutiny. However, he fell one vote short of a majority for this approach, and gender discrimination has never again been subjected to the highest levels of constitutional inquiry. Nevertheless, in *Craig*, he successfully proffered a new intermediate level of scrutiny for sex discrimination, requiring government to have an important, although not a compelling, justification for discriminatory conduct. In the case, the Court invalidated an Oklahoma law that allowed women to buy 3.2 percent beer at age eighteen, but men not until age twenty-one, finding that the law discriminated against males between ages eighteen and twenty-one.

Justice Brennan was very much reflective of the liberal view of the 1960s civil rights era that access to the federal courts to protect individual rights was essential, and that state courts could not always be trusted to have the necessary sensitivity to do the job. The successes with which he met in this realm during the Warren Court were undercut or even overruled during the tenures of Chief Justices Warren E. Burger and William H. Rehnquist. Yet Brennan continued to frame the debate, even after these setbacks.

No opinion by Justice Brennan has received more widespread recognition, nor had more practical effect, than *Baker v. Carr* (1962), which declared for the first time that challenges to the fairness of state legislative apportionments presented legitimate issues under the equal protection clause that could properly be decided in federal courts. Although a classic example of a narrow and carefully crafted opinion, the ruling forced legislatures throughout the country to face the redrawing of fairer district lines and led directly to the subsequent principle of one person, one vote. While the degree of precision required in line-drawing has varied in subsequent decisions, the battles have been fought largely in federal court. Chief Justice Warren remarked later that the ruling was the "most important" of his tenure.

Other efforts by Brennan to expand access to federal courts met with varying degrees of temporary success. His major civil rights decision giving federal courts broad power to issue injunctions to prevent state court interference with First Amendment rights, *Dombrowski v. Pfister* (1965), was substantially undercut in the name of federalism by *Younger v. Harris* (1971), raising the threshold of injury necessary to justify federal court intervention in pending state court proceedings.

The availability of *habeas corpus* for state prisoners in federal court was another roller coaster doctrine for Brennan. *Habeas corpus* is a civil proceeding generally providing post-conviction review of the rights of criminal defendants, and traditionally such review was conducted in the state courts. However, in *Fay v. Noia* (1963), Brennan significantly expanded the availability of federal court review of the fairness of state criminal convictions, allowing federal *habeas* petitions for claims such as unconstitutional confessions or improper searches and seizures. This step gave state prisoners, especially those on death row, a chance to be heard for many years. However, by the late 1970s, the Court was cutting back sharply on this Brennan doctrine, and in *Coleman v. Thompson* (1991), it was expressly overruled after Brennan had left the Court.

Despite significant setbacks to his aspirations for access to the federal courts, Brennan was not to give up. In a seminal article in the *Harvard Law Review* in 1977, and again in his second James Madison lecture in 1986, he urged civil rights lawyers to look to the state courts and state constitutions to protect individual liberties on a broader scale than the United States Supreme Court was willing to do. These urgings helped to spawn an entire constitutional movement toward rediscovery of the guarantees of state constitutions.

Justice Brennan's legacy in the field of equality was not his only contribution to our understanding of the Fourteenth Amendment. He is also directly responsible for the contemporary view that there are "fundamental" rights that are not expressly named in the Bill of Rights, but that are entitled to the highest levels of protection under the equal protection or due process clause. This concept has become an integral one to the body of constitutional law. It was also an important vehicle for expression of the themes of his jurisprudence—reading the Constitution as a twentieth-century document, one that was intended to promote and protect the virtues of human dignity and fairness.

In *Shapiro v. Thompson* (1969), one of the last of the Warren Court decisions, Brennan wrote for the majority that a one-year residency requirement to qualify for local welfare benefits violated the Constitution's right to travel. The decision declared this a fundamental right entitled to the strictest Fourteenth Amendment scrutiny because it directly affected the means of subsistence—"food, shelter and other necessities of life."

The decision by Brennan one year later in *Goldberg v. Kelly*, finding that welfare benefits were protected by the due process clause, was another significant step in this conception of fundamental rights. The decision squarely rejected the long-developing constitutional distinction between rights and privileges, finding that fundamental fairness was required regardless of the label placed on the program. The rigor of the due process required under such circumstances has since been curtailed by the Court, but the basic principle remains intact for government benefits, public employment, and other activities.

No fundamental right has been more controversial than the right to privacy and the related right of women to choose abortion. Here, too, Justice Brennan's influence is significant, although not always in ways that are readily apparent. In *Griswold v. Connecticut* (1965), an opinion by Justice Douglas recognizing a right to marital privacy that protected the use of contraceptives, Brennan worked behind the scenes to provide the rationale for finding privacy implicit in numerous portions of the Bill of Rights. It was Brennan who led the Court to the next step in *Eisenstadt v. Baird* (1972), holding that the equal protection clause prevented treating single women differently than married women for contraceptives.

When the privacy fight moved to yet another field the following year, Brennan once again played a pivotal role. The opinion upholding a right to abortion in *Roe v. Wade* (1973) was written by Justice Harry A. Blackmun, but Brennan was a moving force in internal Court deliberations to find the strongest possible rationale for the newly declared fundamental right. He remained a staunch defender of *Roe*, which remained under fire throughout his tenure, but his support was largely internal, and he never wrote an opinion about the substantive right to abortion.

A final facet of Justice Brennan's jurisprudence is the seemingly simple but important idea that government must be accountable to the people in court. Prior to the ruling in *Monell v. Department of Social Services* (1978), city and county governments were largely immune from lawsuits for damages under the Reconstruction-era federal civil rights law, commonly known as Section 1983, 42 U.S.C.A. 1983. But in *Monell*, Brennan held that local governments may be sued for damages under Section 1983, which provides liability for any deprivation of rights by persons acting "under color of" state law. The decision and others that followed it have prompted a virtual revolution in civil rights litigation.

Similar accountability may apply to federal officials, not under Section 1983, since federal officials never act under color of state law, but directly under provisions of the Bill of Rights. This doctrine, also part of the revolution in accountability, was established by Brennan in *Bivens v. Six Unknown Named Agents* (1971), in which a lawsuit for damages was allowed directly under the Fourth Amendment against federal narcotics agents for an egregious warrantless arrest and search. In *Davis v. Passman* (1979), a similar damages action was allowed against a member of Congress directly under the Fifth Amendment for sex discrimination in employment.

There are a few areas in which Justice Brennan's efforts might be classified as failures, although in some the measure is a subjective one capable of different spins. For example, some critics would consider Brennan's efforts in the gender discrimination arena less than successful because gender bias never achieved equal status with race discrimination. Others argue, however, that the middle level of scrutiny applied to gender bias cases is a significant step forward and that there is no failure there.

Two subjects on which Justice Brennan clearly made fewer inroads than he would have liked are the constitutional status of obscenity and the death penalty.

In Brennan's first term, Chief Justice Warren turned to him for a solution to the legal problem of obscenity. The result was the decision in *Roth v. United States* (1957), holding that obscene materials were not protected by the First Amendment, and offering the first of a number of definitions of obscenity produced over the next decade. This and other attempts to define obscenity in some practical way so that courts could enforce the law proved unworkable, but Brennan led the Court throughout the 1960s in trying to find a solution. He repeatedly rejected the absolutism of Justices Black and Douglas, who believed that the Court should not be in the business of picking and choosing protected speech.

Finally, however, Brennan, too, came to believe that no definition of obscenity could be developed that would allow individuals to conform their conduct to the law with some degree of certainty. He abandoned the definitional effort in a dissenting opinion in *Paris Adult Theatre I v. Slaton* (1973), arguing that obscene materials should be covered within the broad sweep of the First Amendment as long as there is no suggestion of exploiting or selling to minors. This recognition came too late, however, for the First Amendment constituency on the Court had dissipated and on the same day, the majority ruled in *Miller v. California* (1973), that the definition of obscenity and judgments about its prosecution should be left to local community standards.

Thereafter, Brennan dissented from virtually every obscenity decision, including the denial of review by the Supreme Court. Although this forced the Court to confront his position in each instance, it had little substantive impact on the majority.

Brennan's first visible concern with the death penalty came in a dissenting opinion in *McGautha v. California* (1971), in which he expressed strong concerns about the need for fairness in the procedures allowing juries to impose a death sentence. Within a year, however, Brennan had concluded that the death penalty posed not simply due process problems, but was itself inherently a form of cruel and unusual punishment in violation of the Eighth Amendment. This view, expressed in *Furman v. Georgia* (1972), was shared entirely only by Justice Thurgood Marshall. Other justices joined in *Furman* to find the death penalty unconstitutional as then applied in most states, but that coalition was short-lived, and a procedurally acceptable death penalty was reinstated in *Gregg v. Georgia* (1976).

Ironically, the decision in *Gregg* reflected some of the concerns Brennan had expressed in *McGautha*, but by that time he had moved on to the more cosmic view that the death penalty in any form violated the Eighth Amendment. As in the obscenity cases, Brennan dissented thereafter in every death penalty case that came before the Court. His standard "cruel and unusual punishment" dissent had little impact on other justices, but on rare occasions he was able to persuade a majority in a lengthier memorandum of the unfairness of the procedures in a particular case.

Still, Brennan felt as passionately about the death penalty at the end of his tenure as he had almost two decades earlier when he first raised the cruel and unusual punishment argument. As he explained in the Oliver Wendell Holmes lecture at Harvard Law School in 1986:

> As I read them, the Bill of Rights generally and the Eighth Amendment specifically insist that the state treat its members with respect for their intrinsic worth as human beings, and this is true even as the state punishes the commission of the most brutal crimes. . . .
> A punishment is "cruel and unusual" if it does not comport with human dignity. The calculated killing of a human being by the state involves, by its very nature, an absolute denial of the executed person's humanity, and thus violates the command of the Eighth Amendment.

Throughout his tenure, Justice William Brennan had been a constant target of critics who rejected his approach to the Constitution and to the proper role of the courts. These ranged from colleagues on the bench, Justices Frankfurter, Harlan, Black, and Scalia, among them, to luminaries in the academy. For example, Raoul Berger, the retired Harvard Law School scholar, argued in a 1988 article that Justice Brennan "brings his own agenda to the Constitution and is committed to a course that cannot be reconciled with the Constitution or with long established methods of construction." The level of criticism escalated in the 1980s, when the young conservatives who populated the Reagan administration Justice Department treated Brennan as if he were the cause of the deficit, the Cold War, and the rest of the world's ills. Yet Brennan was never fazed by this steady barrage and carried his approach proudly to his last moment on the bench.

While many colleagues and leaders of the profession have paid tribute to his career, two such commentaries spanning a decade sum up his legacy well. Dedicating its annual survey of American law to Justice Brennan in 1981, New York University Law School wrote, "By his strong advocacy of the Bill of Rights, he has changed the very way in which we look at the role of government and government's relation to the individual. Those searching for compassion and humanity in the law need only read the opinions of Justice Brennan."

A decade later in the *Harvard Civil Rights-Civil Liberties Review* of 1991, Justice Blackmun wrote, "By any measure, Justice Brennan must be regarded as one of the great names among those who have served on the Supreme Court of the United States. Whether one makes that evaluation by length of service, influential leadership, or number of significant opinions, the result is the same. Reflection upon Justice Brennan's accomplishments in all three areas makes it inevitable."

—STEPHEN J. WERMIEL

BIBLIOGRAPHY

Justice Brennan's collection of personal Court files is one of the richest ever assembled in Supreme Court annals. Housed at the Library of Congress in Washington, D.C., it is available with his permission to researchers engaged in scholarly pursuits. The collection includes files on thousands of cases, complete with exchanges, memoranda and draft opinions. His most recent files, for the Rehnquist Court, beginning in 1986, will not be open for a number of years.

Other general sources include Stephen J. Friedman, "William J. Brennan," in Friedman and Israel, 4 *Justices* 2849, and Nathan Lewin, "William J. Brennan," in the supplemental volume to that series, at 239. Other useful essays are collected in "The Jurisprudence of Justice William J. Brennan, Jr.," 139 *University of Penn-*sylvania Law Review* 1317 (1991), and "A Tribute to Justice William J. Brennan, Jr.," 104 *Harvard Law Review* 1 (1990).

Finally, some of Justice Brennan's major off-the-bench writings are: "Constitutional Adjudication and the Death Penalty: A View from the Court," 100 *Harvard Law Review* 313 (1986); "The Constitution of the United States: Contemporary Ratification," 27 *South Texas Law Review* 433 (1986); "State Constitutions and the Protection of Individual Rights," 90 *Harvard Law Review* 489 (1977); and "The Bill of Rights and the States," 36 *NYU Law Review* 761 (1961).

DAVID JOSIAH BREWER

BORN 20 June 1837, Smyrna, Asia Minor
[modern Turkey]
NOMINATED to the Court 4 December 1889
by Benjamin Harrison
TOOK seat 18 December 1889
DIED 28 March 1910 in Washington, D.C.

David J. Brewer was born to the Reverend Josiah Brewer, a New England Congregational clergyman noted for his opposition to slavery and war, and Emilia Field, the sister of Supreme Court Justice Stephen J. Field and prominent law reformer David Dudley Field. Brewer was raised in privilege in Wethersfield, Connecticut, and at age fifteen, entered Wesleyan College. He subsequently graduated from Yale University, studied briefly with his uncle, David Dudley Field, and then attended Albany Law School.

Adventurous in spirit and eager to free himself of the overpowering reputation of his uncle, Brewer decided in the late 1850s to launch his professional career in the rough-and-tumble environment of Kansas Territory. He quickly earned a reputation for his skill in representing railroad and business interests. A Republican, he filled several lower political and legal offices in the state before serving on the supreme court of Kansas (1870–1884) and the eighth federal circuit court (1884–1889). In 1890, President Benjamin Harrison elevated Brewer to the Supreme Court, in part because the well-qualified Kansas judge was a reluctant aspirant, a quality that Harrison admired.

A justice of considerable intelligence and energy, Brewer was fated to serve on a court that at various periods of his tenure included Stephen J. Field, John Marshall Harlan, and Oliver Wendell Holmes, Jr., justices genuinely brilliant and even more energetic than Brewer. Brewer nevertheless played a critical role in the history of the Court at the turn of the century. He joined with Rufus W. Peckham to become the intellectual leaders of the conservative bloc. Brewer believed strongly that the Court should limit governmental interference in the economy and permit the marketplace to distribute the inevitable rewards produced by capitalism. Brewer also had an almost unyielding adherence to the idea that the states should be free, under the Tenth Amendment, from federal interference. His orthodox conservatism resulted in more than 200 dissents during his years on the high court. Yet Brewer's views were not altogether predictable. His Congregational, missionary, and antislavery roots meant that he had a sympathetic ear for the disadvantaged.

Brewer's first important majority opinion came in *Reagan v. Farmers' Loan and Trust Co.* (1894), a case that showed clearly that, while the justice might believe in the idea of states' rights, he was wary of giving the states too much authority to interfere in the market place. *Reagan* stemmed from a decision by the Texas Railroad Commission to regulate railroad rates on commerce within the state. Brewer spoke for the Court in finding the regulation violated the rights of investors in the railroad because they were not receiving any return on their invested capital. Brewer's opinion limited the impact of *Munn v. Illinois* (1877), which had provided an opening wedge to state regulatory efforts, and in that respect exposed a philosophical link between the justice and his uncle, Stephen J. Field, who had originally dissented in *Munn* on the grounds that protection of property rights was the highest goal of the Constitution.

Brewer's conservative sympathies appeared most dramatically a year later in *In Re Debs* (1895), in which he wrote a unanimous opinion for the Court upholding an injunction against striking workers at the Pullman Palace Sleeping Car Company. Eugene Debs was the president of the American Railroad Union whose members protested an abrupt reduction in pay by the Pullman company. The strike spread to other unions who called for a general boycott of all Pullman rail cars, an action that disrupted interstate rail transportation and the movement of the mails.

Conservatives denounced the Pullman strike as a harbinger of an even more fearsome general working-class uprising. When the railroad owners refused to drop Pullman cars from service, violence ensued. U.S. Attorney General Richard Olney won an order from the federal district court in Chicago enjoining the strikers from interrupting the flow of the mails. When Debs ignored the injunction, he was found guilty of contempt of court. President Grover Cleveland subsequently broke the strike by dispatching federal troops to restore order and safe passage of the mails. Debs appealed his contempt conviction to the Supreme Court.

Brewer's unanimous opinion affirmed the injunctions and contempt citations against labor leaders accused of conspiring to block interstate commerce. Brewer held that the federal courts had broad powers to issue such injunctions in order to keep interstate commerce moving. Brewer also concluded that the federal government had a duty to protect the general welfare, the execution of which depended on a complementary power to apply to its own courts for assistance. Brewer realized that the best way to dilute the threat of labor unions was to severely restrict the strike as a tool by which to wring concessions from management.

The justice championed conservative property interests in other cases. He took part in the majority opinion in *Pollock v. Farmers' Loan and Trust Co.* (1895) that declared the federal income tax unconstitutional. Brewer's agreement with the majority, over the sharp dissents of four other justices, thwarted the federal government's attempt to impose a tax on income until the adoption of the Sixteenth Amendment in 1913.

He objected on constitutional and philosophical grounds to most other efforts that interfered with economic activity. He was, for example, a silent dissenter in *Holden v. Hardy* (1898). The majority upheld the constitutionality of a Utah law that restricted miners and other workers employed in smelters to an eight-hour day except in case of emergency. The majority sustained the statute based on the scope of the police power of the states to provide for the health, safety, morals, and welfare of their citizenry. In this instance, the Court found the regulations particularly appropriate since they dealt with hazardous occupations. Brewer's silent disagreement with the decision no doubt stemmed from a dilemma in his own thinking. The justice favored the rights of states to manage their internal affairs and at the same time opposed state actions that would strengthen labor unions and weaken employers. He usually chose to honor the latter when forced to choose between these competing principles.

Much the same situation confronted him in the landmark case of *Lochner v. New York* (1905), where he again silently joined the majority. The state of New York had fined Joseph Lochner for violating a labor law prohibiting employment in bakeries for more than sixty hours a week or more than ten hours per day. Lochner appealed his conviction to the high court based on the grounds that he should be free to contract for his wages and working conditions.

Justice Peckham's majority opinion held that the New York law did indeed interfere with Lochner's freedom to contract. While recognizing that the state had lawful police powers, Peckham emphasized that the legislation based on those powers had to be reasonably related to the ends asserted by the state. A majority of the Court held that New York state had failed to show that the hours worked by bakers in excess of the statute endangered either them or the public. The Court concluded that the due process guarantee of liberty under the Fourteenth Amendment outweighed the state's competing interest in protecting an individual from excessive toil. Brewer joined with the majority because he feared that statutes such as the New York bake shop law undermined traditional capitalistic notions, such as the freedom to contract.

Brewer was not altogether blinded by his devotion to capitalism. He was persuaded on occasion, for example, that the power of business could be properly restrained by government when it posed a threat to the market. He provided the decisive vote in *Northern Securities v. United States* (1904), when the justices sustained President Theodore Roosevelt's effort to set aside a merger between two corporate barons of the day, James Hill and J. P. Morgan.

Moreover, Brewer's Congregational background and the missionary experiences of his parents disposed him to a patronizing view of the disadvantaged. For example, his opinion for the Court in *Muller v. Oregon* (1908) seems on first

David Josiah Brewer
Collection of the Supreme Court of the United States.

impression to be at odds with his positions in *Lochner* and *Holden.* In *Muller,* Brewer sustained the constitutionality of an Oregon statute that imposed a ten-hour workday for women, distinguishing this case from *Holden* and *Lochner* on the grounds that they involved male workers. Brewer explained that women required special protection by the state and, arguably, less in the way of protection for their right to contract out their labor. Brewer explained that the ten-hour restriction was altogether appropriate, since "women's physical structure and the performance of maternal functions place her at a disadvantage in the struggle for subsistence." Such paternalistic assumptions about women were the rule and not the exception during his era. Brewer's opinion, for example, reached its conclusion by drawing on much of the argument made in support of it by Louis D. Brandeis, a social and legal reformer otherwise hostile to most of the justice's beliefs.

Brewer also regularly protested the treatment accorded the Chinese. Once again, his behavior on the Court reflected something of his childhood. As the son of a New England clergyman strongly opposed to slavery, Brewer balked at the discriminatory treatment accorded the Chinese under the Chinese Exclusion Acts of 1882 and 1892. These measures imposed strict bureaucratic burdens on Chinese aliens living in the United States and on those seeking to earn resident status. In *United States v. Sing Tuck* (1904), for example, a Chinese alien sued the federal government on the grounds that he had been denied due process in gaining prompt access to the courts. Brewer's powerful dissent in favor of the defendant asked rhetorically: "why should anyone who claims the right of citizenship be denied prompt access to the courts?" He insisted that a denial of due process had occurred because Chinese immigrants had failed to receive adequate administrative procedure to gain resident status. Brewer concluded by admonishing the majority that its position undermined American foreign relations with the most populous nation on earth and demeaned the Chinese people without cause.

Justice Brewer built an impressive record in support of Chinese immigrants, although he usually did so in the minority. For example, he not only dissented from Holmes's opinion in *Sing Tuck,* but in *United States v. Ju Toy* (1905), which denied resident Chinese access to the federal courts to try their claims of citizenship. He disagreed with Justice Harlan's majority opinion in the *Japanese Immigrant Case* (1903), which struck down a Japanese alien's claim for due process in deportation proceedings. He also dissented from the majority in *Fong Yue Ting v. United States* (1893), which involved the use of a pass system for resident Chinese. Brewer strongly believed, given the missionary past of his parents, that Chinese who had been converted to Christianity should also be given better protection under the federal Constitution.

One finds a mixed record where the rights of African Americans were concerned. He shared many of the racist sentiments of his day, affirming that a strong antislavery background did not immediately translate into support for government action designed to promote equality for blacks. In *Berea College v. Kentucky* (1908), for example, Brewer wrote for the Court in upholding a state statute prohibiting private schools and colleges from providing instruction on an integrated basis. He also held in *Hodges v. United States* (1906) that the federal government did not have power to prosecute a gang of whites who had forced blacks to leave their jobs in Arkansas.

Both of these decisions underscored strong states' rights beliefs. In *Berea,* he concluded that the state had total power over the corporations and other entities that it created by law. His reasoning in favor of states' rights was much the same in *Hodges,* where he affirmed that the police power equipped the states to deal exclusively with criminal acts carried out by whites against blacks. The only significant exception was his dissent in *Giles v. Harris* (1903). There he joined Harlan against an opinion by Holmes that sustained the massive disfranchisement of African Americans in the South.

Brewer's states' rights views informed other parts of his jurisprudence. For example, he delivered the opinion of the court in *Kansas v. Colorado* (1907), a case raising the question of whether, under the Tenth Amendment, the federal government was one of delegated powers and, if so, whether those powers not specifically delegated were reserved to the states. In this instance, Kansas had sought to enjoin Colorado from diverting waters of the Arkansas River to the detriment of Kansas. The United States government joined the suit claiming that it had the right under the commerce power to control the waters.

The justice dismissed the position of the federal government on the grounds that the Constitution did not expressly grant to Washington the right to control the waters. Such a right was, according to Brewer, clearly reserved to the states. "The proposition that there are legislative powers," Brewer wrote, "not expressed in the grant of powers, is in direct conflict with the doctrine that this is a government of enumerated powers. . . ." Brewer concluded that under the enumerated powers doctrine, the federal government had no constitutional prerogative to control water simply because of its interstate nature.

Brewer was adamant in his belief that the states controlled the bulk of power in the federal system. In *Leisy v. Hardin* (1908), for example, he dissented when the majority held that the interstate nature of liquor shipped into a state prevented that state from regulating it. The police powers were reserved exclusively to the states, Brewer insisted in a dissent joined by Justices Harlan and Horace Gray. If a state did not wish to have liquor brought across its borders, then the federal government could not make it do so. Brewer had made a similar point five years earlier in *Champion v. Ames* (1903), when he argued in dissent against the constitutionality of a federal law that tried to regulate the sales of lottery tickets across state lines. He had explained that to "hold that Congress has general police power would be to hold that it may accomplish objects not entrusted to the general government, and to defeat the operation of the Tenth Amendment."

His commitment to states' rights even extended to preventing the federal government from outlawing the keeping of an alien woman for the purposes of prostitution. In *Keller v. United States* (1909), Brewer held that the regulation of prostitution was clearly a matter for the states, one that fell within their exclusive police powers. Even though the Constitution gave Congress broad powers over aliens, that authority did not extend to the punishment of crimes. The reasoning here was particularly disingenuous in light of his ruling in *Muller*, since the alien woman in question was not charged with a crime, but rather those persons forcing her into prostitution were criminally liable. Brewer's quest to curb federal power, therefore, yielded somewhat strained results.

David Brewer was a conservative judge with an activist vision of the judge's role. He distrusted most of the popular movements of his day, especially the rise of organized labor, which he viewed as an agent of anarchism and a threat to civilization. In this regard, he was much like Holmes. Yet unlike Holmes, Brewer was eager to join the fray and refused to defer to the legislative branch. He believed that he and his judicial contemporaries should lead not follow in attempting to ensure a free market for capitalism, some appropriate procedural protection for the disadvantaged, and in releasing the states to realize fully their police powers.

Brewer seems antique today. His substantive conservatism on issues of federalism and economic reform disturbs modern-day liberals, while his expansive notion of the power of the judiciary flies in the face of conservatives who believe that judges should defer to the legislative branch. Brewer was an idealist for his conservative times, one sufficiently committed to his beliefs that he thought judicial power an appropriate means of securing them.

—KERMIT L. HALL

BIBLIOGRAPHY

Michael J. Broadhead, "David J. Brewer: A Jurist's Life," (Ph.D dissertation, the University of Kansas, 1991), provides a thorough analysis of Brewer's life and times with a sound discussion of his major opinions. Shorter sketches can be found by Owen M. Fiss in Kermit L. Hall, ed. *The Oxford Companion to the Supreme Court of the United States* (1992), 89–91, and by Arnold M. Paul in Friedman and Israel, 2 *Justices* 1515. Henry J. Abraham, *Justices and Presidents: A Political History of Appointments to the Supreme Court,* 2nd. ed. (1985), provides a thoughtful analysis of the appointment of Brewer to the Court and the political impact on his jurisprudence.

HENRY BILLINGS BROWN

BORN 2 March 1836, South Lee,
Massachusetts

NOMINATED to the Court 23 December 1890
by Benjamin Harrison

TOOK seat 5 January 1891; retired
28 May 1906

DIED 4 September 1913 in New York City

"We consider the underlying fallacy of the plaintiff's argument," wrote Associate Justice Henry Billings Brown for the majority in *Plessy v. Ferguson* (1896), to consist in the assumption "that the enforced separation of the two races stamps the colored race with a badge of inferiority. If this be so, it is not by reason of anything found in the act, but solely because the colored race chooses to put that construction upon it." In this opinion, Brown's most famous and infamous, can be detected the intellectual and social assumptions of the late nineteenth century.

Born into an upper-middle-class family in South Lee, Massachusetts, educated at prep schools and Yale College, and trained in law through apprenticeship and study at the Yale and Harvard law schools, Henry Billings Brown personified the dominant class of his time. A man of ability, a lawyer of talent, and a judge for his era, Brown's life produced a justice who could forthrightly say that separation did not imply the inferiority of blacks. However, Brown could also demonstrate flexibility in his judicial thought, as he did in such cases as *Pollock v. Farmers' Loan and Trust Company* (1895) and *Holden v. Hardy* (1898).

Before joining the court, Brown lived and worked in Detroit, Michigan. In 1860, he became a deputy United States marshall and soon became acquainted with the work of the federal district court in Detroit. Because of the court's location on Lake Erie, he became knowledgeable in admiralty issues. In 1863, President Abraham Lincoln appointed Brown an assistant United States attorney, a position he held until 1868 when he received appointment to the Wayne County circuit court. When he lost his bid to be

elected to that court, Brown entered private practice. In 1875, President Ulysses S. Grant appointed Brown to the federal district court of eastern Michigan, his bench for the next fourteen years.

As a federal district judge, Brown became noted for his control of technical issues and admiralty law. One historian has argued that Brown was "a lawyer's judge," that he disciplined himself to "carefully analyze complex factual situations." This quality of Brown's jurisprudence meant that although he could master the issues and rules in dispute, he was not intellectually disposed to establish new directions for judicial and public policy, as can be seen in *Plessy*, where Brown validated existing discrimination. Using careful planning and politicking, Brown sought a Supreme Court position, and in December 1890, on the death of Justice Samuel Miller, President Benjamin Harrison appointed him to the high court.

Brown disposed of his share of the routine business of the Court. Because of his knowledge of the lower federal courts, Brown often decided cases involving the calculation of fees for lower federal officials and the payment of federal fines, such as in *Massachusetts Benefit Association v. Miles* (1891) and *United States v. Kingsley* (1891). He also penned the usual spectrum of minor cases, such as *Cope v. Cope* (1891), resolving a conflict of laws question, and *Barbed Wire Patent* (1892), resolving the tangled barbed wire controversy on behalf of Joseph Glidden. In addition, because of his admiralty knowledge, Brown often wrote the decisions regarding shipping, such as *The Oregon* (1895).

Although Brown brought important skills to the Supreme Court, what most informed his approach to judging was his background and the dominant intellectual assumptions of his era. Brown viewed the world from a white, male, upper-middle-class perspective which embraced social Darwinism. Social Darwinism held that certain groups had achieved social and economic prominence because, through "natural selection," they had proven to be the most "fit" in the society. America's dominant groups of the late nine-teenth century eagerly adopted this ideology, first, because it justified their control of the society, and second, because the theory made it appear as though their dominance was "natural"; therefore, any attempt to ameliorate the social or economic conditions of "lesser" peoples or races was not only wrong-headed and unscientific, but unnatural.

Although Brown shared these ideas and assumptions, he was not always prepared to press the law into those intellectual channels. For example, when the Court invalidated the income tax in *Pollock v. Farmers' Loan and Trust Company*, Brown dissented. He might have been expected to decide that the tax was a taking from the worthy and a redistribution to the unworthy (as the majority did), but Brown disagreed. Instead, he argued that the income tax was a common instrument used throughout the world as a basis for supporting governments, and by striking down the proposed income tax, the Court had surrendered to the fears of the "moneyed class." Brown would have upheld the income tax as an appropriate governmental policy.

In the 1898 case, *Holden v. Hardy,* which involved Utah's regulation to protect men in a dangerous occupation (hard-rock mining), Brown upheld the power of the states to use their state police power to protect the workers' health and safety. Although the Supreme Court had already built the judicial doctrine of substantive due process as a device to overturn state legislation which interfered with private property rights, in *Holden*, Brown carved out a protected class of persons for which the states could legitimately legislate for—male miners. In cases such as *Holden*, Brown emphasized that the judicial test of a state's statute was whether it was "an exercise of reasonable discretion, or whether its action be a mere excuse for an unjust discrimination, or the oppression, or spoliation of a particular class."

In the *Plessy* case, Brown relied on the reasonableness of the equal but separate doctrine in ruling in favor of Jim Crow railroad cars. In fact, the decision in the case so mirrored the spirit of its times that the decision's announcement failed to generate any controversy. As the most careful student of the *Plessy* case, historian Charles A. Lofgren, has demonstrated, Brown's decision in *Plessy* (though poorly crafted) reflected the era's racial, social, and legal assumptions. Most whites believed that blacks were an inferior race and, therefore, while the Thirteenth and Fourteenth Amendments might have established a rough legal equality between the races, those amendments certainly did not establish social equality. So, if the state of Louisiana separated the races on railroad cars, not only was it free to do so without violating any black rights, but such a policy was a "reasonable regulation" and a valid use of the state's power. If blacks took offense at the separation, in Brown's thinking, it was because blacks were inferior; they failed to understand the true purpose (and benefit for both races) of separation. "If one race be inferior to the other socially," he explained, "the Constitution of the United States cannot put them on the same plane."

When Justice John Marshall Harlan dissented from Brown's opinion, a dissent which remarkably foreshadowed the Supreme Court's reversal of *Plessy* nearly a half-century later in *Brown v. Board of Education* (1954), his was practically the only voice in the country (and the only judicial voice) opposing racial segregation. *Plessy* may offend the sensibility of modern readers, but it is a testament to the changing values of the country and an example of how American law conveys those values into public policy. Although Brown is often censured for his decision in *Plessy*, perhaps he was guilty only of being a "reasonable" American in the Gilded Age.

—THOMAS C. MACKEY

BIBLIOGRAPHY

On Brown and especially the *Plessy* case, see Charles A. Lofgren, *The Plessy Case: A Legal-Historical Interpretation* (1987). Also see Joel Goldfarb, "Henry Billings Brown," in Friedman and Israel, 2 *Justices* 1553; and Robert J. Glennon, Jr., "Justice Henry Billings Brown: Values in Tension," 44 *University of Colorado Law Review* 553 (1973).

WARREN EARL BURGER

BORN 17 September 1907, St. Paul, Minnesota

NOMINATED to the Court 21 May 1969
   by Richard M. Nixon

TOOK seat 10 June 1969; retired 10 July 1986

The influence of a chief justice is difficult to evaluate. Although nominally the leader of the Court, except for administrative matters he has almost no formal power over the Court's decision making. He does decide who writes the Court's opinion, and he can always take the important decisions for himself. Even then, however, he must be among the majority, or he loses the opinion-assignment power to the senior justice on the other side.

The chief justice's ability to use the exalted status of "Chief Justice of the United States" to exercise leadership on the Court thus depends on intangible qualities of character, intellect, persuasiveness, and respect. Whichever of these it was that Warren Burger lacked, he will not be remembered as one of the Court's great leaders. Earl Warren would have been a difficult act to follow under any circumstances, especially by someone chosen to undo much of Warren's legacy while some of the strong figures who were Warren's allies—William J. Brennan, Thurgood Marshall, and William O. Douglas—still sat on the Court. Warren Burger, however, did not even come close.

Nevertheless, Chief Justice Warren Burger had a great impact on American life, if only by exercising the one-ninth of the Supreme Court's enormous power that every justice has. That power was especially important during Burger's tenure, for although it is not generally realized, during his term of service as chief justice, the Court plunged into some of the most controversial aspects of American life. Much that the previous Court did is no longer fought over. *Miranda v. Arizona* (1966), *Mapp v. Ohio* (1961), the apportionment cases, *Brown v. Board of Education* (1954)—these highlights of the Warren Court are now accepted parts of American life and law, despite continued periodic

mutterings about *Miranda* and *Mapp*. But *Roe v. Wade* (1973), the affirmative action cases, the church-state decisions, issues of presidential power, of access to the courts—the subjects of the great cases of the Burger era—are still surrounded by heated controversy.

Warren Earl Burger is one of America's great personal success stories. Born in a working-class family in Minnesota, he attended night school at the St. Paul College of Law. He then practiced law in Minnesota for more than twenty years, and worked with Harold Stassen in Minnesota politics from the 1930s until the 1950s, managing Stassen's unsuccessful presidential campaigns in 1948 and 1952. In 1952, he backed General Dwight D. Eisenhower for the Republican nomination for the presidency and was rewarded by being made assistant attorney general in charge of the civil division of the Department of Justice. There he attained some notoriety by arguing a Supreme Court case defending the use of faceless accusers when the solicitor general, Simon Sobeloff, refused to do so (*Peters v. Hobby,* 1955). In 1955, President Eisenhower nominated him to the court of appeals for the District of Columbia circuit, where he began a bitter lifelong feud with Judge David Bazelon, then chief judge of the court and one of its leading liberals.

After *Miranda v. Arizona* was decided in 1966, Burger became a persistent critic of the decision. Law and order was a major issue in the 1968 election, and Burger's articles and views came to Richard Nixon's attention. Conservative, but not known as an extremist, and very strong on law and order, Burger seemed the ideal person for Nixon to appoint as Earl Warren's successor.

Shortly after becoming chief justice, Warren Burger made it clear that in addition to reducing protection for the rights of the criminally accused, he had at least one other item on his agenda: discouraging the efforts of public interest lawyers and others to go to the federal courts for some kind of redress for social injustice. Stimulated by the *Brown* case, lawyers for women, prisoners, the handicapped, and other disadvantaged groups had turned to the federal courts to obtain the justice they could not get elsewhere. In 1971, Burger told *New York Times* correspondent Fred Graham that young lawyers should not look to the courts for social change and promised them "some disappointments" if they did.

As it happened, however, the first controversial cases to face Burger involved school desegregation. Part of Richard Nixon's southern strategy was to allow southern school boards to continue to resist or evade desegregation. They had managed to do that quite successfully since 1955, but in 1968, the Supreme Court finally ordered that desegregation be achieved "NOW." The federal courts of appeals promptly began to issue orders requiring school boards to comply with plans drawn up by officials of the Department of Health, Education, and Welfare (HEW) under its guidelines.

Some six months after Nixon became president, however, HEW withdrew its guidelines. Southern trial judges, many of whom had always been hostile to the *Brown* ruling, immediately ordered delays in implementing desegregation plans. Within a few months, one of these cases, *Alexander v. Holmes County Board of Education* (1969), was on the Court's calendar as the very first case facing the new chief justice.

The drama of the situation was obvious. For the first time since *Brown*, the Justice Department supported a school board against black litigants, and the entire southern school desegregation effort was at stake. The time usually given for oral argument in the Court was doubled. According to Bob Woodward and Scott Armstrong in *The Brethren*, the case produced a great deal of dispute within the Court, with Burger initially inclined to support the delay. However, the Court ultimately decided to unanimously order immediate desegregation, with Burger going along.

Thereafter, Burger generally supported efforts at school desegregation. During the term after the *Alexander County* case, Burger wrote a major decision for a unanimous Court authorizing federal courts to use busing and other remedies to achieve desegregation *(Swann v. Char-*

lotte-Mecklenburg Board of Education, 1971). Two years later, in 1973, he joined Justice Brennan's opinion for the Court in the Denver school case, setting down certain rules that made it possible to desegregate northern and western schools where, unlike the South, segregation was not mandated by a state statute, but was a result of state or local school board actions *(Keyes v. School District No. 1, Denver, Colorado,* 1973). And six years later, in 1979, in the last of the Court's major school desegregation cases during Burger's tenure, he split his vote in two cases from Ohio, *Dayton Board of Education v. Brinkman* and *Columbus Board of Education v. Penick.*

All in all, Burger's record in school desegregation showed a cautious sympathy. The sympathy was undercut by his joining a 5–4 decision in 1974 in which he chose to write the Court's opinion. In a case involving Detroit and its suburbs, the Court blocked efforts to bring suburbs into the desegregation process, except in rare circumstances *(Milliken v. Bradley,* 1974). The effect on school desegregation efforts verged on the catastrophic. America was increasingly becoming a nation of black central cities and white suburbs, and the ruling made it virtually impossible to prevent the proliferation of impoverished black center-city school districts surrounded by a ring of affluent white districts. The Court's 5–4 decision the previous year in a Texas case refusing to require equalization of state financing, which Burger also joined, only made things worse *(San Antonio Independent School District v. Rodriguez,* 1973).

Oscillation characterized other aspects of Burger's civil rights record. He was the author of what may still be the most important civil rights decision since *Brown, Griggs v. Duke Power Company* (1971). Title VII of the Civil Rights Act of 1964 banned discrimination in employment. In *Griggs*, the Court unanimously interpreted Title VII to prohibit employers from using a hiring method that produced a work force that does not reflect the relevant labor pool unless the employer can show a business necessity for using that method. Whether or not the employer intends to discriminate is irrelevant, Burger wrote.

Warren Earl Burger
Collection of the Supreme Court of the United States.

The Act proscribes not only overt discrimination but also practices that are fair in form but discriminatory in operation . . . that operate as "built-in headwinds" for minority groups and are unrelated to job performance.

This recognition that the problems facing minorities in America are attributable to institutionalized racism and prejudice, as much as to overt intentional discrimination, has been very rare in Supreme Court jurisprudence.

The chief justice was also supportive of efforts to cope with discrimination against minorities in a 1980 decision upholding the authority of the federal government to set aside a certain portion of federal contracts for minority businesses (*Fullilove v. Klutznick, 1980*).

On the other hand, except for *Fullilove*, Burger consistently voted against affirmative action efforts in education and employment, whether in dissent or in the majority. Also, apart from *Griggs*, he usually voted for a narrow interpretation of Title VII's ban on discrimination in employment. And though he wrote the first major decision striking down discrimination against women (*Reed v. Reed, 1971*), he usually voted against efforts to eliminate gender discrimination.

As the years went on, Chief Justice Burger became increasingly conservative. This rightward tilt was not restricted to civil rights. In his last five years, his most frequent ally was the Court's most extreme conservative, William H. Rehnquist, voting with him at least 80 percent of the time. By the time Burger retired, he had become one of the most conservative members of his Court.

Although Chief Justice Burger's record on civil rights was mixed, it was anything but that where access to the courts to redress official injury was concerned. During his seventeen years on the Court, he consistently wrote or joined decisions denying litigants such access, stating that the plaintiffs either did not have enough of an interest to prosecute the action or that in some other way they had not sufficiently demonstrated the existence of the "case or controversy" that a federal court was constitutionally allowed to adjudicate. In many of these, the vote was 5–4, so

that Burger's vote was crucial, and he wrote many of these decisions. In 1972, for example, a 5–4 majority of the Court, in a Burger opinion, refused to allow a challenge to the Army's systematic surveillance of antiwar demonstrations (*Laird v. Tatum*). Two years later, a 5–4 and a 6–3 decision, again both written by Burger, denied citizens the right to assert a constitutional right to see the CIA budget (*United States v. Richardson*), and to block Senator Barry Goldwater and other members of Congress from violating a constitutional ban on serving in both Congress and the military (*Schlesinger v. Reservists Committee to Stop the War*). During the next two years, two other close decisions denied poor blacks and others the right to challenge a housing ordinance that effectively kept them out of a Rochester, New York suburb (*Warth v. Seldin, 1975*), and an Internal Revenue Service regulation that lifted hospitals' incentive to serve poor people (*Simon v. Eastern Kentucky Welfare Rights Organization, 1976*). And ten years later, he joined a 5–3 decision that denied parents of black children the right to challenge the IRS's failure to deny tax exemptions to racially discriminatory private schools (*Allen v. Wright, 1984*). But when the Court wanted to uphold a law encouraging nuclear power, the chief justice had no trouble affirming the federal judiciary's authority to hear the case, even though the standing issue seemed very similar to cases where that authority had been denied (*Duke Power Co. v. Carolina Environmental Study Group, Inc., 1978*).

Despite this virtually unbroken line of hostile decisions, the efforts to deny litigants the opportunity to have a federal court hear their claims appear to have failed. The 1970s saw a burst of consumer, environmental, civil rights, and other social legislation, and in most of these, Congress included a right to go to federal court to enforce the rights created by the legislation. There was little Burger and his allies could do about that.

Chief Justice Burger's determination to undo the Warren Court's legacy in enhancing the rights of the accused was far more successful, though not quite in the way it was originally expected.

The three peaks of the Warren Court's jurisprudence in the criminal justice area were *Mapp v. Ohio* (1961), which required state courts to exclude unconstitutionally obtained evidence from state criminal trials; *Gideon v. Wainwright* (1963), which unanimously ruled that criminal defendants were entitled to a court-appointed lawyer if they could not afford one; and *Miranda v. Arizona* (1966), which required police to warn suspects in custody of their right not to be compelled to incriminate themselves. *Gideon* has been relatively noncontroversial, but *Mapp* and *Miranda* each produced very hostile reactions from police prosecutors and their political allies.

Many, therefore, assumed that when Harry Blackmun joined the Court a few months after Burger, and the law-and-order conservatives had gained a majority on the Court, they would immediately overturn *Mapp* and *Miranda*. The Court did not, and more than a quarter-century later, the decisions are still good law and likely to remain so.

One reason is simply that the decisions have not proven to be much of a hindrance to effective law enforcement. If anything, *Mapp* has probably improved police efficiency. A more significant reason was stated by Chief Justice Burger in one of his earliest efforts to reverse the Court's direction in a case that dealt with the right to sue federal officers for a constitutional violation like wrongly breaking into someone's house. There is no statute that provides compensation in such a case, and in 1971, the Court decided that the Constitution itself authorized such a remedy (*Bivens v. Six Unnamed Police Agents*, 1971). Chief Justice Burger protested. In his dissent, he went beyond the issues in the case to attack the rule excluding unconstitutionally obtained evidence from criminal trials. He tempered his assault, however, with this obviously regretful qualification:

> I do not propose . . . that we abandon the suppression doctrine until some meaningful alternative can be developed. . . . Obviously the public interest would be poorly served if law enforcement officials were suddenly to gain the impression, however, erroneous, that all constitutional restraints had been removed.

These two considerations—the lack of an effective alternative and the possibility of en-

couraging police misconduct by giving the wrong impression—have probably been the main reasons that a fiercely prosecution-oriented Court refrained from overturning *Mapp*.

Instead, the Court continually chipped away and undermined it so that few restraints on police searches and seizures remained. The standard for when the police may search a person or place or arrest someone was diluted and diminished; many exceptions to the exclusionary rule were created or expanded; and privacy interests given constitutional protection were reduced.

As chief justice, Burger participated in all of these developments, and in the few cases where the Court did protect the privacy rights of an accused, he usually dissented. Surprisingly, given the reasons for his appointment, he chose to write infrequently, assigning the opinions in this field to others and contenting himself with simply voting.

The *Miranda* interrogation ruling received the same treatment as *Mapp*—it remained on the books, but much diminished. Creating exceptions, loosening its requirements, and denying it constitutional status drained the decision of much of its significance. Here too, Chief Justice Burger wrote little but simply voted consistently for upholding police action. In one interrogation case involving not *Miranda* but a related doctrine, he did refuse to allow a government informer to circumvent an indicted prisoner's right to counsel and wrote for the Court (*United States v. Henry*, 1980); a few years later, however, he joined a majority that backed off that ruling (*Kuhlmann v. Wilson*, 1986).

Without doubt, the most controversial decision during Warren Burger's tenure was *Roe v. Wade* (1973), which allowed women the right to choose to have an abortion. Seven members of the Court supported Justice Blackmun's opinion, including Burger, who silently went along. Although the ruling immediately came under fire from self-styled right-to-life groups, the decision itself held firm throughout Burger's years on the Court. The attacks came largely in the form of restrictions and obstacles that some states and localities tried to erect in order to prevent women from exercising their right.

The first major challenge occurred in a 1983 case from Akron, Ohio, and here the chief justice joined a majority striking down such restrictions as a requirement that first trimester abortions be performed in a hospital (*City of Akron v. Akron Center for Reproductive Health, Inc.,* 1983). This was practically the only time, however, that Burger voted against restrictions. He joined narrow majorities upholding the right of the federal government and state governments to refuse to fund abortions, and almost all the Rehnquist, White, and O'Connor dissents from decisions striking down restrictions, including the ruling that husbands may not veto abortions. By the time he retired, Burger was considered an automatic vote for virtually any plausible restriction. Indeed, in his last year on the Court he suggested that in light of some of the Court's rulings striking down state and locally imposed regulations, "we should reexamine *Roe*" (*Thornburgh v. American College of Obstetricians and Gynecologists,* 1986). What kind of "reexamination" he had in mind we cannot know, since he left the Court that year, but in view of his consistent support for almost any restriction, it is almost certain that he would at least have joined the Rehnquist opinions in *Webster* (1989) and in *Casey* (1992) significantly diluting *Roe*, though perhaps not the Scalia opinions calling for its overruling.

In light of Burger's post-*Roe* record, it comes as no surprise that in other matters affecting privacy and the family, Burger consistently voted to uphold restrictions or regulation. With a particularly harsh concurring opinion, he joined the Court's 5–4 opinion allowing states to criminalize homosexual behavior; he voted to uphold state restrictions on the distribution of contraceptives, even to adults; and he consistently voted to deny free speech and other rights to children.

Warren Burger's occasionally peculiar mix of positions is nowhere seen better than in his church-state decisions. The 1970s saw a fundamental reconstruction of the law regulating relations between religion and the state, and Burger played a very prominent role, usually writing something, often for a majority, but also many concurrences and dissents.

The Court had first grappled with church-state relationships in *Everson v. Board of Education* (1947). In a Janus-like combination of doctrine and outcome, the decision proved a forerunner of things to come. The opinion by Justice Hugo Black still ranks as one of the strongest statements ever made for a virtually complete separation of religion and the state. Nevertheless, Black and a 5–4 majority of the Court *allowed* substantial assistance to religious schools. As dissenting Justice Robert Jackson put it:

> [T]he undertones of the opinion, advocating complete and uncompromising separation of Church from State, seem utterly discordant with its conclusion yielding support to their commingling in educational matters.

Then, in the 1960s, the Court issued its two decisions banning officially mandated school prayers, *Engel v. Vitale* (1962), and Bible readings, *Abington School District v. Schempp* (1963), which are still among the Court's most controversial and least accepted rulings, at least in some parts of the country and among some groups.

Despite the great significance and impact of these cases, there were relatively few church-state cases during the Warren years. The Court's primary concerns were elsewhere—race, criminal justice, and apportionment. That has changed, and since 1970, hardly a year has passed without at least one or two important church-state separation cases. Chief Justice Burger's influence can be seen in the fact that almost all of these decisions invoke one or the other of his two earliest church-state opinions in decisions that face in very different directions.

In the 1962 school prayer case, the Court stated that to survive a challenge under the establishment clause of the First Amendment, official action must have "a secular legislative purpose and a primary effect that neither advances nor inhibits religion." Then in 1970, Burger's first year on the Court, he was forced to deal with one of the most delicate issues the Court would encounter in its entire church-state jurisprudence: tax exemptions for property used for religious purposes. The Court responded with surprising concord. In an opinion Burger wrote for eight members of the Court (only Justice Douglas dissented), he permitted the exemption. "[An] unbroken practice of according the exemption to the Churches . . . is not something to be lightly cast aside," he wrote in *Walz v. Tax Commission*. In prior cases, history had been used to justify separation of church and state. Now it was being used by the Court to allow state involvement, a tactic that opponents of separation would resort to increasingly over the next twenty years.

The following year, Burger wrote *Lemon v. Kurtzman* (1971), the first of many Burger Court cases involving state grants of money or services to religious schools, and the source of what was to become the controversial *Lemon* test. Pennsylvania and Rhode Island had provided supplemental salary payments to teachers of secular subjects in private schools, most of them religious. In finding these payments inconsistent with the establishment clause, Burger drew on the prior decisions to put together a three-part test that became the standard for state action involving religious entities: (1) the action must have a *secular purpose* (though there may also be a religious purpose); (2) the *primary effect* of the action must not be either the advancement or the inhibition of religion; and (3) ensuring that the action will not promote religion must not *entangle* the government too much in religious affairs.

This *Lemon* test became the dominant criterion. Although continually under fire by both members of the Court and scholars as vague, unhelpful, and confusing, it has lasted for more than twenty years, and as recently as 1992, the Court declined an invitation to abandon it. The best indication of how little guidance it has provided is its own author's record. For though the Court has purported to apply the *Lemon* test in almost all of its establishment clause decisions (with a few notable exceptions), Burger dissented from almost all those that found the state involvement unconstitutional and voted with the majority in all those that upheld the state action. Whether the issue was free services or other aid to parochial schools, a moment of silence for prayer, religious symbols on public property, or tax deductions or credits, Burger almost always

read his three-part test to uphold the state involvement. Most of the time he was in dissent, usually with Justices Rehnquist and White, for during this period, the Court, often by the narrowest of majorities, voted to erect a substantial barrier of separation between church and state.

In justifying his effort to uphold the state action aiding or otherwise involving government in religion, Burger said that he was relying "more on experience and history than on logic," as he did in his very first ruling on the property tax case. "Experience and history" were the basis for his 1984 opinion for the Court in the legislative chaplain case (*Marsh v. Chambers,* 1983), where he wrote for a 6–3 majority of the Court upholding Nebraska's employment of a Presbyterian chaplain because legislative chaplains had existed "from colonial times through the founding of the Republic and ever since."

Chief Justice Burger's two-part legacy to the church-state issue—the *Lemon* test and the reliance on historical practice—is not likely to last. Those who seek more leeway for state involvement and support for religion hope to undo the *Lemon* test. On the other hand, they are not likely to support a substantial reliance on history, for they recognize that this would allow practices that are inappropriate for the society that we are today, regardless of how well-established they were 200 years ago. What Warren Burger did accomplish with the *Lemon* test, probably unintentionally, was to provide a simple-sounding formula synthesizing preexisting tendencies, which was used by the dominant majority of the 1970s and 1980s to erect a substantial wall of separation.

The final area for discussion is one that especially interested Chief Justice Burger: executive power. In retrospect, it is likely that the most momentous decision of Warren Burger's years on the Court was *United States v. Nixon* (1974), the Nixon tapes case. By ultimately providing the smoking gun that proved President Nixon's complicity in the cover-up, it brought down a president. By President Nixon's compliance with the Court's order, which was hardly a foregone conclusion when the suit began, the case established the primacy of the rule of law. And by exploring the nature of executive privilege in the context of both criminal and impeachment proceedings, it was a major statement on the American system of separation of powers.

As told by Woodward and Armstrong in an account that has not been challenged, it was not one of the chief justice's finest hours. Although the opinion in the case appeared over his name, his original draft was rejected by the other justices and the final product was a patched-up compromise to which he contributed relatively little. Compromise over controversial issues is, of course, quite normal, but it is clear that Burger was not much of a leader here. The compromise itself, as set forth in the Court's opinion, seems sound: the president has a constitutionally based executive privilege, but absent sensitive national security, military, or diplomatic considerations, evidence essential to the fair administration of criminal justice must be turned over to a grand jury; a merely general claim of executive privilege will not suffice. Perhaps most importantly, the president must submit to the courts for an adjudication of the matter. He is not above the law.

That Warren Burger was not a great leader of the Court seems generally acknowledged. He is not considered to have run the Court efficiently, and he certainly did not minimize conflict. Few justices apparently respected either his intellect or his character. Some felt that he played fast and loose with Court rules to manipulate the outcome or the assignment of opinions—there are reports of his shifting his position from minority to the majority in order to take advantage of the chief justice's authority to assign the opinion-writing when in the majority. And there have been repeated charges that he breached the Court's confidentiality by discussing pending cases with President Nixon.

History is more likely to rate Warren Burger as a competent and cautious conservative who, despite his conservative instincts and calls for judicial restraint, presided over one of the most activist periods in the Court's history, when it produced results that were anything but conservative. For a man who came to the Court committed to reducing its role in the quest for social

justice, the great irony is that during his tenure the Court greatly enhanced the rights of women, minorities, prisoners, and other disadvantaged groups, erected a relatively high wall of separation of church and state, did not significantly reduce the amount of litigation seeking social change, and wound up drawing the ire of right-wing conservatives at least as much, if not more, than its predecessor. It also contributed to the downfall of the president who appointed almost half of its membership. Neither Richard Nixon nor Warren Burger expected *that* when Richard Nixon made Warren Earl Burger chief justice of the United States.

—HERMAN SCHWARTZ

BIBLIOGRAPHY

There is no biography of Burger, nor are his papers available to scholars. Good overviews of the Court during the Burger years are Vincent Blasi, ed. *The Burger Court: The Counter-Revolution That Wasn't* (1986); Arthur L. Galub, *The Burger Court: 1968–1984* (1986); Charles M. Lamb and Stephen C. Halpern, eds., *The Burger Court: Political and Judicial Profiles* (1991); and Herman Schwartz, ed. *The Burger Years: Rights and Wrongs in the Supreme Court 1969–1986* (1987). An "inside" view of the Court during Burger's early tenure is Bob Woodward and Scott Armstrong, *The Brethren* (1979).

On criminal law, see Jerold H. Israel, "Criminal Procedure, the Burger Court, and the Legacy of the Warren Court," 75 *Michigan Law Review* 1320 (1977); Wayne R. and Jerold Israel, *Criminal Procedure* (1984). For religion cases, see Norman Redlich, "Separation of Church and State: The Burger Court's Tortuous Journey," 60 *Notre Dame Law Review* 1094 (1985). The Nixon case is discussed in the symposium, "United States v. Nixon," 22 *UCLA Law Review* 4 (1974), and for abortion, see Sarah Weddington, *A Question of Choice* (1992).

Burger's views on a number of topics are covered in "Symposium: The Jurisprudence of Chief Justice Warren E. Burger," 45 *Oklahoma Law Review* 1 (1992).

HAROLD HITZ BURTON

BORN 22 June 1888, Jamaica Plain, Massachusetts

NOMINATED to the Court 18 September 1945 by Harry S Truman

TOOK seat 1 October 1945; retired 13 October 1958

DIED 28 October 1964 in Washington, D.C.

Harold Burton was the first of President Harry Truman's four appointments to the Supreme Court. A career politician with no prior judicial experience, Burton brought a pragmatic style of decision making to a Court characterized by ideological conflict. Burton never earned great distinction, but his moderating influence helped to ease the Court through one of its more divisive periods.

Born in a suburb of Boston and educated in eastern schools, Burton decided after graduating from Harvard Law School in 1912 that leaving the East would lead him to greater opportunities for a successful legal career. He ultimately settled in Cleveland, where he established a successful law practice, taught corporate law at Western Reserve University, and served for four years as the city's law director.

Burton's first love was politics, however, and he wasted no time cultivating his ties to the local Republican party organization. From 1935 to 1940, he served as Cleveland's mayor, during which time he lowered the city's crime rate, reduced its deficit, and broke the patronage network. In 1940, Ohio voters easily elected the popular mayor to the United States Senate, where he assumed a moderate stance on domestic issues, while vigorously supporting Franklin Roosevelt's interventionist foreign policy.

On September 18, 1945, President Truman nominated Burton to replace Justice Owen Roberts, who had resigned at the end of the 1944 term. Burton and Truman had worked closely while both were senators and many observers attributed Burton's appointment to the cronyism that characterized Truman's administration, especially since Burton had no prior judicial ex-

perience. In fact, Burton's nomination satisfied several mandates. The retirement of Roberts left Chief Justice Harlan Fiske Stone as the Court's sole Republican member. Burton's appointment, then, met the demands of Republican leaders in Congress that Truman restore some political balance to the Court. At the same time, Burton's moderate and pragmatic politics convinced Truman that Burton would be neither intensely partisan nor fiercely ideological on the Court. Finally, Burton's status as a sitting member of the Senate promised easy confirmation. Truman's calculations proved accurate, for the Senate approved Burton unanimously the day after he was nominated.

During Burton's tenure the Supreme Court was characterized by heated disagreements between judicial activists who favored expansive powers of judicial review, and advocates of judicial restraint, who encouraged deference to legislative judgments. Burton gravitated toward the latter group with opinions that generally upheld legislative enactments and decided cases on narrow procedural grounds.

His restraint was more a product of his political beliefs than a commitment to judicial ideology, however. For example, he supported national security measures because he subscribed to Cold War politics; he favored desegregation because he found racial discrimination personally abhorrent; and he urged restrictions on the right to picket because he feared the effect of organized labor on corporate power. In short, he deferred to legislative judgments because he agreed with them, not necessarily because he believed the political branches had the exclusive power to formulate public policy.

Because Burton's political beliefs closely resembled those of Truman, the president was rarely disappointed with his selection. In several cases, Burton supported the Justice Department's efforts to regulate business through the antitrust statutes. In *Lichter v. United States* (1948), he upheld the government's power to renegotiate wartime contracts to curb fraud and profiteering, a subject that Burton and Truman had investigated when they served in the Senate. In fact, Burton's only significant disagreement with Truman's executive policies occurred in *Youngstown Sheet and Tube Co. v. Sawyer* (1952), which rejected Truman's authority to seize the nation's steel mills in order to avert a strike during the Korean War. Burton's concurring opinion rested on the grounds that the Taft-Hartley Act of 1947 prescribed other methods for resolving labor disputes and specifically reserved to Congress the power to authorize seizure. While generally sympathetic to the exercise of executive power, Burton's congressional experience had instilled in him a respect for the separation of powers, leading him to limit the president's authority when Congress had specifically prohibited certain actions.

Burton's pragmatic approach to adjudication appeared in his decisions regarding national security during the Cold War. Burton usually upheld government regulations against espionage and subversion over claims that they violated First Amendment freedoms. By closely construing the facts of a case to limit the effects of his rulings, however, he occasionally convinced more libertarian justices to join his opinions. For example, in *Beilan v. Board of Education* (1958) Burton upheld the dismissal of a Philadelphia teacher who refused to tell school officials whether he was a member of a Communist organization. Two years earlier, in *Slochower v. Board of Higher Education* (1956), Burton had dissented from a ruling that public employers could not fire workers for refusing to discuss Communist party membership. In *Beilan*, however, Burton convinced two justices from the *Slochower* majority to modify their views. While school boards could not legally infer disloyalty from a teacher's silence, Burton reasoned, they could use the teacher's lack of candor as evidence of professional incompetence.

Similarly, Burton sometimes joined his more libertarian colleagues, but he curbed their activism by focusing on procedural rather than constitutional remedies. In *Joint Anti-Fascist Refugee Committee v. McGrath* (1951), Burton ordered the United States attorney general to remove the names of three allegedly Communist organizations from a list of subversive groups.

Unlike the other four members of the majority, however, who considered the very practice of listing suspected organizations unconstitutional, Burton held only that the attorney general must first offer proof of subversion in a court of law.

Burton's circumspection also dictated his concurrence in *Jencks v. United States* (1957), which involved a perjury conviction of a man who falsely swore that he was not a Communist. Five justices held that a defendant was entitled to examine evidence against him contained in FBI reports, but Burton preferred that the trial judge first screen the files so that information affecting national security could be withheld. Later that year, Congress enacted a statute that regulated the use of FBI records in criminal trials in a manner similar to that recommended by Burton.

Burton's eclectic jurisprudence was not limited to the national security arena. In establishment clause cases, for example, he favored a fairly strict separation of church and state, while permitting some government support of religion. He dissented from Justice Hugo Black's opinion in *Everson v. Board of Education* (1947) because, although he agreed with Black that the First Amendment erected a wall of separation between church and state, he believed that a New Jersey statute that authorized school boards to reimburse parents for transportation to parochial school breached that wall. He then joined Black's opinion in *Illinois ex rel. McCollum v. Board of Education* (1948), which struck down a program that permitted clergymen to provide weekly religious instruction in public school classrooms, but only after Black agreed not to extend his ruling to similar programs that granted students released time to receive off-campus religious training.

In cases involving criminal procedure, Burton generally granted states broad powers to maintain law and order. This pattern was consistent with the political views he had held as mayor of Cleveland, when he had been elected on a platform that promised to rid the city of organized crime. In cases alleging coerced confessions he rarely presumed police misconduct, giving local judges and juries responsibility for determining the reliability of confessions. He also left decisions regarding the appointment of defense counsel in the hands of local jurisdictions.

Despite his support for law enforcement, some of Burton's most libertarian opinions involved criminal cases. Although he usually granted the police broad discretion to obtain evidence, he condemned the use of secret radio transmitters on private property to eavesdrop on a suspect's conversations. His dissent in *Louisiana ex rel. Francis v. Resweber* (1947) forcefully argued that to execute a prisoner after two earlier attempts had failed violated the double jeopardy and cruel and unusual punishment provisions of the Bill of Rights. Burton criticized only the botched attempt at electrocution; he did not challenge the authority of a state to execute its prisoners. He also limited his dissent to the actions taken by prison officials; if state law had permitted repeated attempts he would not have objected.

Burton's civil rights decisions aptly revealed the congruence between his jurisprudential and political beliefs. A member of the Cleveland NAACP, Burton had adopted a moderately progressive stance on race relations, supporting the abolition of poll taxes and the establishment of a fair employment practices commission. Many observers were surprised, therefore, when during his first term, Burton refused to join the otherwise unanimous opinion in *Morgan v. Virginia* (1946), which invalidated a Virginia statute that required segregation on public transportation. In subsequent cases involving the desegregation of graduate and professional schools, however, Burton urged the wholesale reversal of the "separate but equal doctrine" and he heartily supported Chief Justice Earl Warren's efforts to craft a unanimous opinion in *Brown v. Board of Education* (1954). Still, Burton hesitated to invoke constitutional guarantees of equality if narrower remedies were available. His unanimous opinion for the Court in *Henderson v. United States* (1950), for example, relied on the Interstate Commerce Act, rather than the equal protection clause of the Fourteenth Amendment, to void the practice of partitioning railroad dining cars to separate black and white passengers.

By the time Parkinson's disease forced Burton to retire, he had garnered a reputation as a mediocre jurist, generally conservative but never doctrinaire, who made no significant jurisprudential contributions to the Court. Scholars of the Court have concurred in that judgment, but the appraisal is somewhat unfair. Several of his opinions interpreting federal statutes such as the Fair Labor Standards Act and the Taft-Hartley Act remain valid law. His opinion in *American Tobacco Company v. United States* (1946) greatly expanded the government's power under the Sherman Antitrust Act. At the same time, Chief Justice Fred Vinson routinely assigned opinions to wavering justices in order to maintain his slim coalition. This practice gave Burton, a faithful member of the Truman bloc, few opportunities to write important constitutional opinions.

Nevertheless, Burton's style of judging limited his ability to influence his colleagues. During oral arguments he rarely asked questions. He found preparing opinions extremely difficult, yet he insisted on researching precedent exhaustively and writing his own draft opinions, thus limiting his judicial output. His lack of a guiding jurisprudential philosophy and his tendency to decide cases on narrow grounds also hindered his ability to formulate significant constitutional doctrine.

Burton's main contribution to the Supreme Court was to bring a sense of stability to a tribunal that was undergoing a significant transformation. During his tenure he saw five new associate justices appointed to the Court, and he served under three chief justices, two of whom, Warren and Vinson, symbolized the extremes of judicial activism and restraint. His affable personality brought together colleagues who often regarded one another with acrimony. His attention to the technical details of a case often provided solutions when other justices disagreed on the merits. During a period when most members of the Court wanted to avoid political controversy, therefore, Burton proved a reliable ally.

—ERIC W. RISE

BIBLIOGRAPHY

The standard biography of Harold Burton is Mary Frances Berry, *Stability, Security, and Continuity: Mr. Justice Burton and Decision-Making in the Supreme Court, 1945–1958*

(1978), which is useful primarily for its examination of the internal politics of the Court during Burton's tenure. For substantive analysis of the cases that Burton decided, see Ronald Marquardt, "The Judicial Justice: Mr. Justice Burton and the Supreme Court" (Ph.D. dissertation, University of Missouri, 1973). David N. Atkinson provides an intriguing discussion of Burton's work habits, based on interviews with his former law clerks, in "Justice Harold H. Burton and the Work of the Supreme Court," 69 *Cleveland State Law Review* 69 (1978). In "American Constitutionalism under Stress: Mr. Justice Burton's Response to National Security Issues," 9 *Houston Law Review* 271 (1971),

Atkinson assesses the impact of Cold War politics on Burton's jurisprudence. Arthur S. Miller, *Death by Installments: The Ordeal of Willie Francis* (1988), examines the circumstances surrounding one of Burton's most notable dissents.

Justice Burton's papers, including his personal diary and extensive correspondence files, are located in the Library of Congress. This unusually rich collection documents his terms as mayor of Cleveland and United States senator, as well as his judicial career. *The Occasional Papers of Mr. Justice Burton*, edited by Edward C. Hudon (1969), is a compilation of Burton's extrajudicial writings, mostly on the history of the Supreme Court.

PIERCE BUTLER

BORN 17 March 1886, Dakota County,
   Minnesota
NOMINATED to the Court 23 November 1922
   by Warren G. Harding
TOOK seat 2 January 1923
DIED 18 November 1939 in Washington, D.C.

Pierce Butler was born in a log cabin on a
Minnesota farm on St. Patrick's Day, 1866, to
Irish Catholic immigrants who had left Ireland
after the 1848 famine. Graduating from Carleton
College in 1887, he read law and was admitted
to the bar in 1888. That year he cast his first vote
for Grover Cleveland, and remained a Democrat
for the rest of his life. After serving as assistant
county attorney for two years, he was elected
county attorney of Ramsey County, Minnesota,
in 1892. Reelected two years later, he declined
to seek a third term and entered private practice.
A railroad lawyer and an expert in rate and valu-
ation cases, he represented several railroads before the Supreme Court in the *Minnesota Rates
Cases* (1913). Thereafter, he represented the
Canadian government in the Grand Trunk arbitration, in which William Howard Taft was an
arbitrator. The two Americans became friends,
and when President Warren G. Harding nominated Taft chief justice in 1921, Taft and Butler
celebrated the event together.

Anticipating Justice William R. Day's retirement in 1922, Chief Justice Taft surveyed
candidates to recommend to President Harding.
Taft's first choice was John W. Davis, but when
Davis gave no clear sign of interest, Taft considered other possible candidates. Meanwhile,
Martin T. Manton, a judge on the court of appeals for the second circuit, emerged independently as a leading candidate from New York.
Taft thought that Manton's appointment to the
Court would be a "disaster." Manton, in his
view, was "utterly unfit" for the Court. From
what Taft had heard, Manton had been a shady
lawyer, an ambulance chaser who had risen to
the bench entirely through political connections.
When Justice Willis Van Devanter suggested

Pierce Butler, who was also a Catholic and a
Democrat, as a counter-candidate, Taft pursued
the idea vigorously. First, he persuaded Butler
to become a candidate. Then, he advised him to
seek the support of the midwestern and western
Catholic hierarchy, as well as Democrats, the
bench, the bar, and the business community.
Finally, he personally urged Harding to nominate Butler.

Senate progressives strongly opposed
Butler's confirmation, principally because of his
conservative economic views. They also maintained that he lacked a judicial temperament
because, as a regent at the University of Minnesota during World War I, he had taken the lead
in dismissing professors for their "unpatriotic"
views. After examining the evidence against
Butler, a subcommittee of the Senate Judiciary
Committee recommended unanimously that his
nomination be confirmed. The subcommittee
specifically concluded that Butler's economic
views did not disqualify him for the Court. The
vote on Butler's confirmation was sixty-one to
eight, with twenty-seven abstentions.

Butler's confirmation greatly pleased Taft.
It meant that Taft would have a young, strong,
able, and hardworking colleague who would be
a team player. Butler wrote 323 majority opinions in his seventeen years on the Court, aver-
aging nineteen opinions a term, but only a few
of those opinions are of historic significance.
During his early years on the Court, he seldom
dissented. He explained his views on dissent on
the back of one of Justice Stone's slip opinions
as follows: "I voted to reverse. While this sustains your conclusions to affirm, I still think
reversal would be better. But I shall in silence
acquiesce. Dissents seldom aid in the right
development of the law. They often do harm.
For myself I say: 'Lead us not into temptation.'"
Butler's opinions contain few statements as
quotable as the one above, and that was no accident. One of his sons said that Butler carefully
went over each of his opinions with a blue pen-
cil and deleted any statement he thought might
be quotable.

Justice Holmes described Butler in a single word—"a monolith," adding, "there are no seams the frost can get through." Once, after persuading Holmes to acquiesce in a case being discussed in conference, Butler said: "I am glad we have finally arrived at a just decision." Holmes replied, "Hell is paved with *just* decisions." To Butler, principle was everything and could never be sacrificed to expediency. Butler had a system of values that oriented his life and his decisions, and he had articulated those values long before he came to the Court. As one would expect of a lawyer, he prized law, order, tradition, and freedom, but an analysis of his pre-Court public addresses shows that he also highly valued laissez-faire, patriotism, and morality.

Laissez-faire was especially important to Butler. "Contemporaneously with the ever increasing activities of government," he said in 1916, "there is a school of thought leading toward a kind of state socialism. Too much paternalism, too much wet-nursing by the state, is destructive of individual initiative and development. An athlete should not be fed on pre-digested food, nor should the citizens of tomorrow be so trained that they will expect sustenance from the public 'pap.'" It was Butler's view that the state may not transgress "its true function" and become a vast charitable machine, furnishing employment, doling out aid, and meeting the needs of the people. Such a program would ruin the nation, "weaken character and leave the individual man and woman without the motive or hope or inspiration necessary to freedom and morality."

Butler's commitment to patriotism was as strong as his commitment to laissez-faire. In 1915, he said that the strength of the state was limitless when erected by "loving patriotism." Patriotism to Butler was not simply flag waving; he acknowledged such activity was easy and often pleasant, but "real patriotism" required the bearing of the burdens of taxation gladly as well as discharging the other duties of citizenship. The primary duty of citizenship, he said, was undivided allegiance to the nation. "Allegiance to government and protection by it are reciprocal obligations, and, stripped of all sentiment, the one is the consideration for the other; that is,

allegiance for protection and protection for allegiance. Because the citizen is entitled to its protection, he owes allegiance in full measure to his country." This idea, he thought, was implicit in the oaths taken by public officials and aliens, and, though most native citizens took no oaths, they owed the same loyalty. "Thus," he concluded, "it is that all, from the highest to the lowliest of our naturalized citizens, are, by legal obligation strong and binding, held to full and faithful loyalty."

Patriotism and laissez-faire were intimately connected with Butler's central value: morality. "The educated man," he told a Catholic audience in 1915, "whose character is not sound, whose conscience is not well-instructed and whose conduct is not guided by religion or morality, is a danger to the State and his fellowmen." One of his favorite quotations was from Archbishop John L. Spalding: "The end of all worthy struggles is to establish morality as the basis of individual and national life."

Laissez-faire, patriotism, and morality were important in Butler's decisions on the Court. So was his value of tradition, which in the Court meant a strong commitment to precedent. Few justices in the history of the Court have shown stronger resistance to overruling precedents. "Our decisions ought to be sufficiently definite and permanent," he wrote in *Railroad Commission v. Pacific Gas & Electric Co.* (1938), "to enable counsel usefully to advise clients. Generally speaking, at least, our decision of yesterday ought to be the law of today."

No justice in the twentieth century voted more consistently for laissez-faire than Butler. Believing that contracts freely and fairly entered into were "sacred," he never voted against the assertion of a contract right when the Court divided on the issue. Also believing that the government had no right to regulate the hours or wages of workers, he voted accordingly every time the issue arose during his tenure, and he was on the winning side in every such decision until 1937. In *Morehead v. New York ex rel. Tipaldo* (1936), which invalidated New York's law regulating wages for women, Butler wrote the majority opinion. It was one of his most important opinions.

Although Butler valued individual freedom, patriotism almost always prevailed when the two values were in conflict, as in *Schwimmer v. United States* (1929), in which the Court held that a forty-nine-year-old woman was not entitled to become a citizen of the United States because she could not in good conscience swear to bear arms in defense of the nation. Writing for the majority, Butler identified Rosika Schwimmer with pacifists and conscientious objectors during World War I who not only refused to bear arms, but who also refused to obey the laws and encouraged disobedience in others. Pacifists, he wrote, lack a "sense of nationalism"; they do not have the "ties of affection" to the government of the United States that are requisite for aliens seeking naturalization. Butler had expressed similar ideas in public addresses in 1915 and 1916. In every divided decision involving Communists, International Workers of the World, or aliens who refused to swear unqualified allegiance, Butler voted against the individual.

A possible illustration of morality as the basis of Butler's decisions is *Buck v. Bell* (1927), in which the Court upheld the constitutionality of compulsory sterilization of the feeble-minded in Virginia. Holmes, who wrote the Court's opinion, quickly won the approval of all his colleagues, except Butler. "I bet you Butler is struggling with his conscience as a lawyer on this decision," Holmes was quoted as saying to a fellow justice. "He knows the law is the way I have written it. But he is afraid of the Church. I'll lay you a bet that the Church beats the law." Butler dissented without opinion. One might conclude that since Butler was a Catholic, he believed that compulsory sterilization was immoral and for that reason dissented. One might also conclude that he thought that the Virginia sterilization statute was unconstitutional because it deprived persons of liberty in violation of due process of law. So the basis of his dissent is unclear. But there is no doubt that Butler strongly disagreed with Holmes, who wrote for the Court: "It is better for all the world, of instead of waiting to execute degenerate offspring for crime, or to let them starve for their imbecility, society can prevent those who are manifestly unfit from continuing their kind. The principle that sustains compulsory vaccination is broad enough to cover cutting the Fallopian tubes."

Similarly, in *Hansen v. Haff* (1934), Butler also dissented by himself. Hansen, an unmarried alien, had left the United States in the company of a married man with whom she had been having sexual relations for some years. The intimate relationship continued abroad and the woman intended it to continue on her return to the United States until she reached the city of her residence, where she was employed as a domestic. Based on these facts, the immigration authorities refused to readmit her into the country because a federal statute excluded aliens who came to the United States "for the purpose of prostitution or for any other immoral purpose." Butler's colleagues held that the woman was entitled to readmission because her extramarital relations fell short of concubinage, and, at any rate, she was not reentering the country for the purpose of having such relations. Butler countered, citing Webster's definition, that the woman was indeed a concubine. Further, he said, she entered the country for an immoral purpose, and it made no difference whether that purpose was dominant or subordinate.

Although Butler seldom articulated the value of due process in his public addresses prior to his appointment to the Supreme Court, he had a strong commitment to the value. During his tenure on the Court, no justice—not even Louis Brandeis—supported due process claims more than Butler. The fact that he often dissented in favor of due process claims is a measure of the intensity of his commitment to the value. At times, because of value conflicts, loyalty to the opinion of the Court, or respect for those with whom he differed, Butler found it difficult to express his dissenting views, even in defense of due process.

Olmstead v. United States (1928), which upheld the constitutionality of wiretapping, was such a case. Chief Justice Taft, who wrote the Court opinion for a majority of five, saw the problem primarily in terms of his values of law and order. So did Butler, but his early experience at the criminal bar had taught him of unfair police practices, of the zeal of prosecutors to convict, and of the great advantage the state has over the individual in criminal prosecutions. He disliked crime as much as Taft did; but, as he put it in one of his opinions as circuit justice, "Abhorrence, however great, of persistent and menacing crime will not excuse transgression in the courts of the legal rights of the worst offenders." And Butler believed it did not excuse the use of evidence obtained by wiretapping. Thus, he decided to write a dissenting opinion in *Olmstead,* but apparently not without some inner struggle, for he began the opinion by saying he "sincerely regret[ted]" that he was unable to agree with Taft and the majority and concluded with the statement: "With great deference, I think [the defendants] should be given a new trial."

One of Butler's most important due process dissents was in *Palko v. Connecticut* (1937), in which a majority that included such liberal justices as Hughes, Brandeis, Stone, Cardozo, and Black held that a state could try a defendant more than once for the same offense without violating due process of law. Palko had been tried for murder and given a life sentence. Dissatisfied with the sentence, the Connecticut prosecutor tried him again, which state law permitted, and this time Palko received the death penalty. Butler was the sole dissenter, and, as in *Buck v. Bell,* he dissented without opinion, but he expressed his attitude. During the oral argument, he was "very tough" on counsel and shouted at the state's attorney: "What do you want? Blood?"

Supreme Court scholars have questioned Butler's ability. Fred Rodel considered Butler the "least intellectually gifted of the Nine Old Men . . . a second-rate successor, of sorts, to far abler Justice White." William F. Swindler wrote that Butler had "manifest intellectual limitations." There is some evidence that Butler's critics underestimated his ability. Robert H. Jackson recalled Butler as "a man of great ability and devotion to the job as he saw it." The day Butler died, a lawyer remarked that Jackson must be glad not to have Butler on the bench vigorously questioning him when he argued for the government as solicitor general. Jackson replied, "I'm sorry that he is not, for nothing kept our office on its toes as the certainty that our arguments would have to face the scrutiny of Justice Butler." William O. Douglas, who had been Butler's

colleague, said in an unpublished interview in 1961 that Butler was a "very friendly, likeable man. When you crossed swords with Butler you knew you were crossing swords with an expert. He had a very extraordinary mind and great powers of argumentation. He was a great adversary. . . . He has been greatly . . . misunderstood." In his memoirs, William O. Douglas confirmed this assessment of Butler. "While he was extremely conservative," wrote Douglas, "I had great admiration for his intellect . . . Butler was able—very able."

Douglas's statements suggest why Butler was able to keep intact the Court's conservative bloc—the "Four Horsemen"—in the 1930s. As Charles Evans Hughes pointed out, Butler automatically had the vote of the arch-conservative McReynolds, and he had "a strong influence on Justices Van Devanter and Sutherland." Until 1937, Butler was also able to attract Roberts's vote frequently in economic cases, thus forging majorities that invalidated many New Deal laws, which in turn led to a confrontation between Franklin D. Roosevelt and the Court. Butler's success in forging conservative majorities in the 1930s was historically more important than his judicial opinions.

Butler's death in 1939 marked the end of an era in the Court's history. He was the last justice appointed to the Court who had not attended law school. He was also one of the last great champions of substantive due process as a means of protecting property rights, a constitutional doctrine that no longer commanded a majority during his final three years on the Court. Hence it is not surprising that he recorded more dissents in that period than he did in his previous fourteen years on the Court. Finally, Butler's death gave Franklin Roosevelt his fifth Supreme Court appointment, thus bringing into being a new era of constitutional interpretation.

—DAVID J. DANELSKI

BIBLIOGRAPHY

There are no Butler Court papers, but material on his earlier years constitute a small collection at the Minnesota Historical Society in St. Paul. Papers relating to his confirmation are in the University of Washington Library in Seattle.

Material on Butler can also be found in the Robert H. Jackson, Harlan Fiske Stone, and William Howard Taft collections in the Library of Congress.

David J. Danelski, *A Supreme Court Justice Is Appointed* (1964), provides a detailed description and analysis of Butler's appointment. Francis Joseph Brown, *The Social and Economic Philosophy of Pierce Butler* (1945), remains useful for its comprehensive coverage of Butler's judicial opinions. See also David Bruner, "Pierce Butler," in Friedman and Israel, 3 *Justices* 2183.

James Francis Byrnes

Born May 2, 1879, Charleston,
   South Carolina
Nominated to the Court 12 June 1941
   by Franklin D. Roosevelt
Took seat 7 July 1941; resigned
   3 October 1942
Died 9 April 1972 in Columbia,
   South Carolina

Justice Byrnes's memoirs devote but eleven pages to his experience on the Supreme Court, and with good reason: he served only one term. His tenure on the Court was sandwiched between service as a senator from South Carolina and a post bearing the unofficial title of "Assistant President," in which he assisted his close friend Franklin D. Roosevelt with domestic and foreign policy during World War II. Byrnes contributed to the Court mainly by enlivening its social life; he regularly gathered the justices for dinner at his home and led them in post-prandial songs. Byrnes's short service on the Court and impressive political career combined to truncate his judicial legacy. He was impatient with the Court's slow pace while the world was at war: "I don't think I can stand the abstractions of jurisprudence at a time like this."

By today's standards, his legal training, like his formal education, was incomplete. His father died before his birth, and to help his mother support the family, Byrnes quit school at the age of fourteen and began working as a clerk for Charleston lawyers. In a sense, he was a throwback to the early nineteenth century; he read law as an apprentice in the office of a local judge, who eventually sponsored his admission to the bar. His political ambitions surfaced early, and his career in public service began with his election to Congress in 1910.

His most memorable Supreme Court opinion came in *Edwards v. California* (1942). The case involved a California statute that penalized any resident who brought into the state a person known to be indigent—a law obviously aimed at reducing the number of "Okies" emigrating to California during the Great Depression. Byrnes, influenced by Felix Frankfurter, struck down the law on the grounds that the commerce clause protected the right of citizens to interstate travel. Employing an unfortunate analogy, Byrnes concluded that people, like healthy cattle, ought to be free to cross state lines. His reasoning infuriated the civil libertarians on the Court, particularly William O. Douglas, who believed the statute violated the privileges and immunities clause of the Fourteenth Amendment.

In other decisions, Byrnes exhibited an unremarkable disposition to construe strictly the intent of Congress in interpreting federal statutes. In general, he was a judicial conservative who disdained legislating from the bench. In view of his active participation in the New Deal, however, one suspects that a case involving the powers of the executive would have put Byrnes's convictions to the test. He maintained an ideological distance from the more nationalistic New Dealers Roosevelt appointed to the Court and cleaved instead to centrists such as Frankfurter and Chief Justice Harlan F. Stone. In all, he wrote sixteen majority opinions for the court, but no concurrences or dissents, a record that leaves Byrnes's jurisprudence essentially uncharted. But Byrnes eventually revealed his true colors on the major social issue of his day: civil rights. From 1950 to 1955, he served as governor of South Carolina, which furnished one of the cases collectively decided as *Brown v. Board of Education* (1954). As governor, he urged the Eisenhower administration to uphold segregation on the grounds that education was a matter for local authorities to handle, and that forced integration would lead to race riots.

—Victoria Saker Woeste

Bibliography

The only biographical sketch that deals primarily with his Court career is in Friedman and Israel, 4 *Justices* 2517. His memoirs, *All in One Lifetime* (1958), do not shed much light on the Court. There are several biographies of Byrnes, but understandably none give much emphasis to his judicial career or his legal philosophy.

JOHN ARCHIBALD CAMPBELL

BORN 24 June 1811, Washington, Georgia

NOMINATED to the Court 21 March 1853
by Franklin Pierce

TOOK seat 11 April 1853; resigned
26 April 1861

DIED 12 March 1889 in Baltimore, Maryland

John Campbell was a product of the plantation South, and his record on the United States Supreme Court reflected his region's identification with states' rights/strict construction interpretation of the Constitution. The son of a Georgia lawyer-planter, he attended the University of Georgia and West Point before beginning a legal career at the precocious age of eighteen. He relocated to Alabama in 1830 and established himself as a leader of the legal and mercantile community in Mobile.

Although he was twice elected to the Alabama legislature and twice declined appointment to the state supreme court, Campbell's reputation was built primarily on his record as an effective advocate and his thorough knowledge of the law. His personal law library was reputed to be the most extensive in the United States, and his familiarity with the literature of the Anglo-American and continental legal traditions was said to rival that of Joseph Story. Within Alabama politics, Campbell was identified as a Democrat, but as a member of a faction that favored both a strong southern rights position and the commercial development of the state. This group was loosely identified with South Carolina's John C. Calhoun and the cause of southern nationalism. Although Campbell freed his slaves on his appointment to the Supreme Court, and occasionally speculated on the ultimate demise of the peculiar institution, his orientation was generally proslavery.

Campbell was appointed to the Court to replace his fellow Alabaman, John McKinley, who died in July 1852. His nomination was encouraged on the newly inaugurated Pierce by the then current members of the Supreme Court, who had observed Campbell argue six separate cases before them during the December 1851 term. On the eve of his confirmation, a correspondent to the *New York Tribune* wrote of Campbell that he was "a gentleman of shining and profound talents, vast legal attainments and withal is irreproachable in character; but he is a fire-eater [i.e., southern nationalist] of the blazing school."

During his eight years as an associate justice, Campbell wrote 116 opinions, which included ninety-two majority opinions, five concurrences, one statement, and eighteen dissents. He also dissented eleven additional times without opinion. This pattern reflected the generally high degree of agreement on the Taney Court in the 1850s, hardly a surprising fact, given that nine of the ten judges that served on the Court during Campbell's tenure were identified as Jacksonian Democrats at the time of their appointment.

Campbell concurred with the proslavery majority in *Dred Scott v. Sandford* (1857), the best known of the cases in which he participated. He was also thought to be Chief Justice Roger Taney's choice as his successor. However, Campbell's constitutional views differed from those of Taney in important respects. In a number of cases involving the expansion of federal jurisdiction, limitations of state sovereignty and the rights of corporations, Campbell combined with Justices Peter Daniel and John Catron to form a solid states' rights bloc on the Court in contrast to the moderate nationalism that was embraced by most of their colleagues. As such, they constituted the first discrete, multimember faction in the Court's history.

During his first term on the Court, Campbell issued powerful dissents rejecting arguments that a corporation could be treated as a citizen for purposes of federal jurisdiction (*Marshall v. Baltimore and Ohio Railroad,* 1853), and that the contracts clause of the Constitution prohibited a state from repealing a previously granted tax exemption (*Piqua v. Knoop,* 1854). He reiterated these views in his dissent in *Dodge v. Woolsey* (1856). In each case, he was joined in dissent by Daniel and Catron. By one count, the Taney Court decided twenty-one constitutional cases between the time of Campbell's appointment in 1853 and the end of the 1858 term. Daniel and Campbell each dissented in six of these cases, doing so jointly on five occasions and being joined by Catron in four.

A unionist in 1861, Campbell did not resign from the Court immediately on Alabama's January succession, and instead worked for a peaceable resolution of the sectional crisis. However, on April 26, less than two weeks after Lincoln's declaration that an "insurrection" existed, he resigned his position on the Court. During the Civil War, he served as the Confederate assistant secretary of war.

At the end of the conflict, Campbell reestablished himself as one of the South's outstanding lawyers and one of the leading members of the bar of the Supreme Court. He argued at least forty-three cases before his former tribunal, beginning in February 1873 with his representation of the disadvantaged butchers in the *Slaughterhouse Cases* (1873), and concluding with his argument in *Robinson v. Fair* (1888) on October 22, 1888. Had he stayed on the Court during the Civil War, as did his fellow southerners Catron and James Wayne, and remained on the bench until his death, he would have served longer than any justice in the Court's history other than William O. Douglas.

—JOSEPH GORDON HYLTON

BIBLIOGRAPHY

The only full-length biography of Campbell is Henry G. Connor, *John Archibald Campbell* (1920). His role in Alabama politics, which has often not been fully understood, is explored in J. Mills Thornton III, *Politics and Power in a Slave Society: Alabama, 1800–1860* (1978).

BENJAMIN NATHAN CARDOZO

BORN 24 May 1870, New York City

NOMINATED to the Court 15 February 1932 by Herbert Hoover

TOOK seat 14 March 1932

DIED 9 July 1938, Port Chester, Long Island, New York

Benjamin N. Cardozo is generally regarded as being among the most liberal of Supreme Court justices, and that is one of the great ironies of American legal history. A liberal he surely was during his tenure on the Court, but only because his belief in judicial restraint predisposed him to accept congressional statutes regulating the economy. Along with Louis D. Brandeis and Harlan Fiske Stone, Cardozo was one of the three justices most likely to uphold New Deal legislation. But Cardozo's philosophical position was best summed up in the phrase "ordered liberty," which he made famous in *Palko v. Connecticut* (1937). Herbert Hoover had used the same words in his unsuccessful 1932 campaign for reelection, and in important respects, Cardozo's cautious, middle-of-the-road stance, in which order was as important as liberty, was similar to that of the president who appointed him.

Herbert Hoover's nomination of Cardozo to replace Oliver Wendell Holmes, Jr., may have been the most popular act of a president whose reputation was otherwise shattered by his inability to solve the problems of the Great Depression. Throughout his career—first as a lawyer specializing in appellate briefs (from 1891 to 1913), then as a judge (since 1914) and later chief judge (since 1926) of the New York court of appeals—Cardozo, nominally a Democrat, had enjoyed the confidence of all political factions. He was the author of several highly regarded books, the most influential of which was *The Nature of the Judicial Process* (1921). He had received honorary degrees from many universities, including Yale, Harvard, and his alma mater, Columbia. Many of his decisions in such areas as torts, contracts, and liability had influenced judges and courts throughout the United States. Hailed as "a profound scholar, a lucid and courageous thinker and a saintly character," Cardozo was widely regarded as the most suitable successor to the venerable Holmes. As one observer said at the time, "Cardozo is a judge in the fundamental sense of holding the balance even between violently contending shades of thought."

The attempt to hold that balance in the face of the contention surrounding the New Deal would tax even Cardozo's considerable ability. Greatly prizing collegiality and good manners, Cardozo was profoundly hurt by the rancor that increasingly marked the justices' deliberations and unavoidably surfaced in their opinions. But personal considerations also made his years on the Supreme Court the unhappiest of Cardozo's professional career. A bachelor, Cardozo had lived for most of his life with his older sister, Ellen, who needed constant medical attention, but she had died in 1929, leaving him a lonely man. In Albany, he had resided at the same hotel as the other members of the court of appeals, had enjoyed close personal relations with them, and had found it easy to commute to his home in New York City; in Washington, by contrast, he lived and worked by himself, and felt, he often said, as if he were a "homesick exile." Most of the justices did the actual drafting of decisions at their homes, meeting in court only to hear arguments, hold weekly conferences, and deliver their opinions. Cardozo was friendly with Justice Stone, and to a lesser extent, with Owen Roberts. Yet he was dismayed by the icy disdain shown to him, as a Jew, by James C. McReynolds, a notorious anti-Semite.

In 1935 and 1936, when the Supreme Court's conservative majority did most of its damage to the New Deal, Cardozo generally sided with the Roosevelt administration. True, he concurred when the Court, in May 1935, unanimously struck down the National Industrial Recovery Act (NIRA) on the dual grounds that it represented an overly broad delegation of legislative authority and violated the commerce clause. But Cardozo had earlier been the only justice who had been willing to sustain the

NIRA's efforts to raise oil prices by permitting the president to prohibit the interstate shipment of petroleum—so called "hot oil"—produced in excess of an amount prescribed by state authority in *Panama Refining Co. v. Ryan* (1935). The following year, Cardozo wrote dissenting opinions for the liberal minority in three crucial cases: *Carter v. Carter Coal Co.*, which struck down an act establishing minimum wages and maximum hours in the bituminous coal industry; *Jones v. Securities and Exchange Commission*, which restricted the agency's investigative authority; and *Ashton v. Cameron County Water Improvement District I*, which nullified a statute designed to provide bankruptcy relief to state and local governments.

Cardozo was prepared to accept the expansion of federal power under the commerce clause largely because, on his theory of judicial review, the Supreme Court should overturn statutes only when they were clearly arbitrary or oppressive. Nothing better revealed his fundamentally cautious view than another dissenting opinion, also written in 1935, involving a state's right to impose a tax based on a business's gross sales rather than its profits (*Stewart Dry Goods Co. v. Lewis*). In enacting the levy, Cardozo asserted, the legislature had not acted arbitrarily. It had engaged in "no act of sheer oppression, no abandonment of reason, no exercise of the general will in a perverse or vengeful spirit. Far from being these or any of them, it is a pursuit of legitimate ends by methods honestly conceived and rationally chosen. More will not be asked by those who have learned from experience and history that government is at best a makeshift, that the attainment of one good may involve the sacrifice of others, and that compromise will be inevitable until the coming of Utopia."

In 1937, when the Court did an about-face and accepted pivotal New Deal measures, Cardozo's commitment to judicial restraint continued to shape his decisions, which, however, were now written for the majority. In *Helvering v. Davis*, the justices upheld the government's authority to impose taxes on employees and employers in order to fund old-age pensions under the Social Security Act. How, Cardozo asked, was one to decide when Congress was using the spending power in aid of the "general

welfare," as Article I, Section 8 of the Constitution required? "The line must still be drawn between one welfare and another, between particular and general. Where this shall be placed cannot be known through a formula in advance of the event. There is a middle ground or certainly a penumbra in which discretion is at large. The discretion, however, is not confided to the courts. The discretion belongs to Congress, unless the choice is clearly wrong, a display of arbitrary power, and not an exercise of judgment." Cardozo added that the concept of the general welfare necessarily changed over time: "The hope behind this statute is to save men and women from the rigors of the poor house as well as from the haunting fear that such a lot awaits them when journey's end is near."

Cardozo's approach produced a different outcome when the issue before the Court was not economic regulation but individual rights. One such case involved the University of California's requirement that all able-bodied male undergraduates take four semesters of military science. Two students, both devout members of the Methodist Episcopal Church and conscientious objectors to war, petitioned for an exemption on the grounds that training for war was immoral and contrary to their Christian faith. They were suspended, lost an appeal in the California supreme court, and took their case to the Supreme Court. In *Hamilton v. Board of Regents* (1934), the justices unanimously rejected their claim and upheld the requirement. Justice Pierce Butler delivered the majority opinion, but Cardozo wrote a separate concurrence. Conceding that the California Regents' requirement "may be condemned by some as unwise or illiberal or unfair when there is violence to conscientious scruples, either religious or merely ethical," Cardozo nevertheless concluded that "more must be shown to set the ordinance at naught. In controversies of this order courts do not concern themselves with matters of legislative policy, unrelated to privileges or liberties secured by the organic law." To grant the exemption, in effect, would be to exalt the right of private judgment "above the powers and the compulsion of the agencies of government."

In cases involving the criminal law, Cardozo's deference to legislative initiative had

Benjamin Nathan Cardozo
Photograph by Harris and Ewing.
Collection of the Supreme Court of the United States.

similar consequences. An early example was *Snyder v. Commonwealth of Massachusetts* (1934). Herman Snyder had been convicted of murdering a gas station attendant during a holdup. During the trial, the judge had taken the jury, the district attorney, and the defense attorney to "view" the scene of the crime, but had refused to allow Snyder to be present. The question, then, was whether the judge's decision had deprived the defendant of due process of law under the Fourteenth Amendment. Writing for a narrow five-member majority (Brandeis was among the four dissenters), Cardozo held that the risk of injustice to the defendant was, at most, a "shadowy" one. Massachusetts, he continued, "is free to regulate the procedure of its courts in accordance with its own conception of policy and fairness, unless in so doing it offends some principle of justice so rooted in the traditions and conscience of our people as to be ranked as fundamental."

The same viewpoint shaped Cardozo's most famous and influential Supreme Court opinion, *Palko v. Connecticut* (1937). Frank Palka (his name was misspelled in the court briefs) had been accused of murdering a policeman after burglarizing a store in Bridgeport. Connecticut asked for a first-degree murder conviction, but the jury returned a verdict of second-degree murder after the judge had ruled that a confession was inadmissible. Asserting that the judge had erred, the state won a new trial, at which the confession was admitted and Palka was sentenced to death. The questions before the Supreme Court were whether this constituted double jeopardy, and if so, whether it was forbidden by the Fifth Amendment. Writing for the Court in December 1937, Cardozo decided that there was no double jeopardy, but in any event, the federal prohibition did not apply to the states, by reason of the Fourteenth Amendment's due process clause, because protection against double jeopardy was not "of the very essence of a scheme of ordered liberty."

To substantiate his argument, Cardozo had to explain why some provisions of the Bill of Rights were more fundamental than others and consequently were binding on the states. The due process clause, he reasoned, would indeed prohibit a state from abridging freedom of speech, freedom of the press, the free exercise of reli-

gion, the right of peaceable assembly, and the right to benefit of counsel, all of which are "implicit in the concept of ordered liberty." But other rights—such as trial by jury, protection against compulsory self-incrimination, guarantees against double jeopardy—were less deserving of protection. To Cardozo, there was a bright and shining line between the two kinds of rights. With the line clearly drawn, he reasoned, the Court and the people could rest assured that: "The edifice of justice stands, its symmetry, to many, greater than before."

Palko was Cardozo's last Supreme Court decision. Shortly after delivering it, he suffered a heart attack, followed by a stroke in January 1938. In the six months left to him, he was never able to resume his duties. So he did not live to see how the doctrine of judicial restraint, which in the 1930s had served to legitimize New Deal measures, would later become a chief weapon in the arsenal of conservative critics of the Warren Court's activism. Nor, of course, could Cardozo have foreseen that the Warren Court would eventually erase the line he had attempted to draw between rights that were fundamental and those that were not, and would declare that the rights he had considered peripheral were, in fact, essential to American liberty.

—RICHARD POLENBERG

BIBLIOGRAPHY

Most of Benjamin Cardozo's personal papers were destroyed after his death, but some letters may be found in collections at Columbia University and the American Jewish Archives. Cardozo's extrajudicial writings and essays may conveniently be consulted in Margaret Hall, ed., *Selected Writings of Benjamin Nathan Cardozo* (1947). The only biography is George S. Hellman, *Benjamin N. Cardozo: American Judge* (1940), an uncritical but nonetheless informative work. The finest study of Cardozo's jurisprudence is Stanley Charles Brubaker's unpublished doctoral dissertation, "Benjamin Nathan Cardozo: An Intellectual Biography" (University of Virginia, 1979). For an early assessment, see Beryl Harold Levy, *Cardozo and Frontiers of Legal Thinking, with Selected Opinions* (1938). For a modern view, see Richard A. Posner, *Cardozo: A Study in Reputation* (1990).

JOHN CATRON

BORN probably 1786, seemingly
in Pennsylvania

NOMINATED to the Court 3 March 1837
by Andrew Jackson

TOOK seat 1 May 1837

DIED 30 May 1865 in Nashville, Tennessee

Little is certain of John Catron's earliest
years, not even the state or year of his birth. He
grew up poor in Virginia, then Kentucky, moved
to Tennessee's Cumberland Mountains, served
under Andrew Jackson in the War of 1812, and,
seemingly largely self-educated, gained admission to the Tennessee bar in 1815. Therewith his
rapid ascent began.

Relocating to the state capital, Nashville, in
1818, Catron successfully invested in the early
Tennessee iron industry while building a profitable practice centered on land title litigation, then
a massive Tennessee problem. His 1824 appointment to the Tennessee Supreme Court had its
source in legislators' knowledge that he favored
confirmation of de facto landholders despite title
defects. In 1829, he fortified his Jacksonian political credentials statewide by publishing articles
that anticipated Jackson's first presidential message to Congress attacking the Bank of the
United States. Catron was named Tennessee
chief justice in 1831, and during the nullification crisis was instrumental in causing Tennessee to fall in behind Jackson. An 1834 reorgani-
zation of the state judiciary eliminated the chief
justiceship, and, briefly back in private practice,
Catron managed the 1836 Tennessee campaign
for Jackson's designated successor, Martin Van
Buren. On his last day as president, Jackson
nominated Catron to the United States Supreme
Court.

Catron's twenty-eight-year term of Supreme
Court service has been exceeded by only thirteen of the 112 justices appointed since 1789.
During Catron's second year on the Court, Chief
Justice Roger Taney wrote to Jackson: "I have
been impressed with . . . his judgment, legal
knowledge, and high integrity . . . a most valu-

able acquisition to the . . . Supreme Court." Late
nineteenth-century justices still cited Catron's
opinions as did, for example, Stephen Field in
Bowman v. Chicago and North Western Railway
(1888): "The language of Mr. Justice Catron on
this subject . . . is instructive. . . . The learned
justice said . . ."

Scholars have been widely divided over
Catron's jurisprudence. Writing in 1898, Joshua
Caldwell placed Catron in the Taney Court's
doctrinal middle, between "high-toned Federalists" Wayne, McLean, and Curtis, and an anti-
Federalist bloc of Taney, Woodbury, Daniel, and
Nelson. Caldwell found in Catron's opinions a
"leaning toward Federalist principles . . . rather
surprising . . . as he had been a lifelong friend
of Andrew Jackson." Contrariwise, John
Schmidhauser in 1961 placed Taney at the
Court's center and Catron among the pro-southern "extreme justices." More recently, Frank
Otto Gatell described Catron as following "a
reasonable line between . . . federal and state
power, with a preferential bias . . . [for] the latter," whereas John Scheb concluded that
throughout his tenure "Catron was a stalwart
defender of states' rights and of . . . slavery."

Not all these scholars can be on target, and
Caldwell and Gatell come closer than Scheb and
Schmidhauser. The interpretive difficulties stem
less from Catron's politically complex jurisprudence than from missing its underlying ordering
of values. By overfocusing on best-remembered
constitutional decisions, scholars have neglected
other significant "telltale texts," especially
Catron's state opinions concerning slaves and his
federal opinions in other areas prominent on the
nineteenth–century's public agenda. An additional confusion may be in assuming that a justice politically active in "off-duty hours" (which
Catron certainly was) would be a jurisprudential
activist (which Catron frequently was not).

First, one must realize that Catron's support
of slavery fell short of "fire-eating" status. Unlike some southern justices who found threats to
slavery lurking under many a federalism or economic issue, Catron often seemed chiefly driven

by other considerations. Respecting federal powers, these included particularly: (1) sustaining a Jacksonian model of a fairly powerful presidency, and (2) preventing states from trenching unduly on the commerce powers of Congress.

Catron's states' rights jurisprudence poses a complex puzzle. The clue is that he did not entirely share the common states' rights view that less federal power was almost always desirable. Catron's regional reflexes were both new western (when West meant "trans-Appalachian") and old southern. The West wanted geographic expansion and economic modernization, and on issues such as federal admiralty jurisdiction and the disposition of public lands, unlike the old South, sometimes saw federal power as beneficial. However, on one major issue, the contract clause's limitations on state legislatures modifying contracts, the two regions eyed the same enemy—entrenched, northeastern capital—and wanted a weak clause. In contract clause cases, Catron's decision making closely resembled that of his two strongly sectional southern colleagues, Alabama's John Campbell and Virginian Peter Daniel.

Before considering how Catron's western orientation played out in other areas, it is helpful to examine several slavery cases from Catron's Tennessee court years and his related, unique pattern in federal slavery cases. *Bob v. State* (1830) found Catron displaying "textbound" judicial passivism in dissenting from overriding a state circuit judge's refusal to grant a slave's appeal of a death sentence. Catron considered the lower court trials unfair. "I have never known any person convicted . . . upon evidence so slight," he declared, but thought an 1811 statute vested absolute discretion to grant or refuse an appeal in the circuit judge. Catron's colleagues, John Haywood and Jacob Peck, asserting "color, rank, or station can make no difference," decided the circuit judge's discretion was not arbitrary "to do as he pleases, but to discover . . . what is right, . . . otherwise his unrighteous discretion shall be purified."

When not constrained by statute, Catron joined decisions that put the Tennessee court to the left of other southern courts. Thus, a white murderer of a slave was held subject to common

law conviction after acquittal of the statutory crime in *Fields v. State* (1829), a case later scorned by the Georgia court as the "wholly untenable" consequence of "fervid zeal in behalf of humanity to the slave" (*Neal v. Farmer*, 1851). A slave, winning freedom in one suit, was permitted to bring another suit seeking monetary damages in *Matilda v. Crenshaw* (1833).

Telling was Catron's rejection of other slave states' resolutions of a thorny issue: Did the unmentioned children of a slave mother with a bequest of future freedom eventually go free also, or were they doomed to lifelong slavery? The Kentucky and Virginia courts had already adopted the latter answer, but in *Harris v. Clarissa* (1834), Catron stated that "we are not satisfied" with the Kentucky court's reasoning and that the Virginia decision was "a most strict construction, not to say a strained one, in prejudice of human liberty."

Catron's unique approach developed from the first two major Supreme Court slavery cases. He was the only southern justice to find unnecessary a qualifying concurrence with, or a dissent from, northerner Joseph Story's Court opinions in the *Amistad* case (1841), which awarded freedom to black mutineers on a ship engaged in illegal slave trading, and in *Prigg v. Pennsylvania* (1842), which held void state laws that conflicted with exclusive federal power under the fugitive slave clause.

Catron eschewed the southern proclivity for bringing slavery issues into nonslavery cases. In fact, in *Strader v. Graham* (1850) and *Dred Scott v. Sandford* (1857), when slaves unsuccessfully argued that northern sojourns gave them freedom, Catron brought nonslavery issues into slavery cases. Catron's *Dred Scott* concurrence that the 1820 Missouri Compromise was unconstitutional limited its passivist differences with Taney's sweeping opinion to opposing as unnecessary Taney's ruling that blacks could not bring suit in federal court, and to a plaintive reference to a nonslavery implication of Taney's pruning of Congressional power over territories: "It is asking much of a judge, who has for nearly twenty years been exercising jurisdiction . . . to the Rocky Mountains, and . . . inflicting the extreme penalty of death for crimes . . . to agree that he had been all the while acting ... as an usurper."

The better example is *Strader*. It had reached the Court seven years earlier, almost contemporaneously with Catron's taking positions incompatible with Southern extremism—favoring Oregon's admission as a free state, thundering in his Nashville courtroom against southern expansionists bent on invading and extending slavery to Cuba, and holding that the 1850 Fugitive Slave Act, repealing its 1793 predecessor, aborted the pending suit of a slave owner to recover $500 from one who had aided his slave's escape. Taney's *Strader* opinion cited, somewhat misleadingly, one precedent which Catron had authored, *Permoli v. First Municipality of New Orleans* (1845), and another from which Catron had dissented, *Pollard v. Hagan* (1845), and tossed out the entirety of the 1787 Northwest Ordinance as superseded by the Constitution's 1789 ratification. As its third article had prohibited slavery northwest of the Ohio, the ordinance was anathema to ardent slavery supporters who saw the best course as holding precisely what Taney did.

Catron, together with the Court's fiercest opponent of slavery, John McLean, objected that jettisoning the ordinance's other five articles was "*obiter dictum* uncalled for." Catron particularly objected to voiding the fourth article's provision of perpetual rights to free, non-taxed navigation of the Mississippi and St. Lawrence river systems. He saw therein—and liked—the potential for an *intrastate* federal power over navigation, a federal power additional to congressional powers over *interstate* commerce and to the federal judiciary's admiralty powers. Taney, on the other hand, saw the potential for limiting state power—and didn't like it.

That not deciding more than necessary was an independent value for Catron is suggested by its appearance outside the slavery area. Illustrative was his reluctance in *McCracken v. Hayward* (1844) to join in holding contrary to the contract clause an Illinois stay law barring the sale of debtor's property at less than two-thirds of real worth. Catron preferred the narrower course of voiding a circuit court rule that had made the Illinois statute enforceable. Simi-

larly indicative were his criticisms of opinions authored by the Court's chief rivals during his first decade, Taney and Story. Though concurring in *Swift v. Tyson* (1842), Catron criticized Story's opinion for deciding an unnecessary additional issue rather than waiting "until it fairly arose," and correctly predicted some state courts would not follow Story's dictum. When Chief Justice Taney, in *Cutler v. Rae* (1849), rushed to decide an admiralty jurisdiction issue without prior written or oral argument, and unionist Georgian James Wayne called that a regrettable "first" in the Court's history, Catron completely refused to participate in deciding the case.

Catron's capacity for a lonely, nationalist path was well displayed in *Pollard v. Hagan* (1845), a case that Catron "deemed the most important controversy ever brought before this court, either as ... respects the amount of property involved, or the principles." Evaluations of importance change, although twentieth-century legal scholars appear to have overlooked that the majority's ruling contradicts the received wisdom that between *Marbury v. Madison* in 1803 and the Civil War, the Court only once, in *Dred Scott*, ruled a congressional enactment void. At monetary stake was title to Mobile, Alabama, properties created, chiefly by the labors of small landowners, by filling in tidelands. Eight justices held that the "equal footing doctrine" (under which new states were admitted on terms no less favorable than the original thirteen) coupled with an earlier case awarding title to certain oyster beds to New Jersey, as sovereign heir to rights of the British Crown, required upholding the Alabama supreme court's award of title to Alabama, and in turn to other claimants than the fillers-in of the tidal lands.

Catron, objecting that at stake in *Pollard* was United States sovereignty, took a nationalist position similar to the New Deal Court's in the tidal oil lands controversy of the 1940s and 1950s (*United States v. California*, 1947). Catron argued that provisions for federal ownership of these lands written into the 1819 congressional act admitting Alabama to the Union, as well as 1824 and 1836 congressional acts confirming claims deriving from federal title, should be controlling.

Pulsing beneath Catron's *Pollard* opinion was another Jacksonian motivation—preference for the small entrepreneur and diligent settler. It was the same new West disposition to settle title doubts in favor of pioneers that had led to his state court appointment. It burst through the surface of his writing in California controversies pitting eastern corporations' claims under often fraudulent pre-1848 Mexican "floating grants" ("floating" because the boundaries were ill-defined) versus farmer-settlers' claims under federal preemption laws. There was no doubt where lay Catron's populist heart, as can also be seen in his dissent in *Fremont v. United States* (1854): "Cultivators of the soil should . . . [be] safe from the ruin that lurks in a floating claim, familiar to western ploughmen, many of whom remember exhausting litigation in their own families for the paternal hearth, and who relied on the firm and consistent decisions of this court to protect their new homes on the Pacific."

Western and southern interests dovetailed in corporation cases, and Catron often backed his southern colleagues' desire to minimize protective federal jurisdiction extending "person-like" or "citizen-like" status to corporations, as when he dissented with Daniel and Campbell in *Marshall v. Baltimore and Ohio Railroad* (1853). Catron also shared these colleagues' hostility to allowing broad coverage to wealthy or corporate patent holders. Certainly one finds a class-consciousness in his objection to the 5–4 ruling in *Hogg v. Emerson* (1850) that allowed the holder of letters patent on one steam engine improvement to add later, via a patent schedule, what Catron saw as two separate inventions, and then sue for an infringement of the latter. Catron argued that so treating the three as a unity undercut the salutary limiting of patents to single inventions. If three could be run together, any number may be. What would result? And "although the claim may be fictitious, still this does not protect the public from harassment, as usually men using cheap implements cannot afford to litigate in the United States Courts."

When new western aims (that would be enhanced by greater national power) and old southern aims (that would be hindered) diverged, Catron's decision making sometimes stam-

mered—as in federal admiralty jurisdiction, which Hamiltonian proponents of rapid industrialization wanted to expand against the wishes of Jeffersonian agrarians. English law had limited admiralty jurisdiction to tide-affected waters. An inadvertently well-named 1825 decision, *The Thomas Jefferson*, had retained English limits.

The Taney Court majority first ventured in a new direction by accepting evidence of what expansionist Justice Grier sarcastically dubbed "occult tides" invisibly present at inland locations and extending federal jurisdiction to places such as, in *Waring v. Clarke* (1847), a Mississippi River collision scene almost 100 miles north of New Orleans. In 1852, in *The Genessee Chief*, the majority upheld an 1845 act extending federal jurisdiction to the Great Lakes. Where Daniel dissented consistently, Catron either wrote cautious concurrences (as in *Waring*) or voted with the majority (as in *Genessee Chief*). As the Civil War approached, he zigzagged, siding with southerners on some issues and with northern expansionists on others.

Once armed conflict began, Catron's order of values became swiftly clear: Union, national government, West—all first; secession South, last; and the future of slavery, a dependent variable, on the back burner. Catron's wartime actions were hard-line Unionist. When Campbell resigned his seat and joined the Confederacy, Catron hastened to hold circuit court in Kentucky, then on secession's brink. When Taney, back in Baltimore, issued *habeas corpus* for a suspected traitor held in military custody and chastised Lincoln verbally, Catron, holding court in Missouri, refused *habeas corpus* and blistered secessionists in his comments. When Catron returned to his Nashville home in the wake of Tennessee newspaper reports of his Missouri comments, Confederate vigilantes gave him twenty-four hours to resign his Supreme Court seat or get out of town. He chose the latter, though the consequence was confiscation by the rebel government of $90,000 of his property. While declining to uphold the presidential embargo in the *Prize Cases* (1863), Catron went far himself. He issued a writ for arrest of the Kentucky governor and upheld confiscation of a pro-Confederacy newspaper in *United States v. Re-*

publican Banner Officers, an 1863 circuit holding. Catron lived just long enough to see the final surrender of the Confederacy; death came to
the Court's deepest-dyed Jacksonian on May 30,
1865.

—A. E. KEIR NASH

BIBLIOGRAPHY

The scarcity of, and conflict among, secondary sources about even elementary facts of
Catron's life is astonishing, requiring unusual
reliance on deduction from the cases and on the
Catron papers in the Tennessee State Archives
in Nashville. There is also a fair amount of relevant data and sensible interpretation scattered
through Carl B. Swisher, *The Taney Period,
1836–1864* (1974), volume 5, in the Oliver
Wendell Holmes Devise Series.

See also Joshua Caldwell, *Sketches of the
Bench and Bar of Tennessee* (1898); Frank Otto
Gattell, "John Catron," in Friedman and Israel,
1 *Justices* 737; John Schmidhauser, "Judicial
Behavior and the Sectional Crisis of 1837–
1860," *Journal of Politics* (1961); and John M.
Scheb II, "John Catron," in Kermit L. Hall, ed.,
*The Oxford Companion to the Supreme Court of
the United States* (1992). However, none of the
essays specifically on Catron appears to have
proceeded from a thorough reading of Catron's
opinions.

Salmon Portland Chase
Collection of the Supreme Court of the United States.

SALMON PORTLAND CHASE

BORN 13 January 1808, Cornish, New
    Hampshire
NOMINATED as chief justice 6 December 1864
    by Abraham Lincoln
TOOK seat 13 December 1864
DIED 7 May 1873 in New York City

One of ten children born to a New Hampshire farmer-legislator, Chase moved to Ohio in 1820 with his uncle, an Episcopal bishop, three years after his father's death left the family impoverished. He graduated Phi Beta Kappa from Dartmouth College in 1826, briefly considered a career in the ministry, but instead studied law—and politics—in Washington, D.C., as an apprentice to Attorney General William Wirt. Admitted to the bar in Cincinnati, he established a successful practice and then became increasingly involved in various reform causes, especially temperance and antislavery. By the 1840s, Chase's earnest but radical views on slavery and his legal efforts on behalf of runaways earned him the epithet, "Attorney General for the Runaway Negroes."

Although active in Whig and then Liberty party politics from the 1830s, Chase did not hold public office until 1849. The compromise choice of the state legislature for United States senator from Ohio, once in Washington he opposed the Kansas-Nebraska Act and participated in the anti-Nebraska movements that led to formation of the Republican party. Chase returned to Ohio in 1855 and won two terms as governor (1855–57, 1857–59) before gaining election again to the Senate, this time as a Republican. An unsuccessful candidate for the Republican presidential nomination in 1860, he joined the Lincoln administration as secretary of the treasury and skillfully managed wartime finances. Abruptly resigning from the Cabinet in 1864, he considered running against the president, but eventually declined to do so. After the election, Lincoln fulfilled earlier promises to radical Republicans by nominating Chase to succeed the recently deceased Roger B. Taney as chief justice.

Chase's staunch opposition to slavery and his alliance with congressional radicals caused concern among political conservatives, but the new chief justice steered a moderate course. He was, in truth, a one-issue radical. He emphasized the national character of freedom and insisted on equality before the law for all citizens: the Constitution's general welfare provision, the Declaration of Independence, and the Bill of Rights contained individual rights that the nation should protect in the states. On other issues, especially fiscal and monetary matters, Chase held conservative views. A states' rights nationalist, he believed the federal government, although supreme, had no permanent role in state affairs so long as states treated equally all residents engaged in lawful pursuits. Above all, Chase was pragmatic: law, like politics, required compromise. This latter trait especially served him well on the Court.

Few men have become chief justice with a more thorough grounding in the art of governing. Chase needed political skills because he assumed leadership of a weakened Court struggling to regain its stature as an equal branch of government. The self-inflicted wound of *Dred Scott v. Sandford* (1857) had damaged the Court's reputation, and the emergencies of war had shifted power decisively to the president and Congress. At first there appeared to be little opportunity to restore the balance. Trivial issues crowded the docket, much to the dismay of the activist Chase. Missing were the momentous race-centered concerns that occupied the attention of Congress and the president. Also absent were important issues about the nature of a reconstructed union and its impact on prewar understandings of federal-state power.

This state of affairs changed quickly beginning in 1865. While few decisions during Chase's tenure addressed matters of race, questions about Reconstruction loomed increasingly large on the Court's agenda. Also important were economic and social issues given impetus by the Civil War, issues that reflected the nation's nascent transformation from an agrarian to an industrial power. Led by Chase, the justices took advantage of the cases before them. By 1867, the Court had seized a far greater share of federal power than had seemed possible a scant three years earlier. At the time of the chief justice's death in 1873, it had regained near equality with the legislative and executive branches, at times aggressively extending its authority to review state and national actions. Symbolic of this renewed authority was the Court's invalidation of congressional statutes. Before 1865, only two acts of Congress had ever been declared unconstitutional; by 1873, the total was twelve, seven of them since 1869.

Yet for all its assertiveness, a cautious moderation was the dominant tone on the Chase Court. The justices reflected the uncertainties and divisions of the Reconstruction era, when Congress and president vied for the power to set conditions for the rebellious states' reentry into the union. They also sat during a gradual shift from an instrumentalist to a formalist conception of law. Antebellum jurists and commentators had accepted the state legislatures' right to use law as an instrument of social and economic policy, even if it meant abandoning precedent or modifying rights, especially property rights. Although permissive instrumentalism was still the norm in 1865, Civil War experiences tempered its thrust. Not only did war aims emphasize individual and minority rights, but the conflict spurred the creation of a national market and raised constitutional questions about the role of state legislatures in the regulation of business and interstate commerce. Legal theorists increasingly promoted formalism, or an emphasis on formal legal procedures and judicial review, as a means of protecting many kinds of individual rights from legislative interference, including property rights of the corporation, recognized in law as an artificial person. Taken as a whole, the Chase Court's decisions reflected these various conflicts and thus served as a bridge between two political and constitutional eras.

The Chase Court from 1864 to 1873 embodied past and future approaches to politics and constitutional law. No group of justices had ever been as politically oriented; every justice maintained close political connections outside the

Court. More important, the associate justices generally held different conceptions of national power than did the Republican Congress, which took an expansive view of its constitutional authority. Three justices—Robert C. Grier, Nathan Clifford, and Samuel Nelson—were holdover appointees of pro-southern Democratic presidents before the war; they clung to a narrow view of federal constitutional power. Two other justices—John Catron, who died in 1865, and James Wayne—had been appointed by Andrew Jackson and shared his states' rights nationalism. Even most of the justices appointed by Lincoln held more conservative views than Congress, especially its radical Republican bloc. The headstrong Stephen J. Field was a "War Democrat" who supported the union but held an anti-majoritarian, laissez-faire conception of federal power in peacetime. Lincoln's friend and political ally, David Davis, was a moderate Republican who ultimately left the party over the impeachment of Andrew Johnson. Only Noah Swayne and Samuel Miller, together with Chase, were initially sympathetic to the arguments of congressional radicals that the federal government could override state power to achieve Reconstruction policies, or that the Congress's authority in these matters was greater than the president's.

As chief justice, Chase faced several challenges: managing the Court's affairs so as not to create factions among his colleagues; claiming an independent role for the Court in the struggle between the Congress and president over Reconstruction; addressing the changed nature of federal-state relations that resulted from the Civil War; securing the rights of all citizens as promised by the Union victory; and helping the Court to reconcile the constitutional problems posed by the new industrial economy and the shift in law from instrumentalism toward formalism. In all five areas, his political skills proved useful.

Chase was foremost a politician, even while serving as the nation's highest judicial officer. He never hid his interest in politics nor severed his political connections. So strong was his attachment that, in 1868, he actively considered another bid for the Republican presidential nomination. His political experience and connections were not unmixed blessings, however, because his deeply felt commitment to equal rights for African Americans was often at odds with majority public sentiment. Also, at times an aloof and formal personal manner blunted his effectiveness as a conciliator. Still, it is questionable whether a less experienced chief justice could have maneuvered the Court successfully through the politically charged postwar climate.

The dominant issues before the Court during Chase's tenure concerned the scope of national power. Many of the cases, though not all, addressed the constitutionality of wartime and Reconstruction measures. At first—and on an issue that arose from prewar actions—the Court proceeded quietly, extending legal doctrines from the Taney era that upheld national power, while in the process creating doctrines that increased options for the justices. The key case involved bond litigation from Iowa. In Gelpcke v. Dubuque (1864), the Court greatly expanded its review power over state court judgments by requiring Iowa to honor municipal bonds that the Iowa Supreme Court had held to be invalid. The decision was popular with creditors. When combined with the Taney Court's ruling in *Swift v. Tyson* (1842), it allowed federal courts through the 1930s to oversee municipal debts, contracts, and tort liability, among other matters. For Chase, the case sustained the nation's authority in terms reminiscent of his predecessor's views, especially later when the chief justice joined the majority in upholding Taney's innovative use of the Court's mandamus power to compel Iowa's compliance with its decision. It also justified federal judicial restraints on state excesses, an issue that arose often during Reconstruction.

Other actions from 1864 and 1865 also reveal the chief justice and his colleagues working in less visible ways to restore the Court's credibility and to reassert its independence. One of Chase's first acts as chief was to admit a black attorney into practice, the first so honored. Although not predictive of the Court's halting decisions on civil rights, the symbolism of an African American at work where the *Dred Scott* decision had been issued less than a decade earlier was a powerful restorative of public confi-

dence. In another gesture, Chase ordered the clerk to list West Virginia as a state on the Court's docket, thus confirming Lincoln's recognition of its wartime separation from Confederate Virginia. A more substantive action was Chase's brief opinion denying Supreme Court jurisdiction of appeals assigned to it by an 1855 statute establishing a federal court of appeals. Only the fourth time that the Court had invalidated a federal law or a portion of it, the decision foreshadowed the Court's later vigorous use of judicial review, yet avoided a confrontation with either Congress or the president.

The Court in 1866–67 decided against congressional and state laws in three cases that directly involved Reconstruction, although without the full support of its chief. The first significant case with implications for Reconstruction policy was *Ex parte Milligan* (1866), testing the constitutionality of an 1864 military trial and death sentence for an Indiana man convicted of disloyal activities in a state where civilian courts remained open. The justices held unanimously that the military had not followed the requirements of the 1863 Habeas Corpus Act requiring it to report civilian prisoners to the local federal district court. But Chase and three justices differed from the majority on the basic point of whether the judiciary could decide when a crisis justified the use of military courts. To the chief justice, this issue, like Reconstruction policy generally, was political, not legal; it was for Congress and the president to decide, not the courts.

The adverse implications of this decision for Reconstruction became clear a few months later in early 1867 with the *Test Oath Cases* (*Ex parte Garland*; *Cummings v. Missouri*). The justices concluded, 5–4, that congressional and state loyalty oaths required of southern activists and sympathizers violated the federal constitution's ban on *ex post facto* laws and bills of attainder. Chase disagreed with the majority, writing an extended dissent in the Missouri case. Although later calling the state oath "detestable," Chase explained in an 1870 letter that he believed it safer not to interfere with the state's right to regulate its internal concerns. The chief justice thus was able to reconcile his support of radical Reconstruction with his advocacy of "freedom national," the belief that the Constitution protected liberty for all citizens against state restraints. In this instance, the state had withheld the privileges of full civil participation from individuals who acted willfully against its interests. Chase was also concerned that the *Test Oath Cases*, when combined with *Milligan*, sharply diminished the ability of both federal and state governments to prevent ex-rebels from controlling the governments of the reconstructed states.

Chase's support of congressional policies on Reconstruction stemmed from his belief, shared by the Radical Republicans, that the war had changed the American constitutional system. Nowhere was this change more evident than in the 1865 adoption of the Thirteenth Amendment. Although subsequent interpretations restricted its meaning to the elimination of slavery, Chase took a much broader interpretation in the circuit court case, *In re Turner* (1867), when he upheld the Civil Rights Act of 1866 under the Thirteenth Amendment in the course of striking down an apprenticeship law for blacks. He clearly viewed the amendment as the triumph of the abolitionists' broader goal to nationalize the right to freedom. And the amendment also required Congress to enforce this open-ended right, which Chase defined in terms of the Declaration of Independence and Bill of Rights, a definition that suggested the equality of all citizens. Finally, it kept open, perhaps required, the possibility of black suffrage. The vote, Chase believed, gave all men, black and white, the ability to protect his and his neighbor's welfare.

In the *Milligan* and *Test Oath Cases*, the chief justice had balanced his support of congressional reconstruction with his desire to maintain the Court's independence as a coequal branch of government. Rather than challenge Congress, as a majority of his colleagues appeared ready to do—a challenge the Court was sure to lose— Chase argued that reconstructing the Union was a political rather than a judicial process. This pragmatic stance allowed the Court to avoid confrontation while preserving its authority to address future Reconstruction legislation.

Chase's success in winning support for this position can be seen in subsequent Reconstruc-

tion cases. In two 1867 decisions, *Mississippi v. Johnson* and *Georgia v. Stanton*, the chief justice led a unanimous Court in refusing to accept jurisdiction or rule on the constitutionality of the Reconstruction acts of March 1867 establishing military governments in the former Confederate states. Chase, invoking the separation of powers principle in his opinion, recognized the impracticality of issuing an injunction against the president. More important, he wisely kept the Court from using a dubious opportunity to declare the Reconstruction acts unconstitutional, thus isolating it from the brewing conflict between the president and Congress over who would set the terms of Reconstruction.

The same pragmatic assessment of political realities governed the Court's action in subsequent Reconstruction cases during Chase's tenure. In *Ex parte McCardle* (1868), which occurred during and shortly after the impeachment of President Andrew Johnson, a Mississippi editor convicted of writing incendiary articles about Reconstruction questioned the authority of the Congress to establish military tribunals to try civilians. When Chase, speaking for the Court, concluded that it could hear McCardle's *habeas corpus* petition under an 1867 statute, Congress changed the law to prevent the justices from considering this challenge to its authority. A year later the justices unanimously dismissed McCardle's suit, although Chase's opinion emphasized the Court's general power of review.

As the Court considered these cases, Chase faced a different challenge, one that ultimately separated him from many of his former abolitionist colleagues. The House of Representatives impeached President Johnson for violating the Tenure of Office Act, a measure requiring the Senate to approve dismissals of any executive appointee it had confirmed. Chase, as chief justice, was the presiding officer at the trial in the Senate. For some time, Chase had been moving away from positions held by congressional radicals who wanted to use military government to ensure the proper reconstruction of southern states. Early in 1867, he questioned the legitimacy of continued military rule and refused to sit with the circuit court wherever it existed. By the summer of that year he openly advocated a less harsh policy toward the South. Although the Court under his leadership had avoided a direct confrontation with Congress, the McCardle case suggested that differences could not be submerged indefinitely.

Chase prepared diligently for his role as presiding judge, carefully studying the history and law of impeachment. He insisted that the Senate follow court rules and clashed frequently with a prosecution that often proceeded on political grounds. Twice overruled on key evidentiary matters, Chase nonetheless won much sympathy and support for his efforts to require the Senate to conduct itself as a judicial rather than a legislative body. The trial had another effect on the chief justice: it led to his decision to break with his fellow Republicans. After 1868, when he unsuccessfully pursued the Democratic presidential nomination, Chase was much less involved in partisan matters, even though his political interests and ambitions did not wane.

After *McCardle*, the *Test Oath Cases*, and the impeachment trial, Reconstruction issues faded from the Court's docket, at least for the remainder of Chase's tenure. A key exception was *Texas v. White* (1869), in which the reconstructed state government tried to recover bonds sold by the Confederate government to pay for the war effort. For the majority, Chase endorsed the theory of congressional reconstruction as expressed in the Reconstruction acts of 1867, that the Constitution had created a nation, even as it had invested certain powers in the states: "The Constitution, in all its provisions," he wrote, "looks to an indestructible Union, composed of indestructible states." The rebellious states had forfeited their rights. Congress, under its constitutional power to guarantee republican governments, had the power to set the terms for their reentry to the Union. Significantly, Chase pointedly avoided ruling on the constitutionality of the Military Reconstruction Acts, following the Court's previous stance that reconstruction was a political question, not a judicial one.

Late in 1869, the Supreme Court faced another wartime issue, the constitutionality of the Legal Tender Act of 1862, in *Hepburn v. Griswold*. The act, which Chase had supported as a necessary expedient during his days at Treasury, had created a government-issued paper currency, so-called "greenbacks," to finance the war effort. This inflationary currency also could be used to retire debts incurred before 1862, even if the original contract called for repayment in specie, or gold and silver. The justices divided sharply over the case, with Chase leading a 5–4 majority in declaring the act unconstitutional as it applied to contracts made before the measure became law. The decision was highly controversial. Republicans bitterly condemned Chase for reversing his earlier position, whereas Democrats generally applauded. Critics especially feared the Court would extend its ruling to contracts made subsequent to the 1862 law, thus disrupting financial markets.

The controversy heightened when President Grant appointed two new justices, William Strong and Joseph P. Bradley, both assumed to oppose the *Hepburn* decision, and the attorney general moved for a reconsideration of the case. The motion created a bitter dispute among the justices, with Chase pitted against Justice Miller, the leader of the minority in the earlier case. The chief justice made every effort to keep the case from being reopened, but lost. A new 5–4 majority in the *Legal Tender Cases* (1871) held that the notes were valid for repayment of both prior and subsequent debts.

Chase's failing health—he suffered a series of strokes in 1870—limited his activities on the bench for the remainder of his term. Although his condition improved during 1872, he was never able to write effectively, his speech remained partially slurred, and his ability to lead the Court waned markedly. Fittingly, he closed his career by joining the dissent in the *Slaughterhouse Cases* (1873), announced three weeks before his death. His role was minor; he offered no separate opinion. But the case, which limited the scope of the Fourteenth Amendment and restricted the ability of the federal government to protect citizens against the states, offered the chief justice one last chance to reaffirm his belief in equal rights for blacks, a principle that he had promoted throughout his public life.

Chase was a worthy heir to the legacy of his predecessors, Marshall and Taney. The Court under his leadership substantially increased its jurisdiction, influence, and reputation. Chase helped the Court invigorate and extend judicial review, even though at times the justices appeared to differ with Congress over policy, not constitutionality, a result that foreshadowed the actions of subsequent Courts. Under Chase, the Court's Reconstruction decisions—or, more often, its non-decisions—placed the justices squarely in the middle of national politics. But the chief justice led his colleagues to exercise their newfound authority with discretion and always with a pragmatic and essentially conservative view to what was possible. This, indeed, was his greatest achievement and his greatest legacy as a jurist: he skillfully guided the Supreme Court through the trying years of Reconstruction to reclaim its place as a coequal branch of the federal government.

—DAVID J. BODENHAMER

BIBLIOGRAPHY

Important manuscript collections for Salmon Chase exist at the Library of Congress and the Historical Society of Pennsylvania. Edward G. Bourne et al., eds., "Diary and Correspondence of Salmon P. Chase," *Annual Report of the American Historical Association*, vol. 2 (1902), offers a valuable collection of several hundred Chase letters over his entire career. Frederick J. Blue, *Salmon P. Chase: A Life in Politics* (1987), is the latest and best single-volume biography of Chase. Albert B. Hart's *Salmon P. Chase* (1980, reprint of 1899 ed.) was an excellent early biography, although without benefit of recent research and a modern perspective.

Charles Fairman, *History of the Supreme Court of the United States*, vol. 6, *Reconstruction and Reunion, 1864–1888*, part 1 (1971), provides an exhaustive but balanced treatment of the Supreme Court during Chase's tenure as chief justice. Harold M. Hyman and William M. Wiecek, *Equal Justice Under Law, Constitutional Development, 1835–1875* (1982), constitutes a critical yet sympathetic analysis of Chase's role in Reconstruction issues, tying the Court to the Taney Court which preceded it and the Waite Court which followed.

In regard to postwar issues, see also David F. Hughes, "Salmon P. Chase: Chief Justice," 18 *Vanderbilt Law Review* 569 (1965), a careful portrait of Chase's leadership of the Court on the most important Reconstruction questions. Stanley I. Kutler, in *Judicial Power and Reconstruction Politics* (1968), convincingly argues that the Chase Court reasserted judicial independence during Reconstruction.

SAMUEL CHASE

BORN 17 April 1741, in Somerset County, Maryland

NOMINATED to the Court 26 January 1796 by George Washington

TOOK seat 4 February 1796

DIED 19 June 1811 in Baltimore, Maryland

Samuel Chase served on the Supreme Court for only fourteen years and missed all or much of some of those years because of frequent illness. Yet in that time he compiled a lifetime of controversy. He fulfilled the destiny which he had foretold as a riotous leader of the Sons of Liberty in the 1770s. Chase's opposition to the royal governor of Maryland was so extreme that he was branded by the mayor and aldermen of Annapolis as a "busy, restless incendiary, a ringleader of mobs, a foul-mouthed and inflaming son of discord."

Chase supported General George Washington in the Continental Congress from 1775 to 1778, credits on which he would collect in 1796. But in the meantime, his efforts to corner the market on flour forced him to leave Congress in disgrace. He was severely attacked in a pamphlet by Alexander Hamilton, writing as "Publius," no less. In 1778, he survived an attempt to remove him from his position as chief judge of the Maryland criminal court. A majority of the Maryland assembly supported his removal, but not the required two-thirds. Political observers probably were not surprised when Chase became the first, and only, member of the United States Supreme Court to be impeached.

Chase implored President Washington to grant him a federal office because of financial need. Washington considered him for attorney general before appointing him to the Supreme Court. He had, in fact, been a leader of the Maryland opposition to the Constitution, and as recently as 1793 had been violently and publicly anti-British. Yet by the time of his advancement to the Supreme Court he had become equally pro-Federalist and anti-Jeffersonian in his language. Though he was unanimously approved by the Federalist-dominated Senate, he was not welcomed with open arms. Treasury Secretary Oliver Wolcott had "but an unworthy opinion" of Chase. Justice James Iredell's comment provided an accurate, though unintended, forecast of Chase's judicial career: "I have no personal acquaintance with Mr. Chase, but am not impressed with a very favorable opinion of his moral character, whatever his professional abilities may be." Chase's judicial abilities would earn praise for him at the same time that his injudicious temperament brought him condemnation. Joseph Story, who followed Chase on the bench, presented a different picture. He called Chase a "rough, but very sensible man . . . bold, impetuous." When Story compared Chase to Dr. Samuel Johnson, of course, he had Chase's size, appearance, and manner in mind, but Story added that it was "above all" because of Chase's intellect. No less an authority than Edward S. Corwin described Chase as the most notable of any of Chief Justice John Marshall's predecessors.

Despite all of Chase's excess baggage and all the turmoil that was yet to come, few appearances on the Supreme Court have been so auspicious. The constitutionality of state legislation sequestering debts owed by Virginia citizens to British creditors was challenged in *Ware v. Hylton* (1796). Virginia's counsel, led by the young John Marshall, argued that the legislation was unaffected by the protection of British creditors negotiated in the treaty of 1783, because the legislation preceded the treaty by several years. As the junior member, Chase spoke first. His thorough analysis of the case left little for justices William Paterson, James Wilson, and William Cushing to add. Chase's first opinion has been described as the most brilliant Supreme Court opinion prior to *Marbury v. Madison* (1803). Chase laid out every conceivable justification for the Virginia legislation, and then demolished them one by one. Most important, "A treaty cannot be the supreme law," as the Constitution promises, "if any act of a state legislature can stand in its way." *Ware v. Hylton* remains the basic text for future discussions of the supremacy of national treaties over legislation.

The next day, Chase interpreted the direct tax clause of the Constitution in *Hylton v. United States*. His performance here did not compare with *Ware*, and it appears he had focused his best efforts on the treaty case. Chase did, however, offer an *obiter dictum* which was accepted until 1895, when Chief Justice Melville Fuller corrected "a century of error" while ruling a federal income tax unconstitutional. "I am inclined to think," Chase remarked, "but of this I do not give judicial opinion, that the direct taxes contemplated by the constitution, are only two, to wit, a capitation or poll tax simply without regard to property, profession or any other circumstances; and a tax on land." Paterson made the same ruling, with much less hedging, but Chase had said it first.

Chase asserted judicial supremacy in interpreting the Constitution on a variety of occasions. In *Calder v. Bull* (1798), he declared that "An act of the legislature (for I cannot call it a law), contrary to the great first principles of the social compact, cannot be considered a rightful exercise of legislative authority." He was confident that "certain vital principles in our free republican governments . . . will determine and over-rule an apparent and flagrant abuse of legislative power." He assigned full responsibility for interpreting state constitutions to the state judiciaries, which was later confirmed by the Supreme Court in *Cooper v. Telfair* (1800).

His notebook of "Instructions to Grand Jury" contains this powerful charge, probably written in 1799:

If the *Federal* Legislature should, at any time, pass a Law *contrary to the Constitution of the United States, such law* would be *void*; because the Constitution is the *fundamental Law* of the United States, and *paramount* to any Act of the Federal Legislature, whose authority is derived from, and delegated by that Constitution; and which imposes *certain restrictions* on the Legislative Authority that can only be preserved through the . . . Courts of Justice. The *Judicial* power of the United States is

coexistent, co-extensive, and *coordinated* with, and altogether independent of the *Legislature* & the *Executive*; and the Judges of the Supreme and District Courts are bound by the oath of office to regulate their decisions *agreeably to the Constitution.* The Judicial powers, therefore, are the only proper and competent authority to decide whether any Law made by Congress, or any of the State Legislatures is contrary to or in violation of the *federal* Constitution.

John Marshall was an interested observer in 1800 when Chase refused to allow James T. Callender's counsel to argue that the Sedition Act was unconstitutional: "The judicial power of the United States is the only proper and competent authority to decide whether any statute made by Congress (or any of the State Legislatures) is contrary to, or in violation of, the Federal Constitution." This authority is "expressly granted to the judicial power of the United States and is recognized by Congress by a perpetual statute," meaning the Judiciary Act of 1789. He proposed to go a dangerous step farther when he was the only member who argued that Supreme Court justices should rule the Circuit Court Act of 1802 unconstitutional and refuse to return to circuit duty. "The distinction of taking the *Office* from the *Judge*, and not the *Judge* from the *Office*" he considered to be "puerile and nonsensical." Fortunately, calmer heads prevailed in Paterson's *Stuart v. Laird* (1803).

Chase's longest decision, *Calder v. Bull* (1798), is famous for the ruling that the *ex post facto* clause of the Constitution is applicable only to criminal proceedings, which deprived the clause of potential significance as a protection of property against state legislation. This ruling still stands. Chase was most un-Hamiltonian in *Calder* when he ruled that "all the powers delegated by the people of the United States to the federal government are defined, and no *constructive* power can be exercised by it." The states, in contrast, possessed all authorities allowed by the state constitutions, so long as they were "not expressly taken away by the constitution of the United States." This is reminiscent of his remark in *Ware v. Hylton* (1796) that the people grant to state governments "the supreme and sovereign

Samuel Chase
Engraving by H. B. Hall.
Collection of the Supreme Court of the United States.

power of the state" to pass legislation, so long as it does not conflict with the federal Constitution. Chase seemed on the verge of discussing the police power doctrine, which would receive so much attention in the Taney Court.

Ironically, Chase's most memorable circuit decision was quite Jeffersonian in its insistence that there is no federal common law in criminal cases. He ruled in *United States v. Worrall* (1798) in the Pennsylvania circuit court that neither the Constitution nor an act of Congress had conferred common law jurisdiction on the federal courts. Thus it would be "improper to exercise a jurisdiction to make bribery punishable by resort to common law precedent." His precedent was not at the time followed in other circuit courts, but it was upheld by the Supreme Court in *United States v. Hudson and Goodwin* (1812). Where common law could be used, Chase was more consistent than his brethren in following standardized principles of construction and procedure.

Unfortunately, Chase squandered much of the favorable notice gained from these decisions when he became a Federalist "hanging judge" in the sedition and treason trials of 1799–1800. He had openly advocated adoption of the Alien and Sedition Acts, and he intended to see them utilized to fullest effect. Chase sentenced David Brown to a year and a half in jail, the harshest of any sedition sentence. His forceful rulings in the sedition trial of James T. Callender and the treason trial of John Fries, both in 1800, provided the basis of his impeachment in 1804. Counsel for both defendants were so offended by his rulings that they withdrew from the cases. Chase shocked Fries's counsel by showing them his opinion *before* the trial in order to expedite proceedings. He was surprised when they expressed disgust and withdrew. He condemned Fries to death despite his lack of counsel; fortunately, President John Adams pardoned Fries. Most Philadelphia counsel refused to practice before Chase. Even District Judge Richard Peters, a Federalist, complained, "I never sat with him without pain, as he was forever getting into some intemperate and unnecessary squabbles." Even at his worst moments, though, Chase demon-

strated judicial skill. In *United States v. Callender*, he demonstrated more knowledge of libel and slander law and of recent British precedents than his colleagues.

Chase might have avoided impeachment if he had not bitterly attacked Congress's repeal of the Judiciary Act of 1801 in an intemperate jury charge in Maryland on May 2, 1803. He declared that "Mobocracy" threatened to destroy "peace & order, freedom and property." A Maryland legislator demanded that the next Congress "wipe off this defilement from our courts by removing from the bench the obnoxious rubbish which has occasioned it." President Thomas Jefferson relayed the charge to his lieutenant in the House, suggesting impeachment of this "insolent and overbearing man"; having interfered, Jefferson cautioned that "it is better that I should not interfere." Jefferson could not have forgotten that Chase had missed the entire August 1800 term because he was in Maryland campaigning for the reelection of President Adams.

After months of delay, the House of Representatives approved eight charges of impeachment, six of them based on the Callender and Fries trials, by a seventy-three–thirty-two vote. Chase went to trial in the Senate on January 3, 1805, where he anticipated defeat and removal. Yet he assembled a brilliant team of Federalist attorneys who simply overwhelmed John Randolph, the brilliantly erratic but sometimes spectacularly foolish House manager. Five of the eight charges did not even receive a majority, and one received no votes, even though twenty-five of the thirty-four Senators were Jeffersonian Republicans. Six Republicans voted not guilty on all eight charges. The charge based on Chase's conduct in 1803 fared best, with nineteen voting for conviction.

Chase was a changed man in his last six years on the Court, partly because of the chastening experience of impeachment, but more likely because of persistent illness. He was always in need of money, frequently borrowing, and he clung to the bench for his salary despite attacks of gout which left him in misery for his remaining days. He was seldom on duty during 1804–1805, he missed the entire sessions of

1806 and 1810, and there was no 1811 term. Under Marshall, Chase wrote only one opinion of the court (because Marshall had ruled on circuit), a brief concurring opinion, and a dissent against Justice William Johnson's *Croudson v. Leonard* (1808). Johnson's vindictive assessment in 1822 that "Chase could not be got to think or write" was characteristically unfair, but it was not as far afield as some of his other partisan assessments of his Federalist colleagues, so long as it is limited to Chase's waning years.

—DONALD O. DEWEY

BIBLIOGRAPHY

The only full biography, James Haw, Francis F. Beirne, Rosamond R. Beirne, and R. Samuel Jett, *Stormy Patriot, The Life of Samuel Chase* (1980), is thorough and useful, though it bears some of the weight of its many authors and many years in preparation. Irving Dilliard's essay in Friedman and Israel, 1 *Justices* 185 is entertaining and informative. The best account of the impeachment is Jane Elsmere's unpublished doctoral dissertation, "The Impeachment Trial of Justice Samuel Chase" (Indiana University, 1962).

Tom Campbell Clark
Photograph by Harris and Ewing.
Collection of the Supreme Court of the United States.

TOM CAMPBELL CLARK

BORN 23 September 1899, Dallas, Texas

NOMINATED to the Court 28 July 1949
　　by Harry S Truman

TOOK seat 24 August 1949; retired 12 June
　　1967

DIED 13 June 1977 in New York City

During his eighteen years on the Supreme Court Tom C. Clark was not an intellectual leader. He wrote only a handful of memorable opinions and articulated no coherent judicial philosophy. Yet when he retired in 1967, Clark was one of the Court's most widely known and influential members. The reason was his off-the-bench campaign to reform judicial administration. A hobby that became a consuming passion, that crusade even affected his decision making. In adjudicating cases, Clark adhered to a few simple principles that he believed would promote effective judicial management.

That he should have viewed judging with an administrator's eye is understandable, for Clark came to the Court after more than a decade of service in a variety of executive positions within the United States Department of Justice. Born into a family of Texas lawyers, he had attended public schools in Dallas, then enrolled at the Virginia Military Institute, only to drop out after one year to enlist in the army. Following service in an infantry division during World War I, Clark returned home to train for the family vocation at the University of Texas, from which he received a B.A. in 1921 and an LL.B. in 1922. He then joined his father's Dallas law firm. In 1927, Clark was appointed civil district attorney of Dallas County. He returned to private practice in 1933, but although successful, abandoned it again for public service in 1937 when Senator Tom Connally secured him a position with the Justice Department.

Starting there as an assistant to the attorney general assigned to try cases in the war risk litigation section, Clark moved on to the antitrust division, heading up its wage and hour unit and later its New Orleans field office and its West Coast region. Following the Pearl Harbor attack, President Franklin D. Roosevelt appointed him civilian coordinator of the Western Defense Command, in which capacity he handled legal aspects of the relocation and internment of Japanese Americans. Clark then took over the war frauds unit of the antitrust division. He worked closely with Harry Truman, who chaired a Senate committee investigating waste and corruption in defense industries. In 1944 Clark moved up to head the antitrust division, and the following year, when many of its functions were transferred to the criminal division, Attorney General Francis Biddle placed him in charge of that organization. Clark kept in touch with Truman, however, and at the 1944 Democratic convention helped him obtain the vice-presidential nomination. After Roosevelt's death made Truman president in 1945, he selected Clark to replace Biddle.

As attorney general, the Texan retained his interest in antitrust, initiating 160 new enforcement actions and personally arguing a major case before the Supreme Court. He also took an interest in civil rights. Besides pressuring the FBI to investigate lynchings and calling for the enactment of federal legislation to punish them, Clark had his department file an *amicus curiae* brief with the Supreme Court that helped persuade it to declare judicial enforcement of racially restrictive covenants unconstitutional (*Shelley v. Kraemer*, 1948). Exhibiting an interest in fair and orderly administration, he used his position to promote adoption of the Administrative Procedures Act of 1946. Clark also played a large role in the development of the Truman administration's internal security policies. He advocated a loyalty program for federal employees, and under him, Justice drafted the first attorney general's list of allegedly subversive organizations. He secured an expansion of his department's investigative authority that included authorization for the FBI to make greater use of wiretaps. In 1948, despite a dearth of evidence against the accused, Clark personally authorized prosecution of the top leaders of the

American Communist party under the Smith Act.

When Truman nominated him to the Supreme Court in 1949 to succeed libertarian Justice Frank Murphy, liberals and radicals protested the choice; they considered Clark a red-baiting extremist. There were also allegations that he was indifferent to the rights of persons accused of crime. With vastly less justification, critics accused him of being anti-labor and anti-black. Nevertheless, the Senate confirmed Clark by a vote of seventy-three to eight.

He soon demonstrated that concerns about his commitment to individual rights were well founded. Clark became an ally of conservative Chief Justice Fred Vinson; during the four years they served together, he rejected libertarian claims in civil liberties cases 76 percent of the time, only slightly below Vinson's 86 percent. Clark generally supported anti-Communist loyalty-security programs. In *Garner v. Board of Public Works* (1951), for example, he spoke for a 5–4 majority that upheld a Los Angeles ordinance under which city employees had to file affidavits affirming that they were not then, and never had been, members of the Communist party, and to execute loyalty oaths that involved swearing they had not taught or advocated the overthrow of the government.

As John Frank correctly observes, however, Clark was not an arrant red-baiter. When in *Wieman v. Updegraff* (1952) the Court unanimously struck down an Oklahoma law requiring government employees to swear they had not been members of any organization on the attorney general's list during the past five years, Clark wrote the opinion condemning this statute for penalizing even persons who had joined such groups without being aware of their character.

Wieman presaged a brief shift to a more libertarian position that followed Vinson's death and the appointment of Earl Warren as chief justice in 1953. Warren launched a successful drive to increase the number of cases the Court was deciding, an effort in which the administratively minded Clark cooperated gladly. As the Warren Court began to move in a libertarian direction in civil liberties cases, Clark went along. He supported a 1956 ruling that the ex-

istence of the Smith Act precluded states from punishing sedition against the United States, and in *Slochower v. Board of Higher Education* (1956), wrote a majority opinion holding that the dismissal of a Brooklyn College professor under a provision of the New York City charter requiring summary discharge of any employee who invoked the privilege against self-incrimination during an investigation of his official conduct violated the Fifth Amendment.

In 1957, however, Clark became a vigorous dissenter in civil liberties cases. Warren had been drifting closer to the Court's liberal stalwarts, Hugo Black and William O. Douglas, and the 1956 appointment of William Brennan completed the formation of a four-man liberal bloc that Clark perceived as a threat to internal security programs he considered essential. He spoke out first in an intemperate dissent from the Court's May 1957 ruling in *Jencks v. United States* (1957), which held that the government must permit defense attorneys to see written statements furnished to the FBI by prosecution witnesses. The result of this decision, Clark lamented, would be a "Roman holiday for rummaging through confidential information as well as vital national secrets."

On "Red Monday" (17 June 1957), he dissented three more times. In *Yates v. United States* (1957), Clark protested when the majority overturned convictions of California Communist leaders under the Smith Act and rendered a key provision of that law virtually unusable against the Communist party. He also denounced the Court's rulings in *Watkins v. United States* (1957) and *Sweezy v. New Hampshire* (1957), overturning contempt sentences imposed on individuals who had refused to cooperate with federal and state legislative investigations of subversive activities.

Clark continued to dissent the following year, but in cases upholding the dismissals of a teacher and a subway conductor who had refused to answer questions about their involvement in Communist activities, he found himself on the winning side.

Responding to congressional outrage against the Court's recent internal security decisions, Justices Felix Frankfurter and John

Marshall Harlan ceased cooperating with the liberal bloc, and by 1959, Clark was frequently in the majority. He spoke for the Court in *Uphaus v. Wyman* (1959), a decision seemingly inconsistent with *Sweezy*, that rejected a First Amendment attack on a one-man legislative investigation by the attorney general of New Hampshire, declaring that the state's need to unearth subversive activities outweighed any invasion of privacy it might involve. The following year Clark wrote a majority opinion holding Los Angeles County had not denied a temporary employee due process when it fired him for invoking the Fifth Amendment before a congressional committee.

After Frankfurter retired in 1962, the liberal block regained control, and Clark again found himself dissenting in internal security cases. As popular concern about communism abated and the high tribunal devoted more of its attention to other issues, however, he appeared to become more content as a member of the Warren Court. Clark concurred in its pathbreaking ruling in *Baker v. Carr* (1962), subjecting the apportionment of state legislatures to control by the federal judiciary, and he consistently supported its efforts to enhance the rights of African Americans. In *Burton v. Wilmington Parking Authority* (1961), he authored an innovative opinion holding that a private restaurant must comply with the equal protection clause of the Fourteenth Amendment because it rented space from a governmental agency. Clark also spoke for the Court in *Heart of Atlanta Motel v. United States* (1964), when it affirmed the constitutionality of the public accommodations provisions of the Civil Rights Act of 1964, and in *Katzenbach v. McClung* (1964), where it held that, although based on the commerce clause, these provisions could be enforced against a local business having little contact with interstate commerce. Other Clark opinions overturned criminal trespass convictions against sit-in demonstrators and invalidated transfer policies designed to forestall school integration in Knoxville, Tennessee.

While making a number of contributions to the work of the Warren Court in the field of civil rights, Clark was more productive in other areas. Predictably, the former head of the antitrust division became the Court's antitrust specialist. He also produced numerous important opinions on state taxation of interstate business and often spoke for the Court in cases involving other tax issues, interstate commerce, and labor law. He wrote often in immigration cases as well. But his real specialty was criminal procedure. Of the 341 opinions that he authored during his eighteen years on the bench, more than 26 percent dealt with some aspect of that subject. Nearly 20 percent of his majority opinions involved criminal procedure.

Among them was the one he wrote in *Mapp v. Ohio* (1961). It required state courts to join the federal judiciary in excluding evidence that was the product of unreasonable searches or seizures. *Mapp* initiated a constitutional revolution in which the Warren Court made almost all of the criminal procedure provisions of the Bill of Rights fully applicable to the states and dramatically increased the protection they afforded to defendants.

Clark appeared somewhat out of character as the Court's spokesman in that case, for normally he voted against persons convicted of crimes. He was firmly committed to the maintenance of law and order and believed that government could retain the respect of its citizens only if it punished the guilty. As a former prosecutor, Clark identified with those responsible for law enforcement and sympathized with their concerns. Thus, he dissented from the Court's landmark ruling in *Miranda v. Arizona* (1966), requiring police to inform suspects of their rights before attempting to interrogate them. Clark would not vote to reverse a conviction, even where law enforcement personnel clearly had violated the rights of the accused, unless the defendant could prove the violation had contributed to the guilty verdict.

While taking a conditional approach to lapses in pretrial criminal procedure, Clark became an absolutist concerning violations of the right to a fair trial. When first confronted with the problem of prejudicial publicity in criminal cases, he balanced the Sixth Amendment rights of the accused against First Amendment rights of freedom of expression, announcing in a majority opinion in *Irvin v. Dowd* (1961), and a dissent in *Rideau v. Louisiana* (1963), that a defendant was entitled to have a conviction reversed only if he could prove that press coverage had actually biased the jury. While wrestling in *Estes v. Texas* (1965) with the question of whether live television coverage violated the right to a fair trial, however, Clark changed his mind. Ignoring the First Amendment, he adopted an unconditional approach to Sixth Amendment violations that did not require proof of harm. He then followed *Estes* in a notorious pretrial publicity case, *Sheppard v. Maxwell* (1966), presuming harm from the infringement of the defendant's constitutional right to a fair trial. Clark changed his position because he concluded that, as violations of that right (unlike the improper eliciting of confessions) occurred in the courtroom, judges (whom, he believed, should meet higher standards than police officers) could and should prevent them. If jurists appeared to condone violations of the Constitution, public confidence in the judiciary and the fair administration of justice would be undermined. Similar reasoning led Clark to favor requiring state courts to comply with the exclusionary rule; he considered this necessary to ensure the "judicial integrity so necessary to the true administration of justice."

The administration of justice, not the plight of criminal defendants, was his overriding concern. Indeed, this interest was the adhesive that bound the disparate elements of Clark's jurisprudence together. He had no real judicial philosophy. Clark considered flexibility the attribute most essential to success on the Supreme Court, and his opinions reflected common sense rather than commitment to activism, self-restraint, or any other jurisprudential strategy.

Thomas Mengler aptly characterizes the opinion Clark wrote in *School District of Abington Township v. Schempp* (1963), holding that Bible reading in the public schools violated the First Amendment's establishment of religion clause, as designed "for the readership of *Time*, rather than the *Harvard Law Review*." A year earlier the Court had excited a popular outcry by holding unconstitutional the New York regents' recommendation of a prayer to be recited in that state's schools. Disturbed by the reaction to the prayer decision, Clark, a good Presbyterian, determined to reassure the public that the Court was not undermining religion. In *Schempp,* he wrote a short opinion that eschewed sophisticated legal analysis and addressed the concerns of the average citizen. It was, in short, an exercise in public relations.

That is not to say that Clark's decision making was unprincipled. His public relations effort was designed to persuade Americans to accept an exclusion of religious exercises from public schools, which he regarded as constitutionally required. Although devoted to President Truman, Clark concurred when the Court ruled in *Youngstown Sheet & Tube Company v. Sawyer* (1952) that Truman had acted unconstitutionally in seizing the nation's steel mills during the Korean War. He believed the seizure was illegal and that, despite his affection for Truman, duty required him to say so.

Although Clark was a principled man, his approach to opinion writing was pragmatic. A skillful negotiator, he was always willing to conciliate another justice in order to achieve a majority or unanimity, even if doing that required conceding a disputed point. Clark did have convictions to which he adhered firmly, but the principles he implemented most consistently were tenets of judicial administration rather than constitutional law.

These precepts were three in number. The first—based on a belief that once courts had determined a legal issue, even those conscientiously opposed to the result were bound by it—was that he would dissent from a precedent with which he disagreed only in the term in which it was established. The second was that doctrines which embodied bad public policy should be overruled whenever he could persuade four other justices to join him in doing so. Finally, if the Court concluded that a precedent was no longer to be followed, Clark believed it should say so explicitly.

His handling of search and seizure cases illustrates these principles at work. Shortly before his appointment, the Court held in *Wolf v. Colorado* (1949) that the exclusionary rule did not apply to the states. Clark, who had been outraged years earlier when he was unable to prevent the use against one of his first clients of evidence obtained during a particularly heinous search by police in Dallas, disagreed with its position. Yet, when the Court reaffirmed it in *Irvine v. California* (1954), he reluctantly concurred, rather than dissent. Although writing then that *Wolf* remained "the law, and as such . . . entitled to the respect of the Court's membership," he subsequently lobbied his colleagues to persuade them to utilize *Mapp* to overrule the 1949 decision, even though the defendant's attorneys had based their appeal on issues other than whether the exclusionary rule applied to the states.

Clark followed the course he did in these search and seizure cases because he was convinced this was the best way to promote the effective administration of justice. In his opinion, the Court's job was to establish rules for a vast array of social institutions. To avoid confusion at lower levels in the justice system, it had an obligation to make as clear as possible precisely what those rules were. Adherence to his three principles was the best way to achieve that objective, Clark believed.

Achieving clarity was necessary to maximize efficiency, and an efficiently run legal system would provide a higher level of justice. Clark was also convinced that the growth of popular discontent with the courts during the 1960s was due largely to a "breakdown of judicial procedures," and that the way to halt this collapse was to enhance efficiency. Despite his law and order mentality, he became a supporter of decriminalizing victimless crimes. The reason was that cases of this type clogged the courts, impairing their capacity to administer justice promptly.

Ensuring that justice was administered promptly, efficiently, and effectively became Tom Clark's passion during the last two decades of his life. In 1957, he assumed the chairmanship of the American Bar Association's moribund section of judicial administration. For someone who was also a sitting Supreme Court justice, Clark devoted an incredible amount of time to that job. By the end of his term he had revitalized the section, and according to John Frank, "the foundation was laid for the Ameri-

can Bar's modern activities to improve the administration of justice." Clark subsequently played a leading role in the establishment of the Joint Committee for the Effective Administration of Justice, a body that between 1961 and 1964 worked to coordinate the efforts of the ABA section and a number of other organizations active in this field. Besides serving as chair of the joint committee and participating in many of the citizens conferences on court modernization and seminars for judges that it staged, Clark was also instrumental in obtaining a grant from the Kellogg Foundation to fund its operations. Later, he won financial backing from Kellogg for the National College of State Trial Judges, an outgrowth of the joint committee that Clark helped to found and whose board of directors he chaired.

Constantly flying about the country giving speeches and chairing meetings, Clark became in Frank's words "the travelling salesman of justice." For a decade he carried on this sales campaign while also performing his duties as a Supreme Court justice. Clark always gave priority to his Court responsibilities, but meeting them while crusading across the country for the reform of the administration of justice required a travel schedule that would have worn out most men.

Perhaps fortunately for his health, he retired in 1967. Clark stepped down from the Supreme Court so that his son, Ramsey, could become attorney general. President Lyndon Johnson wanted to name Ramsey to head the Justice Department, but because Tom arguably would have to recuse himself from all of the department's many cases before the Court, he hesitated to do so. Clark solved this problem by resigning.

Although willing to step down from the Supreme Court in order to advance his son's career, at sixty-seven and in good health, Tom Clark was not really ready for retirement. He traveled around the country, serving as a trial judge and also becoming the first jurist ever to sit on all of the United States circuit courts of appeal. He also continued his crusade to improve the administration of justice. After Earl Warren got Congress to establish the Federal Judicial

Center, Clark became its first director in March 1968. He also chaired the ABA's special committee on evaluation of disciplinary enforcement and continued to participate in seminars and give speeches. In addition, Clark wrote prolifically on his favorite subject; 95 percent of the articles he published during the latter part of his life addressed problems of court management. "I can categorically state, without fear of legitimate contradiction," his former clerk, Larry Temple, wrote after he died in 1977, "that Tom Clark made a greater favorable impact on the administration of justice than any individual in our legal history."

Clark's influence on that field was far greater than his impact on constitutional law. During his eighteen years on the Supreme Court, he wrote a comparatively small number of really important opinions. *Mapp* was by far the most significant. His *Schempp* opinion, which began the creation of a test the Court would use for two decades to assess alleged violations of the establishment clause, is notable too. *Burton* was an innovative attack on the hoary principle that only government can violate the Constitution, and might have led to this doctrine being severely circumscribed had congressional enactment of civil rights legislation forbidding many private businesses to discriminate not soon rendered such revolutionary judicial action unnecessary. *Heart of Atlanta* and *McClung* were important because they upheld a landmark law, but doctrinally they did little more than underscore what the Justice Department lawyers who drafted the Civil Rights Act of 1964 already knew: Congress can use its power to regulate interstate commerce to do anything it wants. Clark made major contributions to the development of the law governing prejudicial pretrial publicity, and he also produced a significant opinion holding that motion pictures are protected by the First Amendment.

Nothing he did on the bench, however, matched in importance his work to improve the administration of justice. It was this and not his contributions to constitutional law that won him acclaim from the bar and the general public. His efforts on behalf of judicial reform earned him a reputation that redounded to the benefit of the

institution he served. When the Warren Court was under attack for its controversial rulings on race relations, criminal procedure, legislative redistricting, and separation of church and state, Clark was often able to mollify those it had angered.

He was by most standards not a great justice. His memorable opinions were few in number, and he made no significant contribution to the fierce jurisprudential debates that raged within the Supreme Court during the years that he served on it. But, as Temple notes, "When the chronicles of the development and betterment of the administration of justice in this country are recorded, the name of Tom C. Clark will be paramount."

—MICHAEL R. BELKNAP

BIBLIOGRAPHY

Justice Clark's papers are divided between the Harry S Truman Presidential Library in Independence, Missouri, and the Tarlton Law Library of the University of Texas School of Law in Austin, Texas. The material housed in the Truman Library relates to his pre-Court career, while the Texas collection includes both Clark's Supreme Court case files and correspondence and other items reflecting his involvement in efforts to improve judicial administration. There is no biography of Tom Clark. Chapter 5 of John P. Frank, *The Warren Court* (1964), and Richard Kirkendall, "Tom C. Clark," in Friedman and Israel, 4 *Justices* 2665 provide good overviews of his career, but unfortunately the first of these pieces was written while Clark was still on the Court and the second nearly a decade before his death.

Reflecting the intensity of Clark's interest in judicial administration and the importance of his efforts to reform it, there are more articles dealing with this subject than with any aspect of his work on the bench. The most important are John P. Frank, "Justice Tom Clark and Judicial Administration," *Texas Law Review* 46 (1967): 5–56; James A. Gazell, "Justice Tom C. Clark as Judicial Reformer," *Houston Law Review* 15 (1978): 307–29; and Dennis D. Dorin, "Tom C. Clark: The Justice as Administrator," *Judicature* 61 (December-January 1978): 271–77. Marc

Srere, "Note: Justice Tom C. Clark's Unconditional Approach to Individual Rights in the Courtroom," *Texas Law Review* 64 (1985): 421–42; Thomas M. Mengler, "Public Relations in the Supreme Court: Justice Tom Clark's Opinion in the School Prayer Case," *Constitutional Commentary* 6 (1989): 331–49; and Paul R. Baier, "Justice Clark, the Voice of the Past, and the Exclusionary Rule," *Texas Law Review* 64 (1985): 415–19, all provide useful insights into aspects of Clark's jurisprudence. Although short, Larry Temple, "Mr. Justice Clark: A Tribute," *American Journal of Criminal Law* 5 (October 1977): 271–74, is also helpful.

JOHN HESSIN CLARKE

BORN 18 September 1857, New Lisbon, Ohio

NOMINATED to the Court 14 July 1916 by
Woodrow Wilson

TOOK seat 9 October 1916; resigned 18
September 1922

DIED 22 March 1945 in San Diego, California

John Hessin Clarke had been a prominent
railroad and corporate attorney, a newspaper
publisher, an activist in Ohio's Democratic reform politics, and an unsuccessful candidate for
the U.S. Senate when President Woodrow Wilson appointed him to serve as a federal district
court judge in 1914. Two years later Wilson elevated Clarke to the Supreme Court.

As Wilson had hoped, Clarke displayed on
the Court the progressive politics that had characterized his pre-judicial career. Indeed, Chief
Justice Taft complained that Clarke acted "as if
each case was something to vote on as he would
vote on it in the Senate or the House, rather than
to decide as a judge." Clarke's confidence in the
ability of government to solve social problems
was manifest in his voting record in cases involving exercises of federal and state regulatory
power. He dissented in two cases striking down
federal laws regulating the employment of child
labor, *Hammer v. Dagenhart* (1918) and *Bailey
v. Drexel Furniture* (1922). He voted to uphold
the federal Adamson Act's eight-hour day for railway workers in *Wilson v. New* (1917), and joined
the Court's opinion upholding a federal statute
regulating meat packers and stockyards in *Stafford
v. Wallace* (1922). Rejecting the doctrines of substantive due process, which he denounced as
"Fourteenth Amendment nonsense," Clarke voted
to uphold Oregon's minimum wage and maximum hour laws in *Stettler v. O'Hara* (1917) and
Bunting v. Oregon (1917). He endorsed the
Court's opinion sustaining New York's workmen's compensation statute in *New York Central
Railroad Co. v. White* (1917), and joined
Brandeis's landmark fact-intensive dissent from
a decision striking down a Washington statute

regulating the fees charged by employment agencies in *Adams v. Tanner* (1917).

Clarke's sympathy for working people also
led him to resist the use of injunctions to enforce
anti-union contracts in *Hitchman Coal & Coke
Co. v. Mitchell* (1917), to support the right of
employees to picket their employer in *Truax v.
Corrigan* (1921) and *American Steel Foundries*
(1921), and to oppose the use of the antitrust
laws against labor unions in *United Mine Workers v. Coronado Coal Co.* (1922) and *Duplex
Printing Co. v. Deering* (1921). Yet in the leading business antitrust cases of the period—*U.S.
v. U.S. Steel Corp.* (1920), *U.S. v. United Shoe
Machinery Co.* (1918), *U.S. v. Reading Railroad
Co.* (1920), *U.S. v. Lehigh Valley Railroad*
(1920), and *American Column and Lumber Co.
v. U. S.* (1921)—Clarke consistently maintained
a stern trustbusting position.

In Clarke's legal progressivism, however,
diminished solicitude for economic liberty
was not accompanied by an incipient concern for modern civil liberties. He joined
Holmes's landmark opinions upholding federal
prosecutions under the Espionage Act during
World War I in *Schenck v. U.S.* (1919),
Frohwerk v. U.S. (1919), and *Debs v. United
States* (1919), and wrote the majority opinion
in *Abrams v. U.S.* (1919) extending the power
of Congress to punish anti-government speech
even beyond what Holmes was willing to
countenance.

Finding himself dissatisfied with the life of
a justice, Clarke disappointed many liberals by
resigning unexpectedly from the Court in September 1922. He spent much of his time in
retirement promoting the cause of American
participation in the World Court and the League
of Nations. In the 1930s, Clarke joined other
legal progressives in believing that many of the
decisions of the Court declaring New Deal initiatives unconstitutional were unsound. He supported the "Court-packing" plan, and delivered
a national radio address defending its constitutionality. Clarke resisted offers to write his bi-

ography, insisting that his life had not been "sufficiently unusual or important."

—BARRY CUSHMAN

BIBLIOGRAPHY

The definitive biography of Clarke is Hoyt Landon Warner, *The Life of Mr. Justice Clarke: A Testament to the Power of Liberal Dissent in America* (1959). Also useful are David M. Levitan, "The Jurisprudence of Mr. Justice Clarke," 7 *Miami Law Quarterly* 44 (1952), and Carl Wittke, "Mr. Justice Clarke in Retirement," 1 *Western Reserve Law Review* 28 (1949). There is a small collection of correspondence in the Clarke papers at the Western Reserve University Library in Cleveland.

NATHAN CLIFFORD

BORN August 18, 1803, Rumney,
    New Hampshire
NOMINATED to the Court 9 December 1858
    by James Buchanan
TOOK seat 21 January 1858
DIED 25 July 1881 in Cornish, Maine

Soon after starting his legal career in 1827, Nathan Clifford became active in Maine's Democratic politics, serving in the state legislature and as attorney general. In 1839, he entered the House of Representatives and three years later President James K. Polk appointed him attorney general. In 1858, when James Buchanan chose him for the Supreme Court's "New England seat," the nomination raised considerable criticism. Some northern senators objected to him as a "doughface" because of his close links with southern Democrats, his friendship with Chief Justice Roger B. Taney, and his attacks on the abolitionists; other senators considered him merely a party hack. He was confirmed nonetheless, and served as an associate justice for twenty-three years, from 1858 to 1881.

Although Clifford wrote no famous opinions, he did have an impact on the court because he consistently voted according to a strict conservative philosophy which defended states' rights against federal intervention. In the Civil War cases, his political ideology conflicted with the rising policies of nationalism and expansion of federal power, and led to numerous dissents. In the *Prize Cases* (1863), he concurred in Justice Samuel Nelson's dissent, which affirmed that the federal government's seizing of neutral shipping was unconstitutional because the conflict was President Abraham Lincoln's "personal war" until Congress officially declared hostilities. He was with the majority in limiting federal activity in *Ex parte Milligan* (1866), which declared unconstitutional the military commission's trial of civilians outside of the war zone. In *Hepburn v. Griswold* (1870), he voted with the majority against the federal government's power to issue paper money as legal tender even in a time of emergency. When the court reversed itself in *Knox v. Lee* (1871), Clifford wrote a strong dissent of nearly 18,000 words arguing that legal tender must be exclusively gold and silver.

In two Reconstruction cases, Clifford's opinions were unfortunately the voice of the future. *Williams v. Mississippi* (1898) was foreshadowed in his dissent in *United States v. Reese* (1876) when he argued that, although the Fifteenth Amendment strictly limited racial discrimination in voting, other qualifications by cities or states which restricted the franchise were legitimate. Therefore, Lexington's poll tax, used to disenfranchise African Americans, was constitutional. In *Hall v. DeCuir* (1878), a case concerning segregated accommodations on a Mississippi River passenger ship, Clifford coined the phrase "equality is not identity," which was later translated by *Plessy v. Ferguson* (1896) into "separate but equal." He followed this conservative philosophy on racial matters in other cases such as *Strauder v. West Virginia* (1880) and *Ex parte Virginia* (1880), where he joined in the dissent against the Court's invalidating statutes that excluded African Americans from jury service. Jury selection, the dissent contended, was a state prerogative and the majority's declarations were attempts to destroy true dual federalism.

Although the famous cases of this period concerned the Civil War and Reconstruction, most of Clifford's nearly 400 opinions dealt with maritime and commercial law. He became the Court's expert on the assigning of fault and accountability in ship collisions, which were a relatively common occurrence in a commercially expanding nation. Given his being labeled a "doughface," it might seem ironic that he wrote most of the court's decisions upholding the forfeiture of slave ships. His affirmation of the government's seizures had none of the moral indignation of Chief Justice Salmon P. Chase's opinions in regard to slavers, but Clifford strictly applied the laws banning slave importation.

Because he had been sent as a special commissioner to arrange the treaty of Guadaloupe-Hidalgo, which ended the Mexican war, Clifford also specialized in southwestern land disputes. His decisions often favored the appeals of new American claimants rather than those holding the original Spanish land grants.

Although Clifford was a conservative Jeffersonian democrat, his opinions on economic matters strongly supported business expansion. He held firmly for limited liability, "inevitable accident" in maritime cases, a strict interpretation for written contracts, protection for the innocent third party, and an acceptance of the *caveat emptor* principle. He also maintained that "patents for inventions are not to be treated as mere monopolies and, therefore, odious in the eyes of the law; but they are to receive a liberal construction . . . to be so interpreted as to uphold and not to destroy the right of the inventor" (*Turrill v. Railroad Company,* 1863). However, he demanded real novelty for a patent and affirmed that once a patented item was sold, the inventor had no claim whatsoever.

Clifford presided over the commission which determined the 1876 disputed presidential election and naturally, as a staunch Democrat, voted for Tilden. In 1880, he suffered a stroke which ended his active participation in the Court's decisions. Critics suggested that this was no great legal loss because they believed that he had become senile some time before. Even in failing health, Clifford, ever the party stalwart, clung to his position in the hope that a future Democratic president might name his successor. He refused to resign to the bitter end, which came with his death in July 1881.

—WILLIAM BOSCH

BIBLIOGRAPHY

The papers of Nathan Clifford are in the Maine Historical Society. There is no modern biography, but David M. Silver's *Lincoln's Supreme Court* (1956) is a richly researched mother lode from which other authors have mined much on Clifford's character and wartime activities. His later career is considered in Robert Fridlington, *The Reconstruction Court, 1864–1888* (1987).

BENJAMIN ROBBINS CURTIS

BORN 4 November 1809, Watertown,
Massachusetts

NOMINATED to the Court 11 December 1851
by Millard Fillmore

CONFIRMED 20 December 1851; retired
1 September 1857

DIED 15 September 1874 in Newport,
Rhode Island

After receiving degrees from Harvard College in 1829 and Harvard Law School in 1832, Benjamin R. Curtis spent the next seventeen years in law practice in Massachusetts. In 1849, he was elected to the Massachusetts house of representatives and served for two years. President Millard Fillmore, following the advice of his secretary of state, Daniel Webster, then chose Curtis to fill the "New England" seat vacated by the death of Levi Woodbury.

Justice Curtis's six-year tenure was marked by enormous transition in the Court's jurisprudence, particularly with regard to the commerce clause and the Fifth Amendment's guarantee of due process. In his first term, the junior justice forged a valuable consensus in *Cooley v. Board of Wardens of the Port of Philadelphia* (1852), a challenge to a Pennsylvania law which required all vessels using the port of Philadelphia to employ local pilots or pay a substantial fine. Shipmaster Cooley contended on appeal that the statute violated the federal government's "exclusive" commerce clause power to regulate pilotage. Curtis, in a majority opinion noted for its balanced approach to the thorny conflict of national and state concerns, rejected Cooley's argument and upheld the law:

> Either absolutely to affirm, or deny that the nature of this power requires exclusive legislation by Congress, is to lose sight of the nature of the subjects of this power, and to assert concerning all of them, what is really applicable but to a part. Whatever subjects of this power are in their nature national, or admit only of one uniform sys-

tem, or plan of regulation, may justly be said to be of such a nature as to require exclusive legislation by Congress. That this cannot be affirmed of laws for the regulation of pilots and pilotage is plain.

In fact, he continued, Congress had expressly stated in the Judiciary Act of 1789 that such matters should be governed by existing state laws until further congressional enactment. In crafting the "selective exclusiveness" standard later known as the "*Cooley* Doctrine," Curtis set forth a pragmatic method for distinguishing subjects of exclusive federal control from those which might be governed locally or concurrently between the federal government and the states. Although ultimately supplanted by a more flexible balancing approach to delineating the boundaries of the commerce power, the "*Cooley* Doctrine" nevertheless provided a useful analytical transition from the rigidity of earlier commerce clause decisions.

Curtis also influenced the Court's nascent due process jurisprudence. In *Murray's Lessee v. Hoboken Land & Improvement Co.* (1856), he wrote on behalf of a unanimous Court that the Fifth Amendment guarantee of due process applied to the actions of Congress as well as to those of the executive and judicial branches. In so doing, Curtis proffered an instrumental definition of due process as procedures that did not conflict with specific written constitutional provisions or with the "settled modes and usages" of English and early American practice. Other noteworthy opinions authored by Curtis include: *Steamboat New World v. King* (1854), in which the Court broadened the scope of federal admiralty jurisdiction to include inland rivers on the basis of their navigability rather than the ebb and flow of the ocean tides; and *Lafayette Insurance Company v. French* (1856), in which the Court clarified the jurisdictional status of corporations as "citizens" of their state of incorporation.

Aside from Cooley, however, Curtis's most memorable opinion is his forceful dissent in *Dred Scott v. Sandford* (1857). In response to the majority's denial of Scott's appeal on the grounds that Congress was powerless to prohibit slavery and that blacks were not entitled to the privileges and immunities of national citizenship, Curtis methodically, devastatingly, and thoroughly dissected the flaws of the majority's reasoning. Exacerbating the already tense atmosphere of disagreement over the decision, Curtis prematurely released a copy of his dissent to a Boston reporter in the mistaken belief that the majority decision had already been filed. Shortly thereafter, Curtis resigned from the Court, citing the inadequate salary and conflicting "private duties" as his motivations. It is quite likely that his loss of confidence in the Court following the *Dred Scott* decision was a significant contributing factor, as well.

While on the Court, Justice Curtis edited two significant reference works, *Reports of Cases in the Circuit Courts of the United States* (2 vols., 1854), and *Decisions of the Supreme Court of the United States* (22 vols., 1856). The latter accomplishment was one of the earliest compilations of condensed decisions in the history of the Court.

After leaving the bench Curtis devoted the rest of his life to private law practice and argued fifty-four cases before the Court. In 1868, he successfully defended President Andrew Johnson in his senate impeachment trial. After several years of poor health, he died on September 15, 1874, in Newport, Rhode Island.

—MARGARET M. RUSSELL

BIBLIOGRAPHY

Curtis papers are available at both the Library of Congress and the American Antiquarian Society in Boston. *The Life and Writings of Benjamin Robbins Curtis* and *A Memoir of Benjamin Robbins Curtis, LL.D., with Some of His Professional and Miscellaneous Writings*, both edited by the justice's son, Benjamin R. Curtis, in 1879, are wide-ranging collections of Curtis's correspondence, speeches, judicial opinions, and other writings. The most complete study of Justice Curtis to date is an unpublished doctoral dissertation by Richard H. Leach, "Benjamin R. Curtis: Case Study of a Supreme Court Justice" (Princeton, 1951). Portions of this project have been published in three articles: "Benjamin Robbins Curtis: Judicial Misfit," 25 *New England Quarterly* 507 (1952); "Benjamin Robbins Curtis: A Model for a Successful Legal Career," 41 *American Bar Association Journal* 225 (1955); and "Justice Curtis and the *Dred Scott* Case," 94 *Essex Institute Historical Collection* 37 (1958).

WILLIAM CUSHING

BORN 1 March 1732, Scituate, Massachusetts

NOMINATED to the Court 30 September 1789 by George Washington

TOOK seat 1 February 1790; commissioned as Chief Justice 26 January 1796, but declined

DIED 13 September 1810 in Scituate, Massachusetts

William Cushing served longer with minimal effect than any of the fourteen Supreme Court justices whose terms overlapped his. His lengthy judicial career in Massachusetts made him an obvious, almost automatic, choice by President George Washington. Indeed, on paper, he was the most highly qualified of any of his brethren. It was only after his twenty-one uneventful years on the Supreme Court that historians looked back and discovered that there was not a great deal to show for his twenty-nine years on the state bench either—with one possible exception. Legend holds that Cushing proclaimed an end to slavery in Massachusetts in 1783 because it was a violation of the new state constitution. The evidence to support such a claim, however, is scanty and unconvincing.

Cushing seemed to have been born for political influence in Massachusetts. On his mother's side, he descended from the patriarch John Cotton, and his father and grandfather were both judges of the Massachusetts superior court. When John Cushing retired after twenty-three years, he was succeeded by William, who had for the past twelve years been register of deeds and judge of probate for a county in the Maine district, as well as that county's only attorney. Cushing was the only judge who was retained when the new state supreme court was formed in 1775. He had endeared himself to the radicals by refusing his salary from the Crown in 1774, yet also managed to remain on friendly terms with loyalists. He was justly described by contemporaries as "remarkable for the secrecy of his opinions." He was state chief justice from 1777 until his appointment to the United States Supreme Court. Cushing seems to have contributed little enlightenment as a member of the convention which wrote the Massachusetts constitution of 1780, or as vice-president of the state convention which ratified the federal Constitution.

Cushing was officially the senior associate jutice, as well as the oldest of Washington's appointees. John Rutledge was appointed first after the chief justice, but he never occupied the second seat on the Supreme Court. Seniority did not make Cushing more voluble. It may even have had the opposite effect. The justices spoke in reverse seniority, so Cushing preceded only the chief justice. Younger and more creative thinkers would already have expounded on the issues prior to Cushing, so he was often in a position of simply concurring with them. Even before Chief Justice John Marshall persuaded his colleagues to abandon *seriatim* decisions, Cushing could thus rationalize his relative silence. President Thomas Jefferson had Cushing primarily in mind when he proposed that the Court be required to return to *seriatim* decisions, in hopes that it would highlight the weaknesses of the silent majority.

Cushing delivered only nineteen brief opinions during twenty-one years on the bench, and his decisions were direct, non-complex, or as some have said "simple." If succinctness is a blessing, then Cushing was a saint. He wrote only two sentences in *Calder v. Bull* (1798), a case which he considered "clear of all difficulty." He did not even refer to the *ex post facto* clause. This is an extraordinary example, but even his longer opinions generally deal with a single point. In *Ware v. Hylton* (1796), a case involving prewar debts owed to British merchants, he focused entirely on the language of the Treaty of 1783, avoiding the discussions of federal relationships which characterized Justice Samuel Chase's lead opinion. Cushing's first sentence gives an accurate picture of the opinion: "My statement of this case will, agreeable to my view of it, be short." *Chisholm v. Georgia* (1793), which upheld the right of a citizen to sue a state in federal court, is regarded as Cushing's best opinion, but it adds nothing significant to the opinions that had preceded it. He declared that the rights of individuals are "as dear and precious as those of states." He challenged the states that "if the constitution is found inconvenient . . . it is well that a regular mode is pointed out for amendment." Congress and the states quickly initiated that process, which led to the Eleventh Amendment.

Under Marshall, Cushing was called on most often to deal with cases turning on procedural technicalities—frequently issues involving loyalist or British property claims. Sadly, his most impressive later opinion, *McIlvaine v. Coxe's Lessee* (1808), which established guidelines for naturalization policy, was described by a major historian of the Marshall Court as "well beyond his capacities at that time, and perhaps beyond his professional ability even at a younger age." Herbert A. Johnson has speculated that the quality of this opinion, with Cushing's name attached, brings into question "the commonly accepted assumption that *delivery* of a majority opinion implied *authorship* of the opinion."

On circuit in Connecticut, Cushing and Jay were the first federal judges to invalidate a state law for violation of the Treaty of 1783. On the Supreme Court, he took a unique position on the judicial review of state constitutions. In *Cooper v. Telfair* (1800), he was the only justice who thought the Supreme Court could void an act in violation of the Georgia constitution. He added, though, that the case did not warrant judicial review because the authority to banish citizens and to confiscate property were inherent in every government, and were matters for legislative, rather than judicial, determination.

President Washington was obviously not disillusioned by his senior associate justice. Cushing was appointed and confirmed as chief justice on January 26, 1796, after the senate had rejected John Rutledge. Alexander Hamilton and Patrick Henry had also declined before the Cushing appointment, so he was in good company. He kept the commission for a week before declining because of age and ill health. New Hampshire Senator William Plumer was distressed by Cushing's nomination to head the Court: "He is a man I love and esteem. He once

possessed firmness and other qualities for that office, but Time, the enemy of man, has much impaired his mental faculties. When Jay resigned, Cushing was the eldest Justice, and I fear that the promotion will form a precedent for making Chief Justice from the eldest Judge though the other candidates may be much better qualified." Washington next considered Justices William Paterson and James Iredell before looking outside the Court to Oliver Ellsworth. An associate justice would not be advanced to the center chair until 1910, when Edward D. White became chief justice. President John Adams cited the possible offense to Cushing as a reason not to advance Paterson to chief justice in 1801, but that was intended to justify not appointing Paterson rather than to imply serious consideration of Cushing.

Cushing was always dignified, even in his declining years. He was probably the last American judge to wear the full English wig, ceasing only when he realized that this formidable headgear was the reason that scores of New York City boys followed him in the streets. He was well read, both in legal and general literature. His earlier travels to the state courts in a horse–drawn wagon which contained many of the comforts of home, including a library, provisions, and a wife who read to him as they proceeded surely contributed to his knowledge. Distances and roads were such for a Supreme Court justice that he had to travel them by horseback, despite his age.

Cushing was also remarkably dedicated and conscientious, except when his health impeded him. He set a record for responsibility that can never be matched. He was the one justice who was present on the first day that the Court sat in each of the three capitals of the United States. He was in New York with John Jay and James Wilson when the Court first convened on February 1, 1790; he was in Philadelphia with three others when they first met there one year later; and he was the only one who reported for duty at Washington, D.C., at the beginning of February 1801 term.

When Justice Iredell complained about the unfairness of being confined to the distant southern circuit, Cushing characteristically replied that he would do his share, whatever the rotation. He was too optimistic when he consoled Iredell that "the System may ere long meet with a legislative remedy." He suggested that cases should be heard at the capital, rather than at the periphery. This would have placed a severe burden on many litigants and their counsel, while improving the life of six Supreme Court justices. He had been asked by Jay to negotiate with Congress to lessen the burden on the tiring jurists. It is reflective of his sense of duty that in 1790 he delayed the acceptance of his appointment to the Supreme Court so that he could make one last circuit in the state courts to assure that they met.

Generally good spirited both on and off the bench, Cushing was never as partisan as most of his colleagues. His peak of extremism came in 1798, when he warned the grand jury in Virginia about a French "plot against the rights of Nations and of mankind and against all religion and virtue, order and decency."

Sadly, Cushing had no private fortune and was forced to remain too long on the Court in order to maintain his needed salary. He had never been notably successful as an attorney, so he had no legal practice to rely on for survival. Not an outstanding judge either, Cushing re-mained long enough to justify Justice William Johnson's characterization of him twelve years after his death as "incompetent." Perhaps the best assessment of the senior associate justice was expressed fourteen years before Cushing died, by a senator who considered Cushing a friend. William Plumer described the retiring John Blair, who had certainly been no star on the Supreme Court, as "a man of good abilities, not indeed a Jay, but far superior to Cushing."

—DONALD O. DEWEY

BIBLIOGRAPHY

The best published review of Cushing's career is Herbert A. Johnson's essay in Friedman and Israel, 1 *Justices* 57. John Cushing's unpublished doctoral dissertation, "A Revolutionary Conservative: The Public Life of William Cushing, 1732–1810" (Clark University, 1960), is thorough, critical and valuable. His article, "The Cushing Court and the Abolition of Slavery in Massachusetts," 5 *American Journal of Legal History* 118 (1961), takes a dim view of Cushing's leadership on this issue. Dated, but still useful, is Arthur P. Rugg, "William Cushing," 30 *Yale Law Journal* 120 (1920).

Peter Vivian Daniel
Portrait by Thomas Sully.
Collection of the Supreme Court of the United States.

PETER VIVIAN DANIEL

BORN 24 April 1784, Stafford County,
    Virginia
NOMINATED to the Court 27 February 1841
    by Martin Van Buren
TOOK seat 10 January 1842
DIED 31 May 1860 in Richmond, Virginia

Born in Stafford County, Virginia, nearly
midway between Washington and Richmond,
Peter V. Daniel was married twice and had five
children. Daniel was educated by private tutors
and attended the College of New Jersey (later
Princeton) for only a few months. He moved to
Richmond in 1805 to study law with Edmund
Randolph, was admitted to the bar in 1808, and
was elected to the Virginia legislature the next
year. He soon (1812) rose to membership in the
Virginia council of state and became lieutenant
governor in 1818. Daniel was quite active in
leadership of the Old Dominion Democratic-
Republicans, later the Jacksonian Democrats. A
slaveholder, he was never a planter. Within the
strictures of Virginia's slave system, he gave
careful attention to details of fact and to opportunities for mercy in the Virginia council's review of trials of slaves for rape, and of allegations that a slave suspect had been tortured.

Supporting William H. Crawford in 1824
and Andrew Jackson in 1828, Daniel became
Old Hickory's and later Martin Van Buren's
main supporter in Virginia. However, Daniel's
political career was only moderately successful.
When he ran for governor in 1830, he was defeated by John Floyd. By February 1835, he was
off the council, having been defeated for reelection under the new state constitution. Jackson
finally found a way to reward Daniel; in March
1836, the president appointed Daniel federal district judge for the eastern district of Virginia.
Extraordinarily soon after the death of associate
justice Philip Barbour (a Virginian) in 1841,
President Van Buren, with just nine more days
in office, decided to appoint Daniel to the Supreme Court. Whigs mounted a fruitless effort
to obstruct the appointment, but Daniel ascended
to the bench, where he served from January 1842
through the 1858–1859 term. There he wrote
seventy-four majority opinions, filed fifty dissents, and wrote some concurring opinions.

As a justice, Daniel had little lasting influence on the Supreme Court. He wrote more than
twice as many lone dissenting opinions as did
any other justice on the Taney Court. He had to,
if he were to live up to Van Buren's description
of him as "a Democrat *ab ovo*" who was "not
in so much danger of falling off in the true
spirit." States' rights was his unbending position;
hostility to banks and corporations and opposition to internal improvements were his tenets
until his death. The reason that Justice Daniel
frequently was in the minority on the court—
often a minority of one—is his extreme devotion to anti-federalism and agrarianism. There are
some clues concerning his zealous attachment to
states' rights and lingering anti-federalism.
Daniel's first wife was the daughter of Edmund
Randolph, with whom Daniel studied law and
who had displayed ambivalence about the Constitution of 1787. Daniel also came of age and
joined the Old Dominion government when fellow Virginian John Taylor of Caroline was publishing his passionate arguments against mercantile oppression of agriculture through control of
federal power, and when Spencer Roane and
other Virginians challenged the Marshall Court's
decisions concerning federal judicial supremacy.

None of these factors fully explains Daniel's
perseverance in the face of inevitable change,
however. Randolph, Roane, and Taylor could
have had no immediate influence on Justice
Daniel: all were eulogized well before Daniel
joined the Court. While such justices as Roger
Brooke Taney led the Court in reinterpretation
of the Constitution to remove obstacles to early
corporate growth, other members of the bench
and bar expanded the coverage of federal admiralty jurisdiction as steamboats changed the nature of waterborne commerce, corporations and
banks asserted their legal rights in case after federal case, and a minority of northern jurists

looked for ways to employ the power of the federal government against slavery, Daniel fought a rearguard action against corporations and banks, attempted to limit federal admiralty jurisdiction to the traditional tidewater, strenuously opposed internal improvements, and vigorously championed state and federal protection of the peculiar institution. Only in the last two battles did he have a significant number of allies. Had Daniel lived beyond 1860, he would doubtlessly have joined another group—Confederate sympathizers or Confederates—whose cause was lost.

Daniel faced the special uphill battle of anyone who wishes to limit the federal government's power. Where an omission from the Constitution is not obvious and there is no express denial of a power to the federal government, the necessary and proper clause can be cited to claim a federal power. So it was with internal improvements. When the national government offered none of these improvements or services, nor was expressly required to, it was certainly a matter of argument as to whether the Constitution allowed it to. That Daniel held one of the more extreme positions against internal improvement—i.e., *never*—did not place him on the untenable side of the argument. He stood with millions of other Americans. Unelected, Daniel had no constituency, but his point of view did.

Thus Daniel argued in *Searight v. Stokes* (1845) that the Constitution granted no power to the central government to create roads or any other internal improvement within the states. He chose a poor way to emphasize his point. The Constitution did, he admitted, confer on the government the power to establish post roads; but, in a tour de force of denial, he insisted that power did not extend beyond designating routes. Here was a perfect opportunity for someone to respond that the necessary and proper clause gave full power to the central government to build, own, and maintain post roads where there were none, or where existing roads frustrated the delivery of the U.S. mail. By Daniel's implication, however, the sovereign federal government was dependent on state or local governments or on private enterprise to provide the roads by which the mail was to be delivered.

Daniel carried his restrictive interpretation of the limits of federal power into his opinions

in three of the most important regulatory cases that came before the Taney Court. In the *License Cases* (1847), he concurred with the majority that states could regulate the importation of liquor, but, true to form, he did so on the basis of his particularly intense states' right philosophy. He would not be open to later shifts in the Court's position concerning exclusivity of the federal commerce power. Thus Daniel dissented from the majority decision in the *Passenger Cases* (1849) that states could not tax immigrants to finance a hospital for ship passengers. That decision, he declared, was guilty of "trampling down . . . some of the strongest defenses of the safety and independence of the States of this confederacy." Daniel split the difference in his separate opinion in *Cooley v. Board of Wardens* (1852), concurring with the decision, but dissenting from the majority's arguments. The issue was whether pilotage in harbors was within the federal power to regulate commerce. It was not, said five justices, because pilotage was of local rather than national importance. It was not, Daniel averred, because the power to regulate pilotage always had been a state power and admitted neither federal interference nor even tolerance.

Unlike some of his contemporaries, Justice Daniel never explicitly pointed out the connection between the federal regulatory cases and the troublesome question of federal jurisdiction over slavery. But his opinion in *Prigg v. Pennsylvania* (1842), a major fugitive slave case, shows that his attitude towards federal power over commerce was in uneasy harmony with his opinions concerning the domestic institution. He firmly believed that the states had the duty to carry out, by legislation if necessary, the legitimate powers of the central government. In *Prigg*, the court majority appeared to hold any state legislation concerning fugitive slaves to be in conflict with the exclusive power of the federal government to aid owners in the return of their human property. But Daniel believed that state action to aid the capture and return of fugitive slaves upheld—indeed, must uphold—federal power to protect the property rights of owners. He never explicitly acknowledged the extent to which such state aid to the functioning of the federal government would increase federal government power. It increased that power over slavery, of course. But Daniel clearly perceived the practical problem that impelled proslavery people to campaign for adequate assistance from the central government on the question of runaway slaves until the Fugitive Slave Act of 1850 was passed—and after even it proved to be inadequate. There were not enough federal officials in the states to enforce the Fugitive Slave Law of 1793, so state government help was essential to make the fugitive slave provision of the Constitution effective. (Daniel was hardly alone in this dissent from part of Justice Story's opinion for the court: Chief Justice Taney stood firmly with him.)

Daniel's *Dred Scott v. Sandford* (1857) opinion showed his most consistent thinking: he was both proslavery and opposed to the exercise of one kind of federal power, that of Congress over slavery in the territories. (Still, he recognized no right of a state to create a citizen of the national government.) Daniel emphasized the role of Congress as "agent or trustee" of the United States and the people thereof and concluded that Congress could not thereby take upon itself the power to confer on one group of citizens a privilege that it denied to another group. In other words, Daniel argued that Congress had no right to prohibit slave owners from bringing their human property into the area designated by the Missouri Compromise as free when Congress allowed non-slaveholders to bring in other kinds of property. This was discrimination against slaveholders and southerners and therefore went beyond the Constitutional authority of any branch of the federal government. Daniel maintained another kind of consistency. If Congress had no power to legislate concerning slavery in the territories, then how could the Northwest Ordinance's prohibition of slavery be valid? Daniel was the only justice to say it was not—in fact, it was "*ab initio* void." Daniel left nothing to chance in this concurring opinion. He found every way possible to deny federal power over slavery in the territories.

It was in admiralty cases that Daniel became most anachronistic and eccentric. The framers of the Judiciary Act of 1789 took the admiralty clause of the Constitution to mean that the federal courts must have exclusive jurisdiction over admiralty cases. While this left common law cases concerning inland water transportation to state and local courts, it still shifted control of admiralty cases away from the states to the new federal government. The older that government became and the more miles of river and lake that could be covered by migrating people and faster boats, the more many people argued for the extension of admiralty jurisdiction beyond the tidewater to inland waterways, especially those connected with tidewater areas. Daniel had to uphold admiralty jurisdiction over the tidewater, but the moment anyone sought to move beyond that traditional realm, Daniel blocked the way as best he could. As inland, interstate, waterborne commerce grew in complexity, however, problems of jurisdiction began to affect commerce adversely. One commentator stated that purportedly corrective legislation of 1845 granted nothing more than "quasi admiralty jurisdiction" to federal courts because it applied only to lakes and their connecting rivers and relied for its legitimacy on the federal commerce power rather than on admiralty jurisdiction. When the denial of admiralty jurisdiction in *The Thomas Jefferson* (1825) was finally overturned by a nearly unanimous Taney Court in *Propeller Genesee Chief v. Fitzhugh* (1852), Daniel predictably filed the sole dissent, even though the court countenanced jurisdiction only over interstate waterborne commerce. (It may be pointed out that waterborne commerce in other regions of the United States outweighed such commerce in Daniel's native South by four to one.)

It would be a mistake to dismiss Daniel completely because he fought such a manifestly losing battle and exhibited a prickly stubbornness and partisanship seldom seen among the very best jurists. His brothers on the bench took him very seriously because he labored with care over all decisions, expending great time and industry in his research for them and exhibiting great learning in them. His opinion in the *Passenger Cases* is one of his most interesting because his position was almost as credible as those of the rest of the divided court. When he was assigned the writing of opinions for the court, he obviously was in harmony with the majority on the issue at hand. Thus his opinion for the court in *West River v. Dix* (1848) stands out for its clarity and forcefulness. Even on the point of prickly stubbornness one can find something to praise. He was nothing if not independent of the pressure of general opinion, an achievement to be admired in principle in a member of the highest judiciary. That his intellectual independence often pitted him against inevitable change is the tragedy of his career. His stiff backbone attracted little love from friends, but being lovable has never been a requirement for appointment to the supreme tribunal.

—PHILIP J. SCHWARZ

BIBLIOGRAPHY

The most comprehensive judicial biography is John P. Frank, *Justice Daniel Dissenting: A Biography of Peter V. Daniel, 1784–1860* (1964). A succinct account of Daniel's agrarian philosophy is Lawrence Burnette, Jr., "Peter V. Daniel: Agrarian Justice," 60 *Virginia Magazine of History and Biography* 289 (1954). Carl Swisher effectively assesses Daniel's role in the major decisions of the Taney Court in *The Taney Period, 1836–64* (1974), volume 5 of the Oliver Wendell Holmes Devise. The best assessment of Daniel's *Dred Scott* opinion is in Don E. Fehrenbacher, *The Dred Scott Case: Its Significance in American Law and Politics* (1978). There is no major collection of Daniel papers, but important letters are in the Martin Van Buren papers, Library of Congress, and in scattered other collections.

DAVID DAVIS

BORN 9 March 1815, Cecil County, Maryland

NOMINATED to the Court 1 December 1862
    by Abraham Lincoln

TOOK seat 10 December 1862; retired
    5 March 1877

DIED 26 June 1886 in Bloomington, Illinois

The Supreme Court career of David Davis, Abraham Lincoln's friend, campaign manager, and appointee, is most closely identified with one case—*Ex parte Milligan* (1866)—in which the Court challenged the trial of civilians by military tribunals during the Civil War. Davis's fifteen-year career on the Court was, otherwise, relatively undistinguished. Indeed, not only did Davis seek the Liberal-Republican nomination for president while sitting on the Court, but also, when the Illinois legislature elected him to the United States Senate, Davis chose to take the Senate oath. Moreover, Davis's decision to leave the bench disturbed the delicate political balance envisioned for the electoral commission created to resolve the dispute over the presidential election of 1876.

David Davis was born on his maternal grandfather's plantation on Maryland's eastern shore in March 1815, eight months after his father, a young physician, died. At age thirteen, he began studies at Kenyon College; after graduation, Davis moved to Lenox, Massachusetts, to study law with attorney Henry W. Bishop. Less than one year at the New Haven Law School followed, after which Davis returned to Lenox. At the age of twenty, Davis headed west to Illinois, ultimately settling in Bloomington. A successful law practice and an active political life (Davis served in the state legislature in the mid-1840s) led to his election in 1848 as a state judge in the eighth circuit. He held that position until his elevation to the Supreme Court in 1862, two years after orchestrating his close friend Abraham Lincoln's nomination as the Republican presidential candidate in 1860.

One would have to go beyond the opinions written by Justice Davis during his first three years on the Supreme Court to realize that the Union was engulfed in a life-or-death struggle. Of the thirteen decisions he penned during the December 1863 and December 1864 terms (Davis was confined to bed by illness the following term), nine concerned property disputes. But Davis's presence on the high court was significant, for he voted with the mere five-member majority in the *Prize Cases* of 1863, upholding the Lincoln administration's blockade of southern ports, even absent a formal declaration of war.

While fulfilling his circuit court duties, Davis was closer to the exigencies of war. Davis's biographer includes the following excerpt from a grand jury charge issued by the justice from the circuit court bench in Indianapolis: "It is charged that there are secret organizations . . . with 'grips, signs and passwords' having for their objects—resistance to Law, and the overthrow of the Government. . . . If anywhere in this State bad men have combined together for such wicked purposes, I pray you, bring them to light and let them receive the punishment due to their crime." In *Ex parte Milligan*, a case that first came before Davis when he was sitting on the circuit court for the district of Indiana, the issue concerned *where* such disloyal citizens would stand trial to "receive the[ir] punishment."

In May 1865, Davis, along with district judge David McDonald, heard the petition of Lamdin P. Milligan, a Peace Democrat, to be "discharged from an allegedly unlawful imprisonment." Milligan argued there, and (after Davis and McDonald could not agree) before the Supreme Court, that, because he was a civilian, the military commission that tried and convicted him and sentenced him to death by hanging for disloyal activities had no jurisdiction. On December 17, 1866, nine months after extensive oral argument by a group of advocates that included Major General Benjamin Butler (for the government) and David Dudley Field (for the defense), Davis announced a ruling in Milligan's favor.

Davis, who to that point had been circumspect and conservative in his rhetoric as a justice, dramatically noted that the issue posed by

Milligan's challenge "involves the very frame-work of the government and the fundamental principles of American liberty"; indeed, "no graver question was ever considered by this court, nor one which more nearly concerns the rights of the whole people. . . ." Now that the "late wicked Rebellion" was over, constitutional questions regarding the conduct of the Civil War could "be discussed and decided without passion or the admixture of any element not required to form a legal judgment." Thus, Davis's opinion in *Milligan* signals the Court's reassertion of its antebellum role as ultimate arbiter and defender of the Constitution.

Davis concluded that the military commission had no jurisdiction to try or sentence Milligan. The dire conditions of war could not excuse the violation of essential constitutional rights. In the most memorable passage from his entire Supreme Court opus, Davis proclaimed: "The Constitution of the United States is a law for rulers and people, equally in war and in peace, and under all circumstances. No doctrine, involving more pernicious consequences, was ever invented by the wit of man than that any of its provisions can be suspended during any of the great exigencies of government." The price for uttering these noble phrases was, according to Supreme Court historian Charles Warren, "a storm of invective and opprobrium" from Radical Republican quarters. Stung by this reaction, Davis wrote, in private correspondence: "The people can change their Constitution, but until it is done all attempts to evade it, override it, or disregard it, end either in anarchy or despotism." This principle would resurface in Supreme Court history not only in cases specifically concerning military trial of civilians in subsequent wars, but also in the opinions of the Court's conservatives who later struggled against the wave of liberal legislation designed to deliver the nation from the depths of the Great Depression.

Davis's remaining years on the Court would prove to be neither as stormy nor as stimulating, particularly to someone as politically active and interested as he. Much of the Court's work was taken up with problems posed by the outcome and conduct of the Civil War, the relationship between the states and the newly ascendant fed-eral government, and the nation's increasingly complex industrial economy.

One puzzle faced by Davis and his fellow justices was the question of when the war, in fact, ended. In *Burke v. Miltenberger* (1874), for example, the Supreme Court had to decide, in a real property dispute, whether the Provisional Court of Louisiana, established by President Lincoln during the Civil War, maintained its authority as late as June 1865. Davis noted that there was no one event, such as the surrender of Confederate General Kirby Smith (May 26, 1865), that marked the cessation of the war; rather "the war did not begin or close at the same time in all the States, that its commencement and termination in any State is to be determined by some public act of the political departments of the government."

In *United States v. Anderson* (1870), the dispute concerned the effect of a two-year statute of limitations on a claim brought by a loyal citizen in June 1868 under the Abandoned or Captured Property Act. As in *Burke*, Davis refused to identify one universal date for the end of the Civil War. In the absence of clear guidance from Congress, Davis opted for a relatively late date, August 20, 1866, in the process making clear his pro-Union bias: "It is clear the point of time should be construed most favorably to the person who adhered to the National Union, and who has proved the government took his property. . . ."

Although slavery was abolished by the Thirteenth Amendment, the Supreme Court still had to contend with the legacy of the peculiar institution. In *Boyce v. Tabb* (1873), the Court affirmed a federal circuit court holding that a creditor could enforce a promissory note given by a debtor for slaves purchased in 1861. Despite the fact that the Supreme Court of Louisiana had declared such contracts void, Davis, citing the principles of *Swift v. Tyson*, did not feel bound to follow the state's lead, noting that state court decisions "are not conclusive authority, although they are entitled to, and will receive from us, attention and respect."

In an earlier case, *Payne v. Hook* (1869), Davis had also championed federal law, notwithstanding contrary state rulings. In a probate matter brought by a Virginian against a Missouri official, Davis concluded that the equity jurisdiction of federal courts "is subject to neither limitation or restraint by State legislation, and is uniform throughout the different States of the Union."

Still, there was to Davis a limit to judicial power, even of the federal courts. For example, in *Wilmington Railroad v. Reid* (1872), the Supreme Court, in an opinion penned by Davis, thwarted North Carolina's attempt to tax railroad property, despite a provision in the railroad's charter exempting the company "from any public charge or tax whatsoever." The tax exemption provision was deemed "plain and unambiguous"; despite his sympathy for the state's plight, especially since "the necessities of government cannot always be foreseen," Davis concluded that the courts of the country "are not the proper tribunals to apply the corrective to improvident legislation of this character." In this regard, see also *Washington University v. Rouse* (1869), a Davis opinion protecting the school's tax-exempt status.

Another railroad benefited from Davis's jurisprudence in *United States v. Union Pacific Railroad Company* (1875). This time it was the federal government that was seeking payment from the carrier, but the Supreme Court refused to hold the Union Pacific liable for interest on federal bonds before the maturity of the principal. Davis adhered closely to the terms of the 1862 act of Congress authorizing and financing railroad construction and to the realities then prevailing: "Vast as was the work, limited as were the private resources to build it, the growing wants as well as the existing and future military necessities of the country demanded that it be completed." The Court's role was not to "sit in judgment upon [the statute's] wisdom or policy," but merely to "interpret its provisions. . . ." Although Davis privately expressed concern about "railroad mania" in Illinois localities anxious to lend support through bond issues, in the *Union Pacific* case, he did not allow his personal bias to interfere with his judicial obligations.

Davis's years on the Supreme Court were frustrating, exacting, and ultimately unsatisfying. He enjoyed circuit court duties, but confessed privately that he found appellate work "too much like hard labor." In February 1872, Davis received the presidential nomination at the Labor Reform (or National Labor Union) convention in Columbus. His dreams of the White House evaporated two months later when, despite some active campaigning on his behalf, he lost the Liberal Republican nomination to Horace Greeley.

Five years later, Davis had a chance to play a more prominent role in a presidential election, as it was generally expected that, unaligned as he was with the leaders of either party, he would be named to the electoral commission charged with deciding the winner in the Hayes-Tilden contest. Instead, Davis accepted his election to the United States Senate from Illinois and resigned his seat on the Court. He served six years as a senator and, as an independent leader of that body, was named president *pro tem* in 1881. As the first in the line of succession following the death of President James A. Garfield, Davis had finally realized his national political aspirations.

—MICHAEL ALLAN WOLF

BIBLIOGRAPHY

The standard biographical treatment, Willard King, *Lincoln's Manager: David Davis* (1960), is especially strong on Davis's political life. The Davis family papers can be found at the Illinois State Historical Society in Springfield. In addition, an impressive collection of Davis papers and other materials was placed by King into the collection of the Chicago Historical Society. Davis's Court career is skillfully woven into Charles Fairman's broader account in *Reconstruction and Reunion: 1864–88 Part One* (1971), volume 6 of the Holmes Devise. Stanley Kutler's *Judicial Power and Reconstruction Politics* (1968) contains quite a provocative account of the *Milligan* affair.

WILLIAM RUFUS DAY

BORN 17 April 1849, Ravenna, Ohio

NOMINATED to the Court by Theodore Roosevelt 19 February 1903

TOOK seat 2 March 1903; retired 13 November 1922

DIED 9 July 1923 in Mackinac Island, Michigan

Until late in the fourth decade of his life, save for the few years he spent at the University of Michigan, most of William Day's life centered in Ohio. In 1872, he formed a partnership with a locally established lawyer, William S. Lynch, in Canton. Day earned a reputation as a litigator while Lynch built the firm's corporate client base. Lynch introduced Day to his wife and to William McKinley, and Day and McKinley became close friends and remained so until McKinley's death. In 1897, President McKinley brought Day to Washington, and as first assistant secretary of state, secretary of state, and peace commissioner, Day was a key participant in the Spanish-American War. In 1899, McKinley returned Day to Cincinnati, Ohio, as a judge of the sixth circuit, where he sat with two other future members of the Supreme Court, Horace Lurton and William Taft. President Theodore Roosevelt, perhaps to secure the support of the McKinley wing of the party, named Day to the Supreme Court.

In Day's nineteen years on the Court he made a record as a liberal formalist. In an era dominated by government reaction to economic change and judicial scrutiny of such action, Day generally favored government action. The centerpiece of his constitutional faith was the concept of dual sovereignty, especially as expressed in the Tenth Amendment; within limits, he sanctioned government regulation of the economy and life. Day believed that the federal and state governments could extensively regulate the economy, but they could do so only within their proscribed spheres. Thus, Day voted to sustain state use of police powers, yet also favored exercise of limited federal powers.

The states were central to Day's jurisprudence of government action. Under the Tenth Amendment, which reserved to the states the powers not delegated to the central government, Day believed that the states possessed broad police powers. Thus Day dissented in two notable cases where the Court struck down state regulation. He refused to join the majority when it struck down a New York health regulation which limited the working hours of bakers in *Lochner v. New York* (1905). In *Coppage v. Kansas* (1915) the Court struck down, as an infringement of the liberty to contract, a state ban on yellow dog contracts, which made it a condition of employment that the worker not belong or join any union. Day in turn wrote a strong dissent defending the state police power.

Day was not just a dissenter. In *McLean v. Arkansas* (1909), he wrote the opinion for the Court upholding mining safety regulations; likewise, in *Minnesota ex rel. Whipple v. Martinson* (1921), he wrote the Court's opinion sustaining the states' power to regulate drug use. Thus, in Day's jurisprudence, the states could legislate to protect public health, safety, and morals; but he did not believe that the federal government had a similar power.

While the Constitution gives the Congress no general power to legislate in the interest of health and public welfare, many progressives sought such legislation. Reformers hung their proposals on certain constitutional hooks based on the delegated powers. The most important of these was the commerce power, and from the late nineteenth century to the New Deal, it grew dramatically. Day never countenanced the unlimited growth of the commerce power, and was unwilling to expand it beyond its late nineteenth-century bounds. His limitations of the commerce power derived from Chief Justice Melville Fuller's opinion in *United States v. E. C. Knight Company* (1895). In his opinion, Fuller separated manufacturing and commerce, saying Congress could regulate interstate commerce, but it could not regulate manufacturing, which remained a matter for state control.

Day's reading of the commerce clause did not mean that Congress was powerless, but only limited. Day supported federal legislation which regulated those engaged in interstate trade. Thus, to Day, the Interstate Commerce Act, the Sherman Antitrust Act, and the Clayton Antitrust Act were all legitimate. He refused to go along, most notably in his dissent in *United States v. United States Steel Corporation* (1920), with his brethren who limited them. He also allowed the federal government to use its commerce power to ban from transportation impure and harmful products. In *Hoke v. United States* (1913), he even permitted the commerce power—through the Mann Act—to be used to ban the transportation of women across state lines for immoral purposes. But this is as far as Day would go. The limits Day placed on federal action through the commerce power was clearly seen in his opinion for the Court in *Hammer v. Dagenhart* (1918). In a 5–4 decision, the Court struck down a federal ban from interstate commerce of goods made with child labor. To Day, the law was regulation of manufacturing—a subject reserved to the states—and not a legitimate use of the commerce power. The law, Day thought, threatened to eliminate local powers and threatened the federal nature of the nation. Day thus represented a liberal strain of the formalist judicial tradition of the nineteenth century and early twentieth century: he was willing to use government power, but only within the known rules.

—RICHARD F. HAMM

BIBLIOGRAPHY

A good study of Day's judicial career is Joseph E. McLean, *William Rufus Day: Supreme Court Justice from Ohio* (1946), while Stephen B. Wood, *Constitutional Politics in the Progressive Era: Child Labor and the Law* (1968) is the best treatment of the circumstances surrounding his most famous opinion.

WILLIAM ORVILLE DOUGLAS

BORN 16 October 1898, Maine, Minnesota

NOMINATED to the Court 19 March 1939
by Franklin D. Roosevelt

TOOK seat 17 April 1939; retired 12
November 1975

DIED 19 January 1980 in Bethesda, Maryland

Associate Justice William O. Douglas served longer on the United States Supreme Court than any other justice. Irony, variety, and nonconformity were key characteristics of the restless intelligence of this independent-minded man, whose thirty-six-year tenure on the high court spanned major transformations in mid-twentieth-century American society. Justice Douglas was very much a creature of his times. From the New Deal and World War II at the beginning of his judicial career, through the Cold War, the civil rights and environmental movements, to the withdrawal from Vietnam as he retired from the Court, Douglas responded to the challenges of his era.

Douglas's judicial opinions do not fit within any particular school of legal doctrine, although he is associated with the legal realists and considered both an activist and a liberal jurist. In fact, Douglas resisted the very concept of legal doctrine and rejected any foreordained set of propositions from which resolutions of legal controversies could be deduced. Instead, he believed that his job as a justice was to make decisions about particular sets of facts in their particular social, economic, and political contexts. As the situations changed, his decisions changed.

Although he resisted doctrine, Douglas believed passionately in the power of ideas. His judicial opinions sometimes have an oracular style, articulating a wide variety of values and ideals such as democracy, equality, free enterprise, privacy, diversity, and conservation. Especially later in his judicial career, many of his opinions sound like manifestos. Both on and off the court, Douglas tirelessly advocated progressive views and liberal democratic values. Most of all, he believed that each individual should

think for himself. Douglas genuinely despised conformity and fought against the regimentation of individuals by big business or big government.

During his more than three-and-a-half decades on the bench, Douglas wrote more than 1,200 judicial opinions, countless articles and speeches, and thirty-one books, including a two-volume autobiography. After World War II, during Court recesses, Douglas traveled to Russia, China, Burma, India, and other remote parts of the world which he wrote about in popular books and articles. He said that these explorations of diverse societies gave him a fresh perspective on the issues which came before the Supreme Court. For Douglas, theory and life always went together.

In 1939, President Franklin D. Roosevelt nominated Douglas to replace Justice Louis D. Brandeis. Brandeis knew Douglas and was reported to have been pleased by his successor. Roosevelt probably considered Douglas, then the young, vigorous, iconoclastic, and obviously bright chairman of the Securities and Exchange Commission, as insurance against a recurrence of Supreme Court obstruction of New Deal regulatory programs. Forty years old when he was appointed, Douglas was the second-youngest justice to join the Court, after Joseph Story. Moreover, Douglas was from the West, which was demanding representation on the Supreme Court. Hailing from a poor family in Yakima, Washington, Douglas seemed to be the quintessential westerner, and a self-made "common man" to boot. But Douglas came to the Court equipped with more than his often-ridiculed five-gallon western hat. Under that hat was a keen mind sharpened by an eastern legal education at Columbia Law School and service on the law faculties of Columbia and Yale.

In addition to being a New Deal loyalist, Douglas was also one of Roosevelt's personal friends. In fact, Douglas was one of the president's "poker buddies," a group which included such Washington power brokers as Interior Secretary Harold Ickes and Treasury Secretary Henry Morgenthau. Surprisingly, in light of later attempts to impeach Douglas, his confirmation was noncontroversial. No witnesses spoke for or against Douglas's confirmation at the Senate Judiciary Committee hearing. In the Senate, the vote was 62–4, with thirty Senators not voting.

During his first decade or so on the Court, Douglas kept at least one eye on politics. He was considered a possible candidate for the Democratic ticket in 1940. In late 1941, Roosevelt suggested that Douglas resign from the Court and take charge of what became the War Production Board. But Douglas remained on the Court. There are conflicting accounts of how and why Douglas was considered and eventually not chosen to run as vice-president with Roosevelt in 1944. Roosevelt liked Douglas, but left the vice-presidential decision up to the Democratic convention, which chose Harry Truman, who became president when Roosevelt died in 1945. Douglas apparently always felt bitter about not being president of the United States. Although by the 1950s he had turned away from electoral ambition, politics continued to intrude on his judicial life in the form of several unsuccessful politically motivated efforts to impeach him.

Douglas brought to the Court a distinctive approach to law and judging. For Douglas, law was a practical process which operated in a particular political, social, and economic context to serve societal goals. Judging was, in part, applied psychology. As a student and faculty member at Columbia Law School, he adopted what was then called a functional, as opposed to theoretical, view of law. As a member of the Yale Law School faculty from 1928 to 1934, Douglas worked with legal realists who took a dynamic, pragmatic view of law, and insisted on an empirical approach to legal problems in the light of actual social, political, economic, and psychological realities. For realists, concentration on doctrine and precedents perniciously masked the vital actuality of present circumstances. Although Justice Douglas sometimes referred approvingly to "sociological jurisprudence," he avoided describing himself as a legal realist or as a functionalist. He was far too independent-minded to associate himself with anything which sounded like orthodoxy.

Having rejected legal doctrine as a basis for judicial decision making, Douglas gradually developed a distinctive judicial style. In simplest terms, he considered his job to decide cases. Douglas believed he was responsible for making his own decision in each case which came before the Court, and said that he agreed with Thomas Jefferson that each judge should give his individual opinion in every case. That belief may account for Douglas's numerous dissenting and concurring opinions, including his notorious dissents without opinion in tax cases in which he almost invariably voted for the taxpayer because he distrusted big government. During some periods, he filed a separate opinion in every case decided by the Court. Douglas became adept at deciding cases rapidly. Noted for his restlessness on the bench, Justice Douglas was often impatient during oral arguments, when he would write letters or engage in other tasks. He hated to waste time. In his later years on the Court, he complained that Court work, deciding cases, and ruling on petitions and stays only required working four days a week.

Explaining decisions was of secondary importance to deciding cases. Douglas generally avoided established legal doctrine. He said he was opposed to *stare decisis*, the judicial practice of deciding cases based on precedent, because present controversies should be decided on their own terms, rather than by applying past cases. Particularly in constitutional cases, Douglas thought *stare decisis* was an excuse for not making hard choices about how to apply constitutional values to new circumstances. He often said that he would rather create a precedent than find one.

The Douglas approach to judicial decision making has been often criticized as result-oriented: first deciding the result he wanted to reach and then building an argument for the correctness of that outcome. Critics also have disparaged some of his judicial opinions as careless, slapdash polemics. But Douglas was generally unperturbed by criticisms that he was result-oriented or intellectually untidy. For him, life, including law, was just like that. Spinning webs of legal doctrine in order to logically entrap future decisions in foreordained conclusions was

William Orville Douglas, c. 1940s
Collection of the Supreme Court of the United States.

not the role which Douglas thought the Constitution assigned to Supreme Court justices. For him, judicial opinions should provide solutions to real-life problems, not academic dissertations about legal doctrine. Sometimes he gave no reasons at all. Since deciding the case was the point of judging, and supporting reasons were far less important, it is not surprising that he did not often invest a lot of time developing the latter. Professor Vern Countryman, who was Douglas's law clerk and later his literary executor, reports Douglas as saying, "For those who liked the result, it was scholarship."

Douglas had an uncanny ability both to understand what was at issue in complicated cases and to envision new ways of looking at them. A typical Douglas opinion is filled with facts and may even have an appendix or two to provide even more background for his view of the case. Justice Douglas would first focus on the facts at issue and then find a key, pivotal issue at the heart of the legal controversy. In the latter part of his judicial career, he grasped cases especially quickly because he believed that legal controversies, like much of human behavior, fall into cyclical patterns, recurring every decade or so.

Douglas's opinion for the Court in *Griswold v. Connecticut* (1965), which recognized a penumbral right of privacy in the Constitution, provides a typical as well as famous example of Douglas's characteristic approach to judicial decision making. In *Griswold*, the Court held unconstitutional a Connecticut criminal statute prohibiting the use and distribution of contraceptives. Douglas saw the heart of the case as marital privacy: "Would we allow the police to search the sacred precincts of marital bedrooms for telltale signs of the use of contraceptives?" Douglas asked, and then answered: "The very idea is repulsive to the notions of privacy surrounding the marriage relationship." Douglas's opinion found that the penumbras of various constitutional guarantees establish a "right of privacy older than the Bill of Rights," which protects marriage as "a coming together for better or for worse, hopefully enduring, and intimate to the degree of being sacred." His insight into what was really at stake in *Griswold* retains remarkable vitality.

Douglas took seriously the political status of the Supreme Court, which the Constitution places at the head of the judicial branch of government. Just as the executive or the legislative branches, the Supreme Court exercises political power. He felt that, as a justice, he had a political role in deciding cases based on his own understanding of constitutional values. More than once, Douglas described the Supreme Court as "the keeper of the conscience. And the conscience is the Constitution." He felt that it was "very important to have a keeper of the conscience, an independent group, above the storm." Part of the Court's political role under the Constitution was independently to apply constitutional values to keep the other branches in check.

Particularly after Roosevelt's death, Douglas increasingly distrusted executive power. For example, in 1952, the Supreme Court held unconstitutional President Truman's seizure of the steel mills to prevent a lockout in connection with a labor dispute. Justice Douglas concurred in *Youngstown Sheet & Tube Co. v. Sawyer*, but he had his own grounds for holding the seizure unlawful. Seizure of the steel mills was expropriation of private property, which under the Constitution could only be accomplished by legislative action. Justice Douglas warned that "All executive power—from the reign of ancient kings to the rule of modern dictators—has the outward appearance of efficiency." He repudiated the idea that the Constitution gave "the President not only the power to execute the laws but to make some."

Because of his views regarding the political responsibilities of the judiciary, Douglas dissented in numerous cases where the Court dismissed constitutional challenges because those bringing the challenges were found to lack standing to bring the case before the court. *Laird v. Tatum* (1972), in which the Court held that individuals and groups which had been under army surveillance because of anti-war activities lacked standing to complain about it in court, is a good example. Douglas's dissenting opinion asserted that the case involved "a cancer in our body politic" in the form of a dangerously unlawful exercise of executive power which would remain unchecked if the Court did not allow these individuals and groups to bring the case before the court. Douglas explained in his autobiography that his "view always has been that anyone whose life, liberty or property was threatened or impaired by any branch of government . . . had a justiciable controversy and could properly repair to a judicial tribunal for vindication of his rights."

According to Douglas, the Constitution not only established the Supreme Court's political role, but also provided a set of general principles which the Court was to apply. These constitutional principles provided a philosophy which must be interpreted and applied by judges in light of their own lives and experiences. For Douglas, such a dynamic approach to constitutional interpretation was not at all incompatible with strict construction. Douglas considered himself a strict constructionist, like Hugo Black, because he believed strict construction meant not subtracting from or making exceptions to constitutional freedoms. Douglas also considered himself a strict incorporationist, because he believed that all of the rights contained in the Bill of Rights were incorporated into the Fourteenth Amendment's due process guarantee against state and local action which deprives individuals of liberty.

Among the more interesting examples of Douglas's adjustment of constitutional guarantees to contemporary circumstances was his 1946 opinion in *United States v. Causby*. The case was brought by a North Carolina chicken farmer whose property served as a glide path for military aircraft using an adjacent airport during World War II. The farmer sought compensation under the just compensation clause of the Fifth Amendment because the overflights made his property less valuable. Justice Douglas's opinion recognized two important realities. First, modern air transport requires use of the air space above private property as part of the public domain, where airplanes can fly without restriction by those who own the land below. At the same time, the farmer's particular circumstances involved frequent low-level takeoffs and landings. That particular pattern of overflights, so low that they frightened the farmer's chickens literally to death, was a government use of the farmer's land. Since that government use made the farmer's land less valuable, the farmer was entitled to recover just compensation for his loss.

For Douglas, applying constitutional guarantees that the government will not take property without paying just compensation required focusing on what was really at stake: the devaluation of the chicken farmer's land by the government's overflights. In a sense, the decision is result-oriented: big government should bear the financial loss rather than the small farmer. But the opinion's apt focus on the particular circumstances of the case also exemplifies Douglas's characteristic ability to apply the Constitution to new circumstances and technologies.

Psychological aspects of the work of the Supreme Court were also important to Justice Douglas, who believed with the realists that each individual justice brings a unique life experience to bear on making each decision. Douglas's interest in psychology was personal, as well as theoretical. He noted in his autobiography that he undertook psychoanalysis with Dr. George Draper in New York to overcome both migraine headaches and certain fears such as of water and of lightning. Douglas believed that an active life outside the Court was essential both to keep a justice in touch with the realities of the society in which he lived, and also to maintain a psychological balance. He often warned that judges who insulate themselves from life tend to become dried-up husks of human beings, incapable of growth and change.

Change was at once inevitable and beneficial in his view. Unconstrained by commitment to doctrinal consistency, Douglas was notably uninhibited about changing his mind. There are many instances of cases in which he simply admitted that an earlier decision or view was wrong. In the 1940s, the Supreme Court decided a series of cases which involved the constitutionality of compelling school children to salute the American flag. In *Minersville School District v. Gobitis* (1940), Douglas first voted with the majority of the Court that Jehovah's Witnesses children could be compelled to salute the flag, even though doing so violated their religious beliefs. Three years later, in *Board of Education v. Barnette* (1943), he changed his mind and joined Justice Black in a concurring opinion which argued that forced expression contrary to an individual's religious principles violates the First Amendment.

In 1952, Justice Douglas forthrightly declared that he had changed his views with regard to the constitutionality of electronic surveillance. Dissenting in *On Lee v. United States*, a case involving a narcotics agent carrying a hidden microphone, Douglas simply confessed that his earlier tolerance of electronic surveillance in *Goldman v. United States* (1942) had been mistaken. "I now more fully appreciate the vice of the practices spawned by . . . *Goldman*. Reflection on them has brought new insight to me. I now feel that I was wrong in the *Goldman* case," in not voting to overrule *Olmstead v. United States* (1928), which had found wiretapping to be constitutional, over a stirring dissent from Justice Brandeis.

In addition to cases in which Justice Douglas changed his mind and said so, his flexible approach in deciding particular cases greatly annoyed some of his judicial colleagues, especially Felix Frankfurter. The Japanese exclusion cases and the Rosenberg espionage case are two prominent examples. In these cases, which involved highly charged political controversies, Douglas did not see himself or his decisions as inconsistent. In his view, he simply responded to the particular circumstances of various aspects of the cases, to help resolve difficult tensions among strongly held values and interests.

The three Japanese exclusion cases, *Hirabayashi v. United States* (1943), *Korematsu v. United States* (1944), and *Ex parte Endo* (1944), contested the legality of military orders which imposed curfews, relocation, and detention of Japanese on the West Coast after the attack on Pearl Harbor. Douglas filed a concurring opinion in *Hirabayashi* which upheld the legality of a curfew order against persons of Japanese ancestry. He voted with the majority in *Korematsu*, in which the Supreme Court upheld an order excluding persons of Japanese ancestry from military areas of the West Coast and providing for their relocation and detention. Although Douglas opposed racial and ethnic discrimination and said so repeatedly in his opinions, he thought that the wartime circumstances presented by the *Korematsu* and *Hirabayashi* cases involved a genuine national emergency sufficiently grave to warrant interference with

individual civil rights. Douglas's sense that the nation was in imminent danger was probably particularly acute, because during this time Douglas was a frequent visitor at the White House, where the fear of Japanese invasion of the West Coast must have been palpable. However, Douglas's opinion for the Court in *Ex parte Endo* focused on the conceded fact that Mitsuye Endo was a loyal American citizen who posed no danger to the war effort or national security. Douglas's context-bound realist view saw that the government's exclusion of Ms. Endo was unjustified and, therefore, unconstitutional.

In the Rosenberg espionage case, Douglas's shifting votes apparently outraged Frankfurter and Robert H. Jackson, who saw his shifts as irresponsible political grandstanding for Douglas's civil libertarian constituencies. Julius and Ethel Rosenberg had been convicted of conspiracy and violations of the Espionage Act for giving atomic and military secrets to the Soviet Union, and were sentenced to death by the judge in the case. In reacting to numerous petitions brought to the Supreme Court on behalf of the Rosenbergs, Douglas seems to have thought that he was just considering each petition, as he considered any other petition, on its own merits. First, he voted to deny a hearing before the Supreme Court, then dissented from such denial and eventually granted a last-minute stay of execution after the Court had adjourned. That final extraordinary stay was immediately overturned by the full Court meeting in special session in *Rosenberg v. United States* (1953). Douglas was undoubtedly ambivalent about the situation. A militant anti-Communist, he was also concerned about individual rights and procedural fairness. Although not a consistent opponent of the death penalty, Douglas strongly believed in strict enforcement of constitutional protection of the rights of people accused of crimes.

As he considered the various Rosenberg petitions, he apparently began to sense that the sensationalized prosecution of the Rosenbergs had deprived them of a fair trial. In granting the emergency stay of execution, Douglas did not feel constrained to be consistent with earlier decisions on different petitions, even though they involved the same case. In deciding this particular petition, Douglas became convinced that under provisions of the Atomic Energy Act, the Rosenbergs could not legally be executed without a jury recommendation of the death penalty. Whether he was subconsciously swayed by the public controversy on all sides of the Rosenberg case is difficult to determine. In later speeches and articles, Douglas insisted that the Supreme Court was and should be above the storm of public pressures. He always maintained that he had been unaffected by the public outcry and protest marches for and against the Rosenbergs and merely decided the legal issues in the petitions presented to him.

Douglas's many decisions in cases involving the economy reflected his roots in legal realism. His views about economics generally favored free enterprise, although early opinions often favored the regulatory power of government. A bankruptcy expert and corporate regulator before he came to the Court, Douglas insisted that corporate directors, officers, and controlling shareholders have fiduciary duties of care and fairness with regard to their investors and creditors.

Although over time Douglas came to fear too much power on the part of regulatory agencies, many of his decisions favored economic regulation. Among his more famous decisions regarding economic regulation was his opinion for the Court in *Federal Power Commission v. Hope Natural Gas Co.* (1944). This decision greatly enhanced the discretion of regulatory agencies to set the rates utility companies charge their customers. Douglas's majority opinion held that "fixing of 'just and reasonable' rates involves a balancing of the investor and the consumer interests," by the regulatory agency, with very little role for the courts in reviewing the reasonableness of the rates.

Like Louis Brandeis before him, Douglas was wary of big business and believed in vigorous enforcement of the antitrust laws. Echoing the populism of his times, Douglas was skeptical about the power of large business and financial interests over the economy and especially over small businesses and small investors. For example, he dissented in *United States v. Columbia Steel Co.* (1948), in which the majority found

no violation of the Sherman Act when the nation's largest unfinished steel producer acquired the largest independent steel fabricator on the West Coast. "We have here the problem of bigness," Douglas insisted. "Industrial power should be decentralized. It should be scattered into many hands so that the fortunes of the people will not be dependent on the whim or caprice, the political prejudices, the emotional stability of a few self-appointed men."

From his childhood, when he overcame the debilitation of polio by hiking in the Cascade mountains, Douglas loved the natural world. The outdoors provided a source of personal strength and comfort for the restless justice, even though an accident while horseback riding nearly cost him his life in 1949. An avid naturalist, conservationist, hiker, and rider, Douglas actively promoted environmental causes, such as the preservation of the C & O Canal in and near Washington, D.C., which in 1977 became a national historic park named after him. Some of his most impassioned non-judicial writing, such as *A Wilderness Bill of Rights* (1965), concerned the environment. It is therefore somewhat surprising that Justice Douglas did not write a great many judicial opinions dealing with the environment.

Significantly, the last opinion Douglas filed as a Supreme Court Justice was a concurring opinion in *Northern Indiana Public Service v. Walton* (1975), where, in addition to voicing concern about unconstrained discretion on the part of an administrative agency, Douglas expressed grave concern about the environmental hazards of nuclear power.

Douglas's famous dissenting opinion in *Sierra Club v. Morton* (1972) suggested a whole new strategy for bringing environmental problems before the courts. The majority had held that the Sierra Club lacked standing to object to government approval of a recreational resort in the Mineral King Valley in the Sierra mountains of California. Douglas's dissenting opinion, its footnotes and its appendix, are filled with examples of threatened environmental destruction. He argued that natural features and creatures, from trees and rivers to mountains and woodpeckers, should be allowed to bring their own legal actions, through guardians, to prevent destruction of their ecological systems.

Douglas also wrote important opinions supporting land use regulation. His opinion in *Berman v. Parker* (1954) upheld the urban renewal powers of government to condemn whole neighborhoods, including blighted and not-so-blighted properties, to make way for rebuilding a more attractive and healthy community. He also wrote the majority opinion in *Belle Terre v. Boraas* (1974), in which the Court approved a zoning regulation which restricted occupancy of single family residences by groups other than traditional families. Even though dissenting Justice Thurgood Marshall thought that rights of association were violated by the restriction, Douglas did not think that freedom of association was involved in the case at all. Justice Douglas was concerned about "The regimes of boarding houses, fraternity houses, and the like [which] present urban problems. More people occupy a given space; more cars rather continuously pass by; more cars are parked; noise travels with crowds." In Douglas's view, "A quiet place where yards are wide, people few, and motor vehicles restricted are legitimate guidelines in a land-use project addressed to family needs." The power to regulate land use "is not confined to elimination of filth, stench, and unhealthy places. It is ample to lay out zones where family values, youth values, and the blessings of quiet seclusion and clean air make the area a sanctuary for people." Environmental quality was of such great importance to him because he knew from personal experience that a healthy environment is essential for the development of strong, independent individuals.

Much of William O. Douglas's judicial philosophy focused on the importance of individual freedom and equality. Even his economic and environmental interests were frequently based on his overriding belief in the importance of the independent, self-reliant individual. Douglas's insistence on individual freedom and equality, including his own personal independence of mind and spirit, was legendary. In his 1958 book, *Right of the People,* he declared, "Our Society is built upon the premise that it exists only to aid the fullest individual achievement of which each of its members is capable. Our starting point has always been the individual, not the state."

Douglas's concerns about individual freedom were mostly focused on threatened government oppression, although he sometimes also expressed misgivings about domination of independent entrepreneurs by what he called the unelected "industrial oligarchy." Early in his judicial career he was sometimes willing to subordinate individual rights to broader government interests. For example, in the emergency circumstances of World War II, Douglas thought it constitutionally acceptable to sacrifice the rights of individuals of Japanese ancestry in the interests of national security.

In the early 1950s, he became increasingly concerned about the dangers posed by government regimentation of individual freedom. He came to believe that one of the most important purposes of the Constitution was to restrain government. Dissenting in *Laird v. Tatum* (1972), Douglas declared, "The Constitution was designed to keep government off the backs of the people. The Bill of Rights was added to keep the precincts of belief and expression, of the press, of political and social activities free from surveillance." In Douglas's view, "The aim [of the Bill of Rights] was to allow men to be free and independent and to assert their rights against government."

Douglas provided the most comprehensive discussion of his views regarding individual freedoms guaranteed by the Constitution in connection with the 1973 abortion cases, *Doe v. Boulton* and *Roe v. Wade*, in which the Supreme Court invalidated Georgia and Texas abortion statutes on privacy grounds. In his concurring opinion in *Boulton*, he described what he called "a reasoning" about individual rights which are guaranteed by the Bill of Rights, and are included within the right to liberty protected against state government interference under the Fourteenth Amendment to the Constitution. Douglas suggested three concentric circles of individual rights: "First is the autonomous control over the development and expression of one's intellect, interests, tastes, and personality." Douglas saw these rights, including freedom of conscience and free exercise of religion, as aspects of freedom of thought and conscience which were absolutely protected under the First Amendment without any exceptions or qualifications. In this absolutely protected area, Douglas also placed the right to remain silent under the Fifth Amendment.

"Second, is freedom of choice in the basic decisions of one's life respecting marriage, divorce, procreation, contraception, and the education and upbringing of children." These fundamental rights, including the right of privacy involved in *Griswold* and the abortion cases, were outside the absolute protection of the First Amendment and were therefore subject to some reasonable control by the regulatory power of government. But any regulation had to be narrowly drawn and supported by a compelling state interest. "Third is the freedom to care for one's health and person, freedom from bodily restraint or compulsion, freedom to walk, stroll, or loaf." These rights protected individuals as they interacted with others out in the world where the individual, although not exactly immune from government regulation, nevertheless retained certain rights to be let alone by the government, even in relatively public circumstances.

The particular individual freedom with which Justice Douglas is most closely associated is the right of privacy. Douglas derived many of his views about protecting individual privacy against government interference from his predecessor on the Court, Louis D. Brandeis. But Douglas nearly always referred to a right "of" privacy, rather than Brandeis's right "to" privacy. Moreover, Douglas's right of privacy was solely focused on governmental threats to privacy. Douglas rejected imposing damage liability for invasions of privacy by the news media, which Brandeis had suggested many years earlier. For example, dissenting in *Public Utilities Commission v. Pollak* (1952), Douglas argued that when the government forced a "captive audience" of riders on the publicly licensed street cars in the District of Columbia to listen to radio broadcasts, such action infringed the privacy rights of individuals to be let alone by the government. After repeatedly calling for recognition of a constitutional right of privacy in a series of dissenting

opinions, Douglas eventually persuaded a majority of the Court to adopt his views about privacy in *Griswold*. In that case, Douglas characterized the right of privacy as based on "several fundamental constitutional guarantees," of individual freedom, including the First Amendment right of association, the Third Amendment's prohibition of quartering soldiers, the Fourth Amendment's prohibition of unreasonable searches and seizures, and the Fifth Amendment's prohibition of compelled self-incrimination. Douglas's opinion for the Court found the right of privacy in the penumbras of these constitutional guarantees. In Douglas's view, "specific guarantees of the Bill of Rights have penumbras, formed by emanations from those guarantees that help give them life and substance. Various guarantees create zones of privacy."

For Douglas, the right of privacy was part of the meaning of the Constitution, even though the word "privacy" does not appear in the text. One had but to open one's eyes and one's mind to see it. Douglas believed that the right of privacy is consistent with strict construction of the Constitution, because it is part of what the Bill of Rights means. Since he also believed that all of the guarantees of individual freedom in the Bill of Rights are included as aspects of the liberty protected against state action under the due process clause of the Fourteenth Amendment, states such as Connecticut were constrained to respect the right of privacy along with the rest of the Bill of Rights. Douglas did not believe that the right of privacy was the same thing as substantive due process, which he rejected as simply fastening extra-constitutional personal views and economic preferences of particular justices on the Constitution. The right of privacy was, for Douglas, part and parcel of the Constitution itself.

Justice Douglas came to agree with Justice Black that First Amendment guarantees of freedom of expression and religion permit no governmental regulation of any kind with regard to speech, press, religion, conscience, or association. Douglas dissented in obscenity cases such as *Roth v. United States* (1957), in which he stated, "The First Amendment, its prohibition in terms absolute, was designed to preclude courts as well as legislatures from weighing the values of speech against silence. The First Amendment puts free speech in the preferred position." Even though Douglas was a victim of obnoxious press accounts of his own personal life, he believed that awarding damages for defamation or invasion of privacy was unconstitutional because it involved penalizing the media for disseminating information. For example, Douglas concurred in rejecting the invasion of privacy action in *Time v. Hill* (1957), which involved a sensationalized magazine account of a family's experience as hostages of escaped criminals. He was concerned that the possibility of having to pay damages might discourage publication.

Because he believed in the intrinsic worth of each individual, Douglas consistently favored equality of opportunity. A case involving a special admissions program for minority applicants to the University of Washington Law School, *DeFunis v. Odegaard* (1974), presented a particularly difficult equal protection question. The majority found the case moot because the nonminority plaintiff was in his last semester of law school and would graduate no matter what the court decided. Douglas thought the Court should decide the case. Repeatedly insisting on racial neutrality and decrying racial, religious, and ethnic quotas, Douglas took a hard look at law school admissions practices. After carefully considering the circumstances, Douglas concluded that the law school's special admissions process was constitutional because, in his view, it was designed to individualize and to equalize the treatment of applicants from minority backgrounds. "I think a separate classification of these applicants is warranted, lest race be a subtle force in eliminating minority members because of cultural differences," Douglas wrote. At the same time, he also insisted that "There is no constitutional right for any race to be preferred." For Douglas, equal protection, like many constitutional values, involved a complex balancing of the realities of the situation. Individualized treatment in this instance satisfied Douglas's understanding of the spirit of equal protection.

Douglas's concerns about individual equality are also reflected in his application of equal protection guarantees to strictly scrutinize legislative classifications which affect fundamental rights. Among the most interesting examples of this approach to equal protection guarantees was Douglas's inventive 1942 opinion for the court in *Skinner v. Oklahoma*. His opinion describes Oklahoma's Habitual Criminal Sterilization Act at issue in the case as "legislation which involves one of the basic civil rights of man. Marriage and procreation are fundamental to the very existence and survival of the race. There is no redemption for the individual whom the law touches. . . . He is forever deprived of a basic liberty." Therefore, the opinion concludes, the Court should apply "strict scrutiny of the classification" which differentiated between those convicted of grand larceny and others convicted of such similar property crimes as embezzlement. Careful scrutiny was required "lest unwittingly, or otherwise, invidious discriminations are made against groups or types of individuals in violation of the constitutional guaranty of just and equal laws." Since Oklahoma provided no reasons why it needed to sterilize people who had been three times convicted of grand larceny, but not people who had been three times convicted of embezzlement, the statute was unconstitutional. "The equal protection clause would indeed be a formula of empty words if such conspicuously artificial lines could be drawn," when such fundamental individual rights as the right to have children is at stake. Douglas later applied this strict scrutiny approach in invalidating Virginia's $1.50 annual poll tax as a condition for voting in state elections in *Harper v. Virginia State Board of Elections* (1966). Douglas's idea that legislative classifications which affect fundamental individual rights must be strictly scrutinized by the courts has proved to be both powerful and enduring.

Of course, the individual with whom Douglas was most familiar was himself. A self-conscious nonconformist, Douglas saw himself as a unique individual who, through native ability, self-reliance, and hard work, had overcome adversity and challenge, to make his own way in the world. By 1970, when then-Representative Gerald Ford sought to impeach Justice Douglas, it was in part on the basis of William O. Douglas's independent life-style, as well as his association with the Parvin Foundation. Much to the disapproval of conventional society, Douglas had been divorced three times while sitting as a justice and was, at the age of sixty-seven, happily married to a twenty-three-year-old fourth wife. His off-the-bench activities included leading environmental protest marches and travel to strange and faraway places. At times he seemed to have his own foreign policy, including opposition to the Vietnam War. As long as he did his Court work, he reasoned, he could live as he liked.

Much of Douglas's sense of his own unique individuality was founded on his relationship with the natural world. He thrived in the outdoors and relished strenuous hikes, particularly in remote places of wild beauty, such as his vacation home at Goose Prairie, Washington. He valued the natural world as a source of personal challenges, which brought individual satisfaction as well as growth. For Douglas, wilderness was an essential environment where, by literally getting lost in nature, he could find his own unique individuality. He counted his own life-span in terms of the destruction of the American wilderness.

William O. Douglas's judicial work was as eclectic as it was prolific. People tend to strongly agree or equally strongly to disagree with his independent-minded judicial philosophy, much as they intensely liked or disliked the blunt-spoken and impatient man. Some of his judicial opinions have a remarkable resonance and eloquence. Some are political tracts. Still others appear to have been carelessly thrown together. Through it all, Douglas had an insight into the American spirit, an ability to articulate constitutional values, and a power to provoke thought and argument which few Supreme Court justices have equalled.

—DOROTHY J. GLANCY

BIBLIOGRAPHY

Extensive Douglas papers are in the Library of Congress in Washington, D.C. Melvin I. Urofsky, ed. *The Douglas Letters* (1987) contains an intriguing selection of those private papers, such as letters, memoranda, and personal files. William O. Douglas, *Go East, Young Man: The Early Years* (1974) and *The Court Years:*

The Autobiography of William O. Douglas (1980), comprise Douglas's autobiography. Douglas also wrote twenty-nine additional books on subjects which varied from the environment to international travel to political freedom.

James Simon, *Independent Journey* (1980), provides a readable and thought-provoking account of the essential qualities of Douglas's character as they developed over the course of his long life.

There have been a number of analyses of Douglas's judicial career, and these include Howard Ball and Philip J. Cooper, *Of Power and Right: Hugo Black, William O. Douglas and America's Constitutional Revolution* (1992); Bernard Wolfman, Jonathan L.F. Silver, and Marjorie A. Silver, *Dissent Without Opinion: The Behavior of Justice William O. Douglas in Federal Tax Cases* (1975); and Stephen L. Wasby, ed., *"He Shall Not Pass This Way Again": The Legacy of Justice William O. Douglas* (1990), which contains a useful collection of essays and commentary about Justice Douglas from nearly thirty legal scholars and historians.

Vern Countryman, a former law clerk to Justice Douglas and literary executor of Justice Douglas's estate, has written a number of books about Douglas. One of the more interesting is *The Judicial Record of Justice William O. Douglas* (1974), which was written in reaction to the last impeachment effort brought against Douglas. Professor Countryman has also published selections of Douglas opinions, including *Douglas of the Supreme Court* (1959) and *The Douglas Opinions* (1977).

G. Edward White's *The American Judicial Tradition* (1988) contains a very provocative chapter regarding Justice Douglas entitled "The Anti-Judge: William O. Douglas and the Ambiguities of Individuality." For a contrary view, see Melvin I. Urofsky, "William O. Douglas as a Common Law Judge," 41 *Duke Law Journal* 133 (1991).

At least two plays have been written about Justice Douglas's colorful life. Douglas Scott's *Mountain* (1990) enjoyed success off-Broadway in New York. A biographical monodrama, *Douglas*, by Robert Litz, was presented in Seattle, Washington, in September 1992.

GABRIEL DUVALL

BORN 6 December 1752, near Buena Vista in Prince George's County, Maryland

NOMINATED to the Court by James Madison on 15 November 1811

TOOK seat 3 February 1812; resigned 14 January 1835

DIED 6 March 1844, in Prince George's County

Gabriel Duvall was nominated to the Supreme Court to fill the vacancy created by the death of Samuel Chase of Maryland. On the same day, Joseph Story was named to the seat left vacant by the death of William Cushing. Both were confirmed only three days later. The striking contrast between the two nominees suggests a presidential stratagem by which Duvall's confirmation could be cast as balancing Story's. While both had served in their state legislatures and in the House of Representatives, at the time of their nominations, Story had just turned thirty-two, while Duvall was nearly fifty-nine. Story had no judicial experience, while Duvall had served for six years as chief judge of the Maryland general court and recorder of the mayor's court. Certainly, their ages and backgrounds gave no hint either to the length of their tenures or to the extent of their jurisprudential legacies.

Notwithstanding his prior experience as a judge, Duvall sat quietly in the Supreme Court; in twenty-three years, he penned opinions in only seventeen cases. All were nicely crafted examples of the judicial art, but none were of much significance other than to the parties involved. Formerly the first comptroller of the treasury, Duvall wrote most often for the Court in disputes arising from audits of public accounts.

Duvall's most frequently cited opinion appears in *Walton v. United States* (1824), where the Court held that a bill of exceptions (the formal list of objections made at trial) properly prepared at, or immediately following, trial was the jurisdictional *sine qua non* of appeal. In another frequently cited case, *Boyd's Lessee v. Graves* (1819), he adopted for the high court the rule that a boundary line marked out and honored by the parties over many years prevails over the terms of a land patent with which it varies.

In *Prince v. Bartlett* (1814), a federal marshal, in pursuit of goods against which to levy a federal judgment, burgled the storehouse in which they had been placed by a county sheriff after execution of a state writ of attachment. Notwithstanding the provocative facts of the case, the Court eschewed a ruling on federalism and found lacking the statutory conditions for affording priority to the federal claim. Subsequently, courts have relied on *Prince v. Bartlett* for the distinction drawn by Duvall in that case between bankruptcy and mere insolvency.

In *United States v. January* (1813), Duvall fashioned the federal rule that the ordinary practice permitting first the debtor and alternatively the creditor to designate to which among competing obligations a payment should be applied did not pertain when different sureties, under distinct obligations, were interested.

During Duvall's entire tenure on the bench, John Marshall headed the high court. In only two cases did Justice Duvall offer for the record a dissent from the position taken by the great chief justice. In the famous case of *Trustees of Dartmouth College v. Woodward* (1819), Duvall dissented without offering a full opinion, entering in the record only a brief note calling attention to the apparent consensus of French lawyers in 1786 that, had a royal charter been properly issued to the French East India Company, it would have been irrevocable.

Duvall's most moving opinion came in *Mima Queen v. Hepburn* (1813), when he alone disagreed with Marshall's opinion refusing admission in the courts of the District of Columbia of hearsay evidence to prove a person was not a slave. The chief justice wrote for the Court with great sympathy for the plight of petitioners and others in their condition, but failed to see any distinction between freedom cases like this and others "in which a right to property may be asserted." Duvall rested his dissent on the practice of admitting hearsay in such cases by the courts of Maryland (the laws of which were supposed by act of Congress to be adopted in the courts for that part of the District formerly part of Maryland) and on the more serious consequences for "persons of color" of excluding hearsay in freedom cases than in other boundary, pedigree, custom, and prescription disputes in which hearsay exceptions were already widely recognized.

—JOHN PAUL JONES

BIBLIOGRAPHY

There is very little written on Duvall. See, however, Irving Dillard, "Gabriel Duvall" in Friedman and Israel, 1 *Justices* 419, and G. Edward White, *The Marshall Court and Cultural Change, 1815–35* (1988), 321–27.

OLIVER ELLSWORTH

BORN 29 April 1745, Windsor, Connecticut

NOMINATED to the Court 3 March 1796
by George Washington

TOOK seat 8 March 1796; resigned
16 October 1800

DIED 26 November 1807 in Windsor,
Connecticut

Oliver Ellsworth was a thoroughgoing Calvinist who experienced his election by God for salvation. Born into a prosperous (though not wealthy) Connecticut farming family, his parents intended him for the ministry, and he was educated by famous new divinity divines before and after he graduated from the College of New Jersey (now Princeton) in 1766. But Ellsworth found his calling in law and politics. He became—in the Calvinist parlance of his times—a "Righteous Ruler."

After marrying the daughter of a prominent Connecticut family, Ellsworth developed a lucrative law practice and entered politics. From 1773 to 1789, he was a state legislator and then a judge. He also was an active and influential delegate, first to the Continental Congress and later the Constitutional Convention, after which he became Connecticut's most effective advocate for ratification. Ellsworth then represented Connecticut in the Senate and was the Federalist senators' de facto floor leader until he became chief justice of the United States in 1796.

None of his contemporaries—save John Marshall—had a more profound and long-lasting influence upon the federal judicial system. At Philadelphia he was a member of the Committee of Detail that wrote the Constitution's judicial article. More significantly, in the First Congress, he personally drafted and was widely recognized as the "leading projector" of the Judiciary Act of 1789 that established and prescribed the federal courts' judicial powers. Finally, he concluded his national public service as chief justice of the Court that he had helped to create.

Ellsworth was a gifted politician and quite self-disciplined. William Vans Murray, who served with Ellsworth on a diplomatic mission to France in 1800, wrote that Ellsworth "has a head of iron—just iron—that works with the precision of a mill, without its quickness and giddy manner. I profoundly admire the neatness and accuracy of his mind." Ellsworth also thoroughly understood the art and utility of political compromise. He believed human events to be absolutely predestined by God according to a perfect plan that was beyond human comprehension. His teachers had taught him that even evil was part of God's plan and served a divine purpose. Because he had experienced his personal salvation, he knew that his own conduct was righteous. At the same time, he could accept political compromises as part of God's unknowable plan. These psychological dynamics added up to an immensely confident man who acted from principle, but who nevertheless could enthusiastically embrace compromise as a desirable component of political life.

Ellsworth's ability to craft workable compromises played a major role in the drafting and enactment of the Judiciary Act. He was adamant on the need for vesting the federal courts with plenary power over a comparatively narrow range of litigation, including revenue collection cases, criminal prosecutions, and prize cases. He warned that "there will be Attacks on the General Government that will go to the Very Vitals of it [and state] Judges may Swerve." Without adequate revenues and effective criminal laws, the government could not defend itself. To obtain these absolutely essential powers, Ellsworth agreed to exclude the federal courts from trying many other suits that implicated important but lesser national interests.

As chief justice, Ellsworth revisited the major themes of the Judiciary Act. In *Wiscart v. Dauchy* (1796) and *Turner v. Bank of North America* (1799), he reaffirmed Congress's extensive powers to limit the federal courts' jurisdiction. In *United States v. La Vengeance* (1796), he significantly expanded the federal admiralty judges' authority to enforce federal revenue laws without the intercession of juries.

Chief Justice Ellsworth also took an active role in the vigorous enforcement of criminal law.

Oliver Ellsworth
Painting by William Wheeler after Ralph Earl.
Collection of the Supreme Court of the United States.

He believed that God had predestined human history to bring order out of chaos and that the federal government was obviously part of God's plans. He instructed grand juries that "national laws ... are the means by which it pleases heaven to make of weak and discordant parts, one great people; and to bestow upon them unexampled prosperity." But he also believed in original sin and had a pessimistic view of human nature. "Numerous are the vices," he warned, "and as obstinate the prejudices, and as daring as restless is the ambition, which perpetually hazard the national peace." He therefore urged "constant vigilance" in the enforcement of federal criminal law. "No transgression is too small, nor any transgressor too great, for animadversion."

Given this concern for the enforcement of criminal law, it comes as no surprise that in 1799, his last year of service on the Court, Ellsworth delivered a grand jury charge providing the most comprehensive explanation and justification of the federal courts' controversial enforcement of federal common law crimes. Similarly, that same year, Ellsworth wrote one of the early Supreme Court's most controversial opinions in the common law prosecution of Isaac Williams. In *United States v. Williams,* he insisted that the federal common law of crimes extended even to conduct outside the United States by an individual who had renounced his American citizenship and became the naturalized citizen of a foreign country.

In addition to his contributions to federal criminal law, Chief Justice Ellsworth was an effective administrator who convinced his fellow justices to accept a significant change in the structure of the Court's public opinions. Before Ellsworth's time, the Court followed the English practice in which each justice would deliver his own opinion *seriatim.* Under Ellsworth, however, the Court followed the Connecticut practice of pronouncing a single opinion presenting the majority's view together with dissenting opinions, if any. During Ellsworth's tenure, *seriatim* opinions were delivered in only one case in which he participated in the Court's decision. Ellsworth's new practice of delivering a single majority opinion has continued to the present and has enormous implications for the Court's role as the ultimate expositor of constitutional law. Instead of multifarious pronouncements from the individual justices, Ellsworth's idea of a single majority opinion permits the Court to speak with a single voice.

Like Chief Justice John Jay before him, Ellsworth spent the last months of his judicial tenure as a diplomat. In 1799, he sailed to Europe to negotiate a conclusion to the United States' undeclared naval war with France. Following the conclusion of successful negotiations, he resigned his office on the grounds of ill health. Ellsworth spent the rest of his life in Connecticut where he was an active participant in state politics.

—WILLIAM R. CASTO

BIBLIOGRAPHY

William Garrott Brown, *The Life of Oliver Ellsworth* (1905) is the best biography of Ellsworth, but is quite out of date in terms of the author's style and access to primary sources. "Biographical Sketch of Chief Justice Ellsworth," 3 *Analectic Magazine* 382 (1814), is an insightful and reasonably frank sketch by Gulian Verplanck, who knew Ellsworth. The various volumes of *The Documentary History of the Supreme Court of the United States, 1789–1800* (1985 *et seq*) provide the best tools for tracing Ellsworth's drafting of the Judiciary Act and his subsequent service as chief justice.

Stephen Johnson Field
Collection of the Supreme Court of the United States.

STEPHEN JOHNSON FIELD

BORN 4 November 1816, Haddam, Connecticut

NOMINATED to the Court 6 March 1863 by Abraham Lincoln

TOOK seat 20 May 1863; resigned effective 1 December 1897

DIED 9 April 1899 in Washington, D.C.

Stephen J. Field, the justice with the second longest tenure in Supreme Court history, spent his early youth in Connecticut and Massachusetts; he then lived in Europe for several years with a sister and brother-in-law before returning to Massachusetts to attend Williams College in the early 1830s.

Field was part of a large and accomplished family, which most likely helped to stoke his ambitious and independent spirit. After college graduation, he read law in the office of his eldest brother, David Dudley Field, Jr., a noted New York attorney who would later gain prominence for his Field Code, an effort to provide a streamlined codification of New York law. Stephen Field's bar preparation was interrupted briefly by a disabling accident, after which he resumed studies in the Albany office of John Van Buren, then the attorney general of New York. He was admitted to practice in New York in 1841. For the next six years, Field practiced law with his brother David, ending the partnership to return to Europe in 1848. Intrigued by tales of fame and fortune from the burgeoning gold-rush territory, Field decided in 1849 to move to California, where he was to spend the remainder of his prominent pre-Court career.

After sailing to San Francisco, Field quickly became active in both political and business affairs. Within three weeks of his arrival in California, he had helped to found the town of Marysville at the junction of the Yuba and Feather Rivers, had purchased a significant amount of property, and had been elected as the town's alcalde, a quasi-political, quasi-judicial office which entailed service as both mayor and chief civil magistrate. By Field's own account, he used this position to establish Marysville as a "model town" through a combination of bold leadership and legal acumen. When the office of alcalde was abolished by the adoption of the 1850 California constitution, Field moved on to establish a successful law practice in town and to win election to a Democratic seat in the California legislature, in which he assumed a critical role in drafting the new state's civil and criminal codes. After leaving the legislature to unsuccessfully seek election to the state senate in 1851, Field returned to law practice for six years before winning election to the California supreme court in 1857. He was elevated to the position of chief justice in 1861.

In his turbulent half-decade on the California supreme court, Field honed a reputation for personal brashness, frontier spirit, and stubborn independence that would later also characterize his lengthy tenure on the United States Supreme Court. Self-confident and outspoken, Field developed during this period well-publicized friendships with Leland Stanford and other famous tycoons of industry; such conspicuous connections to California business both catalyzed his professional success and fueled public criticism of him as arrogant and corrupt. Ultimately, however, the more positive aspects of Field's reputation prevailed; in 1863, when Congress added a tenth seat to the Supreme Court to ensure a majority of pro-Union votes and to avail itself of a westerner's likely expertise in land and mining cases, Field handily won unanimous acclamation from Stanford and the California congressional delegation as the best jurist to represent the new Pacific Coast circuit.

From his earliest years on the Court, Field's opinions displayed tenacity, clarity, and boldness of vision; he was an ardent critic of governmental—especially federal—interference in private business, and never hesitated to be a lonely or even lone dissenter when his tireless powers of persuasion had failed to win over his colleagues. Field's admonition shortly before his death that judges must speak out with "absolute fearlessness" was evidently embraced throughout his judicial career; from a prolific lifetime oeuvre of 640 opinions on the Court, he authored dissenting opinions in eighty-six cases, dissented a total of 220 times, sixty-four times alone. As he proclaimed in departing from the Court's judgment in the *Second Legal Tender Cases* (1871): "The only loyalty which I can admit consists in obedience to the Constitution and the laws made in pursuance of it." Such avowed singularity of vision, however, can also foster intellectual myopia, and Field's jurisprudence may be characterized by his adherence at least as often to his own peculiar brand of judicial dogmatism as to the Constitution itself.

Field's first ten years on the Court involved significant challenges, not only to the exercise of federal executive and legislative authority in the wake of the Civil War, but to the nature and scope of postbellum judicial review as well. Certainly, the Court's tragic decision in *Dred Scott v. Sandford* (1857) was a "self-inflicted wound" to its own legitimacy during this period, and as Edward S. Corwin noted: "During neither the Civil War nor the period of Reconstruction did the Supreme Court play anything like its role of supervision, with the result that during the one period the military powers of the President underwent undue expansion, and during the other, the legislative powers of Congress. The Court itself was conscious of its weakness. . . . [A]t no time since Jefferson's first administration has its independence been in greater jeopardy than between 1860 and 1870."

Into this arena of ambivalence entered Field, who sought to puncture any assumptions regarding the politically precarious circumstances of his own wartime appointment as the "tenth justice" by resolutely determining "to apply the Constitution as strictly as though no war had ever existed." (In fact, Field was not the "tenth justice" for long; Justices John Catron's death in 1865, James M. Wayne's death in 1867, and Robert C. Grier's resignation in 1870 gradually reduced the Court's membership to seven, and the Court was not restored to a newly fixed full membership of nine until 1870.) In *Ex parte Milligan* (1866), Field joined a unanimous Court in holding that President Abraham Lincoln had acted unconstitutionally by permitting military commission trials for civilians in nonwar areas in which civil courts had continued to function, and joined a 5–4 majority in holding that even Congress and the president acting together during wartime lacked the constitutional power to authorize such tribunals. Such clear-cut Court repudiations of presidential and congressional authority were not well received, and Field soon became the target of venomous public criticism for his views.

Consternation over the *Milligan* opinions was further heightened by the controversial *Test Oath Cases* (*Cummings v. Missouri* and *Ex parte Garland*, 1867), in which Field wrote for each 5–4 majority in striking down laws requiring retrospective Union loyalty oaths as conditions of employment. In *Cummings*, the Court invalidated a Missouri regulation requiring persons in the professions to swear past and present loyalty to the Union; in *Garland*, the Court struck down a federal statute imposing a similar oath on attorneys seeking to practice law in the federal courts. In declaring both test oath laws invalid under the bill of attainder and *ex post facto* provisions of the Constitution, Field demonstrated a willingness to exercise fully and seriously the Court's power of review, even in the face of vociferous objections from both Congress and the public. In an intriguing harbinger of future jurisprudential concerns, Field's majority opinions also focused particularly on the importance of preserving the individual's inalienable right to pursue a lawful occupation free from government restraint—a central tenet which would be invoked frequently by Field in the decades to come. In the meantime, Congressional and public reaction to the unfavorable decisions in both *Milligan* and the *Test Oath Cases* ranged from legislative proposals for impeachment of the majority justices to press condemnation of the decisions as "Dred Scott Number Two" and "Dred Scott Number Three."

Despite—or perhaps because of—such trenchant criticism so early in his Court career, Field began to carve a niche for himself on the Court and in the national spotlight. Nominated for the presidency by the California delegation at the Democratic National Convention of 1868, he was hailed as "a wall of fire against the encroachments of Radical domination" and "the guardian of the Constitution of his country against all the power of the Radical party. . . ." Field's paltry showing in convention ballots quashed any such possibilities; however, his willingness to be considered for the presidency so early in his Court career may be viewed perhaps as a revealing indication not only of his lingering pre-Court political ambitions, but also of the power and influence he hoped to wield in shaping the direction of the Court itself.

Field's first Court decade drew to a close with a series of cases concerning Reconstruction era legislation, which starkly illustrate both the tenuous nature of the postbellum Court and the ready iconoclasm with which Field criticized the views of his brethren. In *Ex parte McCardle* (1869), the Court considered a southern editor's *habeas corpus* petition for release from military imprisonment for obstructing Reconstruction efforts. The case was first heard by the Court in its 1868 term; however, shortly after oral argument, Congress—fearing that McCardle's appeal would afford the Court the opportunity to declare the Reconstruction Acts unconstitutional—began to consider legislation which would revoke the Court's jurisdiction over *habeas corpus* appeals, including McCardle's. When a majority of the Court agreed to a stay of the case until Congress had voted on the jurisdiction-stripping bill, Field joined Justice Robert Grier's acerbic dissent from what they termed the Court's "shameful" abdication of judicial responsibility. Nevertheless, Field's dismay did not affect his ultimate position regarding the proper procedural disposition of the case. When Congress eventually voted to pass the bill, Field and Grier, without comment, joined the rest of the Court in dismissing the appeal.

A final example of Field's outspokenness during this era was his unswerving criticism of the Congressional legal tender acts, wartime statutes authorizing the substitution of "greenbacks," or paper money, for gold and silver in the payment of debts. In two decisions in the 1870 and 1871 terms concerning the constitutionality of these acts, Field displayed a characteristically staunch determination to hold fast to his position, even as politically-driven shifts in the Court's composition transformed it from the majority to the minority viewpoint. In *Hepburn v. Griswold* (1870), the first of these challenges, the Court heard oral arguments in both the 1867 and 1868 terms, but because of strong pressures, both internal and external, it was unable to reach a decision until late 1869; even then, the Court's tentative preliminary vote of 5–3 to strike down the acts quickly unraveled when an ailing and confused Grier absentmindedly voted in conference first to uphold the acts and then to strike them down. Field persuaded Grier to resign because of his failing health, and Grier left the bench on February 1, 1870.

On February 7, 1870, the Court issued a decision in *Hepburn*, voting 4–3 to invalidate the acts as both an abrogation of Congressional powers and an impairment of freedom of contract as applied to debts incurred before their passage. That same day, President Ulysses S. Grant nominated William Strong, a Pennsylvania state judge, and Joseph P. Bradley, a New Jersey attorney, to fill the vacancies which had been created by Wayne's death and Grier's retirement from the Court. Strong and Bradley were confirmed and seated on the Court in March, and within weeks of their seating, the Court agreed to reconsider the constitutionality of the legal tender acts. This second challenge, *Knox v. Lee* and *Parker v. Davis* (known as the *Second Legal Tender Cases*), was argued in the 1870 term and concerned the same central issue—the power of Congress to enact the acts and apply them to preexisting debts.

With the brand-new addition of Strong and Bradley, the Court voted 5–4 to overrule the *Hepburn* decision of fifteen months before. Field issued a lengthy and vehement dissent, arguing that the acts authorized the repudiation of debts, a "dishonor" and "public crime" unwarranted by the Constitution; moreover, Field contended, invoking natural law principles in support of his method of constitutional interpretation, "It is only by obedience [to the Constitution and its dictates] that affection and reverence can be shown to a superior having a right to command. So thought our Master when he said to his disciples: 'If ye love me, keep my commandments.'"

Other significant opinions authored by Field in his first decade on the Court include *Low v. Austin* (1872), in which a unanimous Court held that the constitutional ban on state taxes on imports or exports prohibits state taxes on goods brought in from foreign countries only if those goods retain their character as "imports"; and *Bradley v. Fisher* (1872), in which the Court recognized the doctrine of judicial immunity, ruling that judges may not be sued in their official capacities, regardless of the error of their actions.

Although Field quickly established a bold judicial style in his first few years as associate justice, he did not fully develop his nascent judicial philosophies until his second decade on the Court. During the next fifteen years, many of his inchoate leanings would coalesce into a distinctive jurisprudence, rendering this period by far the most prolific and influential phase of his Supreme Court career. A critical factor in the development of his jurisprudence during this period was the emergence of the Civil War amendments: the Thirteenth Amendment, ratified in 1865, which officially abolished slavery; the Fourteenth Amendment, ratified in 1868, which prohibited the exercise of state action to deny persons the equal protection and due process of the law, and the privileges or immunities of national citizenship; and the Fifteenth Amendment, ratified in 1870, which forbade states to deny anyone the right to vote on the basis of race, color, or previous condition of servitude. Understood in the context of the Civil War/Reconstruction era in which they were promulgated, these amendments were clearly intended to limit state encroachment on individual liberties in order to undo the evils of slavery, and to effect far-reaching goals of racial equality; yet, in their first several decades of implementation, they were construed by the Court in such a narrow and crabbed fashion that they were virtually unrecognizable as constitutional guarantees in this regard.

Field's unique contribution to this interpretive debate lay not in his refusal to view the Civil War amendments as guarantors of personal liberty, but rather in his consistently broad application of the amendments to protect economic and property interests as core human rights, while at the same time endorsing an extremely constricted interpretation of the applicability of the amendments to the eradication of racial discrimination—the original purpose for which the amendments had been enacted. These constitutional perspectives, forcefully advanced in both majority opinions and in dissents, provided the Court with interpretive tools which would continue to affect its jurisprudence concerning the Civil War amendments throughout the next half-century.

The Court's first definitive statement on the meaning and scope of the Fourteenth Amendment emerged in the *Slaughterhouse Cases* (1873), cases which had nothing to do with the vestiges of slavery or with the civil rights of blacks. Rather, the cases concerned a challenge by a group of New Orleans butchers against the state of Louisiana's decision to grant a monopoly on the slaughterhouse business in New Orleans to one company; such an arrangement, the butchers contended, interfered with their right to do business and violated guarantees under both the Thirteenth Amendment and the Fourteenth Amendment's privileges or immunities, equal protection, and due process clauses. By a vote of 5–4, the Court rejected the butchers' argument, holding that their "right to do business" was neither a "privilege or immunity" of United States citizenship nor a "property" interest protected by the due process clause. Defending a narrow interpretation of the privileges or immunities clause as protecting only those limited preexisting rights which had previously been recognized as concomitants of federal rather than state citizenship, Justice Samuel Miller wrote on behalf of the majority that any broader interpretation would allow the Court to be "a perpetual censor upon all legislation of the States on the civil rights of their own citizens."

Field's dissent in the *Slaughterhouse Cases* is an intriguing exemplar of both his increasing concern with the subject of economic liberty and his use of natural law principles in defense of his constitutional reasoning. He opined that the privileges or immunities clause of the Fourteenth Amendment should be interpreted to protect the right of man "to pursue his happiness by following any of the known established trades and occupations . . . subject only to such restraints as equally affected all others." Moreover, he asserted, the Fourteenth Amendment should be read broadly to protect such "inalienable rights, rights which are the gift of the Creator, which the law does not confer, but only recognizes." Despite the implications of such hortatory language concerning "inalienable rights," however, Field's forthcoming decisions in interpreting the Civil War amendments would reveal an overarching concern not with the recognition of individual civil (i.e., social and political) rights, but rather with the protection of individual and corporate property rights, economic freedoms, and other forms of private enterprise.

Field's sharply circumscribed definition of "inalienable rights" in social and political terms may be seen in a series of cases throughout the 1870s and early 1880s. In *Bradwell v. Illinois* (1873), a ruling announced the day after the release of the *Slaughterhouse* opinions, Field joined with the 8–1 majority in rejecting Myra Bradwell's privileges or immunities clause challenge to the state of Illinois's refusal on the grounds of gender to license her to practice law in its courts; in the context of a female's "right to do business," Field agreed with the Court's holding that the right to practice law was not a privilege or immunity of American citizenship. Similarly, a few years later, in *Minor v. Happersett* (1875), Field joined a unanimous Court in holding that the privileges or immunities clause of the Fourteenth Amendment does not guarantee women the right to vote; the Court stated, "[T]he Constitution of the United States does not confer the right of suffrage on anyone."

Even when considering challenges concerning Congressional authority to protect blacks' suffrage rights—a constitutional mandate directly traceable to the history and language of the Fifteenth Amendment—Field shared the rest of the Court's refusal to recognize an expansive definition of federally protected individual civil rights under the Civil War amendments. In *United States v. Reese* (1876), Field agreed with the Court's 8–1 majority in holding that Congress had exceeded its power to enforce the Fifteenth Amendment in enacting a statute which penalized state officials who denied or otherwise obstructed the right of blacks to vote; the Court held that the Fifteenth Amendment guaranteed not the right to vote, but only the right to be free from racial discrimination in the exercise of the state-created right to vote.

In the companion case of *United States v. Cruikshank* (1876), the Court unanimously dismissed federal indictments brought against Louisiana citizens charged with using fraud and violence to prevent blacks from exercising their right to vote; the Court held that because the indictments at issue had not explicitly averred the existence of racial animus on the part of the defendants, they were therefore not truly federal offenses under the Fifteenth Amendment.

In *Ex parte Siebold* (1880), Field dissented from the Court's decision upholding the convictions of two state election officers under federal laws for interfering with federal elections, arguing for a narrower construction of Congressional power. Although Field occasionally acceded to a broader interpretation of Congressional authority under the Fifteenth Amendment's enabling clause, for example in *Ex parte Yarbrough* (1884), his overarching philosophy endorsed severe limitations on the use of the Fifteenth Amendment to protect blacks in the exercise of the franchise.

Field's position with respect to constitutional protections of the civil rights of blacks in other areas was similarly stinting. In the companion cases of *Strauder v. West Virginia* and *Ex parte Virginia* (1880), Field dissented from two of the few decisions of the era in which the rights of blacks were upheld in challenges under the Civil War amendments. In *Strauder*, the Court reversed the conviction of a black defendant who had unsuccessfully petitioned during his state court trial for removal to federal court on the grounds that West Virginia's statute excluding blacks from juries deprived him of equal protection of the laws; the majority noted that not only was the impartial selection of a jury a "legal right" protected by the Fourteenth Amendment, but also that congressionally authorized removal from state to federal court under such circumstances of invidious discrimination was "an ordinary mode of protecting rights and immunities conferred by the Federal Constitution and Laws."

In *Ex parte Virginia*, the Court upheld a provision of the Civil Rights Act of 1875 which prohibited racial discrimination in jury selection, affirming that the purpose of the Fourteenth Amendment was indeed to eliminate state bias on the grounds of race and color. Field dissented from both decisions, asserting that "the equality of protection assured by the Fourteenth Amendment to all persons . . . does not imply that they shall be allowed to participate in the administration of its laws . . . or to discharge any duties of public trust."

Finally, in a devastating blow to Congressional attempts under the Civil War amendments to reach and prohibit private racial discrimination, Field joined the 8–1 majority in the *Civil Rights Cases* (1883), holding that neither the Thirteenth nor the Fourteenth Amendments authorized Congress to ban discrimination against blacks in privately owned public accommodations. In so doing, Field agreed with the Court's conclusions both that private racial bias did not constitute a badge of slavery or involuntary servitude impermissible under the Thirteenth Amendment, and that private racially discriminatory acts were unreachable under the Fourteenth Amendment absent state action.

In salient contrast to his narrow construction of the Civil War amendments with regard to individual civil rights in such areas as the franchise and jury selection, Field vigorously advanced a broadly expansive interpretation of the amendments with respect to the protection of economic liberties and private enterprise concerns. Indeed, Field's jurisprudence of "property rights" as developed in the 1870s and 1880s has led many historians to label him the most prominent and successful proponent of laissez-faire economics in Court history. Certainly Field forged a clear-cut impression of pro-business, anti-statist predilections during this era which render the laissez-faire label both apt and accurate today.

Field's dissent in the *Slaughterhouse Cases* provided an early indication of the importance with which he regarded economic freedom as a core right enshrined with constitutional protections. Field further developed this concept in *Bartemeyer v. Iowa* (1874), in which he asserted that both the due process and privileges or immunities clauses of the Fourteenth Amendment

should be interpreted to protect an individual's right to use, enjoy, sell, and dispose of property free from governmental interference. In *Munn v. Illinois* (1876), as well as in the other so-called "Granger Cases" concerning the constitutionality of state legislation regulating the rates to be set by grain elevator owners, Field dissented from the majority view, which deemed such laws to be permissible exercises of state police power so long as the use of the grain elevators was "affected with a public interest"; he wrote, "I deny the power of any Legislature under our government to fix the price which one shall receive for his property of any kind."

In the *Sinking Fund Cases* (1879), two cases involving the validity of a 1878 congressional statute which had required two Pacific railroads (one incorporated by Congress, the other by the state of California) to set aside portions of their earnings in a "sinking fund" to ensure the payment of their debts, Field issued a particularly vehement and detailed dissent to what he viewed as an impairment of contract and a violation of the due process clause, warning:

> The decision will, in my opinion, tend to create insecurity in the title to corporate property in the country. . . . Where contracts are impaired, or when operating against the government are sought to be evaded and avoided by legislation, a blow is given to the security of all property. If the government will not keep its faith, little better can be expected from the citizen. If contracts are not observed, no property will in the end be respected; and all history shows that rights of persons are unsafe where property is insecure. Protection to one goes with protection to the other; and there can be neither prosperity nor progress where this foundation of all just government is unsettled. "The moment," said the elder Adams, "the idea is admitted into society that property is not as sacred as the laws of God, and that there is not a force of law and public justice to protect it, anarchy and tyranny commence."

Thus, through a combination of forceful rhetoric and unrelenting adherence to his views,

Field effectively used the vehicle of the dissenting opinion to promulgate notions of "substantive due process" in the realm of economic rights—notions which would gradually gain credence among his brethren and which would be recognized decades later by a majority of the Court. Therefore, in assessing Field's influence on the Court's jurisprudence during this period, it is instructive to note not only his majority opinions and concurrences, but his dissents and his opinions while "riding circuit" in his role as designated justice for the ninth circuit court of appeals, as well.

A classic example of his influence in the latter regard was his statement in the ninth circuit case of *San Mateo v. Southern Pacific R.R. Co.* (1882), in which the court ruled unconstitutional under the equal protection and due process clauses a tax imposed by the state of California on its railroads. Despite the lack of clear Supreme Court precedent supporting such a result, Field held that the Fourteenth Amendment's protection of "persons" should be interpreted to include the protection of corporations and corporate property; he observed, "It would be a most singular result if a constitutional provision intended for the protection of every person . . . should cease to exert such protection the moment the person becomes a member of a corporation."

Apparently, Field's new interpretive addition to "Ninth Circuit law" concerning the Fourteenth Amendment found a sympathetic ear with the rest of the Court; by the time a similar challenge reached the U. S. Supreme Court a few years later, in *Santa Clara County v. Southern Pacific Railroad Co.* (1886), the Court summarily noted in dictum that the Fourteenth Amendment's protection of "persons" applied to corporations as well as individuals.

Other notable opinions written by Field during this period were *Pennoyer v. Neff* (1878), in which Field spoke for an 8–1 majority in a landmark decision delineating the constitutional and procedural bases under the Fourteenth Amendment for a state's exercise of personal jurisdiction over a noncitizen, nonresident defendant who is not physically present in the state at the time of service; and *Mugler v. Kansas* (1887), in which Field dissented from the majority decision upholding a Kansas law which forbade the manufacture and sale of intoxicating liquor in the state as a valid exercise of state police power to protect public health and morals.

Finally, full consideration of Field's evolving judicial philosophy during this era bears some mention of his ongoing political interests, activities, relationships, and possible aspirations to elective office. Life as a member of the Supreme Court had enhanced rather than diminished his prestigious social circle of friendships with such well-known figures as Leland Stanford and Collis P. Huntington, and rumors about his prospects as a presidential candidate continued to percolate throughout the 1870s and much of the 1880s. When a special commission was appointed in 1877 to resolve a bitter dispute over electoral votes in the presidential election of 1876, Field was one of five members of the Court chosen to serve; when the electoral commission ruled, after heated partisan deliberations, that Republican Rutherford B. Hayes had won the electoral count by one vote, Field showed his indignance at the result and his support for the Democratic cause by absenting himself from Hayes's inauguration ceremonies. Still, at the Democratic Convention of 1880, Field received a mere sixty-five votes on the first ballot—a showing which clearly established the unrealistic nature of any political ambitions he may still have harbored at that time. By the mid-1880s, his viability as a candidate for electoral office had waned even further; at the 1884 Democratic state convention in California, Field's adopted "home" state overwhelmingly refused to support his candidacy, and his name was not proposed at all at that year's national convention. By the late 1880s, as Field reached his early seventies, he abandoned all serious presidential aspirations and turned instead to the further solidification of his influence on the Court and to his hopes of someday garnering an appointment as chief justice.

Field's last ten years on the Court were marked by high drama, great disappointment with respect to personal ambitions, and ultimately the tremendous satisfaction of seeing many of his maverick conservative judicial views gain ascendancy. In 1888, Field's longtime hope of becoming chief justice was dashed when President Grover Cleveland instead chose Melville W.

Fuller to fill the vacancy created by the death of Morrison R. Waite. Field apparently regarded Cleveland's rejection of him as a great personal insult and never forgave him for the slight.

That same year, while serving as ninth circuit judge in California, Field became embroiled in a bizarre personal feud with litigants in his courtroom which nearly cost him his life. The complicated imbroglio began when David S. Terry, former chief justice of the California supreme court and an old enemy of Field's, appeared in Field's court with his wife, Sarah Hill, in a dispute concerning an alleged secret marriage contract between Hill and the late William Sharon. In response to several comments made in open court by Field about Hill's character, both Terry and Hill noisily objected and were promptly held in contempt and sentenced to jail by Field. As a result, Terry waged a bitter vendetta against Field, and Field was advised not to resume his circuit court duties in California.

In 1889, Field did return to California, accompanied by his deputy marshal and bodyguard, David Neagle. By happenstance, Field and Neagle encountered Terry and Hill while dining in a restaurant; Terry lunged at Field and attacked him, and Neagle drew a gun in defense of Field and shot Terry to death. In the ensuing state criminal proceedings against Neagle, the federal circuit court issued a writ of *habeas corpus*, which was in turn challenged before the United States Supreme Court. The Court (sitting without Field) upheld the writ as a proper exercise of federal power in *In re Neagle* (1890), on the ground that the attorney general's order to Neagle to protect Field was "a law of the United States." Ironically, despite its odd and idiosyncratic factual underpinnings, the case remains a leading precedent concerning the scope of federal executive and judicial powers.

In his waning years on the Fuller Court, Field quite possibly was able finally to enjoy the quiet triumph of realizing that his decades-old defenses of private property rights and other conservative ideologies were, with increasing frequency, no longer minority viewpoints. Field's nephew, Justice David J. Brewer, appointed in 1890 by President Benjamin Harrison, shared many of Field's beliefs with respect to economic concerns and appeared ready to carry those beliefs into the next century's jurisprudence. In Field's view, much remained to be accomplished; in one of his final opinions, a concurrence in the Court's decision to strike down the federal income tax in *Pollock v. Farmers' Loan & Trust Co.* (1895), Field warned:

> If the provisions of the Constitution can be set aside by an act of Congress, where is the course of usurpation to end? The present assault on capital is but the beginning. It will be but the stepping-stone to others, larger and more sweeping, till our political contests will become a war of the poor against the rich—a war constantly growing in intensity and bitterness.

By 1896, Field's health was frail, and his inability to fulfill his judicial duties was increasingly apparent to his colleagues. According to Charles Evans Hughes, various justices thought that Field would surely be encouraged to retire if he were reminded of his own role in persuading the aging Justice Grier to retire some twenty-six years earlier:

> Justice Harlan was deputed to make the suggestion. He went over to Justice Field, who was sitting alone on a settee in the robing room apparently oblivious of his surroundings, and after arousing him gradually approached the question, asking if he did not recall how anxious the Court had become with respect to Justice Grier's condition and the feeling of the other Justices that in his own interest and in that of the Court he should give up his work. Justice Harlan asked if Justice Field did not remember what had been said to Justice Grier on that occasion. The old man listened, gradually became alert and finally, with his eyes blazing with the old fire of youth, he burst out: "Yes! And a dirtier's day work I never did in my life!" That was the end of that effort of the brethren of the Court to induce Justice Field's retirement; he did resign not long after.

In fact, Field's lingering last months on the Court were undoubtedly prolonged by his determination to break the record of thirty-four-plus years of service set by Justice John Marshall in

1835. By early 1897, it was clear that he would, so Field announced that his resignation would take effect on December 1. On that date, Field retired after a total of thirty-four years, eight months, and twenty days—a record which has since been surpassed only by Justice William O. Douglas.

Field died on April 9, 1899, in Washington, D.C. Perhaps the most fitting epitaph for his irascible spirit, fervently held convictions, and lifetime of public service can be found in his own words, written in his last year on the Court:

> Timidity, hesitation and cowardice in any public officer excite and deserve only contempt, but infinitely more in a judge than in any other, because he is appointed to discharge a public trust of the most sacred character. To decide against his conviction of the law or judgment as to the evidence, whether moved by prejudice, or passion, or the clamor of the crowd, is to assent to a robbery as infamous in morals and as deserving of punishment as that of the highwayman or the burglar; and to hesitate or refuse to act when duty calls is hardly less the subject of just reproach.

—MARGARET M. RUSSELL

BIBLIOGRAPHY

The writings of Justice Stephen Field include the following: *Personal Reminiscences of Early Days in California with Other Sketches* (1893); "The Supreme Court of the United States, Centennial Celebration of the Organization of the Federal Judiciary," 134 U.S. 729 (1890), and "The Centenary of the Supreme Court of the United States," 24 *American Law Review* 351 (1890), two retrospectives on the work of the Court; and "The Late Chief Justice Chase," 11 *Overland Monthly* 305 (October 1873). By far the most informative of the four works is the first, Field's relatively informal recollections of his early life and work; the others are more carefully tailored and staid presentations of his opinions and judicial perspectives.

Carl Brent Swisher, *Stephen J. Field: Craftsman of the Law* (1930), is considered by many to be the definitive study of Field's life. Numerous competent general studies of Field's life and career may be found, including Chauncey F. Black and Samuel B. Smith, eds., *Some Account of the Work of Stephen J. Field, as Legislator, State Judge, and Justice of the Supreme Court of the United States* (1895); Calvin Durfee, "Stephen Johnson Field," in *Williams Biographical Annals* 503–504 (1871); Orrin K. McMurray, "Field's Work as a Lawyer and Judge in California," 5 *California Law Review* 87 (1917); and Robert McCloskey, "Stephen J. Field," in Friedman and Israel, 2 *Justices* 1069.

Field's judicial philosophy, particularly as a proponent of laissez-faire and other conservative economic ideologies, is discussed at great length in the following works: Robert Goedecke, "Justice Field and Inherent Rights," 27 *Review of Politics* 198 (1965); Howard J. Graham, "Justice Field and the Fourteenth Amendment," 52 *Yale Law Journal* 851 (1943); William C. Jones, "Justice Field's Opinions on Constitutional Law," 5 *California Law Review* 108 (1917); Robert G. McCloskey, *American Conservatism in the Age of Enterprise: A Study of Summer, Field, and Carnegie* (1951); Charles W. McCurdy, "Justice Field and the Jurisprudence of Government-Business Relations: Some Parameters of Laissez-Faire Constitutionalism, 1863–1897," 61 *Journal of American History* 970 (1975); and Wallace Mendelson, "Mr. Justice Field and Laissez-Faire," 36 *Virginia Law Review* 45 (1950).

ABE FORTAS

BORN 19 June 1910, Memphis, Tennessee

NOMINATED to the Court 28 July 1965 by
Lyndon B. Johnson

TOOK seat 4 October 1965; nominated as
chief justice by Lyndon B. Johnson
26 June 1968; nomination withdrawn
10 October 1968; retired 5 May 1969

DIED 5 April 1982 in Washington, D.C.

Abe Fortas is remembered more for the circumstances surrounding his abortive nomination as chief justice and his subsequent resignation than for his judicial opinions. This is unfortunate. Trained as a Washington lawyer during the 1930s, and later trusted as a close advisor to President Lyndon Johnson, Fortas, perhaps more than any other justice, provided a link between Franklin Roosevelt's New Deal and Johnson's Great Society. Though his tenure was brief and controversial, Fortas played a significant role in shaping some of the most important cases handed down by the Warren Court.

Abe Fortas was born into a modest, working-class family steeped more in the cultural than the religious traditions of Judaism. From his father, an amateur musician, Fortas inherited a deep and abiding love of music, and became an avid violinist; he later came to count Pablo Casals and Isaac Stern among his friends and clients.

An outstanding student, Fortas won scholarships both to Southwestern College in Memphis and to Yale Law School. At Yale, Fortas served as editor-in-chief of the *Yale Law Journal* and came under the influence of two powerful exponents of legal realism: Thurman Arnold and William O. Douglas. After graduating in 1933, Fortas joined Yale's faculty while also accepting a position with Jerome Frank in the New Deal's Agricultural Adjustment Administration. In 1937, while serving at the Interior Department, Fortas befriended a young Texas Congressman named Lyndon Johnson.

In the 1940s, Fortas left government service, but remained in Washington and founded a law firm with Thurman Arnold and Paul Porter. Fortas came to exemplify the Washington lawyer of the postwar era. An able and aggressive advocate, trained in government by the New Deal, he effectively navigated clients through the intricacies of federal policies and programs. Always drawn to men of power and influence, Fortas maintained his friendship with Lyndon Johnson during the 1950s, serving as his lawyer and close advisor until Johnson, as president, nominated his old friend to the Court in 1965.

On the Court, Fortas developed a reputation as a liberal in civil rights and a conservative in areas involving government regulation of business. His opinions demonstrate an instrumental approach to the law but reveal no coherent legal philosophy. This is not to say Fortas was unprincipled, though some accused him of this, but that true to his education in legal realism, he saw the law as a tool to achieve specific results.

Fortas's experience as a corporate lawyer led him to take a dim view of judicial interference in business matters. For example, in *Baltimore & Ohio Railroad v. United States* (1967), Fortas in dissent argued that the Court had no business questioning the informed decision of the Interstate Commerce Commission to allow a merger of two railroads.

Fortas's greatest concern, however, lay in protecting the rights of minorities, the disenfranchised, and the powerless. He fiercely championed the rights of criminal defendants, especially their Fifth Amendment right against self-incrimination. In *In re Gault* (1967), Fortas wrote a strong opinion that effectively created a "Bill of Rights" for juvenile criminal offenders by extending certain basic Fourteenth Amendment due process rights into juvenile courts. Writing in a realist vein, Fortas relied more on historical, sociological, and psychological studies of the juvenile justice system than on legal precedent to support his holding.

Free speech was an area of special concern for Fortas, especially in the era of civil rights and anti-Vietnam War demonstrations. He was not, however, a First Amendment absolutist. To the contrary, he could not abide disruptive civil disobedience or symbolic speech that violated valid laws merely to dramatize dissent. The musician in him cherished harmony and decorum. He allowed for tension and conflict but insisted it be contained or structured. Thus, in *Brown v. Louisiana* (1966), Fortas found a Louisiana breach of the peace statute unconstitutional as applied to several blacks who conducted a peaceful sit-in of a segregated public library. But in *Street v. New York* (1968), Fortas, in a stinging dissent, drew the line at flag burning, declaring that "protest does not exonerate lawlessness." Yet in his landmark opinion in *Tinker v. Des Moines School District* (1969), Fortas held unconstitutional a school's prohibition on black arm bands worn by certain students to protest the Vietnam War. Echoing his support for juvenile rights enunciated in *Gault*, Fortas declared that students did not surrender their First Amendment rights upon entering a school. Wearing the arm bands, he asserted, was akin to "pure speech" that did not involve "aggressive, disruptive actions" and did not interfere with the school's work.

Fortas also had a very strong commitment to privacy as a constitutional right. Indeed, he saw the right to privacy as a significant limitation on freedom of the press. Consistent with his free speech cases (and with his deep personal antipathy toward the press), Fortas refused to extend First Amendment protections to press activities he considered to be intrusive or disruptive. See, for example, his dissent in *Time v. Hill* (1967).

After only three years on the Court, President Johnson nominated Fortas to replace the retiring Earl Warren as chief justice. It was an honor from which he never recovered. The con-

firmation hearings took place after Johnson had decided not to seek reelection and had become a lame duck. Fortas soon became the target of a conservative backlash against the activism of the Warren Court and Johnson's Great Society programs. Revelations of his ongoing business connections with millionaire businessman Louis Wolfson didn't help matters any. By October, Johnson was forced to withdraw Fortas's name. One year later, amid further allegations of improper business dealings, Fortas resigned from the Court, although he maintained his innocence of any wrongdoing. Back in the private sector he was rebuffed by his old law firm, but continued to practice law until his death in 1982.

—JONATHAN KAHN

BIBLIOGRAPHY

Fortas's own views can be found in his *Concerning Dissent and Civil Disobedience* (1968), a fascinating look into his ideas on the nature and limits of free expression in a civil society, made even more interesting by the fact that he wrote it while sitting on the Supreme Court.

There are two major biographies. Laura Kalman, *Abe Fortas: A Biography* (1990), and Bruce Allen Murphy, *Fortas: The Rise and Fall of a Supreme Court Justice* (1988). The latter is an incisive study that concentrates on Fortas's life as a Washington insider, and is primarily a political biography. Kalman's is a solid study of Fortas's life and the first to be based on complete access to Fortas's private papers. Her work is therefore more complete than Murphy's, yet lacks a certain critical distance. Kalman does, however, provide a good review of the development of Fortas's legal ideas.

FELIX FRANKFURTER

BORN 15 November 1882, Vienna, Austria

NOMINATED to the Court 5 January 1939
by Franklin D. Roosevelt

TOOK seat 30 January 1939; retired
28 August 1962

DIED 22 February 1965 in Washington, D.C.

Closely identified with the social and economic reforms of President Franklin D. Roosevelt's New Deal, and long associated with liberal causes and organizations ranging from the American Civil Liberties Union to *The New Republic* magazine, Felix Frankfurter generated fear and paranoia among conservatives when the Senate considered his nomination in 1939. Elizabeth Dilling, author of *The Red Network*, a volume published at her own expense and highly recommended by the American Legion, warned members of the Senate Judiciary Committee that the nominee had "long been one of the principal aids of the 'red' revolutionary movement in the United States."

A spokesman for the American Federation Against Communism, while denying any anti-Semitic intentions, cautioned "in America, an anti-Jewish sentiment is growing by leaps and bounds. ... To place, at this time, upon the highest court another one of that race is not only a political mistake but a social one." The national director of the Constitutional Crusaders wondered why the president had not chosen "an American from Revolutionary times instead of a Jew from Austria just naturalized," to which Senator George Norris, a Frankfurter ally responded, "an American from Revolution times would be too old."

New Dealers and liberals, on the other hand, greeted Frankfurter's nomination and confirmation with euphoria. Secretary of the Interior Harold Ickes pronounced it "the most significant and worth-while thing the President has done." The *Nation* magazine believed "no other appointee in our history has gone to the Court so fully prepared for its great tasks. ... There will be no Dred Scott decisions from a Supreme Court on which he sits." *Newsweek* predicted the newest justice would be "a magnificent champion of the underdog."

Supreme Court justices have a habit of disappointing, amazing, and confounding the presidents who selected them, as well as the groups and individuals who supported and opposed their appointment. There are few clearer examples of this axiom than Felix Frankfurter, the vibrant Harvard Law School professor, who arrived at the Court with a resume attesting to three decades of participation in some of the most controversial social, legal, and political battles of his generation. As a teacher, author, public servant, litigator, and adviser to presidents, he had usually thrown his considerable energy and intellect into the fray on the side of what contemporaries called the progressive direction of affairs.

Joining the Harvard faculty shortly before World War I, Frankfurter pioneered the development of courses in administrative law and federal jurisdiction and fired the imagination of three generations of students to serve the public interest rather than private gain. As one of the federal government's chief labor administrators during the Great War, he sought protection for union members and pushed for improved working conditions, including an eight-hour day in the steel industry. He severely criticized California's prosecution of Tom Mooney, a militant labor organizer sent to prison on dubious evidence, and later leveled similar charges against Massachusetts authorities in the Sacco-Vanzetti case.

Frankfurter condemned Attorney General A. Mitchell Palmer and the postwar red scare, opposed American military intervention against the Bolsheviks in Russia, represented alien Communists threatened with deportation, and argued for the constitutionality of a federal minimum wage law in the famous case of *Adkins v. Children's Hospital* (1923). In the pages of *The New Republic*, he regularly criticized the judicial vetoes of the Supreme Court under Taft and Hughes. His fingerprints were all over landmark pieces of legislation in the 1930s, including the Norris-LaGuardia anti-injunction law, the Securities Act of 1933, and the Public Utility Holding Company Act of 1935. By the time of his appointment, Frankfurter's students, often labeled "Felix's hot dogs," played key roles in many New Deal departments and agencies.

Frankfurter's intimate association with Oliver Wendell Holmes, Louis Brandeis, and Benjamin Cardozo, members of the Court who had displayed the greatest judicial toleration for social reform, as well as concern for safeguarding civil liberties, also encouraged his supporters to predict that he would follow much the same path. Archibald MacLeish, a former Frankfurter student, noted that the late 1930s marked a major watershed in the nation's constitutional history as the Court approved New Deal reforms, permitted more latitude to the political branches on economic measures, and became more assertive with regard to issues that touched civil liberties and civil rights. MacLeish predicted Frankfurter would do likewise, a point of view shared by Yale law professor Walton Hamilton: "Frankfurter defends Holmes and Cardozo alike when they elevate the authority of the legislature above freedom of contract, yet make it yield before freedom of speech."

MacLeish, Hamilton, and other observers made the faulty assumption that Holmes and Brandeis shared a common vision about civil liberties and that Frankfurter stood shoulder to shoulder with them. In fact, Brandeis displayed far more regard for individual rights in the First Amendment area and elsewhere than Holmes, who treasured civil liberties far less than legislative discretion to regulate a splintered, fractious society. And before joining the Court, Frankfurter usually sided with Holmes. He backed the latter's dissent in *Meyer v. Nebraska* (1923), when the majority, including Brandeis, struck down a law that prohibited public school instruction in the German language. Holmes's position, he noted to Learned Hand, might encourage legislative attacks against "despised minorities," but "we are back at the old issue of the denial of power because of the potentiality of its abuse."

Two years later, he again sided with Holmes when the other justices invalidated an Oregon statute intended to ban education in private, church-run schools. Writing in *The New Repub-*

lic under the heading, "Can the Supreme Court Guarantee Toleration?" Frankfurter concluded in the negative. "We expect our Courts to do it all," he lamented. Had Frankfurter's supporters paid closer attention to his pre-Court views about judicial power and civil liberties, they would not have been so shocked by his later stand in similar cases. He remained throughout his life a quintessential Bull Moose progressive, who believed in strong, energetic government to promote the general welfare. He read from the book of Rousseau, not Locke, a classical republican who placed the interests of the commonwealth above private rights, economic or otherwise.

As a young lawyer fresh from Harvard Law School in 1906, Felix Frankfurter joined the Wall Street firm of Hornblower, Byrne, Miller and Potter. Soon after his arrival, a senior partner suggested that he might rise faster there if he anglicized his name. Recalling his mother's admonition to "always hold yourself dear," he politely but firmly refused. Later in life, as a justice of the United States Supreme Court, he expressed anger when told that one of his former Jewish students, faced with the same decision, had chosen to do otherwise. Although a descendant of several generations of Central European rabbis, he seldom set foot in a synagogue or temple after adolescence and usually described himself as a "reverent agnostic."

Much to his mother's chagrin, he married a Congregational minister's daughter. He followed Brandeis into the Zionist crusade more out of fealty to the former than out of deep devotion to the latter. He insisted that his funeral be conducted without a rabbi, but wanted the *kaddish*, the ritual prayer for the dead, read by a former law clerk, a practicing, orthodox Jew. "I came into this world a Jew and although I did not live my life entirely as a Jew," he told playwright Garson Kanin, "I think it is fitting that I should leave as a Jew."

Of all the justices who ever served on the Supreme Court of the United States, Felix Frankfurter, it can be argued, was both the least and the most influenced by his ethno-cultural heritage. Among the most secular of our jurists, he displayed an almost Enlightenment faith in the powers of reason. But he was also, in the shrewd

Felix Frankfurter
Photograph by Harris and Ewing.
Collection of the Supreme Court of the United States.

assessment of one recent scholar, "first and fore-most a teacher in the rabbinic style," who relished "complexities, balanced truths, entertained questions, and understood puzzles."

Instead of the Torah, however, he quoted copiously and endlessly from the opinions of Holmes and Brandeis, much to the annoyance of his brethren on the bench. "We would have been inclined to agree with Felix more often in conference," Justice William Brennan once remarked, "if he quoted Holmes less frequently to us."

A Jew, an immigrant, and a naturalized citizen, Felix Frankfurter never attempted to conceal these attributes, but his own journey from New York's Lower East Side to the Supreme Court of the United States shaped his almost mystical faith in assimilation, in the transforming powers of American culture, especially public education, to forge what St. Jean de Crevecoeur had called in 1782 "the American . . . a new man . . . who leaving behind him all his ancient prejudices and manners, receives new ones from the new mode of life he has embraced, the new government he obeys, and the new rank he holds. . . . Here individuals of all nations are melted down into a new race of men, whose labors and posterity will one day cause great changes in the world. . . ."

Frankfurter's robust belief in cultural assimilation, in the melting pot, in the ideal of a meritocratic social order where talent, brains, and energy counted for more than race, religion, or class led him to employ the Court's first black law clerk in 1948, William Coleman, Jr. And it inspired perhaps his greatest contribution to American law: helping Chief Justice Earl Warren forge a unanimous Court to strike down segregated public schools in *Brown v. Board of Education* in 1954.

In addition to Coleman, he actively promoted the careers of other black lawyers, notably Charles H. Houston, the chief legal strategist of the NAACP, and William Hastie, the first black named to the federal bench by Roosevelt, and later dean of the Howard University Law School. But Frankfurter also wrote the Court's 1950 opinion in *Hughes v. Superior Court of California*, which upheld an injunction prohibiting blacks from picketing at supermarket in order to secure for them-selves a certain percentage of its jobs. California had no law against racial hiring quotas, but the local court and Frankfurter found the goals of the picketing to be inimical to the state's policy of nondiscrimination.

A longtime supporter of the NAACP's original program of nondiscrimination and the ideal of "a color-blind" legal order, Frankfurter did not move beyond that position during his lifetime. A decade after the *Hughes* case, as the civil rights struggle escalated in the South, Frankfurter expressed grave doubts about the militant tactics of young black college students and the court's response to the first sit-in demonstrations. In Louisiana and elsewhere, black protestors in department stores, theaters, amusement parks, and restaurants had been jailed for trespass on private property. Following a heated conference about one of these cases, he told Hugo Black, another skeptic: "It will not advance the cause of constitutional equality for Negroes for the court to be taking short cuts to discriminate as partisans in favor of Negroes or even to appear to do so."

Although felled by illness before the final decision in *NAACP v. Button* (1963), Frankfurter was prepared to sustain a Virginia law that forbade solicitation of clients by an agent of an organization that litigates cases in which it is not a party and has no pecuniary interest. The NAACP argued that the Virginia legislature had aimed the statute explicitly at their organization and other civil rights groups that advised persons about their legal rights and remedies. Frankfurter, however, argued "there's no evidence . . . this statute is aimed at Negroes as such," and he concluded, "I can't imagine a worse disservice than to continue being the guardians of Negroes." Aside from *Hughes*, he never faced the dilemma of affirmative action programs, but it does seem likely that his views would have been closer to those of Antonin Scalia than to Thurgood Marshall's.

The same commitment to assimilation, derived from his own successful experience as a Jew, an immigrant, and a naturalized citizen, had other less happy consequences, as well. Who can doubt that they profoundly shaped his views in *Meyer v. Nebraska* (1923) and *Pierce v. Society of Sisters* (1925) before he joined the Court, or in *Gobitis v. Minersville School District* (1940) at the start of his judicial career, and *Braunfeld v. Brown* near its end?

In *Gobitis*, the first flag salute case, he affirmed the power of school officials to compel children to salute the flag against the claims of a religious minority that such coerced participation violated the free exercise of their faith. In *Braunfeld*, he concurred in rejecting claims that Sunday closing laws were both a forbidden establishment of religion and an interference with religious liberty. In Felix Frankfurter's universe, secular public policies and rituals, when backed by a strong popular consensus, always trumped narrow sectarian religious beliefs, however passionately held. Neither Jehovah's Witnesses nor Orthodox Jews, he believed, could escape the common burdens and shared responsibilities of American citizenship.

Like most mortals, Felix Frankfurter was a person of paradox and contradiction, someone who frequently acted and thought in ways that were not always consistent. Warm, charming, and supportive with his law clerks, he could be rude, abrasive, and petty with his brethren on the Court. Because of his intimate relationship with Justice Brandeis, probably no person came to the Court with greater inside information about how that institution functioned and about the importance of collegial relations among its members. Yet he failed to put what he knew into practice. Always critical of those like Justice Black who read constitutional provisions in absolute terms, he could be a strict constructionist when it came to issues of church and state or the Fourth Amendment. No one denounced with more fervor the extrajudicial activities of his colleagues, while himself engaging furiously in off-the-bench politics and policy making.

Frankfurter's extrajudicial political activities, especially during the Second World War, require some extended discussion, because they raise troubling questions about his fidelity to the important principle of the separation of powers. He was not, of course, the first sitting justice to dabble behind the scenes in the affairs of the legislative and executive branches. John Jay advised President George Washington on his

State of the Union address and served as a commissioner of the mint. Under various pseudonyms, the great John Marshall pilloried his Jeffersonian critics in the press. Joseph Story drafted federal bankruptcy legislation and encouraged friends in Congress to sponsor it. Roger Taney helped pen Jackson's message vetoing the recharter of the Second Bank of the United States.

But even in light of these historical precedents, Frankfurter's extrajudicial efforts were unusual in scope and volume. They have no parallel until the Abe Fortas-Lyndon Johnson relationship during the 1960s. Frankfurter assisted White House lawyers with the drafting of the executive agreement that transferred American destroyers to England in exchange for leases on British naval bases. He authored sections of the Lend-Lease Act and suggested to congressional allies that it bear the title of H.R. 1776. Fortunately for Frankfurter, legal issues touching on these matters never came before the justices. The same cannot be said of his role in the famous case of the Nazi saboteurs.

In the summer of 1942, the German government landed eight saboteurs at locations on Long Island and Florida with the assignment of blowing up bridges, factories, and other military installations. The scheme failed miserably. The saboteurs and their few American confederates were quickly apprehended by local police, the FBI, and military intelligence. President Roosevelt ordered them tried by a special military tribunal. He also issued a proclamation closing the federal courts to any enemy alien then in custody on charges of sabotage. Seeking advice on how to constitute the military tribunal, Secretary of War Henry L. Stimson consulted his old protégé, Felix Frankfurter, who recommended that it be composed solely of regular officers and exclude any civilian leaders from the department. Justice Frankfurter also took Stimson's side when the secretary became embroiled in an argument with Attorney General Francis Biddle over permitting press coverage of the trial. Frankfurter opted for secrecy.

Henry Stimson's diary entries probably reveal only a fraction of Frankfurter's conversations with him about the saboteurs' case. It seems very likely that the justice also discussed the issues regularly with John McCloy, his newest confidant in the War Department, who lived near Frankfurter in Georgetown and who took walks with him regularly in the evening. Having helped the government structure its proceedings against the German spies, Frankfurter then became the most vigorous defender of the administration's position when the accused sought judicial relief in the federal courts. Frankfurter played a major role in shaping Chief Justice Harlan F. Stone's opinion that rejected their *habeas corpus* plea and sealed their fate in *Ex parte Quirin* (1942).

Frankfurter's extrajudicial activities ended abruptly with Roosevelt's death in 1945 and the conclusion of the war, when he lost access to both the White House and key agencies of the executive branch. They resumed briefly but significantly during the long struggle over school desegregation in the Eisenhower years, when he regularly advised his former clerk, Philip Elman, then in the office of the solicitor general, about the administration's strategy in both *Brown I* and *Brown II*.

Were Frankfurter present today to defend his actions during the war and the desegregation cases, he would no doubt claim that he only stepped over the bounds of judicial neutrality on behalf of two noble causes: defeating Nazi Germany and assuring an effective strategy for ending racial segregation in the public schools. His critics might respond that Mr. Justice Frankfurter, normally uncompromising when it came to questions of process, seldom argued that the ends justified the means. Or, at the very least, they would wish he had displayed more charity toward those of his judicial colleagues who dabbled, often less effectively than he, in affairs beyond the Court.

His law clerks called him affectionately, "The Little Judge." Most of them recalled Frankfurter bouncing (he apparently never walked) down the corridors of the Supreme Court building while he whistled (usually off key) "Stars and Stripes Forever," the sextet from "Lucia di Lammermoor," or the adagio from Mozart's great clarinet quintet. Bursting into their office after a long conference with the other justices,

he regaled them with amusing stories about the behavior of his brethren: when Justice Stanley F. Reed, nicknamed "Dopey," said something especially absurd; when Justice Charles E. Whittaker, unable to make up his mind, switched his vote for the third time; or how Chief Justice Warren, grappling with the issue of the foreseeability of lightning in a torts case, finally threw up his hands in despair and said: "Oh, hell, how can I know if it's foreseeable? I don't know that much about lightning. We don't have much lightning in California!"

Dean Acheson, who often walked to work with Justice Frankfurter in the early 1950s, spoke of "the general noisiness of the man," an opinion shared by Court staff and clerks who often heard his voice piercing above others from the justices' private conference room. Just being Felix Frankfurter, wrote one journalist, "is in itself a violent form of exercise."

He often tested his clerks' intellectual mettle by goading them into long arguments over legal history, current events, constitutional doctrine, and music: name ten milestones in Anglo-American law and defend your choices. Who was Home Secretary in the Atlee government? Who was the greater composer, Bartok or Bruch? To win these debates, he did not hesitate to intimidate his younger opponents by invoking his seniority or his intimate knowledge of the persons and events under discussion. Sometimes sensing defeat, he would bolt from the office in disgust, leaving a shaken clerk behind. But next morning, within earshot of the same clerk, he would tell his secretary: "Wasn't that a terrific argument last night? Wasn't Al just great. Did you hear what he said to me?"

With less affection, attorneys who appeared before the Supreme Court from the late 1930s until the early 1960s recalled how Frankfurter peppered them with vexing questions. Perched forward on his high-backed chair, looking at times like a brittle, bespectacled, irritated sparrow, he turned the proceedings into a law school seminar. He could be especially brutal in his interrogation of former students and clerks, who often became targets for their mentor's display of judicial impartiality. "How," he asked one lawyer about a jurisdictional issue, "did you get to our Court?" "I came in on the Baltimore & Ohio, Mr. Justice," was the befuddled reply.

For twenty-three years on the bench, in chambers, and in conference, Frankfurter's judicial colleagues suffered his wit, learning, vanity, and fury. "If you had gone to the Harvard Law School," he once quipped to the brilliant Robert Jackson, "there would have been no stopping you." Chief Justice Fred Vinson, he noted, had made only two contributions to the rhetoric of jurisprudence: the expressions "for my money" and "in my book." During one heated exchange with Earl Warren, he shouted: "Be a judge, God damn it, be a judge."

After another tense conference battle, Justice Black told his son: "I thought Felix was going to hit me today, he got so mad." No doubt speaking for others, Warren told a friend, wearily: "All Frankfurter does is talk, talk, talk. He drives you crazy." "When I came into this conference," Justice Douglas said on one occasion, "I agreed in the conclusion that Felix has just announced, but he's talked me out of it."

His first law clerk and longtime friend, the late Joseph L. Rauh, Jr., once observed that Felix Frankfurter's historical reputation would have been more secure had he never served on the Supreme Court of the United States. It is difficult to imagine that statement being made about many of the other 107 individuals nominated and confirmed for our nation's highest judicial tribunal since 1789. For virtually all of them, service on the Supreme Court became the capstone of a career and the arena of public life that most clearly defined their place in American history. But for his tenure on the Supreme Court, John Marshall would be remembered as simply another diplomat and secretary of state; Roger Taney as a partisan politician and treasury secretary; Hugo Black as a loyal New Deal senator from Alabama; Earl Warren as a moderately progressive three-term governor and vice-presidential candidate; and William J. Brennan as an able appellate jurist from New Jersey.

History, often unsympathetic to those on the losing side, has not been kind to Mr. Justice Frankfurter. The publication of his Court diaries and letters in the 1970s revealed a man of enormous insecurities, one frequently consumed and crippled by anger, vanity, and self-pity. Apart from Justice James McReynolds, it is difficult to recollect a member of the Court who had worse personal relations with his colleagues.

There is now almost universal scholarly consensus that Frankfurter, the justice, was a failure, a jurist who, in Joseph Lash's memorable phrase, became "uncoupled from the locomotive of history" sometime during World War II and left little in the way of an enduring doctrinal legacy. He would have made a superb contribution to the Court in an earlier era when its rampant activism often thwarted the creation of the modern welfare state, but his brand of judicial restraint became an anachronism when the nation's agenda shifted to the expansion of civil rights and civil liberties. Like the judicial conservatives of the New Deal years, Frankfurter saw many of his cherished constitutional structures demolished during his own lifetime—notably in the case of the exclusionary rule and legislative reapportionment. And unlike the two jurists he admired most—Holmes and Brandeis—his dissents assumed less significance over time.

Frankfurter's appointment in 1939 simply confirmed the triumph of New Deal jurisprudence, especially its deference to social and economic legislation. His retirement in 1962, however, fundamentally altered the course of constitutional development. When Arthur Goldberg took Frankfurter's seat, he gave Chief Justice Warren a dependable fifth vote and opened the most expansive era in the Court's defense of civil rights and civil liberties. In pending cases that challenged portions of the Immigration and Nationality Act in *Kennedy v. Mendoz-Martinez* (1962) and *Rusk v. Cort* (1962), the contempt powers of the House Un-American Activities Committee in *Russell v. United States* (1962), and the authority of Florida to compel certain disclosures by the NAACP in *Gibson v. Florida Legislative Investigation Committee* (1963), Frankfurter had been prepared to sustain the government in each instance. Goldberg tipped the balance in the other direction.

In the following decade, a majority of the justices spurned virtually all of Frankfurter's views on justiciability, political questions, due process, incorporation, and the speech clause of the First Amendment. Many of the neo-conservatives who resisted the new judicial activism in the 1970s and 1980s attempted simultaneously to claim him as their own, but had great difficulty doing so in view of Frankfurter's defense of government economic regulation, his frequent stance against capital punishment, and his near-absolute position on both the Fourth Amendment and the establishment clause. He became almost a jurist without jurisprudential progeny.

When seeking to reconstruct Frankfurter's judicial world, scholars have employed a range of intellectual tools. Conventional legal analysis stresses his links to a tradition of judicial restraint from James Bradley Thayer to Holmes and Brandeis. Those who have utilized social-psychological or social-cultural explanations emphasize his immigrant background, unresolved identity crisis, and desire for acceptance by a Protestant establishment symbolized by Harvard, Henry Stimson, Holmes, and Franklin Roosevelt. Robert Burt offers the most severe indictment. In his view, Frankfurter was the Jewish insider, the parvenu who "struggled against acknowledging his outcast status . . . and always remained homeless in spite of himself." By failing to accept his own marginal status, Burt concludes, "Frankfurter lost all sympathy for outsiders anywhere."

That judgment is probably unduly harsh and reductionist. It fails to take into account numerous instances in Frankfurter's judicial career where, despite having reached the pinnacle of "insider" status, he manifested deep sympathy for outsiders and outcasts—most notably in his sustained opposition to capital punishment from the case of *Chambers v. Florida* in 1940 to *Culombe v. Connecticut* two decades later. Arthur Culombe, a thirty-three-year-old illiterate with a mental age of nine who had been in trouble with the law since adolescence, had been convicted of murder and sentenced to death on the basis of a confession secured after five days of continuous and isolated interrogation by the police. No one can read Frankfurter's concurring opinion reversing this conviction without sensing both his outrage at the police tactics and his sympathy for Arthur Culombe.

Even more revealing is Frankfurter's dissenting opinion in the little-noted capital murder

case from the District of Columbia in 1947, *Fisher v. United States.* The defendant, a Negro janitor, had been convicted and sentenced to death for killing his white employer during an argument and brawl. Led by Justice Reed, the Court majority affirmed this conviction, despite powerful evidence that Fisher had been provoked, fought in self-defense, and that the trial judge had failed to properly instruct the jury on the issue of premeditation. Frankfurter's scathing dissent noted the judge's incompetence, highlighted the long history of conflict between Fisher and his boss, and stressed that the fight had started when the employer called Fisher "a black nigger." This section of the opinion outraged the other justices, who urged Frankfurter to delete the racial slur from his opinion. He refused. President Truman also refused to commute Fisher's death sentence, despite a personal appeal from the justice.

Time and again over the course of his judicial career, Frankfurter spoke out in capital cases where outsiders faced execution under circumstances that suggested to him their accusers had played fast and loose with the basic rules of criminal justice—notably in the cases of Julius and Ethel Rosenberg, convicted atomic spies, and Caryl Chessman, California's alleged "red light" bandit.

Finally, one should note several instances during the Warren years where resident aliens, accused of subversive activities, faced deportation by the government of the United States. One might have expected the insider, parvenu justice to don his patriotic attire and sanction the government's conduct. But in *Carlson v. Landon* (1952), Frankfurter dissented against the proposition that Congress could deny bail to five alien Communists pending a final decision. And in *Rowoldt v. Perfetto* (1957), he provided the fifth and decisive vote to reverse the deportation of an elderly Jewish alien who had briefly joined the Communist party in the 1930s. Earl Warren, ironically, always pointed to *Rowoldt* as an example of Frankfurter's failure to practice judicial restraint when his personal sympathies got the better of him! "I think Frankfurter is capable of a human instinct now and then," Warren told one of his clerks. "Frankfurter really obviously just felt sorry for this poor old immigrant. . . . I think Frankfurter may well have thought that there but for the grace of God go I."

While virtually all of his important constitutional decisions failed to survive the judicial revolution of the 1960s and 1970s, Frankfurter left us a number of critical legacies that merit emphasis in the 1990s—the importance of judicial restraint in a democratic society, the value of federalism, the necessity for the Court to articulate an evolving conception of due process, and a passionate belief in the role of the courts and in something called the rule of law.

Courts, he told us, are not the only or the primary institutions of government in this society. They could not, he often repeated, guarantee toleration where that spirit had withered among the people at large. If his greatest failing on the Court was an all-too-eager deference to majorities, it sprang from a unique historical context where the judiciary had for decades thwarted the popular will and from a passionate belief in the virtues of self-education through the trial-and-error of messy democratic politics. The pre-New Deal judiciary often confused disputes over policy with debates over constitutional fundamentals. Reacting to those judicial excesses, Frankfurter sometimes forgot that the Constitution does articulate basic values and that it is the duty of the Court to give preference to them over the competing policy choices of transitory majorities.

As one of FDR's closest advisers, he eagerly embraced the social and economic reforms of the New Deal. But among post-New Deal justices, he became something of a rarity in resisting the spirit of economic nationalism that would have swept away state regulatory power under the broad banner of the commerce clause. He did not believe, for example, that Congress intended to oust the states from their primary role in policing the insurance industry or managing the underwater resources of the outer continental shelf. His judicial brethren scorned these views, but Congress confirmed them in later legislation. He rejected the notion that the marketing of milk required a single, uniform national rule. He sought to preserve the fiscal integrity of the states by demolishing the vast array of tax immunities erected by judicial decisions.

Frankfurter's robust state-centered federalism was vividly demonstrated in cases touching the interpretation of state laws and state constitutions by local courts. "The state courts belong to the States," he wrote in *Flornoy v. Wiener* (1944). "Not only do we not review a case from a state court that can rest on a purely state ground, but we do not even review state questions in a case that is properly here from a state court on a federal ground." Of course, such deference to federalism can perpetuate injustice, but civil libertarians and environmentalists who today look to state courts and state constitutional provisions to defend individual rights and save local resources by invoking "independent state grounds" owe a debt to Felix Frankfurter.

Long identified with the ideal of judicial restraint, Frankfurter was, in fact, an activist when it came to the due process clause, where he believed the Court had a special constitutional obligation to articulate the community's evolving moral consensus toward more civilized standards of conduct and human relations.

"Due process of law," he wrote in *Wolf v. Colorado* (1949), "conveys neither formal nor fixed nor narrow requirements. It is the compendious expression for all those rights which the courts must enforce because they are basic to our free society. But basic rights do not become petrified as of any one time, even though, as a matter of human experience, some may not too rhetorically be called eternal verities. It is of the very nature of a free society to advance in its standards of what is deemed reasonable and right. Representing as it does a living principle, due process is not confined within a permanent catalogue of what may at a given time be deemed the limits or the essentials of fundamental rights."

His great constitutional adversary, Justice Black, who wished to cabin due process within the specific boundaries of the Bill of Rights, denounced Frankfurter's approach as dangerously subjective: "this stretching-contracting meaning of due process" or "the accordion-like meaning of due process." Black feared it would produce a judicial despotism reminiscent of the pre-New Deal Court. But Frankfurter's more open-ended, evolutionary approach to due process allowed him to strike down racial segregation in the District of Columbia, even without an equal protection clause in the Fifth Amendment, and it did not run aground when the Court was called upon to vindicate rights not explicitly catalogued in the Bill of Rights. Here, Frankfurter's approach to due process, carried on by Justice John Harlan, and more recently reaffirmed in the Pennsylvania abortion decision (*Planned Parenthood of Southeastern Pennsylvania v. Casey*, 1993), has helped to advance the revolution in human rights.

Frankfurter, the apostle of judicial restraint, nonetheless claimed for the judiciary an activist role with respect to due process. And here one perceives another major contradiction in his conception of the institutional function of courts in American society. He preached *ad nauseam* the virtues of judicial restraint and judicial humility with respect to legislative policy choices and ultimate constitutional questions. At the same time, he possessed one of the most exalted conceptions of the judiciary's competence and importance of any jurist in the modern era.

He seldom voted to invalidate a legislative choice. But he also rarely reversed a judicial contempt order. That power, he wrote in *Offutt v. United States* (1954), "is a mode of vindicating the majesty of law." In conflicts between the press and the courts, disputes that usually pitted the First Amendment against the Fifth or Sixth Amendments, he normally sided with the judges. And he reserved his greatest scorn for judges—Webster Thayer in the Sacco-Vanzetti case, Harold Medina in the Smith Act prosecutions, Irving Kaufman in the Rosenberg trial—who dropped the veil of judicial impartiality to engage in blatant political partisanship. They destroyed confidence in "the majesty of the law" as surely as reckless newspapers during a murder trial, defiant mine workers who ignored judicial decrees, or blacks engaged in massive civil disobedience.

Shortly before his final illness in 1962, Frankfurter attended a performance of Robert Bolt's play about Thomas More, *A Man for All Seasons*. He sat with Garson Kanin, Ruth Gordon, and Howard Beale, the Australian ambassador to the United States. At a crucial moment in the drama, More warns his future son-in-law, William Roper, not "to cut a great road through the law to get after the Devil." When Roper insists that the ends may sometimes justify the

means, More snaps back: "Oh? And when the last law was down, and the Devil turned round on you—where would you hide, Roper, the laws being flat? Yes, I'd give the Devil benefit of law, for my own safety's sake."

According to Beale, Frankfurter was enthralled by the speech and kept jabbing him in the ribs.

"That's the point!" he said. "That's it, that's it!"

Indeed, that was the final point for Justice Frankfurter, a true romantic, who could speak without irony about something called "the majesty of the law." He never accepted the proposition of legal realists that law was simply a manifestation of arbitrary human desires, perhaps the residue of what a particular judge had for breakfast or lunch. And he surely scorned the Fascist or Communist notion that law came from the barrel of a gun.

Sometimes, in pursuit of this ideal—the rule of law—Felix Frankfurter defied the better angels of his own nature. The results could be disastrous, as they were in the flag salute cases, or his concurrence in *Dennis v. United States* (1951), affirming the conviction of American Communists under the Smith Act. Sometimes, off the bench, temporarily shedding his judicial robes, he did not always practice what he preached. He aspired to be Thomas More, but he sometimes acted like William Roper, ready "to cut a great road through the law to get after the Devil," especially when the Devil happened to be the Nazi regime or racial segregation. But the alternative to that ideal—no rule of law and a judiciary swept away by a blind faith in its own rectitude—could be equally fatal to the health of a democratic society. That, too, Felix Frankfurter knew.

—MICHAEL E. PARRISH

BIBLIOGRAPHY

Felix Frankfurter's pre-Court papers are housed at the Library of Congress, and his judicial papers are available at the Harvard Law Library. Several volumes of Frankfurter's essays have been edited; see Archibald MacLeish and E.F. Pritchard, Jr., eds., *Law and Politics: Occasional Papers of Felix Frankfurter, 1913–*

1939 (1939); Philip H. Kurland, ed., *Felix Frankfurter on the Supreme Court: Extrajudicial Essays on the Court and the Constitution* (1970), and Philip Elman, ed., *Of Law and Men: Papers and Addresses of Felix Frankfurter, 1939–1956* (1956).

Melvin I. Urofsky has written the best short biography, *Felix Frankfurter: Judicial Restraint and Individual Liberties* (1992). On Frankfurter's pre-judicial career, see Michael E. Parrish, *Felix Frankfurter and His Times: The Reform Years* (1982). Two provocative psychological interpretations of Frankfurter are offered by Harry N. Hirsch, *The Enigma of Felix Frankfurter* (1981), and Robert A. Burt, *Two Jewish Justices: Outcasts in the Promised Land* (1988). Frankfurter offered an interpretation of his own

life in an oral memoir published as *Felix Frankfurter Reminisces* (1960), Harlan Philips, ed. His own diaries, focusing on the Court years, have been edited with an insightful introduction by Joseph P. Lash, ed., *From the Diaries of Felix Frankfurter* (1975).

For sympathetic accounts of Frankfurter's jurisprudence, see Sanford W. Levinson, "The Democratic Faith of Felix Frankfurter," 25 *Stanford Law Review* 430 (1973), and Mark Silverstein, *Constitutional Faiths: Felix Frankfurter, Hugo Black, and the Process of Judicial Decision-Making* (1984). Frankfurter's complex relationship with Hugo Black is well explored in James F. Simon, *The Antagonists: Hugo Black, Felix Frankfurter and Civil Liberties in Modern America* (1989).

Melville Weston Fuller
Photograph by Harris and Ewing.
Collection of the Supreme Court of the United States.

MELVILLE WESTON FULLER

BORN 11 February 1833, Augusta, Maine

NOMINATED to the Court 30 April 1888
by Grover Cleveland

TOOK seat 8 October 1888

DIED 4 July 1910 in Sorrento, Maine

After spending his childhood in Augusta, Maine, Melville Weston Fuller entered Bowdoin College in September of 1849. He was active in a debating society and pursued his strong interest in literature. Graduating from Bowdoin in 1853, Fuller promptly began his legal studies. As was then the common practice, he received most of his legal training by apprenticeship. In the fall of 1854, however, Fuller entered Harvard Law School, where he attended lectures for six months. Admitted to the Maine bar in 1855, Fuller moved back to Augusta and began to practice law with an uncle. Notwithstanding advantageous family contacts in Augusta, Fuller abruptly decided to move to Chicago in 1856. Like many New Englanders of his generation, Fuller felt that Chicago, which was emerging as the commercial center of the middle west, offered attractive business and professional opportunities.

On his arrival in Chicago, Fuller formed a series of short-lived partnerships with other attorneys. Although he appeared regularly in court and earned recognition as a skillful appellate advocate, Fuller found it difficult to establish a financially successful law practice. Fuller also became active in Democratic party politics and was a supporter of Stephen A. Douglas. The outbreak of the Civil War put Fuller in an awkward political position. Loyal to the Union, he favored military action to crush secession. At the same time, Fuller opposed abolitionism and grew increasingly unhappy about the Lincoln administration's conduct of war. Fuller did not serve in the military. Instead, he was elected to the Illinois constitutional convention of 1862 and also served in the Illinois house of representatives during the 1863 legislative session. He supported a proposed state constitutional amendment to deny blacks the right to vote,

denounced the Emancipation Proclamation, and assailed Lincoln's suspension of *habeas corpus*. Notwithstanding this controversial political record, Fuller excelled in establishing harmonious personal relations with persons of diverse legal and political views. He was possessed of a genial nature, with an urbane sense of humor and unfailing courtesy.

Fuller's professional status was substantially enhanced by each of his two marriages. He inherited land in Chicago from his first wife, who died after six years of marriage. In May of 1866, Fuller married Mary Ellen Coolbaugh. Her father was a wealthy banker and president of the Union National Bank, the largest financial institution in Chicago. Aided by his father-in-law's contacts, Fuller developed a large and successful practice focused on real estate and corporate law. He began to represent the Union National Bank, and frequently appeared on behalf of other Illinois banks. In addition, Fuller defended railroad companies in personal injury litigation arising out of railroad accidents. Although Fuller increasingly appeared on behalf of Chicago's business elite, he also served as counsel for municipal bodies such as the South Park commissioners. Similarly, he handled various legal matters for the city of Chicago, including the famous case involving ownership of lakefront land along Lake Michigan.

In time, Fuller became one of the busiest attorneys in Chicago, trying approximately 2,500 cases during his career. He was also a skillful appellate advocate; in 1872, he argued his first of many cases before the United States Supreme Court. Before his appointment to the bench, Fuller had a wide experience with many diverse fields of law. Fuller secured professional recognition as well as financial success, and was elected president of the Illinois State Bar Association in 1886.

The death of Chief Justice Morrison R. Waite in March of 1888 opened the door for Fuller's surprise appointment to the nation's top judicial post. After considering other individuals, President Grover Cleveland, the first Democrat in that office since the Civil War, selected Fuller as chief justice. Fuller was an enthusiastic backer of the Cleveland administration and the president had consulted Fuller concerning the distribution of political patronage in Illinois. Indeed, Cleveland had earlier unsuccessfully asked Fuller to accept the post of solicitor general. With his strong ties to Chicago, Fuller was reluctant to accept the nomination to the Court, but he acquiesced to the president's wishes. The Republican-controlled Judiciary Committee delayed action on Fuller's nomination for months in the hope of preventing a confirmation vote until after the upcoming presidential election. In July 1888, however, after a brief debate which centered on Fuller's conduct during the Civil War, the Senate confirmed the appointment by a vote of 41–20.

By any standard, Fuller was eminently successful as a judicial administrator. His initial task was to exert leadership over his colleagues. A likeable man, Fuller soon succeeded in establishing warm personal relations and proved a masterful social leader of the Court. Despite sharp divisions in some important cases and inevitable personality conflicts, Fuller's skills as a mediator prevented destructive personal feuds. As part of his effort to foster harmonious working relations, Fuller introduced the practice of requiring each justice to shake hands with the other justices before hearing arguments or meeting in conference. He hoped that this custom, which has endured to the present, would minimize personal rifts among the justices.

Fuller also skillfully managed the Supreme Court's business. He expedited the handling of cases, and presided with dignity over public sessions and oral arguments. Fuller's easy manners and genial temperament served him well in managing judicial conferences. He softened differences among the justices and used humor to dispel tension.

As chief justice, Fuller was responsible for assigning the preparation of opinions when he was in the majority. Early in his tenure Fuller kept some of the major opinions, such as *Pollock v. Farmers' Loan and Trust Co.* (1895), for himself. Thereafter, he generally assigned significant cases to others. This assignment policy reflected Fuller's self-effacing nature, as well as his desire to promote judicial harmony. There is no evidence that Fuller used assignments to reward or punish colleagues for their views. An indefatigable worker, Fuller shouldered far more than his share of opinions for the Court. He tended to author unglamorous opinions dealing with jurisdictional and procedural matters, or commercial transactions. Like many of his colleagues, Fuller's prose style was verbose and diffuse. He wrote only a handful of dissenting opinions, and these usually came in cases where Fuller sought to protect state autonomy from federal encroachment.

When Fuller became chief, the operations of the Supreme Court were hampered by an antiquated federal court structure and a staggering workload. Fuller helped to secure passage of the 1891 Evarts Act establishing the modern circuit courts of appeals system. In so doing, he demonstrated effective political skills and became the first chief justice to lobby Congress for legislation reforming the federal judicial system. Fuller also ably discharged a variety of extrajudicial duties, and twice served as a member of arbitration panels dealing with international disputes.

Fuller led the Supreme Court during an era of sweeping social and economic transformation. The growth of large-scale corporate enterprise, rapid urbanization, and the emergence of a national market posed vexing questions for the Court. Fuller did not have a systematic judicial philosophy when he became chief. He was markedly influenced, however, by the Jacksonian political legacy with its insistence on limited government, preservation of states' rights, and opposition to paternalism. Fuller's success in the practice of law reinforced his acceptance of such principles. Hence, the key to understanding Fuller's judicial outlook is his persistent attachment to Jacksonian principles. He exemplifies the link between Jacksonian democracy and the emergence of laissez-faire constitutionalism in the late nineteenth century.

Faith in state autonomy, dedication to the rights of property owners, and attachment to free trade among the states formed the cornerstone of Fuller's constitutional thought. He was, therefore, prepared to read national power broadly in order to protect economic rights under the due process clause of the Fourteenth Amendment and the dormant commerce power. Still, Fuller was willing to allow the states wide latitude in shaping social policy with respect to race relations, criminal justice, and public morals.

Fuller's reverence for private property was a crucial ingredient of his jurisprudence. Like many nineteenth-century Americans, Fuller regarded the right to acquire, possess, use, and transfer property as among the most important individual liberties. Freedom was defined largely in economic terms. Fuller was convinced that the Constitution and Bill of Rights erected barriers against majoritarian rule to protect economic liberty. Moreover, Fuller believed that private property and other types of individual liberty were inseparable. Respect for property rights, therefore, safeguarded individuals by limiting the reach of legitimate government authority. Under Fuller's leadership, the Court sought to protect private property as a personal right. Anchoring this commitment to property ownership was Fuller's awareness of the vital role of investment capital in the economic transformation of the United States. He was eager to safeguard capital formation and to facilitate the development of a national market.

The chief issues before the Court during Fuller's tenure concerned the rights of property owners and the extent to which Congress or the states could control economic activity. Throughout the nineteenth century the justices had defended property and contractual rights from legislative infringement. But the appointment of Fuller as chief justice marked a dramatic shift in the formulation of constitutional doctrine. The Fuller Court took an activist role in protecting the rights of property owners, striking down both federal and state economic legislation. In so doing, Fuller had no trouble supporting a host of bold constitutional innovations. Thus, the Court adopted a substantive interpretation of the due process clause in *Chicago, Milwaukee & St. Paul Railway Co. v. Minnesota* (1890), fashioned the novel liberty of contract doctrine in *Allgeyer v. Louisiana* (1897), and placed constitutional limits on rate regulation in *Smyth v. Ames* (1898).

Fuller provided the fifth vote for *Lochner v. New York* (1905) in which the Court struck down a state statute regulating the hours of labor in bakeries as an interference with the liberty of contract. The rationale of *Lochner* made the Court the overseer of state regulatory laws.

Likewise, Fuller favored an expansive use of injunctions by federal courts in order to secure effectively property rights. Thus, he joined his associates in upholding a ground-breaking injunction against interference by strikers with interstate commerce in *In re Debs* (1895), and in affirming the issuance of injunctions to prevent state officials from enforcing unconstitutional laws in *Ex parte Young* (1908). In another important step, the justices in *Chicago, Burlington and Quincy Railroad Company v. Chicago* (1897) held that the just compensation requirement of the Fifth Amendment was an essential element of due process as guaranteed by the Fourteenth Amendment. Just compensation became, in effect, the first provision of the Bill of Rights to be applied to the states. This decision set the stage for the gradual extension of other provisions of the Bill of Rights in the twentieth century. In short, a profound commitment to property and private economic ordering gave a distinct cast to the jurisprudence of the Fuller years.

Yet Fuller was no doctrinaire adherent to laissez-faire philosophy. Fuller frequently invoked the state police power and sustained legislation which he perceived as protecting the health, safety, and morals of the public. For example, Fuller supported decisions which sustained state laws limiting the hours of employment in mines, mandating payment of wages in cash, and imposing licensure requirements on certain businesses. In *Muller v. Oregon* (1908) Fuller agreed that a state could restrict the working hours for women in factories and laundries. Despite its reputation as a conservative economic bastion, the Court under Fuller validated much more regulatory legislation than it overturned. In practice, the liberty of contract doctrine was employed sparingly.

Fuller was well aware that there was a political dimension to constitutional adjudication. In such sensitive areas as race relations and public morals, Fuller and his associates were disinclined to challenge popular attitudes. Even in the sharply contested economic terrain, where some of his rulings were assailed by Populists and Progressives, Fuller was usually in harmony with the dominant currents of political thought. Indeed, there was a forward-looking dimension to Fuller's handling of economic issues. Fuller identified with burgeoning industrial capitalism, and the Court, under his direction, was more receptive to the new realities of American economic life than many other sectors of the polity.

Overshadowed by such highly visible justices as Stephen J. Field and Oliver Wendell Holmes, Fuller never gained intellectual ascendancy over his colleagues. Yet he was adept at massing the Court behind zealous defense of the rights of property owners. Fuller exercised considerable leadership through informal consensus building.

Fuller authored relatively few of the leading constitutional decisions handed down during his tenure. Perhaps his most famous opinions were written in connection with *Pollock v. Farmers' Loan and Trust Co.* (1895) in which Fuller, speaking for a majority of five, invalidated the 1894 income tax. Distinguishing earlier authority which upheld the Civil War income tax, he ruled that an income levy was a direct tax, which under the Constitution had to be apportioned among the states according to population. Fuller was motivated in part to protect accumulated capital and to preserve the existing balance in state-federal relations. He instinctively realized that an income tax would expand federal revenue and power as well as portend further moves to reallocate wealth. Although Populists fiercely denounced the *Pollock* decision, there is evidence that the outcome was in line with public sentiment. Nor it is convincing to portray Fuller as a champion of the wealthy. He voted to sustain both state and federal inheritance taxes.

Fuller's handling of the commerce power reflected unresolved tensions between the needs of a national industrial market and the persistence of localism and state rights sentiments. He consistently championed free trade among the states and joined numerous decisions holding

that state regulations unreasonably burdened interstate commerce. At the same time, Fuller was reluctant to recognize broad congressional authority to regulate commerce.

In *United States v. E.C. Knight Company* (1895), the first case under the Sherman Antitrust Act to reach the Supreme Court, the justices accepted the constitutionality of the measure but restricted congressional power to prevent manufacturing monopolies. Speaking for a majority of eight justices, Fuller followed the established view that manufacturing was local in nature and subject to state control. He drew a sharp line between manufacturing and the sale of goods in interstate markets. The *E.C. Knight* decision narrowed the reach of the Sherman Act and hampered antitrust enforcement. To modern eyes there is an air of economic unreality about Fuller's opinion. His distinction between manufacturing and commerce appears to ignore the basic interdependence of economic activity.

But to Fuller, the issues transcended the threat of business consolidation and went to the very foundation of the constitutional scheme. Consistent with his dedication to a limited federal government, Fuller insisted that large areas of economic life remained outside the authority of Congress. He did not read the commerce clause as a comprehensive grant of power because such a step would upset the federal system and leave the states with little economic activity to control. If Fuller took a narrow view of congressional power, he nonetheless voted to apply the Sherman Act in several cases. Moreover, in *Swift and Company v. United States* (1905) Fuller supported the stream of commerce doctrine which extended the federal commerce power to local enterprises which were an integral part of interstate transactions. Despite this development, the line between manufacturing and commerce drawn by Fuller in *E.C. Knight* endured until the New Deal and the constitutional revolution of 1937.

Fuller could not consistently marshall a majority behind the principle of limited government. This was made evident in *Champion v. Ames* (1903), in which the justices, by a vote of 5–4, construed congressional commerce authority broadly to uphold legislation suppressing the interstate transportation of lottery tickets. In perhaps his best-known dissenting opinion, Fuller pointed out that Congress was, in effect, seeking to exercise a police power to regulate public morals. He argued that this was inconsistent with the intent of the framers, and threatened to upset the constitutional balance between the national and state governments.

One of Fuller's most far-reaching opinions came in *Loewe v. Lawlor* (1908). At issue was a private damage suit under the Sherman Act against union officials for instituting a secondary boycott against the plaintiff employer. Speaking for a unanimous court, Fuller maintained that the Sherman Act prohibited any combination which obstructed the free flow of commerce. Accordingly, the law applied to union activities. Although controversial with labor unions, who feared large damage suits, Fuller followed the prevailing view that the Sherman Act reached all combinations which restrained trade.

Despite his preoccupation with economic issues, Fuller also made contributions in other areas of law. He authored several opinions which helped to define the Supreme Court's original jurisdiction. In *Virginia v. West Virginia* (1907), Fuller concluded that the Supreme Court had jurisdiction over an original action by Virginia seeking to allocate part of its pre-Civil War debt to West Virginia. He occasionally demonstrated concern over civil liberties. Fuller filed an eloquent dissent in *Fong Yue Ting v. United States* (1893), arguing that the Constitution protected resident Chinese aliens against summary deportation. Again in dissent, Fuller contended in the insular cases that the Bill of Rights extended to overseas territories on their acquisition by the United States. Fuller joined the opinion in *Twining v. New Jersey* (1908), which intimated that some of the personal guarantees in the Bill of Rights might be effective against the states. This paved the way for eventual nationalization of procedural rights for criminal defendants. In addition, Fuller demonstrated sympathy for the plight of injured workers. He regularly voted to restrict application of the fellow servant rule, which protected employers from liability for injury to their workers. In *Johnson v. Southern Pacific Company*

(1904), Fuller insisted that the Safety Appliance Act should be liberally construed to secure the safety of railroad employees. Lastly, in *United States v. Shipp* (1909), he vigorously used the contempt power to punish law officers who connived in the lynching of a black prisoner despite the issuance of a stay pending appeal. This was the first instance of a contempt proceeding being instituted by the Supreme Court, and Fuller's ringing condemnation of this incident served to focus national attention on the practice of lynching.

Over time, many of Fuller's judicial achievements have been eclipsed. The nation no longer adheres to a constitutional order based on the principles of limited government, states' rights, and respect for private property. Thus, Fuller's attempts to cabin congressional tax and regulatory authority ultimately proved futile. Indeed, after a lacerating struggle over the New Deal program, the Supreme Court largely abandoned its longstanding concern with economic rights in 1937. To modern eyes, much of Fuller's handiwork seems to belong to another era.

For this reason, few scholars would place Fuller among the great justices. Yet Fuller left his mark on American jurisprudence and has perhaps received inadequate attention. He saw the federal judiciary as an active participant in governance and greatly strengthened its role in American life. Many of the doctrinal innovations associated with his name have continuing vitality. Contrary to popular conception, the Supreme Court has never really abandoned a substantive interpretation of the due process clause. The doctrine is currently employed as a safeguard for noneconomic rights rather than property interests. Expansive use of federal equity power in the late twentieth century has built upon precedent from the Fuller era. Further, many of the issues which predominated during Fuller's tenure—the reach of regulatory authority, the rights of property owners—have re-emerged in recent years. Renewed scholarly and judicial interest in economic rights suggest enduring recognition that property ownership and individual liberty are linked. Fuller was a major contributor to the ongoing debate over the place of property in American constitutional law.

—JAMES W. ELY, JR.

BIBLIOGRAPHY

The Fuller papers are divided between the Library of Congress and the Chicago Historical Society. The standard, although somewhat outdated, biography is Willard L. King, *Melville Weston Fuller: Chief Justice of the United States, 1888–1910* (1950); Fuller's leadership of the Court is also explored in Robert J. Steamer, *Chief Justice: Leadership and the Supreme Court* (1986), and Jeffrey B. Morris, "The Era of Melville Weston Fuller," 1981 *Yearbook of the Supreme Court Historical Society* 37.

Studies of the Court and its doctrine during the Fuller years include: Loren P. Beth, *The Development of the American Constitution, 1877–1917* (1971); David P. Currie, *The Constitution in the Supreme Court: The Second Century, 1888–1986* (1990); Arnold Paul, *Conservative Crisis and the Rule of Law: Attitudes of Bar and Bench, 1887–1895* (1960); and John E. Semonche, *Charting the Future: The Supreme Court Responds to a Changing Society, 1890–1920* (1978).

For studies focusing more on doctrinal issues, see James W. Ely, Jr., *The Guardian of Every Other Right: A Constitutional History of Property Rights* (1992); Herbert Hovenkamp, *Enterprise and American Law, 1836–1937* (1991); Paul Kens, *Judicial Power and Reform Politics: The Anatomy of Lochner v. New York* (1990).

RUTH JOAN BADER GINSBURG

BORN 15 March 1933, Brooklyn, New York

NOMINATED to the Court 14 June 1993
by Bill Clinton

TOOK seat 10 August 1993

When President Jimmy Carter nominated Ginsburg to the court of appeals for the District of Columbia in 1980, the American Bar Association rated her "exceptionally well qualified." Conservative Senator Strom Thurmond voted against her. Thirteen years later, on her nomination to the Supreme Court, he beamingly presented her with a pocket-sized Constitution.

Thurmond's gift was indicative of the solid reputation she had made as a highly competent, non-ideological judge who emphasized procedure and objectivity. Her approach was based on a firm commitment to popular democracy and protection of individual rights, a philosophy developed during her early years and honed as a young lawyer.

Ruth Bader, the daughter of a small clothing store owner, received her early education in the public schools of Brooklyn. A bright and outgoing student who was both a cheerleader and an editor of her high school newspaper, Bader was much influenced by the mother who took her to the public library and stressed the achievement and independence possible to citizens of a democracy. In 1950, however, her mother died of cancer after a four-year illness and a life spent in a society that denied her the access to a career available to men. Bader would accept nomination to the Court praying "that I may be all that she would have been had she lived in an age when women could aspire and achieve and daughters are cherished as much as sons."

Graduating Phi Beta Kappa from Cornell University in 1954, she married fellow prelaw student Martin Ginsburg, gave birth to a daughter, and entered Harvard Law School in 1956—one of nine women in a class of more than 500. She was chosen for the *Harvard Law Review*, but moved to New York when her husband got a job there. Continuing her legal education at Columbia, she became a member of its law review and graduated at the top of her class. In spite of high recommendations, Supreme Court Justice Felix Frankfurter would not hire her because she was a woman. Neither could she find a job with any New York law firm, a circumstance she attributed to her being a woman, a Jew, and a mother.

She clerked for district court judge Elmund Palmieri and then taught at the Rutgers Law School, where she wore her mother-in-law's larger clothing because she feared the school would fire her if it realized that she was pregnant with her second child. Rutgers granted her tenure in 1969.

Ginsburg began litigating gender discrimination cases while at Rutgers and continued to do so when she became Columbia's first tenured woman law professor in 1971, creating and directing the American Civil Liberties Union's Women's Rights Project. Between 1973 and 1976, she argued six major women's rights cases before the Supreme Court on behalf of the project, winning five of them—*Frontiero v. Richardson* (1973); *Edwards v. Healy* (1975); *Weinberger v. Weisenfeld* (1975); *Califano v. Goldfarb* (1977); and *Duren v. Missouri* (1979)—remaking the law of gender equality in the process.

Her opinions as a circuit judge reflected her conviction that majority rule worked best when most issues were left to the "political" branches of government. Rules regarding standing and access to the court system should be applied liberally, such as in *Loe v. Heckler* (1985) and *National Coal Association v. Lujan* (1992), so that the courts could fulfill their responsibility of acting when the people's elected representatives showed themselves unwilling to do so, or violated individual rights. Her approximately 350 opinions relied heavily on deference to precedent (*Save Our Cumberland Mountains v. Hodel*, 1987) and to Supreme Court rulings (*Mosrie v. Barry*, 1983, or *Quiban v. Veterans Administration*, 1991).

She nevertheless felt free to express her disagreement with it (*Mosrie v. Barry*, 1983) and

Ruth Joan Bader Ginsburg
Photograph by Richard Strauss, Smithsonian Institution.
Courtesy of the Supreme Court of the United States.

rejected the idea of "original intent" (*In re Sealed Case,* 1988). Her concurring opinions, such as in *Doe v. Casey* (1986), typically emphasized the areas of agreement between the majority and the dissenters, in keeping with her belief in dialogue as the key to both democracy and good judging. She was sufficiently open to new ideas, and to the people who held them, to call highly conservative judge Antonin Scalia "the best colleague I've ever had." Scalia returned the compliment by naming her as the legal figure with whom he would most want to be stranded on a desert island.

Judge Ginsburg's opinions suggested that affirmative action might be acceptable even without a showing of past discrimination (*O'Donnell v. District of Columbia,* 1992). She usually upheld the right of the individual in First Amendment cases, as in *Goldman v. Secretary of Defense* (1984) and *Petroleum Information Corporation v. Department of Interior* (1992). *Action for Children's Television v. FCC* (1988) demonstrated her tendency to support the government's power to regulate; *DKT Memorial Fund v. AID* (1989) was typical of her rejection of governmental power to limit the constitutional rights of those accepting government benefits. She decided so frequently for business in antitrust cases that the *Wall Street Journal* rejoiced at her nomination to the high court.

During hearings before the Senate Judiciary Committee at the time of her nomination to the Supreme Court, Ginsburg spoke approvingly of *Baker v. Carr* (1962), the reapportionment case, as an instance in which the courts had acted because of failure by the elected branches to do so, and expanded on some earlier criticism of *Roe v. Wade* (1973). Noting that by 1973 states had begun rethinking antiabortion statutes, she argued that the Court should have based its decision on equal protection grounds and struck down the overly restrictive antiabortion statute at issue as sexually discriminatory, without imposing a detailed scheme for regulating abortions at different points in a pregnancy. That would have enabled the dialogue in the states to continue, and society would have been able to reach a consensus. Ginsburg deplored the ambiguity of many statutes, however, and reiterated the position she had stated in law review articles that the

solution to the overcrowding of the Supreme Court's docket lay not in the creation of additional courts, but in a greater assumption of responsibility by legislatures. If the elected branches performed their jobs with precision and proper attention to the needs and constitutional rights of the people, the courts would be able to minimize their involvement in policy making.

Ginsburg had stated in a law review article that the greatest judges were "independent-thinking individuals with open but not drafty minds, individuals willing to listen and, throughout their days, to learn . . . above all, they have exhibited a readiness to reexamine their own premises." "They set a model," she wrote, "I strive to follow."

Ginsburg seemed to be adhering to this model during her first few months on the Supreme Court. The questions with which she peppered attorneys during oral arguments, her suggestions in oral argument and in concurring opinions of fully formed criteria for deciding cases, and her reliance in opinions on a wide reading of the legal literature reflected independence, a willingness to listen, and a clear sense of comfort with the demands of her new position.

One of the more convoluted cases decided during the October 1994 Term required the Court to define sexual harassment, which it had ruled was an aspect of employemnt discrimination forbidden by the Civil Rights Act of 1964 (*Meritor Savings Bank v. Vinson,* 1986). Lower courts subsequently had wrestled with *Meritor*'s definition of sexual harassment as an "abusive working environment" so "severe or persuasive" as to "alter the conditions" of the victim's employment. Attempting to apply that standard, a lower court had ruled that a plaintiff in a harassment suit had to prove that she suffered "severe psychological injury." Even the employer in the suit had rejected that criterion by the time *Harris v. Forklift Systems* (1993) reached the Supreme Court, but the briefs of the parties and amici demonstrated confusion over the appropriate standard.

Ginsburg perhaps relied upon her familiarity with gender discrimination cases when she suggested in oral argument that harassment could be defined simply as a situation in which "one sex has to put up with something that the other sex doesn't have to put up with." Justice Sandra Day O'Connor's opinion for the Court relied instead on the criterion of a work environment that "would reasonably be perceived, and is perceived, as hostile or abusive." In a brief concurrence, Ginsburg reiterated the standard she had enunciated during oral argument and indicated that she read the Court's decision as "in harmony" with her view.

She again concurred alone when the Court decided that two trial judges' definition of "reasonable doubt" as "an abiding conviction, to a moral certainty, of the truth of the charge" and "an actual and substantial doubt . . . as distinguished from a doubt arising from mere possibility" raised no due process problem (*Victor v. Nebraska,* 1994, and *Sandoval v. California,* 1994). Ginsburg suggested that other elements of the judges' charges were not acceptable and referred state courts to a definition of reasonable doubt proposed by the Federal Judicial Center. When the court held that the government's disclosure of home addresses of federal civil service employees to their collective bargaining union constituted a "clearly unwarranted invasion" of privacy under the Freedom of Information Act (*United States v. Federal Labor Relations Authority,* 1994), Ginsburg concurred alone to note that until a Supreme Court decision in 1989 (*Department of Justice v. Reporters Committee*), every court that considered the issue held that the Privacy Act did not bar disclosure. The Supreme Court held otherwise in 1989, finding such disclosure inconsistent with congressional intent in the Freedom of Information Act. Disagreeing that the Court's statutory interpretation then and in the FLRA case were necessarily correct and concerned that the decision "denied federal-sector unions information accessible to their private-sector counterparts," Ginsburg nonetheless deferred to a unanimouse court and to "the pull of precedent," which she agreed was "strongest in statutory cases." She hinted, however, that Congress might consider amending the FOIA.

Her opinions for the Court were primarily in areas of statutory construction (*Ratzlaf v.*

United States [1994]; *John Hancock v. Harris Trust & Savings Bank* [1993]; *Northwest Airlines v. County of Kent* [1994]; and *United States v. Granderson* [1994]). In a 1994 Fourth Amendment case, she reiterated and applied an earlier Court holding (*Griffith v. Kentucky,* 1987) that its decision about the conduct of criminal investigations was to be applied retroactively to all state and federal cases pending at the time of the decision (*Powell v. Nevada*).

Her opinions in general relied heavily on precedent. In most cases in which she did not write an opinion, she concurred with the majority. As she reached the halfway mark in her first term as a justice, her capability, conscientiousness, and intelligence were apparent. Unsurprisingly, the kind of judicial record she would create was not.

—PHILIPPA STRUM

BIBLIOGRAPHY

Ginsburg's thoughts about the role of the courts and their relationship to other branches of government are in "A Plea for Legislative Review," 60 *Southern California Law Review* 995 (1987); "Reflections on the independence, good behavior, and workload of federal judges," 55 *University of Colorado Law Review* 1 (1983); and "Inviting Judicial Activism: A 'Liberal' or Conservative Technique?" 15 *Georgia Law Review* 539 (1981). She discusses the role of concurring and dissenting opinions in "Styles of Collegial Judging," 39 *Federal Bar News & Journal* 199 (1992), and "Remarks on Writing Separately," 65 *Washington Law Review* 133 (1990).

Her view of the equal protection clause and privacy in litigation about gender equality and abortion can be found in "Some Thoughts on Autonomy and Equality in Relation to *Roe v. Wade,*" 63 *North Carolina Law Review* 375 (1985), and "Remarks on Women Becoming Part of the Constitution," 5 *Law & Inequality* 17 (1988). Deborah L. Markowitz, "In Pursuit of Equality: One Woman's Work to Change the Law," 11 *Women's Rights Law Reporter* 73 (1989), summarizes Ginsburg's work as a litigator.

ARTHUR JOSEPH GOLDBERG

BORN 8 August 1908, Chicago, Illinois

APPOINTED to the Court 31 August 1962
by John F. Kennedy

TOOK seat 1 October 1962; resigned
25 July 1965

DIED 19 January 1990, Washington, D.C.

Nominated by John F. Kennedy to fill the seat of the more conservative Felix Frankfurter, Arthur J. Goldberg became the justice who completed the Warren Court. Serving on the Court for only three years, Goldberg never achieved the reputation for judicial craftsmanship of his predecessor, but he nevertheless made a significant mark on the history of the Court and of the country by joining Earl Warren, Hugo Black, William Douglas, and William Brennan to provide a majority for what became known as the Warren Court agenda: judicial reinforcement of constitutional rights and civil liberties, particularly the equality rights of minorities, the rights of those suspected or accused of crime, and the freedom to differ.

Goldberg's career began early. He galloped through college and law school, and was admitted to the bar of Illinois in 1929, at the age of twenty. He then practiced law in Chicago for some twenty years, representing a number of labor unions, before becoming general counsel to the Congress of Industrial Workers and then the United Steel Workers. After moving to a Washington law firm in the 1950s, Goldberg helped to effect the merger of the AFL and CIO, and then became special counsel to the AFL-CIO industrial union department. It was in this capacity that he met and began to advise John F. Kennedy during the 1960 presidential campaign. From January 1961 to September 1962, Goldberg served as an outspoken secretary of labor, advocating an enhanced federal role in mediating labor disputes, and also on foreign affairs.

After joining the Court in October of 1962, Goldberg predictably took an active role in cases involving labor law and antitrust, often writing opinions interpreting federal legislation like the Sherman Act and Clayton Act to permit an expansive role for the federal government in these areas (see, *e.g.*, *United States v. Loew's, Inc.,* 1962; *Silver v. New York Stock Exchange,* 1963; and *United States v. Ward Baking Co.,* 1964).

But Goldberg's most significant contribution to the Court was his conviction that individual rights frequently outweigh countervailing governmental interests and concerns about federalism. Goldberg joined and often created majorities deciding that particular Bill of Rights guarantees should be incorporated and applied in state proceedings. In *Malloy v. Hogan* (1964), he supported the claim that the Fifth Amendment privilege against self-incrimination applies to the states; *Pointer v. Texas* (1965) incorporated the right to confront witnesses; and in the landmark decision in *Gideon v. Wainwright* (1963), the Court ruled that the Sixth Amendment right to counsel, including obligation to provide assigned counsel for indigent defendants, applies to the states. Goldberg also proved willing to expand the scope of particular rights, such as the right to counsel; *Massiah v. United States* (1964) held that the Sixth Amendment right to counsel attaches at the beginning of formal judicial proceedings and prohibits the police or prosecutors from "deliberately eliciting" information from a defendant in the absence of counsel.

Goldberg's belief in the importance of the right to counsel during the accusatory stage of a criminal proceeding led him to write an opinion for a bare majority in one of the Warren Court's most controversial opinions: *Escobedo v. Illinois* (1964). Goldberg's opinion, declaring a right to counsel during police interrogation, even before the commencement of formal proceedings, led law enforcement officials to fear that the Court's expanding view of the Sixth Amendment would severely curtail the utility of interrogation as an investigatory technique. Civil libertarians, on the other hand, forecast an end to inherently coercive police tactics. After Goldberg had departed, however, the Court found a compromise in the Fifth Amendment rule of *Miranda v. Arizona*

(1966) instead of building on the rationales Goldberg had offered in *Escobedo*.

Goldberg also supported or wrote opinions designed to improve the access of indigent criminal defendants to full and fair appeals; *Douglas v. California* (1963) extended the right to counsel on appeal, while *Lane v. Brown* (1963) provided indigents free transcripts. Joined by Justices Douglas and Brennan, Goldberg expressed some of the Supreme Court's first serious doubts about the constitutionality of a state's use of the death penalty, dissenting from the Court's refusal to hear *Rudolph v. Alabama* (1963). His prescient dissent in *Swain v. Alabama* (1965) argued for a right to be free from racial discrimination in jury selection, and anticipated that peremptory challenges would have to be limited in the interest of equal protection, a realization that commanded a majority on the Court only two decades later.

With Goldberg's participation, the Warren Court also sought to promote civil rights by protecting civil rights demonstrators. *Cox. v. Louisiana* (1965) reversed convictions of demonstrators on First Amendment grounds, while *Heart of Atlanta Motel, Inc. v. United States* (1964) affirmed the power of Congress to enact powerful civil rights legislation. In one of the landmark cases of the century, the Court equalized voting power through reapportionment (*Reynolds v. Sims,* 1964).

Goldberg's commitment to the principle of equality is documented in his book, *Equal Justice* (1971), published after he had left the Court. But his opinions show an equally fervent commitment to other constitutional guarantees, including the First Amendment. In a concurring opinion in *New York Times Co. v. Sullivan* (1964), a case limiting libel actions brought against public figures, Goldberg stated his view that the First Amendment confers "an absolute, unconditional privilege to criticize official conduct despite the harm which may flow from excesses and abuses." His generous interpretation of the First Amendment also led him to argue against restrictions created by obscenity prosecutions or ideological restrictions on the right to travel.

Goldberg's last opinion, a concurrence in *Griswold v. Connecticut* (1965), argued that a constitutional right of privacy, protecting such decisions as the right to use contraceptives, exists in part because of the Ninth Amendment's guarantee that the people retain rights not enumerated in the Constitution. This opinion, like many others Goldberg wrote, reflected his conviction that it is the constitutional role of the courts to vindicate equality or liberty rights of minorities who are unlikely to command the support of legislatures, and his disagreement with the frequent Warren Court dissenters, John Marshall Harlan, Tom Clark, Potter Stewart, and Goldberg's fellow Kennedy appointee, Byron White, who believed that the Supreme Court should play a more modest role in deference to Congress and to state legislatures.

In July of 1965, President Lyndon Johnson asked Goldberg to leave the Court to replace Adlai Stevenson as ambassador to the United Nations. Anxious to pursue his interest in international relations, Goldberg agreed. Goldberg is quoted as having described the difference between his role on the Court and at the United Nations as being captured in four words: "It is so ordered." After serving as ambassador until 1968, Goldberg returned to private practice, teaching, and an unsuccessful campaign to become governor of New York. Before his death on January 9, 1980, Arthur Goldberg was awarded the President's Medal of Freedom, capping a legal career that began when Goldberg became interested in the law while watching Clarence Darrow, another champion of equality, justice, and the underdog.

—SUSAN N. HERMAN

BIBLIOGRAPHY

After leaving the Supreme Court, Arthur Goldberg wrote prolifically on the topics that had been important to him on the Court, publishing several books on the constitutional issues that had dominated the Warren Court. See *Equal Justice: The Warren Era of the Supreme Court* (1971); *The Evolving Constitution: Essays on the Bill of Rights* (1989), and dozens of articles in law reviews and other publications about criminal justice, the death penalty, and other constitutional issues, including the First Amendment. Goldberg's tenure on the Court also left him with an interest in the Supreme Court and in judicial administration generally. He wrote extensively on these topics, and was a frequent contributor to symposia evaluating the work of other justices and judges. He also maintained his interest in labor law and international affairs, writing and speaking frequently on these topics, as well. Biographies of Goldberg include Dorothy Goldberg's *A Private View of a Public Life* (1975) and Victor Lasky's *Arthur J. Goldberg: The Old and the New* (1970).

Horace Gray
Photograph by Handy Studios.
Collection of the Supreme Court of the United States.

HORACE GRAY

BORN 24 March 1828 in Boston,
    Massachusetts
NOMINATED to the Court 19 December 1881
    by Chester A. Arthur
TOOK seat 9 January 1882
DIED 15 September 1902 in Nahant,
    Massachusetts

Graduating at seventeen from Harvard, Horace Gray learned during a European tour soon after that his Boston family's wealth—ample since the 1790 return from China to Salem harbor of a profitably tea-laden ship—had abruptly disappeared.

No other Supreme Court justice was quite so "well-born." In the early 1800s, his grandfather, William Gray, was the richest New Englander. Though suffering from Jefferson's 1808 embargo, French and British seizures of his ships, and the War of 1812, he strongly supported the war effort. Becoming a Jeffersonian, he was twice Massachusetts lieutenant governor. Out of his own pocket, he provided daily relief to the poor and, when the government was nearly broke, paid for refurbishing the U.S.S. "Constitution" so she could fight. After William Gray's 1820 death, Horace Gray's father (also Horace) ran the family's businesses well for two decades, but then shifted too much capital from shipping into high-risk iron mill investments that folded during a business slump.

Thus jolted, young Gray studied law assiduously at Harvard and joined the antislavery Free Soil party in 1848. Soon after he had a stroke of luck (or rather, of luck and family connections). At twenty-six, while building a profitable legal practice, he was appointed reporter of the Massachusetts supreme judicial court. He continued both activities for nine years, joining the Republican party and gaining wide attention for an 1857 *Monthly Law Review* article that devastated the historical contentions of Roger Taney's proslavery *Dred Scott* opinion.

In 1864, he was appointed to the Massachusetts high court, and in 1873 became its chief

justice. There he sat and wrote 1,367 opinions, only one of which was in dissent. On recommendations from Gray's longtime friend, Massachusetts Senator George Hoar, and from Justice Samuel Miller, President Chester Arthur nominated Gray to the United States Supreme Court. There, while maintaining three homes (in Washington, Boston, and on the Massachusetts seashore), he sat for twenty-one years and wrote 451 opinions. He penned only ten dissents—a circumstance which later led to misassessment of his judicial influence by scholars who overlooked when he did, and when he did not, join in the dissents of others.

At Gray's 1902 funeral, Chief Justice Melville Fuller likened Gray's accomplishments to those of Massachusetts Chief Justice Lemuel Shaw and two earlier holders of Gray's Supreme Court seat, Joseph Story and Benjamin Curtis: "He will be ranked with them without appreciable interval." In 1909, Harvard law professor Samuel Williston, a former Gray law clerk, repeated the prediction. History has been somewhat less appreciative. In 1961, Stephen Mitchell put Gray "just below the top rung in the judicial ladder." In 1992, John Semonche seemed more impressed by Gray's formalism in manners and writing style than by his substantive contribution. Gray's constitutional opinions—staples of legal textbooks well into the New Deal era—have almost vanished from recent casebooks, whereas Story's and Curtis's continue therein.

Gray's constitutional opinions had three main themes. One was support of substantial and effective national governmental power, but not too much. He endorsed congressional power in both wartime and peacetime to make paper money legal tender in *Julliard v. Greenman* (1884); held that Congress may by statute override an earlier treaty and provide for summary detention and expulsion of aliens in *Fong Yue Ting v. United States* (1893); and ruled that Congress had power without regard to the Fourteenth Amendment's state action limitation to provide for punishing persons who deprive citizens in the custody of federal marshals of their civil rights in *Logan v. United States* (1892). But he drew the line when Congress attempted to enact a peacetime income tax (*Pollock v. Farmers' Loan and Trust*, 1895), or tried to exert commerce clause power over manufacturing that only indirectly affected interstate commerce (*United States v. E.C. Knight Co.*, 1895).

Another theme was that states had fairly ample police powers to regulate the economy. In the absence of contrary federal law, a state could require nondiscriminatory railroad rates on journeys beginning within the state even if the destination were out-of-state (concurrence with Bradley dissent in *Wabash, St. Louis, and Pacific Railway v. Illinois*, 1886); prohibit importation and sale of liquor (dissent in *Leisy v. Hardin*, 1890); and could levy a tax based on the railroad's in-state proportion of total track mileage, regardless of how much or little its cars traveled in state (*Pullman Palace Car Co. v. Pennsylvania*, 1891). But here, also, Gray would not allow states unlimited powers. A state could not, after the railroad built a bypass, require an interstate passenger express to go three miles out of its way on the old track to stop at a county seat (*Illinois Central R.R. v. Illinois*, 1896). Nor would mandamus lie to compel a railroad to put a stop where it passed through a Washington county seat—Yakima—after the railroad decided it could make more money by platting a new town four miles away on its own land, stopping trains there instead, and depopulating Yakima (*Northern Pacific Ry. v. Washington*, 1892).

A third theme pertained to individual rights. Under the Fourteenth Amendment, persons born in the United States, except Indians living in tribes or separately but not taxed, were citizens regardless of race. Congress could not, pursuing an anti-Chinese immigration policy, deny reentry to the San Francisco-born son of Chinese aliens (*United States v. Wong Kim Ark*, 1898).

Gray also insisted that the government respect Indians' treaty-acquired property interests. In lengthy 1863 negotiations, Chippewa Chief Moose Dung expressed a desire for a 640-acre set-aside for him and his heirs: "I have taken the mouth of Thieving River as my inheritance." The federal negotiator, a Minnesota senator, seemingly exasperated, or thinking the United States was "thieving" enough Indian land for the day,

directed the interpreter, "Tell him I don't care anything about the mouth of Thieving River. He can have it." Whereupon Moose Dung optimistically said, "I accept . . . because . . . I am going to be raised from want to riches . . . to the level of the white man." Gray held that an 1894 congressional resolution giving the secretary of the interior power to oversee the rental terms of said land (by then urbanized and valuable) collapsed before the vested right of Moose Dung's son (known as Moose Dung the younger) to lease as he pleased (*Jones v. Meehan*, 1899).

While Gray agreed with *Plessy* that state-required racial segregation in intrastate rail transportation was constitutional, a local practice of excluding African Americans from state court grand juries, neither prohibited nor prescribed by state law, was unconstitutional (*Carter v. Texas*, 1900). For Gray, due process pertained primarily to criminal procedures, and he initially viewed the doctrine of substantive due process as unsound (*Head v. Amoskeag Manufacturing*, 1885). The Fourteenth Amendment's due process clause did not incorporate the Bill of Rights and make all its provisions applicable to states, who therefore could reduce jury size from twelve to eight. But in federal trials, the Seventh Amendment's guarantee of a trial by jury meant what it historically did in English law—twelve jurors and a judge (*Capital Traction v. Hof*, 1899). Nor should a judge tamper with historically mixed allocations of powers to decide questions of law and fact by instructing jurors in a way that limited their freedom in deciding whether the circumstances indicated murder or manslaughter (sixty-page dissent in *Sparf v. United States*, 1895).

Many Gray positions (particularly regarding government and the economy) were more consistent with New Deal views of good constitutional results than with the strong laissez-faire judicial activism of the *Lochner* era. Why, therefore, did the apparent slide in Gray's perceived importance occur? One reason is that some decisions thought important at the time were analytical derivations from another judge's earlier "head" opinion, which survives better. For example, *Logan* largely derives from Miller's opinion in *Ex parte Yarbrough* (1884), a "structural" argument that, quite apart from Fourteenth and

Fifteenth Amendment demands for fair, nondiscriminatory state behavior in elections, the Constitution's requirement of periodic federal elections entails sufficient federal power to reach individuals' discriminatory behavior hindering other citizens' voting therein.

A second reason relates to the point that it is not Gray's methods and substantive jurisprudence that have changed, but rather succeeding generations' standards of greatness. Standards of late nineteenth-century elite lawyers, trained when Langdellian legal analysis searched for scientifically objective, formal symmetries thought to underlie the case law, fit well with Gray's preferred decision-making method. His seemingly neutral method soft-pedaled cases' public policy implications. Late twentieth-century standards tend to prize policy-explicitness in the constitutional interpretations of both activist and passivist judges.

Relatedly, a third reason pertains to the fields of law thought more and less important. For Williston in 1909, race relations and labor rights scarcely rose to the level of consciousness, whereas international law, the law of charitable trusts, and admiralty law were close to center stage. Much of Gray's contribution lay in the latter fields.

Gray's preferred method and fields of interest were well displayed in what Williston considered two great Gray opinions—*Liverpool and Great Western Steam v. Phenix Insurance* (1889), and *Hilton v. Guyot* (1895). Gray sought out precedents exceedingly far back and then wrote exceedingly lengthy historical essays finding the answers in those precedents. *Liverpool* took sixty-seven pages and citations of more than eighty American, British, French, Dutch, and Italian cases and commentators to "find" that American law (which held invalid clauses in shipping contracts exempting a common carrier from liability for employee negligence) prevailed over British law (which held the opposite) where the bill of lading was drawn up in New York by a British ship company's agent for goods bound therefrom to Liverpool but lost when the ship sank in a Welsh bay just short of its destination.

Gray's majority opinion in *Guyot* held that since the French judicial system treated other "civilized" countries' court judgments as *prima*

facie evidence in—but not conclusive on—related French court proceedings, then American courts could retry on the merits French judgments on American-owned companies with Paris offices. Gray produced a 100-page examination of a 1629 French royal ordinance down through two and a half centuries of the cases and commentaries of twenty-two countries.

Like his predecessor, Morrison Waite—who once wistfully wrote to Gray, "Can't you tell me the secret of your *style*. I wish I had it"—Melville Fuller was frequently persuaded by Gray's meticulous analytic powers. His character, despite its stiffness, attracted several other justices. Harlan joked to Waite that Gray's idea of a vacation was searching for precedents in British Columbia. But Waite at age sixty-nine really wanted the company of Gray (a keen hiker) and General Sherman (good at expeditions) on an 1883 Montana trip where they "slept . . . on the ground. . . . The thermometer went . . . below freezing . . . had breakfast at five . . . eggs and lambchops . . . superb morning."

Gray in fact had considerable power within the Court. Vacationing in Europe, one of the clearly great justices, Stephen Field, wrote to another, Joseph Bradley, about unwanted Gray impact on their colleagues' thinking. Field urged that Bradley pen a very strong dissent in the Pullman-Pennsylvania tax case, and pledged "to co-operate with you . . . to defeat the manifest purposes of Gray to overturn our interstate commerce decisions." He also vowed "to purchase a one-horse landau" so that he and Bradley could have strategy chats going to and from Court conferences.

But how much power did Gray have, and to what societal ends did he use it? One scholarly misconception infers from Gray's low number of written dissents relatively low power. A misreading of primary sources led one scholar to state that Gray's "closest friends . . . found attitudes which bordered on prejudice . . . [but] never so far as can be discovered, committed . . . to writing." The friends, however, probably were not referring in modern fashion to ethnic prejudice (which most of Gray's Brahmin friends shared) but rather, in nineteenth-century usage, to Gray's being opinionated. In any event, Gray's prejudices or, better, his Anglocentered point of view can be found, with a little searching, in Gray's writing—e.g., in an unintentionally funny opinion about customs duties on imported tomatoes.

In *Nix v. Hedden* (1893), the importer argued tomatoes were fruits and should enter duty-free. The government insisted they were vegetables, and imposed a 10 percent tariff. Gray's favored 100-page historical solution wouldn't work, as only one dubious precedent was available—beans were not seeds in a pod (*Robertson v. Salomon,* 1889). Into Court came dictionaries and experts. Discussion was inconclusive. Then Gray had one of his most original—if Anglo-culture-bound—jurisprudential ideas. Look not to definitions or botany, but to the tomato's societal functions. Said he, tomatoes "are usually served at dinner in, with, or after the soup, fish, or meats which constitute the principal part of the repast, and not, like fruits generally, as dessert." Tomatoes, *q.e.d.*, are vegetables and taxable.

Gray wrote this cultural-anthropological silliness a few days before his *Fong Yue Ting* majority opinion further displayed his underlying social attitudes (and not just, it appears, his deference to Congress). Fuller, Field, and David Brewer dissented, the latter saying: "In view of this enactment of the . . . foremost Christian nation, may not the thoughtful Chinese disciple of Confucius fairly ask, 'Why do they send missionaries here?'"

Of course, these justices were prejudiced by today's standards. The significant question is what else came with, or offset, these upper-class Anglo-Saxon prejudices and also drove their decision making. Comparing Gray on this score with Brewer (generally now remembered only as the Court's staunchest advocate of substantive due process), Henry Billings Brown (author of *Plessy*, who later said he thought Harlan's dissent might have been right), and Bradley (who, dead before *Plessy*, joined Harlan's dissent in its 1890 precursor, *Louisville, New Orleans, & Texas Railroad Company v. Mississippi*), suggests a final cause of Gray's reputational decline—his lack of empathy for less fortunate mortals, his icy, precedent-cloaked judicial passivity.

Thus, where Gray let the Northern Pacific Railway devastate Yakima economically, Brewer in dissent objected that the railroad "locates its depot on the site of a 'paper town;' and for private interests, builds up a new place at the expense of the old. . . . A railroad corporation has a public duty to perform as well as a private interest to subserve. . . . I never before believed that the courts would permit it to abandon the one to promote the other."

With respect to First Amendment freedoms, one searches Gray's jurisprudence in vain for anything like Bradley's lone dissent in the Court's earliest free speech case, *Ex parte Curtis* (1882). Objecting to an 1876 statute prohibiting federal employees from soliciting, giving, or receiving money for electoral campaigns, Bradley said bluntly: "The freedom of speech and of the press, and that of assembling together to . . . discuss matters of public interest . . . are expressly secured by the Constitution." Congress could thus impose as a condition of taking employment entire silence on political subjects, which struck him as "absurd. Neither men's mouths nor their purses can be constitutionally tied up in this way." Instead, one finds an 1896 obscenity prosecution, *Swearingen v. United States*, in which the Court majority held the publication not obscene, while Gray and three others voted it was, but without explanation.

With respect to treatment of nonwhite ethnic groups, there is nothing in Gray's opinions like Brown's condemning the army for firing on unarmed Native Americans in a forced relocation march. *Conners v. United States* (1901).

Finally, with respect to the rights of whites far below the justices' economic station in life, despite Gray's historical legal learning, there is nothing like Brown's essay in *Holden v. Hardy* (1898) upholding Utah's eight-hour maximum workday for miners, with its sweeping sense of American law's dynamism over the course of the nineteenth century, its realization that changes in industrial techniques required changes in worker-protective legislation, and its realistic analysis of corporation-labor relations.

More typical of Gray's judicial activities as they bore upon less fortunate groups and on how the costs and profits of industrialization should be distributed among Americans was his role concerning expansion or contraction of the "fellow servant rule," then a hotter social justice issue than hours legislation. Gray's Massachusetts predecessor, Lemuel Shaw, had held in 1842 that each worker, and not the employer, assumed the risk for the negligence of his coworkers ("fellow servants")—a very convenient rule for the entrepreneurial class, but not for the injured worker whose negligent fellow servant was usually too poor to pay much of a recompense. By the 1870s, state legislatures were overturning this judge-made rule. Indeed, Gray, while on the Massachusetts court, originated a countertending rule making the employer liable for unsafe working conditions (*Coombs v. New Bedford Cordage,* Massachusetts, 1869).

Gray's Supreme Court role respecting the fellow servant rule was different. It has, seemingly, been camouflaged by the received scholarly wisdom about dissent on the Court of the Gilded Age that, looking only at written dissents, characterizes Harlan and Field as the "great dissenters." This overlooks both the tactical value of mutely joining others' dissents and the difference between the self-expressive value of a solo dissent and the strategic value of appearing a consensus-builder, rather than a cantankerous loner, by only dissenting when at least one other justice wants to do so.

Limiting the analysis to cases with two or more dissenters, a different picture of the Court during Gray's first half-decade emerges. Counting the number of times one justice paired with another justice in multiple-dissent cases, Gray appears as the leader of the dissenter pack. Gray joined in thirty-seven dissenting pairs, followed by Harlan joining in thirty-four pairs, Bradley in thirty-one, Chief Justice Waite in twenty-nine, and Field—exactly in the Court middle—in twenty-eight. During the first half of the 1890s, however, Gray's frequency of pairing in dissent dropped to the Court middle, while the dissent-pairings of the only two Civil War and Reconstruction era appointees still alive in 1895 (Field and Harlan) leapt to the top.

What was happening? First, Gray's persuasive impact was seemingly becoming even stronger than when Field had written worriedly to Bradley. Second, a frequent cause of dissent pairings on the later Waite Court had been occasioned by Field's limiting the scope of the fellow servant rule over the objections of Bradley (on this they disagreed) joined by Gray and two other 1880s appointees. By the 1890s, as the Civil War era appointees died, Gray's viewpoint was winning out. By 1897, he was ready to move from debate in chambers and concurring in dissents, to penning an expansion of the rule. In *Alaska Treadwell Gold Mine v. Whelan,* Gray ruled that a foreman (even if he had the power of hiring and firing employees under him) was not a company supervisor but a "fellow-servant" of the worker whom he first ordered to break rock and add it at the top of a full chute, then seriously injured by forgetfully opening the chute-gate at the bottom. Thereupon down had tumbled rock and worker and all. Gray overruled the Alaskan jury and the appeals court, and returned to the mining company the award to the injured worker.

Such—a half century distant from Gray's 1848 days in the Free Soil Party—was Gray's purportedly neutral 1890s' jurisprudence. Too much was morally gray in it, and too little in him was William Gray.

—A. E. KEIR NASH

BIBLIOGRAPHY

Samuel Williston, "Horace Gray," in William Draper Lewis, ed., *Great American Lawyers* 3: 189 (1909), is the best commentary by Gray's contemporaries. John C. Semonche offers a different view in his very brief piece in Kermit Hall, ed., *Oxford Companion to the Supreme Court of the United States* (1992). Stephen Robert Mitchell's unpublished dissertation, "Mr. Justice Horace Gray" (University of Wisconsin, 1961), is the best single secondary source, but is analytically a bit wooden and often has too little distance from the biographical primary sources, including their wording.

ROBERT COOPER GRIER

BORN 5 March 1794, Cumberland County,
Pennsylvania

NOMINATED to the Court 3 August 1846
by James K. Polk; confirmed
4 August 1846; retired 31 January 1870

DIED 25 September 1870 in Philadelphia,
Pennsylvania

Robert C. Grier entered Dickinson College
in 1811 and received his degree a year later. After studying law with a local lawyer and gaining
admission to the Pennsylvania bar in 1817, Grier
spent the following sixteen years in legal practice.
A Jacksonian Democrat, he received a patronage
appointment to a state court judgeship in 1833, a
position he held for the following thirteen years.
After a Court vacancy of more than two years
caused by the death of Henry Baldwin in 1844
and the subsequent inability of President John
Tyler to gain approval for his nominees, Grier was
nominated by James K. Polk and confirmed by
the Senate on August 4, 1846.

Early in his tenure on the Court, Grier assumed a pivotal and outspoken stance on the
complex issue of state infringement on the federal commerce power. In the *License Cases*
(1847), Grier concurred separately in the Court's
decision to uphold three state laws regulating
liquor sales as a valid exercise of state police
power. Grier vigorously defended a state's prerogative to protect its general health and morals
by excluding an article of trade such as liquor
from its own commerce. Two years later, however, Grier wrote separately in the *Passenger
Cases* (1849) to emphasize the limits of state
police power. In the *Passenger Cases*, the Court
struck down New York and Massachusetts laws
which had levied head taxes on each alien passenger brought into their ports. Grier asserted
that Massachusetts had exceeded its power by
adopting a tax which could directly affect foreign commerce, the regulation of which belonged to Congress alone. Thus, in holding that
state police power must not interfere with for-

eign commerce, Grier struck a careful balance
which would continue in his alliance with the
majority's reasoning in *Cooley v. Board of Wardens of the Port of Philadelphia* (1852).

On other matters pertaining to states' authority, Grier was similarly influential. In *Cook v.
Moffat* (1847), he wrote the majority opinion rejecting a Maryland businessman's effort to use his
state's insolvency laws to escape debts from another state, reasoning that a state should honor
another state's otherwise valid bankruptcy laws
only as it chose under comity. In *Peck v. Jenness*
(1849), Grier spoke for a unanimous Court in
upholding a New Hampshire state court's judgment under an 1841 federal bankruptcy act as the
valid decision of a tribunal "equal and independent" to the courts of the United States. In 1851,
Grier dissented on behalf of himself and the
Court's three most vociferous states' rights advocates in *Woodruff v. Trapnall* (1851), and decried
the majority's denial of the state of Arkansas's
right to refuse acceptance of state bank notes proffered by the former state treasurer.

Grier also aggressively defended state autonomy in a number of pre-Civil War cases concerning slavery, and was sternly criticized in
abolitionist circles. In *Moore v. People of Illinois* (1852), Grier wrote the majority opinion
sustaining an Illinois fugitive slave statute over
the objection that such laws were exclusively
within federal jurisdiction, on the grounds that
states entertained the authority to "repel from
their soil a population likely to become burdensome and injurious, either as paupers or criminals." In a peculiar turn of events, Grier assumed
a critical—and ethically improper—role in the
disposition of the Court's most infamous slavery
case, *Dred Scott v. Sandford* (1857). In the spring
of that year, after an inappropriate letter inquiry
from president-elect James Buchanan about the
progress of the as-yet-unreleased *Dred Scott*
decision, Grier responded with a detailed account
of the pending case and a promise to work
closely with other justices in the majority to
minimize the breadth of dissent in the final opin-

ions of the Court. In the final decision, Grier wrote briefly to concur both with Justice Nelson's view that Missouri law should determine Scott's status, and with Chief Justice Taney's opinion that the Missouri Compromise was unconstitutional.

Despite his earlier affirmations of states' rights against abolitionist challenges, Grier's majority opinion in the *Prize Cases* (1863), expressed a compelling defense of wartime presidential power to quell Confederate resistance. In the *Prize Cases*, the Court was charged with determining the constitutionality of the Union blockade of Confederate ports instituted by President Abraham Lincoln in April 1861, several months before Congress met and approved the action. Grier upheld the president's authority to act immediately to address Confederate insurrection, reasoning that a formal declaration of war by Congress was unnecessary for a war "which all the world acknowledges to be the greatest civil war known in the history of the human race."

Significant cases in the remaining years of Grier's Court service include: *Ex parte Milligan* (1867), in which Grier joined the Court in rejecting the assertion of wartime government power to authorize military tribunals to try civilians in areas with functioning civil courts; and *Texas v.*

White (1869), in which Grier joined Justices Swayne and Miller in dissenting from the majority opinion upholding the status of Texas as a "state" which could not have seceded from the Union. Grier also strongly opposed the Court's one-year postponement before passing upon the constitutionality of the Reconstruction acts in *Ex parte McCardle* (1869). In a statement joined by Justice Field, Grier protested as a dereliction of duty the Court's decision to delay its ruling until Congress had passed a law stripping it of appellate jurisdiction.

After an extended period of declining health in the late 1860s and accompanying widespread criticism of his judicial competence, Grier retired on January 31, 1870, at the urging of his colleagues on the Court. He died on September 25 of that year in Philadelphia.

—MARGARET M. RUSSELL

BIBLIOGRAPHY

There is a relatively small body of writing on Grier's life and judicial career. The most complete sources include: David P. Brown, "Robert Cooper Grier, LL.D," 2 *Forum* 91 (1856); Salmon P. Chase, "Resignation of Mr. Justice Grier," 75 U.S. vii (1870); and Frank Otto Gatell, "Robert C. Grier," in Friedman and Israel, 2 *Justices* 871.

JOHN MARSHALL HARLAN

BORN 1 June 1833, Boyle County, Kentucky

NOMINATED to the Court 17 October 1877 by
    Rutherford B. Hayes

TOOK seat 11 December 1877

DIED 14 October 1911 in Washington, D.C.

When Justice John Marshall Harlan sat down in late 1910 to write up a list of his most important decisions, he chose many of those which one would expect. For example, his renowned dissents in the *Civil Rights Cases* (1883) and *Plessy v. Ferguson* (1896) are there. But also listed are a great many decisions concerned primarily with economic issues, and some, such as bond repudiation cases, few would have anticipated. What seems to have bound the various cases together in Harlan's mind was their importance in promoting nationalism. While Harlan's favorite opinions on civil rights aimed to achieve a nationalized standard of rights, many of his economic cases strove to encourage and protect a national economy, one in which trade flowed freely among the states without regional barriers or discriminations. He believed that the great corporations which arose in the Gilded Age threatened to wipe out the individual entrepreneur trying to do business in that national market. As a result, Harlan backed the federal agencies and legislation which aimed at controlling the power of these corporations, and so found himself both honored and vilified during the Progressive Era.

In part, this commitment to nationalism was an inheritance from Harlan's father, a Whig politician. But Harlan's Civil War experience as a unionist in the border state of Kentucky confirmed this tendency and made it into one of the primary concerns of his judicial career. Harlan was born to an elite Kentucky family of lawyering Whigs who held slaves. He first went to Centre College in Danville, Kentucky, then completed his legal studies at Transylvania University at Lexington. He was admitted to the bar in 1853 after working and studying in several law offices, including his father's. He joined the Whig party and was recognized as a gifted stump speaker immediately. In 1858, Harlan won election as judge of the county court of Franklin County for one year, his only judicial experience before being appointed to the Supreme Court. He ran for a seat in the United States House of Representatives in 1859 and lost. From 1863 to 1867, he served as attorney general of Kentucky, and in 1871 and 1875, ran unsuccessfully for governor under the Republican banner. Harlan's shift in political allegiance from the Whig to the Republican party and his abandonment of the institution of slavery occurred after the Civil War. From the time of secession through the end of the war, Harlan was part of a shifting pro-Union, anti-emancipation coalition which existed under various names in Kentucky. When war broke out, Harlan organized and led a regiment for the Union army, but he resigned his commission in 1863 after his father's death left the family law office with no competent head. Throughout this time he counseled gradual emancipation, and as late as 1865 condemned the Thirteenth Amendment as an unrepublican assault on the property rights of white slaveholders.

The Harlans were never abolitionists; they defined forbearance from the physical abuse of power and goodwill between the races as essential to honorable behavior for white men. The Republican party rejected the white supremacy which had existed hand in hand with this paternalistic ethos, and Harlan found the GOP's embrace of legal equality far more palatable than the racial terrorism of the Democrats. Still, Harlan would never shake free of paternalism with its assumptions of racial hierarchy and separation.

Harlan's journey to the Court began in 1876 when he threw the Kentucky delegation to the Republican presidential convention behind the candidacy of Rutherford B. Hayes. The new president appointed him to the Louisiana commission which was sent down to decide the disputed state election of 1876. When Hayes nominated Harlan for an associate justiceship in October of 1877, some Republicans complained because they still did not trust Harlan to be true to the party's principles.

If they were worried about his devotion to the constitutional amendments which the Civil War had produced, they did not know their man. Justice Harlan's record on civil rights, while it betrays the taint of paternalism, was by far the most favorable to blacks and other minorities of any member of the high court during the Gilded Age. Harlan rejected the majority's notion that the Fourteenth and Fifteenth Amendments only applied to the acts of the states or their officials. These jurists did have a point, since the Fourteenth Amendment used the words "No State shall . . . " in declaring its prohibitions and the Fifteenth contained similar language. Yet Congress, made up of many of the same men who had approved of the Civil War amendments, passed laws which punished individuals for their attacks on persons trying to exercise their civil rights, and the Court struck them down. In *Baldwin v. Franks* (1887), Harlan disagreed with a decision involving persecuted Chinese immigrants of the Pacific Coast. He insisted in dissent that "the rights therein granted or guaranteed might be guarded and protected against lawless combinations of individuals, acting without the direct sanction of the states." Similarly, he dissented in *James v. Bowman* (1903), when the Court held that the Fifteenth Amendment did not protect blacks from private assaults made upon them for trying to vote.

In applying the Thirteenth Amendment, Harlan was not hampered by the state-action doctrine because it read simply, "neither slavery nor involuntary servitude, except as punishment for crime . . . shall exist within the United States." Thus, its ban on slavery was universal. Harlan invoked this amendment, as well as the Fourteenth, in the two dissents for which he is best remembered—the *Civil Rights Cases* (1883) and *Plessy v. Ferguson* (1896). The first decision tested the constitutionality of the Civil Rights Act of 1875, a federal statute which decreed "that all persons within the jurisdiction of the United States shall be entitled to the full and equal enjoyment of the accommodations" in inns, public transportation, places of amusement, and the like. Harlan had opposed the law as a gubernatorial candidate in 1875, but now, from his protected judicial position, he came out in its defense. In *Plessy*, which was little noticed by the public, the Court reviewed a Louisiana state law which segregated the races on public railroads. The question in both cases was whether the Thirteenth and Fourteenth Amendments to the Constitution prohibited racial segregation.

In both instances, the majority of the Court decreed that the Thirteenth Amendment's prohibition on slavery did not extend to racial segregation. Justice Bradley asked in the *Civil Rights Cases* "what has [the denial of public accommodation] to do with the question of slavery?" Similarly, Justice Brown wrote in *Plessy*, "A statute which implies merely a legal distinction between the white and colored races—a distinction which is founded in the color of the two races . . . has no tendency to destroy the legal equality of the two races, or reestablish a state of involuntary servitude." Harlan, in contrast, argued in *Plessy* that the Civil War amendments had "removed the race line from our governmental systems." "Our Constitution is color-blind," he declared, warning that: "The destinies of the two races, in this country, are indissolubly linked together, and the interest of both require that the common government of all shall not permit the seeds of race hate to be planted under the sanction of law."

Segregation in public accommodation was a badge of slavery, wrote Harlan, which had been used during antebellum times to mark even free blacks out as members of a slave race. Harlan admonished his brethren for failing, as he put it in the *Civil Rights Cases*, "to compel the recognition of the legal right of the black race to take the rank of citizens." He dissented for similar reasons in other cases, including *Louisville, New Orleans, & Texas Railroad Company v. Mississippi* (1890) and *Chiles v. Chesapeake & Ohio Railway Co.* (1910).

Yet even in his two famous dissents, there were suggestions of limits on the egalitarianism of Harlan's racial thought. In *Plessy*, for example, he began with a complaint that segregation prevented a white man from having his

John Marshall Harlan
Painting by Pierre Troubetzkoy.
Collection of the Supreme Court of the United States.

colored servant with him during a train trip, and in the *Civil Rights Cases*, Harlan did not deny the legitimacy of the dubious notion of social rights, but settled for declaring them irrelevant. In other decisions, he failed to follow the color-blind rule which, one presumes, would have prohibited the mere mention of race in statutes. In *Pace v. Alabama* (1885), the Supreme Court concluded that a state law which punished inter-racial adultery more harshly than same-race adul-tery was not a violation of the equal protection of the laws, because both partners of the inter-racial couple were punished equally. Harlan did not dissent from this legal sophistry. Also, he made a point of not giving an opinion as to the legality of segregation in the public schools when he very well might have in *Cumming v. Richmond County Board* (1899).

Similarly, his off-the-bench activities as a Presbyterian elder suggest the ambiguity of his position on race. As a member of the standing committee on freedmen at the Presbyterian gen-eral assembly of 1905, he assented to the state-ment in their report that "Assimilation is as de-structive as it is repugnant." Destructive, possibly, because romantic racialism held at this time that each race possessed a distinct spiritual genius worth preserving; repugnant, undoubt-edly, because of racist distaste for interracial sexual relations. In that same year, Harlan fought hard but unsuccessfully against a proposal to allow individual Presbyterian churches to limit themselves to one race exclusively. The front page of the *New York Age* of April 20, 1905, recorded his position "against separate presbyteries for whites and blacks even if the whites and blacks were to agree mutually to have them," which he voiced at a public meeting led by black clergymen.

He asked his fellows to be color-blind and race blind. In *Berea College v. Kentucky* (1908), Harlan was outraged when the majority of the Court allowed the state to prohibit interracial teaching in a private school. "Have we become so inoculated with the prejudice of race," he asked, "that an American government, pro-fessedly based on the principles of freedom, and charged with the protection of all citizens alike, can make distinctions between such citizens in

the matter of their voluntary meeting for inno-cent purposes simply because of their respective races?" Perhaps Harlan emphasized the inno-cence because he remembered *Pace*. Surely he remembered *Cumming* when he emphasized in *Berea College* that he spoke only of private schools. These actions leave us wondering how he could incorporate his forceful stand against the official imposition of segregation with an acquiescence to some forms of voluntary and involuntary social separation. Perhaps he was trying to create a biracial (not an interracial) society in an egalitarian polity. The habits of thought bred into a slaveholder may have been impossible to shake.

While Harlan worked on a way to integrate free black citizens into the political community, he also fought a rearguard action against the progressive technocrats who wanted to decrease all citizen participation in government. Harlan's concern for popular participation in civic affairs was at the root of his decision to support the idea that the due process clause of the Fourteenth Amendment incorporated all the protections found in the first eight amendments to the Con-stitution. This idea, called incorporation theory or the nationalization of the Bill of Rights, was first voiced by Harlan in dissent in *Hurtado v. California* (1884).

Hurtado had been tried and convicted of murder in California, but he had not been in-dicted by a grand jury; he complained, therefore, that he had been denied his rights as guaranteed in the Fifth Amendment and applied to state action by the Fourteenth Amendment. The Court majority, although it admitted some exceptions, held that according to the rules of constitutional draftsmanship, no clause may repeat another; so the term "due process" in the Fifth Amendment could not also signify all the other protections also in the Fifth Amendment, such as a grand jury indictment in felony cases. Therefore, since a given term must mean the exact same thing each time it is used, the due process clause of the Fourteenth Amendment could not encompass all those other protections named in the Fifth Amendment, either. Harlan threw aside the rules of draftsmanship as technicalities which camou-flaged the awful fact that the Court was willing to allow the states to abandon elements of criminal procedure which the founders had conceived of as essential to republican government. Many states were experimenting with simplified criminal procedures and Harlan considered California to be the thin edge of a wedge. By the 1890s, there was a full-scale battle among legal writers over whether the entire jury system should be discarded because of its inadequacies.

Harlan pursued the doctrinal logic of his *Hurtado* dissent and championed the nationalization of all of the protections found in the first eight amendments of the Bill of Rights. He tried unsuccessfully to have the Court apply to the states the Eighth Amendment's ban on cruel and unusual punishment in *O'Neil v. Vermont* (1892), the Fifth Amendment's traditional grand and petit jury procedures in *Maxwell v. Down* (1900), the First Amendment's freedom of speech protection in *Patterson v. Colorado* (1907), and the Fifth Amendment's protection against self-incrimination in *Twining v. New Jersey* (1908). His colleagues gave Harlan a small victory in *Chicago, Burlington & Quincy Railroad Company v. Chicago* (1897) by allowing him to deliver an opinion which applied to the states the Fifth Amendment's requirement for fair compensation for property taken for public use. They would not, however, let him use it to bolster his position in any of the other cases, despite his complaint that the brethren seemed to value civil rights only when property was involved.

After the Spanish-American War, Harlan found himself again fighting for the idea that the full protections of the Bill of Rights was applicable to all persons subjected to governmental authority. Harlan had supported the war as a battle against tyranny and a way to soothe the old wounds of the Civil War by giving the North and South a common enemy. But Congress and the administration did not feel that the Filipinos or the Puerto Ricans measured up to the responsibilities of citizenship, and so made them into colonies instead of granting them independence. The question of whether Congress could treat those territories differently than territories destined for statehood brought the first of the so-called *Insular Cases* before the Court in 1901. In *Delima v. Bidwell* (1901), Harlan found himself on the winning side when the Court declared that Puerto Rico was not a foreign country. Unfortunately, on the same day he also had to dissent in *Downes v. Bidwell* (1901), in which the majority declared that Congress could pass special tariff laws applicable only to Puerto Rico, something it might not do to a state.

Intertwined with the tariff question was that of what rights the island inhabitants might claim from the federal government. Many white Americans believed Congress might pick and chose which rights would be granted. Harlan's dissent in *Downes* expressed his fear that the Court would allow Congress to rule the new territories as it pleased without regard to the limits of its constitutionally enumerated powers. "I confess," he wrote in *Downes*, "that I cannot grasp the thought that Congress which lives and moves and has its being in the Constitution and is consequently the mere creature of that instrument" could exclude its creator from the islands.

It was not enough in his eyes for Americans to congratulate themselves, as Justice Brown did in writing for the majority, that "there are certain principles of natural justice inherent in the Anglo-Saxon character which need no expression in constitution or statutes to give them effect." Harlan pointed out that "the wise men who framed the Constitution, and the patriotic people who adopted it, were unwilling to depend for their safety upon . . . 'certain principles of natural justice inherent in the Anglo-Saxon character.'" "They well remembered," as some of the brethren had apparently forgotten, "that Anglo-Saxons across the ocean had attempted, in defiance of law and justice, to trample upon the rights of Anglo-Saxons on this continent."

Harlan would continue his unsuccessful effort in *Hawaii v. Mankichi* (1903). There he declared that in 1898 "when the flag of Hawaii was taken down . . . and in its place was raised that of the United States," every provision of the Constitution went into force. He continued to protest in silent dissents to *Gavieres v. United States* (1910) and *Dowdell v. United States* (1910). Harlan never reconciled himself to the American empire. When he used the vocabulary of colonialism, he always put the words "dependencies" and "subjects" in quotation marks. He blamed imperialism on the greed of the commercial interests.

Just as Harlan tried to bind the nation together after the Civil War by extracting a national standard of citizenship rights from the Civil War amendments, so he attempted to open to all citizens a national marketplace. Interstate economic ties could strengthen national feeling. Harlan wanted goods to travel freely, and for a contract between a buyer on one side of the country and a seller on the other side to be enforced in the courts. Like his brethren, Harlan invoked the clause which gave to Congress sole power to "regulate Commerce . . . among the several states," but he surpassed them by spotting unconstitutional burdens on commerce where they did not. In fact, Harlan defended interstate commerce in the broadest practical sense of the term, even when state regulation was not involved.

In municipal and state bond repudiation decisions, Harlan's devotion to commercial nationalism becomes clear. He tended to favor creditors in order to preserve the integrity of the national and international market in local American bonds. In *Antoni v. Greenhow* (1882), Harlan foretold "disastrous consequences which would result both to the business interest and to the honor of the country" if the state succeeded in defying its creditors. Although some legal scholars believe that judges of the Gilded Age who found repeatedly for property holders were prejudiced by class interest, in Harlan's case, commercial nationalism was responsible.

In the bond case found on his list of favorites, *Presidio County, Texas v. The Noel-Young Bond & Stock Company* (1909), Harlan made it clear that the Court held the county responsible for the promises which its bonds recited on their face because such promises had made sale of those bonds to far-off purchasers possible in the first place. The Court followed this logic usually, but Harlan's concern led him to dissent when they did not, as he did in *City of Brenham v. German American Bank* (1892), where he warned that in light of the "enormous" amounts of similar bonds in circulation, "a declaration by this court that such notes are void . . . will, we fear, produce incalculable mischief." However,

Harlan swerved from his interpretation that the Eleventh Amendment did not protect the states from being sued on their bonds in *Ex parte Young* (1908), after railroad attorneys began to put his doctrine to an entirely different, pro-corporation use. But so long as the issue was localism versus nationalism, his position was clear.

Despite Harlan's devotion to the commerce clause, he also had great respect for the states' police powers, so long as commercial localism was not involved. He spoke for the majority in *Reid v. Colorado* (1902), which allowed Colorado to punish anyone who did not hold out-of-state livestock off the market for ninety days in order to prevent the spread of Texas fever. Harlan also supported state efforts to protect the people from the immoral effects of liquor in *Mugler v. Kansas* (1887), and dissented when the rest of the Court proved less concerned in *Bowman v. Chicago & Northwestern Railway Company* (1888), *Rhodes v. Iowa* (1898), and *Adams Express Company v. Iowa* (1905).

He had a similarly clear but only partially successful record on the regulation of lottery tickets. In *Leisy v. Hardin* (1890), he joined Horace Gray's dissent when the Court refused to allow a state to prohibit such tickets, while in *Champion v. Ames* (1903), he managed to deliver a majority opinion which allowed Congress (not the states) to ban such tickets from interstate commerce. His record on the regulation of margarine displayed a similar high-minded moralism. In *Powell v. Pennsylvania* (1888) and in *Plumley v. Massachusetts* (1894), Harlan upheld laws prohibiting the sale of oil products treated to pass for dairy products. But finally, in *Schollenberger v. Pennsylvania* (1898), he met defeat and dissented while the majority of the Court declared margarine an inherently healthy product which a state might not regulate out of existence.

Harlan's dissent in *Lochner v. New York* (1905), a decision which struck down a labor law for bakers, should be understood in terms of his respect for the police powers of the state where no commercial localism was present. After all, he supported liberty of contract in *Adair v. United States* (1908) when he spoke for the majority in striking down the Erdmann Act, which made it a criminal offense for an interstate railroad to fire a worker because of union membership. Harlan held that such membership had no necessary connection to interstate commerce, while bakers' working conditions had a clear connection to health.

Harlan's respect for state police powers ended at the point where their exercise might amount to a discrimination against out-of-state goods. Speaking for the Court, he condemned the localism displayed in a wharfage fee laid only on ships carrying out-of-state goods in *Guy v. Baltimore* (1879). In his dissent to *Transportation Company v. Parkersburg* (1882), he displayed his dislike of all state-imposed burdens on interstate commerce even when they fell equally on in-state and out-of-state goods. He tried unsuccessfully to have the Court strike down inspection fees for out-of-state fertilizer in *Patapsco Guano Company v. North Carolina Board of Agriculture* (1898). Harlan also dissented in several cases where the Court allowed states to place embargoes on livestock or people because of the threat of disease; *Smith v. St. Louis & Southwestern Railway Company* (1901) and *Compagnie Francaise de Navigation a Vapeur v. Louisiana State Board of Health* (1902). Apparently, Harlan was so suspicious of localism that he wished the Court to make the states allow both cows and people a chance to prove their good health.

Harlan was more successful when states tried to close their borders to out-of-state meat in a heavy-handed manner. In *Minnesota v. Berber* (1890) he carried the Court with him in striking down a law which made it practically impossible for anyone to sell out-of-state meat in Minnesota markets. He had similar luck in *Brimmer v. Rebman* (1891), where Virginia placed an inspection fee on all meat slaughtered 100 miles from Norfolk.

Statutory discrimination against out-of-state products was only the tip of the iceberg of localism in Harlan's eyes. He wanted to improve the status of foreign (i.e., out-of-state) corporations. In *Hooper v. California* (1895) and *Nutting v. Massachusetts* (1902), Harlan tried but failed to convince the Court that insurance policies should fall under the constitutional defini-

tion of commerce. He always objected to stipulations made by the states that foreign corporations exchange their right to resort to the federal courts for permission to enter; he joined Justice Day's dissent to that practice in *Blake v. McClung* (1898). The Court's willingness to tolerate the statutory sniping which the states directed at one another's foreign corporations provoked his dissents in *Philadelphia Fire Association v. New York* (1886) and *New York v. Roberts* (1898). Harlan was vindicated late in life by three decisions involving foreign corporations which he delivered, *Western Union Telegraph Company v. Kansas* (1910), *Ludwig v. Western Union Telegraph Company* (1910), and *International Textbook Company v. Pigg* (1910). The year 1910 seems to have marked the beginning of the end for unconditional requirements laid upon foreign corporations in exchange for permission to enter a state.

More than other brethren, Harlan feared that state taxation would burden interstate commerce. When he stood before his constitutional law class at the Columbia (now George Washington University) Law School on January 8, 1898, he confided to his students one absolute certainty: "that there is not a state in this union which would not, if it had the power, support its government from top to bottom by levying tribute or taxes upon the commerce among the states; they have all tried to do it." His accuracy and disapproval was born out in decisions involving the issue of taxing property used in interstate commerce where he dissented (sometimes with others) from the Court's less strict standard of judgment: *Pullman's Palace Car Company v. Pennsylvania* (1891), *Maine v. Grand Trunk Railway Company* (1891), *Horn Silver Mining Company v. New York State* (1892), *Ficklen v. Shelby County Taxing District* (1892), *Adams Express Company v. Ohio State Auditor* (1897), *Pittsburgh, Cincinnati, Chicago and St. Louis Railway Company v. Backus* (1894), *Kidd v. Alabama* (1903), and *Postal Telegraph-Cable Company* (1904). There were only occasional victories, such as *Louisville & Jeffersonsville Ferry Company v. Kentucky* (1903), where Harlan convinced the majority of the Court that the state had tried to tax property which was not actually within its control.

It is perhaps this zeal for an unrestricted flow of commerce among the states that explains Harlan's support for that most controversial of Gilded Age doctrines—substantive due process—whereby the Court set itself up as a kind of superagency passing on the reasonableness of railroad and other rates set by state legislatures and state commissions. Harlan explained in his law lecture for April 23, 1898, that:

> since the adoption of the 14th amendment there have been a great many decisions in the country as to what constitutes due process of law, and you will never hear the last of that phrase as long as this is a free country because there are varying circumstances arising and the judges are put at their wits' ends to know whether this, that or the other act transcends the provision of the Constitution.

Harlan's contribution to defining due process were two decisions: *Covington & Lexington Turnpike Road Company v. Sandford* (1896), and more importantly, *Smyth v. Ames* (1898), where he held that the judiciary was best suited to act as an evenhanded dispenser of justice between the corporation's property rights and the public's right to service. He offered a formula for judges to consult in estimating the fair value of the property and thus the proper rate of carriage. For this, he brought down on his head the opprobrium of a good many constitutional scholars who do not believe the judiciary constitutionally qualified or institutionally capable of playing such a role. However, this opinion, with its careful balancing of the interests of farmers and merchants on the one hand, and of the rail lines on the other, contains a logic which is often overlooked.

Substantive due process is the doctrine most often cited as proof of the Gilded Age judiciary's favoritism of property holders at the expense of the general population. While Harlan may have had a hand in creating the legal framework for a marketplace which gave rise to the national corporations that seemed to threaten the country with plutocracy, he was clearly more supportive of federal action to counter such a threat than any of his brethren. He dissented in the *Income Tax Case* (1895), where the Court struck down the tax on the grounds that as a direct tax it should have been apportioned among the states according to population. "No such apportionment can possibly be made without doing gross injustice to the many for the benefit of the favored few in particular States," he complained, and then urged the populace to amend the Constitution—which it did.

Harlan also supported the Interstate Commerce Commission in a string of cases where the majority of the Court gutted its powers, including *Texas v. Pacific Railway Company v. ICC* (1896), *ICC v. Cincinnati, New Orleans & Texas Pacific Railway* (1897), and *ICC v. Alabama Midland Railway Company*, (1897). Harlan complained in this last dissent that "taken in connection with other decisions defining the power of the Interstate Commerce Commission, the present decision, it seem to me, goes far to make that commission a useless body for all practical purposes, and to defeat many of the important objects designed to be accomplished."

Similarly, he believed that the Court's interpretation of the Sherman Antitrust Act of 1890 in *United States v. E.C. Knight Company* (1895) went a long way toward preventing the federal government from controlling monopolies. The Court distinguished between commerce, which Congress might regulate, and manufacturing, which it might not, and held that the sugar monopoly fell into the latter category. Harlan dissented silently from other decisions which limited the scope of the law, such as *Hopkins v. United States* (1898) and *Anderson v. United States* (1898).

Such decisions led to Harlan's being called "The Great Dissenter," but he was victorious in *Northern Securities Company v. United States* (1903), where he held that the Sherman Act authorized the attorney general to stop railroad tycoons J. P. Morgan and James J. Hill from consolidating their roads. The government's effort, he explained, would prevent the public from finding itself "at the absolute mercy of the holding corporation." *Northern Securities* popularized both Harlan and the antitrust effort; he again came to public notice in the 1911 trust cases, *Standard Oil v. United States* and *United States v. American Tobacco.* While Harlan supported the Court's finding that the government had a case against both monopolies, he feared that references to the "rule of reason" were the majority's way of "usurp[ing] the constitutional functions of the legislative branch of the Government." He feared that in the future, judges might use their discretion to decide that some restraints of trade created by such monopolies were not unreasonable, and then disallow efforts to prosecute such corporations. Harlan reminded his brethren that when the Sherman Act was passed:

> the conviction was universal that the country was in real danger from . . . the slavery that would result from aggregations of capital in the hands of a few individuals and corporations controlling, for their own profit and advantage exclusively, the entire business of the country, including the production and sale of the necessaries of life.

That Harlan could use the language of slavery so vividly almost fifty years after the Civil War is one indication of how closely his imagination was bound up with that war's transformative effects. Harlan never shook off completely the habits of his antebellum life, but he came to see nationalism as the central organizing principle of political and constitutional thought when he sat on the bench from 1877 to 1911

—LINDA C. A. PRZYBYSZEWSKI

BIBLIOGRAPHY

There are two large collections of private papers which contain Court-related materials, one at the Library of Congress and the other at the University of Louisville Law School.

There is only one full-length biography of Harlan, Loren Beth's *John Marshall Harlan: The Last Whig Justice* (1992), a book which covers all the important legal issues, but which is less analytical than one might have desired. An early dissertation by Floyd Barzilla Clark, "The Constitutional Doctrines of Justice Harlan" (Johns Hopkins, 1915), degenerates into a list at

times. A more analytical dissertation is Lewis Isaac Maddocks, "Justice John Marshall Harlan: Defender of Individual Rights" (Ohio State University, 1959). The best piece on Harlan's pre-Court political career is Louis Hartz's "John Marshall Harlan in Kentucky, 1855–1877," 14 *Filson Club Quarterly* 17 (1950). Before the civil rights movement flourished, there were several attempts to defend Harlan as a man before his time. See, for example, Edward F. Waite, "How 'Eccentric' was Mr. Justice Harlan?" 37 *Minnesota Law Review* 173 (1953), and Richard F. Watt and Richard M. Okiloff, "The Coming Vindication of Mr. Justice Harlan," 44 *Illinois Law Review* 13 (1949)

After *Brown v. Board of Education* (1954), many scholars turned to Harlan's civil rights decisions and the *Kentucky Law Journal* devoted its Spring 1958 issue to Harlan with articles by Henry J. Abraham, Florian Bartosic, David G. Farrelly, and Alan F. Westin. Probably the best article on civil rights, the seed of a never-finished biography, is Westin's, "John Marshall Harlan and the Constitutional Rights of Negroes: The Transformation of a Southerner," 66 *Yale Law Journal* 637 (1957). Monte Canfield, Jr., tried to use Harlan's approach to the state-action doctrine in "'Our Constitution is Color-Blind': Mr. Justice Harlan and Modern Problems of Civil Rights," 32 *University of Missouri at Kansas City Law Review* 292 (1964). Perhaps the only piece which looks closely (and caustically) at Harlan's economic decisions is Mary Cornelia Aldis Porter, "John Marshall Harlan the Elder & Federal Common Law: A Lesson From History," 1972 *Supreme Court Review* 1.

Several works which explore important decisions include: David G. Farrelly, "Justice Harlan's Dissent in the Pollock Case," 24 *Southern California Law Review* 174 (1951); J. Morgan Kousser, "Separate But Not Equal: The Supreme Court's First Decision on Racial Discrimination in the Schools," 46 *Journal of Southern History* 17 (1980); and Charles A. Lofgren, *The Plessy Case: A Legal-Historical Perspective* (1987).

John Marshall Harlan II
Photograph by Harris and Ewing.
Collection of the Supreme Court of the United States.

JOHN MARSHALL HARLAN II

BORN 20 May 1899, Chicago, Illinois

NOMINATED to the Court 8 November 1954
by Dwight D. Eisenhower

TOOK seat 28 March 1955; retired
23 September 1971

DIED 29 December 1971 in Washington, D.C.

John Marshall Harlan was the son of John Maynard Harlan and Elizabeth Palmer Flagg Harlan. His family was distinguished in the law. His great-grandfather was a lawyer; his grandfather, for whom he was named, was a justice of the United States Supreme Court for thirty-four years; his father was a lawyer; and an uncle was a member of the Interstate Commerce Commission.

Harlan studied at Princeton University (A.B., 1920), and was a Rhodes scholar for three years at Balliol College, Oxford, where he began the study of law and formed lifetime attachments. Harlan completed his legal education at New York Law School (LL.B., 1924), and was admitted to practice in New York in 1925.

Harlan began his career with Root, Clark, Buckner & Howland, a large Wall Street firm. When a senior member of the firm, Emory R. Buckner, was appointed United States attorney for the southern district of New York in 1925, Harlan became his assistant. During this period Harlan participated in several noted matters, including the prosecution of Harry M. Daugherty, former U.S. attorney general, for official misconduct and of Thomas W. Miller, former alien property custodian, for fraudulent conspiracy.

Harlan was made a partner in the Root, Clark firm in 1931 and, after the death of Buckner in 1941, he became its leading trial lawyer. Harlan's practice had unusual range and complexity. For example, he represented the New York City Board of Higher Education in litigation involving the appointment of free-thinking Bertrand Russell to teach in City College; he handled the will of Miss Ella Wendel, involving an extensive fortune and a host of claimants—at least one of whom was subsequently convicted of fraud; and he represented heavyweight champion Gene Tunney in a contract action.

During World War II, Harlan rendered conspicuous service in England as head of the operational analysis section of the Eighth Air Force, which was composed of hand-picked civilians in the fields of mathematics, physics, electronics, architecture, and law, to furnish advice on bombing operations. Harlan was awarded the United States Legion of Merit and the Croix de Guerre of Belgium and France.

On return to private practice in 1945, Harlan was soon recognized as a leader of the New York bar. He participated in a large number of important matters, arguing several appeals before the United States Supreme Court, including one case that became a landmark in corporate law and civil procedure.

Although private practice was his professional love, Harlan soon was again called to public service. From 1951 to 1953, he acted as chief counsel for the New York State Crime Commission, which Governor Thomas Dewey had appointed to investigate the relationship between organized crime and state government. Harlan was also active in professional organizations, serving as chairman of the committee on the judiciary and vice-president of the Association of the Bar of the City of New York.

In January 1954, Harlan was appointed a judge of the United States court of appeals for the second circuit. He served less than a year before President Eisenhower appointed him to the Supreme Court.

Throughout most of his years on the Supreme Court, Justice Harlan provided a form of resistance to the dominant liberal motifs of the Warren Court. He did this in a way that was intelligent, determined and, above all, principled. But it would be a mistake to conceive of Harlan solely in this conservative light. To a surprising degree, Harlan concurred in the liberal activism of the Court, picking his spots carefully and above all seeking to be true to his core judicial values. In all his work he exhibited outstanding professional competence, leading Judge Henry Friendly to write that "there has never been a Justice of the Supreme Court who has so consistently maintained a high quality of performance or, despite differences in views, has enjoyed such nearly uniform respect from his colleagues, the inferior bench, the bar, and the academy."

Harlan's two principal judicial values were federalism and proceduralism, both directed to keeping the "'delicate balance of federal-state relations' in good working order." On many occasions, Harlan in dissent criticized the Court's entry into political matters, as in *Reynolds v. Sims* (1964), or into state procedures, as in *Henry v. Mississippi* (1965), as inconsistent with the demands of the federal structure. His view of federalism is perhaps best summarized in a dissenting opinion by Justice Stephen Field in *Baltimore & Ohio Railroad v. Baugh* (1893), which Harlan quoted approvingly:

> The Constitution of the United States . . . recognizes and preserves the autonomy and independence of the States. . . . Supervision over either the legislative or the judicial action of the States is in no case permissible except as to matters by the Constitution specifically authorized or delegated to the United States.

Harlan applied federalism principles to restrict the so-called state action doctrine that permits expansion of federal court authority. He thought that such expansion over activities that are properly the responsibility of state government simultaneously impairs "independence in their legislative and independence in their judicial departments." Thus, despite his strong commitment to racial equality, Harlan did not believe that land bequeathed in trust to a Georgia city as a "park and pleasure ground" for white people was unconstitutionally administered merely because a state court replaced public trustees with private ones and the park was municipally maintained (*Evans v. Newton,* 1966). And in a nonracial context, Harlan dissented from a holding that a privately owned shopping mall was the equivalent of a company town and was thus barred from prohibiting peaceful picketing of a supermarket in the mall, in *Amalgamated Food Employees Union 590 v. Logan Valley Plaza, Inc.* (1968).

It is of special importance that Harlan saw federalism not only as part of our constitutional design, "born of the necessity of achieving

union," but as "a bulwark of freedom as well." In one of his speeches he declared:

> We are accustomed to speak of the Bill of Rights and the Fourteenth Amendment as the principal guarantees of personal liberty. Yet it would surely be shallow not to recognize that the structure of our political system accounts no less for the free society we have. Indeed, it was upon the structure of government that the founders primarily focused in writing the Constitution. Out of bitter experience they were suspicious of every form of all-powerful central authority and they sought to assure that such a government would never exist in this country by structuring the federal establishment so as to diffuse power between the executive, legislative, and judicial branches.

Harlan also viewed federalism as essential for preserving pluralism and local experimentation. No other political system "could have afforded so much scope to the varied interests and aspirations of a dynamic people representing such divergencies of ethnic and cultural backgrounds," and still "unify them into a nation." Addressing government power to regulate obscenity, Harlan said: "One of the great strengths of our federal system is that we have, in the forty-eight States, forty-eight experimental social laboratories."

Harlan's dedication to proceduralism was equally firm. "Proceduralism" refers not only to rules that govern trials and appeals, but also to issues that determine when the judicial power will be exercised. In his dissent in *Reynolds v. Sims* (1964) from the Court's "one person, one vote" decision, Harlan stated his basic philosophy. He rejected the view:

> that every major social ill in this country can find its cure in some constitutional "principle," and that this Court should "take the lead" in promoting reform when other branches of government fail to act. The Constitution is not a panacea for every blot on the public welfare, nor should this Court, ordained as a judicial body, be thought of as a general haven for reform movements.

Thus, Harlan urged the Court to steer clear of "political thickets," lest "the vitality of our political system, on which in the last analysis all else depends, is weakened by reliance on the judiciary for political reform; in time a complacent body politic may result."

Harlan embodied his view of the limited role of the courts in a series of doctrines. First, he jealously guarded the Supreme Court's appellate authority, which he believed should be used "for the settlement of [issues] of importance to the public," and "should not be exercised simply 'for the benefit of the particular litigants.'" He repeatedly called on the Court to follow a number of practices designed to avoid unnecessary or premature judicial intervention, such as allowing administrative processes to run their course, not passing on the validity of state statutes which have neither been enforced nor interpreted by state courts, avoiding issues not considered below, and refusing to hear appeals of nonfinal orders.

Second, Harlan urged the Court to show deference to other decision-making authorities. For example, perhaps growing out of his experience as a trial lawyer, Harlan believed strongly in deference to the fact-finding of trial courts, saying that "appellate courts have no facilities for the examination of witnesses; nor in the nature of things can they have that intimate knowledge of the evidence and 'feel' of the trial scene."

Finally, Harlan was committed to the stable and predictable development of the law. He protested when the Court resolved important issues by way of summary disposition. For example, in the 1971 Pentagon Papers case (*New York Times Co. v. United States*), Harlan in dissent recounted the "frenzied train of events" whereby, within one week from the date of lower court decisions, the Court heard argument and issued a decision. He identified several difficult issues and noted that the "time which has been available to us, to the lower courts, and to the parties has been wholly inadequate for giving these cases the kind of consideration they deserve."

In light of his commitment to federalism and proceduralism, we may now look more closely at Harlan's dissents from the principal civil liberty themes of the Warren Court. Perhaps

the most central of these is "equality," an idea that as Archibald Cox put it, "once loosed . . . is not easily cabined." Harlan vigorously opposed egalitarian rulings of many kinds. He was most vehement in condemning the reapportionment decisions, first in *Baker v. Carr* (1962), in which the Court authorized federal jurisdiction to decide the issue whether state legislative districts were malapportioned, then in *Reynolds v. Sims*, in which the Court established the one person, one vote rule, and in the many sequels to these rulings. Harlan never became reconciled to what he regarded as a wholly unjustified encroachment into the political realm, saying in *Reynolds* that "it is difficult to imagine a more intolerable and inappropriate interference by the judiciary with the independent legislatures of the States."

Closely related to the reapportionment cases are those dealing with the right to vote. Harlan dissented from the ruling that invalidated Virginia's poll tax, from a decision that opened school board elections to a man who was neither a parent nor a property holder in the district, and from the decision upholding Congress's power to extend the franchise to eighteen-year-olds.

The poll tax case illustrates an aspect of the Court's egalitarianism to which Harlan especially objected: its acceptance of the idea that government has an obligation to eliminate economic inequalities as a way to permit everyone to exercise human rights. The leading case in this regard was *Griffin v. Illinois* (1956), in which a sharply divided bench held that where a stenographic trial transcript is needed for appellate review, a state violates the Fourteenth Amendment by refusing to provide the transcript to an impoverished defendant who alleges reversible errors in his trial. Harlan's dissent maintained that "all that Illinois has done is to fail to alleviate the consequences of differences in economic circumstances that exist wholly apart from any state action." He later dissented in *Douglas v. California* (1963), where the Court held that a state had to provide counsel to a convicted indigent seeking to appeal.

Another example of this genre was Harlan's protests at efforts to transform welfare payments into an entitlement. Harlan maintained in dissent that states could deny such payments to otherwise eligible welfare applicants who had not resided in the state for a year or more (*Shapiro v. Thompson,* 1969).

Harlan also found himself out of step with the prevailing view on criminal procedure in state trials, where the Warren Court rewrote the book, transforming the law relating to confessions and lineups, the privilege against self-incrimination, jury trials, wiretapping and eavesdropping, and the admissibility of illegally obtained evidence. Harlan vigorously dissented from almost all of the key decisions, asserting that a healthy federalism was inconsistent with the assertion of national judicial power over state criminal justice.

Harlan also objected in the interests of federalism to extensions of congressional power. In the two most significant cases, he protested when the Court adopted broad theories in sustaining the authority of Congress to invalidate state English-language literacy tests for voting as applied to individuals who completed the sixth grade in Puerto Rican schools (*Katzenbach v. Morgan,* 1966), and to punish private (as distinguished from state) interference with constitutional rights (*United States v. Guest,* 1966).

At the same time, Harlan, contrary to the majority, deferred to congressional judgments that resulted in an impairment of civil liberties. For example, he conceded broad authority to Congress over citizenship, rejecting any constitutional right to prevent involuntary denationalization in *Afroyim v. Rusk* (1967), protesting a softening of the immigration law that provided for deportation of an alien who had ever been a member of the Communist party, however nominally, in *Rowoldt v. Perfetto* (1957), and opposing a constitutional right to travel abroad in *Kent v. Dulles* (1958). In these cases he refused to overturn actions of the elected branches of government that resulted in severe and arguably unjustified harm to individuals.

In addition to these dissents from many of the Warren Court's key liberal decisions, there were many important cases in which Harlan was part of a majority that rejected constitutional theories supported by the liberal justices. For example, he wrote the prevailing opinions that rejected First Amendment claims by individuals who were held

in contempt by the House Un-American Activities Committee (*Barenblatt v. United States,* 1959), were denied admission to the practice of law for refusing to respond to questions concerning Communist activities (*Konigsberg v. State Bar,* 1961), and sentenced to prison because of membership in the Communist party (*Scales v. United States,* 1961). He also agreed with rulings that permitted states to question suspects of crime without regard to the privilege against self-incrimination, and that denied women the right to serve on juries equally with men.

The Warren Court ended in mid-1969, but Harlan remained for two more terms, a brief period in which he was the leader of the Court. Possessing seniority and an unmatched professional reputation, he took advantage of the replacement of Earl Warren and Abe Fortas by Warren Burger and Harry Blackmun to regain the position of dominance that Felix Frankfurter and he shared until Frankfurter retired in August 1962. Thus, against Harlan's average of 62.6 dissenting votes per term in the period between 1963 and 1967, he cast only twenty-four such votes in the 1969 term and eighteen in the 1970 term.

This new situation meant that Harlan could reassert conservative themes in his own opinions or join such expressions in the opinions of others. For example, during this period he adhered to his longstanding opposition to expansion of the constitutional rights of poor people to public assistance in the leading case rejecting welfare as an entitlement in *Dandridge v. Williams* (1970).

Similarly, he prevailed in a series of criminal justice decisions, including those that denied a right to jury trial in juvenile delinquency proceedings, and permitted the closing of such hearings to the public, in *McKeiver v. Pennsylvania* (1971), and authorized capital sentencing without guidelines in *McGautha v. California* (1971). And Harlan joined the opinion sustaining the power of caseworkers to make unannounced visits to the homes of welfare recipients to check their eligibility and provide rehabilitative assistance. *Wyman v. James* (1971).

In the First Amendment area Harlan also maintained longstanding positions, but here he was more often in dissent. The most notable occasion was *New York Times Co. v. United States* (1971), where he would have permitted the prior restraint of newspaper publication of the Pentagon Papers, an extensive and politically embarrassing history of the Vietnam War. He also dissented in an important libel case, *Rosenbloom v. Metromedia, Inc.* (1971), and in two decisions restricting the authority of bar examiners to probe into the associations of applicants, *In re Stolar* (1971) and *Baird v. State Bar* (1971). But he prevailed in another bar admission case, recalling issues from earlier days, that upheld questions about Communist associations (*LSRRC v. Wadmond,* 1971), and he was part of the majority that sustained an important obscenity prosecution in *United States v. Reidel* (1971).

But these conservative opinions and votes are far from the whole story. Justice Potter Stewart, one of Harlan's closest colleagues, recognized this when he said at a memorial service after Harlan died: "I can assure you that a very interesting law review article could someday be written on 'The Liberal Opinions of Mr. Justice Harlan.'" In virtually every area of the Court's work, there are cases in which Harlan was part of the Warren Court consensus and, indeed, in which he spoke for the Court.

Harlan joined *Brown v. Board of Education II* (1955) and *Cooper v. Aaron* (1958), decisions instrumental in protecting the principle of school desegregation. He also joined every opinion decided while he was on the Court that rejected other sorts of state-enforced segregation.

He concurred in *Gideon v. Wainwright* (1963), the pathbreaking case granting a right to counsel to accused felons, and he wrote the opinion of the Court in *Boddie v. Connecticut* (1971), which held that a state could not deny a divorce to a couple because they lacked the means to pay the judicial filing fee. Although both these cases were decided under the due process clause, they amounted at bottom to judicially mandated equalization of economic circumstance in situations where Harlan concluded that it would be fundamentally unfair to deny poor people what others could afford.

In the criminal procedure area, while opposing the rule that excluded illegally seized evidence in state prosecutions, he consistently supported a strong version of the Fourth Amendment protection against unreasonable searches and seizures by federal authorities, as in *Jones v. United States* (1958) and *Giordenello v. United States* (1958), including application of the principle to wiretapping and eavesdropping (*Katz v. United States,* 1967). He also supported the ruling that extended criminal due process protections to juveniles accused of delinquency (*In re Gault,* 1967).

One also finds many important cases in which Harlan supported the right of free expression. For example, he wrote the opinion in *NAACP v. Alabama* (1958), which held that freedom of association protected the right of individuals to join unpopular civil rights groups anonymously. He joined *New York Times Co. v. Sullivan* (1964), which first imposed limits on libel judgments against the media, and some (though not all) of the sequels to that case. He joined opinions that barred states from refusing to seat an elected legislator because of his sharply critical views on the Vietnam War (*Bond v. Floyd,* 1966), and from convicting a leader of the Ku Klux Klan for "seditious" speech (*Brandenburg v. Ohio,* 1969). And he wrote for the Court to protect the right of a black man, unnerved by the shooting of a civil rights leader, to sharply criticize the country while burning the flag (*Street v. New York,* 1969). Harlan also wrote opinions, all curbing variants of McCarthyism, that nominally were decided on nonconstitutional grounds but rested on First Amendment principles (*Cole v. Young,* 1956; *Service v. Dulles,* 1957; *Yates v. United States,* 1957; and *Maisenberg v. United States,* 1958).

Freedom of religion also showed Harlan as frequently, but not invariably, protective of constitutional guarantees. He joined decisions that prohibited organized prayer in the public schools (*Engel v. Vitale,* 1962), and that invalidated a requirement that state officials declare a belief in God (*Torcaso v. Watkins,* 1961). And while approving state loans of textbooks to church schools (*Board of Education v. Allen,* 1968), he balked when tax-raised funds were used to reimburse parochial schools for teachers' salaries, textbooks, and instructional materials (*Lemon v. Kurtzman,* 1971). Similarly, while unwilling to grant constitutional protection to adherents to sabbatarian faiths who objected to Sunday closing laws in *Braunfield v. Brown* (1961), and to unemployment compensation laws that required Saturday work in *Sherbert v. Verner* (1963), Harlan wrote a powerful opinion during the Vietnam War declaring that a statute that limited conscientious objection to those who believed in a theistic religion offended the establishment clause because it "accords a preference to the 'religious' [and] disadvantages adherents of religions that do not worship a Supreme Being" (*Welsh v. United States,* 1970).

In these cases, Harlan emphasized that "the attitude of government towards religion must . . . be one of neutrality." Harlan was sophisticated enough to appreciate that neutrality is "a coat of many colors." Nevertheless, as Professor Kent Greenawalt has observed, "no modern justice has striven harder or more successfully than Justice Harlan to perform his responsibilities in [a neutral] manner."

A final area of civil liberties, sexual privacy, is of particular importance because Harlan produced the most influential opinions on this subject written by anyone during his tenure on the Court. In the first case, a thin majority led by Justice Frankfurter refused to adjudicate, on the ground that there was no threat of prosecution, the merits of a Connecticut law that criminalized the sale of contraceptives to married and unmarried people alike (*Poe v. Ullman,* 1961). Harlan's emotional opinion—a rarity for him—not only differed with this conclusion, but extensively defended the proposition that Connecticut's law violated the due process clause of the Fourteenth Amendment, a position that soon prevailed in *Griswold v. Connecticut* (1965), the case that first recognized a right to sexual privacy. It is impossible to know whether Harlan would have extended this reasoning to support the result in *Eisenstadt v. Baird* (1972), which held that a state could not punish the distribution of contraceptives to unmarried persons, or the recognition of abortion as a personal right in *Roe v. Wade* (1973), both decided soon after he retired. But I am confident that, at a minimum, he would have protected the right of a married woman to proceed with an abortion that was dictated by family considerations.

Harlan's participation in the major thrusts of the Warren Court was not confined to civil liberties and civil rights. In economic cases, too, he sometimes went along with the majority's support of government regulation of business, despite the fact that his private practice often involved the defense of antitrust and other actions involving the government.

Harlan fortified his formidable conservative record under Chief Justice Warren Burger after the Warren Court ended. But he nevertheless adhered to a balanced judicial profile by supporting some of the Court's liberal activist rulings. Thus, in the equality area, he maintained his support for desegregation, and he joined the new chief justice's opinion expanding remedies against discriminatory employment tests in *Griggs v. Duke Power Co.* (1971), and he continued his deep concern for Fourth Amendment rights in *Coolidge v. New Hampshire* (1971). The opinion in *Boddie*, which invalidated a state statute that denied poor couples the right to a divorce because they could not afford court filing fees, came during this period. Harlan's reliance on the due process clause to reach this result was criticized, and the doctrine has not survived, but the case stands as a rare example of Harlan's reaching out to right an economic imbalance that prejudiced poor people in American society. In the First Amendment field, he wrote a widely cited opinion that protected the display on a jacket in a state courthouse of a "scurrilous epithet" ("fuck the draft"), in protest against conscription (*Cohen v. California,* 1971).

What should one conclude from the many decisions in which Justice Harlan, a conservative, supported constitutional rights, often in highly controversial cases in which the Court was split? That he was in step with the majority of the Warren Court? Plainly not. There are too many instances where he marched separately. That he was essentially a civil libertarian? No again. Not only are there too many cases to the contrary, but at a basic level, that is not the way Harlan reacted to injustice. This is not to say that he was insensitive to human suffering or unmoved by evidence of arbitrariness. It is rather that something else was at the core.

That something was Harlan's deep, almost visceral, desire to keep things in balance, to resist excess in any direction. Many times during my year as one of his clerks he said how important it was "to keep things on an even keel." To me, that is the master key to Harlan and his jurisprudence. One recalls Castle, the hero of Graham Greene's novel, *The Human Factor*, as he muses on those who are "unable to love success or power or great beauty." Castle concluded that it is not because these people feel unworthy or are "more at home with failure." It is rather that "one wanted the right balance." In reflecting on some of his own perplexing and self-destructive actions, Castle decided that "he was there to right the balance. That was all." Harlan was not a man who avoided success or power or, if one knew Mrs. Harlan, great beauty, but nevertheless, in his own eyes, he was there to right the balance. It is significant that he entitled a major speech at the American Bar Association "Thoughts at a Dedication: Keeping the Judicial Function in Balance."

There is evidence of balance not only in the decisions discussed above, but in his elaborate views on doctrines of justiciability. These are closely related to his frequent preoccupation with judicial modesty or, put negatively, his opposition to excessive judicial activism, which in turn is linked to the central theme of his judicial universe—federalism. Several years ago, I suggested that "his pervasive concern has been over a judiciary that will arrogate power not rightfully belonging to it and impose its views of government from a remote tower, thereby enervating the initiative and independence at the grass roots that are essential to a thriving democracy."

On the other hand, reflecting his balanced approach, Harlan wrote or joined many opinions that expanded the Court's jurisdiction. One was *Poe v. Ullman* (1961), where he vigorously dissented from Justice Frankfurter's reasoning in dismissing an early challenge to Connecticut's birth control law on the ground that the statute was not being enforced. Again, in *NAACP v. Alabama* (1958), the first case explicitly recognizing a freedom of association, his opinion for the Court overcame difficult procedural obstacles involving the doctrines of standing and independent and adequate state grounds. In the first school prayer case, *Engel v. Vitale* (1962), and again in the ruling that ordered the House of Representatives to seat Adam Clayton Powell,

Powell v. McCormack (1969), both cases of unusual sensitivity, Harlan joined majority opinions that rejected substantial procedural defenses.

Stare decisis is another area relating to legal process and the judge's role in which Harlan sometimes manifested an activist spirit. He recognized that the doctrine "provides the stability and predictability required for the ordering of human affairs over the course of time and a basis of 'public faith in the judiciary as a source of impersonal and reasoned judgments.'" And while the principle should not be "woodenly applied," and "no precedent is sacrosanct,"

> surely if the principle of *stare decisis* means anything in the law, it means that precedent should not be jettisoned when the rule of yesterday remains viable, creates no injustice, and can reasonably be said to be no less sound than the rule sponsored by those who seek change, let alone incapable of being demonstrated wrong.

There are, therefore, many cases where Harlan vigorously protested the overruling of precedent.

But there are also many contrary instances which betoken Harlan's flexibility. Thus, Harlan wrote separately in *Gideon v. Wainright* (1963) to give *Betts v. Brady* (1942), "a more respectful burial than has been accorded" by the Court. In *Marchetti v. United States* (1968), he spoke for the Court in overruling a decision that denied the privilege against self-incrimination to gamblers prosecuted for failing to register and pay taxes. In *Moragne v. States Marine Line, Inc.* (1970), a celebrated opinion, he overruled a case that "rested on a most dubious foundation when announced, has become an increasingly unjustifiable anomaly as the law over the years has left it behind, and . . . has produced litigation-spawning confusion in an area that should be easily susceptible of more workable solutions."

Finally, one may point to a series of cases in which Harlan exhibited a trait familiar to all of his law clerks—his exceptional open-mindedness and willingness to listen to new arguments. In these cases he dissented from the Court's refusal to hear oral argument on constitutional claims, although in each of them he was not predisposed to endorse the merits of the appeal. Thus, he joined Justice Douglas's dissent from the refusal to hear a plea that a group was improperly ordered to register as a Communist front organization (*Veterans of the Abraham Lincoln Brigade v. Subversive Activities Control Bd.*, 1965). And in perhaps the most far-reaching action, he would have set down for oral argument a complaint that challenged the legality of the Vietnam War, *Massachusetts v. Laird* (1970), although he ordinarily accorded great deference to the elected branches of government on matters of war and peace.

The pattern of decisions provides ample proof that Harlan was not a one-dimensional justice. What is less obvious is the source of his drive to keep things in balance, to eschew an extreme ideology.

Two possibilities may be suggested. The first is the familiar notion that, in any society, patricians (like Harlan) are concerned less with results in particular controversies, and certainly less about pressing any group against the wall, than with assuring the smooth functioning of institutions without the precipitation of volatility or deep-seated enmities. This means that dissent should be allowed an outlet, that minorities should be able to hope, that political power should not become centralized and therefore dangerous. Thus Harlan's decisions supporting desegregation, a strong federal presence, and law and order. Thus also his fears about court-dominated legislative reapportionment and about the "incorporation" of the Bill of Rights through the Fourteenth Amendment that enhanced judicial authority and represented too dramatic a break with established doctrine. But thus also Harlan's willingness to take reformist steps, to overrule outdated precedent selectively and before a problem worsened, and above all to listen closely to many voices.

These traits are consistent with Harlan's warm embrace of federalism principles. It should be recalled that the idea of federalism itself is a kind of balance—a way of dividing governmental authority to prevent a too-easy dominance of public life by a single institution or faction. The Federalist Papers are explicit in extolling, as a "guard against dangerous encroachments," the division of power "between two distinct governments" so that the "different governments will control each." Years ago I reflected on whether

the national government or states and local governments are the securer bulwark of—or the greater threat to—civil liberty.

Local units are closer to the people but offer more opportunity for undetected discrimination and repression. The national government acts more visibly and with more formal regard for minority interests, but its vast power is a civil liberties time bomb that in this century has brought us the Palmer Raids, McCarthyism, and Watergate.

Whatever the proper resolution of this question, it is clear that Justice Harlan believed, as much as he believed in any principle, that federalism was "a bulwark of freedom."

A second source of Harlan's overall philosophy is legal process theory, which had its heyday during almost exactly the period that he served on the Supreme Court. In the early 1950s, Henry Hart produced a draft of the work that he and Albert Sacks published at Harvard Law School in a "tentative edition" in 1958 (it was also the final edition). The moderate philosophy embodied in these materials, entitled "The Legal Process: Basic Problems in the Making and Application of Law," was tailor-made to Harlan's personality. It emphasized the central role that procedure plays in assuring judicial and legislative objectivity and argued that "just" policies will result when each branch of government works within its assigned role. In this way courts through "reasoned elaboration" of decisions, and legislatures through the public-seeking interpretation of statutes, will assure maximum fulfillment of society's expectations.

Not surprisingly, Harlan was attracted to this theory, which enabled him to take constitutional steps as long as they were not too long or jarring, while simultaneously offering him ample institutional reasons for resisting excessive judicial authority. This approach was often enlisted in opinions that were inhospitable to civil liberties, but Harlan's reliance on legal process also led him at times to the protection of individual rights and the overruling of outmoded precedent.

By 1971, when Harlan left the Supreme Court, legal process theory, buffeted by events in society at large, was beginning to lose its hold, even at Harvard, and the more extreme philosophies of law and economics and critical legal studies soon moved to the forefront. The struggle within the Court became ever more polarized as in succeeding years strong civil libertarians, which Harlan was not, waged battle with doctrinaire conservatives, which he also was not.

It fell to John Marshall Harlan, by nature a patrician traditionalist, to serve on a Supreme Court which, for most of his years, was rapidly revising and liberalizing constitutional law. In these circumstances, it is not surprising that Harlan would protest the direction of the Court and the speed with which it was traveling. He did this in a remarkably forceful and principled manner, thereby providing balance to the institution and the law it generated. Despite this role, Harlan joined civil liberties rulings on the Court during his tenure to the degree that his overall jurisprudence can fairly be characterized as conservative primarily in the sense that it evinced caution, a fear of centralized authority, and a respect for process.

—NORMAN DORSEN

BIBLIOGRAPHY

Justice Harlan's papers are deposited in the Seeley G. Mudd Manuscript Library at Princeton University. Tinsley E. Yarbrough, *John Marshall Harlan: Great Dissenter of the Warren Court* (1992), is the only comprehensive biography, and provides considerable information on Harlan's life as well as his career on the Supreme Court. A biographical note cites to several doctoral dissertations on the justice. David L. Shapiro, ed., *The Evolution of a Judicial Philosophy: Selected Opinions and Papers of Justice John M. Harlan* (1969), is a compilation of opinions, speeches, and tributes through June 1968, carefully selected and edited by a former law clerk.

Various articles and symposia worth consulting include: Henry J. Bourguignon, "The Second Mr. Justice Harlan: His Principles of Judicial Decision Making," 1979 *Supreme Court Review* 251; Centennial Conference in honor of Justice John Marshall Harlan, 36 *New York Law School Law Review* 1 (1991) includes contributions by judges, former law clerks, and scholars on Harlan as a judicial conservative, Harlan and the Bill of Rights, and Harlan's legal process; "Comment, The Legitimacy of Civil Law Reasoning in the Common Law: Justice Harlan's Contribution," 82 *Yale Law Journal* 258 (1972); Norman Dorsen, "The Second Mr. Justice Harlan: A Constitutional Conservative," 44 *New York University Law Review* 249 (1969); Daniel A. Farber, "Civilizing Public Discourse: An Essay on Professor Bickel, Justice Harlan, and the Enduring Significance of *Cohen v. California*," 1980 *Duke Law Journal* 283; and "Mr. Justice Harlan," 85 *Harvard Law Review* 369 (1971), consisting of articles on the occasion of his retirement by Earl Warren, J. Edward Lumbard, John E. F. Wood, Henry J. Friendly, and Charles Nesson.

Oliver Wendell Holmes, Jr.
Photograph by Harris and Ewing.
Collection of the Supreme Court of the United States.

OLIVER WENDELL HOLMES, JR.

BORN 8 March 1841, Boston, Massachusetts

NOMINATED to the Court 11 August 1902
by Theodore Roosevelt

TOOK seat 8 December 1902; retired
12 January 1932

DIED 6 March 1935 in Washington, D. C.

Oliver Wendell Holmes is the best known Supreme Court Justice in history, and has consistently been ranked by commentators as one of the "great" justices to sit on the Court. Holmes is also notable in engendering more literature, both scholarly and popular, than any other justice. More than 150 years after his birth, his life and career continue to be objects of fascination.

Holmes had literary aspirations as an undergraduate at Harvard, but they were postponed in the spring of his senior year, when the Civil War began. Holmes left Harvard and enlisted in the Twentieth Regiment of Massachusetts Volunteers, in which he eventually secured a commission as a lieutenant in July 1861.

Holmes's Civil War service was one of the memorable episodes in his life. He served until June 1864, and was wounded three times, in the chest, neck, and heel. The first two wounds were life-threatening, with only the fortunate trajectory of the bullets sparing him. For the remainder of his life Holmes thought of his experiences in the Civil War as especially vivid and meaningful. He claimed that his generation had been uniquely favored ("touched with fire") in being the first to participate in the "crusade" of the Civil War. He romanticized the experience of participating in war (as opposed to war itself, which he once described as "horrible and dull.") In 1895, he wrote an essay, "The Soldier's Faith," in which he characterized the attitude that made a soldier throw his life away for a cause that he could not comprehend as "true and adorable."

After his wartime service, Holmes returned to Boston, attended Harvard Law School, and after several years of practicing law, writing essays on legal history and jurisprudence for the *American Law Review* (of which he was coedi-

tor from 1870 to 1873), editing a volume of James Kent's *Commentaries on American Law*, writing his influential book, *The Common Law* (1881), and briefly teaching on the Harvard law faculty, Holmes was appointed an associate justice of the supreme judicial court of Massachusetts in December 1881. Holmes had always wanted to be a judge, feeling that academic life was "half life" and law practice was insufficiently theoretical. By 1901, he was chief justice of the Massachusetts court.

For all of Holmes's dedication to his work and satisfaction on being a judge, however, the demands of the Massachusetts court were not sufficient to meet his intellectual energies. During the twenty years he served, he continued to write scholarly articles and to make speeches and addresses, publishing them in a volume, *Speeches*, whose first edition appeared in 1891. "The Soldier's Faith" was one such address. It came to the attention of Governor Theodore Roosevelt of New York in the late 1890s, who was impressed with its apparently jingoistic sentiment. In the summer of 1902, Roosevelt, now president of the United States, nominated Holmes to the United States Supreme Court.

Cautious to the end, Holmes did not resign from the Massachusetts court until the Senate had formally confirmed him. He and Fanny then moved to Washington to start a new life. In the early months of his tenure, Holmes wrote friends of his wonder and delight in the magnitude of the task: the capacities of his fellow judges, the breadth of the legal questions, the energized political atmosphere of Washington.

Ten years later, Holmes no longer felt that the work of a Supreme Court justice was completely absorbing. He had found that he could easily keep up with the work of the Court, being able to dash off his assigned opinions and help recalcitrant justices with their work. He turned increasingly in his leisure time to his life-long hobbies of reading and correspondence, and as his personal contacts narrowed, his correspondence friendships increased. After 1912, the circle of his friends changed, as his older contemporaries began to die out. In their place he increasingly sought the company of a younger generation of intellectuals, among them Felix Frankfurter, Harold Laski, Learned Hand, Herbert Croly, Walter Lippmann, and Zechariah Chafee.

In seeking out the company of new friends, Holmes was seeking recognition. As surprising as it may currently appear, Holmes in 1912, after ten years on the Court, was still essentially unknown, not only to the lay public, but to all but a handful of lawyers. To the extent he had developed a reputation, it was with a handful of "progressive" intellectuals who had found in his dissent in the 1905 case of *Lochner v. New York* (1905), which tested the constitutionality of a state statute fixing minimum hours of work in the baking industry, the outlines of an appropriately deferential judicial attitude toward reformist social legislation. Beyond *Lochner*, which had only begun to be celebrated by 1912, many Court watchers found Holmes enigmatic and his opinions obscure.

A tally sheet of Holmes's major opinions during the first fifteen years of his tenure, 1902–1917, produces a record that seems at variance with subsequent images of Holmes as a judge. Not only was Holmes a largely unrecognized figure during those years, the principal attributes of his later images—that he was an enlightened judge in his deference to "progressive" legislation and that he was a supporter of civil liberties—are hard to square with the thrust of his decisions.

The best evidence of Holmes's attributed "enlightenment" can be found in a series of decisions, including *Lochner*, in which he made it clear that judges should not supersede the policies of legislatures on questions of economic policy. He had announced this posture in his very first opinion for the Court, *Otis v. Parker* (1902), a case testing the constitutionality of a California statute prohibiting contracts for the sales of shares of corporate capital stock on margin. "It by no means is true," Holmes wrote, "that every law is void which may seem to the judges who pass on it excessive, unsuited to its ostensible end, or based on conceptions of morality with which they disagree." A similar posture

marked his dissent in *Lochner* and his dissents in *Adair v. United States* (1907), *Noble State Bank v. Haskell* (1911), and *Coppage v. Kansas* (1914), all of which protested against judicial use of the doctrine of "liberty of contract," ostensibly derived from the Fourteenth Amendment's due process clause, to invalidate social legislation. In all those dissents Holmes deferred judgement on the wisdom of the legislation in question, while reiterating that, as he put it in *Haskell*, "judges should be slow to read into the [Constitution] a [mandate to void] . . . the legislative power."

Such opinions identified Holmes as having a clear and consistent approach to the scope of constitutional review in cases of social legislation. He was opposed to judicial glosses on the constitutional text, such as "liberty of contract," as a means of substituting the ideology of judges for that of legislators, so long as legislative decisions were arguably rationally based. Judicial intervention, in his view, was reserved for the case of the overwhelming constitutional mandate, as where a statute offended against the exact text of the Constitution. The opinions were not, however, necessarily supportive of any ideological position on the legitimacy of social legislation. While Holmes's results in the cases were endorsed by "progressives," who supported regulation of the industrial marketplace to foster desirable social ends, Holmes did not necessarily share that attitude.

Beyond that line of decisions and *Swift and Company v. United States* (1905), where Holmes found that an agreement among shippers of fresh meat to fix prices came within the reach of the Sherman Antitrust Act of 1887, there were few that early twentieth-century "progressives" would have found congenial. In the most celebrated case of Holmes's early tenure, *Northern Securities Co. v. United States* (1904), he was conspicuously on the "wrong" side. The Roosevelt administration had sought to apply the Sherman Antitrust Act, which outlawed "every contract, combination in the form of trust or otherwise, or conspiracy, in restraint of trade among the several states," against a holding company capitalized from the stock of competitor railroads. A bare majority of the Court found that the creation of the holding company violated the act. Holmes dissented, arguing that the meaning of the terms "contract," "combination," and "conspiracy" in the act could only be the technical meaning at common law, otherwise any two-party agreement between competitors of any size would violate the law. For this arguably common-sensical position he received the enmity of Roosevelt, who said that Holmes had been "a bitter disappointment . . . on the bench."

Similarly, in *Dr. Miles Medical Co. v. Park & Sons Co.* (1911), Holmes declined to apply the Sherman Act to an agreement between a manufacturer of proprietary medicines and representatives of drugstores in which the prices of patent medicines were fixed. In dissenting from a majority opinion that the price-fixing scheme violated the act, Holmes said that "I think . . . it is safe to say that the most enlightened judicial policy is to let people manage their own business in their own way, unless the ground for interference is very clear." He then went on to say that in his view, the meaning of the term "fair price" was the "point of most profitable returns." That point "marked the equilibrium of social desires" and determines the fair price. This was an astonishingly "unprogressive" statement in its espousal of judicial noninterference with the economic marketplace and its assumption that whatever was "profitable" in that marketplace was "fair."

If Holmes's early decisions on social legislation permit him to be labelled a "progressive" judge only with strain, his early decisions on civil liberties were equally inconsistent with a later stereotype of Holmes as a "liberal." Here, context is again important. Early twentieth-century "progressives," concerned primarily with redressing economic inequalities, did not address minority rights beyond the sphere of industrial relations. The oft-described tension in American "liberal" thought between support for governmental regulation and solicitude for minority rights did not surface until later in the century.

Even so, Holmes's early decisions were notably unsympathetic to minority rights. In the midst of widespread discrimination against blacks in the early decades of the twentieth century, the Court regularly supported the positions of black claimants who sought relief against government-supported racial discrimination. Holmes, however, was not usually part of the Court majorities who upheld minority claims. In *Bailey v. Alabama* (1911), for example, the Court invalidated an Alabama statute that made the breach of a contract *prima facie* evidence of fraud as inconsistent with the Thirteenth Amendment's prohibition of slavery. The Court reasoned that such statutes, invariably applied to contracts between black farm laborers and their employers, effectively prevented laborers from terminating their contracts except in the unlikely event that they were able to repay advanced wages at the time of termination. Holmes, dissenting, argued that given the tendency of black laborers "to remain during a part of the season, receiving advances, and then to depart at the period of need in the hope of greater wages at a neighboring plantation," the statute was a reasonable device to ensure the performance of labor agreements. "The power of the states to make breach of contract a crime," he asserted, "is not done away with by the abolition of slavery."

In *United States v. Reynolds* (1914), however, Holmes joined a decision invalidating a comparable arrangement, the criminal-surety practice. Under that practice, persons convicted of minor offenses, and ordered to pay fines, could enter into arrangements with other persons to have their fines paid in exchange for labor. Evidence in Alabama and Georgia, which permitted the arrangements, was that they were used overwhelmingly in cases involving black farm laborers, and often resulted in laborers being subject to what the Court called "an ever-turning wheel of servitude." A unanimous Court concluded that the practices amount to peonage and invalidated them.

Holmes wrote a separate concurrence revealing his motivation in supporting the Court's position. After reiterating his view that the Thirteenth Amendment did not prevent states from criminalizing breaches of contract, Holmes indicated that he thought the application of the criminal-surety practice to contracts involving black laborers particularly unfortunate. "Impulsive people with little intelligence," he said, "may be expected to lay hold of anything that affords a relief from present pain even though it will cause greater trouble by and by. The successive [surety] contracts, each for a longer term than the last, are the inevitable, and must have taken to have been the contemplated outcome of the Alabama laws."

Holmes's posture in *Reynolds* amounted to a scrutiny of the motives of legislation and a conclusion that those motives were race conscious. This was an unusual posture for Holmes, given his deferential stance toward legislation and his indifference to claims based on racial discrimination. Yet Holmes's position in *Reynolds* amounted to the exception that the proved the rule, for his scrutiny was precipitated by his conviction that the system was deliberately designed to take advantage of the "impulsiveness" of black laborers. Ordinarily, Holmes eschewed paternalism in economic relationships, but in *Reynolds* he inclined toward paternalism because he accepted the stereotype of black "impulsiveness." His race consciousness was a consciousness based on white supremacy.

Holmes's general indifference to the claims of minorities surfaced even more starkly in his decisions involving aliens, in which he allowed the United States and individual states sweeping powers over aliens. In three cases, *United States v. Sing Tuck* (1904), *United States v. Ju Toy* (1905), and *Patsone v. Pennsylvania* (1914), Holmes wrote majority opinions for the Court denying the constitutional claims of aliens. The first two cases involved efforts on the part of Chinese petitioners to prove that they were citizens of the United States. Holmes upheld as constitutional federal administrative proceedings requiring the testimony of two witnesses that a petitioner had been born in the United States, and making the determinations of immigration officials on the question of an applicant's citizenship conclusive without provision for judicial review.

Not only could the federal government summarily exclude aliens from the country, states had apparent impunity to discriminate against aliens who resided within their borders. That was the message of Holmes's decision in *Patsone v. Pennsylvania*. The Pennsylvania legislature, in the wake of labor unrest, had passed a statute making it unlawful for any unnaturalized for-

eign-born resident to kill wildlife, and thus prohibited resident aliens from owning or possessing firearms. The statute, enacted a month after an agreement between Pennsylvania coal mine operators and mine workers had expired, was clearly an effort on the part of the legislature to reduce the possibility of violence in the coal mines. Pennsylvania made absolutely no effort to show that aliens, as a class, were more dangerous to wildlife than citizens. The legislation had nothing to do with the dangers aliens posed to wildlife; it had everything to do with the dangers aliens in the labor force purportedly posed to the public at large.

It is easy enough to critique *Patsone*, but seen from the perspective of judicial review, Holmes's *Patsone* opinion is instructive. He may have believed that, given principles of sovereignty, states could exclude aliens entirely from their borders. He may have felt that, given the mandates of sovereignty, legislative pronouncements in an area in which legislative supremacy was unquestioned were in effect unreviewable. That was a consistent and defensible position, but it obliterated the impact of constitutional clauses designed to restrict legislative power. If a state could invoke its sovereignty as a basis for the most arbitrary sort of classification, it was hard to know the meaning of "equal protection" as a constitutional principle.

Not much in Holmes's early career on the Court, then, lends support for the characterization of him as a civil libertarian, any more than for the characterization of him as a "progressive" or "liberal" judge. The case for Holmes in those capacities has rested largely on two features of his later years on the Court. The first of those features was his continued dissenting posture in "liberty of contract" and other cases in which conservative majorities used doctrinal glosses on constitutional provisions to limit the scope of social legislation. The second was his emergence, after 1919, as a champion of free speech.

One way to resolve the apparent contradiction between Holmes's image and his early decisions is to suggest that his judicial stance changed with time, that he became more "liberal" as he aged. There is some support for this suggestion. Holmes's new set of friends, the group of younger "progressive" intellectuals, became his principal intellectual constituency, and through them he became acquainted with the issues that "progressives" thought important. Strong evidence exists that in the area of free speech, Holmes's "progressive" friends had a direct impact on the way he conceptualized speech issues in the last years of his tenure.

Nonetheless, the suggestion, on balance, must be rejected. Holmes's jurisprudence, even taking free speech issues into account, remained largely of a piece during his career on the Court. He was only accidentally a "progressive," and a "liberal" only with respect to certain kinds of speech issues. The emergence of his image as a "progressive" and "liberal" judge rests largely on the selective publicization of others and on the fortuitous affinity between Holmes's extremely limited theory of judicial review and the social goals of "progressives." Even Holmes's allegedly libertarian posture on speech, which emerged very late in his career, arguably rests more on a few memorable sentences in his opinions than on a consistent jurisprudential theory.

Two sets of cases illustrate the above conclusions. The first set is composed of Holmes's opinions between 1917 and 1931 on cases testing the constitutionality of social legislation, such as *Hammer v. Dagenhart* (1918), *Truax v. Corrigan* (1921), *Pennsylvania Coal Co. v. Mahon* (1922), *Adkins v. Children's Hospital* (1923), *Tyson & Brother v. Banton* (1927), and *Buck v. Bell* (1927). The second set is composed of Holmes's free speech opinions, ranging from his early decisions in *Patterson v. Colorado* (1907) and *Fox v. Washington* (1915) through his 1919 decisions testing the constitutionality of the Espionage Act of 1917, *Schenck v. United States* and *Abrams v. United States*, to his notable later statements about free speech in *Gitlow v. New York* (1925) and *United States v. Schwimmer* (1929).

The first set of cases does not establish Holmes as an ideological "progressive": it merely provides additional evidence of his opposition to substantive judicial readings of open-ended clauses in the Constitution. *Hammer* and *Adkins* were eloquent critiques of the doctrine of "liberty of contract," reinforcing the position

Holmes had previously advanced in *Lochner, Adair,* and *Coppage.* In all those decisions Holmes sustained state regulatory power, which he supported because of his positivist inclinations, not because he cared about the evils of child labor (*Hammer*), the level of wages paid hospital workers (*Adkins*), or the regulation of theater ticket prices (*Banton*).

Mahon and *Buck v. Bell* are less easily reconciled with a "progressive" ideological agenda, although both were arguably consistent with Holmes's own ideological instincts as a judge. In *Mahon,* a coal company had sold off its surface land rights for development, retaining its subsurface mineral rights. When Pennsylvania forbade subsurface mining in areas where public buildings, thoroughfares, or private houses were located, the company challenged the statute as a violation of its property and contract rights. In his majority opinion, Holmes maintained that the contract and due process clauses imposed limits on the capacity of legislatures to take property without compensation. He seems to have been motivated by commonsensical propositions. The company had retained subsurface rights, and, given its business, the principal value of the land to it lay in those rights. Those who acquired land from the company could have acquired the subsurface rights as well. Moreover, the contract and due process clauses were strong textual mandates for constitutional limitations on legislative conduct.

Holmes's "progressive" friends declined comment on *Mahon.* The opinion, however, has had nothing of the notoriety over the years of Holmes's decision in *Buck v. Bell*, in which he sustained the constitutionality of a Virginia statute providing for compulsory sterilization of certain inmates in state mental health institutions. The statute established a procedure by which inmates were labeled "mentally deficient" and sterilized so as to keep them from "perpetuating their kind" and adding to the burden on state facilities. The inmates did not have much opportunity to demonstrate their ineligibility for sterilization, nor did the state advance a convincing justification for why only inmates of state facilities, rather than "mental defectives" in the general population, were singled out for sterilization.

Holmes summarily dismissed both the due process and equal protection arguments. He felt that compulsory sterilization was akin to compulsory vaccination, and that "three generations of imbeciles," a label he mistakenly applied to Carrie Buck and her family, were "enough." He downplayed equal protection as "the usual last resort of constitutional arguments." *Buck v. Bell*, in contrast to many of Holmes's decisions, was not a case where he exhibited indifference toward the social policy embodied in the statute he was sustaining. He was an enthusiast for eugenics, the movement that had precipitated the *Buck* statute. Eugenics was a "reform" for which many "progressives" exhibited great enthusiasm. The movement became somewhat tarnished by its Nazi adherents, but in the 1920s, those dimensions of "population control" had not yet been anticipated.

On balance, Holmes's later decisions on social legislation exhibited the same consciousness as his earlier ones. He began with a presumption that legislatures, being majoritarian and positivist institutions, could do what they wanted: the scope of judge-created constitutional review was narrow. He was at bottom a Darwinist, a Malthusian, and a fatalist, so his enthusiasm for reformist legislation was extremely limited. He believed that the idea that judges were constrained by some disembodied, transcendental entity called "the law" was nonsense. Judges, he concluded, had ample opportunities to be creative lawmakers, and consequently should be loath to write their views on public policy into constitutional doctrine. Since a constitution was made "for people of differing views," judges should avoid substituting their doctrinal glosses for the text.

A generation of early twentieth-century intellectuals sought to make Holmes a "progressive" judge for their own purposes, and the label so attached itself to him that it took forty years, and the more searching scrutiny of a later generation puzzled by Holmes's apparent indifference to civil liberties, to complicate matters and begin a new phase in Holmesian historiography. But there was one dimension of his jurisprudence that has appeared as resolutely "progressive" or "liberal," his apparent sympathy for

dissident, "unpopular" speakers, and his apparent championing of what he called "the principle of freedom for the thought we hate."

Here again Holmes has been widely misunderstood, as commentators, seduced by the power of his rhetoric, have ignored the pattern of his decisions. But there are complicating factors. In contrast to his decisions on social legislation, where Holmes immediately adopted and followed a consistent jurisprudential posture, his opinions on free speech underwent a process of change distinctly in the direction of speech-protectiveness. By the end of his career, Holmes treated freedom of speech issues as raising the most serious constitutional questions, whereas earlier he had apparently assumed that the First and Fourteenth Amendments added little to the doctrinal status of speech at common law.

Up to the end of World War I, Holmes's views on free speech were orthodox and restrictive. In *Patterson v. Colorado* and *Fox v. Washington*, he summarily dismissed free speech claims by newspaper editors who had criticized the motives of Colorado judges and championed the cause of public nudity. In *Patterson* he stated that First Amendment protection only applied to prior restraints on speech, not speech that had been published. In both cases he indicated that speech could be suppressed if it had a "tendency" to encourage illegal or undesirable conduct, even if there had been no showing that such conduct had actually occurred. The decisions treated the First Amendment as adding nothing to the common law, which held objectionable speech as no different than any other socially undesirable act.

In 1919, Holmes confronted the scope of Congressional power to suppress speech in four cases testing the constitutionality of the Espionage Act of 1917 and the Sedition Act of 1918, the most sweeping effort on the part of the federal government to restrict "subversive" speech since the Alien and Sedition Acts of 1797. Those statutes criminalized expressions having the effect of causing insubordination in the armed forces or of obstructing the recruitment or enlistment of soldiers, and expressions advocating any "curtailment of production" of the war effort.

Holmes wrote opinions in all the cases, the leading two of which, doctrinally, were *Schenck* and *Abrams,* and the most popularly celebrated of which was *Debs v. United States,* which involved the incarceration of Eugene Debs, a prominent Socialist politician, for declaring his opposition to the war. In all the cases, Holmes laid down an apparently consistent doctrinal position: the constitutional test "in every case" for whether allegedly "subversive" speech could be criminally prosecuted was whether it created a "clear and present danger" that the evils described by the statute would occur. In laying down the "clear and present danger" test, Holmes explicitly abandoned his position in *Patterson* that the First Amendment's protection was confined to prior restraints, and intimated that the "clear and present danger" test was intended to supplant the "bad tendency" test he had employed in *Patterson* and *Fox.*

In actuality the situation was far less clear. After mentioning the "clear and present danger" test in upholding the legislation in *Schenck,* Holmes did not refer to it again in either *Frohwerk v. United States* or in *Debs,* even though the facts of those cases suggested that the expressions were too remotely related to interference with the war effort to make out a "clear and present danger." Then, in *Abrams,* Holmes, this time in dissent, appeared to deviate from his previous opinions in his understanding of "clear and present danger." The *Abrams* case involved the convictions of Russian-speaking immigrants, sympathetic to the anti-Bolshevik forces in Russia, who distributed leaflets to munitions workers urging them not to manufacture weapons that were going to be used against their Russian comrades. Holmes rephrased the "clear and present danger test" to read "clear and imminent danger," and argued that the leaflets were too inept in their syntax and content to have any serious effect. He then declared that "we should be eternally vigilant against attempts to check the expression of opinions that we loathe and believe fraught with death, unless they so imminently threaten immediate interference with the lawful and pressing purposes of the law that an immediate check is required to save the country." This was a much more speech-protective reading of the "clear and present danger" formula than Holmes had previously made.

From *Abrams* on, one could chart a progression of Holmesian First Amendment decisions in which speech received greater and greater protection, including *United States ex rel. Milwaukee Social Democratic Publishing Co. v. Burleson* (1921), *Gitlow,* and *Schwimmer.*

In *Burleson,* Holmes argued in dissent that the postmaster general could not summarily deny second-class mail privileges on the basis of a publication's content, a marked departure from an earlier opinion of Holmes on the Supreme Judicial Court of Massachusetts, *McAuliffe v. New Bedford* (1892). There, a policeman had been dismissed for political campaigning, and Holmes had argued that since New Bedford could decline to hire policemen at all, it could establish the terms of their employment. In *Burleson,* he conceded that the United States could terminate its postal service. But that "greater power" did not apparently subsume the "lesser power" to condition access to that service on the content of publications.

Gitlow and *Schwimmer* went even further. In *Gitlow,* the New York legislature had provided criminal penalties for speech advocating the overthrow of the government, and had subsequently convicted Gitlow for circulating "The Communist Manifesto," a document that called in general terms for "revolutionary mass action," but specifically recommended only "mass political strikes." Even though there was no evidence that the publication of the "Manifesto" had "any effect," a majority of the Court held this fact immaterial because the statute proscribed advocacy itself. In such situations the "clear and present danger" test did not apply because the legislature had predetermined that certain types of advocacy imminently threatened the body politic.

Holmes dissented, and his dissent contained some startling statements. "Every idea is an incitement," he declared, and the "only difference" between the expression of an opinion and "an incitement in the narrower sense" is "the speaker's enthusiasm for the result." He went on that "if in the long run the beliefs expressed in proletarian dictatorship are destined to be accepted by the dominant forces of the community, the only meaning of free speech is that they be given their chance and have their way." These two comments appeared to endorse a view of speech well beyond that embodied in the "clear and present danger" test. That test had implicitly distinguished between "speeches" and "incitements," with the latter a category of speeches that bore a close enough connection to danger to the state that they could be suppressed. In suggesting that the only difference between a "speech" and an "incitement" was the speaker's "enthusiasm for the result" Holmes seemed to be suggesting that "clear and present danger" was a subjective rather than an objective formulation, which robbed it of its utility. One could hardly let a speaker decide whether his or her speech posed a danger to the state if there were to be any restrictions on speech.

Even more puzzling were Holmes's comments about "the only meaning of free speech." They suggested that the test for whether "the beliefs of proletarian dictatorship" were legitimate was their eventual acceptance or rejection by "the dominant forces of the community," not their initially incendiary character. The logic of this statement led to complete protection for all speech, with the "market," as signified by the views of "dominant forces," being the ultimate determinent of legitimacy. Some speech might not eventually "have [its] way," but all speech needed to be "given [its] chance." The "dominant forces," however, could eventually suppress any speech they disapproved of. As interpreted, the statement seemed inconsistent with all of Holmes's free speech decisions since *Schenck*, in which he had assumed that the First Amendment placed some limits on majoritarian repression of "unpopular" speech.

If Holmes's dissent in *Gitlow* is read as a libertarian document, his progression from a restrictive to an ultra-libertarian conception of free speech was completed in *Schwimmer*, where he applied the First Amendment in a context where it had never before been applied. That context was the deportation of resident aliens, a class of persons, Holmes had argued in *Sing Tuck* and *Ju Toy*, that were afforded no constitutional protection.

In *Schwimmer*, a forty-nine-year-old citizen of Hungary who had been a resident of the United States for several years filed an application for American citizenship. On her application form she declined to give an affirmative answer to a question as to whether she would take up arms in the defense of the United States, citing her belief in pacifism. The Immigration and Naturalization Service summarily denied her application. When she challenged that denial, a federal appellate court held that the denial was improper because as a forty-nine-year-old woman she would not be asked to take up arms. A majority of the Supreme Court reversed and instituted the original denial of citizenship.

Holmes, in dissent, repeated the argument that Schwimmer's pacifism was irrelevant because she would not be asked to take up arms. He then went on, however, to suggest that *Schwimmer* was a free speech case. "If there is any principle of the Constitution that more imperatively calls for attachment than any other," he said, "it is the principle of free thought—not free thought for those who agree with us but freedom for the thought we hate. I think that we should adhere to that principle with regard to admission into, as well as to life within this country." The oddity of that statement was that there was no requirement for Congress to adhere to the First Amendment, or any other constitutional provision, in naturalization cases. Congress had the undoubted power to condition American citizenship on the avowal of certain beliefs, just as it had the power to condition citizenship on health requirements. Holmes had made much of that sovereign power in his earlier alien decisions. Now he was suggesting that the constitutional principle of free speech ought to apply "with regard to admission into, as well as life within this country."

It is hard to imagine that by the time he wrote *Schwimmer* in 1929, Holmes had reconsidered his position on sovereignty and alien rights and concluded that the Constitution, after all, did apply to aliens. *Schwimmer* was an example of Holmes's tendency, not only in free speech cases but throughout his opinions, to prefer a memorable, sweeping phrase to analytical or doctrinal consistency. Doctrinally, *Patterson*, *Schenck*, *Abrams*, *Gitlow*, and *Schwimmer* were irreconcilable: Holmes had successively announced a battery of "tests" and conceptions of the impact of the First Amendment in "subversive" speech cases, and the tests and conceptions could not be squared with one another. Only in

Schenck had Holmes explicitly rejected one of his earlier conceptions: in *Schwimmer* he said that the "position and motives" of the petitioner were "wholly different from those of Schenck" as if the two cases should be decided in the same constitutional framework. That suggestion was analytically bizarre.

The *Patterson-Schwimmer* sequence suggests that it is not very fruitful to approach Holmes's free speech opinions seeking doctrinal or even philosophical consistency. Even what might be called a progression in those opinions of greater solicitude for speech requires qualification in light of some other decisions, such as *Gilbert v. Minnesota* (1920), or the companion cases of *Meyer v. Nebraska* and *Bartels v. Iowa* (1923), in which Holmes either permitted state restrictions on speech in circumstances where a "clear and present danger" did not seem to have been demonstrated, or failed to conceptualize the cases as raising free speech issues at all. In the *Meyer-Bartels* cases, certain states had attempted to prohibit the teaching of foreign languages before the eighth grade, apparently on the grounds of patriotism and anti-German sentiment. While Holmes conceded such statutes infringed on the "liberty of teacher and scholar," he thought them constitutional. He either did not see the "liberty" to receive information about a foreign language or culture as raising First Amendment issues or he thought the states' interest in promoting "a common tongue" compelling. That position was impossible to square with *Schwimmer*.

On balance, Holmes's free speech opinions were not so much evidence of a "progressive" or "liberal" sensibility as they were evidence of the unique complex of values which composed his judicial posture. Holmes was extremely interested, as a judge, in exploring the philosophical foundations of legal issues and identifying his philosophical stance toward those issues. He was far less interested in doctrinal or analytical consistency, and his philosophical views, rendered in terms of the political ideologies of his day, did not easily mark him as a "progressive," a "liberal," or a "conservative."

Free speech was the sort of issue that Holmes enjoyed ruminating about. He had first conceived speech as no different from any other social act, and thus entitled to no greater protection than "unpopular" conduct. As he was forced to think more about speech in the context of the wartime subversive speech cases, he began to recognize a strong social interest in encouraging even "unpopular" speech as part of the process by which persons exchange ideas in a democratic society. He thus disengaged speech from an older "liberty" framework, which had included "liberty of contract" and of which he was highly skeptical, and began to conceive of it as a philosophical principle of "freedom" in a democracy—freedom to protest, to express one's individuality, to articulate "fighting faiths." He began to associate this principle with his deterministic views on majoritarian power and historical change, and concluded that suppressing speech was wrongheaded and ultimately fruitless. In so doing he was not endorsing the substance of unpopular views: he continued to express indifference toward them, as he had toward "progressive" social legislation. In short, free speech for Holmes was a complicated and important philosophical puzzle. Addressing such puzzles was one of the things he liked best to do as a judge.

Another thing Holmes liked to do as a judge was to write his opinions "with style." "Style" for Holmes meant an emphasis on the pithy, arresting, often cryptic or ambiguous aphorism. Such Holmesian aphorisms have a capacity to linger in the memories of readers. It is far easier to summon up their language than to explain them. In the area of free speech, Holmes experimented with a number of memorable phrases, and while they vividly encompassed some of the philosophical complexities of free speech issues, they did little to clarify those issues or, for that matter, Holmes's position on them. To affirm the principle of "freedom for the thought we hate" or to suggest that "the only meaning of free speech" is that unpopular doctrines may ultimately "have their way" is to state, in memorable fashion, one of the central philosophical rationales for protection for speech in a society committed to democratic forms of change.

When one asks what follows from the statements for lawyers and judges charged with analyzing and deciding free speech issues, the statements evaporate. Holmes was not particularly interested in that dimension of judicial decision making, nor in the political labels others attached to his work. An irony of Holmes's career is that so few commentators have granted him his preferences. As a judge, he said to Canon Patrick Sheehan in 1912, he wanted "to put as many new ideas into the law as I can, to show how particular solutions involve general theory, and to do it with style." He pursued those goals avidly and successfully throughout his judicial career. One may be frustrated by the dimensions of judging that his blueprint leaves out. One should, nonetheless, resist trying to recast his jurisprudential sensibility.

—G. EDWARD WHITE

BIBLIOGRAPHY

The Oliver Wendell Holmes, Jr., papers, in the Harvard Law School Library, have been issued in a microfilm edition by University Publications of America (1985). The Holmes papers contain about 29,000 items, the bulk of which is correspondence. Several of Holmes's correspondences, including those with Harold Laski, Frederick Pollock, Lewis Einstein, Clare Castletown, Morris Cohen, Canon Patrick Sheehan, Franklin Ford, and John C. H. Wu, have been published. The major unpublished correspondence collections in the Holmes papers are those with Felix Frankfurter, Mr. and Mrs. John Chapman (Nina) Gray, and John Wigmore. Other items in the Holmes papers include travel and Civil War diaries, a list of his yearly readings, engagement calendars, and a sparse collection of judicial papers. Two excellent collections of Holmes's writings are Max Lerner, *The Mind and Faith of Justice Holmes* (2d ed., 1988), and Richard A. Posner, *The Essential Holmes* (1991).

Biographies of Holmes include Liva Baker, *The Justice From Beacon Hill* (1991), a reliable and well-written trade biography that is sparse and derivative in its discussion of Holmes's work as a scholar and judge; Catherine Drinker Bowen, *Yankee From Olympus* (1944), a blend of fact and fiction about Holmes and his family, captivating reading if one is unconcerned with accuracy; Mark DeWolfe Howe, *Justice Oliver Wendell Holmes: The Shaping Years* (1957) and *Justice Oliver Wendell Holmes: the Proving Years* (1963), the authorized biography, and a masterful treatment of Holmes's early life and career through the publication of *The Common Law*, lamentably cut short by Howe's death in 1967; John S. Monagan, *The Grand Panjandrum: The Mellow Years of Justice Holmes* (1988), a delightful account of Holmes's later life, based on interviews with persons who knew him well; Sheldon Novick, *Honorable Justice* (1989), the first nonfictional trade biography covering Holmes's entire life, based on the Holmes papers, but erratic in its coverage and insights; and G. Edward White, *Justice Oliver Wendell Holmes: Law and the Inner Self* (1993), an analysis of Holmes's life and work and the relationship between them.

Robert W. Gordon, ed., *The Legacy of Oliver Wendell Holmes, Jr.* (1992), is a collection of recent essays on Holmes, including some accomplished treatments of various phases of his career. In addition, one should consult Yosal Rogat, "Mr. Justice Holmes: A Dissenting Opinion," 15 *Stanford Law Review* 3, 254 (1963), a major revision of Holmes's image as a civil libertarian, focusing on cases involving aliens and blacks, and Rogat, "The Judge As Spectator," 31 *University of Chicago Law Review* 213 (1964), a brilliant analysis of Holmes as a detached, Brahmin figure, comparing him with his contemporaries, Henry James and Henry Adams.

Edmund Wilson's essay on Holmes in Wilson's collection of writings on the Civil War, *Patriotic Gore* (1963), remains one of the most insightful and best-written analyses of Holmes, demonstrating that one need not have professional legal training to produce lucid evaluations of legal figures.

CHARLES EVANS HUGHES

BORN 11 April 1862, Glens Falls, New York

NOMINATED to the Court 25 April 1910 by William Howard Taft

TOOK seat 10 October 1910; resigned from the Court 10 June 1916 to accept the Republican party nomination for president; nominated to the Court as chief justice 3 February 1930 by Herbert Hoover; took seat 24 February 1930; retired 1 July 1941

DIED 27 August 1948 on Cape Cod, Massachusetts

Charles Evans Hughes was born during the Civil War in a small town in upstate New York. He was the only child of a preacher and of a rigidly devout Baptist mother who believed implicitly in the hot fire of Hell and the looming wrath of a just God. Together, they inculcated in their child the stark discipline of hard work and moral diligence, and the paramount importance of order. From such seemingly parochial beginnings would emerge one of the most outstanding, influential, and urbane figures of twentieth-century American law.

A prodigy with a photographic memory and compulsive attention to detail, the young Hughes matured prematurely. At three, he was reading English; at eight, he was reading Greek and German. Six years old and less than a year into first grade, he persuaded his parents to let him leave school by drafting and sending to them a detailed agenda for assiduous study at home. At thirteen, he earned a high school diploma, and a year later enrolled in Madison (later Colgate) University, dutifully following his parents' plan for him to prepare for the ministry. But here a spark of rebellion appeared, and sixteen-year-old Charles transferred to Brown University in search of broader horizons. His preoccupation with order in an orderly universe remained, but now in a more secular context: he chose law. At the age of twenty-two, he graduated from Columbia Law School, immediately began practice with one of the leading law firms in New York City, and became a partner three years later.

Hughes's rejection of his father's calling evoked from his parents desperate anxiety "that," as his father wrote, "you may be turned from the path of rectitude by the influence of your worldly associates." They needn't have worried. Most of the stern habits that ordered his life during his childhood tutelage endured powerfully into his old age. At least twice, they would drive him close to physical and mental breakdowns, and induced a recurrent bleeding ulcer. They would decisively shape the way he would approach his duties in his truly remarkable public career. "Whatever I do, wherever I go," Hughes once wrote, "when the question of right or wrong comes up, it is decided by what Pa or Ma will say if I did it."

Never a profound thinker, but always a meticulously systematic thinker, Charles Evans Hughes forged for himself one of the most extraordinary careers a man of the law might ever hope for. In a society that formally invested authority in law rather than in persons, that meant high place, public honor, and exceptional opportunity to influence his society's structure of power. During the first half of his life, he earned wealth and widespread respect as a practicing attorney who also willingly gave his time and talents to public service. During the second half he was elected governor of New York; was appointed associate justice of the United States Supreme Court (1910–16); resigned to become the Republican party's candidate for president in 1916 and very nearly unseated the incumbent Woodrow Wilson; served as president of the American Bar Association; was appointed secretary of state (1921–25); served on the Permanent Court of International Justice, or World Court (1928–29); and finally was appointed a second time to the Supreme Court—a unique achievement—this time as chief justice (1930–41). In short, this man, whose intellect was so profoundly shaped by the rigid discipline of early nineteenth-century rural American Protestant fundamentalism, would become one of the most influential figures of twentieth-century pluralist, urban America.

During the eighty-six years that he lived, Hughes's country was dramatically transformed in almost every way. The post–Civil War political settlement provided the framework for a more centralized or national constitutional order. Local and regional economies were even more clearly absorbed into a national matrix by the transportation and industrial revolutions. Small unit private proprietary business enterprise yielded to large-scale multidivisional, multifunctional public corporations as the dominating force and defining feature of the American business system.

It is not clear that Charles Evans Hughes understood the significance of these changes better than most. As a member of the Court, however, he did understand two things that would help bring American law and constitutional jurisprudence into line with those changes. The first was the paramount need for social and political order. The second was the importance of preserving the integrity of the Court itself as the vital arbiter of conflicting and sometimes mutually exclusive claims on justice that are inevitable in a complex and fast-changing society. "We secure our peace and confidence," he remarked, "by loyal acceptance of the decisions of our umpires."

Consistent with that idea were the immortal words that Hughes, when he was governor of New York, ad-libbed during an address—words which he came to regard as a plague: "The Constitution," he said, "is what the judges say it is." As he explained later, he intended no denigration of the Constitution nor a complaint about judges. What he meant was that because judges play such a pivotal role in declaring the Constitution's meaning, they should stay out of the business of reviewing the fact-findings of government regulatory agencies. That would, he said, place them too "close to the public impatience." Because the courts are indispensable for protecting "our liberty and . . . our property under the Constitution," and since the judges determine what the Constitution says, it is essential that the public continue to regard judges as demigods. Don't weaken them, he pleaded, by exposing them to the public pressures implicit in fact-finding. Keep the judges "for . . . questions of property rights," to sustain the "constitutional right to hold property and not to be deprived of it without due process of law."

Hughes was too sophisticated to believe that judges either did or should disinterestedly apply the principles of law to particular cases of fact without regard to favored social outcomes. He would himself suffer (probably fair) criticism for allegedly tailoring his judicial opinions to outcomes he favored. But in his mind it was the myths of an aloof judiciary and of inalienable property rights that sustained liberty in a democratic polity; those myths represented for him the vital buttresses of the good society. He worked hard throughout his career to protect the strength of those myths, even as his meticulous attention to detail and to facts impelled him to factor the real, everyday consequences of legal decisions into his judicial opinions.

Hughes's concern for order, and perhaps most of all his remarkably profound, inner-directed sense of right, often moved Hughes to digress from legal reasoning shaped before the transportation, industrial, and corporation revolutions. Always acutely conscious of the need to maintain the perception of stability in the law, he strove nevertheless to apply a juridical logic that accommodated to modern times. And there were two important long-term outcomes of Hughes's efforts.

The first was to enhance the power of government at both the state and federal levels to regulate American life. In contemplating cases requiring a fine-line interpretation of the commerce or contract clauses of the Constitution, Hughes usually sought outcomes that empowered Americans to use their government to make social and economic policy commensurate with the vast changes they were experiencing. Once on the Court, Hughes usually was inclined to favor strong public direction of economic behavior. As one writer has noted: "Hughes's judicial opinions consistently manifested . . . a desire for some central ordering force to supplant the inadequate ordering of markets and contracts."

The second important result of Hughes's work was to give substance to the Constitution's restraints on government when it came to protecting the personal and communicative rights emphasized in the first six amendments. Justice Oliver Wendell Holmes, Jr., usually is assigned credit for shaping doctrine that would infuse

Charles Evans Hughes
Photograph by Harris and Ewing.
Collection of the Supreme Court of the United States.

federal jurisprudence with meaningful limits on the power of government to abridge speech, press, and lawful assembly. His and Justice Louis D. Brandeis's repeated dissents in civil liberties cases during the 1920s surely did build the case for confining such power to circumstances wherein the alleged offense presented "a clear and present danger" to public safety or national security. But it was not until the Court presided over by Chief Justice Hughes in the 1930s that the Holmesian principles began to emerge as those of the Court's majority, with Hughes himself writing key opinions.

Some of Hughes's actions during his first Court tenure (1910–1916) in the era of Taft and Wilson foreshadowed the achievements of the Court over which he would later preside. From the beginning, Hughes showed a tendency to uphold social legislation that, as he put it in a case concerning state regulation of the hours of labor for women, had a "reasonable relation to a proper purpose." *Miller v. Wilson* (1915). The purpose he usually had in mind concerned civil order, the integrity of government authority, and (though he would have denied it) his own standards of justice. On behalf of federal regulation, he tended to give broad scope to the power granted to Congress in the Constitution to regulate interstate commerce.

When Hughes first came on the Court, as well as during his chief justiceship, that was still fiercely in dispute. In *United States v. E.C. Knight Co.* (1895), fifteen years before Hughes began his first tenure, the Court had found that a sugar refining company whose raw sugar came entirely from out of state, and most of whose refined sugar found markets outside the state, nevertheless lay beyond Congress's control within its power to regulate interstate commerce. Notions of "state sovereignty" dominated constitutional law, except where judges deemed state legislation "confiscatory" or somehow in violation of "due process"—which usually meant in violation of the judges' view of the prerogatives of private property.

As the youngest member of the Court, Hughes moved cautiously. Yet he moved effectively toward augmenting government's regulatory powers. In the much celebrated *Minnesota Rate Cases* (1913), he asserted the power of the states to control intrastate transportation even where it might seriously affect interstate commerce, as long as Congress had not already acted in the field. But in the same opinion, Hughes insisted that all commerce had become so intricately dependent that Congress might well preempt intrastate rules in order to effectively regulate interstate commerce.

Shortly afterward came the most famous of his early opinions. "Congress is empowered to regulate," Hughes wrote. "That is, to provide the law for the government of interstate commerce; . . . 'to promote its growth and insure its safety.' . . . Its authority . . . necessarily embraces the right to control the operations in all matters having such a close and substantial relation to interstate traffic that the control is essential or appropriate to the security of that traffic, [and] to the efficiency of the interstate service" (*Shreveport Rate Cases,* 1914). In shaping what came to be known as "The Shreveport Doctrine," Hughes argued that the states' regulatory power must yield to that of Congress whenever the conduct of even purely intrastate commerce might adversely affect interstate conduct.

Hughes was willing, moreover, to extend this principle to Congress's jurisdiction over businesses when there was "actual movement" of their goods or services across state lines. "In determining whether commerce is interstate or intrastate," he insisted, "regard must be had to its essential character" (*Pennsylvania R.R. Co. v. Clark Bros. Coal Mining Co.,* 1915) These opinions appeared to contrast sharply with the Court's earlier rulings, especially that in the *Knight* case.

Hughes did not remain entirely consistent on such matters. The Court on which he sat did not overturn *Knight,* and in any case, Hughes himself would later join in supporting comparably narrow decisions. In an opinion that he wrote shortly before resigning to accept the Republican nomination for president in 1916, Hughes sustained an injury liability claim against an interstate railroad that was validated by state law, although under federal law, no such claim could stand. In *Chicago, Burlington & Quincy R.R. Co. v. Harrington* (1916), while noting that the injury victim had been loading coal brought entirely from outside the state, Hughes could find no "close or direct relation to interstate transportation," although in another case that same year Hughes had no difficulty in holding that federal law controlled a railroad's liability if merely the goods involved in the accident had crossed state lines (*Southern Railway v. Prescott*). Such apparent contradictions led critics to see Hughes's jurisprudence as focusing less on principle than on favored results—albeit results that contrasted with his brethren's more common solicitude for corporate business immunity from government regulation or civil tort actions.

Like Justice Holmes, whom he greatly admired, Hughes refused to accept "liberty of contract" or the sanctity of contract as absolutes. The first, he believed, did not preclude state action to protect certain classes of workers from accepting unduly burdensome contracts. Nor did the second preclude the state from modifying or abrogating contracts that it determined obstructed legitimate legislative objectives.

In several cases, sometimes in dissent, Hughes argued that a state or city retained the power to revoke a franchise on the grounds that "a tacit condition [is] annexed to grants of franchises that they may be lost by mis-user or non-user"; and that the grant of a franchise does not preclude the government from subsequently regulating rates or services (*New York Electric Lines Co. v. Empire City Subway Co.*, 1914).

On the other hand, Hughes would not permit a state to enforce a contract that imposed unconstitutional burdens on an individual. In 1911, for example, Hughes wrote for the Court an opinion that struck down a statute that compelled an employee to work off his debt to a creditor by stipulating that refusal to do so ipso facto constituted a criminal offense as a fraudulent violation of contract. Such a law violated the Constitution's ban on involuntary servitude, Hughes wrote, because it was a crude form of coercion—forcing a person to choose between performing involuntary services or facing criminal charges—an instrument especially effective "against the poor and ignorant, its most likely victims" (*Bailey v. Alabama*, 1911).

Hughes's solicitude for personal rights also emerged early in his first Court tenure. He wrote for the Court in overturning an Arizona statute that limited the number of aliens a single em-

ployer could hire. Although he usually granted legislatures wide scope in determining means for protecting the public welfare, in this case he saw that the language of the statute showed that "discrimination against aliens [is] . . . an end in itself." That made it an unconstitutional intrusion on "the right to work for a living." Since Congress had full power to invite immigrants to the nation, a state could not effectively nullify that power by forcing an alien into penury (*Truax v. Raich*, 1915).

Similarly, he wrote for a bare majority of the Court an opinion that declared unconstitutional a part of an Oklahoma statute permitting railroads to provide luxury cars for whites, but none for nonwhites. While accepting the doctrine of "separate but equal" laid down in *Plessy v. Ferguson* (1896), Hughes insisted that even if only one Negro required a luxury car, the railroad must bear the cost of providing it. "The constitutional right [to such a car does] not depend upon the number of persons who may be discriminated against. . . . The essence of the constitutional right," wrote Hughes, "is that it is a personal one" (*McCabe v. Atchison, Topeka & Santa Fe Ry. Co.*, 1914). This was probably the first legal victory in the twentieth century for African Americans after decades of reverses that effectively nullified the intent of the Fourteenth and Fifteenth Amendments to secure the freedmen's civil rights and guarantee them equal protection of the law. Unfortunately, because Hughes also found that the plaintiffs in the case did not have standing, because they were not the individuals denied access to a luxury car, Hughes's *obiter dictum* about the personal essence of a constitutional right assertion served merely as an invitation for future litigation. And it was not until 1941, Hughes's last year as chief justice, that the Court finally made the principle stick.

Hughes's concern for civil liberties showed up most clearly after he left the Court. Following his defeat for president in 1916, he returned to private practice and, in that capacity, he represented many large corporations, sometimes before his former colleagues on the Supreme Court. But his most distinguished service occurred in 1920 when, on his own initiative, he volunteered his services on behalf of five duly elected New York assemblymen who had been peremptorily denied their seats because they belonged to the Socialist party. In the bigoted American postwar environment following the Bolshevist triumph in Russia, Hughes's efforts proved as futile as comparable good-citizen actions of the McCarthyite era of the 1940s and 1950s. But it was a gesture that would eventually help build civil liberties into an important feature of American democracy.

In 1931, Chief Justice Hughes wrote the Court's opinion in *Stromberg v. California*, a decision Harry Kalven, Jr., has called "the first case in the history of the Court in which there was an explicit victory for free speech." Even so, Hughes did not move the law very far. He ordered reversal of a conviction on grounds that a part of the California law under which a young Miss Stromberg was convicted was unconstitutional because it was too vague, while he explicitly upheld the constitutionality of another part of the law which made it a felony to use provocative flags or symbols that might serve as "an invitation or stimulus to anarchistic action or as an aid to propaganda that is of a seditious character." The Court evidently was not yet prepared to regard "anarchistic action" or "seditious character" as at all vague, to say nothing of what might constitute "an invitation" or "an aid to propaganda."

Hughes and his brethren continued to regard government authority as superior to most private rights, at least when those rights concerned lifestyle or political expression. In 1934, a unanimous Court rejected a Methodist's conscientious objection to serving in a university's reserve officer training corps, then required of all able-bodied male students. Even the Court's three most liberal members, Benjamin Cardozo, Harlan Stone, and Brandeis, joined in a concurring opinion that pointedly rejected the claims of private conscience to some measure of immunity from state command. "The right of private judgment," Cardozo wrote, "has never yet been so exalted above the powers and compulsion of the agencies of government" (*Hamilton v. University of California Regents*, 1934).

It would not be until after 1937 that the Court began moving civil liberties into the center of modern liberal law. And that would come primarily after numerous Court vetoes of New Deal economic legislation brought about a major political crisis, and after resignations from the Court permitted Franklin Roosevelt to appoint new justices. Until that time, Hughes's record as chief justice was spotty on this issue.

Hughes's nomination in 1930 to replace William Howard Taft was strongly opposed by progressives who thought of Hughes mainly as a Republican lawyer for corporations. The Senate confirmed his nomination by a small majority, with twenty-six opposed and eighteen abstaining. Nor did Hughes begin auspiciously. His first public statement after confirmation, a speech to the American Bar Association, emphasized the importance of preserving states' rights against federal encroachment—at a time when the country faced a national economic calamity.

Once his term began, Hughes joined again and again with the conservatives—in particular, the four fiercely anti-reform justices, Van Devanter, Sutherland, Butler, and McReynolds—in overturning state and federal measures designed to alleviate the country's critical conditions. In one case, against even his own declared principles that the courts should refrain from second-guessing the fact findings of regulatory commissions, he contrived to find that the courts could properly review the facts ascertained by the commission charged with administering a workman's compensation act (*Crowell v. Benson*, 1932). In another case, ostensibly out of solicitude for state court jurisdiction, he joined those four again, plus Justice Roberts, in throwing out a case against six top executives of the American Tobacco Company who had bilked the corporation for millions of dollars in "bonuses" and sold themselves stock for a fifth of its market value. As Justices Stone and Brandeis noted in dissent, Hughes revealed (untypically) an almost willful blindness to the obvious interstate character of modern corporate business. *Rogers v. Guaranty Trust Co.* (1933).

What was going on? A fair guess is that Hughes was troubled by the popular outcry against American business that followed on the stock market crash of 1929 and the devastating Depression that followed. His keen concern for order led him to "tilt" against what appeared to be a movement toward radical change that would, among other things, undermine the security of private business property. Like many fundamentally conservative people at the time, Hughes seems to have believed in the nearness of revolution.

His celebrated opinion in *Home Building & Loan Assn. v. Blaisdell* (1934), for a 5–4 majority, revealed this clearly. In upholding a Minnesota law that suspended foreclosures on indebted properties, Hughes acted in line with his earlier opinions on the legitimate power of states to alter or abrogate contracts. But in this case, instead of emphasizing, as Stone, Cardozo, and Brandeis wanted him to, that the states have plenary power to determine the balance between private rights and public welfare (a phrasing Hughes did take from Cardozo to include in his opinion), Hughes preferred to highlight the temporary nature of the act, and to stress how it helped to preserve the public's faith in a just and orderly government amid emergency conditions. Hughes's acknowledgment of the emergence of the state in America as an entity independent of the multiple social forces that made demands on it was an important contribution to modern political thinking. But Cardozo and Stone let it be known at the time that by failing to emphasize the plenary powers of the state to treat the allocation of economic advantages, the Court thereby missed an opportunity to bring Constitutional law fully into the twentieth century.

In one other case in 1934, Hughes joined in sustaining a state's regulatory power. In *Nebbia v. New York*, the Court, with Roberts writing for a 5–4 majority, upheld New York's right to counter "destructive competition" by regulating milk prices. "There is," wrote Roberts, with Hughes joining in an expansive assertion of government's power to regulate, "no closed class or category of businesses affected with a public interest.... The phrase ... can ... mean no more than that an industry, for adequate reason, is subject to control for the public good." But for the next two years, Hughes would be found mostly on the other side, going a long way toward eviscerating the federal government's major programs for coping with the Depression.

On what came to be called "Black Monday," May 27, 1935, a unanimous Court overturned the National Industrial Recovery Act, the measure that some regarded as the heart of the New Deal, in *Schechter v. United States*, as well

as the Frazier-Lemke Act, a farm mortgage relief measure, in *Louisville Jt. Stock Bank v. Radford*. The latter case was not critical because it fell mostly on its careless wording. Brandeis, for the Court, stressed that though government may alter contracts for good public purpose, as Hughes had successfully argued during his first Court tenure, the poor wording of the act seemed to give government the right to take property without compensation.

But in the case of the NIRA, much more was at stake. And Hughes again split with his more progressive colleagues where his earlier record might have indicated he would do otherwise. The key to the case for Brandeis, Cardozo, and Stone was the virtually unlimited and unstructured delegation of government power to private trade associations for setting prices, wages, and production levels. The example of fascism, which was then vigorously ascending in Europe and in theory featured a superficially similar form of syndicalism, played a strong role in the brethren's view of the NIRA. It was not altogether unreasonable in those years to fear the spread of authoritarian regimes, even in the liberal democracies. But Hughes seemingly had a more antiquated concern for states' rights. He threw his support to a distinction between "direct" effects on interstate commerce that Congress could regulate and "indirect" effects that he insisted it could not. That line of reasoning brought the Court back to 1895 with *E.C. Knight* and the sugar trust.

The next year, Brandeis, Cardozo, and Stone found themselves alone again, this time in dissent, when Hughes's Court threw out the New Deal's Agricultural Adjustment Act in *United States v. Butler*. Here, Justice Roberts wrote a truly astonishing opinion for the 6–3 majority that Hughes joined. The opinion asserted, first, that although Congress did have the power to tax and spend for the general welfare, it could not do so for purposes reserved to the states, namely, to regulate agriculture—notwithstanding the plain interstate and international character of modern agriculture; second, that "A tax ... has never been thought to connote the expropriation of money from one group for the benefit of another"—notwithstanding that nearly all taxation does that; third, that by tying receipt of such benefits to specific regulations, Congress was engaged in "coercion by economic pressure"—notwithstanding that the law required no one to accept the benefits and thereby the regulations, and that nearly all government largesse is conditioned by some required behavior; and, fourth, that if the federal government could thus purchase compliance by offer of grants, one could foresee a condition whereby "the independence of the individual states [will be] obliterated, and the United States converted into a central government exercising uncontrolled police power in every state of the Union, superseding all local control or regulation of the affairs or concerns of the states."

Justice Stone, with Brandeis and Cardozo concurring, dispatched such blather with a brief, sharp dissent: "The suggestion that [the government's power of the purse] must now be curtailed by judicial fiat because it may be abused by unwise use hardly rises to the dignity of argument. So may judicial power be abused. . . . Courts are not the only agency of government that must be assumed to have capacity to govern." The Court and the American people, Stone concluded, would benefit most from "the frank recognition that language, even of a constitution, may mean what it says: that the power to tax and spend includes the power to relieve a nationwide economic maladjustment by conditional gifts of money."

But the Court majority remained incorrigible. By a 5–4 margin, with Hughes concurring, it followed the AAA decision by overthrowing a congressional act that sought to stabilize prices and wages in the troubled bituminous coal industry. In *Carter v. Carter Coal Co.*, Hughes once again seemingly returned to the *Knight* doctrine: "If the people desire to give Congress the power to regulate industries within the state, and the relations of employers and employees in these industries," he pontificated in a concurring opinion, "they are at liberty to declare their will in the appropriate manner, but it is not for the Court to amend the Constitution by judicial decision." As one law school dean complained that year: "What we face now is the question, not how governmental functions shall be shared, but whether in substance we shall govern at all."

By this time, the Hughes Court's collision with Franklin Roosevelt's New Deal program

had attracted criticism across the country, and not altogether on partisan political or strictly ideological grounds. A widespread sentiment had formed that the Court, made up mostly of aging men deep into their 70s and 80s, was out of touch with reality and was engaging in blunt political acts aimed at blocking every effort of the Roosevelt administration to deal with the modern corporate economy realistically, and to end the crisis of the Depression. Why Hughes was participating in this obstructive course is still not clear. It is true he was a lifelong Republican who may well have resented his much younger, shallow, patrician-born Democrat neighbor from downstate New York. But then, Harlan Stone was also a New York Republican who distrusted the New Deal experiments and had no personal fondness for Roosevelt. Perhaps the best answer is that Hughes was always profoundly conservative, and his departures from the old came mainly—and usually grudgingly—when he feared that to do otherwise would put order into jeopardy.

Following the Coal Act decision, the Hughes Court in 1936 would take one more dramatic step toward provoking disorder when it overturned a New York minimum wage law. This time, Hughes voted with the minority in the 5–4 decision. But the damage was done. Even conservative students of the law exclaimed their disapproval. Stone, in his dissent, denounced the "economic predilections" of the Court's majority. Calls for revamping the Court grew.

That November, FDR won a landslide re-election victory in which he made "the Republican Supreme Court" a campaign issue. Thinking the time ripe, he asked Congress to pass a reform bill that would have permitted the president to name an additional justice to the Court for every sitting justice over the age of seventy (six of them were). Roosevelt's plan misfired. Although Congress had changed the number of seats on the Supreme Court several times before, this time even a large number of the president's own party in Congress rose in opposition. So great had the Supreme Court's authority grown in Americans' sense of nationhood, so important had the myth of its nonpartisanship become, that even in the face of the manifest partisanship of at least the consistently united four conservatives on the Court, the public recoiled from what the press quickly dubbed "Courtpacking." FDR found his plan attacked as if he had challenged the importance of motherhood, religion, and apple pie. To make matters worse, he chose to sidestep the political reasons for the proposal and disingenuously argued the need to relieve the workload of the superannuated justices.

That eased the task of his enemies. Although Hughes wished to avoid a direct confrontation with the administration on what he recognized was a proper political issue, FDR's claim that the aging Court members needed help gave him his opening. He responded to FDR's proposal in two ways. The first was to pick apart, in his well-practiced fashion of providing detailed data, the president's contention that the Court's aging members needed relief. Taking cues from Democratic Senator Burton Wheeler, he addressed a letter to the Senate Judiciary Committee as if in answer to a factual inquiry. Hughes easily showed that the Court had had no more trouble handling its full load of cases than had any previous Court. Hughes spoke for himself, but claimed that the letter was "in accord with the views of the Justices," although in fact he had consulted only with Van Devanter and Brandeis. Had he consulted all, he would have risked revealing division among the brethren on the issue. And the others, miffed though some were by their chief's presumption, declined to expose the Court to the embarrassment and controversy that a public challenge would entail. FDR's congressional opponents used Hughes's letter well in their successful campaign to sink the plan.

Although he would forever after deny it, Hughes's second response to the "Court-packing" controversy was essentially to change his judicial posture. The year 1937 marked the beginning of a nearly complete reversal of the Hughes Court's earlier positions on reform legislation, with Hughes and Roberts joining Brandeis, Cardozo, and Stone for a new 5–4 majority in the 1937 term.

By that margin, only months after voiding New York's minimum wage law, the Court upheld Washington State's minimum wage law in *West Coast Hotel Co. v. Parrish*, and explicitly reversed the decision in the New York case and the main precedent cited in that case, the infa-

mous *Adkins v. Children's Hospital* (1923). Only weeks later, Hughes gave the New Deal its greatest victory when he and the same four others upheld the National Labor Relations Act in *NLRB v. Jones & Laughlin Steel Corp.* To do so, he almost cavalierly waved aside his own position in the NIRA, AAA, and Bituminous Coal cases, as if rediscovering his earlier view that "regard must be had to [the] essential character" of the stream of commerce to determine Congress's jurisdiction. Justice McReynolds had every right to protest in his dissent: "Every consideration brought forward to uphold the [National Labor Relations] Act . . . was applicable to support the Acts held unconstitutional in cases decided within [only the past] two years."

The NLRB decision represented something new in modern American government. Until 1935, the growth of a government regulatory regime had responded almost entirely to demands made by various elements within the business community. With passage of the NLRA in 1935, a major piece of federal regulatory law emanated from concerns of the state itself to establish a controllable order in industrial relations, as well as in response to demands from among nonbusiness interests within the society for the kind of statutory protection from adverse market outcomes that different business groups commonly enjoyed. In upholding the act and in recognizing collective bargaining as a "fundamental right," the Hughes Court dramatically altered the employer-employee relationship, restoring to the state a large part of the mediating role it had had before nineteenth-century changes in law created a free-labor market that underwrote industrial capitalism. The restoration of government's active role in regulating industrial relations won firm standing in 1941, the last year of Hughes's stewardship. With the Court largely restructured by six resignations and deaths, Hughes reluctantly joined in a unanimous validation of the Fair Labor Standards Act of 1938, which reversed several precedents that had denied Congress's full power to regulate interstate commerce and the labor and goods that produced that commerce.

Before the end of 1938, the Court clearly indicated that it would henceforth presume the legitimacy of legislative efforts to govern the economy. In an obscure case, *United States v. Carolene Products Co.*, Justice Stone, for the Hughes Court, declared: "The existence of facts supporting the legislative judgment [in economic matters] is to be presumed." Then, in what became a famous footnote, Stone added that "legislation which restricts . . . political processes . . . is to be subjected to more exacting judicial scrutiny." Stone included among such restrictions the right to vote, to assemble, to organize politically, and in general, "restraints upon the dissemination of information."

In a vital way, this development marked the maturing of modern liberalism. Traditional liberalism had placed private property at the center of its emphasis on individual liberty, reasoning that from the immunity of property from arbitrary constraint or expropriation all other elements of individual liberty followed. Modern liberalism placed personal freedom—life-style, speech, assembly, religious choice, etc.—at the center of its concern for individual liberty, recognizing that the industrial and corporation revolutions, by bringing about a concentration of propertied power, had impaired the function of private property to protect individual liberty.

It is among the less featured facts about the Hughes Court that it set the first important precedents for developing a civil liberties jurisprudence. In *DeJonge v. Oregon* (1937), in which the Court unanimously overturned the conviction of a man for attending a Communist party meeting, Hughes declared loudly and clearly, "Peaceable assembly for lawful discussion cannot be made a crime." In *Herndon v. Lowry* that same year, for the first time the Court put Justice Holmes's test of "clear and present danger" into a majority opinion that overturned a conviction for illicit speech. In this case, a black organizer for the Communist party had been convicted for inciting insurrection. Justice Roberts for the Court declared the law under which the state had obtained the conviction "a dragnet which may enmesh anyone who agitates for a change of government," and "an unwarrantable invasion of the right of free speech." In *Hague v. C.I.O.* (1939), the Hughes Court found a municipal ordinance requiring permits for citizens to hold peaceful public meetings to be an unconstitutional burden on free speech and assembly. Simi-

larly, in *Thornhill v. Alabama* (1940), the Court held a statute banning peaceful picketing to be "invalid on its face," interfering as it did with the free discussion "indispensable to the effective and intelligent use of the processes of popular government to shape the destiny of modern industrial society." In all these cases, the Hughes Court set apart certain rights and immunities having to do with the communicative freedoms that no government could abridge without establishing some impelling reason of safety or order. Although a thorough protection for civil liberties still had a long way to go, the Hughes Court prepared a solid base.

There remains finally an assessment of the reputation of Charles Evans Hughes as a jurist. Most public accounts of the man's career have treated him with high honor. One scholar called the body of opinions by Hughes to be the most important since those of the great John Marshall. Others also extolled his administrative abilities as chief justice. Some contemporaries even cited his great sense of humor—a quality not obvious from either the character of his writings, including his autobiographical notes, or his public image. The man's very appearance, perhaps most of all his full, well-groomed but imperious beard, suggested a formidable authoritative presence. He appeared indeed the very embodiment of a "Great Judge." That he was the last of the major public figures in the United States to sport a beard added to the apartness that he cultivated as the chief "umpire" in American constitutional contests. "He radiated authority," which he exerted "by the artistic mastery with which he presided," wrote Justice Felix Frankfurter.

On the other hand, private opinions of Hughes by many of his contempoaries, including some of the same colleagues who publicly extolled him, differ sharply. The papers of Harlan Stone, who succeed Hughes as chief justice, are full of scorching judgments of both the man's legal opinions and his conduct as chief. "At conference," Stone wrote about one case, "the case was presented by the Chief Justice in his usual fashion of greatly over-elaborating the unimportant details of the case and disposing, by ipsi dixit, in a sentence or two, of the vital question." Others found his opinions verbose, often obscuring the critical issues. Some contemporaries jibed that Hughes, who coveted a reputation as a liberal like Holmes and Brandeis, usually chose not to speak for the Court when he joined conservative opinions, while assigning himself the Court's voice when he could agree on a liberal decision. Many stressed his inconsistency, and conservatives especially deplored his results-oriented activism. Archibald Cox of the Harvard Law School gave faint praise in saying that the Hughes Court did "appreciably less violence" than did the Warren Court "to the ideal of a coherent, growing, yet continuing body of law."

Perhaps it may best be said that Charles Evans Hughes presided over the United States Supreme Court at a time when great things were happening in constitutional law, and that they probably happened as much in spite of Hughes as because of him.

—RICHARD M. ABRAMS

BIBLIOGRAPHY

The Hughes papers are in the Library of Congress. The most complete biography remains Merlo J. Pusey, *Charles Evans Hughes* (2 vols., 1952), which is very much an "official" work. David J. Danelski and Joseph S. Tulchin have edited *The Autobiographical Notes of Charles Evans Hughes* (1973), which provides the most intimate image of Hughes we are likely to get.

For various interpretations of the man, see Paul A. Freund, "Charles Evans Hughes as Chief Justice," 81 *Harvard Law Review* 4 (1967); Samuel Hendel, *Charles Evans Hughes and the Supreme Court* (1951), a balanced account that pays more attention than most to Hughes's record on civil liberties; in this regard, see Merle William Loper, "The Court of Chief Justice Hughes: Contributions to Civil Liberties," 12 *Wayne Law Review* 535 (1966). The best and most succinct account of Hughes's first tenure on the Court is an anonymous note, "Governor on the Bench: Charles Evans Hughes as Associate Justice," 89 *Harvard Law Review* 961 (1976). Michael E. Parrish provides a critical account of the Hughes Court in "The Great Depression, the New Deal, and the American Legal Order," 59 *Washington Law Review* 723 (1984). One should also consult Alpheus T. Mason, *Harlan Fiske Stone: Pillar of the Law* (1956), which provides an intensive examination of the Hughes period, and a rare less-than-wholly favorable treatment of the chief justice.

WARD HUNT

BORN 14 June 1810, Utica, New York

NOMINATED to the Court 3 December 1872 by
    Ulysses S. Grant; retired 27 January
    1882

DIED 24 March 1886 in Washington, D.C.

Ward Hunt's nine-year term on the Supreme Court was generally undistinguished; he
is known in law schools today only because of
a vigorous dissent on a still troubling jurisdictional question, and he deserves the limited attention of legal historians because of a brief but
eloquent dissent from the Court's abdication of
civil rights principles.

Little is known of Hunt's life, although
basic data can be gleaned from public records
and contemporary newspapers. Born into a comfortable middle-class milieu, Hunt was groomed
for a legal career, graduating with honors from
Union College and studying law with James
Gould in Litchfield, Connecticut. He was politically active, aligning himself with Martin Van
Buren's Jacksonian branch of the New York
Democratic party. In 1844, he was elected
mayor of Utica. Opposition to slavery led him
to leave the Democrats, and in 1855–56, he
became a founder of the Republican party in
New York. At the close of the Civil War, he was
elected to the New York court of appeals, becoming chief judge in 1868. He was still serving as New York's chief judicial officer when
President Grant named him to the Supreme
Court. The nomination was apparently at the
behest of Senator Roscoe Conkling, a fellow
Utican and longtime friend. His nomination
proved uncontroversial and he was confirmed
within a week.

Hunt's jurisprudential production (152
opinions, seven dissents) may seem scant for a
justice who served nearly a decade on the Court.
However, Hunt was stricken by a paralytic
stroke in 1878; during the next four and a half
years he remained an associate justice, but did
not participate in any of the Court's proceedings.
Hunt lacked an independent income, and was
only willing to retire after Congress enacted a
special bill granting him an early pension.

Hunt's most noble contribution came in the
form of a dissent to the Court's 1876 decision
to gut the Enforcement Act of 1870, which
implemented the Fifteenth Amendment's guarantee of the right to vote for African-American
citizens. In extraordinarily twisted and attenu-
ated reasoning, Chief Justice Waite, writing for
all but Hunt in *United States v. Reese*, found the
congressional act unconstitutional because it
was not, in its penalty provisions, limited to
denial of the right to vote "on account of race."

In fact—as Hunt correctly demonstrated—
the statute did incorporate such a limitation. The
Supreme Court's majority was animated not by
fidelity to the laws they were sworn to uphold,
but by baser political motives. The Compromise
of 1877, marking an end to Reconstruction and
the rise of the era of Jim Crow throughout the
South, was already in preparation, and the
Court's majority was making its contribution to
the betrayal of the South's new citizens. Hunt
distinguished himself by refusing to participate
in this charade.

The balance of Hunt's opinion consisted of
a forceful statement of the Radical Republican
principles behind the Fifteenth Amendment.
Congress had intended to grant the freed slaves
the full measure of rights that had been enjoyed
by white citizens up to that date. He found that
this guarantee plainly extended the right to vote
to state as well as federal elections and that it
had become part of the "republican form of
government" promised by the Union to the citizens of the states. In the end, Hunt somberly
noted, the majority's intent was to render all the
Civil War amendments "impotent."

Regrettably, Hunt stood quietly by as
Waite's steamroller proceeded to devastate the
legal protections granted the freedmen; he seems
to have regarded *Reese* as a form of *stare decisis*
to which he was bound. In *Cruikshank v. United
States* (1876), he went along with a ruling that
in effect held that vigilantism and terrorism
designed to intimidate African Americans from

voting were "rights guaranteed to the people by the Constitution," and in *Hall v. DeCuir* (1878), he silently assented to a ruling striking down a Louisiana law guaranteeing former slaves and freemen access to railroads without discrimination as an "unconstitutional interference with interstate commerce." These opinions collectively may represent the most odious chapter in the history of Supreme Court jurisprudence.

Law students today are most likely to come across Hunt through his dissent to the intriguing case of *Pennoyer v. Neff* (1877). In that case, the Supreme Court invalidated a money judgment rendered against an absentee landowner on the grounds that the state court's exercise of jurisdiction was unconstitutional. The plaintiff had made use of a state statute allowing service by publication if the defendant owned property in the jurisdiction and providing for attachment of the property. Such jurisdiction is called *quasi in rem* today because it rests on the fictional notion that the *res*, in this case the real property, is the subject of the litigation. The Court held that the exercise of jurisdiction was unconstitutional because the property had not been attached first. Hunt found this distinction trifling; more significantly, he demonstrated that the Court's opinion rested on mere *obiter dicta* in the cases cited, that is, language which was not necessary to the holding. In opposition, Hunt compiled an impressive assemblage of cases whose holdings squarely contradicted the majority. While *Pennoyer* is still correct law, Hunt won lasting admiration for his forceful and persuasive argument on a close legal point.

Hunt was more favorably disposed than his immediate successors on the Court toward the exercise of state regulatory authority on economic questions. He joined in *Munn v. Illinois* (1877), authorizing the state to fix a ceiling on storage charges in grain silos; and in the *Slaughter House Cases* (1873), he voted to sustain a state-authorized monopoly. In another series of opinions, he regularly supported bondholders who challenged the attempts of governmental authorities to welch on their obligations (*Commissioners of Johnson Cty. v. Thayer,* 1877; *Randolph Cty. v. Post,* 1877; and *Burlington Township. v. Beasley,* 1877). In these and most other opinions, Hunt did not stand out from his colleagues; he seems very much a man of his times, and he offers us little which is of more than historical interest.

—SCOTT HORTON

BIBLIOGRAPHY

Stanley I. Kutler's "Ward Hunt" in Friedman and Israel, 2 *Justices* 1221, is the only serious biographical treatment.

JAMES IREDELL

BORN 5 October 1751, Lewes, England

NOMINATED to the Court 8 February 1790
by George Washington

TOOK seat 3 August 1790

DIED 20 October 1799 in Edenton,
North Carolina

James Iredell had gained a reputation as a prominent North Carolina Federalist prior to his Supreme Court appointment in 1790. Although he began his career as an official of the colonial government—he served as collector of customs in Edenton and, after studying law, was appointed deputy king's attorney—he wrote several tracts during the 1770s that established him as sympathetic to the revolutionary cause.

During the Revolutionary War, Iredell served as a member of a committee charged with reviewing state statutes (1776); as a superior court judge (1777–78); and as state attorney general (1779–81). Returning to private practice, Iredell was able to give vent to his strongly held opinions concerning the fundamental nature of constitutional law and the importance of judicial review. In his *Instructions to Chowan County Representatives* (1783), he argued that fixed salaries for judges were necessary, for "otherwise they cannot be truly independent, which is a point of the utmost moment in a Republic where the Law is superior to any or all the Individuals, and the Constitution superior even to the Legislature, and of which the Judges are the guardians and protectors." As an attorney in the case of *Bayard v. Singleton* (1787), he successfully argued that a state confiscation act violated the North Carolina constitution because it denied a jury trial to litigants challenging the confiscation. Iredell's efforts in favor of adoption of the Constitution during North Carolina's ratifying conventions of 1788 and 1789 brought him to the attention of President Washington, who named him to the high court in 1790.

As a justice, Iredell proved himself to be conscientious and careful. His opinions, in which he usually raised and answered the arguments of the parties in methodical fashion, often took a tack independent of his brethren. He was sensitive to the impact that the Court's decisions might have in the larger world, and he frequently expressed his reluctance to decide important or constitutional questions unnecessarily (although he was quite willing to engage in extraneous discussions that would now be termed dicta). His primary concerns, as revealed in his opinions, were the principles of separation of powers and judicial review and, perhaps most importantly, his concern for the interests of the states vis-à-vis the federal government.

Early in his career on the Court, Iredell had the opportunity to act on his beliefs in separation of powers and judicial review of legislation. In 1792, Congress passed the Invalid Pensions Act, assigning to the federal circuit courts the task of determining whether veterans who claimed to have been injured in the Revolutionary War were eligible for pensions. The act made the determination of the court subject to review by the secretary of war. Shortly after the act's passage, circuit courts around the country (which at that time were composed of one or two Supreme Court justices and the local district judge) confronted the statute, and all found it defective.

Iredell, sitting on the circuit court for the district of North Carolina, and district judge John Sitgreaves sent a letter to George Washington setting out their views on the statute. Because they had no case before them, the letter amounted to an advisory opinion. By the terms of the Constitution, they said, each department—legislative, judicial, and executive—must remain separate. Because the act authorized the secretary of war to review the court's decision, it in effect set up an arm of the executive branch as an appellate court—without investing the secretary of war with life tenure, as required by Article III. Thus, the act subjected the court's decision to "a mode of revision which we consider to be unwarranted by the Constitution." Essentially, the judges were expressing their conclusion that the act was unconstitutional because it violated the guarantee of separation of powers.

An even clearer statement of Iredell's belief in judicial review of legislation came in *Calder v. Bull* (1798), the first case in which the Supreme Court confronted the meaning of the constitutional prohibition against *ex post facto* laws. While agreeing with the rest of the justices that the Connecticut law at issue was not an *ex post facto* law because it was civil rather than criminal in nature, Iredell observed that if any federal or state act violated a constitutional provision, it was "unquestionably void"—adding that, "as the authority to declare it void is of a delicate and awful nature, the Court will never resort to that authority, but in a clear and urgent case."

Undoubtedly, Iredell's most famous opinion is his dissent in *Chisholm v. Georgia* (1793)—the case that precipitated the Eleventh Amendment to the Constitution, which bars federal courts from hearing suits brought by individuals against states other than their own. *Chisholm* was a suit brought by citizens of South Carolina against Georgia for nonpayment of a debt contracted during the Revolution. Georgia, claiming sovereign immunity, refused to enter an appearance, and the plaintiffs moved for a default judgment. In separate opinions issued in February 1793, four of the five justices then on the Court found no constitutional barrier to the suit; on the contrary, they held that suits against states were authorized by Article III, Section 2, which conferred federal jurisdiction over suits "between a state and citizens of another state." Iredell alone dissented.

Having first encountered the case in 1791 while sitting on the circuit court for the district of Georgia—where he dismissed the suit on the ground that the circuit court lacked jurisdiction, but implied that it might be allowable in the Supreme Court—Iredell had had ample time to formulate his views. He presented the question in the narrowest possible terms: would an action of *assumpsit* (an action for damages for the nonperformance of an oral or written contract) lie against a state? Vehemently rejecting the plaintiffs' suggestion that judicial authority could be derived directly from the Constitution, without the benefit of any enabling legislation, Iredell turned to the Judiciary Act of 1789 for clarification. The fourteenth section of that act, he noted, authorized the issuance of all writs *"agreeable to the principles and usages of law."* The "law" referred to, he concluded, could only

be "the common law"—that is, the law *"as it existed in England, (unaltered by any statute) at the time of the first settlement of the country."* Iredell proceeded to examine the common law of England regarding suits against the Crown, explaining that "every State in the *Union* in every instance where its sovereignty has not been delegated to the *United States*, I consider to be as compleatly sovereign, as the *United States* are in respect to the powers surrendered."

Iredell then embarked on a lengthy disquisition on English case law, which led him to the conclusion that the only method of proceeding against the king in the case of debt was by petition, and was dependent on his consent. By analogy, the only remedy against a state in the case of debt was by petition to the legislature. Iredell went on to reject the argument that a state could be analogized to a corporation. As he had done earlier in his opinion when rejecting the idea that judicial power could be derived directly from the Constitution, Iredell set out a sharp division between the spheres of the courts and the legislature: to apply the law of corporations to the very different situation of states would be tantamount to engaging in lawmaking, "when the *application* of law, not the *making* of it, is the sole province of the Court."

In conclusion, Iredell observed that his decision made it unnecessary for him to consider whether the Constitution itself authorized federal courts to entertain suits against states, noting that "it is of extreme moment that no Judge should rashly commit himself upon important questions, which it is unnecessary for him to decide." However, he continued, since so much had been said on the subject of the Constitution, "it may not be improper to intimate that my present opinion is strongly against any construction of it, which will admit, under any circumstances a compulsive suit against a State for the recovery of money." His last sentence rang ominously: "I pray to God, that if the Attorney General's doctrine, as to the law, be established by the judgment of this Court, all the good he predicts from it may take place, and none of the evils with which, I have the concern to say, it appears to me to be pregnant."

Iredell's opinion, as it turned out, was more in keeping with the mood of the country than

James Iredell
Artwork by Albert Rosenthal.
Collection of the Supreme Court of the United States.

were those of his fellow justices. The day after the opinions came down, a constitutional amendment to overturn the result was introduced in the House, and a similar amendment passed both houses of Congress the following year. By 1795, the requisite number of states had ratified the amendment, although, because of bureaucratic errors, the ratification was not made official until 1798.

Some commentators, such as Griffith J. McRee—the first editor of Iredell's letters—have seen in Iredell's dissent the germ of what later became known as the doctrine of states' rights. Others, noting Iredell's strong Federalist record and judicial support for such unpopular displays of Federalist might as the Alien and Sedition Acts, have disputed this view. Jeff B. Fordham has written that what Iredell did "was simply to state a legal opinion instead of writing a political tract." Unwilling to embark on new and uncharted territory when it "was of no great importance to the effectuation of the purposes of the union," Iredell chose the road of caution. Christopher T. Graebe has offered a more instrumentalist analysis of Iredell's dissent, pointing out that a number of its legal arguments do not hold water: "Iredell knew the result that the country needed in light of growing Southern discontent with federal power, and he found the requisite law to achieve his political goal." Certainly, Iredell was influenced by an awareness of the political difficulties inherent in the majority's decision. In a draft of part of the opinion that Iredell ultimately omitted, he considered the impossibility of enforcing a judgment against an unwilling state. Turning on its head the adage that "where there is a right, there is a remedy," Iredell suggested that "where no remedy can be found, there is no right."

Iredell again displayed his concern for state prerogatives in *Ware v. Hylton* (1796), another politically charged case. The suit involved a debt contracted before the Revolution; the debtor was a Virginian, the creditor British. In 1777, Virginia passed a sequestration act, allowing citizens who owed money to British creditors to discharge their debts by paying them to the state. In 1780, the debtor took advantage of this statute to discharge part of the debt, but when peace was negotiated in 1783, the treaty provided that creditors on either side should "meet with no lawful impediment" to the recovery of debts contracted before the Revolution. Relying on the treaty, the British creditor sued the Virginia debtor for recovery of the debt—including that part of the debt that had been paid to the state.

Four justices, in separate opinions, held that the 1783 treaty nullified the Virginia sequestration act. As in *Chisholm*, Iredell was the only one to disagree. Having decided the case in circuit court, he took no actual part in the decision, but he felt sufficiently strongly about the case that he chose to read his circuit court opinion from the bench. In Iredell's view, the provision of the treaty at issue was executory, requiring legislative action to give it effect. Once the Constitution was ratified, the supremacy clause served to repeal the Virginia sequestration act, but "*everything done under the act while in existence*, so far as private rights at least were concerned," was unaffected by the repeal. Thus the defendant was no longer a "debtor" as to that part of the debt paid over to the state, and the words of the treaty could not apply. This reasoning ignored the political reality that the treaty was expressly directed at allowing British creditors to surmount legal obstacles such as state sequestration and confiscation acts. But Iredell—who appeared to recognize the shaky legal ground on which his argument rested—chose to defer to another political reality, namely, the hostility of the states to this provision of the treaty.

Although Iredell's reading of the law in these cases was influenced by pragmatism, he was far from unprincipled. If he can be said to have defended "states' rights," he did so only when no great harm would result to the interests of the federal government. Indeed, given his generally staunch defense of federal power— most evident in the charges he delivered to grand juries while riding circuit—it is likely that his dissents were motivated by a desire to preserve the Union by mollifying those states, including his own, whose fierce independence threatened to tear it apart.

—NATALIE WEXLER

BIBLIOGRAPHY

Regrettably, there is no modern full-length biography of James Iredell. A brief but informative biographical sketch of Iredell is Fred L. Israel, "James Iredell," in Friedman and Israel, 1 *Justices* 121. Thoughtful analysis of Iredell's opinion in *Chisholm v. Georgia* can be found in Christopher T. Graebe, "The Federalism of James Iredell in Historical Context," 69 *North Carolina Law Review* 251 (1990), and, to a lesser extent, in Jeff B. Fordham, "Iredell's Dissent in *Chisholm v. Georgia*," 8 *The North Carolina Historical Review* 155 (1931).

The bulk of Iredell's papers are in the Charles E. Johnson collection at the North Carolina State Department of Archives and History, while others are deposited at Duke University. Both collections contain some items relating to Iredell's judicial career. Griffith J. McRee, *Life and Correspondence of James Iredell* (1857, 1949), is dated and somewhat unreliable, but contains transcripts of a number of letters that have since been lost. Many documents and letters relating to Iredell's tenure on the Supreme Court can be found in the volumes of Maeva Marcus, ed., *The Documentary History of the Supreme Court, 1789–1800* (1985–). For information on Iredell's early life, see Don Higginbotham, ed., *The Papers of James Iredell* (1976).

HOWELL EDMUNDS JACKSON

BORN 8 April 1832, Paris, Tennessee
NOMINATED to the Court 2 February 1893
    by Benjamin Harrison
TOOK seat 4 March 1893
DIED 8 August 1895 in West Meade,
    Tennessee

History considers the central event in the public life of Howell Jackson to be the ironic irrelevance of a judicial vote which he had overcome serious illness and great distance to cast. A deeper irony, however, may be that history has misunderstood both iterations of *Pollock v. Farmers' Loan and Trust Co.* (1895), and Jackson's support of the small income tax there held unconstitutional.

Howell Jackson's legal work as an eminent corporate lawyer and Democrat opposed to state debt repudiation led to his election to the United States Senate and important alliances with Grover Cleveland and Benjamin Harrison. It is a measure of Jackson's political skill that he was appointed to the federal appellate bench by the former, and to the Supreme Court by the latter, during the period of their own presidential rivalry.

Like most of the era's judges, Jackson carved no new directions in either economic or civil rights policies. He voted with the majority in *Fong Yue Ting v. United States* (1893), which denied a resident alien due process protection to challenge his deportation under the Chinese Exclusion Act. In *Brass v. North Dakota* (1894), Jackson concurred in David J. Brewer's dissent from a ruling upholding the constitutionality of state regulation of grain elevators. In *Mobile & Ohio R.R. v. Tennessee* (1894), Jackson invalidated under the contracts clause a Tennessee effort to repudiate the tax exemption provision in a state-granted charter. In 1894, Jackson contracted tuberculosis, and his illness prevented his participation in the Court's narrow interpretation of the Sherman Antitrust Act in *United States v. E.C. Knight Co.* (1895), and its support of the labor injunction in *In re Debs* that same year. The evidence, however, suggests that he would have strongly supported both rulings.

But for his role in the income tax cases, therefore, this representative of mainstream legal assumptions would have seemed to progressives a typical member of the rogues' gallery of reactionaries that populated the Court during the era. Returning to the capital after the first *Pollock* ruling, which had held the tax unconstitutional as applied to income from land, Jackson appeared to be the swing vote for the tax on the remaining questions which had deadlocked the Court. Yet, after the final hearing, the Court held the entire income tax unconstitutional, with Jackson in vocal dissent, generating the view that a "vacillating jurist" must have switched his vote.

Jackson's *Pollock* opinion is his most celebrated, yet a careful reading integrates it with his centrist premises. His problem with the decision was not that a genuinely redistributive law had been thwarted, but rather that precedent and the traditional "practice of the government" had been abandoned. The decision was less a slap at the poor than "the most disastrous blow ever struck at the constitutional power of Congress."

Progressives and legal realists who argued for a judicial approach based in social facts and policy results criticized the Court for frustrating a genuinely reformist law. On this view, Jackson's vote gave him a "liberal" cachet, despite his lifelong corporate associations. Recent scholarship has argued that lawmakers across the political spectrum sought to maintain the existing order against economic and political upheaval. This view makes Jackson's career, his brief tenure on the Court, and his most celebrated opinion more easily reconcilable.

—ROBERT STANLEY

BIBLIOGRAPHY

The primary biographical source is still Irving Schiffman, "Howell E. Jackson," in Friedman and Israel, 2 *Justices* 1603. For a discussion of progressive interpretive assumptions and recent departures, see Robert Stanley, *Dimensions of Law in the Service of Order: Origins of the Federal Income Tax, 1861–1913* (1993).

Robert Houghwout Jackson
Photograph by Harris and Ewing.
Collection of the Supreme Court of the United States.

ROBERT HOUGHWOUT JACKSON

BORN February 13, 1892, Spring Creek,
     Pennsylvania
NOMINATED to the Court 12 June 1941
     by Franklin D. Roosevelt
TOOK seat 11 July 1941
DIED 9 October 1954 in Washington, D.C.

In February 1941, Justice James McReynolds, the last of the conservative "Four Horsemen" who had tried to block key New Deal programs, resigned from the Supreme Court, and President Roosevelt named his attorney general, Robert Jackson, as McReynolds's replacement. Jackson had provided Roosevelt with legal advice at several important junctures, including FDR's Court-packing plan and the "lend-lease" program, which had circumvented a congressional prohibition to provide key military equipment to Great Britain.

Jackson joined the Court during a transition period. After the so-called "switch in time" in 1937, when Justice Roberts changed his position on key issues, a new majority of the Court had begun to embrace the modern regulatory state. By the time of Jackson's appointment, all of the justices except Stone and Roberts were Roosevelt appointees. Although the direction of change was clear, the new doctrines had not yet received their decisive formulations. Having abandoned the effort to protect economic rights from government regulation, the Court was also just beginning to find a new role for itself as a defender of civil liberties. Jackson helped create the modern doctrinal rules governing judicial review of economic regulations. He also participated in the process by which the Court became the guardian of free speech and other individual rights.

Jackson was something of a maverick. He served with Justices Black and Frankfurter, who created, respectively, the intellectual bases for the Warren Court and for its critics. Unlike those justices, however, Jackson's votes could not be easily predicted on the basis of his general judicial philosophy. His opinions have a far more personal touch than those of most judges of the

period, or even today. They combine vivid metaphors with a sometimes sardonic humor. Many of his opinions are forgotten now because the evolution of the law took a different path. But some of his opinions took root, and seem as fresh today as when they were written. For instance, his opinion in the second flag salute case provided the foundation for the Court's important and controversial flag-burning opinions nearly fifty years later.

Born on a western Pennsylvania farm, Jackson was a fourth-generation Democrat with strong rural roots, whose great-grandfather had been a staunch supporter of Andrew Jackson. His father operated a livery stable and country hotel. Although he attended law school for one year, Robert Jackson was self-educated, holding neither an undergraduate nor a law degree. He was the last justice to have qualified as a lawyer by "reading law" rather than through formal legal education. He briefly attended Albany Law School only because he had decided to set up a small practice in Jackson, New York, and many of the leading lawyers in that town had studied at Albany. Later, his clients included businessmen, labor unions, and farmers. He was active in New York politics, became an advisor to then-governor Franklin Roosevelt, and in the 1932 presidential election campaigned for Roosevelt through New York State.

At the age of forty-two, Jackson moved to Washington, D.C., where he worked for the rest of his life as a government lawyer and then as a judge. As general counsel to the Bureau of Internal Revenue (where he successfully brought tax evasion proceedings against Andrew Mellon, former secretary of the treasury), then as solicitor general and later attorney general, Jackson was considered a staunchly loyal New Dealer. He would describe the period of his service as solicitor general as the happiest part of his life.

Jackson's horizons were not limited to the judiciary. He was considered a serious possibility for the Democratic party's presidential nomination in 1940 in the event that Roosevelt decided not to run again. He also received international acclaim for his role as chief prosecutor in the Nuremberg War Crimes trial. During World War II, Jackson had felt removed from the great events of the period; he remarked that on the Monday after Pearl Harbor, the Court had heard arguments about the taxability of greens fees at country clubs. He thus welcomed the opportunity to participate in the Nuremberg trials. Although he took the Nuremberg assignment against the advice of Chief Justice Stone, his successful prosecution helped establish important new principles of international law. Jackson later viewed the Nuremberg prosecution as his most important professional achievement.

Unfortunately, at the close of the trials, Jackson learned that for a second time, he would be passed over for the position of chief justice. His response was swift and savage. He publicly proclaimed that the Court was split by ideological differences and that his nomination as chief justice had been blocked by the civil libertarian wing of the Court, in particular by Hugo Black. The repercussions of this ugly public fight between the justices poisoned Jackson's later years on the Court.

Jackson's most famous opinion is undoubtedly *West Virginia State Board of Education v. Barnette* (1943). In June of 1940, before Jackson joined the Court, *Minersville School District v. Gobitis* had been decided. In an opinion by Justice Frankfurter, the Court held that a Jehovah's Witness could be expelled from school for refusing to salute the flag for religious reasons. It may be no coincidence that this opinion was announced at a time when the European picture was gloomy indeed. In the same month as *Gobitis* was decided, the British were evacuating Dunkirk, and the Germans were closing in on Paris. Nor, at that time, did the Court have a robust history of defending free speech. It is little wonder, under the circumstances, that Frankfurter wrote for an 8–1 majority in support of national unity. Only Harlan Stone dissented.

By 1943, it was clear that *Gobitis* had dubious prospects. Justices Black, Douglas, and Murphy took advantage of another case involving the Jehovah's Witnesses to make an extraordinary public announcement that they no longer supported the *Gobitis* ruling. Justice Rutledge, who was appointed in 1943, was also known to oppose *Gobitis* because of a dissent he had written as a court of appeals judge in another case involving the Witnesses.

Justice Jackson wrote the opinion overruling *Gobitis*. Because this was probably his most notable opinion, it is worth detailed consideration. The opinion begins with several pages carefully reviewing the facts of the case. After *Gobitis*, the West Virginia legislature had enacted a requirement that all schools present courses on civics. Two years later, the state board of education had adopted a resolution ordering all students and teachers to salute the flag, "provided, however, that refusal to salute the Flag be regarded as an act of insubordination, and shall be dealt with accordingly." The penalty for this insubordination was expulsion, with the added result that the child was considered a truant, so that he or she could be sent to a reformatory as a delinquent and the parents could be prosecuted criminally.

Jackson begins his analysis with the premise that the flag salute, though not verbal, is nevertheless a form of communication. As he observed, "objection to this form of communication when coerced is an old one, well known to the framers of the Bill of Rights." An accompanying footnote points out that William Tell was sentenced to shoot the famous apple on his son's head "for refusal to salute a bailiff's hat." Jackson then observes that censorship of speech, under the Court's precedents, could be allowed only if the speech created a clear and present danger. "It would seem," he added, "that involuntary affirmation could be commanded only on even more immediate and urgent grounds than silence." But in reality, the state had not even purported to identify a clear and present danger of any kind. Thus, Jackson said, sustaining the West Virginia rule would imply "that a Bill of Rights which guards the individual's right to speak his own mind, left it open to public authorities to compel him to utter what is not in his mind."

Jackson then turned to the *Gobitis* precedent. He noted that the opinion in that case had focused on the question of religious exemption, assuming that the mandatory flag salute was otherwise constitutional. Notably, Jackson declined to follow *Gobitis* in deferring to state authorities. As to the role of school boards as representatives of the local community, he said in a frequently quoted passage that:

> The very purpose of a Bill of Rights was to withdraw certain subjects from the vicissitudes of political controversy, to place them beyond the reach of majorities and officials and to establish them as legal principles to be applied by the courts. One's right to life, liberty, and property, to free speech, freedom of worship and assembly, and other fundamental rights may not be submitted to vote; they depend on the outcome of no elections.

Nor was Jackson persuaded by the argument that school boards had greater expertise than judges in educational matters, for "we act in these matters not by authority of our competence but by force of our commissions."

This brought Jackson to the heart of the case. In an apparent reference to the Nazis, he said that "those who begin coercive elimination of dissent soon find themselves exterminating dissenters." Compulsory uniformity, in the end, "achieves only the unanimity of the graveyard." The opinion then closes with a passage that has become famous to generations of law students and scholars:

> The case is made difficult not because the principles of its decision are obscure but because the flag involved is our own. . . . But freedom to differ is not limited to things that do not matter much. That would be a mere shadow of freedom. The test of its substance is the right to differ as to things that touch the heart of the existing order.
>
> If there is any fixed star in our constitutional constellation, it is that no official, high or petty, can prescribe what shall be orthodox in politics, nationalism, religion, or other matters of opinion or force citizens to confess by word or act their faith therein.

Barnette historically marked the Court's shift from the protection of economic interests to individual rights. Today, First Amendment doctrine is a complicated skein of rules and standards. Judicial opinions today are more likely to discuss the appropriate standard for judicial review than to revisit the basic values underlying

the first amendment. *Barnette* did not break new ground in the sense of articulating a new test; it essentially retained the existing "clear and present danger" test. But in a sense, all of the current doctrinal complexities are no more than a series of footnotes to Jackson's resounding affirmation of freedom of thought and speech.

Barnette today overshadows Jackson's other, less powerful first amendment opinions. For example, in *Terminiello v. Chicago* (1949), the Court reversed the conviction of a vituperatively anti-Semitic, anti-Catholic speaker. The Court held that the jury instructions were fatally flawed, because they allowed conviction for speech that "stirs the public to anger, invites dispute, brings about a condition of unrest, or creates a disturbance." Jackson dissented. He saw more at stake than just a street-corner demagogue. Rather, he saw a replay of the street battles of the Weimar Republic, which culminated in Hitler's rise to power. The influence of his Nuremberg experience is evident here. But *Terminiello* also reflects Jackson's general willingness to distinguish between the suppression of ideas, of the kind he rejected in *Barnette*, and responses to concrete harms, which he usually found tolerable. For example, he was willing to uphold a ban on door-to-door solicitation by Jehovah's Witnesses, in order to protect the privacy of residents (*Douglas v. City of Jeannette*, 1943, dissenting opinion).

Apart from *Barnette* Jackson's most important opinions involved structural constitutional issues—federalism and separation of powers—rather than individual rights. Perhaps because of his extensive experience in government, he was able to make a lasting contribution to the law in these areas.

Jackson wrote a seminal opinion in the steel seizure case, *Youngstown Sheet & Tube Co. v. Sawyer* (1952). Although only a concurring opinion, Jackson's test was later cited more often than Justice Black's majority opinion as the governing test.

The case arose during the Korean War. To head off a nationwide strike of steel workers, which was thought to be a threat to the war effort, President Harry S Truman issued an executive order directing the secretary of commerce to take charge of most of the steel mills. The order was based on "inherent presidential power" rather than on any specific statutory authority. This order presented the Court with difficult and unprecedented questions regarding the scope of presidential power.

For Justice Black, this was a simple case. No express constitutional provision gave the president the power to seize the steel mills. Rather than granting the president the authority to formulate public policy, the Constitution gave Congress the lawmaking power. For Justice Black, no more needed to be said.

Although it is formally the "opinion of the Court," Justice Black's majority opinion reflected a frail consensus. Each justice who joined Black's opinions also felt called upon to file a concurring opinion; Justice Clark agreed only with the result but not with Black's opinions; while Vinson, Reed, and Minton dissented. The reason for the dissatisfaction with Black's opinion was probably that, while accurately reflecting the constitutional text, it entirely ignored the evolution of the presidency over the course of almost two centuries since the founding.

Jackson's influential concurrence begins with a candid disclosure that his experience as a presidential counselor probably had colored his views more than conventional legal sources. In light of that experience, he rejected Black's formalistic approach. For, as Jackson said, the "actual art of governing under our Constitution does not and cannot conform to judicial definitions of the power of any of its branches based on isolated clauses or even single Articles torn from context."

In order to provide guidance in analyzing the tangled relationships between the branches of government, Jackson offered what he called a "somewhat over-simplified" classification of presidential actions. He distinguished three categories of presidential acts. First, Congress may have authorized the presidential action, either implicitly or explicitly. In this situation, the president's power is at its peak, since he acts by virtue of the combined powers of both branches. Second, when Congress has been silent on the subject, the president must rely on the independent constitutional powers of his office, but "there is a zone of twilight" in which those powers overlap with congressional authority. Here, "any actual test of power is likely to depend on the imperatives of events and contemporary

imponderables rather than on abstract theories of law." Third, when Congress has forbidden the presidential action, "his power is at its lowest ebb." In this situation of direct conflict between the two branches, the president's claim must be scrutinized with special caution, lest the "equilibrium" of the constitutional system be upset.

Clearly, the steel seizure did not belong to the first category of specifically authorized actions. As to the second category, Jackson could find no basis for a claim of inherent presidential power. He specifically rejected the government's claim that the first clause of Article II, vesting the executive power in the president, was a general grant of all executive powers. Nor was he willing to accept the view that the president had broad inherent powers, beyond those in the constitutional text, to deal with emergencies. After reviewing recent European history, he concluded that "emergency powers are consistent with free government only when their control is lodged elsewhere than in the Executive."

In closing, Jackson remarked on the evolution of presidential powers:

> The Constitution does not disclose the measure of the actual controls wielded by the modern presidential office. That office must be understood as an Eighteenth-Century sketch of a government hoped for, not as a blueprint of the Government that is. . . . Subtle shifts take place in the centers of real power that do not show on the face of the Constitution.

Given the amount of power that had gravitated to the White House already, Jackson saw no reason for the Court to further aggrandize the presidency.

The consequences of recognizing a broad presidential power to respond to national emergencies were, in Jackson's view, unforeseeable. Acknowledging such a presidential power might erode the very basis of the rule of law, for "with all its defects, delays and inconveniences, men have discovered no technique for long preserving free government except that the Executive be under the law, and that the law be made by parliamentary deliberations."

More than twenty-five years later, in a case arising from the Iranian hostage situation, the

Court turned to Jackson's concurrence as a guiding framework for analyzing presidential power (*Dames & Moore v. Regan,* 1981).

Jackson came to the Court in a period when the relationships between the federal government and the states were in flux. He authored an opinion that crystallized the new understanding of the scope of federal power. *Wickard v. Filburn* (1942), involved wheat quotas adopted under the Agricultural Adjustment Act. The statute was designed to stabilize wheat production through the use of quotas, which were subject to approval by the farmers themselves in a referendum. Filburn owned a dairy and poultry farm in Ohio. He raised a small amount of wheat, sold part, and used the rest for livestock feed, home consumption, or as seed the following year. The question before the Court was whether, as applied to the wheat Filburn used himself rather than selling, the statute was a valid regulation of interstate commerce.

Jackson's opinion for the Court in *Wickard* is a ringing affirmation of national power. Prior decisions had suggested that Congress could regulate interstate sales and transportation, but not such "local" activities as production or consumption. Jackson rejected the concept that these local activities are beyond the commerce power. By producing wheat for his own use, Filburn was reducing the demand in the interstate market for wheat. Admittedly, the effect of his individual activities was minuscule. But Congress had the power to regulate his activities because "his contribution, taken together with that of many others similarly situated, is far from trivial." This test paved the way for the later adoption of the 1964 Civil Rights Act, which was based on Congress's power to regulate interstate commerce.

The obverse side of congressional power consists of limits on state power. Although the commerce clause, on its face, is simply a grant of power to Congress, since the early days of the republic it has also been considered a limitation on the powers of the states. Here again, Jackson took a strongly nationalist stand. He believed passionately in the importance of free trade between the states, and he viewed the commerce clause as mandating a national common market. *H.P. Hood & Sons, Inc. v. Du Mond* (1949), is one of his strongest judicial statements of this philosophy. Hood supplied milk to Boston, and

wanted to make additional purchases in New York state for the Boston market. Under New York law, Hood needed a state license to open an additional facility for receiving milk from farmers. The New York statute required the state agriculture commissioner to determine "that the issuance of the license will not tend to a destructive competition in a market already adequately served." The commissioner denied the license on the grounds that the dairy market was already adequately served and that Hood's purchases would divert milk from local consumption.

As Jackson pointed out, the dairy industry was heavily regulated and had already given rise to several Supreme Court opinions regarding state interference with interstate commerce. In one of those earlier cases, Justice Cardozo had remarked that the Constitution was "framed upon the theory that the peoples of the several states must sink or swim together." As Jackson pointed out, one of the primary flaws of the Articles of Confederation had been the existence of trade barriers among the states. The Constitution therefore established the "principle that our economic unit is the Nation."

Jackson's description of the commerce clause culminates in a powerful endorsement of free trade among the states:

Our system, fostered by the Commerce Clause, is that every farmer and every craftsman shall be encouraged to produce by the certainty that he will have free access to every market in the Nation, that no home embargoes will withhold his experts, and no foreign state will by customs duties or regulations exclude them. Likewise, every consumer may look to the free competition from every producing area in the Nation to protect him from exploitation by any. Such was the vision of the Founders, such has been the doctrine of this Court which has given it reality.

He concluded that New York, by attempting to protect local buyers of milk from interstate competition, was directly flouting this basic principle of a national common market.

Jackson remains a somewhat enigmatic figure. Some of his opinions helped lay the foundations for important doctrinal developments. Others seem quaint or even quirky. The latter category is illustrated by his dissent in *Beauharnais v. Illinois* (1952), in which Jackson endorsed the general principle of treating racist speech as "group libel," but argued that the defendant was entitled to a jury trial regarding the truth of his racist credo. Today, this seems a somewhat eccentric position.

Jackson's best opinions, however, are a unique addition to the Court's jurisprudence. Their distinguishing feature is their bold effort to enunciate broad principles. While Jackson related those principles to the intent of the framers and earlier precedents, he was also candid in admitting that they reflected value judgments based on history and contemporary experience. This technique could misfire when Jackson misjudged the values toward which society was moving. But when it worked—when he called upon values that were to prove basic and enduring—his opinions provided a strong foundation on which other, more legalistic, justices could build.

—DANIEL A. FARBER

BIBLIOGRAPHY

The Jackson papers are in the Library of Congress, and there is a large and important memoir in the Columbia University oral history collection. Eugene Gerhart, *America's Advocate: Robert H. Jackson* (1958) is uncritical, and relies heavily on a lengthy autobiographical sketch Jackson wrote to defend his point of view in the imbroglio over the chief justiceship.

Jackson's *The Struggle for Judicial Supremacy* (1941) expresses Jackson's view of the Court's evolution as an institution, with particular reference to the *Lochner* era and the 1937 "switch-in-time" that upheld the New Deal. His ideas on the Court are well explained in Glendon Schubert, *Dispassionate Justice: A Synthesis of the Judicial Opinions of Robert H. Jackson* (1969).

For other analyses, see Felix Frankfurter, "Mr. Justice Jackson," 68 *Harvard Law Review* 938 (1955), an appraisal by a judicial ally; the symposium, "Mr. Justice Jackson," in 8 *Stanford Law Review* (1955); Louis Jaffe, "Mr. Justice Jackson," 68 *Harvard Law Review* 940 (1955), a thoughtful overview of Jackson's opinions and legal writings; and G. Edward White, *The American Judicial Tradition: Profiles of Leading American Judges* (1976), which includes a thoughtful essay about Jackson's jurisprudence.

JOHN JAY

BORN 12 December 1745, New York City

NOMINATED to the Court as chief justice 24
    September 1789 by George Washington

TOOK oath 19 October 1789; resigned 29 June
    1795; nominated again by John Adams
    18 December 1800; confirmed by
    Senate, but commission returned by Jay

DIED 17 May 1829 in Bedford, New York

The war for American independence cata-
pulted dozens of young, barely seasoned politicians and lawyers into positions of extraordinary
power and influence. Among them was the reserved, eminently capable John Jay of New
York—the first chief justice of the United States.

Early experiences powerfully shaped Jay's
conception of the "good" political society and
the role of judicial statesmen in republics. The
eldest son of the wealthy Peter and Mary Van
Cortlandt Jay, John followed the path dictated by
his parents' social class and connections within
the New York mercantile community. He was
educated privately until 1760, when he matricu-
lated at King's College (now Columbia University) to deepen his mastery of the classics, natural science, public law, and philosophy
(including political economy).

Jay decided to take up the study of law only
in his final year at university, partly (as was
customary among gentlemen) in preparation for
public service. After graduation with honors, he
took up an apprenticeship in the law office of
eminent attorney Benjamin Kissam where, as
assistant to the chief clerk, Jay chafed under piles
of tedious copy work. When city lawyers struck
in 1765 in support of colonial protests of the
Stamp Act, Jay happily fled to the family estate
in Rye, New York, where he immersed himself
in the classics, philosophy, and political theory.

After the Stamp Act crisis in 1766, young
Jay returned to Kissam's firm as chief clerk; two
years later, Jay gained admission to the New
York bar and opened law offices in the city with
his old schoolmate, Robert Livingston, Jr. There,
he threw himself into work, the whirl of high

society, debating clubs, and conservative state
political groups. In 1769, he accepted his first
public office as a commissioner to settle a
boundary dispute between New York and New
Jersey.

Jay's generation soon confronted adversity.
By 1774, the streets and wharves of American
port cities rumbled with rebellious talk about the
Intolerable Acts, King George III's abrogations
of his coronation oath, and ministerial violations
of the ancient English constitution. At first, Jay
resisted independence: he helped formulate the
conciliatory olive branch petition of 1774, and
seriously considered moving to London as an
alternative to treason. But, by 1775, the transat-
lantic volley of exchanges about the status of
colonies and the merits of continued membership
in the British union powerfully attracted an up-
and-coming expert in political economy and foreign affairs. Jay feared, too, that the Crown no
longer could protect colonial property and
trade—in Jay's view, the "great and weighty
reasons" underlying genuinely useful alliances
and political unions.

Jay therefore remained in New York to
serve the cause, both in his home state and in
the First and Second Continental Congresses. He
sat on state committees of correspondence and
safety, synchronizing intercolonial protests and
providing a semblance of government as the
British magistracy collapsed. Jay helped draft the
New York state constitution; until 1779, he also
served (erratically and without distinction) as
chief justice of the New York superior court.

Independence proved to be a watershed in
Jay's career. In the space of a few months, he
found himself starring—without much of a
script—in the drama of national establishment.
In 1778, while still sitting on the state bench, and
only three days after his arrival in Philadelphia
as a New York delegate to the general government, Jay was elected president of Congress. A
year later, he became minister plenipotentiary to
Spain; in 1782, he was one of five commissioners sent to Europe to negotiate what would become the Paris Peace Treaty with Great Britain.

These rapid-fire experiences were formative: Jay quickly came to believe that his original, gloomy assessment of American prospects for success had been appallingly accurate. As a weak quasi-executive in Congress, Jay helplessly watched the confederation collapse. Americans were experiencing growing pains—the invention of modern party politics, for example, and the flexing of capitalist muscle; Jay saw only degenerate partisan bickering, demagoguery, excessive "leveling," logjams in Congress, a dangerous tendency to fetter diplomats, drifts of worthless paper currency, and interstate competition for trading alliances. In Europe, Jay personally guaranteed repayment of war loans and encouraged entrepreneurs to invest in America; privately, he despaired of Americans' capacity for virtue and Congress's ability to navigate the rapids between independence and nationhood.

When Jay returned to New York in July 1784, he turned down ambassadorships to Britain and France in favor of law practice and state politics. But the respite was brief. Within weeks, Congress drafted Jay to be secretary of foreign affairs, an office held until 1789; he continued to serve until March 1790 as secretary of state *ad interim*, awaiting Thomas Jefferson's return from Europe.

As Jay struggled to prevent disaster in Congress and abroad, his anxieties about the "degraded" condition of New World republicans, and about American prospects for survival in the hurly-burly of international exchange, gave rise to a stringently conservative scheme for unification and stabilization. As early as 1784–85, he advocated the creation of a coercive, departmentalized federation with enhanced executive prerogative, a Congress capable of ensuring economic growth and the security of property, and a superior federal judiciary possessed of strength sufficient to immobilize self-serving states. On the question of federal power, Jay (with Alexander Hamilton) epitomized high federalism: in 1785, he told John Adams that, in a perfect world, he would have the states "considered . . . in the same light in which counties stand to the States," as mere administrative "districts to facilitate the purposes of domestic order and good government," not as separate seats of sovereignty.

By 1788, observers viewed Jay as a linchpin in the drive to secure ratification of the new federal constitution. Because of illness, he wrote only five Federalist Papers (Nos. 2–5 and 64) in areas of particular expertise—foreign affairs, federal treaty powers, relations between domestic stability and long-term prosperity, and the utility of well-enforced federal laws as Americans struggled to persuade Europeans of republican reliability. Jay fretted about vaguely worded reservations of state power in the federation, and so supported subsequent calls for revisionary constitutional conventions. But, after federation, Jay gladly accepted a commission as the republic's first chief justice (and, as it turned out, as a judge of the eastern circuit established by the first federal congress); on February 2, 1790, he called his new Court to order with a quorum of four judges.

Jay's acceptance of the chief justiceship seems odd. Why would a man known widely as an indispensable (if not particularly imaginative) political economist and diplomat, and only secondarily as a lawyer, agree to preside over an untested, controversial tribunal, years before the articulation of the Supreme Court's implied power to review acts of Congress? In the late eighteenth century, legitimacy and prestige attached most completely to firmly established ideas and institutions; the high court boasted no history, no case law or procedure separate from British law practice, no distinguished bar, no clear role in governance beyond responsibility to decide certain limited categories of legal disputes. Jay himself had exhibited scant interest in his state judgeship or the minutiae of legal research. Why, then, did he leave the political spotlight, abandon a lucrative law practice, and preside over a docketless court in borrowed chambers at the New York City Stock Exchange?

Jay's decision makes sense when viewed in light of his experience and priorities. The years between 1787 and 1803, to borrow historian Bernard Bailyn's phrase, might be termed a "soft ambiguous moment" in the history of the judiciary. No chief justice, then or now, could make of the high court whatever he wished; but, within the vague outlines sketched in Philadelphia and in the 1789 Judiciary and Process Acts, the Court (perhaps for the last time in its history) could be

John Jay
Painting by Gilbert Stuart.
Collection of the Supreme Court of the United States.

pressed into service in decidedly unmodern ways, to reflect the interests and assumptions of the diplomat seated as chief justice. Washington chose a friend he knew to be schooled in the law of nations, economy, and Burkean political philosophy; moreover, as the president put it in 1794, Jay had been "personally conversant" with signatories of the 1783 peace treaty, served as foreign affairs secretary, and helped frame republican constitutions, thus fitting himself for judicial statesmanship at a dangerous moment in American history.

How did John Jay envision the chief justiceship and the Supreme Court's role in government? A staunch Federalist might be expected to hope—and Jay did—that federal courts might be used as a hedge against "Laws dictated by the Spirit of the Times not the Spirit of Justice." But Jay's vision amounted to more than a mindless attempt to impose order. By 1790, Jay believed that the pressing issue of the day was American survival within a skeptical global community; the republic needed to escape unhealthy economic dependence in relations with Europeans (including a heavy debt load), and move toward healthy, reciprocal trading alliances. Only then, said Jay, could Americans be "honest and grateful to our allies, but . . . think for ourselves." In Jay's judgment, national prosperity—his long-term and most important "object of state"—depended entirely on refurbishing a tarnished reputation and persuading Europeans that Americans would protect property, create stable currencies, and make good on the terms of contracts and treaties.

Jay pinned his hopes for the realization of his objects on the federal judiciary and effective deployment of relevant bodies of federal law. By enforcing contracts and treaties, judges could construct images of reliability; they also could force states to accept federal guidelines in the creation of uniform economic legislation. While Jay did not object to the notion of implied powers of judicial review (and indeed encouraged his colleagues to exercise review powers on circuit), he probably did not envision a Marshall-style Supreme Court aimed primarily at domestic development and consolidation: as more than one scholar has noted, Jay was a cosmopolitan rather than provincial figure, with one eye trained perpetually on Europe. Instead, he hoped to use the Court to ensure domestic stability *so that* America might experience prosperity as a trading nation.

Federal courts also would expose citizens to the moralizing principles embedded in the bodies of law Jay particularly admired—notably the law of nations, which he took to be a virtual codification of God's will. In this way, imperfect republicans eventually might achieve the perfection which the framers, in a fit of republican zeal, wrongly imputed to the electorate. As Jay explained in 1793, society was not yet "so far improved, and the Science of Government [so perfected] that the whole nation could in the peaceable course of law, be compelled to do justice." Federal courts would educate as well as control the citizenry by means of grand jury charges and the swift execution of well-made laws.

Jay's vision proved chimerical. The associate justices complained incessantly about onerous circuit-riding duties, thus eroding morale; and, while grand jury charges provided a welcome occasion to instruct jurymen and newspaper readers on the fine points of the federal government, Jay had too few occasions to use his new court as an instrument in pursuit of "great objects."

On the one hand, Jay's contributions probably were more substantial than scholars recognize: the justices laboriously hammered out rules of practice and evidence, established a federal bar, and, by pointedly relying on *state* practice whenever possible, chipped away at Republican charges of Federalist tyranny. Jay also modestly strengthened the Court's shaky position within the general government. In a 1792 New York circuit court hearing on a writ of mandamus in *Hayburn's Case*, he defended the separation of powers by refusing to allow federal courts to pass judgment, as federal statute required, on claims of invalid pensioners; the decision (reinforced in 1794 by suggestive language in *Glass v. The Sloop Betsey*) paved the way for later attempts to garner implied review powers.

Finally, Jay was able to wield federal judicial power in defense of the Treaty of Paris and American sovereignty in relations with Europe.

His dissent on circuit in *Ware v. Hylton* anticipated high court insistence on adherence to treaty provisions in a 1796 appeal of the same case; and in the *Sloop Betsey* case, Jay ruled against France's use of its American consul as a prize agent, thereby shoring up the United States precarious claim of sovereignty.

On the other hand, the Court fell far short of its chief justice's expectations: by 1793, Jay decided to pursue his "objects" through diplomacy and other executive posts. The proximate cause of Jay's dejection was the state of Georgia and, more particularly, its insistence in the 1793 case of *Chisholm v. Georgia* (the first constitutional law case decided by the Supreme Court) on the ongoing utility in republics of the old monarchical doctrine of sovereign immunity.

The circumstances bear repeating. In 1792, Chisholm, a Carolinian and the executor of the estate of one Farquhar, sought state payment on a war supply contract. He invoked the Court's original diversity jurisdiction in suits between citizens of different states, or between states and noncitizens. The state of Georgia returned the summons, claiming sovereign immunity from federal process. Also in 1792, the Court heard arguments in *Georgia v. Brailsford,* a bill in equity in which Georgia appeared willingly as complainant, hoping to recover the amount of a debt originally owed to South Carolinian Loyalists and a Briton whose property had been either confiscated or sequestered (justices disagreed on the point) during the Revolution.

The amount had become the object of an injunction; although his colleagues urged otherwise, Jay continued the restraining order (dissolved in 1794, when Georgia brought and lost an action at law), partly so that Jay could exploit Georgia's voluntary appearance in his *Chisholm* opinion. Both disputes generally addressed state obligations to settle Loyalist claims fairly, as the Paris Treaty required; hence, they also tested whether federal courts might be useful to Jay in restoring America's reputation in Europe. If "national regularity" depended on "attention and obedience to those rules and principles of conduct which reason indicates and which morality and wisdom prescribe," said Jay, Georgia's recalcitrance threatened not only the union, but

also American prospects on an international stage.

In separate opinions (the Court's usual practice before the advent of John Marshall), Jay and Justice James Wilson contended that the whole people, not the states, had compacted to form a federation and so could hold a state accountable for behavior damaging to the nation. The relevant clause in Article III of the federal Constitution, after all, did not exclude suits by citizens of other states, nor did it require state consent for such suits. By the same logic, the sovereign people surely could summon states. Jay pointed to *Brailsford*: were federal courts mere conveniences, to be heeded only when states benefited from decisions?

The Court's 1793 ruling by default (because Georgia refused to appear) against the state claim of sovereign immunity seemed to render depleted state treasuries vulnerable to the claims of war suppliers and traitors. If the Jay Court had its way, moreover, other states soon would eat humble pie: on February 20, 1793, process had been returned and the state ordered to appear at the next term in *Oswald v. New York*. Simultaneously, the Court awarded a subpoena in *Grayson et al. v. Virginia*; five months later, William Vassal, a Loyalist victim of Massachusetts's confiscation statute, was granted a subpoena, which inspired Governor John Hancock to deliver a speech warning his countrymen of the perils of runaway judicial federalism.

Because these cases and many others threatened a flood of litigation against states and insupportable pressure on state treasuries, Jay's decisions in the Georgia cases caused widespread alarm. On December 14, 1792, the Georgia assembly had resolved not to be bound by an unfavorable Court ruling; after *Chisholm*, a Georgia grand jury formally presented a grievance to Governor Edward Telfair, who in turn urged passage of a statute (enacted two weeks later) affirming state sovereign immunity. On March 18, Massachusetts legislators in special session spearheaded a movement encouraging Congress to adopt the Eleventh Amendment, which made it impossible for federal officers to summon states as defendants. Virginia officially condemned Jay for attacking the reserved sov-

ereignty of states; Georgians toyed with hanging federal officers, should they again try to force
a state appearance. In 1798, when the amendment took effect, the clerk of the Supreme Court
painstakingly entered a list of reversals in the
minute book (including *Chisholm*) for "want of
jurisdiction."

The comparative ease with which the states
humiliated the highest court in the land caused Jay
to despair of its potential as an effective agency
of government. In 1794, while still seated as chief
justice, he sailed to England as *envoy
extraordinaire* to defuse tensions with Britain over
unpaid debts, sequestration of Loyalist estates by
state governments, and New World trading rights.
The Jay Treaty established mixed commissions to
resolve economic disputes, granted trade concessions to Britain, and shifted responsibility for
payment of defaulted loans to Congress. While
resistance to the treaty was formidable, the Senate ratified it in 1795. Jay was relieved: "Should
the treaty prove . . . beneficial," he wrote, "justice
will *finally* be done. If not, be it so—my mind is
at ease." In a revealing letter, Jay told Edmund
Randolph that the treaty's debt-related sixth article
addressed "that justice and equity which judicial
proceedings may, on trial, be found incapable of
affording"; commissioners could do "exactly what
is right."

Having been elected governor of New York
in absentia, Jay resigned as chief justice in 1795.
When President John Adams asked him to resume
his judicial post in 1800, Jay demurred on the
ground that he yearned for retirement and still
perceived the Court to be destitute of "energy,
weight and dignity." In 1801, he retired to his farm
in Westchester County, New York. Jay had no
taste for Jeffersonian America; he particularly
deplored the public fascination with Jacobinism
and weak government. Yet his favored maxim
always had been "Fortitude founded on Resignation." Despite poor health, he devoted the rest of
his life to the Episcopal Church, an extensive
correspondence, and abolitionism.

More completely perhaps than any of his
Federalist allies, Jay believed that evil stalked
humankind, that order prevailed only within firm
legal structures, and that Republicans lacked virtue, wisdom, and discipline. Thus, when Alexander Hamilton advocated manipulation of election returns in 1800 to defeat Thomas Jefferson,
Jay quietly wrote off both Hamilton and Federalism; better to sacrifice individuals and party
than moral principle. Jay probably died without
changing his mind about the inadequacy of republicanism. Having witnessed the failure of his
conception of judicial statesmanship at the hand
of licentious states, he simply could not foresee
American success. Surely the republic would
succumb to anarchy, he warned in *Chisholm*, if
a "pleasure to obey or transgress with impunity
should be substituted in the place of a sanction
to its laws." Benjamin Kissam's chief clerk,
Lindley Murray, said of the young Jay that he
had been notable for "strong reasoning powers,
comprehensive views, indefatigable application,
and uncommon firmness of mind"; in mid-life,
these traits crystallized into a sophisticated but
rigidly legalistic conservatism. Historian Richard Morris perhaps said it best: "[Jay's] tireless
effort to endow the national government with
energy, capacity, and scope . . . attest to his vision, courage, and tenacity," he wrote in 1967.
"It remained for others to spell out the safeguards
for individual liberties and the limitation on national power . . . essential to the maintenance of
a democratic society."

—SANDRA F. VANBURKLEO

BIBLIOGRAPHY

The Jay papers are in the Columbia University libraries, and various portions are available
in a variety of editions. Biographical studies of
Jay include Irving Dilliard's sketch in Friedman
and Israel, 1 *Justices* 3, a gracefully written essay, only slightly impatient with the Jay Court's
decidedly unmodern appearance and behavior;
and Herbert Johnson, *John Jay, 1745–1829*
(1970), an older empathetic description of the
life, flawed by limited exposure to critical documents and the literature of the Revolution.

The best brief study of Jay's stint on the
bench is Richard Morris, *John Jay, the Nation,
and the Court* (1967), although it is flawed by its
anachronistic determination to rescue Jay by transforming him into a pale imitation of John
Marshall. For fuller accounts of the early Court,
see Maeva Marcus, et al., eds., *Documentary*

History of the Supreme Court of the United States, 1780–1800 (1985–), an invaluable guide to the Supreme Court's business with a sound biographical sketch of Jay; and Julius Goebel, *History of the Supreme Court of the United States: Antecedents and Beginnings to 1801* (1971), the first volume of the Holmes Devise, the most consistently useful compilation of information about the Court's first decade in doctrinal and institutional terms, but staunchly anti-Jay and not particularly sensitive to the context of legal development.

Specialized studies of particular aspects of Jay's career include: Jerald Combs, *The Jay Treaty* (1970), a balanced account of the negotia-tion and ratification process; Doyle Mathis, "Chisholm v. Georgia: Background and Settlement," 54 *Journal of American History* 19 (1967), a now-classic corrective to erroneous received wisdom, to be read in conjunction with Clyde Jacobs, *The Eleventh Amendment and Sovereign Immunity* (1972), a detailed study of the early Supreme Court's most humiliating moment; and Sandra F. VanBurkleo, "'Honour, Justice, and Interest': John Jay's Republican Politics and Statesmanship on the Federal Bench," *Journal of the Early Republic* 239 (1984), an article critical of earlier attempts to restore Jay to the judicial pantheon by modernizing him.

THOMAS JOHNSON

BORN 4 November 1732, Calvert County,
   Maryland

NOMINATED to the Court on a temporary
   commission 5 August 1791
   by George Washington

TOOK seat 6 August 1792; resigned
   16 January 1793

DIED 26 October 1819 in Frederick,
   Maryland

Thomas Johnson's most significant contributions to the development of the new American nation would not necessarily include his service on the bench of the Supreme Court, although in his very brief tenure he participated in a number of interesting cases. Johnson played a major role in the success of the American Revolution and in the establishment of the capital of the United States in the District of Columbia. An attorney, Johnson soon began to pursue public office and served in the lower house of the assembly in Maryland from 1762 to 1774. Because of his ardent support of American rights, Johnson was elected to the Annapolis committee of correspondence and to the First and Second Continental Congresses. He returned to Maryland as commander of its militia; was elected to three one-year terms (1777–1780) as the first governor of the state of Maryland; became a member of the Maryland house of delegates (1780–1782, 1786–1788), as well as of the state's convention to ratify the federal constitution. In 1790, the governor appointed him chief judge of the Maryland general court, and it was that position from which Johnson resigned to become an associate justice of the Supreme Court.

Initially reluctant to serve on the Court because of the duty of riding circuit imposed on the justices by the Judiciary Act of 1789, Johnson overcame his reservations and accepted the temporary commission sent to him by President Washington on August 5, 1791. The Senate, out of session in August, confirmed him, on November 7, to a permanent position. Johnson, however, missed the February 1792 term of Court and did not take his seat on the Supreme Court until August 6, 1792. His entire career on the federal bench consisted of holding a circuit court in Virginia in the fall of 1791, attending the Supreme Court in August 1792, and riding the southern circuit in the fall of 1792. (While holding the court in South Carolina, however, Johnson indicated his belief in judicial review by refusing to allow the court to proceed under the Invalid Pensions Act passed by Congress in 1792.) After that experience, Johnson decided the burdens of circuit riding were too much for him and resigned his position on January 16, 1793. He retired to his estate in Frederick, Maryland.

Despite his presence at only one term of the Supreme Court, Johnson had the opportunity to examine two very important issues. In *Hayburn's Case* (1792), the Court heard argument as to whether the attorney general had authority *ex officio*, without the specific permission of the president, to move for a mandamus to the United States circuit court for the district of Pennsylvania requiring it to hear the petition of William Hayburn. The Court divided equally on the question, so the motion was denied. Johnson joined those members of the Court who thought the attorney general should be permitted to proceed on his own. Had his views prevailed, elements of federal procedure might look very different today.

Johnson also participated in the initial stage of the case of *Georgia v. Brailsford* (1792). The state of Georgia asked the Supreme Court to issue an injunction to prevent Brailsford, a British subject, from receiving the money owed him as a result of a judgment in the United States circuit court for the district of Georgia. Georgia believed the money belonged to it by virtue of a state statute authorizing sequestration of British property during the Revolution. If an injunction were granted, all the parties' interests could be adjudicated in the Supreme Court. The majority voted in favor of issuing the injunction; Johnson, in dissent, stated that Georgia was not entitled to an injunction, because her "right to the debt in question . . . may be enforced at common law." Georgia eventually lost her battle with Brailsford in a jury trial in the Supreme Court (1794) in which the justices unanimously indicated, in a charge to the jury, that they thought that the peace treaty ending the Revolutionary War superseded a state sequestration statute. When this verdict was rendered, Johnson had already left the Court.

—MAEVA MARCUS

BIBLIOGRAPHY

Letters pertaining to Thomas Johnson's Supreme Court service are published in the volumes of Maeva Marcus, ed., *The Documentary History of the Supreme Court of the United States, 1789–1800* (1985–). Edward S. Delaplaine's *The Life of Thomas Johnson* (1927) remains the only full-length biography. A short informative essay about Johnson, written by Herbert Alan Johnson, appears in Friedman and Israel, 1 *Justices* 149.

WILLIAM JOHNSON

BORN 27 December 1771, near Charleston,
St. James Goose Creek Parish,
South Carolina

NOMINATED to the Court 22 March 1804
by Thomas Jefferson

TOOK seat 8 May 1804

DIED 4 August 1834 in Brooklyn, New York

William Johnson, the great dissenter of the early republic, embodied the American dream. Born to blacksmith William Johnson and Sarah Nightingale Johnson, young William went to grammar school in Charleston, completed studies at Princeton University by 1790, read law with South Carolina's renowned lawyer-diplomat Charles Pinckney, and, in 1793, gained admission to the Charleston bar. Johnson rose to power with dazzling speed. Once admitted to the bar, he was elected to the South Carolina house of representatives; by March 1794, he had married and established himself as a society figure, a reliable, colorful Jeffersonian Republican, and a confidante of the master of Monticello. Johnson served as house secretary, speaker, and judge of the South Carolina constitutional court; at age thirty-two, he accepted Thomas Jefferson's nomination to the U.S. Supreme Court, replacing the ineffectual North Carolinian, Alfred Moore.

John Marshall's young associate relished a good scrap; but he also found it necessary to cooperate with his brethren. As he explained in an 1822 letter, "I found that I must either submit to circumstances or become such a cypher . . . as to effect no good at all. I therefore bent to the current." In 1807, Johnson infuriated Jefferson by relying on (and thus granting credence to) Marshall's *Marbury* v. *Madison* ruling to protest the Court's grant of a writ of mandamus in the treason trial of Aaron Burr. A year later on circuit, Johnson—apprehending presidential overreach—refused in *Gilchrist v. Collector of Charleston* to allow the detention of Gilchrist's vessel, as Republican embargo policies required. Family legend has it that Johnson personally boarded several vessels and issued sailing orders. In his decision of 28 May 1808, he insisted that federal officers never were justified, at the bidding of the executive, to increase "restraints upon commerce"; presidents and collectors were "equally subjected to legal restraint" and so "equally incapable" of "an unsanctioned encroachment upon individual liberty."

Attorney General Caesar Rodney promptly denounced Johnson as a Jeffersonian imposter suffering from "leprosy of the bench," but that judgment was premature. During and after the War of 1812, Johnson came to blows repeatedly with Joseph Story; within a few years, the two men barely spoke. By Story's lights, republicanism required a sturdy, if mutable system of federal law (including an energetic system of admiralty courts and federal criminal jurisdiction) to ensure public morality as capitalists and crooks swarmed over the American continent. Johnson preferred to rely on state courts in criminal cases, and feared federal tyranny (symbolized for him by the specter of admiralty courts in places like Louisville, Kentucky) more than the moral corruption associated with scrambles for wealth. Thus, in *United States v. Hudson and Goodwin* (1812), he refused to grant federal jurisdiction in criminal cases; Story dissented and ignored *Hudson* on circuit. Similarly, in *Ramsey v. Allegre* (1827), Johnson resisted attempts to modify the English "ebb and flow of the tide" doctrine (limiting admiralty jurisdiction to salt water) in order to expand federal authority to inland waterways without the constitutional amendment demanded by critics.

Johnson also perceived tyranny in the attempt by business corporations to persuade judges of their organizational identity with stockholders, whose collective rights and immunities then could be ascribed to a corporate "person." Johnson contended, for example, in his 1808 *Bank of the United States v. Deveaux* circuit court opinion, that banking corporations possessed neither standing nor a right to sue in federal courts. He went along with John Marshall in *McCulloch v. Maryland* (1819); five years later, in *Osborn v. Bank of the United States*, he supported Congressional power under the necessary and proper clause to create a bank, in part because he exalted Congress—described by him in *Anderson v. Dunn* (1821) as a "deliberate assembly, clothed with the majesty of the people."

Yet even as he acknowledged congressional power to erect a bank in *Osborn*, he blasted Marshall's partial grant of rights and immunities to artificial persons; indeed, as his *Osborn* position makes clear, Johnson distinguished continually between mindless support for malignant combinations (runaway government, corporations, banks), and support for congressional aid to free-wheeling capitalism. He particularly encouraged national legislation to empower states, maintain social stability, break down barriers between regions, facilitate free trade, and build transportation networks (the "arteries" and "veins" of an extensive body politic). He therefore denounced James Monroe's veto of the Cumberland Road Act in 1822 and joined the centrist majority in *Martin v. Hunter's Lessee* (1816), with its ringing affirmation of the Court's authority under Section 25 of the 1789 Judiciary Act to review state court decisions whenever they touched federal statutes or treaties. Johnson also acquiesced in Marshall's anti-Jacksonian *Cherokee Nation v. Georgia* (1831), which condemned Indian removal policies and state meddling with settled indigenous communities protected by treaty.

Johnson laid out some of the elements of this selectively nationalist philosophy in his concurring opinion in *Gibbons v. Ogden* (1824)—the "steamboat case" testing the validity of a New York grant of monopoly to the Fulton-Livingston company to run boats exclusively on the Hudson River. Brushing aside state warnings about the imminent collapse of the republic, Marshall toyed with but ultimately rejected Daniel Webster's "exclusivity" principle—the idea that Congress, under the commerce clause, might regulate new commercial subjects (like steamboats), and persons (possibly including fugitive slaves), as well as interstate exchange of goods. Marshall feared southern resistance to exclusivity and so held, less radically, that steamboat traffic on interstate rivers fell easily within Congress's established power to control "navigation."

The South Carolinian felt no such inhibition. Heedless of southern opposition and armed to the teeth with constitutional convention proceedings and the law of nations, Johnson chided Marshall for unwarranted timidity: "The power of a sovereign state over commerce . . . must be exclusive," residing in only "one potentate; and hence the grant of this power carries with it the whole subject, leaving nothing for the state to act upon."

As the *Gibbons* opinion suggests, Johnson was ambivalent about complete state control over slavery—perhaps because (as he said in the steamboat case) he opposed absolute state authority over labor and other resources; nor did he worry, with Americans a decade later, that Congress might wield regulatory power to aid fugitive slaves or destroy property rights in persons. Interestingly, the slaveholder Johnson opposed abolition as well as the inhumane treatment of Africans, whether free or bonded. In 1822–24, he tarnished his reputation in South Carolina by sharply criticizing state denial of due process to slave rebel Denmark Vesey; in his 1823 circuit court opinion in *Elkison v. Deliesseline*, Johnson declared South Carolina's Negro Seaman Act (which barred African-American sailors from Charleston and other harbors) a violation of the civil rights of free blacks seeking trade in South Carolina; later, he courted extreme disfavor by opposing South Carolina's notorious nullification of the Tariff of Abominations, again (as he explained in *Osborn*) because he viewed the federal constitution as an economic document designed to eradicate the Confederation's "Congress of Ambassadors" as well as an unfruitful localism in commerce.

In cases involving the contract clause, Johnson exhibited a markedly thinner skin. Before the Panic of 1819, Marshall had written opinions in contract cases to accommodate dissenting views; thus, Johnson could join the majority in *Dartmouth College v. Woodward* and *Sturges v. Crowninshield* (both decided in 1819). But, as a state rights rebellion gained force in the west and south, Johnson sounded an alarm. In 1823, he wrote a poignant, politically devastating concurrence in *Green v. Biddle*, in which Story and Bushrod Washington wielded the contract clause against Kentucky's occupying claimant laws in order to force state compliance with an agreement struck between Kentucky and Virginia in 1792. In *Green*, Johnson distinguished between the law of the case (which, he grudgingly concluded, supported the result) and the decidedly anti-republican tenor of a bench that refused to forge rules appropriate to new, non-English situations. On the one hand, he pointed to provisions of the *state* constitution outlawing the taking of property without due process or compensation as solid ground for invalidating the occupant laws; the Court was overreaching for no good reason. On the other hand, he condemned his colleagues for destroying the property rights of *occupants* without jury trial. Ever the champion of free-trading republicanism, Johnson simply could not abide Court support for the anti-republican bankers, speculators, and corporatizers served so well by *Green*; moreover, federal jurisdiction had been expanded at the expense of an assembly rightly concerned about its lack of control over land titling.

In *Green*, Johnson probably reached the end of his unionist tether. While "groping [his] way through the labyrinth" of land and contract law toward his brilliant *Green* opinion, he began to cut himself loose from juridical convention. After 1819, his opinions evince a sea change, away from abstract reasoning rooted in international law, political theory, and natural law, toward a concrete, community-centered jurisprudence capable of reflecting diverse measures of fairness without collapsing into relativism.

Johnson, in other words, unwittingly began to pave the way for the economic policies and "dual federalism" of the later Taney Court. Not surprisingly, he often did so in dissent. His apprehensions about judicial support for bankers and other unproductive "nabobs," and his conviction that public morality in economic life depended to a great extent on local control over remedial legislation, underlay his opinion in *Ogden v. Saunders* (1827) in which he supported, to Marshall's horror, a state prohibition of endless claims by creditors against insolvents; characteristically, and in the name of union, he drew the line at New York's discharge of obligations to out-of-state creditors.

The prolific Johnson served almost three decades on the federal bench; not counting circuit court rulings, he penned 112 opinions for majorities, twenty-one concurring opinions, thirty-four dissents, and five *per curiam* opinions. Only Marshall and Story outdid him. He was castigated regularly—by Federalists for his support of state legislative power, and by Jeffersonians for attacks upon executive "tyranny" or radical anti-unionism.

Johnson surely could be a loose cannon: as his remarkable *Ogden* and *Green* concurrences make clear, he viewed opinions as occasions for experimentation, admitted impetuousness, and often devoted days or weeks to land speculation or non-judicial writing (such as a two-volume biography of Nathanael Greene). Yet he was also an engaged and engaging jurist with an uncommon capacity for surprise; only enemies like John Quincy Adams thought of him as "restive, turbulent, hot-headed, [and] flaringly independent."

In the end, it is of small moment that Johnson alienated Court reporters or pigheadedly refused to admit obvious mistakes. Johnson's legacy rests with written evidence of a formidable legal imagination—in opinions, in his richly technical correspondence with Jefferson, and in published replies to critics. Arguably, Johnson established the dissent as a legitimate component of American constitutional discourse. He also articulated a strikingly modern, rights-centered vision of the role of federal courts. When Rodney publicly shredded Johnson's *Gilchrist* opinion, the judge took to his pen; no better summary of his philosophy exists than the one written in self-defense. "In a country where laws govern," said Johnson, "courts of justice necessarily are the medium of action and reaction between the government and the governed. The basis of individual security and the bond of union between the ruler and the citizen must ever be found in a judiciary sufficiently independent to disregard the will of power, and sufficiently energetic to secure to the citizen the full enjoyment of his rights."

—SANDRA F. VANBURKLEO

BIBLIOGRAPHY

The standard biography is Donald G. Morgan, *Justice William Johnson: The First Dissenter* (1954); short sketches include Morgan, "William Johnson," in Friedman and Israel, 1 *Justices* 355, and Sandra F. VanBurkleo, "William Johnson," in Kermit Hall, ed., *Oxford Companion to the Supreme Court of the United States* (1992), 449–450.

For Johnson within the context of the Marshall Court and his times, see the two volumes in the Holmes Devise, George Haskins and Herbert Johnson, *Foundations of Power: John Marshall, 1801–1815* (1981), and G. Edward White, *The Marshall Court and Cultural Change, 1815–1835* (1991).

ANTHONY McLEOD KENNEDY

BORN 23 July 1936, Sacramento, California
NOMINATED to the Court 30 November 1987
    by Ronald Reagan
TOOK seat 18 February 1987

A graduate of Stanford University and the Harvard Law School, Anthony Kennedy spent more than a decade in private practice before President Gerald Ford appointed him to the United States court of appeals for the ninth circuit in 1975. When he left Sacramento for Washington at the time of his Supreme Court nomination, he carried the reputation of a devoted family man, a devout Roman Catholic, and a loyal Republican.

During Kennedy's dozen years with the ninth circuit, he took part in more than 1,400 decisions and wrote more than 400 opinions. Often in dissent in the circuit recognized as the nation's most liberal, Judge Kennedy nevertheless wrote many influential opinions. His opinion for the court in *American Federation of State, County, and Municipal Employees v. Washington* (1985), holding that federal employment discrimination law did not require the state to base its compensation scheme on a theory of comparable worth, was widely followed in other circuits. In *Pacemaker Diagnostic Clinic of America, Inc. v. Instromedix, Inc.* (1984), he presented a theory for determining the extent of congressional discretion to shift claims from Article III courts to other government tribunals; it was adopted by the Supreme Court in 1986, a year before he joined the Court. His advocacy of a good faith exception to the exclusionary rule in 1983 in *Harvey v. United States* presaged its adoption by the Supreme Court a year later, and his opinion for the court in *Chadha v. INS* (1978), that a one-house congressional veto for administrative decisions was unconstitutional, was affirmed five years later.

Kennedy's nomination to replace the retired Lewis F. Powell, Jr., followed the senate's rejection of Judge Robert H. Bork after a spirited ideological debate, and the withdrawal of Dou-

glas H. Ginsberg after public exposure of controversial facts about his personal life. That Judge Kennedy would fall third on the short list prepared by Ronald Reagan and Ed Meese, an intimate from Reagan's term as California governor who had been named his attorney general, could be attributed to White House perception that Judges Bork and Ginsberg were more committed to the president's version of conservative ideology. That evaluation has proven out. While Justice Kennedy has taken conservative positions in many important constitutional areas, he has also shown a streak of independence which has caused him to part company occasionally with those at the core of the Rehnquist Court's right wing, the chief justice and Justices Scalia and Thomas.

Justice Kennedy is clearly no champion of affirmative action. In *City of Richmond v. J.A. Croson Co.* (1989), he joined the Court in holding unconstitutional the city's program for setting aside a portion of its public contracts for minority businesses. He espoused the view that government programs said to be violations of the equal protection clause because they discriminated against whites ought to be judicially assessed by the same strict standard employed in assessing programs said to discriminate against minorities. He wrote separately to insist that federal programs be treated the same way as state programs, notwithstanding the difference in the text of the Fifth and Fourteenth Amendments, a position he returned to the following year dissenting in *Metro Broadcasting, Inc. v. FCC* (1990).

Kennedy has contributed to the erection of new barriers to securing the Great Writ. He wrote for the Court in *McClesky v. Zant* (1991) that a prisoner was entitled to only one *habeas corpus* review unless he could satisfy the court that a subsequently raised claim of constitutional error could not have been included in his earlier petition. Justice Kennedy supplied the swing vote in *Murray v. Giarratano* (1989), which reversed a decision that the Constitution required states to appoint counsel for indigent death row prisoners pursuing state *habeas* review.

Anthony McLeod Kennedy
Photograph by the National Geographic Society.
Collection of the Supreme Court of the United States.

Perhaps his most influential contribution lies in the area of the First Amendment's establishment clause. In *County of Allegheny v. ACLU* (1989), Kennedy wrote for a plurality holding that permitting religious groups to display a crèche and a menorah in the courthouse during the Christmas and Hanukkah seasons was not forbidden by the establishment clause. According to Justice Kennedy, the establishment clause does not stop government from endorsing religion so long as government does not favor one religion over another and so long as government does not coerce persons into participating. He reiterated this view recently in *Lamb's Chapel v. Center Moriches Union Free School District* (1993), in which the Court held unconstitutional a school district's policy which discriminated against religious groups applying for use of school facilities after hours.

In *County of Allegheny*, Kennedy had acquiesced in applying the test for establishment clause constitutionality found in *Lemon v. Kurtzman* (1971). According to that Burger Court–era test, government action is unconstitutional if its primary purpose is to aid religion, if its primary effect aids religion, or if its consequence is excessive government entanglement in religious matters. By 1993, however, Kennedy was willing to join Justices Scalia and Thomas in *Lamb's Chapel* in condemning the *Lemon* test as unworkable. Later in the same term, he supplied the swing vote in *Zobrest v. Catalina Foothills School District* (1993), in which the Court held that a school district did not violate the establishment clause if it paid for a sign language interpreter to accompany a student to classes at a Roman Catholic high school. Mention of *Lemon v. Kurtzman* was conspicuously absent from *Zobrest*, which could reasonably be said to tacitly overrule it.

If Justice Kennedy has substantially lived up to expectations that he would supply the fifth vote for the right wing of the Rehnquist Court, he has occasionally proven a maverick. His most notorious deviation came in *Planned Parenthood v. Casey* (1992), when he and Justices O'Connor and Souter formed a plurality of the not-so-reactionary in refusing to overrule *Roe v. Wade* (1973). The three insisted on continued constitutional recognition for the right to an abortion, but called for a much relaxed standard in assessing state laws curtailing its exercise. If their position continues to dominate abortion cases, more ardent conservatives will be denied a categorical rejection of *Roe v. Wade*'s fundamental principle and be forced to argue the facts in every challenge to local abortion laws.

It might also be said that Justice Kennedy frustrated ideological expectations in *Texas v. Johnson* (1989), when he supplied the swing vote for a decision that a protestor's conviction for burning an American flag during a political demonstration violated constitutionally guaranteed freedom of speech.

In the context of Anthony Kennedy's general inclination to vote with the Court's right wing and his apparent antipathy for group rights in affirmative action, his positions in *Planned Parenthood* and *Texas v. Johnson* suggest a slightly more individualistic or libertarian form of conservative jurisprudence than the far right of the Rehnquist Court. He has refused to join in Justice Scalia's campaign to make tradition the sole determinant of due process, and he has insisted that the due process clause is a source for otherwise unenumerated rights pertaining to the individual. His independence is certainly not surprising for a jurist of his experience, and probably does not surprise Ed Meese.

—JOHN PAUL JONES

BIBLIOGRAPHY

Good profiles of Kennedy are in Richard C. Reuben, "Man in the Middle," 12 *California Law* 34 (1992), and David G. Savage, *Turning Rights: The Making of the Rehnquist Court* (1992). For analyses of Kennedy's decisions and his role on the court, see the annual reviews in the *National Law Journal* of 31 Aug. 1992 and 23 Aug. 1993.

JOSEPH RUCKER LAMAR

BORN 14 October 1857, Ruckersville, Georgia

NOMINATED to the Court 12 December 1910
    by William Howard Taft

TOOK seat 3 January 1911

DIED 2 January 1916 in Washington, D.C.

Descended from two distinguished Georgia families, Joseph Rucker Lamar was a product of the Southern establishment. His paternal side in particular had a heritage of public service, with Merabeau Lamar serving as president of the Republic of Texas, and Lucius Quintus Cincinnatus Lamar as associate justice of the United States Supreme Court. Lamar lived up to this heritage. Educated in the South, he attended Richmond Academy, the University of Georgia, Bethany College, and Washington and Lee Law School before studying law in the office of a prominent Georgia attorney. On passing the Georgia bar, Lamar built his reputation as a corporate lawyer. He served in the state legislature from 1886 to 1889, and in that year was selected to a commission rewriting the Georgia civil code. While practicing law he also wrote extensively on Georgia legal history. In 1903, Lamar took a seat on the Georgia supreme court, but returned to private practice in 1905, where he stayed until President Taft nominated him to the Supreme Court.

Lamar served on the Supreme Court just five years, writing only 113 majority opinions. Generally thought of as a conservative on economic matters, his most significant opinion represented a setback for labor unions and civil liberties. Writing in *Gompers v. Bucks Stove & Range* (1911), Lamar ruled that an antitrust order prohibiting the American Federation of Labor from organizing a secondary boycott through the publication of "unfair" and "we don't patronize" lists did not infringe on the First Amendment freedom of expression. Other of Lamar's opinions tended to reinforce this conservative image. Taking a narrow view of the state's regulatory power in *Smith v. Texas* (1914), he ruled that a law requiring that train conductors have previous exprience as brakemen violated liberty

of contract. Also, in *Kansas City Southern Railway v. Anderson* (1914), he dissented from a decision allowing double damages to be paid to a plaintiff when a railroad refused to pay for livestock killed on its tracks.

Lamar's attachment to laissez-faire economics was even more evident in *German Alliance Insurance Co. v. Luis* (1914). There, in one of his few dissents, Lamar disagreed with a majority decision upholding state regulation of insurance rates. Insurance, he maintained, was not "a business affected with public interest" and therefore should not be subject to state regulation. Lamar predicted that the expansion of regulation would become all pervading. He warned that citizens would then hold their property and their individual right of contract and of labor under legislative rather than constitutional guarantee.

In contrast to the cases of state regulation, Lamar seemed willing to give more latitude to federal agencies than is usually associated with the conservative thinking of his time. In *United States v. Grimaud* (1911), for example, he wrote an opinion expanding Congress's authority to delegate rule-making authority to administrative agencies. He also joined the majority that expanded the Pure Food and Drug Act in *Hipolite Egg Company* (1911), and extended the authority of the Interstate Commerce Commission in the *Minnesota Rate Cases* (1913).

In matters of civil rights, Justice Lamar's record was mixed. He concurred in the result of *McCabe v. Atchison, Topeka & Santa Fe Railway Co.* (1914), upholding an Oklahoma law that required separate coaches for Negro passengers. Yet he voted with the majority in invalidating a peonage law in *Bailey v. Alabama* (1911), wrote the opinion invalidating a special tax that discriminated against Chinese laundries in *Ouong Wing v. Kirkendall* (1912), and protected the Choctaw and Chickasaw tribes from Oklahoma's attempt to withdraw a tax exemption on their lands in *Choate v. Trapp* (1912).

A forceful dissent in *Diaz v. United States* (1912) hinted that Lamar also had a broader view of criminal justice and civil liberties than might have been expected. There he argued that the constitutional guarantees that an accused has a right to confront witnesses and a right not to be placed in jeopardy twice for the same crime should apply to a case tried in the Philippines. Lamar appeared to have a special disdain for conspiracy laws. In 1912, he joined Holmes dissenting in two cases that upheld conspiracy convictions. Later, in *United States v. Holte* (1915), he dissented from a decision that upheld a woman's conviction for "conspiring to cause her own transportation in interstate commerce for purposes of prostitution." Such a construction of the law would make every victim guilty of conspiracy, he argued. "Even that elastic offense cannot be extended to cover such a case."

When he was being considered for appointment, Joseph Rucker Lamar was described as a man with "no entanglements or extreme tendencies of thought." As moderate as it was conservative, his record as a justice of the Supreme Court appears to bear out that assessment.

—PAUL KENS

BIBLIOGRAPHY

The best available biography is Leonard Dinnerstein, "Joseph Rucker Lamar," in Friedman and Israel, 3 *Justices* 1973. Clarinda Pendleton Lamar, *The Life of Joseph Rucker Lamar 1857–1916* (1926), is a biography written by Lamar's wife. A small amount of Lamar correspondence is held by the University of Georgia.

LUCIUS QUINTUS CINCINNATUS LAMAR

BORN 17 September 1825, Eatonton, Georgia

NOMINATED to the Court 6 December 1887
by Grover Cleveland

TOOK seat 18 January 1888

DIED 23 January 1893 in Macon, Georgia

In *Profiles in Courage*, John F. Kennedy analyzed such well-known political leaders as John Quincy Adams and Daniel Webster, but he also looked at L.Q.C. Lamar. As a symbol of his age, Lamar served his state, his section, and the country in a long political and legal career culminating with service on the United States Supreme Court. Although best known as a politician, Lamar affected the Supreme Court through his devotion to the separation of powers, his interest in interstate commerce, and his suspicion of executive power.

Lamar attended Emory College and apprenticed law in Macon, Georgia. As a young man, he lived in Mississippi and Georgia and dabbled in politics, winning a congressional seat from Mississippi in 1857. In Congress, he worked with the secessionist wing of the Democratic party, becoming friends with Jefferson Davis and his cousin, Justice John A. Campbell. Lamar left Congress at secession and aided in the establishment of the Confederacy. He served briefly in the Confederate army before becoming Confederate commissioner to Russia, but although he traveled to London, he never reached Russia. Lamar returned in 1863 and completed the war as a colonel and judge advocate.

After the war, Lamar became a professor of law at the University of Mississippi while pursuing a private practice. Once again elected to Congress in 1872, Lamar became a symbol of those southerners willing to accept the results of the war while opposing Reconstruction. Calling for national reconciliation, Lamar's short but impassioned 1874 eulogy for Charles Sumner was "one of the great speeches in the history of the House" and it made him an overnight sensation. Elected to the senate in 1876, Lamar participated in the major policy debates regard-

ing the end of Reconstruction and the tariff question. When Democrat Grover Cleveland became president in 1884, Lamar became interior secretary. With the death of Justice William B. Woods in May 1887, Cleveland nominated Lamar to the Supreme Court.

The nomination was not without controversy. Because Lamar was the first southerner nominated to the Court since the Civil War and because of his age (sixty-two when nominated, the second oldest appointment made), the Republican-dominated Senate Judiciary Committee reported his nomination to the full senate with a negative vote. Although the senate confirmed Lamar, 32–28, his nomination emphasized just how sensitive sectional feelings remained in Gilded Age America.

Although starting slowly, Lamar came to be a force on the bench, particularly in 1890 and 1891. While he also handled routine cases against the federal government for recovery of monies, such as *United States ex rel. Redfield v. Windom* (1891), most of Lamar's decisions dealt with land boundaries, tort issues, and contracts; he wrote for the Court in *Southern Development Corporation v. Silva* (1888), *Hannibal and St. Joseph Railroad Company v. Missouri River Packet Company* (1888), and *Clement v. Packer* (1888), among others.

Legal historian Arnold Paul defined Lamar's judicial style as "constitutional formalism." In cases of important public policy, Lamar construed statutes narrowly, and especially so in matter of separation of powers. Lamar believed that the Court should enforce the separation of powers between the branches of the federal government in order to avoid tyranny by any particular branch.

His commitment to the separation of powers can also be discerned in his dissent in *In re Neagle* (1890), joined by Chief Justice Melville Fuller. Growing out of a complex fact situation from California, the Court's majority in *Neagle* read executive branch powers broadly. The attorney general's office had appointed a bodyguard to defend Justice Stephen J. Field from personal attack, but Congress had not authorized the bodyguard. The attorney general's office defended its action as inherent in the president's constitutional duty "to take care that the laws be faithfully executed." But Lamar was not convinced. Since Congress had not authorized the appointment of the bodyguard, he argued, the executive department could not read into a constitutional phrase executive powers which Congress had not approved. This dissent demonstrates both Lamar's attachment to the separation of powers and his suspicion of executive power.

Lamar also strengthened federal regulation of interstate commerce relative to regulations by the states. In the *Chicago, Milwaukee, and St. Paul Railway Company v. Minnesota* (1890), Justice Samuel Blatchford, for a six-person majority, struck down as unconstitutional the strong railroad commission of Minnesota on the grounds that the statute did not provide adequate judicial review of the "reasonableness" of the maximum railroad rates set by the commission. Justices Joseph P. Bradley, Horace Gray, and Lamar dissented, arguing that reasonableness was not a judicial issue but a legislative one and therefore the statute should be upheld. Although written by Bradley, the dissent has Lamar's concurrence because of implied judicial restraint—

courts ought not interfere with the formation of public policy.

Lamar's position regarding interstate commerce is best seen in *McCall v. California* (1890). Although three justices dissented from Lamar's majority opinion, *McCall* elaborated the rule that a state tax on an agency of an interstate corporation was an unconstitutional burden on interstate commerce. This position parallels his strict separation position because the states and the federal government possess clearly defined powers in the regulation of commerce and the courts ought to enforce the separation of those powers.

Lamar died while visiting Georgia in the winter of 1893. His life can be read as an accommodation to the changing needs of the South, which he served first, and the nation, which he served well and with honor later.

—THOMAS C. MACKEY

BIBLIOGRAPHY

Lamar's life received full treatment in James B. Murphy, *L.Q.C. Lamar: Pragmatic Patriot* (1973). Also useful are Arnold M. Paul, "Lucius Quintus Cincinnatus Lamar," in Friedman and Israel, 2 *Justices* 1431, and John F. Kennedy, *Profiles in Courage* (1955).

HENRY BROCKHOLST LIVINGSTON

BORN 25 November 1757, New York

NOMINATED to the Court 13 December 1806 by Thomas Jefferson

TOOK seat 2 February 1807

DIED 18 March 1823 in Washington, D.C.

Born into one of New York's wealthiest and most powerful eighteenth-century families, Henry Brockholst Livingston received his education at the College of New Jersey and, after graduating in 1774, joined the Continental army at the outbreak of the Revolution. After the war, he read law under Albany's Peter Yates, gained admission to the bar in 1783, and soon won a seat in the New York assembly. Despite favoring the ratification of the nation's new Constitution and developing a professional association with Alexander Hamilton, Livingston became a Jeffersonian during the 1790s. In 1802, after a decade and a half of involvement in state politics, he was appointed to the New York supreme court, where he served alongside the venerable chancellor James Kent. Five years later, on the death of Justice William Patterson of New Jersey, Thomas Jefferson appointed Livingston to the Supreme Court, primarily because of political and geographical considerations.

Livingston's appointment came at an important time in American constitutional history, as Jefferson was attempting to stifle the power of the Federalist-dominated Supreme Court. Despite an impressive record as a state judge, however, Livingston offered little resistance to the Court's prevailing course and seemed to fade into obscurity among the likes of John Marshall and Joseph Story. While Livingston had been accustomed to writing separate opinions on the New York bench, he hesitated to challenge John Marshall's policy of having the Court speak in a single voice; moreover, he rarely dissented, even when he privately disagreed with his brethren. For example, after writing a strongly-worded circuit opinion in 1817 affirming the constitutionality of state insolvency legislation applied retroactively (*Adams v. Storey*), Livingston kept silent in *Sturges v. Crowninshield*

(1819), where the Court held that similar legislation violated the Constitution's contract clause. Moreover, while he expressed some doubts about the Court's decision in *Dartmouth College v. Woodward* (1819), the most important contract case decided by the Marshall Court, Livingston voted with the majority on learning that his former colleague, Chancellor Kent, favored the Court's position. Livingston's reticence in such instances was characteristic of his Supreme Court career as a whole. As a justice for seventeen years, he wrote only forty-nine opinions, none of which related to the central constitutional questions of the day.

Much of Livingston's work on the Court dealt with commercial issues—the law of promissory notes, bills of exchange, and insurance, for example. In such cases, indicative of his acceptance of the Marshall Court's Federalist position, Livingston tended to take the side of creditors. In *Lennox v. Prout* (1813), he held that, in the event of default by the maker of a promissory note, the endorser of that note was not entitled to the protection of a court of equity. Instead, the holder of the unpaid note could bring an action against either the endorser or the maker. Consistent with this line of reasoning, in *Dugan v. United States* (1818), Livingston held that in all cases involving contracts with the United States, the national government had the right to enforce the performance of the contract or to recover damages for its violation. "It would be strange," he reasoned, "to deny to them a right which is secured to every citizen of the United States." Again, in light of his support for retroactive bankruptcy legislation while on circuit, Livingston's strict view of the enforcement of contracts in these cases points to the important influence of the Court's Federalist majority on his judicial behavior.

Aside from commercial law, Livingston also made his mark in maritime and prize cases. One of his most notable opinions was *United States v. Smith* (1820), which involved the scope of a congressional piracy statute. In the case, American citizens had been convicted under the law for the capture and robbery of a Spanish ship on the high seas. In dissent, Livingston argued that the act failed to define "piracy" specifically, in accordance with congressional power to do so under the Constitution. Because of the statute's imprecision, he favored the release of the defendants. *Smith* was one of the few cases in which Livingston refused to assent to the majority position.

Despite his scant judicial record, Livingston earned the respect and friendship of his fellow justices, particularly Joseph Story, with whom he carried on a lengthy correspondence. Story described Livingston as "a very able and independent judge," who was "luminous, decisive, earnest, and impressive on the bench." Such comments, coming from a jurist of Story's caliber, speak well for Livingston's abilities. Yet, Livingston's opinions—few in number and terse in style—have perhaps misrepresented his juristic talents and helped make him one of the most obscure justices in Supreme Court history.

—TIMOTHY S. HUEBNER

BIBLIOGRAPHY

There is no major collection of the justice's papers, although some materials do exist in the large collection of Livingston family papers in the New York Historical Society. Some of the correspondence between Livingston and Joseph Story has been published; see *Life and Letters of Joseph Story* (1971), and Gerald T. Dunne, "The Story-Livingston Correspondence," 10 *American Journal of Legal History* 224 (1966). The best overall sketch of Livingston is by Gerald Dunne in Friedman and Israel, 1 *Justices* 387.

HORACE HARMON LURTON

BORN 26 February 1844, Newport, Kentucky

NOMINATED to the Court 13 December 1909
 by William Howard Taft

TOOK seat 3 January 1910

DIED 12 July 1914 in Atlantic City,
 New Jersey

Horace Lurton was one of the last persons appointed to the Supreme Court to have served in the Civil War. Although only eighteen years of age when war broke out, he joined the Fifth Tennessee Regular Infantry. Captured in 1862, he escaped from a Union prison and joined the guerrilla forces led by General John Morgan. Morgan's Raiders harassed Union forces and raided supply installations until July 1863, when most of the unit was captured. Once again Lurton found himself a prisoner of war. Suffering from a lung disease, he was released shortly before the war's end.

On his release, Lurton embarked on a career as prudent as his youth had been daring. After completing his education at Cumberland Law School in 1867, he entered a successful practice in his home town of Clarksville, Tennessee. Lurton served a short stint as a trial judge in 1875–78, returned to private practice, then was elected to the Tennessee supreme court in 1886. He had just become chief justice of that court in 1893 when President Grover Cleveland selected him for the federal court of appeals. Lurton served on the sixth circuit with future Supreme Court justice William Day, and future president and chief justice William Howard Taft. It was there that he had his most productive years. Certainly he was highly regarded. Theodore Roosevelt seriously considered Lurton, a southern Democrat, for the Supreme Court in 1906, but opted instead for a nominee from his own party, William H. Moody. Four years later, however, Taft made Lurton his first appointment to the high court.

At the time of his appointment, Lurton was sixty-six years old. He served on the Court for only four years, writing just ninety-seven opinions, none of which were landmark cases. Lurton rarely expressed a written dissent or concurrence.

Both on the sixth circuit and in the Supreme Court, however, cases assigned to him often involved complex questions of financial relations or antitrust. Demonstrating respect for precedent, his opinions tended to trace earlier case law in detail. Professionalism muted expression of a personal philosophy in his writing which, if anything, reflected a tempered conservatism.

That conservatism was apparent in opinions involving economic regulations. In *Heaton-Peninsular Button-Fastener* (1896), a circuit court case, Lurton discounted the argument that certain contracts could be against public policy. "If there is one thing which, more than another, public policy requires," he wrote, "it is that men of full age and competent understanding shall have utmost liberty of contracting." His language left little doubt that Lurton subscribed to liberty of contract, a theory the Court used to oversee state regulations. Yet he was not quick to invalidate state regulations. On the circuit court, for example, he upheld statutory mechanics' and materialmen's lien laws against charges that they violated liberty of contract. On the basis of his voting record, Justice Lurton appeared even more sympathetic to federal economic regulation. He voted with a majority that upheld a federal employer liability insurance statute in the *Second Employer Liability Case* (1912), strengthened the Pure Food and Drug Act in *Hipolite Egg Co.* (1911), and expanded the power of the Interstate Commerce Commission in the *Minnesota Rate Cases* (1913).

Lurton's most significant opinions dealt with antitrust. *Henry v. A.B. Dick Co.* (1912) involved the sale of patented duplicating machines. As a condition of sale, the Dick company required purchasers to use only ink and supplies it made. Henry, who sold another company's ink, claimed that this condition amounted to a restraint of trade. Justice Lurton disagreed. The company had a patent on the machine, he reasoned. The very purpose of patent law is monopoly, and the sale of ink is closely enough linked to the patented product to be justified. Where *A.B. Dick* restricted the impact of antitrust laws, other of his opinions, such as *United States v. Terminal Railroad Assn.*

and *Park v. Hartman* (1907), demonstrated that Lurton was willing to enforce antitrust law in many circumstances.

Although the record is slim, Lurton's conservative inclination was more evident in civil rights matters. *Karem v. United States* (1903) invalidated a federal statute which made it a crime to conspire to keep black citizens from voting. The statute, Lurton reasoned, was inappropriate under the Fifteenth Amendment because it governed acts of individuals rather than those of the state. Later, in *Bailey v. Alabama* (1911), he joined Justice Holmes in dissent when the majority overruled a state peonage law.

What stands out most in Horace Lurton's record, however, is moderation. Not even his most significant opinions broke new legal ground. By the time he applied it in *Karem*, for example, the state action doctrine was well established. Rather than an innovative application of antitrust law, *Henry v. A.B. Dick* reflected a judicious weighing of the purpose of antitrust against the purpose of patent law. By all accounts, Horace Lurton was the consummate professional judge.

—PAUL KENS

BIBLIOGRAPHY

The best available biography is James F. Watts, Jr., "Horace Harmon Lurton," in Friedman and Israel, 3 *Justices* 1847. A collection of Justice Lurton's correspondence is held by the Library of Congress.

Joseph McKenna

BORN 10 August 1843, Philadelphia,
Pennsylvania

NOMINATED to the Court 16 December 1897
by William McKinley

TOOK seat 26 January 1898; retired
5 January 1925

DIED 21 November 1926 in Washington, D.C.

At age twelve, Joseph McKenna's Irish-Catholic immigrant parents moved to Benicia, California. At fifteen, McKenna, whose parents had already invested in his education by sending him to Catholic school, became the head of the family upon his father's death. While supporting the family through odd jobs he managed to study law on his own, well enough to pass the bar exam in 1865. But law held less of an allure for McKenna than politics, and except for a brief period, he never practiced as a private lawyer. Rather, he became a staunch Republican politician. From 1865 on, McKenna was either a candidate or an elected office holder until appointed to the bench. He served in the House of Representatives from 1885 to 1892, where he displayed the knack of gaining the support of powerful figures; Leland Stanford and William McKinley both found him to be a useful ally and played a part in his political rise. Stanford suggested his name to President Benjamin Harrison for a vacancy on the ninth circuit court of appeals in 1892. After his election to the presidency, McKinley named McKenna his attorney general and then, within the year, nominated him to the Supreme Court to fill the seat of Justice Stephen Field, who had finally been persuaded to retire after thirty-four years on the Court.

McKenna would also serve a long time, and his twenty-six-year tenure broke into three periods: an early period of learning his new role; a middle period where he was an important (though somewhat erratic) member of the Court; and a late period of failing abilities limiting his effectiveness. His career, especially his middle period, essentially showed him as a politician dressed in judicial robes.

At the time of his appointment there were complaints that McKenna was unsuited for the Court. While politically motivated, there was a germ of truth in them. Nothing in his background, including his legal positions, prepared McKenna for the Court. He was a poor lawyer and knew it, spending time in the Columbia University law library to ready himself. But the cramming did little good, and a Court librarian later commented that as a new justice, McKenna was overwhelmed by the duties. McKenna's tentativeness as a justice was reflected in opinions; his early ones, e.g., *Magoun v. Illinois Trust and Savings Bank* (1898), were weighed down with heavy loads of precedent and irrelevant case law. Nor did he have a clear philosophy to guide him, and despite his long tenure, he never developed one.

Throughout his career and across many different issues, McKenna proved inconsistent in his decisions and reasoning. Typical of his lack of consistency were his votes and opinions in cases concerning state and federal regulation of working conditions. He was with the majority in *Lochner v. New York* (1905) when the Court struck down a New York health regulation which limited the working hours of bakers. But in the 1908 case, *Muller v. Oregon*, he joined the unanimous majority in upholding the state's hours regulation for women industrial workers. Also, in *Wilson v. New* (1917), McKenna was in the majority upholding the federal Adamson Act which set an eight-hour day for railroad workers. A belief in dual federalism cannot explain this shift, since in *Bunting v. Oregon* (1917), McKenna's majority opinion sustained a state law mandating a ten-hour day that was in effect a minimum wage law. Then, in *Adkins v. Children's Hospital* (1923), he joined the majority in striking down federal minimum wage legislation for women in the District of Columbia, thus returning to where he had started in *Lochner* case.

While McKenna never developed a consistent judicial stand he did adapt his politician's skills to his new role. In the middle of his career, especially in the second decade of the twentieth century, his writing style returned to a more natural form and he expressed his opinions in strong, clear phrases. His opinion in *United States v. United States Steel Corporation* (1920) is a brief and direct statement of the application of the rule of reason (that not all restraints of trade were unreasonable and therefore illegal) to the Sherman Antitrust Act. Moreover, his sensitive political antenna had earlier picked up the strong support for federal action under the commerce power. His opinions for the Court in *Hipolite Egg Company v. United States* (1911) upholding the constitutionality of the Pure Food and Drug Act, and *Hoke v. United States* (1913) upholding the Mann Act, reflected both his political awareness and maturing judicial powers. Both opinions are lucid and forceful statements of the federal government's power to use the commerce power to promote the general welfare. Moreover, both opinions upheld popular laws passed in the face of supposed national emergencies.

This same pattern emerged in the McKenna's votes and opinions in the free speech cases that grew out of the federal and state legislative attempts to limit expression during World War I. In a number of cases, beginning with *Schenck v. United States* (1919), and ending with *Gilbert v. Minnesota* (1920), McKenna joined with the majority in upholding these popular laws. In the *Gilbert* case, McKenna asserted that while the freedom of speech was inherent it was not absolute. In time of emergency, like a war, broad restrictions and limitations could be placed on speech despite the First Amendment.

The wartime speech cases were his swan song. In the 1920s, he stayed on the Court even though he no longer had the ability to understand the issues. Chief Justice William Taft, after McKenna's mental decline, dismissed him as a "Cubist" on the bench, and several times had to ask McKenna to rework his opinions so they would reflect the accordance of the majority. His colleagues suggested he retire and he refused. In 1924, as an expedient, the brethren—under the chief justice's direction—agreed not to make any decisions in cases in which his vote would be the deciding one. Whether it was the pressure of colleagues, his realization of his decline, or his wife's death, McKenna finally decided to retire in 1925.

—RICHARD F. HAMM

BIBLIOGRAPHY

The standard biography is Matthew McDevitt, *Joseph McKenna: Associate Justice of the United States* (1946), which is sympathic but honest in its treatment. For McKenna's decline, see Alpheus T. Mason, *William Howard Taft: Chief Justice* (1964).

JOHN MCKINLEY

BORN 1 May 1780, Culpeper County, Virginia

NOMINATED to the Court 22 April 1837
    by Martin Van Buren

TOOK seat on 9 January 1838

DIED 19 July 1852 in Lexington, Kentucky

McKinley migrated with his parents from Virginia to Kentucky, where he spent his boyhood and young adulthood. In 1800, he was admitted to the bar and practiced law in Frankfort and Louisville until 1818, when he moved to Huntsville, Alabama. Soon after Alabama achieved statehood in 1819, McKinley stood for election as one of the state's new circuit judges. Although he was defeated in that election, within a year he was elected a member of the state legislature. In 1822, he was an unsuccessful candidate for the United States Senate, but in 1826, he was elected to fill the vacancy in Alabama's other Senate seat caused by the incumbent's death. Failing reelection in 1830, McKinley returned to the state legislature in 1831 where his status as a former senator gave him a prominent role. Within a year he was again representing Alabama in Washington, this time as a member of the House of Representatives. At the end of the term, McKinley declined to run again, but returned to the Alabama legislature in 1836, and was once again chosen to serve as senator. Before his term began, however, he was appointed by Martin Van Buren to the Supreme Court.

McKinley had begun his fifteen years' service in the state and national legislatures as a supporter of Henry Clay, a former Kentucky acquaintance, but by 1826 acknowledged himself a Jackson man. In another era or another state, McKinley's conversion might have courted suspicion, but political consistency was not the rule in Alabama politics in the 1820s. And McKinley's attitudes toward public lands, internal improvements, and the Bank of the United States all bore the Democratic stamp.

As a justice, McKinley continued to adhere to Democratic principles, but his difficult circuit duties and poor health caused frequent absences from sessions of the Court. Appointed to the ninth circuit, which included parts of Alabama, Mississippi, and Louisiana, and all of Arkansas, for the first years of his service McKinley had a route of 10,000 miles and a docket of nearly two-thirds of the cases pending in all of the federal circuit courts. His circuit opinions were never published, and his limited attendance in Washington resulted in few Supreme Court opinions—eighteen majority, two concurring, and two dissenting.

McKinley missed the initial cases of the judicial "revolution" of 1837 when the era of the Marshall Court ended and that of Chief Justice Roger B. Taney began. Yet McKinley, as a junior member of the Court, soon informed the more senior members of his Democratic position on states' rights with regard to corporations. On circuit in 1838, he decided *Bank of Augusta v. Earle*, a case involving the right of a bank chartered out-of-state to operate in Alabama. The defendant, refusing to pay a bill of exchange, pointed to the Alabama constitutional provision prohibiting "foreign" banks from doing business in the state. McKinley decided in favor of Earle, citing the state constitutional prohibition and arguing that comity (respect for the laws of another jurisdiction) did not apply. The Bank of Augusta appealed, and the case was paired with two similar cases.

The Supreme Court heard the cases in January 1839, amid the financial difficulties brought about by the Panic of 1837. The concerns in *Bank of Augusta v. Earle* also resonated with the political issues raised in 1832 over the recharter of the Bank of the United States. McKinley's circuit court opinion had excited commercial and banking interests throughout the country. Joseph Story wrote Charles Sumner that McKinley's decision had "frightened half the lawyers and all of the corporations of the country out of their proprieties." Arrayed before the Court were the cream of the Supreme Court bar arguing on behalf of the banks, while James Kent, former chancellor of New York and a leading legal commentator, contended in an article in the *Law*

Reporter that McKinley's decision had no support in English or international commercial law.

Chief Justice Taney, writing for the majority, reversed McKinley's lower court decision and found for the bank, holding that comity granted foreign corporations the right to operate in other states unless specifically forbidden to do so. Since the Alabama constitutional provision had not forbidden out-of-state corporations negotiating bills of exchange, the bank was entitled to collect against Earle. McKinley was the lone dissenter.

Three other cases of the 1840s show McKinley's adherence to state powers. In *Groves v. Slaughter* (1841), McKinley, in a dissenting opinion reminiscent of *Bank of Augusta*, held the Mississippi constitutional prohibition of slaves from other states was self-executing. The majority, however, found that in order to be effective the provision required specific legislation.

As a dissenter in *Lane v. Vick* (1845), McKinley found the majority's decision overruling the Mississippi Supreme Court's construction of a will gave too much power to federal courts. According to McKinley, in the absence of a need for national uniformity, state court interpretations should be followed.

In *Pollard's Lessee v. Hagan* (1845), McKinley expounded for the Court the compact theory and its relationship to the disputed ownership of submerged land. Here he found that the national government only held federal lands as the agent of the states and could not exceed its commission as agent. Since territories were to be admitted to the Union on an equal footing with the original states, the national government could not continue to maintain sovereignty over submerged lands.

In the *Passenger Cases* (1849), McKinley surprisingly found that the statutes of New York and Massachusetts regulating the arrival of alien passengers were unconstitutional. Whether his opinion was predicated on the un-Democratic concept that Congress had exclusive power over interstate commerce, or on the belief that the statutes conflicted with existing federal immigration laws, is unclear. Even the justices themselves failed to reach consensus, as eight wrote separate opinions.

With the exception of the *Passenger Cases*, McKinley's few opinions of his fourteen years on the high court reflect his political stance before his arrival on the bench. He propounded the typical Democratic attitudes of his region which for most of his tenure were shared by Jacksonians in the White House and Congress. But McKinley's intermittent attendance in Washington left others to influence contemporary legal attitudes. His death occasioned little notice.

—ELIZABETH BRAND MONROE

BIBLIOGRAPHY

McKinley's judicial career has excited little research. The most extensive treatment is Frank Otto Gatell's essay in Friedman and Israel, 1 *Justices* 769. Carl Swisher addresses McKinley's limited contributions in the context of the Taney Court in *The Taney Period, 1836–1864* (1974), volume 5 of the Holmes Devise *History of the Supreme Court*.

JOHN MCLEAN

BORN 11 March 1785, Morris County,
New Jersey
NOMINATED to the Court 6 March 1829
by Andrew Jackson
TOOK seat 7 March 1829
DIED 4 April 1861 in Cincinnati, Ohio

Despite his long tenure, hard work, and national prominence during his lifetime, John McLean was never a very important justice and his impact on law was minimal. Although he wrote 247 opinions of the Court, McLean was neither a scholar nor a theorist, and with a few exceptions, his majority opinions are virtually forgotten. Those few that are remembered, such as *Wheaton v. Peters* (1834), *Briscoe v. Bank of Kentucky* (1837), and *Pennsylvania v. Wheeling Bridge Co.* (1852), are recalled more for the parties involved, the high political issue at stake, or the important economic issue in question than for the importance of McLean's opinion. Furthermore, despite his dissent in *Dred Scott v. Sandford* (1857) and fifty-nine other separate opinions, concurrences, and dissents, he did not leave a record of prophetic dissents or concurrences. Few justices have worked so hard, for so long, with such little impact.

McLean was born in New Jersey, the son of Scotch-Irish immigrants, but was raised on the frontier in the Ohio valley. McLean had little formal education, but studied law with Arthur St. Clair, the son of the former governor of the Northwest Territory. In 1807, he began practicing law in Lebanon, Ohio. From 1813–1816, he was a congressman, vigorously supporting Madison's war policy, and then became a judge of the Ohio supreme court from 1816 to 1822. While on this court, McLean ruled in *Ohio v. Carneal* (1817) that masters could not employ slaves in Ohio, but that they could probably travel through the state with their slaves. President James Monroe appointed McLean as a commissioner of the General Land Office in 1822 and as postmaster general in 1823. McLean's brilliant administrative skills and adept political

maneuvering enabled him to retain his position under President John Quincy Adams. Always politically agile, during the election of 1828, McLean refused to use his office and immense patronage powers to help Adams. Although he had not worked for Jackson, the president-elect rewarded McLean for his silent "nonpartisan" support. Two days after his inauguration, Jackson nominated McLean to the bench, and one day later the Senate confirmed him.

Although Jackson's first Supreme Court appointee, McLean was not truly a Jacksonian Democrat. He opposed Jackson's wholesale removals of officeholders in order to distribute patronage, and he supported protective tariffs and internal improvements. While on the bench McLean persistently dabbled in politics, and seemed available to any party. He was, at various times, discussed as a presidential nominee by the Anti-Masonic Party, Free Soil Democrats, the Whigs, and in 1856 and 1860, the Republicans. McLean never saw any impropriety in continuing to be a politician while on the Court. In this sense he was no different than many others on and off the bench at this time.

Despite his early affiliation with the Democrats, McLean's jurisprudence lay more in the Federalist-nationalist tradition of Marshall and Story than the emerging Jacksonian jurisprudence of Chief Justice Roger B. Taney. Three elements characterized that jurisprudence: an inclination to stimulate and allow new economic enterprises through the release of creative energies; a deference to state power and state sovereignty; and strong proslavery tendencies. McLean distanced himself from Taney in the first two of these areas, and whenever possible—within his notion of proper jurisprudence—he opposed slavery.

In *Charles River Bridge v. Warren Bridge* (1837), Taney held that the franchise to build a new bridge did not abrogate the rights of the stockholders of the older bridge company. McLean's dissent explicitly rejected older English doctrine that protected virtually all existing enterprises from competition, and to this extent he

accepted some of the Jacksonian ideals of enhanced competition. But he was unwilling to
apply the Jacksonian ideas to this case. On the
substantive issues, McLean agreed with the Federalist jurisprudence of Joseph Story. The
creation of the new Warren Bridge unconstitutionally violated the contract clause of the Constitution by abrogating the Charles River Bridge
Company's charter, which was clearly a contract
between the state and the proprietors.

However, unlike everyone else on the
Court, McLean did not believe the Court had
jurisdiction in the case. His view of the jurisdictional issue also reflected some of the Jacksonian
deference to the states. McLean did not want the
Supreme Court micromanaging the emerging
dynamic economy.

Unlike Taney and other Jacksonians, in a
number of commercial cases McLean was ready
to intervene in state affairs to strengthen national
power. In the *License Cases* (1847) he joined the
majority to uphold the challenged regulations of
the sale of liquor as legitimately within the scope
of a state's police power. However, McLean
also reaffirmed that in the area of interstate commerce, the power of Congress was "supreme."

McLean applied the implications of his
License Case opinion to the *Passenger Cases*
(1849). As the senior judge in the majority, Mc-
Lean wrote the lead opinion in this case in which
every judge wrote something, and the Court split
5–4. McLean wrote to strike down state laws
requiring that ship captains pay a fee for every
immigrant they landed. He construed this fee
to be a tax and found that any tax on imports,
whether "upon tonnage, merchandise, or passengers" was a "regulation of commerce, and cannot be laid by a State, except under the sanction
of Congress." Chief Justice Taney, favoring state
power over national power, led four hard-core
states' rights dissents.

In *Cooley v. Board of Wardens of the Port
of Philadelphia* (1852) the Jacksonian majority
on the Court upheld Philadelphia's regulation of
its port, which included a requirement that most
ships hire local pilots. McLean did not dispute
the utility of this legislation, but believed it violated Congress's power to regulate commerce.
He expressed concern that a majority of the

Court had now subscribed to the notion that "a
State may regulate foreign commerce, or commerce among the States." McLean feared a "race
of legislation between Congress and the States"
that would produce chaos in interstate and international commerce.

Consistent with his neo-Federalist view
of national power, McLean wrote the majority
opinion in *Pennsylvania v. Wheeling Bridge
Co.* (1852) ordering that the Wheeling Bridge be
raised so it not interfere with commerce on the
Ohio River. Here Taney, and the extreme states'
rights advocate, Peter V. Daniel, dissented.

McLean's jurisprudence on slavery is complex. McLean was personally and politically opposed to slavery, and the antislavery lawyer and
politician Salmon P. Chase was a good friend and
political ally. In 1848, Chase told Charles Sumner
that McLean was "the most reliable man, on the
slavery questions, now prominent in either party."
As Robert M. Cover noted, from a free soil perspective, McLean was "sound on slavery, politically and personally, if not judicially."

McLean heard a number of fugitive slave
cases in his role as circuit justice, and he also
reviewed fugitive slave and other slavery-related
cases on the Supreme Court. His early jurisprudence was clearly antislavery. In 1841, he joined
Story's opinion in ordering the release of the
Amistad captives. This result was a direct slap
at the proslavery policies of Jackson's successor, Martin Van Buren. *Groves v. Slaughter*
(1841) pitted McLean's Federalist commercial
jurisprudence against his antislavery views. The
case turned on a Mississippi constitutional
provision which prohibited the importation of
slaves. McLean noted that the "necessity of a
uniform commercial regulation, more than any
other consideration, led to the adoption of the
federal Constitution" and denied that the states
had concurrent power to regulate commerce in
the absence of congressional legislation. This put
him squarely in the Federalist-nationalist-Whig
tradition and clearly in opposition to the Taney-
Jacksonian views of commerce. This analysis
seemed to lead to the conclusion that Mississippi
could not prohibit the importation of slaves as
articles of commerce. But that would have undermined his antislavery views and the laws of

most of the North. Instead, in a concurring opinion, McLean declared that slavery was purely a creature of local law and thus, using his home state as an example, McLean asserted that while Ohio could not prohibit the importation "of the cotton of the south or the manufactured articles of the north . . . no one doubts its power to prohibit slavery."

Prigg v. Pennsylvania (1842) also forced McLean to chose between a nationalist jurisprudence and an antislavery jurisprudence. Here he broke ranks with both Story and Taney. Story's majority opinion struck down all state personal liberty laws on the grounds that the federal fugitive slave law of 1793 preempted all state regulation of the return of fugitive slaves. The proslavery, states' rights Jacksonians, let by Taney and Daniel, agreed with the result in this case, but they wanted to allow the states to be proactive in aiding the return of fugitive slaves. McLean, on the other hand, abandoned his normal support for a strong national government. In the only dissent in the case, he argued, consistent with his opinion in *Groves*, that slavery was local and thus the states could constitutionally intervene in the return of fugitive slaves to protect free blacks.

Although he dissented in *Prigg*, McLean accepted the will of the majority of his brethren. Thus, in a number of subsequent circuit court cases, he usually (but not always) ruled in favor of masters and against those who wanted to help fugitive slaves. In *Norris v. Newton* (1850) he charged an Indiana jury to find for the slaveholding plaintiff, reminding the jurors, that "the law, and not conscience, constitutes the rule of action." McLean's circuit court opinions in *Jones v. Van Zandt* (1843), *Norris*, and *Miller v. McQuerry* (1853) continued to disappoint his friends, as did his failure to dissent from Levi Woodbury's opinion when *Jones v. Van Zandt* reached the high court in 1847.

While obligated by his notion of *stare decisis* to support fugitive slave renditions, McLean remained opposed to slavery. In *Dred Scott v. Sandford* (1857) McLean wrote a thirty-five-page critique of Taney's opinion. As he had throughout his career, McLean argued that slavery was "emphatically a state institution." The only exception to this, he asserted, involved the Constitution's fugitive slave clause. Also consistent with his lifelong views, McLean supported the power of the national government, in this case to regulate affairs in the territories. McLean's dissent was admirable, but is often forgotten because of Justice Curtis's sixty-eight-page attack on Taney's opinion. At the time, however, McLean's dissent led to renewed interest in him as a presidential candidate. In 1860, Thaddeus Stevens, among others, backed him for the presidential nomination, but the presidency was no longer a realistic possibility for the seventy-five-year-old jurist. Moreover, his home state of Ohio backed a more viable candidate, Salmon P. Chase. McLean remained on the Court during the secession crisis, but died a month after Abraham Lincoln's inauguration.

—PAUL FINKELMAN

BIBLIOGRAPHY

Francis P. Weisenburger, *The Life of John McLean: A Politician on the United States Supreme Court* (1937), the only scholarly biography of McLean, is dated and overemphasizes his political interests and career. An excellent short summary of McLean's life, followed by some of his opinions, is Frank Otto Gattel, "John McLean," in Friedman and Israel, 1 *Justices* 535.

Robert M. Cover, *Justice Accused: Antislavery and the Judicial Process* (1975), discusses the dilemmas of judges like McLean who opposed slavery but felt obligated to enforce the constitutional provisions protecting the institution. Paul Finkelman, *An Imperfect Union: Slavery, Federalism, and Comity* (1981), places much of McLean's jurisprudence on slavery in the context of federalism.

Harold M. Hyman and William M. Wiecek, *Equal Justice Under Law* (1982), is the best book available on the constitutional history of antebellum America. Carl B. Swisher, *The Taney Period, 1836–1864* (1974), volume 5 of the Holmes Devise *History of the Supreme Court* is a classic history of the Taney Court.

James Clark McReynolds
Photograph by Harris and Ewing.
Collection of the Supreme Court of the United States.

JAMES CLARK MCREYNOLDS

BORN 3 February 1862, Elkton, Kentucky

NOMINATED to the Court 19 August 1914
by Woodrow Wilson

TOOK seat 5 September 1914; retired
1 February 1941

DIED 24 August 1946 in Washington, D.C.

In the annals of United States Supreme Court history, James Clark McReynolds is as well-known for his disagreeable nature as for his conservative, even reactionary, opposition to the New Deal programs of President Franklin Roosevelt. Like Woodrow Wilson, the president who appointed him, McReynolds was a southerner and a gold Democrat. In fact, both men received legal training at the University of Virginia in the early 1880s. Unlike Wilson, however, McReynolds took to the law and made it his career, a career that culminated in federal service as attorney general (1913–1914), and as an associate justice for twenty-six of the most dynamic years in the history of the nation.

McReynolds, of Scotch-Irish descent, grew up on the family plantation in Elkton, Kentucky, near the Tennessee border; his father had served as a surgeon in the Confederate army. McReynolds excelled at Vanderbilt University (valedictorian, B.S., 1882), and studied with the legendary John Minor and others at the University of Virginia (LL.B., 1884). On graduation, McReynolds served briefly as a secretary to Senator Howell E. Jackson of Tennessee, then moved on to a successful law practice in Nashville. While there, McReynolds taught commercial law at Vanderbilt's law school, serving with then-circuit court Judge Horace Lurton, the man whose seat on the Supreme Court McReynolds would later occupy.

From 1903 to 1907, McReynolds served in the Theodore Roosevelt administration as assistant attorney general, specializing in antitrust law. He divided the next several years between private practice in New York City and service as a special federal prosecutor in the American Tobacco antitrust case. In 1913, President Wilson, after vehement opposition arose to his idea of appointing Louis Brandeis as attorney general, named McReynolds. Although McReynolds appears to have filled that job competently, his term was marked by an embarrassing incident concerning the postponement of a Mann Act prosecution of the son of a Democratic politician, and by friction with other members of the administration. When Justice Lurton died in July 1914, Wilson went with another southern Democrat, despite some concern over McReynolds's irascible temperament.

In the years before the New Deal, McReynolds disagreed with the progressive-leaning majority, siding instead with those who championed private property interests in cases such as *Block v. Hirsh* (1921, supporting rent control), and *Village of Euclid v. Ambler Realty Company* (1926, upholding zoning).

During these pre-New Deal years, McReynolds also revealed, despite his record as a strong trustbuster, an impatience with government regulation of business. For example, in *Federal Trade Commission v. Gratz* (1921), McReynolds spoke for the majority that overturned the FTC's complaint against a cotton bagging manufacturer: "Nothing is alleged which would justify the conclusion that the public suffered injury or that competitors had reasonable ground for complaint. . . . If real competition is to continue, the right of the individual to exercise reasonable discretion in respect of his own business methods must be preserved."

McReynolds's record in the realm of civil liberties is somewhat enigmatic. In *Berger v. United States* (1921), and *Stromberg v. California* (1931), for example, he disagreed with the majority's tolerance. In *Berger*, a case involving the prosecution of German- and Austrian-born Socialist dissenters under the Espionage Act, the Supreme Court was faced with the allegation that Judge Kenesaw Mountain Landis was "prejudiced and biased against [some] defendants because of their nativity." The majority of the Supreme Court concluded that Judge Landis had "no lawful right or power to preside as judge on the trial of the defendants upon the indictment." In dissent, McReynolds—who throughout his judicial tenure demonstrated his own prejudice against Jews, African Americans, and female professionals—was more understanding of Landis: "Intense dislike of a class does not render the judge incapable of administering complete justice to one of its members. . . . And while 'an overspeaking judge is no well-tuned cymbal,' neither is an amorphous dummy unspotted by human emotions a becoming receptacle for judicial power." These words came from a man who was openly racist and anti-Semitic and who declined to appear at functions attended by Justices Cardozo and Brandeis.

In *Stromberg*, McReynolds dissented when the majority overturned the conviction of a Communist woman charged with flying a red flag at a summer camp for children, finding the state statute under which she was prosecuted to be "repugnant to the guarantee of liberty contained in the Fourteenth Amendment." Yet, only eight years before, McReynolds had articulated an expansive view of the nature of liberty, and in the process led the Court as it overturned a state law that forbade teaching reading in the German language. The case was *Meyer v. Nebraska* (1923), and McReynolds's rhetoric is a memorable challenge to the state's police power. "Without doubt," McReynolds wrote concerning liberty guaranteed by the Fourteenth Amendment, "it denotes not merely freedom from bodily restraint but also the right of the individual to contract, to engage in any of the common occupations of life, to acquire useful knowledge, to marry, establish a home and bring up children, to worship God according to the dictates of his own conscience, and generally to enjoy those privileges long recognized as essential to the orderly pursuit of happiness by free men."

Two years later, in *Pierce v. Society of Sisters* (1925), McReynolds wrote for the Court as it ruled unconstitutional a compulsory public school attendance statute. He cited *Meyer* and concluded that the act "unreasonably interferes with the liberty of parents and guardians to direct the upbringing and education of children under their control."

On the foundation of *Meyer* and *Pierce* were cases like *Griswold v. Connecticut* (1965) and *Roe v. Wade* (1973) built by later, more liberal, justices.

It was during Franklin Roosevelt's presidency that McReynolds, aligned with Pierce Butler, Willis Van Devanter, and George Sutherland (the "Four Horsemen"), would earn his reputation as the Supreme Court's most reactionary member. In case after case, McReynolds registered his disagreement as the majority increasingly gave support to radical efforts by state and federal governments to rescue the nation from the Great Depression. One observer of the Court noted that, as the Court became more liberal, McReynolds replaced Justice Brandeis as the "great dissenter."

In *Home Building & Loan v. Blaisdell* (1934), he joined Justice Sutherland who, dissenting from the Court's approval of Minnesota's mortgage moratorium law, warned of "future gradual but ever-advancing encroachments upon the sanctity of private and public contracts." In *Nebbia v. New York* (1934), he fumed as the majority upheld the state's milk price-control scheme: "If now liberty or property may be struck down because of difficult circumstances, we must expect that hereafter every right must yield to the voice of an impatient majority when stirred by distressful exigency. . . . Certain fundamentals have been set beyond experimentation; the Constitution has released them from control by the state." He asked skeptically whether "the milk business [is] so affected with a public interest that the Legislature may prescribe prices for sales by stores?" He searched in vain for a "reasonable relation" between means and ends. He ended with the observation that "the highest duty intrusted to the courts" was "zealously to uphold" the "dominance of the Constitution."

In 1935, in a series of decisions known as the *Gold Clause Cases*, McReynolds offered his most memorable dissent, but not in the pages of the *United States Reports*. In the early days of the New Deal, after the nation left the gold standard and the gold content of the dollar was reduced, Congress, by joint resolution, had canceled the gold clause included in private contracts and government bonds as insurance against inflation. The printed version of McReynolds's objections to the majority's failure to negate this "confiscation of property rights and repudiation of national obligations" can be found following the holding in *Norman v. Baltimore & Ohio Railroad* (1935), and by reference in two subsequent cases. His tone was caustic: "Just men regard repudiation and spoilation of citizens by their sovereign with abhorrence," two policies he regarded as unauthorized for a "federal government . . . of delegated and limited powers," and as contrary to the intent of the framers. His prediction for the future was dire indeed: "Loss of reputation for honorable dealing will bring us unending humiliation; the impending legal and moral chaos is appalling."

There are varying accounts of what McReynolds said from the bench when he read aloud his dissent. According to one report, he warned that "shame and humiliation are upon us" and that "anarchy and despotism are at the door." Others quote the angry justice as declaring, "This is Nero at his worst. The Constitution is gone!" The exact phrases are not as important, however, as the spirit in which they were offered. To the conservative members of the Supreme Court, these were dire times for the constitutional republic.

As the New Deal progressed, so did McReynolds's pattern of protest at the excesses of government. His was the lone dissenting voice in *Ashwander v. Tennessee Valley Authority* (1936). While the majority approved the plan for the sale of surplus power from the Wilson Dam, McReynolds characterized the TVA's program as disingenuous and illegal: "If under the thin mask of disposing of property the United States can enter the business of generating, transmitting, and selling power . . . with the definite design to accomplish ends wholly beyond the sphere marked out for them by the Constitution, an easy way has been found for breaking down the limitations heretofore supposed to guarantee protection against aggression."

One year later, in *West Coast Hotel Co. v. Parrish* (1937), a case in which the Court upheld a state of Washington minimum wage law for women, the victim of the Court's excessive deference was the "liberty of contract" advanced by *Adkins v. Children's Hospital* (1923). In *West Coast Hotel*, McReynolds joined Justice Sutherland (the author of the Court's opinion in *Adkins*) in reiterating the power of the Supreme Court to declare such statutes repugnant to the

Constitution. The power base of the Court had shifted to the left, marginalizing McReynolds and the other conservatives as the New Deal built up steam.

McReynolds's dissent in *National Labor Relations Board v. Jones & Laughlin Steel Corporation* (1937), best represents the rapidity of the Court's shift. In an opinion for the "Four Horsemen" objecting to the sweep of the National Labor Relations Act, McReynolds noted that the majority's holding "departs from well established principles followed in" two cases in which the Court had checked the New Deal program: *Schecter v. United States* (1935), and *Carter v. Carter Coal Company* (1936). As if to add special emphasis to the Court's about-face, McReynolds, in a departure from proper citation form, included the months and years of those two, now-rejected precedents. McReynolds reacted against a "view of congressional power [that] would extend it into almost every field of human industry." "Any effect on interstate commerce by the discharge of employees shown here would be indirect and remote in the highest degree," wrote McReynolds, rejecting the majority's expansive "stream of commerce" rationale.

McReynolds remained on the Court for another four years, and died five years later. During World War II, the cantankerous ex-justice adopted thirty-three British war children, corresponding with them and providing financial support. In his will, the lifelong bachelor left significant bequests to various charities. Even in death, McReynolds remained an enigma.

—MICHAEL ALLAN WOLF

BIBLIOGRAPHY

The McReynolds papers are collected at the University of Virginia Library in Charlottesville. Justice McReynolds's Supreme Court memorial, 334 U.S. v (1948), contains some helpful details concerning McReynolds's life, but little in the way of criticism or analysis of his judicial philosophy. Alexander Bickel provides some perceptive insights in *The Judiciary and Responsible Government: 1910–1921 Part One* (1984), volume 9 of the Holmes Devise. Bickel relied in part on Barbara Barlin Schimmel's dissertation, "The Judicial Philosophy of Mr. Justice McReynolds" (Yale, 1964).

John Marshall
Artwork by Elson and Company.
Collection of the Supreme Court of the United States.

JOHN MARSHALL

BORN 24 September 1755, Germantown,
Fauquier County, Virginia

NOMINATED to the Court 20 January 1801
by John Adams

TOOK seat 4 February 1801

DIED 6 July 1835, Philadelphia, Pennsylvania

John Marshall was born on the Virginia colonial frontier to one of the leading families in
Fauquier County. His father, Thomas, a militia
officer and surveyor, served as Fauquier's delegate in the House of Burgesses, as a vestryman
for Leeds Parish, and as county sheriff. His employment as a surveying assistant to his boyhood
friend, George Washington, identified the family
with the future president and ultimately involved
his son in the purchase of a substantial portion of
the Fairfax estate that Washington and Thomas
Marshall surveyed. John Marshall's mother, Mary
Keith Marshall, was the daughter of a clergyman
who had married into the prominent Randolph
family. Through her the future chief justice was
distantly related to Thomas Jefferson.

Tutored at home by his mother and local
clergy, Marshall studied for a time with the
Reverend Archibald Campbell of Westmoreland
County. At nineteen, he was appointed lieutenant in the Culpeper Minute Men, and saw action
at the battle of Great Bridge in southeastern
Virginia (9 Dec. 1775). From August 1776 to the
spring of 1780, Marshall served as first lieutenant and captain in the Virginia Continental Line,
with additional duties as a judge advocate. He
was present during the battles of Brandywine,
Germantown, and Stony Point, and he endured
the harsh winter encampment at Valley Forge.

After military service, Marshall studied law
with George Wythe, the newly appointed professor of law and police at the College of William and Mary, and was admitted to practice law
in Fauquier County Court on 28 August 1780.
Shortly after his marriage to Mary Willis "Polly"
Ambler in January 1783, he shifted the locus of
his law practice and political life to Richmond,
where in addition to service in the house of delegates, he also spent three years as the recorder
of the Richmond city hustings court, the only
judicial position he held before his nomination
to the United States Supreme Court.

As a delegate to the Virginia convention that
ratified the Constitution, Marshall supported the
pro-ratification cause and delivered a persuasive
speech on the need for a federal judiciary in the
proposed government. After the new government
was in operation, he declined several offers of
federal office, preferring to remain in private practice. He was particularly prominent in defending
Virginia planters against their British creditors,
and it was in this context that he argued his only
Supreme Court appeal, *Ware v. Hylton* (1796).

Marshall came to national prominence as a
result of his membership in a mission to France
in 1797–98, in the course of which he and his
colleagues soundly rejected French demands that
the United States pay tribute to the French Republic before a treaty of amity could be negotiated. With the publication of their correspondence with the French agents (named Messrs. X,
Y, and Z), they became the focal point of partisan debate between the Jeffersonian and Federalist political parties. On Marshall's return from
France, and at the urging of former President
George Washington, he ran for the Richmond
seat in the House of Representatives. Elected as
the only Federalist congressman from Virginia,
he served in the House until his appointment as
secretary of state in May 1800. During the last
months of the Adams administration, Marshall
served concurrently as secretary of state and
chief justice of the United States.

The federal judiciary came under heavy attack when the Jeffersonian Republican party came
into power in March 1801. President Jefferson and
his supporters in Congress were strongly opposed
to the establishment of new federal trial courts.
They were even more critical of the composition
of the circuit courts, the judges having been selected from among the most loyal members of the
Federalist party. Many federal judges, including
some of John Marshall's colleagues on the high
court, had been overbearing and unprofessional in
their conduct of criminal trials designed to stamp
out political opposition. When the Jeffersonian

majority in Congress repealed the Judiciary Act of 1801, the justices of the Supreme Court reluctantly resumed their riding circuit to preside over the traditional circuit courts. In *Stuart v. Laird* (1803), decided within a few days of *Marbury v. Madison*, the Court upheld the authority of Congress to abolish the circuit courts established under the 1801 Judiciary Act.

Against this background, Chief Justice Marshall delivered his famous decision in *Marbury v. Madison* (1803), which held a section of the Judiciary Act of 1789 null and void since it conflicted with provisions of the Constitution. The statute granted the Supreme Court jurisdiction to issue a write of mandamus which, but for Marshall's invalidation, would have been available to command delivery of William Marbury's commission as a justice of the peace.

Ostensibly, the Court's decision was a formal rejection of jurisdiction, and since it did not require enforcement, it was self-executing. However, *Marbury* brought earlier American jurisprudence concerning judicial review into the precedents of the Supreme Court, and thus it represented an important step in establishing the Court as a primary expositor of American constitutional law. *Marbury* also demonstrated the manner in which the Court, through deciding cases concerning its own jurisdiction, could gain institutional power within the federal union. While judicial nullification of congressional statutes was used sparingly before 1890, courts thereafter would expand the concept of judicial review and assert that the Supreme Court was the sole expounder of constitutional law in the United States, as in *Cooper v. Aaron* (1958).

Marbury drew on diverse strands of constitutional thought: first, the concept of a written constitution which implied a sovereign act of the people which was superior to statutes passed by the legislature; second, the implication of the Constitution that federal courts were of limited jurisdiction; third, a corollary on separation of powers doctrine which asserted that judges in administering the law were required by their oath to uphold the Constitution, and thus were independent of both legislative and executive control.

Equally important to the American federal union was the conferral upon the Supreme Court of a limited power to hear appeals from the highest courts of each state in certain federally related cases. In 1816, the Commonwealth of Virginia defied the Court's mandate in a case involving the Fairfax proprietaries; since Marshall had a personal financial interest in the litigation, he did not participate in the decision, but his close confidante on the bench, Joseph Story, wrote a strong defense of the proposition that for the Union to function, such an appeal was proper and must be binding upon the various states (*Martin v. Hunter's Lessee,* 1816).

Five years later, Chief Justice Marshall decided that matters pending in state courts that were otherwise subject to Supreme Court review might be appealed from the highest state court having jurisdiction of the case. *Cohens v. Virginia* (1821) involved a Virginia criminal statute imposing a fine for selling lottery tickets. Cohens had sold a ticket issued by the District of Columbia lottery managers pursuant to a district statute. He was convicted before the hustings court of Norfolk, and under state procedural law there was no right to appeal to Virginia's highest court, the court of appeals. Marshall upheld the validity of the appeal from the Virginia trial court, based on the fact that the lottery was authorized by a statute passed by Congress. In 1824, when the case was argued on the merits, Cohens lost because the Court viewed the district statute authorizing the lottery as a mere local regulation, not intended by Congress to be supreme over state law.

Cohens demonstrates Marshall's insistence that the Supreme Court exercise broad authority in reviewing state laws that conflicted with the Constitution, or the laws and treaties made pursuant to it. He believed this essential to the smooth functioning of the constitutional system, a necessary instrument for the implementation of foreign treaties and agreements, and a manifestation of federal supremacy. Consequently, no state should be permitted to so structure its appellate system that federal questions were shielded from appellate review, and the Supreme Court might make its own decisions of fact when its jurisdiction depended upon such a decision.

In *McCulloch v. Maryland* (1819), the chief justice spoke for the Court in explaining the scope of the necessary and proper clause in Article I, Section 8, of the Constitution. This had been debated since the 1792 disagreement between Thomas Jefferson and Alexander Hamilton over the chartering of the first Bank of the United States. Essentially, Marshall in *McCulloch* adopted the Hamiltonian position—that the powers of the federal government were delimited by Constitution, but that under the necessary and proper provision, whatever was useful or efficacious in implementing those powers was constitutional. This contrasted with Jefferson's view that the clause permitted only those additional powers as were essential to functioning within the enumerated grants of power.

McCulloch is a good example of Marshall's preference for effectiveness in the exercise of governmental power. He was deeply concerned that political leaders should possess adequate authority to carry out their duties. He drew a distinction between policy decisions, which in his opinion were to be left to the executive and Congress, and matters touching on private individual rights, which courts should protect against overbearing or confiscatory governmental action. Deference to the political decisions of the president and Congress is implicit in the Marshall Court's acceptance of Jefferson's imposition of the embargo as an instrument of foreign policy. However, Marshall was quick to intercede when governmental action threatened the constitutional rights of individuals or groups, as evidenced by his opinions in *Fletcher v. Peck* (1810), *Dartmouth College v. Woodward* (1819), and *Worcester v. Georgia* (1832).

Marshall's opinion in *McCulloch* was based on the supremacy of the federal government within its constitutional sphere. The case involved Maryland's attempt to tax the notes issued by the Bank of the United States branch in Baltimore. The chief justice pointed out that such a tax imposed a burden on a federal activity. While some equitably imposed taxes might be constitutional, this particular tax operated to place the Bank of the United States at a competitive disadvantage within Maryland. Hence, it was contrary to the Constitution's Sixth Article, which made the laws of the United States the supreme law of the land, and thus subordinated state statutes and taxes to the provisions of congressional acts. Like many Marshall Court opinions in other fields, *McCulloch* merely initiated the process of defining

the tax immunities which existed between the federal and the state governments. Its clear and emphatic assertion of federal supremacy, however, remains Marshall's most enduring contribution to American constitutional law.

Although Marshall has frequently been described as a pro-capitalist judge, he is best seen as a strong nationalist who sought the prosperity of the United States through economic diversification and legal safeguards for private property. In general, he favored free competition, but was not unwilling to use governmental subsidies to encourage new forms of commercial or industrial activity. Commercial activity between the states should not be subjected to artificial mercantilist obstructions, and monopolies were to be regarded with suspicion.

Like many of his contemporaries, Marshall wished to see the United States develop into a free trade area where goods and services might be bought and sold across state boundaries with virtually no restriction. His most famous opinion in this area is *Gibbons v. Ogden* (1824), which involved efforts by the New York state legislature to restrict steamboat navigation in New York harbor and on the Hudson River to vessels operated by the Fulton-Livingston monopoly. Observing that trade among the states included navigation of the waterways, Marshall held that the New York statutes and monopoly violated the Constitution. That document gave Congress the right to regulate commerce among the states, and the New York legislation conflicted with that federal constitutional grant. In addition, Congress, in the Federal Coasting Licensing Act of 1793, had already exercised its power to regulate commerce in the waters covered by the New York statutes, preempting the states from making rules for the regulation of commerce. Undoubtedly one of the most encyclopedic of Marshall's opinions, *Gibbons* remains the cornerstone of the federal commerce power to this day. It anticipated future cases that would apply an economic test to determine what was burdensome to the flow of commerce, and it guaranteed that the commerce clause of the Constitution would become one of the focal points of federal power in the nineteenth and twentieth centuries.

In a nation as undeveloped as the United States was in the first three decades of the nineteenth century, foreign investment was essential to economic prosperity. Investment in turn depended on the legal system's support for the institution of private property. Building on earlier case law which developed legal safeguards for vested property interests, Marshall shaped the contract clause into an additional instrument for controlling state tendencies to trample on private property rights. This was accomplished through a broad, and now antiquated, view of contract. Originally, the Constitution's prohibition against states abridging the obligation of contracts was directed toward seizure of accounts payable in commercial transactions, as had been done in the case of British creditors during the American Revolution, or state laws which favored debtors and impeded creditors from collecting their accounts.

Marshall began his creative work on the contract clause in *Fletcher v. Peck* (1810) by treating a Georgia state land grant as if it were a contract between the grantor state and the grantees, who had bribed the legislature and secured the vast Yazoo land grant which included the rich farmlands of the future states of Alabama and Mississippi. The subsequent reform-minded legislature enacted a statute repealing the land grant, but Marshall held that while a legislature would not normally be bound by the actions of its predecessor, when private rights arose as a consequence of a legislative act, those property interests could not be infringed without violation of the contract clause.

In *Dartmouth College v. Woodward* (1819), Chief Justice Marshall viewed contract in a more general and equitable context. The pre-Revolutionary charter to Dartmouth College was viewed as the origin of property rights in those who received the charter (that is, the trustees), the Crown which granted the charter, and those who gave property to the college in reliance upon the charter's terms. Marshall reasoned that these arrangements prevented the state of New Hampshire from seizing the assets and books of the college and making it a state university. As the legal successor to the English Crown, the state was bound by its contractual relation with the trustees and the donors. While the broad application of the contract clause to business, as well as charitable corporations, was somewhat restricted by the

Marshall Court, it was left to the Taney Court to assert countervailing rights reserved to states when corporate charters were vague.

John Marshall's most serious dissent from his colleagues involved the contract clause and its application to state insolvency laws. The 1819 economic depression found many mercantile firms in financial difficulty and some sought refuge in insolvency, a process whereby creditors agreed not to imprison the debtor provided his or her assets were made available for distribution among them. Although the Constitution authorized Congress to enact a uniform law of bankruptcy, it had not done so, except for a short-lived statute in effect from 1800 to 1803. Marshall and his Court faced the question whether the enactment of an insolvency law that discharged a preexisting debt violated the contract clause in *Ogden v. Saunders* (1827). A majority of the Court held that state insolvency laws did not abridge the obligations of contract, but simply altered the remedies available to creditors. Marshall dissented, asserting that the parties entered into a contract for payment, and that no state action infringing upon those agreed rights was permissible. By this point in Marshall's career it appears that he viewed contract rights as arising under natural law by virtue of the private agreement of the parties. In opposition, his associates saw contractual rights arising from private agreement, which in turn was subject to the applicable state law. Consequently, for Marshall's associates, certain contractual rights and obligations might, under some circumstances, be legislatively altered without violating the constitutional mandate.

Marshall's growing acceptance of natural law principles in regard to the contract clause cases began to shape his approach to individual rights in the last decade of his chief justiceship. However, pragmatism and caution limited his resort to abstract principles of natural law. Despite English precedents, including the famous *Somerset's Case* (1772), which held that slavery was contrary to natural law and hence could exist only by virtue of express municipal law, Marshall preferred a positivist approach. In *The Antelope* (1825), he was asked to rule on the status of Africans captured from a slave trading ship off the American coast. He rejected the invitation to consult the law of nations or some abstract theory of natural justice. Rather, he sought express provisions in the municipal law of the states involved to determine whether the purported slaves were held and transported illegally. Absent proof that the nation of the ship's registry had abolished the slave trade, Marshall felt compelled to surrender both the ship and its human cargo to the owners of the vessel.

In regard to Indian land titles, the chief justice, in *Johnson v. McIntosh* (1823), considered the various tribes to hold a mere possessory interest which did not restrict the right of the Crown, the commonwealth of Virginia, or its grantee, the United States, to confer title to the land. Thus the post-Revolutionary grant of Illinois land extinguished possessory rights held by those claiming under Indian deeds. Subsequently, in *Cherokee Nation v. Georgia* (1831), he asserted that the Cherokee tribe was neither a separate sovereign nation nor a state of the United States. Thus it lacked standing to obtain an injunction from the Supreme Court against Georgia legislation which undermined the independence of the Cherokee people. Since the Cherokee were living within the limits of the United States, they were subject to state and federal law. They were a dependent domestic nation, and once they surrendered possession of their land, it became available for grant by the states or federal government. Furthermore, Marshall pointed out that the State of Georgia had civil authority over the Cherokee lands, and the Court would exceed its authority by restraining that state's legislature from acting on Indians subject to its jurisdiction.

In deciding *Cherokee Nation,* Marshall indicated that in an appropriate case the Supreme Court might intervene to protect Indian rights. This proved to be the situation when Indian rights arose from agreements incorporated in federal treaties. Such a case arose the following year in *Worcester v. Georgia* (1832). Samuel Worcester, a missionary appointed by the American Board of Commissioners for Foreign Missions and approved by the president of the United States as a resident within the Cherokee territory, was convicted under a Georgia criminal law prohibiting residence without a state license. Citing treaties between the tribe and the federal government granting self-government to the tribe, Worcester asserted that he was not subject to Georgia law. Relying on those treaty provisions, Marshall declared the Georgia statute null and void, and contrary to the authority of Congress to regulate trade with the Indian nations. Since the treaties were in the nature of contracts between the Cherokee and the United States, and since they also involved the supremacy of the United States under the commerce clause, Marshall's firm holding in favor of the Indians was inevitable. Unfortunately, it was to be of no practical value, since President Andrew Jackson refused to enforce the decree; the "Trail of Tears" that would carry a large portion of the Cherokee to the Oklahoma Territory continued to operate, and white settlers from Georgia poured into Cherokee lands that contained some gold deposits and the rich alluvial soil necessary for cotton production.

Perhaps more than any other chief justice, John Marshall was responsible for altering the manner in which the Supreme Court conducted its business. Within the first years of his tenure he succeeded in convincing the other justices to accept a unitary "opinion of the Court" as the preferred way of announcing decisions. This was not a novel practice, since under Marshall's predecessor, Oliver Ellsworth, a number of Supreme Court opinions had been issued *per curiam.* However, these were on relatively minor points, and the practice of *seriatum* opinions persisted for major cases. In the *seriatum* opinion, based on English practice, each judge stated his individual view of the case, and the law of the case had to be extracted from the points on which a majority of the justices seemed to agree.

Agreement on the content of "opinions of the Court" moved the Supreme Court in the direction of unanimity. This was enhanced by Marshall's efforts to have all justices room together in one hotel, where they ate at the same table and discussed the cases pending before them. While the influx of new associate justices appointed by Thomas Jefferson and Andrew Jackson began to undermine these arrangements, Chief Justice Marshall remained a dominant figure on the Court until about 1825, when his influence began to wane. For almost a quarter of a century, he delivered well over 50 percent of the opinions of the Court, most of them bearing clear marks of his authorship and judicial philosophy.

Marshall's leadership of the Supreme Court was marked by political astuteness and exceptional skill in human relations. When the Court was under attack by a hostile president and Congress, he used jurisdictional holdings as a way to defer decision of cases that might prove inflammatory. Such was the case of *Marbury v. Madison* and *Cherokee Nation v. Georgia*. After Marshall joined the Court there were relatively few original jurisdiction cases involving the states, but there was growing resort to the Court's appellate jurisdiction over state courts construing the Constitution, or federal statutes and treaties entered into pursuant to the Constitution. A substantial portion of the Court's work involved cases arising in the District of Columbia, where no state interests were involved. In these ways, the probability of conflict with state authority was limited, and the Supreme Court became less controversial in a political sense.

Within the Court, Marshall used his skills at human relations to bring his associates into agreement with his view of the Court as the principal institution for interpretation of the Constitution. He was a robust and outgoing person with a quick sense of humor. In Richmond and in Washington he gained a reputation for modesty in dress and behavior, and his female relatives were frequently appalled at his disregard for the fashionable conventions of the day. From his days as a Continental Line officer he exhibited a rare ability to soothe ruffled feelings and compromise arguments. Generous in his treatment of others, he could count as personal friends virtually all who opposed him politically. The single noteworthy exception to this statement was his kinsman, Thomas Jefferson, who suspected Marshall of a malevolent and calculating disposition toward him and his policies. While the chief justice was not unaware of these feelings, he joined a group of subscribers pledged to raise money for Jefferson's support in the last years of his life.

Marshall's correspondence with Joseph Story and his concern for the health of Justices Bushrod Washington and Gabriel Duvall demonstrate his involvement in the well-being of his colleagues. This extended to Henry Baldwin, a Jacksonian appointee plagued with fits of insanity during his service on the Marshall Court. Both Baldwin and Jefferson's first appointee, the fiery William Johnson, were treated with tolerance and respect. Despite serious health problems in the last five years of his life, the chief justice continued to carry out his duties, fearing that President Jackson would undo much of his work through the appointment of his successor.

Marshall left to the United States Supreme Court a legacy of respect and stature that ensured its continuance as a major institution in American life. His constitutional law articulated clear principles of federal supremacy and laid the legal foundation for economic prosperity and growth in the decades before the Civil War. In thirty-four years on the Supreme Court bench he succeeded in erecting a structure for constitutional government that would dominate the Court's work until at least the Civil War, and in many cases, well beyond.

—HERBERT A. JOHNSON

BIBLIOGRAPHY

Marshall's papers are being published in Herbert A. Johnson, Charles T. Cullen, and Charles Hobson, eds., *The Papers of John Marshall* (1974–) 6 vols. to date.

The classic biography is Albert J. Beveridge, *The Life of John Marshall* (4 vols., 1916–1919). A more recent biography is Leonard Baker, *John Marshall: A Life in Law* (1974), which provides a good readable description of his life and activities. Francis N. Stites, *John Marshall: Defender of the Constitution* (1981), is a brief, readable survey of Marshall's life with a helpful selective bibliography.

Two volumes of the Holmes Devise cover the Marshall era, George L. Haskins and Herbert A. Johnson, *Foundations of Power: John Marshall, 1801–1815* (1981), and G. Edward White, *The Marshall Court and Cultural Change, 1815–1835* (1988).

Robert K. Faulkner, *The Jurisprudence of John Marshall* (1968), is the definitive treatment of Marshall's judicial philosophy, while Robert L. Clinton, *"Marbury v. Madison" and Judicial Review* (1989), is a revisionist study of *Marbury*, tracing the historical development of the modern concept of judicial review from Marshall's perception of the doctrine.

THURGOOD MARSHALL

BORN 2 July 1908, Baltimore, Maryland

NOMINATED to the Court 13 June 1967
by Lyndon B. Johnson

TOOK seat 2 October 1967; retired
27 June 1991

DIED 24 January 1993 in Washington, D.C.

President Lyndon Johnson appointed Thur–good Marshall to the Supreme Court because, in Johnson's words, it was "the right thing to do, the right time to do it, the right man and the right place." Marshall was the first African American to sit on the Supreme Court. His nomination came at the right time because by 1967, the Democratic party's commitment to civil rights required representation of African Americans in high office. Marshall was the right man not only because he had been the strategist of the legal challenge to school segregation that culminated in *Brown v. Board of Education* (1954), and was the nation's most prominent African-American lawyer, but also because he was committed to the implementation, through constitutional law, of the Great Society vision.

When Marshall arrived at the Court, he joined a solid liberal majority that shared that vision. The Court's composition changed rapidly, though, and Marshall spent most of his career on the Court holding up the banner of a vision about which the nation had become increasingly skeptical.

After graduating from Lincoln University in Pennsylvania, Marshall enrolled in Howard University's law school, from which he graduated first in the class of 1933. Dean Charles Hamilton Houston of Howard took Marshall as a protégé, and Marshall referred throughout his life to the lessons Houston taught him. For Houston, law was a method of social engineering. He urged his students to work through law to improve the legal and social conditions of the African-American community.

Marshall became the leader among African-American lawyers because he took Houston's message to heart. After a brief attempt to sus-tain a private practice in Depression-racked Baltimore, Marshall moved to New York in 1936, where he joined Houston on the staff of the National Association for the Advancement of Colored People (NAACP). In 1939, after Houston left New York, Marshall became the NAACP's chief lawyer, a position he held until 1961. Marshall was one of the NAACP's leading speakers and organizers, but his main contribution came through his work as a lawyer.

The NAACP's legal staff grew from two when Marshall joined it to around a dozen when he left. Marshall's responsibilities as a manager made it difficult for him to sustain his work as a trial lawyer, but his early experience at trials gave him a sense, which infused his work as a judge as well, of how the abstract legal rules appellate judges define actually work in the courtroom. Marshall also was the NAACP's leading appellate advocate. He developed a casual and informal style of argument that worked quite effectively before courts, like the Supreme Court in the late 1940s and 1950s, that were inclined Marshall's way but needed assurance that the course he wanted to pursue was acceptable both legally and morally. When he argued against school segregation in *Brown v. Board of Education*, his conversational style contrasted dramatically, and favorably, with the more oratorical style of his great adversary, John W. Davis. And, even when the Court rejected Marshall's argument for rapid desegregation in its decision on the appropriate remedy in *Brown II* (1955), his insistence that constitutional rights were "present and personal" made the justices appropriately uncomfortable with their own actions.

In 1961, President John F. Kennedy appointed Marshall to the court of appeals for the second circuit, where he served four years. In 1965, President Lyndon Johnson named Marshall solicitor general, intending to elevate him to the Supreme Court when the opportunity arose. Two years later, Johnson created a vacancy on the Court by appointing Ramsey Clark attorney general, which led Tom Clark, Ramsey's father, to retire from the Court.

Marshall arrived at the Supreme Court when it was in the full flush of the Warren Court's liberal activism. Like most new justices, though, Marshall did not write many significant opinions in his first years on the Court. By the time Marshall had enough seniority, the Court's composition had changed: President Richard Nixon's four appointments destroyed the powerful liberal coalition and, although occasionally a majority could be knit together for a liberal result, Marshall's abilities were not those of a coalition builder. His main contributions to constitutional law thus came in his dissents. The Court's further transformation in the 1980s simply reinforced this situation.

In *Stanley v. Georgia* (1969), for example, Marshall wrote an opinion drawing together free speech and privacy concerns to find it unconstitutional to punish a person for possessing obscene material in his home. In sympathetic hands, Marshall's analysis might have led the Court to ban all regulation of obscene materials, but when the Court confronted the fundamental free speech question in 1973, a new conservative majority allowed local communities to apply their own standards to suppress obscenity; Marshall was, of course, among the four dissenters.

For most of Marshall's tenure, his colleagues respected him for the role he had played in making constitutional law with the NAACP, and for the unique perspective he brought to the Court. Their respect, however, did not translate into making Marshall influential within the Court. His contributions to the Constitution took the form, first, of his work with the NAACP and, second, of the public and academic reception of his dissents.

Marshall's jurisprudence embraced Houston's belief that law was a method of social engineering, but without the scientific or systematic overtones that Houston's term has. Rather, Marshall approached legal problems with a practical orientation born of his experience as a lawyer. For him, legal issues were practical problems of social organization, and the right legal answers were those that provided the most sensible solutions to the problems. Marshall's experience led him to rely not on expert advice, but on his own judgment to determine what the most sensible

solution was. In *Powell v. Texas* (1968), for example, Marshall rejected the position, advanced by most liberals of the time, that alcoholism was a disease that could not be punished through the criminal process. He was skeptical about the claims made on behalf of experts in a rather thin record but, more important, he emphasized that, as society was then organized, no real solution to the problem of public drunkenness seemed available except through the admittedly unattractive use of police to help alcoholics "dry out."

Another early decision, and its ultimate fate, illustrates Marshall's jurisprudence and place on the Court. The NAACP's lawyers had struggled for years to eliminate racial discrimination by private parties like homeowners and restaurant operators. Their constitutional claims were impeded by the state action doctrine, which required some participation by state officials in enforcing discrimination before the discrimination became unconstitutional. Marshall had argued one of the Court's restrictive covenant cases, and his argument in *Shelley v. Kraemer* (1948) drew on his insistence that the Constitution had to take social reality into account. As a justice, Marshall found "state action" in the activities of operators of modern shopping malls, which he described as the modern equivalents of Main Street in *Amalgamated Food Employees v. Logan Valley Plaza* (1968). The opinion made social reality the basis for what Marshall regarded as sensible constitutional law. Again, however, the Court's new majority first undermined the decision in *Lloyd Corp. v. Tanner* (1972) and then formally overruled it in *Hudgens v. NLRB* (1976).

Marshall's pragmatism led him to develop his most enduring contribution to constitutional law, the "sliding scale" approach to equal protection cases. The Court's majority purported to follow a rigid scheme in which the crucial step involved classifying a challenged statute as implicating either a fundamental right or a suspect class; if the statute involved either, it was almost always held unconstitutional. According to Marshall, that approach failed to appreciate the way in which rights and classifications could interact: The practical and normative impact of a statute that involved a not-quite-suspect class *and* a

Thurgood Marshall
Photograph by Joseph Lavenburg, National Geographic Society.
Collection of the Supreme Court of the United States.

not-quite-fundamental right, Marshall argued, could be as problematic as the statutes the Court's majority regularly held unconstitutional. Rather than using a rigid classifying approach to equal protection cases, Marshall argued, the Court should balance the severity of the statute's impact on groups and on rights against the goals government was trying to promote. Although the Court purported to reject Marshall's approach, some of its decisions are best understood as adopting it, as, for example, in *City of Cleburne v. Cleburne Living Center* (1985). Academic commentators almost uniformly believe that Marshall's approach is sounder than the majority's.

Marshall's "sliding scale" or balancing approach allowed him to incorporate his sensitivity to the practical impact of law, particularly its impact on the poor, into constitutional law. When the Court upheld a fifty-dollar filing fee for bankruptcy cases in *United States v. Kras* (1973), Marshall objected to Justice Blackmun's casual suggestion that it would be relatively easy for poor people to raise that sum: "No one who has had close contact with poor people can fail to understand how close to the margin of survival many of them are." Suggesting that the Court would not uphold "compulsory visits to all American homes for the purpose of discovering child abuse," Marshall dissented from a decision allowing social workers to make unannounced searches of welfare recipients' residences in *Wyman v. James* (1971). He objected to the Court's use of a "relentlessly formalistic catechism" to uphold Congress's denial of funding for abortions to women receiving Medicaid, noting that the denial had "a devastating impact on the lives and health of poor women" (*Harris v. McRae*, 1981).

Most of Marshall's career with the NAACP had been devoted to attempts to persuade the Court that race discrimination pervaded society, but could be eliminated through law. He continued that effort as a justice, even as the Court's conservative majority became skeptical about both parts of the argument. Dissenting from the majority's refusal to find unconstitutional a city's decision to close a street through an exclusively white neighborhood to keep out "undesirable

traffic," Marshall applied what he called "a dab of common sense" to explain why the decision was discriminatory in *City of Memphis v. Greene* (1981). His experience as a member of a racial minority allowed him to explain why race discrimination could persist even in communities with a majority of racial minorities: "Successful" members of minority groups, he wrote, "frequently respond to discrimination . . . by attempting to disassociate themselves from the group," but the point of the anti-discrimination doctrine was to avoid "broad overgeneralizations concerning minority groups" (*Casteneda v. Partida*, 1977).

Marshall's concern for individual rights might have posed a problem for him in affirmative action cases. Adhering to a Great Society notion of affirmative action, Marshall consistently voted to uphold affirmative action programs. His opinions, though, endorsed affirmative action as a remedy for prior discrimination, not as a means of allocating social benefits to minority groups. He was, of course, more willing than the Court's majority to find that past discrimination continued to affect present conditions. But he always connected affirmative action to discrimination.

Marshall's affirmative action opinions also contain a second theme. After the Court held segregation unconstitutional, it gave state governments time to work out programs to eliminate segregation. The Court, in short, deferred to the judgment of local authorities as they tried to respond to what they, and the Court, understood to be a difficult social problem. Marshall saw affirmative action in much the same way: It too was a difficult social problem, and local authorities should be given substantial leeway in developing their responses. Thus, although Marshall never suggested that the Constitution required governments to adopt affirmative action programs, he always voted to uphold the programs they did adopt.

Great Society liberalism generally had a strongly nationalizing impulse and, despite Marshall's willingness to defer to legislatures in the affirmative action area, his experience made him skeptical of "states' rights" claims made to insulate local governments from national regulation. He was an active supporter of the War-ren Court's innovations in constitutional crimi-nal procedure, one of his earliest opinions being one of the Court's important decisions applying Bill of Rights guarantees to the states in *Benton v. Maryland* (1969). These decisions imposed national standards of police conduct and over-rode claims that states should be free to develop their own approaches to law enforcement. In Marshall's eyes, local police practices were too often directed at racial and economic minorities. Marshall dissented in *Florida v. Bostwick* (1991) when the Court upheld the practice of "working the buses," where police officers board buses and "request" permission to search passengers' be-longings. For Marshall, the practice did not give the people who used buses any real choices; they tended to be people who could not afford trains or airplanes, and Marshall's opinion suggested that, as in the bankruptcy filing fee case, the majority failed to understand what it was like to be relatively poor. The theme he sounded in criminal procedure cases was the demand for a realistic appreciation of what one observer said Marshall's questions to lawyers asked for, "what really happens between the cops and a criminal suspect in a squad car, or the way social work-ers really treat welfare clients."

Marshall drew on his life's experience when he became, along with Justice William Brennan, one of two justices who argued that capital pun-ishment violated the Constitution's ban on cruel and unusual punishments. As a practicing law-yer, he had represented defendants executed for capital crimes, and he always believed that, be-cause "death is so lasting," even a small risk of error was intolerable.

His analysis of the constitutional question had two elements. First, as he argued in *Furman v. Georgia* (1972), capital punishment no longer served any acceptable social purpose. Retribu-tion, which he called "vengeance," was simply an appeal to "our baser selves." No convincing case for the death penalty's deterrent effect had been made out. And, in an approach that re-vealed the importance Marshall gave to experi-ence, he argued that the death penalty was "mor-ally unacceptable to the people of the United States," despite widespread legislative approval of capital punishment. The reason for that judg-ment, Marshall explained, was that "people who were fully informed as to the purposes of the penalty and its liabilities" would find it "shock-ing, unjust, and unacceptable." An important component of this judgment, to Marshall, was the fact that the death penalty "falls upon the poor, the ignorant, and the underprivileged mem-bers of society," who find it difficult to get their voices heard in legislatures. For Marshall, the courts—staffed by people experienced in law, as he was—were the places that these people could get a fair hearing.

The second element in Marshall's approach to the death penalty also relied on his experience, this time as a lawyer who knew how the law was actually administered. After the Court allowed states to reinstitute capital punishment, Mar-shall's dissents regularly pointed out how unfair-ness infected capital trials. His most astringent comments were reserved for the question of competency of counsel. When in *Strickland v. Washington* (1984), the Court adopted a strict test for determining when counsel's performance was unconstitutionally ineffective, requiring that the lawyer's performance had to be both well below what professional norms required *and* prejudicial to the defendant, Marshall com-mented, "How under the sun can a deficient performance not register in the defense?"

Marshall was a Great Society liberal in an-other way. Although he was not sympathetic to claims by local governments, he did try to insu-late some intermediate institutions—those stand-ing between individuals and governments—from government regulation. This was a part of the Great Society's institutional settlement in which such intermediate groups, through bargaining in a pluralist political system, could shape public policy and thereby become committed to the existing order.

Labor unions were among the most impor-tant of these intermediate institutions, at least in the ideological universe of Great Society liber-als. Marshall tended to support the power of centralized labor unions against challenges from individual members. Perhaps most dramatically, he wrote the Court's opinion in *Emporium Capwell Co. v. Western Addition Community*

Organization (1975), finding no violation of federal labor law when an employer fired four African-American workers who had created a minority caucus outside their union, and tried to bargain with the employer. Marshall's opinion argued that separate bargaining would "divid[e workers] along racial or other lines," thereby reducing the bargaining power of all workers.

Marshall's concern for preserving the authority of intermediate groups was also expressed when he became the Court's liberal specialist in Native American law. His opinions regularly sought to insulate Native American populations from state regulation, and developed standards for interpreting federal law that, while conceding the *power* of the national government to do whatever it wanted with respect to those populations, routinely found that Congress had not tried to exercise its power in a way that severely undermined them. Again, a case lying at the intersection of concern for intermediate groups and attention to minority interests shows Marshall's concerns more clearly. *Santa Clara Pueblo v. Martinez* (1978) involved a rule defining membership in the pueblo, which had significant consequences for a person's entitlement to federal benefits, in a way that discriminated against women. Marshall's opinion for the Court refused to find that Congress, in enacting the 1968 Indian Civil Rights Act, meant to allow lawsuits in federal court to challenge such rules. The challenger's only remedy, Marshall said, was within the Native American system of courts.

That Marshall implemented the liberal vision associated with President Johnson's Great Society does not mean, therefore, that he adhered to positions taken by those labeled "leading liberals" in the media. He supported Johnson in the Vietnam War, for example, at one point issuing an extraordinary order dissolving a stay Justice William O. Douglas had issued against continued bombing of Cambodia in *Schlesinger v. Holtzman* (1973). Marshall was also more skeptical than some liberals about some versions of affirmative action as they developed in the 1980s, and never found black nationalists like Malcolm X attractive.

Great Society liberalism, though, might be acceptable as a political vision but not as a constitutional one. The most basic criticism of Marshall's approach to constitutional law emerged in the dialogue between him and the Court's majority over the choice between the majority's rigid approach to equal protection law and Marshall's "sliding scale" approach. Proponents of the majority's approach argued that some rigidity was essential to confine judicial discretion; otherwise, judges who "balanced" competing interests would both duplicate what occurred in the political branches and enact their own policy preferences into constitutional law. Similarly, critics were concerned about Marshall's insistence on a "realistic" appreciation of what happened outside the Court; some degree of abstraction, they argued, was necessary because each judge's assessment of what "really" happened would be shaped by his or her personal perspective, an inadequate basis on which to rest constitutional law.

Precisely because Marshall did not find it important to work out in general terms an overall approach to constitutional law, he never addressed these concerns directly. His deep commitment to his realistic and pragmatic approach, though, showed that he rejected these arguments. Here too he relied on his experience. For Marshall, perhaps judges whose careers had been confined to the academy or to elite law practice might not truly understand how constitutional law operated in police stations or welfare offices. Marshall, though, was not such a judge. His career had carried him from a struggling private practice, to trial and appellate work in ordinary cases and in celebrated constitutional ones, to the solicitor general's office where he had an overview of the federal government's litigation, to the Supreme Court. And, of course, unlike any of his colleagues, he had lived the life of an African American in a racially divided society. His range of experience gave him confidence in his assessment of reality. His confidence was bolstered, as well, by the trajectory of his career, not just by the range of his experience. As Marshall saw it, he had succeeded as a lawyer and judge because, at each stage in his career, his judgment had been vindicated—for example, when the Supreme Court held segregation unconstitutional and when President Johnson selected him for the Supreme Court.

Marshall's approach to constitutional adjudication thus fit comfortably with his sense of himself and his career. An open and friendly man who found it difficult to have harsh words with or say harsh words about people he worked with, Marshall tried to treat his colleagues on the Court as if they ought to have the same degree of confidence in their ability to exercise sound judgment, to develop sensible solutions to the practical problems that law presented, as he had in his own ability. Within the Court, even those who consistently voted to reject Marshall's positions said that they respected the experience he brought to the conference table. Still, Marshall may not have appreciated, though, that his colleagues, however much they respected him for his achievements, might not be willing to base the edifice of constitutional law solely on the sound good sense of whoever happened to be the justices of the Supreme Court.

For all the misgivings critics might have about directing judges with less experience and generosity of spirit simply to exercise good judgment in making constitutional law, Marshall's career as a practicing lawyer and as a justice does exemplify how far good judgment can take a person.

—MARK TUSHNET

BIBLIOGRAPHY

The Marshall papers are in the Library of Congress, and were opened shortly after the justice's death. Mark Tushnet, *Making Civil Rights Law: Thurgood Marshall and the Supreme Court, 1936–1961* (1993), deals with Marshall's career with the NAACP. Roger Goldman with David Gallen, *Thurgood Marshall: Justice For All* (1992), is a compilation of tributes to Marshall, with an essay on and excerpts from his opinions.

For examinations of his opinions on specific subjects, see Victor Kramer, "The Road to *City of Berkeley*: The Antitrust Positions of Justice Thurgood Marshall," 32 *Antitrust Bulletin* 335 (1987); Mark Tushnet, "Change and Continuity in the Concept of Civil Rights: Thurgood Marshall and Affirmative Action," 8 *Social Philosophy & Policy* 150 (1991); Jonathan Weinberg, "Thurgood Marshall and the Administrative State," 38 *Wayne Law Review* 115 (1991); and Tracey Maclin, "Justice Thurgood Marshall: Taking the Fourth Amendment Seriously," 77 *Cornell Law Review* 723 (1992).

STANLEY MATTHEWS

BORN 21 July 1824, Lexington, Kentucky
NOMINATED to the Court 14 March 1881
     by James A. Garfield
TOOK seat 17 May 1881
DIED 22 March 1889 in Washington, D.C.

Even the most conventional public figures of the past century occasionally led lives of color and seeming paradox. An antislavery Democrat in Cincinnati in the 1840s, Stanley Matthews was by 1858 a federal district attorney responsible for the prosecution of violators of the Fugitive Slave Act; a Union veteran of the Civil War, he was a key author of the Compromise of 1877, which handed the presidency to his friend, Rutherford B. Hayes, in return for the removal of federal troops from the South; a devout Presbyterian, Matthews opposed religious instruction in public schools; an eminent Republican railroad attorney, as senator from Ohio he favored inflation of the currency and opposed the Chinese Exclusion Act.

One biographer thus found in Matthews "an unusual combination of liberal and conservative premises," yet neither Matthews nor his generally admiring contemporaries found inconsistencies in his views or rulings. Progressive writers have charged Matthews and the other bearded and remote legal figures of the age with manipulating judicial formalism—rigid reliance on precedent and deduction from vague natural law assumptions—in order to prevent reform. Recent scholarship has argued that judges of the era across the political spectrum sought to preserve the existing social order against transformation by the forces of industrialism and political upheaval.

Matthews stands as preeminently a representative of classical legal consciousness, committed to controlling change through the careful definition of spheres of private rights and public powers. Matthews sketched no alternatives to the course of industrial policy or civil rights, voting with the majority to extend Fourteenth Amendment protection to corporations in *Santa Clara County v. Southern Pacific Railroad* (1886), to expand their protection from state regulation in *Wabash, St. Louis and Pacific Railroad Co. v. Illinois* (1886), and to thwart congressional power to oppose racial discrimination in the *Civil Rights Cases* (1883).

To modern eyes, Matthews's most important opinions were rendered in *Hurtado v. California* (1884), where he found the grand jury indictment clause of the Fifth Amendment unavailable to defendants in state criminal proceedings, and in *Yick Wo v. Hopkins* (1886), where Matthews held unconstitutional a San Francisco ordinance requiring permits to operate laundries in wooden buildings, because permits were denied to all Chinese applicants, but not to others. Matthews ruled that a facially neutral law "administered by public authority with an evil eye and an unequal hand" violated equal protection.

It is emblematic of both Matthews's time and his place in it that his most celebrated opinion policed the boundaries of state power and read the common law to defeat the threat of economic turmoil. In *Poindexter v. Greenhow* (1885), Matthews ruled that states lacked authority to repudiate their debts under the contract clause, and that while the Eleventh Amendment protected the states themselves from suits challenging repudiation, state officials could be sued for trying to enforce such illegal acts.

Precisely this kind of legalistic distinction without a "realistic" difference, seemingly designed to protect the wealthy, persuaded progressive writers of Matthews's "conservatism," while cases like *Yick Wo* sounded "liberal." On the whole, however, it is Matthews's overall similarity to other and more progressive judges of his era, rather than his particular differences from them, that merits attention.

—ROBERT STANLEY

BIBLIOGRAPHY

The primary biographical source is still Louis Filler, "Stanley Matthews," in Friedman and Israel, 2 *Justices* 1351. The best general introduction to recent interpretive scholarship is

Elizabeth Mensch, "The History of Mainstream Legal Thought," in David Kairys, ed., *The Politics of Law: A Progressive Critique* (2d ed., 1990). The most fully developed interpretive departure is Charles W. McCurdy, "Justice Field and the Jurisprudence of Government-Business Relations: Some Parameters of Laissez-Faire Constitutionalism, 1863–1897," in Lawrence M. Friedman and Harry N. Scheiber, eds., *American Law and the Constitutional Order* (1978).

SAMUEL FREEMAN MILLER

BORN 5 April 1816, Richmond, Kentucky

NOMINATED to the Court 16 July 1862
   by Abraham Lincoln

TOOK seat 21 July 1862

DIED 13 October 1890 in Washington, D.C.

Justice Samuel Freeman Miller arrived on the Supreme Court bench in 1862, strongly endorsed by his fellow Iowa Republicans, but without any formal legal training or previous experience in public office higher than justice of the peace and member of the county court in his native Kentucky. Despite this seeming lack of proper credentials, Miller's strength of character, strong pragmatic bent, aggressiveness, analytical ability, and enormous faith in his own intellect proved him worthy of the nation's high bench. Chief Justice Salmon P. Chase labeled this Lincoln appointee the Supreme Court's "dominant personality." During his twenty-eight years of service, Miller wrote 616 opinions, more than any previous Supreme Court justice. Miller would leave his mark on American constitutional law, most notably in his construction of the Fourteenth Amendment.

Law was the second career choice for Miller. He attended medical school at Transylvania University at Lexington, graduated in 1838, then served as a country doctor for about ten years. He had married Lucy Ballinger and established a family before his avid participation in the Barbourville debate club convinced him that law and politics suited him better than medicine. Miller read law and passed the bar exam in 1847. He left Kentucky in 1850, persuaded that his abolitionist tendencies would be more acceptable elsewhere. He relocated in Keokuk, Iowa, where he joined a prominent law firm and quickly became one of the area's leading attorneys. A former Whig, Miller joined the Republican party at its inception and worked hard for its success, although he was unsuccessful in his bid for state senator in 1856 and passed over for party nomination for governor in 1861. A strong Lincoln man, Miller was unknown outside Iowa. Reor-

ganization of the federal judicial circuits after the Civil War broke out, however, fostered his chances for appointment to the Supreme Court. He had little competition west of the Mississippi River. Fellow Iowans lobbied intensely for Miller's appointment; their efforts paid off when Lincoln chose Miller as the first Supreme Court justice appointed from west of the Mississippi to represent the newly created ninth circuit, the first circuit which lay entirely west of the Mississippi. Lincoln's faith in Miller was rewarded by strong support for the president's war efforts.

Miller's conduct on the bench during the Civil War was strongly nationalistic. He voted with the 5–4 majority in the *Prize Cases* (1863), for example, to uphold the constitutionality of Lincoln's blockade of southern ports. This opinion, perhaps the most significant of the cases approving Lincoln's wartime policies, enabled the government to treat the war as a conventional war for purposes of foreign policy while continuing to maintain that it was an insurrection for purposes at home. Miller went along with the Court's refusal to interfere with the wartime suspension of *habeas corpus* and military trials for civilians. When the fighting was over and the danger to the Union was past, however, he joined a belated censure of the wartime military trials in *Ex parte Milligan* (1866). But where the majority decided that neither the president nor Congress had authority to authorize military trials of civilians when the civilian courts were open, Miller agreed with a concurring opinion which stated that Congress possessed such power, but had not used it.

Miller's early postwar record demonstrated a similar regard for governmental authority which was often at odds with his judicial brethren. When 5–4 majorities found in *Ex parte Garland* (1867) and *Cummings v. Missouri* (1867) that federal and state required test oaths violated the Constitution as *ex post facto* laws and bills of attainder, Miller dissented. He insisted that the oath was not a punishment but simply another requirement for the privilege of practicing law or serving as a minister. It was absurd to Miller that in one case the Court found the Constitution "to confer no power on Congress to prevent traitors practicing in her courts, while in the other it is held to confer power on this court to nullify a provision of the Constitution of the State of Missouri, relating to a qualification required of ministers of religion." In Miller's estimation, the court had clearly overstepped the bounds of judicial review.

Miller registered a biting dissent against the majority's tender regard for the property rights of creditors in *Hepburn v. Griswold* (1870), another 5–4 decision. The issue was the constitutionality of paper money or "greenbacks" as legal tender. Invoking the "spirit" of the contract clause, which in fact restrains the states rather than the federal government, Chief Justice Chase found greenbacks unconstitutional for repayment of debts contracted prior to the law. The Legal Tender Act also violated the Fifth Amendment, according to Chase, as a deprivation of property without due process of law. Miller, on the other hand, was convinced that the Constitution granted Congress ample power to define and regulate the money supply. He stressed wartime necessity and opposed "substituting a court of justice for the National Legislature."

Within fifteen months, Miller's dissenting opinion became constitutional law when *Knox v. Lee* (1871) overturned *Hepburn*. President Grant appointed William Strong and Joseph Bradley to the court on the same day that the first legal tender decision was announced. Thus a new majority favorable to administration policy reopened the issue with Miller, as he put it to his brother-in-law, serving "as leader in marshalling my forces, and keeping up their courage against a domineering Chief, and a party in court who have been accustomed to carry everything their own way." Miller's aggressiveness and determination paid off in the second legal tender decision written by Strong.

Miller's reaction to congressional Reconstruction policies contrasted sharply to his nationalistic support for the war effort. For its initial interpretation of the rights of citizens under the Fourteenth Amendment, the Supreme Court chose, ironically, a case which involved white butchers rather than the former slaves. That the Fourteenth Amendment had made some changes

in the rights of citizenship seemed clear, but its precise meaning was surrounded with uncertainty. What changes, if any, had the amendment made in federal-state relationships? What were the privileges and immunities associated with national citizenship? Did the amendment nationalize the Bill of Rights? The backlog of civil rights cases in the South demanded answers to these tough questions, but the Supreme Court refused to address the issues in Enforcement Act cases, and chose the *Slaughterhouse Cases* (1873) instead. Why so strange a choice? The justices of the Supreme Court obviously recognized that precedent made in these cases would hold enormous implications for the civil and political rights of the freedmen. It seems safe to argue, therefore, that the Court deliberately chose a case which would depoliticize the explosive legal questions involved. The butchers' case enabled the high court to decide some of the controversial issues regarding Reconstruction without seeming to decide them at all. If the *Slaughterhouse Cases* were about white butchers, they nevertheless foredoomed the establishment of a broad nationalization of rights for black Americans.

The carpetbag government of Louisiana had established a monopoly of butchers in New Orleans. Although the law would ordinarily fall under the police powers of the state, the other butchers sued on the grounds that it violated the Thirteenth and Fourteenth Amendments. John A. Campbell, a former Supreme Court justice who had resigned to follow his state into the Confederacy, argued that the state monopoly was a form of servitude outlawed by the Thirteenth Amendment. More important, it violated the "privileges and immunities" guaranteed to citizens by the Fourteenth—the right to follow the vocation of one's choice being one of those privileges.

Miller spoke for a closely split majority. Recognizing that "no questions so far reaching and pervading in their consequences . . . have been before this court during the official life of any of its present members," he quickly rejected the Thirteenth Amendment argument and turned to the Fourteenth. Miller seemed genuinely surprised to think that the Reconstruction amendments, written to benefit blacks, could be con-

Samuel Freeman Miller
Photograph by Handy Studios.
Collection of the Supreme Court of the United States.

strued to uphold the rights of white citizens. But Miller's interpretation of national citizenship gave the former slaves little reason to cheer. This previously nationalistic judge rendered an opinion grounded in traditional notions of dual federalism. National citizenship, for Miller, was separate and distinct from state citizenship. The basic rights of citizenship remained where they had always been, under the protection of the states. Miller listed a number of privileges and immunities he considered a part of national citizenship, most of which were of little use to the freed slaves. The United States could protect its citizens on the high seas and in foreign countries, Miller decided, but not in the states where they lived. That the Fourteenth Amendment was intended "to transfer the security and protection of all the civil rights . . . from the States to the Federal government," he emphatically denied. It was impossible, he thought, that the Congress meant to make such a drastic change in the basic nature of the federal system.

Miller's tortured construction aroused bitter dissent among four of his brethren. Justice Field maintained, for example, that the fundamental rights of citizenship were no longer dependent on citizenship in a state. If the amendment meant no more than the majority said, it had "most unnecessarily excited Congress and the people on its passage." The dissenting opinions recognized what Miller denied, that rights were no longer to be "separate and exclusive" but "complementary and concentric," allowing the federal government to protect the rights of its citizens when the states failed to do so.

Miller may have been willing to sacrifice the rights of the freedmen, as William Gillette has suggested, to preserve the states' right to regulate business, thus postponing judicial support for big business. Letters to his brother-in-law indicate, however, that Miller was no proponent of equality for blacks. While he was unwilling to leave the freedmen to the tender mercies of the former Confederates, he feared that Republican Reconstruction policy risked "the eventual destruction of some of the best principles of our existing constitution." Miller's opinion in *Slaughterhouse* went a long way to preserve the "existing constitution." If Miller's opinion postponed federal protection for vested property rights, the dissenting opinions of Bradley and Field embraced substantive due process and the laissez-faire principles which pointed the court's way to the future.

United States v. Cruikshank (1876) reiterated the principles of *Slaughterhouse* in terms of rights for black citizens. Miller voted with the majority in a case involving a massacre of some 100 blacks in Louisiana. Following Miller's logic in *Slaughterhouse*, Chief Justice Waite stated that people must "look to the states" to protect their individual rights. The Fourteenth Amendment had added "nothing to the rights of one citizen as against another." The Supreme Court had allowed the narrow interpretation of national citizenship in *Slaughterhouse* to circumscribe the meaning of the amendment for those people for whom it was intended to bestow all the benefits of citizenship.

In the *Civil Rights Cases* (1883), the Court once again employed a constricted view of the Fourteenth Amendment. At issue was the constitutionality of the Civil Rights Act of 1875, which attempted to secure equality of social rights, including equal access to privately owned public facilities. Since there was no state action—no discriminatory state law—the national government had no right to intervene. "Individual invasion of individual rights," Justice Bradley insisted for the majority, "is not the subject of the amendment." The law was clearly unconstitutional, according to this interpretation. Consistent with his interpretation of Fourteenth Amendment in *Slaughterhouse*, Miller voted with the majority in these cases, as well as in *Cruikshank*.

While the conduct of Justice Miller and the Supreme Court in the area of civil rights is disappointing by today's standards, it should be noted that very few Americans were committed to genuine equality for black people during the Reconstruction era. Although the Republican majority in Congress provided amendments and laws sufficient to establish a broad nationalization of civil and political rights, they failed to follow up with the necessary funds to finance the increased caseload in the lower federal courts and the military force necessary to subdue the recalcitrant South. After the election of 1874 returned a Democratic majority to Congress, signaling that the American people had grown weary of the never ending racial problems in the southern states, federal Reconstruction efforts were in full retreat. Whether the Supreme Court led that retreat beginning with the *Slaughterhouse Cases*, or merely followed the lead of the legislative branch, it is too much to expect that the third branch of government with no powers of enforcement could establish the full citizenship of the four million freed people.

If Miller's estimation of the Fourteenth Amendment was disappointing, he displayed a stronger regard for the voting rights of blacks. He went along with the Court in *United States v. Reese* (1876), deciding that the Fifteenth Amendment did not grant freedmen the right to vote but rather the right not to be discriminated against in the franchise on the grounds of race. The case struck down two sections of the Enforcement Act of 1870, but nevertheless suggested that the federal government had power to prosecute both state officials and private individuals who interfered with the suffrage on grounds of race.

Ex parte Yarbrough (1884) marked a resounding victory for the voting rights of black Americans. The case involved conspiracy to deprive a black citizen of the franchise on account of race. Speaking for the majority, Miller construed the Fifteenth Amendment broadly and then went on to hold that neither the case nor the Enforcement Act depended on the Fifteenth Amendment, which forbid only those denials of the franchise which were because of race. Congressional authority to protect voters in national elections derived from Article I. "If this government is anything more than a mere aggregation of delegated agents of other States and governments, each of which is superior to the general government," Miller ruled, "it must have the power to protect the elections on which its existence depends from violence and corruption." Congress had broad powers to protect blacks in federal elections against both private persons and state officials; since state and local elections were generally held at the same time, the power extended to state elections, as well. It was a decision worthy of Miller's Civil War nationalism.

As one of the Republican justices to serve on the electoral commission to settle the disputed presidential election of 1876, Miller had a part in bringing about the official end of Reconstruction. Like all the other participants, he voted his party preference, giving Rutherford B. Hayes a majority of one in the commission and securing the presidency for the Republican party.

Outside the arena of civil rights, Miller withstood the efforts of big business and his judicial brethren to write laissez-faire economic theory into constitutional law through the Fourteenth Amendment. He had turned a deaf ear to the substantive due process arguments in *Slaughterhouse*, preserving the states' right to regulate. Otherwise, he noted, the Court would become a "perpetual censor" of state legislation. The Supreme Court held firm in the Granger cases. Miller voted with the majority to allow state regulation of railroads and grain elevators, establishing a public interest doctrine in *Munn v. Illinois* (1877). But Chief Justice Waite conceded even in *Munn* that "under some circumstances" a state regulatory statute might be so arbitrary as to be unconstitutional. Such a concession was all that business needed to keep pounding the Court with a substantive reading of the due process clause. Miller complained in *Davidson v. New Orleans* (1877) that the Supreme Court docket was "crowded with cases in which we are asked to hold that state courts and state legislatures have deprived their own citizens of life, liberty, or property without due process of law." This "strange misconception of the scope of this provision" of the Fourteenth Amendment soon overtook the justices. Miller fought a losing battle. If his initial construction had postponed the protection of vested interests through the Fourteenth Amendment, the Supreme Court had by 1886 made corporations "persons" entitled to equal protection under the amendment intended to protect the citizenship rights of black Americans. And shortly before Miller's death in 1890, the Court expressly adopted substantive due process, with Miller concurring.

Miller made a similar stand against judicial protection of vested interest in a long line of dissenting opinions in state and municipal bond repudiation cases beginning with *Gelpcke v. Dubuque* (1864). However valid the grounds for repudiation seemed to state courts, the nation's high court generally held that a contract, once made, could not be broken. Miller, however, was unwilling to make the taxpayers suffer for the wrong judgement of their officials. He thought that state law should be construed by the state courts. It was a "painful matter," Miller complained in a letter to his brother-in-law, that these cases compelled him "to take part in a farce whose result is invariably the same, namely to give more to those who have already, and to take away from those who have little, the little that they have." Miller spoke for the majority for a change when *Loan Association v. Topeka* (1875) invalidated a Kansas law which authorized spending tax money for private purposes.

While the Supreme Court was becoming more deeply entrenched in its determination to protect property rights, it was becoming increasingly apparent to the American people that regulation of big business—and railroads in particular—was necessary at some level of government. Yet the attempts of the various states to regulate intrastate commerce could be seriously detrimental to the smooth flow of interstate commerce. When the constitutionality of an Illinois statute outlawing long haul–short haul rate differentials was before the Court in *Wabash v. Illinois* (1886), Miller seized the opportunity to sound a clear call for national regulation. Speaking for the majority in one of his most important decisions, Miller struck down the state law as a violation of the commerce clause. Refusing to speak to the "justice or propriety" of the Illinois regulation, Miller maintained that "regulation can only appropriately exist by general rules and principles, which demand that it should be done by Congress of the United States under the commerce clause." Miller's exhortation led directly to the Interstate Commerce Act of 1887. That neither the Congress nor the Supreme Court was willing to clothe the Interstate Commerce Commission with enough authority to regulate effectively was not the fault of Samuel Miller.

During his twenty-eight years on the nation's high bench, Justice Miller stood firm for the right of government to govern. He lacked the fear of government action and overriding respect for private property which entrenched his brethren in laissez-faire economic policy. Unfortunately, he stood for the right to regulate at too high a cost to black Americans. Justice Miller left his mark on constitutional law. Although Miller was bitterly disappointed when Grant passed him over for the center seat in 1874, the *Albany Law Journal* labeled him in 1890 "the real chief in any court in which he might have sat."

—LOU FALKNER WILLIAMS

BIBLIOGRAPHY

Charles Fairman, *Mr. Justice Miller and the Supreme Court* (1939), the standard biography of Miller, is a model of careful scholarship, although Fairman's penchant for getting all his information into print often overrides organization and analysis. Fairman also treats Miller extensively in two articles, "Justice Samuel Miller: A Study of a Judicial Statesman," 50 *Political Science Quarterly* 15 (1935), and "Samuel F. Miller, Justice of the Supreme Court." 10 *Vanderbilt Law Review* 193 (1957), as well as the two volumes he wrote for the Holmes Devise, *Reconstruction and Reunion*, parts 1 and 2 (1971, 1987), which is the most exhaustive treatment of the Reconstruction court. For a short biographical sketch, see William Gillette, "Samuel Miller," in Friedman and Israel, 2 *Justices* 1011, an excellent, succinct analysis of the justice and his contribution to the law.

For comparative studies, see Paul Albert Weidner's unpublished dissertation, "Justices Field and Miller: A Comparative Study in Judicial Attitudes and Values" (University of Michigan, 1957), and G. Edward White, "Miller, Bradley, Field, and the Reconstructed Constitution," in *The American Judicial Tradition: Profiles of Leading American Judges* (1988 ed.).

SHERMAN MINTON

BORN 20 October 1890, Georgetown, Indiana

NOMINATED to the Court 15 September 1949
by Harry S Truman

TOOK seat 12 October 1949; retired
15 October 1956

DIED 9 April 1965 in New Albany, Indiana

Sherman Minton, the first Supreme Court justice from Indiana, was President Harry Truman's final appointment to the Court. As a member of the conservative "Truman bloc," led by Chief Justice Fred Vinson, Minton supported the broad exercise of executive and legislative power and approved the restriction of civil liberties in the name of national security. More than any other Truman nominee, however, Minton was ideologically committed to the philosophy of judicial restraint, providing a theoretical grounding for the rulings of his more politically inclined colleagues.

Minton's judicial philosophy grew out of his political experiences during the Great Depression. In 1934, he was elected to the United States Senate, where he befriended another freshman senator, Harry Truman. Minton vigorously supported Franklin Roosevelt's economic policies and when the Supreme Court invalidated New Deal legislation, he harshly attacked the tribunal for substituting its own political judgment for that of Congress. He introduced legislation that would have required the vote of seven justices to declare a federal statute unconstitutional and he championed Roosevelt's Court-packing scheme before a skeptical Senate. In 1940, after Minton lost his bid for reelection, Roosevelt invited his supporter to join the White House staff. Six months later, when a vacancy appeared on the U. S. court of appeals for the seventh circuit, which included Minton's home state, Roosevelt rewarded him with a judicial appointment.

Following Justice Wiley Rutledge's death in 1949, Truman nominated his old friend to the Supreme Court. The nomination followed Truman's pattern of naming political allies to the bench, although in this case the criticism was somewhat muted because Minton had more judicial experience than any of Truman's previous nominees. Perhaps because of a growing concern for judicial professionalism, however, Minton was the last member of Congress to be named to the Court. During the confirmation hearings in the Senate Judiciary Committee, several Republicans questioned Minton's fierce Democratic loyalties while other members wondered whether he could fairly serve on a tribunal that he had so recently criticized. After the committee reported the nomination favorably, the senate voted to confirm, 48–16, with most of the opposition coming from Republicans.

Guided by his frustration with the judicial activism of economic conservatives during the Great Depression, Minton adopted a philosophy of judicial restraint. The duty of the Court, he believed, was simply to determine whether the Constitution granted the political branches the power to enact certain policies, not to judge the wisdom of those policies. Thus Minton adhered strictly to precedent, interpreted statutes and constitutional provisions narrowly, and deferred to the judgment of the other branches. This practice comported with the views of Truman's other appointees—Harold Burton, Tom Clark, and Chief Justice Fred Vinson—and Stanley Reed, who often joined the Truman bloc. These justices, however, used judicial restraint more as a vehicle for political conservatism than as a coherent philosophy of adjudication. Minton was more faithful to the values of Felix Frankfurter, the Court's leading theorist of judicial restraint, although Frankfurter's concern for the independence of the judiciary and his willingness to look beyond the formalistic application of precedent often led him to disagree with Minton.

In addition to professing judicial restraint, Minton also emphasized to his colleagues the importance of acting as a unified deliberative body. He believed that a judicial opinion should reflect the judgment of the Court, not the personal views of its author, and he willingly altered passages in his opinions if another justice threatened to dissent. He disdained concurring opinions, writing only three in his entire career, because they obscured the singular reasoning of the majority. When writing for the majority, Minton ignored countervailing arguments, so that his opinions resembled the advocacy of an appellate attorney more than the jurisprudential musings of a justice like Frankfurter.

Minton's approach to judging was evident in one of his earliest and most controversial opinions, *United States ex rel. Knauff v. Shaughnessy* (1950). Under the authority of a 1941 statute that permitted the executive branch to exclude aliens who posed a security risk, the attorney general prohibited Ellen Knauff, the German-born wife of an American soldier, from entering the country. Knauff claimed that she had been denied due process because the government had not conducted a hearing. Minton held that the president's inherent power to conduct foreign affairs included the authority to exclude aliens, placing those decisions outside the scope of judicial review. *Knauff* not only demonstrated Minton's deference to other branches, particularly when national security issues were involved, it also revealed his cramped view of statutory interpretation. The War Brides Act of 1945 had relaxed the criteria for admitting the alien spouses of American veterans, yet Minton dismissed its relevance because it had not specifically limited the 1941 statute.

Because of his belief that the political branches of government were best equipped to assess national security interests, Minton also upheld the power of Congress and state legislatures to combat subversion by limiting the freedom of expression and association. In *Adler v. Board of Education* (1952), a teacher challenged New York's "Feinberg Law," which permitted school boards to fire teachers for disloyalty if they belonged to certain organizations. Praising the law's goal of shielding children from dangerous ideas, Minton upheld the use of group membership as evidence of disloyalty because "one's reputation [is] determined in part by the company he keeps." He denied that the law infringed on teachers' freedom of association because they were free to choose between public employment or membership in a subversive organization.

Decisions like *Adler* disappointed civil libertarians, especially since Minton had promised

when he joined the Court to "work fiercely for the enforcement of the Bill of Rights." Actually, Minton compiled a libertarian record in free expression cases unrelated to national security issues by supporting the right of speakers to espouse unpopular views without governmental interference. These opinions were the product not only of a genuine concern for First Amendment freedoms but also of a respect for precedents established in the 1930s and 1940s. In *International Brotherhood of Teamsters v. Hanke* (1950), for example, Minton dissented from Frankfurter's majority opinion, which upheld restrictions on labor picketing, because earlier cases had clearly held that picketing was a form of speech protected by the First Amendment.

In criminal procedure cases, however, he permitted the government wide latitude to control criminal behavior. His most important opinion in this area, *United States v. Rabinowitz* (1950), held that the Fourth Amendment's warrant requirement and its prohibition against unreasonable searches were separate provisions, meaning that searches incident to arrest were to be judged by the reasonableness of the search rather than the reasonableness of obtaining a warrant. This ruling overturned a three-year-old precedent that required police officers to obtain search warrants, when practicable, before searching a suspect. Minton also narrowly interpreted the right to counsel, the privilege against self-incrimination, and the availability of federal *habeas corpus* relief for state prisoners. He was especially loath to grant relief when defendants alleged technical errors rather than asserted their innocence.

Minton's deference to legislative judgment did not extend to race relations. He opposed all forms of government-sponsored discrimination, as evidenced by his vigorous support of the school desegregation cases. He considered *Brown v. Board of Education* (1954) to be the most significant case in which he participated. In his majority opinion in *Barrows v. Jackson* (1953), he extended the holding of *Shelley v. Kraemer* (1948), which forbade the judicial enforcement of restrictive covenants, by prohibiting courts from awarding damages to property owners who sued their neighbors for violating restrictive covenants.

Consistent with his judicial philosophy, however, Minton strictly interpreted the Constitution's "state action" doctrine, which limited the application of the Fourteenth and Fifteenth Amendments to discriminatory practices that were directly authorized by state legislatures or government officials. In *Brotherhood of Railroad Trainmen v. Howard* (1952), for example, Justice Hugo Black held that a white union, bargaining under the authority of the Railway Labor Act, could not infringe on the rights of other workers by inducing a railroad to replace black porters with the union's members. Minton's dissent, joined by Vinson and Reed, countered that the union, as a private association, could conduct negotiations in any manner it pleased. Similarly, in a lone dissent in *Terry v. Adams* (1953), he insisted that the preprimary elections conducted by the private Jaybird Democratic Association, which excluded black members, did not constitute state action, even though the Jaybird primary had governed the selection of local Texas leaders for half a century. Private discrimination, however objectionable, could only be forbidden by the courts if the government directly enforced it.

When an anemic condition forced Minton reluctantly to retire, he predicted that "there will be more interest in who will succeed me than in my passing." His remarks were prescient, as he left no judicial legacy. He emerged as a leader of the Truman bloc, forging compromises that fostered the public's image of institutional stability, but his influence waned significantly after Earl Warren became chief justice. His opinions lacked the elegant reasoning that characterizes great jurists. Most important, as a proponent of judicial restraint, he lacked Felix Frankfurter's ability to transcend the more doctrinaire aspects of the philosophy. Minton's jurisprudence sprang from his experience during the New Deal, when activist judges attempted to preserve a laissez-faire economy in the face of massive societal dislocation. By the time Minton reached the Court, however, his approach, particularly his reverence for precedent, deprived him of the opportunity to lead a Court that increasingly employed activist principles to protect individual rights and liberties from governmental interference.

—ERIC W. RISE

BIBLIOGRAPHY

No book-length biography of Justice Minton has been published, but see Elizabeth A. Hull's unpublished dissertation, "Sherman Minton and the Cold War Court" (New School for Social Research, 1977). For an excellent discussion of Minton's career prior to joining the Court, which also examines the origins of his judicial philosophy, see David N. Atkinson, "From New Deal Liberal to Supreme Court Conservative," 1975 *Washington University Law Quarterly* 361. The most comprehensive account of Minton's tenure on the Court, written by one of his law clerks, is Harry L. Wallace, "Mr. Justice Minton—Hoosier Justice on the Supreme Court," 34 *Indiana Law Journal* 145, 377 (1959). While perhaps overly sympathetic to Minton, Wallace ably assesses Minton's contribution to the jurisprudence of the Vinson Court. David Atkinson has published several law review articles examining Minton's views on specific constitutional issues, the most perceptive of which is "Justice Sherman Minton and the Protection of Minority Rights," 34 *Washington and Lee Law Review* 97 (1977). Minton destroyed most of his papers, but a small collection of documents pertaining to opinions that he authored is housed in the Harry S Truman Library in Independence, Missouri.

WILLIAM MOODY

BORN 23 December 1853, Newbury, Massachusetts

NOMINATED to the Court 3 December 1906 by Theodore Roosevelt

TOOK seat on 17 December 1907; resigned 20 November 1910

DIED 2 July 1917 in Haverhill, Massachusetts

Born and raised in Massachusetts's Merrimac valley, Moody excelled at physical, not mental, activity until his third year at Harvard. While he never lost his love of sports—especially baseball—and the outdoor life, Moody became a man of some learning and an aggressive, able lawyer. In 1878, he began practicing corporate law in Haverhill. He soon entered local politics and became a typical Yankee Republican reformer. He was a protégé of Henry Cabot Lodge and through Lodge met Roosevelt. With their backing, he quickly rose politically, serving as a state district attorney (he was one of the prosecutors of Lizzie Borden), federal representative, secretary of the navy, and attorney general. In the latter office, Moody vigorously carried out Roosevelt's policies of punishing "bad" trusts under the Sherman Antitrust Act and rebating railroads under the Elkins Act of 1903. Thus, Roosevelt elevated him to the Court in the hopes of making that body more receptive to the progressives' use of government power.

A key to his jurisprudence is found in his dissent in the *First Employers Liability Case* (1908). In a 5–4 decision, the Court struck down the 1906 Employers' Liability Act, which made all common carriers engaged in interstate commerce liable for injuries sustained at work by their employees. The majority—committed to the theory of dual sovereignty of state and nation—held the law as too broad and as such an interference with the states' right to control intrastate commerce through their police powers. Moody, speaking of the Constitution's commerce clause, wrote, "its unchanging provisions are adaptable to the infinite variety of the changing conditions of our National life." Thus, because "the forces of steam and electricity" had "so wonderfully aided" the development of interstate commerce, it was natural to Moody that the federal commerce power should also modernize to keep pace.

But, like many progressives, Moody did not intend to allow the central government to ride outside of all constitutional limits and obliterate the states. Thus, he supported the states' police power to regulate the economy and daily life. In *Tilt v. Kelsey* (1907), for instance, Moody wrote the opinion which declared the states had the sovereign authority to determine rules for the succession of property upon death. Further, in *Twining v. New Jersey* (1908), Moody wrote the Court's opinion which stated that the Fourteenth Amendment did not extend the Bill of Rights to the states. Moody assumed that state action would be enough to protect liberties; if people thought they did not, they should seek redress at the ballot box and not in the federal courts. Thus, in his brief career on the bench, Moody showed himself a true Rooseveltian progressive.

Illness, however, kept Moody from fulfilling Roosevelt's ambition for him. Almost as soon as he took his seat, rheumatism began to affect Moody, and he only participated in two judicial terms. After 1909, his failing health kept him from attending the sessions. Following Congress's conferring upon him special retirement benefits, he resigned.

—RICHARD F. HAMM

BIBLIOGRAPHY

The Moody papers, dealing mostly with his pre-Court career, are housed at the Library of Congress. James F. Watts, Jr., "William Moody," in Friedman and Israel, 3 *Justices* 1801, is a short but sensitive treatment of Moody's life and Court career.

ALFRED MOORE

BORN 21 May 1755, Brunswick County,
North Carolina

NOMINATED to the Court 4 December 1799
by John Adams

TOOK seat 21 April 1800; retired
26 January 1804

DIED 15 October 1810 in Bladen County,
North Carolina

Alfred Moore is among the least-known justices ever to sit on the Supreme Court, and his lack of notoriety is well deserved. Though he played a small part in one of the most important decisions of the Court, *Marbury v. Madison* (1803), he himself wrote only one opinion during his four years as a justice.

Before his appointment to the Court, however, Moore had been a prominent North Carolina Federalist. After a notable career during the Revolutionary War, he served the state as a legislator and as attorney general. Most important, he successfully defended a state law that required the dismissal of all suits contesting the title of land confiscated from Tories. In doing so, he challenged the legitimacy of judicial review even though an initial verdict against him is often cited as a precedent for the *Marbury* decision. Moore's active support of the Federalists and his success as a treaty negotiator brought him to the attention of President Adams, and when North Carolinian James Iredell died in 1799, Adams appointed Moore to the high court.

The quasi-war with France provided Moore his only opportunity to draft an opinion. *Bas v. Tingy* (1800) arose out of the frequent seizure of American merchant ships by French privateers. A statute specified that the owner of an American ship captured by "the enemy" and recaptured after more than ninety-six hours had to pay one-half the value of the ship and its goods to the recapturer as salvage. But if the ship had not been taken by the "enemy," the owner only had to pay one-eighth the value as salvage.

The American ship "Eliza" had been captured by the French and then recaptured twenty days later by an armed American vessel. The Court had to decide whether to consider the French an "enemy" within the meaning of the act. Like his colleagues, who all issued their own opinions, Moore decided that a state of war did exist between the United States and France. "And how can the characters of the parties engaged in hostilities of war, be otherwise described than by the denomination of enemies," he asked rhetorically. The former owner of the "Eliza" had to pay half the value of the ship and its goods for salvage.

Moore's only other major judicial contribution came when tardiness forced him to miss the arguments in the *Marbury* case. As a result, he did not take part in the decision, and voiced no opinion on judicial review, even though he had resisted it as North Carolina attorney general. Chief Justice John Marshall, however, was criticized for going ahead with the case and not waiting for Moore and Justice William Cushing, who also missed the arguments.

Citing fears of ill health caused by the rigors of circuit riding, Moore resigned from the Court in 1804, creating the vacancy to which Thomas Jefferson appointed the first Republican justice, William Johnson of South Carolina. Moore spent the final years of his life helping to establish the University of North Carolina.

—MICHAEL GROSSBERG

BIBLIOGRAPHY

There is practically nothing written on Moore other than the sketch by Leon Friedman in Friedman and Israel, 1 *Justices* 267.

Francis (Frank) William Murphy
Collection of the Supreme Court of the United States.

Francis (Frank) William Murphy

Born 13 April 1890, Sand [now Harbor] Beach, Michigan

Nominated to the Court 4 January 1940 by Franklin D. Roosevelt

Took seat 18 January 1940

Died 19 July 1949 in Detroit, Michigan

The appointment of Frank Murphy in 1940 gave President Franklin D. Roosevelt a crucial fifth vote on a Supreme Court that had been dominated for two decades by a reactionary "horse-and-buggy" approach to the Constitution. Roosevelt tried to reshape the Court as a New Deal agency, but several of his eight nominees, most notably Felix Frankfurter, shed their liberal politics and veered to the right on the bench. Frank Murphy, however, began and ended his entire public career as a consistent, committed liberal. He is arguably the most liberal—even radical—justice ever to serve on the Supreme Court. His judicial opinions, often written in dissent, swept aside technical "niceties" in a quest for justice and "human dignity." Often accused of voting with his heart, Murphy pleaded guilty to a visceral jurisprudence. "The law knows no finer hour," he wrote, "than when it cuts through formal concepts and transitory emotions to protect unpopular citizens against discrimination and persecution."

Unlike many of his colleagues, there is no mystery to Frank Murphy, no disparity between his upbringing and his judicial philosophy. But there were differences within his family that help to explain the demons that afflicted Murphy during his entire life. His father was a small-town lawyer, a Democrat and freethinker in the Republican bastion of northern Michigan. Murphy's Irish heritage affected him in two very different ways. His great-grandfather was hanged by the British as an insurrectionist, and his father was jailed as a youth in Canada for Fenian sympathies. Murphy adopted his father's radical politics, but he also absorbed his mother's devout Catholicism. This was not just parish piety; she instilled an equally radical religious vision that would not allow Murphy, he later wrote, to "remain silent in the face of wrong."

The conflicts of Murphy's early years offer a clear guide to those of his judicial career. In high school and college, he loved debating and hated exams. He was popular, but had few close friends. He courted many women, but never married. Murphy was renowned for his generosity, and equally noted for his egocentricity. He acted for the people, and looked first at his press clippings. There was nothing about Murphy that was not calculated. He differed from other judges who gave their votes to the government because of his sympathy for those who "have been burned at the stake, imprisoned, and driven into exile in countless numbers for their political and religious beliefs."

Murphy viewed law and politics as inseparable, and pursued an ambitious political career, with the White House as the ultimate goal. First elected as a Detroit criminal judge in 1923, he reformed an archaic system. Clarence Darrow, who tried a racially charged case before Murphy, called him "the kindliest and most understanding man I ever happened to meet on the bench." Murphy courted labor and minority groups, and was elected Detroit's mayor in 1930. Faced with massive unemployment, he instituted a welfare program that strained city finances but alleviated poverty.

Murphy helped Franklin Roosevelt win the White House in 1932, and was rewarded with the post of governor general of the Philippines. Murphy became popular by supporting the independence movement and bringing money from Washington for jobs and welfare. The political bug lured him back to Michigan in 1936; his inauguration as governor was followed by immediate crisis. Militant auto workers began "sit-down" strikes that company and local officials met with judicial injunctions. Murphy called out national guard troops to maintain peace while he labored behind the scenes to head off industrial warfare. The irony of his success was that both sides accused him of favoring the other, and Murphy lost his reelection battle in 1938.

To repay his political debt, Roosevelt appointed Murphy as attorney general in 1939. His major achievement was to set up the civil liberties unit, whose lawyers dusted off unused federal laws to prosecute local officials who abused—and even murdered—blacks and labor organizers. Murphy's crusading zeal made enemies, many of them Democrats; moving him to the Supreme Court allowed Roosevelt to find a more pliable replacement. Murphy did not want to join the Court; he lobbied for appointment as secretary of war, feeling he lacked the legal skill for the job Roosevelt forced him to accept. "I am not too happy about going on the Court," he wrote a friend. "I fear that my work will be mediocre up there while on the firing line where I have been trained to action I could do much better." Although several senators agreed with Murphy's self-assessment, and others considered him too radical, Roosevelt's clout secured his confirmation without objection.

It is not surprising that Justice Murphy arrived at the Court with an inferiority complex; he was joining such legal luminaries as Chief Justice Charles Evans Hughes, who presided with Jovian firmness; Harlan Fiske Stone, former Columbia law dean; Felix Frankfurter, who lectured his colleagues like the Harvard law students he had taught; and William O. Douglas and Hugo Black, dissimilar in temperament but liberal allies on the bench. Murphy, in fact, had more prior judicial experience— eight years as a criminal judge—than any sitting justice, but his knowledge of constitutional law was sketchy and he had never written an appellate opinion. But neither had Stone, Frankfurter, Douglas, or Black before they joined the Supreme Court. Like most junior justices, Murphy learned by on-the-job training, assisted by colleagues and bright law clerks. More than most justices, he relied on his clerks to draft opinions, which caused some grumbling from those who considered him lazy.

Three years before Murphy joined the Court, the "Constitutional Revolution" of 1937 had ended the reign of the judicial reactionaries who struck down most of the New Deal recovery measures Roosevelt had pushed through Congress. The following year, the Court had shifted its agenda from property rights to human rights. The famous "footnote four" of Justice Stone's opinion in the *Carolene Products* case proposed a "searching judicial inquiry" of laws that were challenged as violating any of "the first ten Amendments" or as discriminating against racial or religious minorities. Murphy embraced the so-called "strict scrutiny" doctrine and the related position that First Amendment rights occupied a "preferred place" in the Constitution.

New justices are allowed to pick their first opinion, and Murphy's choice reflected his concerns for labor and free speech. The case, *Thornhill v. Alabama* (1940), challenged a state law that banned virtually all picketing by union members. Judges had often agreed that even peaceful picketing was not speech, but a form of intimidation. Murphy broke new ground in extending the First Amendment to picketers. He made a point of citing the *Carolene Products* footnote, and he struck down the statute "on its face" as violating the First Amendment. He also took note of "the circumstances of our time" in holding that "the dissemination of information concerning the facts of a labor dispute must be regarded as within that area of free discussion that is guaranteed by the Constitution." Implicit in his opinion was Murphy's recognition that workers had fewer weapons in battles for public support than employers, who often controlled local newspapers. Picket signs helped to answer hostile news coverage and editorials.

Murphy's first major opinion turned out to be one of his most influential and enduring. *Thornhill* has been cited in more than 300 later opinions, and Justice Tom Clark wrote in 1969 that it was "the bedrock upon which many of the Court's civil rights pronouncements rest." Critics have complained that *Thornhill* was phrased too broadly, and limited the power of officials to protect streets and sidewalks from disruption. But Murphy effectively buried the ancient doctrine that picketing was unlawful in any form.

Murphy's commitment to *Carolene Products* and its protection of minorities was shaken by a case decided six weeks after *Thornhill* in June 1940. With war clouds looming, the Court in *Minersville v. Gobitis* upheld the expulsion from public school of a Jehovah's Witness student who refused on religious grounds to salute the American flag. Only Justice Stone dissented from the majority opinion of Frankfurter, who wrote that "national unity is the basis of national security." Murphy first prepared a dissent, but withdrew it to show his patriotic colors. Even more than Frankfurter, Murphy had a bad case of war fever. He shocked his colleagues by trading his judicial robe for a uniform in 1942, reporting for infantry training at Fort Knox.

This short army stint, however, did not keep Murphy from deserting Frankfurter's judicial platoon. Along with Douglas and Black, and a new recruit, Justice Wiley Rutledge, he joined Stone, now chief justice, in overruling *Gobitis* in 1943. Concurring in *West Virginia v. Barnette*, Murphy answered Frankfurter in writing that "the real unity of America" rested not on coercion or conformity, but on religious freedom. "Reflection has convinced me," he added, "that as a judge I have no loftier duty or responsibility than to uphold that spiritual freedom to its farthest reaches." The *Barnette* case split the Court into hostile factions. Frankfurter felt betrayed and derided Murphy as a conspirator in a judicial "Axis" that undermined political and military authority. Changing his mind from *Gobitis* to *Barnette* did not mean that Murphy had no judicial compass. It showed, rather, his growing ability to separate personal emotions from the Constitution's dictates. In this regard, he displayed greater maturity and discipline than Frankfurter, who remained a war hawk.

Murphy showed his commitment to principle by consistently supporting the Jehovah's Witnesses, who bitterly attacked his beloved Catholic church. He dissented when the Court upheld in 1944 a state law that barred minors from selling religious literature on public streets. Murphy cited the Witnesses in *Prince v. Massachusetts* as "living proof of the fact that even in this nation, conceived as it was in the ideals of freedom, the right to practice religion in unconventional ways is still far from secure." He noted that Witnesses "have suffered brutal beatings; their property has been destroyed; they have been harassed at every turn by the resurrection and enforcement of little used ordinances and statutes." Theological disputes aside, Murphy knew that Witnesses and Catholics had both suffered for their faith. "If Frank Murphy is ever sainted," one colleague said, "it will be by the Jehovah's Witnesses."

Even more than religious bigotry, Frank Murphy hated racism. As a criminal court judge, he knew that black defendants were treated more harshly. As mayor of Detroit, he saw the punishing impact of the Great Depression on minorities. During his army training in southern states, he witnessed all-black chain gangs and observed the demeaning customs of segregation. Murphy was determined, he wrote a friend, to redress the reality that "people of color" were denied "constitutional rights and any kind of social justice."

When Murphy was forced to choose, however, between his wartime fervor and revulsion at racism, he succumbed to judicial paralysis. He faced this choice in *Hirabayashi v. United States* (1943), which produced a dramatic clash between the Constitution's "war powers" and its prohibition of racial discrimination. The case began with the Japanese attack on Pearl Harbor in December 1941. More than 100,000 Americans of Japanese ancestry—two-thirds of them native-born citizens—became the victims of wartime hysteria and racism. Fueled by sensational (but false) reports of sabotage and espionage, military officials persuaded President Roosevelt to sign an executive order in February 1942 that authorized the removal of "any or all persons" from the West Coast. Congress backed the order with criminal penalties, and army troops herded the entire Japanese-American population into "relocation centers" in isolated desert and swamp areas. Even liberals such as Earl Warren, then California's attorney general, supported this "ethnic cleansing" program.

Only three young men, acting separately, had the courage to challenge the military curfew and exclusion orders that preceded the mass evacuation. They were arrested and convicted in brief trials, and appealed their sentences to the Supreme Court. The justices first addressed the curfew orders in the cases of Gordon Hirabayashi, a University of Washington student, and Minoru Yasui, an Oregon lawyer and reserve army officer. Chief Justice Stone wrote for the Court in both cases, addressing the major issues in the *Hirabayashi* opinion in June 1943. "Distinctions between citizens solely because of their ancestry," he admitted, "are by their very nature odious to a free people whose institutions are founded upon the doctrine of equality." Wartime pressures, however, allowed officials to place "citizens of one ancestry in a different category from others." Stone blamed Japanese Americans for their plight; decades of discrimination resulted in "little social intercourse between them and the white population." The chief justice deferred to military authority and ignored his *Carolene Products* footnote on racial discrimination.

Murphy was appalled by an opinion he considered "utterly inconsistent" with American ideals, and drafted a stinging dissent. He denied that the Constitution allowed "one law for the majority of our citizens and another for those of a particular racial heritage." And he said the internment of Japanese Americans "bears a melancholy resemblance to the treatment accorded to members of the Jewish race" by the Nazis. Justice Frankfurter was offended by suggestions the Court was "behaving like the enemy" and pleaded with Murphy to withdraw his dissent. As he had in *Gobitis*, Murphy yielded. But his *Hirabayashi* concurrence retained the analogy to Nazi persecution and said the mass internment "goes to the very brink of constitutional power."

Again, Murphy repented his vote with a vengeance. But this time he remained in the minority. In December 1944, the Court upheld the military exclusion orders in *Korematsu v. United States*. Fred Korematsu was a shipyard welder in California who violated the exclusion order because he wanted to stay with his Caucasian fiancée. But someone recognized him and called the police. Justice Hugo Black wrote for the Court in affirming his conviction. Like Stone, Black agreed that laws which "curtail the civil rights of a single racial group" were subject to "the most rigid scrutiny." And like Stone, he exempted from scrutiny military claims that Japanese Americans posed a security threat and that it was impossible to separate "the disloyal from the loyal" in this racial group.

Murphy was the only member of the liberal "Axis" to dissent in *Korematsu*. He charged the Court with plunging over the brink of constitutional power "into the ugly abyss of racism." His carefully documented opinion showed that belief in "racial guilt rather than bona fide military necessity" had motivated the officials who urged the internment program. Murphy quoted the West Coast army commander who said all Japanese Americans belonged to "an enemy race" and the farm leader who admitted "wanting to get rid of the Japs" so that "white farmers can take over and produce everything the Jap grows." And he accused the Court's majority of adopting "the cruelest of the rationales used by our enemies to destroy the dignity of the individual" and of opening the door "to discriminatory actions against other minority groups in the passions of tomorrow." Murphy simply could not stomach, he said, "this legalization of racism."

Justice Murphy's dissent in *Korematsu* stands as his most powerful opinion. His marshalling of the facts—which Black ignored or distorted—belies charges that Murphy lacked the skills of legal craftmanship. It should be noted that he won vindication four decades later when federal judges vacated the convictions in the wartime internment cases. The judge who cleared Gordon Hirabayashi added more documentation to Murphy's charges that racial bias had motivated government officials. He hoped these facts would "stay the hand of a government again tempted to imprison a defenseless minority without trial and for no offense." And the judge in Fred Korematsu's case echoed Murphy in writing that "the shield of military necessity and national security must not be used to protect governmental actions from close scrutiny and accountability." Murphy would have relished these posthumous tributes to his legal skills.

The bedrock principle of Murphy's view of the Constitution was that no person remained outside its protection, however unpopular or even hated. Communists, aliens, accused spies, even war criminals deserved all the rights of the most respected citizen. Murphy held government officials, from policemen to the president, to the highest standards of behavior. For example, he dissented in 1945 from a decision overturning the federal conviction of a Georgia sheriff for beating to death a black prisoner. The Court held in *Screws v. United States* that a Reconstruction era law making it criminal to act "under color of law" in depriving anyone of constitutional rights required strict proof of intent. Writing for a bare majority, Justice Douglas found insufficient evidence that Sheriff Claude Screws intended to deprive Robert Hall of a specific federal right when he killed the handcuffed prisoner with a tire iron.

Murphy was the only justice who voted to uphold both the law and the conviction. He faulted the majority for ignoring the clear language of the Fourteenth Amendment, "which firmly and unmistakably provides that no state shall deprive any person of life without due process of law." Robert Hall "has been deprived of the right to life itself," he wrote. "That right was his because he was an American citizen, because he was a human being." It required only "common sense" to understand that a policeman who has "beaten and crushed the body of a human being" has violated the clearest demand of the Constitution.

In two politically charged cases, Murphy protected an admitted Communist from denaturalization and an alleged party member from deportation. Federal officials tried in 1939 to strip William Schneiderman of American citizenship on grounds that his Communist activities showed he was not "attached to the principles of the Constitution" when he was naturalized in 1927. Opposed to loyalty tests in general, Murphy objected to this retroactive test in particular. Writing for the Court, he blasted the government for seeking "to turn the clock back twelve years" and to deprive Schneiderman of the "priceless benefits" of citizenship for acts that were perfectly lawful. Murphy would grant to every new citizen—even Communists—the right "to think and act and speak according to their convictions, without fear of punishment or further exile so long as they keep the peace and obey the law" (*Schneiderman v. United States,* 1943).

The government tried even harder to deport Harry Bridges, the controversial leader of West Coast maritime workers. Bridges came from Australia in 1920 and never applied for citizenship. He freely admitted his radical sympathies but denied Communist membership. Efforts to deport Bridges began in 1934 after a bloody waterfront strike in San Francisco, but several panels found no evidence he belonged to the Communist party. Congress finally passed a law in 1940 allowing deportation of aliens who had at any time been "affiliated" with the party. Its sponsor proclaimed his "joy" that the govern-

ment "should now have little trouble in deporting Harry Bridges and all others of similar ilk." Government witnesses at a new hearing testified that Bridges agreed with Communist policies, and he was again served with a deportation order. The Supreme Court reversed the order in *Bridges v. Wixon* (1945), ruling narrowly that key witnesses had given "untrustworthy" testimony. But the Court declined to decide whether "affiliation" with the Communist party could justify deportation.

Although he agreed with the outcome, Murphy was outraged at this evasion of the constitutional issue. He put his most passionate language into a concurring opinion. "The record in this case will stand forever as a monument to man's intolerance of man," he wrote. "Seldom if ever in the history of this nation has there been such a concentrated and ruthless crusade to deport an individual because he dared to exercise the freedom that belongs to him as a human being and that is guaranteed to him by the Constitution." The final sentence of his opinion set out Murphy's vision of the Constitution: "Only by zealously guarding the rights of the most humble, the most unorthodox and the most despised among us can freedom flourish and endure in our land."

General Tomoyuki Yamashita was probably the "most despised" person who ever appealed to the Supreme Court. There was no doubt the Japanese troops he commanded in the Philippines committed unspeakable atrocities. There was considerable doubt, however, that Yamashita ordered or even knew of these atrocities. But he was sentenced to hang by an American military tribunal for violating the American "Articles of War." His appeal, prepared by U.S. Army defense lawyers, raised issues of due process, international law, and American treaty obligations. Chief Justice Stone urged the justices to take a "hands off" position on military authority. All but Rutledge and Murphy agreed, and Yamashita's execution quickly followed the Court's decision.

His years in the Philippines gave Murphy a special sympathy for those who suffered "brutal atrocities" at the hands of Japanese troops. But he had a greater attachment to the Constitution. His dissenting opinion catalogued at length the procedural flaws in Yamashita's hasty trial. Due process guarantees applied to "any person" accused of crime. "No exception is made as to those who are accused of war crimes," Murphy wrote. Yamashita was "rushed to trial under an improper charge" and deprived of basic rights. Murphy put the Bill of Rights in universal terms. "The immutable rights of the individual," he wrote, "belong to every person in the world, victor or vanquished, whatever may be his race, color, or beliefs. They rise above any status of belligerency or outlawry. They survive any popular passion or frenzy of the moment. No court or legislature or executive, not even the mightiest army in the world, can ever destroy them" (*In re Yamashita*, 1946).

Not surprisingly, Murphy's last opinion was a dissent. And, not surprisingly, it dealt with another "despised" person, an accused Soviet spy named Gerhart Eisler who had fled the country to avoid imprisonment. The Court voted to dismiss his pending appeal, but Murphy disagreed. The issues before the Court, he wrote, "did not leave when Eisler did." *Eisler v. United States* (1949). Within weeks of this opinion, Murphy died of a heart attack. The inscription on his grave marker, in his Michigan birthplace, is simple. "Frank Murphy/ Justice United States Supreme Court/ 19 July 1949."

But the final paragraph of Murphy's final opinion offered a fitting epitaph: "Law is at its loftiest when it examines claimed injustice even at the instance of one to whom the public is bitterly hostile. We should be loath to shirk our obligations, whatever the creed of the particular petitioner. Our country takes pride in requiring of its institutions the examination and correction of alleged injustice whenever it occurs. We should not permit an affront of this sort to distract us from the performance of our constitutional duties. I dissent."

—Peter Irons

Bibliography

The Frank Murphy papers are in the Michigan historical collections, University of Michigan, Ann Arbor, and contain virtually all of Murphy's Court papers and correspondence. The Eugene Gressman papers, also in the Michigan historical collections, are a valuable supplement to Murphy's papers. Sidney Fine, *Frank Murphy: The Washington Years* (1984), is the definitive account of Murphy's Supreme Court career. Two prior volumes in this massive biography cover the earlier parts of his public life. See also J. Woodford Howard, Jr., *Mr. Justice Murphy: A Political Biography* (1968), an earlier biography that is less detailed but somewhat more critical than Fine's work. Harold Norris, *Mr. Justice Murphy and the Bill of Rights* (1965), includes many of Justice Murphy's opinions. Two worthwhile articles are Eugene Gressman, "The Controversial Image of Mr. Justice Murphy," 47 *Georgetown Law Review* 631 (1959), an admiring but insightful memoir by a former law clerk and longtime friend, and Archibald Cox, "The Influence of Mr. Justice Murphy on Labor Law," 48 *Michigan Law Review* 769 (1950), an excellent review of Murphy's labor opinions.

SAMUEL NELSON

BORN 10 November 1792, Hebron, New York

NOMINATED to the Court 14 February 1845
by John Tyler

TOOK seat 5 March 1845; retired
28 November 1872

DIED 13 December 1873 in Cooperstown,
New York

Samuel Nelson attended Middlebury College in Vermont, apprenticed in a law office in Salem, New York, and was admitted to the New York bar in 1817. He then built a successful litigation and commercial law practice, and also served as postmaster in Cortland, New York, from 1820 to 1823. From 1823 to 1831, he served on the state supreme court's sixth circuit, presiding over the suits in equity brought in the nine counties of the jurisdiction. From 1831 to 1837, he served as an associate judge on the New York supreme court, becoming chief judge in 1836, a position held until 1845 when he was sworn in as associate justice on the Supreme Court of the United States.

Although he was President Tyler's third nominee to fill the Supreme Court vacancy, Nelson proved a wise choice. In his twenty-seven years on the Court, Nelson was one of the most prolific justices, producing 347 opinions (323 majority opinions, nineteen dissents, five concurrences). Although he wrote on a broad range of legal topics in these opinions, his most noteworthy contribution was the influence he brought to bear in resolving the difficult legal issues arising before and during the Civil War.

Nelson was originally to have been the author of the majority opinion in *Dred Scott v. Sandford* (1857), but his proposed proslavery opinion held only that Missouri's slavery laws determined Scott's status after he returned from Illinois, a free jurisdiction in which he had resided with his master. Chief Justice Roger Brooke Taney believed that a stronger statement was needed to counter the antislavery dissents, and took on the writing of the majority opinion. Taney went further than Nelson's more temperate views, holding the Missouri Compromise

void and that an African American could never be a citizen of the United States. Nelson filed a separate concurrence.

Two years later Taney wrote for a unanimous Court in *Ableman v. Booth* (1859). Wisconsin's Supreme Court had released Sherman Booth, who had allegedly assisted a fugitive slave to escape from his pursuing master, after a hearing on a writ of *habeas corpus*. Taney's opinion characterized the state court's action as a great abuse of power. Yet Taney had joined a Nelson dissent in the earlier decision of *In re Thomas Kaine* (1852), in which Nelson had extolled the liberal use of the writ of *habeas corpus*, stating a preference "to follow the free and enlarged interpretation always given, when dealing with it by the courts of England." Indeed, "so liberally do the courts of England deal with this writ, . . . that the decision of one court or magistrate upon the return to it, refusing to discharge the prisoner, is no bar to the issuing of a second, or third, or more, by any other court or magistrate having jurisdiction of the case."

Taking the opinions together, the views of Nelson and Taney seem to be far more lenient in the case of a fugitive from justice (i.e., Thomas Kaine, arrested in the United States on a charge of murder committed in Ireland and examined before a United States commissioner) than in the case of an American citizen (Booth) who has been accused of assisting a fugitive slave to escape to freedom. While numerous motives for the difference in perspective on the two kinds of fugitives might be defended, both the date of each case and its proximity to the Civil War undoubtedly bore some influence.

Nelson wrote a number of opinions regarding the capture of ships and their cargos as war prize. In the *Prize Cases* (1863), the majority held legitimate the July 1861 taking of four ships attempting to run a Union blockade President Abraham Lincoln had declared the previous April. In a powerful dissent concurred in by Taney, Catron, and Clifford, Nelson declared that only Congress and not the president could declare war. Since Congress had not declared war in July 1861, he believed the seizures invalid.

In *The Circassion* (1864), a Union ship had captured a British merchant steamer close to Havana, Cuba, on May 4, 1862, on evidence that its ultimate destination was New Orleans, then under blockade. The majority opinion upheld the ship's capture as prize even though New Orleans had been taken by federal troops on May 2, 1862. Nelson dissented, claiming "the defect in the case, on the part of the captors is that no blockade existed at the port of New Orleans at the time the seizure was made."

The facts in *The Siren* (1868) were more complicated, involving a steamer captured by Union forces. While being taken to Boston, "The Siren" collided with a sloop, sinking the sloop with its cargo of iron. After "The Siren" was sold as lawful prize, the sloop's owners filed a claim against the proceeds for damages. The majority decided this claim should be honored; Nelson dissented, stating that under the principle of sovereign immunity, the sloop's owners could not sue the United States government. With its capture, "The Siren" had become government property, and the fact that it was later sold changed nothing.

Justice Nelson joined with the majority in two other noteworthy Civil War cases, both concerning the jurisdiction and powers of military commissions during the War. In *Ex parte Vallandigham* (1863), a commission had imprisoned a civilian in Ohio for public speech disloyal to the Union. The Court held this decision was not reviewable and denied the writ of certiorari. But in *Ex parte Milligan* (1866), the Court reversed a military commission decision to hang an Indiana civilian convicted of various treasonous acts during "the late wicked Rebellion," and held that Milligan deserved a jury trial in either state or federal court.

Samuel Nelson was truly craftsmanlike in his work, with an "elevated conception of justice and of right" as stated in a letter from members of the Supreme Court bar after his retirement. In several respects he could be considered a precursor of his twentieth-century brethren on the Court: his opinions were lucid and logical; he frequently cited authority for specific points (Chancellor Kent being one of his favorites); and his opinions were quite succinct by comparison with many other nineteenth-century judicial pronouncements. But he was also a gentleman, and thus would have been horrified by some of the personal attacks engaged in by late twentieth-century members of the Court toward each other.

Nelson's combined years of service on state and federal courts covered half a century, an era of unprecedented change in America. Old age and failing health forced his retirement from the Court in November 1872 and he died a year later. Far less has been written about this quietly competent jurist than his more flamboyant and controversial judicial brethren. This probably says more about Supreme Court observers than it does about Samuel Nelson.

—JENNI PARRISH

BIBLIOGRAPHY

There is no full-length authoritative biography on Samuel Nelson and no single collection of his papers in existence. The following round out what little there is in print on the man. Edwin Countryman, "Samuel Nelson," 19 *The Green Bag* 329 (1907) (probably the single best biographical source on Justice Nelson to date); Richard Leach, "The Rediscovery of Samuel Nelson," 34 *New York History* 64 (1953), which includes excerpts from Justice Nelson's correspondence; Jenni Parrish, "Justice Samuel Nelson," *New York Notes* (1987), useful for discussion of cases during his tenure on the New York State Supreme Court. Numerous biographical directories include basic descriptions of Justice Samuel Nelson. Possibly the most ubiquitous is in 13 *Dictionary of American Biography* 422 (1928).

SANDRA DAY O'CONNOR

BORN 26 March 1930, El Paso, Texas
NOMINATED to the Court 7 July 1981
  by Ronald Reagan
TOOK seat 25 September 1981

Sandra Day O'Connor, the 102nd justice and the first woman appointed to the United States Supreme Court, spent her early years on the family cattle ranch on the Arizona-New Mexico border. She went to elementary and high school in El Paso, living with her maternal grandmother, Mamie Scott Wilkey, and then attended Stanford University and Stanford Law School, graduating third in her law school class. (First in her class was future Chief Justice William Rehnquist.)

Despite her stellar academic credentials, O'Connor received no offers from the law firms she interviewed with in Los Angeles and San Francisco, which had never hired a woman as a lawyer. Concentrating on the public sector where the opportunities for women lawyers were better, she found work as a law clerk and deputy county attorney in the San Mateo County attorney's office. After spending two years in Frankfurt, West Germany, where her husband, John O'Connor, served in the Judge Advocate General's Corps, and she worked as a civilian lawyer for the United States Army, the pair returned to Arizona. John O'Connor joined a Phoenix law firm and Sandra O'Connor, now a mother, opened a small law practice with another lawyer in a suburb of Phoenix. Active in Republican politics, in 1965 Sandra O'Connor became an assistant attorney general. She was appointed to the Arizona state senate to fill a vacancy in 1969 and subsequently was elected to two full terms, becoming senate majority leader in 1973. In 1974, she won election as trial judge on the Maricopa County superior court, and in 1979, she was appointed to the Arizona court of appeals. In 1981, President Ronald Reagan nominated her to fill the vacancy created by Justice Potter Stewart's retirement.

The jurisprudence of Sandra Day O'Connor has been followed with interest, in part because of her status as the first woman to serve on the Supreme Court, but perhaps more importantly as the first of five justices appointed by the Republican presidents Ronald Reagan and George Bush over their combined twelve-year occupancy of the White House (1980–1992). As succeeding Republican appointees joined the bench, Court watchers with hope or fear awaited the day when a solid conservative majority would be in a position to undo much of the product of the preceding, more liberal era. What was witnessed, instead, was the evolution of a moderate center on the Court, judicially conservative in its respect for precedent and in its unwillingness to make law outside the bounds of the cases put before them. Justice O'Connor has served as the seed around which this center has crystallized, especially in the areas of federalism, religion, and abortion rights.

Perhaps influenced and informed by her experiences as an assistant state attorney general, state legislator, and state appellate court judge, Justice O'Connor has been a consistently powerful advocate for the states as independent sovereigns within the federal system. Often, but not always, in the minority, O'Connor has stood as a defender of a core of state sovereignty into which the broad powers granted the federal government do not penetrate, a core thus protected by the Tenth Amendment to the United States Constitution. "The true 'essence' of federalism," she stated in dissent in *Garcia v. San Antonio Metropolitan Transit Authority* (1985), "is that the States as States have legitimate interests which the National Government is bound to respect even though its laws are supreme."

O'Connor has been particularly wary of federal statutory schemes that seemed to force state governments into the role of mere tools in effectuating a federal agenda. In *Federal Energy Regulatory Commission v. Mississippi* (1982), for example, a federal statute provided that in order to continue regulating in a particular area, the relevant state agencies would have to consider whether to adopt certain federal standards—and follow certain procedures in making the decision. O'Connor argued in dissent that the statute impermissibly "conscript[ed] state utility commissions into the national bureaucratic army." She reasoned that a state's sovereign power "to make decisions and set policy . . . embraces more than the ultimate authority to enact laws; it also includes the power to decide which proposals are most worthy of consideration, the order in which they should be taken up, and the precise form in which they should be debated." In *South Dakota v. Dole* (1987), in which the Court upheld the conditioning of federal highway funds on a state having a minimum drinking age of twenty-one, O'Connor, again in dissent, argued that to be valid under the congressional spending power, conditions on federal grants to states should relate directly to how the funds would be spent; "otherwise, the Congress could effectively regulate almost any area of a State's social, political, or economic life."

After protesting mightily against the incursions into state sovereignty upheld in the above cases, Justice O'Connor won a majority for the proposition that the Tenth Amendment provided at least the limitation that "Congress may not simply commandeer the legislative process of the States by directly compelling them to enact and enforce a federal regulatory program" (*New York v. United States,* 1992). The case invalidated a provision of the Low-Level Radioactive Waste Policy Amendments Act of 1985 that would have forced any state that had not developed disposal facilities by a certain deadline to take title to and possession of the waste privately generated in the state. "In this provision, Congress has not held out the threat of exercising its spending power or its commerce power; it has instead held out the threat, should the States not regulate according to one federal instruction, of simply forcing the States to submit to another federal instruction." O'Connor supported the Court's ruling with historical evidence indicating that the framers envisioned a constitutional structure in which the federal government would implement its regulations directly rather than employ the states to do so. Moreover, she observed that when Congress is not allowed to commandeer state governments to execute federal regulatory schemes, the identity of the ultimate government decision maker is made clearer, and thus the political accountability of state and federal governments is enhanced.

O'Connor's sensitivity to state governments is reflected not only in those cases directly focused on the implications of the Tenth Amendment; rather, it is a concern that plays a role in a wide range of contexts. In the area of federal *habeas corpus*, for example, she has been a leader more often than a dissenter, and the Court's *habeas* jurisprudence has been strongly influenced by her respect for state courts and state judicial procedures. Federal *habeas* proceedings provide collateral review of state court criminal convictions for constitutional error. In a series of decisions strengthening the requirement that state court remedies be exhausted before a *habeas* petition is heard by a federal court, and narrowing the circumstances under which a *habeas* claim that was not heard by a state court due to a claimant's procedural default will ever be entertained by a federal court, Justice O'Connor has observed that "it would be unseemly in our dual system of government for a federal district court to upset a state court conviction without an opportunity to the state courts to correct a constitutional violation" (*Rose v. Lundy,* 1982). In O'Connor's view, adopted by the Court in *Engle v. Isaac* (1982), "the Great Writ imposes special costs on our federal system," because "federal intrusions into state criminal trials frustrate both the States' sovereign power to punish offenders and their good-faith attempts to honor constitutional rights." More recently, in an opinion reinforcing the obstacles to federal *habeas* review of a claim that, due to procedural default, was not reviewed by the state courts, O'Connor began the opinion for the Court thus: "This is a case about federalism" (*Coleman v. Thompson,* 1991).

O'Connor's respect for the role of state courts and state court procedures, while substantial, has not been applied mechanically to justify a wholesale retreat from federal *habeas* relief. In cases such as *Brecht v. Abrahamson* (1993) and *Keeney v. Tamayo-Reyes* (1992), she dissented from holdings that made federal *habeas* relief more difficult to obtain, noting that federalism concerns do not support "the proposition that denying relief whenever possible is an unalloyed good."

One of the very few bright spots in the disarray of the Court's current establishment clause jurisprudence is the "endorsement" test that Justice O'Connor first developed in her concurrence in *Lynch v. Donnelly* (1984), and has applied and

Sandra Day O'Connor
Photograph by National Geographic Society.
Collection of the Supreme Court of the United States.

refined in a series of cases since. Receiving the praises of numerous scholars, and assuming an ever-greater role in the Court's establishment clause analyses, the endorsement test may be the Court's one hope for a reasoned, useful consensus in this area.

Lynch v. Donnelly involved an establishment clause challenge to the city of Pawtucket's inclusion, in a private park in the midst of the shopping district, of a crèche as part of an elaborate Christmas display. In evaluating the challenge, the opinion for the Court applied the test developed in *Lemon v. Kurtzman* (1971), under which a court inquires into "whether the challenged law or conduct has a secular purpose, whether its principal or primary effect is to advance or inhibit religion, and whether it creates a excessive entanglement of government with religion." Chief Justice Burger's opinion for the Court, following a glowing description of many of the "countless [examples] of the Government's acknowledgment of our religious heritage," found that the inclusion of a crèche with "among other things, a Santa Claus house, reindeer pulling Santa's sleigh . . . a Christmas tree . . . cutout figures representing such characters as . . . a teddy bear . . . [and] a large banner that reads 'Seasons Greetings,'" served the secular purpose of celebrating a national holiday and did not impermissibly advance or require government entanglement in religion.

Justice O'Connor, concurring in the opinion of the Court, wrote separately to "suggest a clarification of our establishment clause doctrine."

> The Establishment Clause prohibits government from making adherence to a religion relevant in any way to a person's standing in the political community. Government can run afoul of that prohibition in two principal ways. One is excessive entanglement with religious institutions. . . . The second and more direct infringement is government endorsement or disapproval of religion. Endorsement sends a message to nonadherents that they are outsiders, not full members of the political community, and an accompanying message to adherents that they are insiders, favored members of the political community.

Under her refinement of the *Lemon* test based on this understanding of the establishment clause,

> The purpose prong of the Lemon test asks whether government's actual purpose is to endorse or disapprove of religion. The effect prong asks whether, irrespective of government's actual purpose, the practice under review in fact conveys a message of endorsement or disapproval. An affirmative answer to either question should render the challenged practice invalid.

Applying this formulation to the Pawtucket display, O'Connor found that the display neither was intended to nor did communicate a message of endorsement of the Christian beliefs represented by the crèche. "Although the religious and indeed sectarian significance of the crèche . . . is not neutralized by the setting, the overall holiday setting changes what viewers may fairly understand to be the purpose of the display—as a typical museum setting, though not neutralizing the religious content of a religious painting, negates any message of endorsement of that content."

The following year, O'Connor elaborated on her proposal in her concurrence in *Wallace v. Jaffree* (1985), in which the Court struck down Alabama's "moment of silence" statute. Noting that the many other state statutes that allow for a moment of silence in public schools for voluntary meditation or prayer are not necessarily invalid, she observed that "the crucial question is whether the State has conveyed or attempted to convey the message that children should use the moment of silence for prayer. . . . This question cannot be answered in the abstract, but instead requires courts to examine the history, language, and administration of a particular statute to determine whether it operates as an endorsement of religion."

In subsequent cases, Justice O'Connor has demonstrated the applicability of her endorsement analysis in other establishment clause contexts, including a state statute mandating that an employer honor an employee's sabbath in *Estate of Thorton v. Caldor, Inc.* (1985) and Title VII's exemption for religious organizations, *Corporation of Presiding Bishop of Church of Jesus Christ of Latter-day Saints v. Amos* (1987), both cases in concurrences. Also during this time, analyses that focused on the question of government endorsement were finding their way into opinions of the Court in such cases as *Edwards v. Aguillard* (1987) and *School District of Grand Rapids v. Ball* (1985).

In a 1989 case revisiting the very issue raised in Lynch—government-sponsored displays of religious symbols—a majority of the Court adopted Justice O'Connor's endorsement analysis in *County of Allegheny v. ACLU* (1989). The case involved two distinct displays featured on government property during the Christmas season. One was a creche displayed at the grand staircase of the county courthouse, the "main," "most beautiful," and "most public" part of the courthouse. The other display, located a block away at the entrance to the city-county building, featured a forty-five-foot Christmas tree decorated with lights and ornaments, an eighteen-foot Hanukkah menorah, and a sign bearing the mayor's name and entitled "Salute to Liberty." The Court found the crèche display to be violative of the establishment clause, but the "Salute to Liberty" display constitutional. (Only Justices Blackmun and O'Connor advocated this precise result, however; Justices Brennan, Marshall, and Stevens argued that both displays offended the establishment clause, while Justices Kennedy, Scalia, White, and Rehnquist argued that neither did.) Although the case produced a particularly tangled set of opinions, a majority of the Court agreed that "in recent years, we have paid particularly close attention to whether the challenged governmental practice either has the purpose or effect of 'endorsing' religion, a concern that has long had a place in our establishment clause jurisprudence."

What are the perceived merits of an endorsement test? The test recognizes the crucial importance in establishment clause analysis of the symbolic significance of government acts. Moreover, it is believed to offer the Court an opportunity to chart a reasoned middle course of "liberal neutrality" in its establishment clause jurisprudence, avoiding the extremes of rigid separation from, or undiscriminating accommodation to, the many religious elements in our pluralistic society. Whether the Court will fully embrace this opportunity, and whether greater consensus on the Court will result, remains to be seen.

Justice O'Connor's jurisprudence is marked by a firm insistence that law be developed and applied with a full appreciation of the particular factual context of each case. On several issues she has found the adoption of a sweeping bright-line rule that avoids the difficult task of balancing competing rights and interests in the particular case to be an abdication of the Court's responsibility in the constitutional structure. Logically following from this principle is an obligation to rule narrowly, keeping to the question presented by the facts of the case to the extent consistent with the Court's duty to provide guidance to lower courts, and refusing to reach out to decide constitutional issues unnecessary to resolution of the particular case. Moreover, a jurisprudence committed to a balancing of concerns in the particular case has provided opportunities to stake out a logical middle ground between more rigid positions to the left and right.

The cases discussed above demonstrate these characteristics. Thus, when the Court overruled *National League of Cities v. Usery* (1976), claiming that its protection for "traditional governmental functions" was an "unworkable" Tenth Amendment standard, Justice O'Connor dissented, and argued that while "it has been difficult for this Court to craft bright lines defining the scope of the state autonomy . . . it is and will remain the duty of this Court to reconcile [federalism and commerce power concerns] in the final instance" (*Garcia v. San Antonio Metropolitan Transit Authority,* 1985). In her establishment clause jurisprudence, her analyses are extremely sensitive to the factual context of each case. In *Allegheny*, for example, O'Connor was one of only two justices who could differentiate between the elaborate nativity scene holding a place of honor in the grand stairway of the county courthouse, and a menorah displayed as part of a "Salute to Liberty" in front of another government building a block away.

Her principles of judging are also well illustrated in *Employment Division v. Smith* (1990), in which the Court, in an opinion penned by Justice Scalia, held that a neutral criminal statute of general applicability may not be subject to a claim that it burdens an individual's free exercise of religion. Although she concurred in the result, O'Connor found this "single categorical rule," with its "sweeping result," to be in direct conflict with free exercise precedents that required the government to demonstrate that application of the particular prohibition to the religious objector was necessary to achieve a compelling state interest. "To me, the sounder approach—the approach more consistent with our role as judges to decide each case on its individual merits—is to apply this test in each case to determine whether the burden on the specific plaintiffs before us is constitutionally significant and whether the particular criminal interest asserted by the State before us is compelling." She concluded that the Court's ruling was unnecessary because the state criminal provision at issue in that case—a prohibition on peyote use—served a compelling government interest in restraining drug abuse and therefore could be upheld on that ground alone.

These elements—a suspicion of sweeping categories, a preference for standards sensitive to the facts of each case, a reluctance to reach out to issues not squarely presented by the case at hand, and positions that stake a middle ground between warring factions on the Court—are all illustrated by Justice O'Connor's abortion opinions.

Not long into her tenure on the Court, dissenting in *Akron v. Akron Center for Reproductive Health, Inc.* (1982), O'Connor issued a stinging critique of the trimester framework for abortion regulation set out in *Roe v. Wade* (1973). Under that framework the extent of permissible state regulation varied with the trimester of the pregnancy, based on the increasing state interest in maternal health and potential human life as the pregnancy progressed. "The *Roe* framework . . . is clearly on a collision course with itself," she asserted. "As the medical risks of various abortion procedures decrease, the point at which the State may regulate for reasons of maternal health is moved further forward to actual childbirth. As medical science becomes better able to provide for the separate existence of the fetus, the point of viability is moved further back toward conception."

O'Connor argued that the state's interests in maternal health and potential human life exist throughout the pregnancy, and that only those regulations that impose an "undue burden" on the fundamental right to abortion should be subjected to strict scrutiny by the Court.

Because it had not been challenged by either party, Justice O'Connor did not revisit the basic holding of Roe that a woman's decision to terminate her pregnancy was a fundamental liberty protected by the Fourteenth Amendment. However, in *Webster v. Reproductive Health Services* (1989), the state did call for the Court to reconsider—and overrule—Roe. O'Connor declined the invitation, much to Justice Scalia's distress. She found the abortion regulations at issue consistent with the Court's past decisions, and therefore saw no need to reexamine the validity of those cases. "Where there is no need to decide a constitutional question, it is a venerable principle of the Court's adjudication processes not to do so. . . . Neither will it generally formulate a rule of constitutional law broader than is required by the precise facts to which it is to be applied."

The question presented to the Court, and the makeup of the Court, was dramatically different three years later when *Planned Parenthood v. Casey* (1992) was argued. The Pennsylvania statute at issue in that case, while not outlawing abortions entirely, contained certain informed consent and notification provisions that could not be squared with *Roe* and its progeny. And since *Webster*, two of the most stalwart defenders of *Roe*—Justices Brennan and Marshall—had retired and had been replaced by Republican appointees Souter and Thomas. Many anticipated that this case would mark the death of *Roe v. Wade*.

Instead, in an opinion jointly authored by O'Connor, Anthony Kennedy, and David Souter, the Court explicitly reaffirmed the central holding of *Roe* that a woman has a constitutional right to choose to have an abortion before fetal viability. *Stare decisis* called for *Roe's* essential holding to be reaffirmed, because, among other reasons, for two decades "people have organized intimate relationships and made choices that define their views of themselves . . . in reliance on the availability of abortion in the event that contraception should fail." "The ability of women to participate equally in the economic and social life of the Nation has been facilitated by their ability to control their reproductive lives," the justices observed.

While reaffirming the essential holding of *Roe*, the three justices adopted O'Connor's "undue burden" test for state regulation of abortion procedures. Applying that standard, the three upheld most of the challenged Pennsylvania regulations (joined in this part of the judgment by those justices who wished to overrule *Roe*), but struck down a provision requiring a married woman to notify her husband before obtaining an abortion (joined in this part of the judgment by Justices Blackmun and Stevens, who also found most of the other challenged provisions unconstitutional).

Although adhering to the trimester framework he had crafted in *Roe v. Wade*, Justice Blackmun nonetheless commended the joint opinion as "an act of personal courage and constitutional principle." Commentators also viewed the joint decision as important, marking the coalescence of a centrist block on the Court that could be the determining factor in its judgment in the years ahead.

—JOAN I. GRECO

BIBLIOGRAPHY

There has been only one biography, and that directed at younger readers, but it is nonetheless quite good, Peter Huber, *Sandra Day O'Connor: Supreme Court Justice* (1990). The number of articles on O'Conner and her opinions is increasing each term. See especially Donald L. Beschle, "The Conservative as Liberal: The Religion Clauses, Liberal Neutrality, and the Approach of Justice O'Connor," 62 *Notre Dame Law Review* 151 (1987); M. David Gelfand and Keith Werhan, "Federalism and the Separation of Powers on a 'Conservative' Court: Currents and Cross-Currents from Justices O'Connor and Scalia," 64 *Tulane Law Review* 1443 (1990); William P. Marshall, "'We Know It When We See It': The Supreme Court and Establishment," 59 *Southern California Law Review* 495 (1986); Kathleen Sullivan, "The Supreme Court 1991 Term: Foreword: The Justices of Rules and Standards," 106 *Harvard Law Review* 22 (1992); and Christopher S. Nesbit, "Note: County of Allegheny v. ACLU: Justice O'Connor's Endorsement Test," 68 *North Carolina Law Review* 590 (1990).

William Paterson
Portrait by James Sharples.
Collection of the Supreme Court of the United States.

WILLIAM PATERSON

BORN 24 December 1745, County Antrim,
    Ireland
NOMINATED to the Court 27 February 1793
    by George Washington
TOOK seat 11 March 1793
DIED 9 September 1806 in Albany, New York

William Paterson left a major imprint on the United States judiciary, but it was based largely on his achievements before he was appointed to the Supreme Court. Paterson supported an independent judiciary at the Philadelphia Convention of 1787. His New Jersey Plan of Union proposed to amend the ineffective Articles of Confederation by adding "a federal Judiciary . . . to consist of a supreme Tribunal" and providing that acts and treaties established under the new Constitution "shall be the supreme law of the respective States . . . and that the Judiciary of the several States shall be bound thereby." Much of the rest of his life was devoted to implementing the "supreme law" clause which he had introduced.

Two years later, as a member of the first United States Senate, Paterson was second only to Oliver Ellsworth as principal author of the Judiciary Act of 1789, legislation which for a century provided the framework of the federal judiciary, and much of which is still determinative. The first nine sections of the manuscript, those which establish the structure of the federal courts, are in Paterson's hand. He argued strenuously in the Senate for lower federal courts, rather than leaving local jurisdiction entirely to state courts. Ironically, President Washington attempted to withdraw Paterson's nomination the day after he had submitted it, because of the Judiciary Act. On February 28, the President wrote the Senate that "It has since occurred that he was a member of the Senate when the Law creating that office was passed, and that the time for which he was elected is not yet expired. I think it my duty therefore, to declare that I deem the nomination to have been null by the Constitution." Paterson was, nevertheless, confirmed four days later.

Although Paterson had never previously been on the bench, he brought a wealth of courtroom experience to the Supreme Court. As attorney general for New Jersey from 1776 to 1783, he was accustomed to long horseback rides from court to court. This may have been the best possible preparation for the arduous circuit court duties which seemed to consume the lives of early Supreme Court justices; in 1800, Paterson complained of riding "over stones and rocks and mountains" to get to court in New Hampshire. Paterson had compiled the *Laws of the State of New Jersey* and "Paterson's Practice Laws," a compendium of New Jersey procedures and practices in common law and chancery courts. Even though he did not take his seat until 1794, Paterson was the first holder of the second seat (intended to be that of the senior associate justice) to give substantive service. Paterson declined the opportunity for an early exit when Washington wished to appoint him as secretary of state in 1796.

Paterson's devotion to the integral part the judiciary would play in preserving the Constitution can be found in a lengthy charge to the federal grand jury in the Pennsylvania circuit court in 1795. There he offered one of the finest and most extensive justifications for judicial review prior to *Marbury v. Madison* (1803). The superiority of the Pennsylvania constitution to state legislation was at stake in *Van Horne's Lessee v. Dorrance*, but Paterson's powerful argument would extend as well to federal legislation. "I take it to be a clear proposition," he declared, "that if a legislative act oppugns a constitutional principle the former must give way, and be rejected on the score of repugnance. I hold it to be a position equally clear and sound that in such a case, it will be the duty of the court to adhere to the constitution and to declare the act null and void." He showed little concern for the tender feelings of legislatures. They are merely "creatures of the constitution; they owe their existence to the constitution, it is their commission and, therefore, all their acts must be conformable to it, or else they will be void." Lest the jury remain in doubt, he admonished that "there can be no doubt that every act of the legislature repugnant to the constitution is absolutely void." This powerful charge soon gained wide attention in pamphlet form. In *United States v. Lyon* (1799), Paterson informed the jury that the constitutionality of the Sedition Act was a matter for judges to determine, not juries.

Paterson had been a confirmed nationalist from the time in the Constitutional Convention that he had succeeded in establishing a secure place for New Jersey (and other small states) within the Union. This was shown in his first Supreme Court decision, *Talbot v. Jansen* (1795) when he ruled that state law could not affect United States citizenship: "Allegiance to a particular state is one thing; allegiance to the United States is another. . . . The sovereignties are different." A system of "sovereignties moving within a sovereignty" requires great care lest "a slight collision may disturb the harmony of the parts and endanger the machinery of the whole."

He went a huge step farther in *Penhallow v. Doane's Administrators* (1795), when he declared that the states had never been recognized as sovereign. He ridiculed the idea that the states could have any power of war and peace. He saw the United States as one great political body, with Congress "the directing principle and soul." Some in the gallery must have marveled at this imaginative paean to the repudiated Continental Congress: "Congress was the general, supreme, and controlling council of the nation, the centre of the nation, the centre of the union, the centre of force, and the sun of the political system."

One of four Supreme Court justices who had participated in the writing of the Constitution, Paterson twice took advantage of his status as a Founding Father. He argued persuasively in *Hylton v. United States* (1796) that the direct tax clause of the Constitution was intended to apply only to a capitation tax and a land tax. He asserted that it was "obviously the intention of the framers of the Constitution, that Congress should possess full power over every species of taxable property, except exports," since they had been painfully aware of the failings of the requisition system under the Articles of Confederation. He took a further step in *Calder v. Bull* (1798). After remarking that the Convention had

intended that the *ex post facto* clause apply only to criminal cases, not to civil cases, he added that he, personally, felt differently, implying that this was an issue on which he had lost in the secrecy of the last few days of the 1787 convention. In the same session as *Hylton v. United States* Paterson also participated in the vitally important *Ware v. Hylton*, but he added little to Justice Samuel Chase's masterful exposition.

As with most of the other Founding Fathers, Paterson strongly disapproved of political parties. Yet like so many of his peers, he too became extremely partisan. His intense respect for authority and stability, his aristocratic view of society, made him a natural ally of the Hamiltonian Federalists. He quickly displayed blatant Federalism in circuit trials of several participants in the so-called Whiskey Rebellion. Trials under the Sedition Act of 1798 brought out the worst in him. Even his admiring biographer describes him as an unjust "hanging judge" who merited the abuse of his Republican critics in 1799–1800. Following the prosecution of Matthew Lyon for sedition in 1799, Paterson proceeded to rule before Lyon's counsel could present a defense. When they protested, he "politely sat down." But Paterson's instructions demolished Lyon's defense and the Vermont congressman was convicted within an hour, the first conviction under the Sedition Act. Paterson sentenced him to four months in jail and fined him $1,000. He likewise undermined the defense of Anthony Haswell, who had defended Lyon so strenuously that he, too, was convicted of sedition.

Paterson became a special hero to the high Federalists with a charge to the Portsmouth, New Hampshire, grand jury in May 1800. He branded the Jeffersonian Republicans as Jacobins who were "the disorganizers of our happy country, and the only instruments of introducing discontent and dissatisfaction among the well-meaning part of the Community." His admirers hoped to reward him by persuading or coercing President John Adams to appoint Paterson as Chief Justice Oliver Ellsworth's successor. The Federalist-dominated Senate briefly held up Marshall's confirmation in hopes that Adams would relent, but the president had no desire to reward someone who was so popular among those Federalists who had so persistently undermined his administration. Federalist friends sent him spiteful remarks about Adams and his refusal to appoint him as chief justice which would have merited prosecution for sedition if they had been supporters of Jefferson rather than of Hamilton.

"I will not nominate him," Adams declared. After offering the position again to John Jay and unsuccessfully sounding out other nominees, Adams finally turned to Secretary of State John Marshall, shortly before the position would have fallen by default to President Jefferson. This was a dramatic turning point in American judicial history. If Paterson had been appointed, Thomas Jefferson would have been able to appoint a new chief justice in 1806, when Paterson died. Marshall, on the other hand, outlasted the Jefferson, Madison, Monroe, and John Quincy Adams administrations, and most of Jackson's as well. Paterson sent a warm letter of congratulations to Marshall and was a valued ally in the short time that they were together on the bench.

Ironically, nonpartisan statesmanship became the hallmark of Paterson's last few years on the Supreme Court. His last significant decision proved also to be his most important one. In *Stuart v. Laird* (1803), he upheld the constitutionality of the Circuit Court Act of 1802. The seeming partisanship of the Judiciary Act of 1801, by which the lame duck Congress attempted to create lifetime judicial sinecures for "deserving Federalists," while seeking the more worthy goal of relieving Supreme Court justices from their arduous circuit duties, caused President Jefferson to respond in kind. In addition to withholding some commissions from lesser lights such as William Marbury and others, the Republicans took the more important step of deleting the new circuit courts and, with them, the new circuit judges. The Supreme Court justices, all Federalists, received two concessions from the Republican Congress following the repeal of the Judiciary Act of 1801. Only one justice would be required in each circuit court, and the Supreme Court would meet for one four-week session each year, rather than for two sessions of two weeks each. This had the politically beneficial impact, from the Republican standpoint, of keeping the Court from convening until February 1803. Ironically, it was probably also fortunate timing for the Court. It gave them time to discuss the judicial reforms before ruling on whether

Congress had acted constitutionally in removing judicial positions from judges who had theoretically been appointed for a lifetime tenure. Only Justice Samuel Chase insisted that the members should refuse to continue riding circuits.

Paterson ruled in *Stuart v. Laird* because Marshall had already ruled on the question on circuit. Paterson's four brief paragraphs agreed essentially with Marshall's findings. Paterson conceded that Congress could assign Supreme Court justices to circuit duty. They had performed such duties from the beginning, and this practice had "fixed the construction" so that it is "too strong and obstinate to be shaken or controlled." The question is at rest, he admonished, and it ought not now to be revived. Congress has the "constitutional authority to establish from time to time such inferior tribunals as they may think proper; and to transfer a cause from one tribunal to another." Paterson did not add, if he even knew, that Chief Justice John Jay had questioned the constitutionality of circuit riding in September 1790. The Supreme Court justices' wisdom in accepting a setback in their politics and in their personal comfort, rather than challenging the dominant Republicans, has been described as the ultimate "example of the nonpartisanship of the American judiciary." Just the week before, the Court had chosen a much less dangerous case, *Marbury v. Madison* (1803), through which to challenge Congress and the Jefferson administration.

Justice William Johnson, whose term overlapped with Paterson's for barely two years, unjustly described Paterson in 1822 as "a slow man" who "willingly declined the Trouble" of writing opinions. This despite the fact that Paterson, not Johnson, was the first to write a dissent from a Marshall opinion, in *Simms v. Slacum* (1805). Paterson was seriously injured in a carriage accident in 1804, was nearly immobile for weeks, and he missed both Court and circuit assignments. Severe illness forced him to leave the New York circuit in August 1806, where he was contending that the court should subpoena President Jefferson and Secretary of State James Madison, to answer allegations of defendants being prosecuted for participation in Francisco Miranda's attack on Venezuela. His departure left the field to district judge Matthias Tallmadge, who opposed this affront to the executive. Justice Paterson died shortly afterward at the home of his daughter in Albany, New York. Justice Johnson could scarcely have known the colleague whom he criticized for partisan reasons sixteen years later.

—DONALD O. DEWEY

Bibliography

John E. O'Connor, *William Paterson, Lawyer and Statesman, 1745–1806* (1979), is admiring of Paterson's career, yet properly critical of his partisan decisions. His life is ably and briefly profiled in Michael Kraus's essay in Friedman and Israel, 1 *Justices* 163. Gertrude S. Wood's doctoral dissertation, "William Paterson of New Jersey, 1745–1806," (Columbia, 1933) was privately published in condensed form in 1940. Julian P. Boyd in Willard Thorpe, ed., *The Lives of Eighteen from Princeton* (1946) utilizes the *Van Horne* case to justify entitling his essay on Paterson, "Forerunner of John Marshall." Leonard B. Rosenberg's unpublished doctoral dissertation, "The Political Thought of William Paterson" (New School for Social Research, 1967) helps us understand his judicial career.

RUFUS WHEELER PECKHAM, JR.

BORN 8 November 1838, Albany, New York

NOMINATED to the Court 3 December 1895
by Grover Cleveland

DIED 24 October 1909 in Altamont,
New York

Rufus Wheeler Peckham, Jr., was born into
one of New York's oldest and most prominent
upstate families in 1838. While in later life he
relished the mantle of judicial impartiality, his life
was filled with intense partisan furor, and there
can be little doubt that this fact exercised a tremendous influence over Peckham's judicial philosophy. Peckham's father, Rufus Wheeler
Peckham, Sr., was a Democratic party stalwart
who served in the House of Representatives and,
like his son, on the New York supreme court and
court of appeals. Rufus Jr. was strongly influenced
by his father's political and philosophical views
and was so similar to his father in mannerisms and
appearance that the two were occasionally confused by their contemporaries. Peckham's brother,
Wheeler H. Peckham, was a president of the state
bar and himself a nearly successful candidate for
a seat on the Supreme Court.

Peckham's judicial philosophy was strongly
shaped by the two preoccupations of his pre-
judicial career, namely, struggling with Tam-
many Hall for control of the state Democratic
party machinery and representing major corporate interests, particularly railroads. In the political arena, Peckham aligned himself closely with
Grover Cleveland, who came to view Peckham
as a key ally. On the corporate stage, Peckham
developed a reputation as a zealous, if not brilliant or inventive, advocate for the captains of
industry. Although Peckham himself was never
the target of charges of serious corruption, there
can be little doubt that Peckham's excellent political connections were useful to his clients and
contributed to his success in practice—judges in
New York are elected and in the second half of
the nineteenth century these elections were
fiercely partisan.

As the nineteenth century drew to a close,
America's tycoons were under attack from an
array of groups seeking to reign in the industri-
alists' unfettered control over the market and the
workplace. Reformers sought to bust monopolies, develop more humane working conditions,
end child labor, and protect consumers. To industry's defense rose Rufus Peckham, and great
titans of industry such as George F. Baker, Jim
Fisk, Jay Gould, James J. Hill, J. Pierpont Morgan, William Rockefeller, James Speyer, and
Cornelius Vanderbilt became his clients, friends,
and confidants.

While Peckham's best known Supreme
Court opinion is *Lochner v. New York* (1905),
the views in that case are stated much more vigorously in a dissent Peckham authored while on
the New York court of appeals, to which he was
elected in 1886 with Grover Cleveland's solid
support. In *People v. Budd* (1889), New York's
efforts to fix rate levels for grain elevators were
attacked as unconstitutional. The court upheld
the statute, but Peckham issued an impassioned
dissent, which contains one of the clearest and
earliest statements of substantive due process.
Directing stinging criticism at his colleagues for
their political partisanship, he observed that "all
men, however great and however honest, are
almost necessarily affected by the general belief
of their times." Yet Peckham, even more than
his colleagues, was driven by a political credo.
He believed that allowing the government to
intervene in the economy would "wholly ignore
the later and as I firmly believe the more firmly
correct ideas which an increase of civilization
and a fuller knowledge of the fundamental laws
of political economy, and a truer conception of
the proper functions of government have given
us at the present day."

Curiously, Peckham saw the political controversy in terms of an almost Marxist class struggle.
In his mind, the government could not be permitted to involve itself in a struggle between one
"class" (impoverished farmers) against another
("capitalist" grain factors), since this would lead
to "a new competition for the possession of the
government so that legislative aid may be given
to the class in possession thereof in its contests
with rival classes or interests in all sections or

corners of the industrial world." For Peckham, the Constitution formed a bulwark against governmental interference in favor of the underprivileged: the statute was an abridgement of "the most sacred rights of property and the individual's liberty of contract" and was entitled to no presumption of validity. Freedom of contract and the takings clause thus invalidated such legislation which, moreover, was "not only vicious in its nature, communistic in its tendency and in my belief wholly ineffective to permanently obtain the results aimed at, but illegal."

In 1895, the death of Justice Howell E. Jackson created a vacancy that President Cleveland was quick to fill with the nomination of his Albany protégé, Rufus Peckham. The confirmation process was uneventful. During his thirteen-year tenure on the Court, Peckham authored 303 opinions, nine dissents and two concurring opinions, only one of which is generally still reckoned to be of importance, *Lochner v. New York* (1905).

From his arrival, Peckham belonged to the Court's ultraconservative wing. He joined in what was perhaps the Court's most pernicious case after *Dred Scott*, *Plessy v. Ferguson* (1896), endorsing the "separate but equal" doctrine, and he dissented in nearly all the handful of cases, most notably *Holden v. Hardy* (1898) and *Jacobson v. Massachusetts* (1905), in which reform legislation was sustained. By 1905, Peckham was finally able to muster a 5–4 majority on the Court for his viewpoint.

In *Lochner,* the Court was presented with a challenge to New York's law limiting the number of hours that an employee could work in a bakery to sixty per week. Peckham declared that the right of employee and employer to contract freely for performance of labor is fundamental to the Fourteenth Amendment, and any state power of intervention narrowly circumscribed. If the state chooses to invoke its police power in a way that potentially infringes freedom of contract, the Court must inquire: "Is this a fair, reasonable, and appropriate exercise of the police power of the state, or is it an unreasonable, unnecessary, and arbitrary interference of the right of the individual to his personal liberty, or to enter into those contracts in relation to labor which may seem to him appropriate or necessary

for the support of himself and his family?" So phrased, there could be little doubt as to the anticipated outcome. The effect of *Lochner* was to elevate the Supreme Court to the status of a superlegislature authorized to reconsider the wisdom of legislation and to strike down offensive acts as an abridgement of the "sacred freedom of contract."

Peckham and his colleagues maintained that the Civil War amendments had one essential purpose: to further individual economic rights, and particularly the freedom of contract. They simultaneously denied or undermined what clearly had been the major purpose of those amendments, to protect the fundamental civil and human rights of the recently emancipated slaves. Thus, in the hands of the Court's conservative majority, these constitutional provisions had the effect not only of frustrating the efforts of Progressive reformers to enact and enforce legislation protecting consumers, promoting health, and improving safety in the workplace, but also of offering no protection to black southerners feeling the oppressive hand of the Ku Klux Klan and its sympathizers in state government, or to individuals facing criminal procedures clearly at odds with the Bill of Rights. Peckham was forthright in acknowledging that his purpose in introducing substantive due process was to protect America's industrial sector, the mainspring of America's economy, against the regulatory barrage of the Progressive movement. Peckham acknowledged a single exception—for women. In his paternalistic view, women were the "weaker sex" and required protection from the exploitation of men (*Muller v. Oregon,* 1908).

Peckham was also an active writer on cases challenging the Sherman Antitrust Act. His opinions in this area reveal strong sympathies for antitrust legislation for the protection of small business. "It is not for the real prosperity of any country that such changes should occur which result in transferring an independent business man, the head of his establishment, small though it might be, into a mere servant or agent of a corporation selling the commodities which he once manufactured or dealt in, having no voice in shaping the business policy of the company and bound to obey orders issued by others" (*United States v. Trans-Missouri Freight Association,* 1897). In *Addyston Pipe & Steel Co. v. United States* (1899), he succeeded in breathing new life into the Sherman Act by rejecting the argument hitherto advanced by manufacturers that proof of total monopoly was necessary to sustain an action. Higher prices alone constituted sufficient evidence, Peckham reasoned. Still, in the most important antitrust case of the period, *Northern Securities Co. v. United States* (1904), he sided with the conservative majority in urging a narrow reading of the Sherman Act, so that it applied only against *unreasonable* restraints of trade.

A significant number of Peckham's other contributions on the Court were in the area of criminal procedure. With only a few exceptions, Peckham, the former Albany County prosecutor, revealed his disdain for the "mere technicalities" of criminal procedure which are the bedrock of the Bill of Rights (*White v. United States,* 1896). He was vehement in the conviction that the Bill of Rights protections of the criminal justice system, while grudgingly applicable in federal courts, should not apply to the states (*Maxwell v. Dow,* 1900).

Today we know Peckham principally through the devastating critique of Oliver Wendell Holmes, Jr., whose *Lochner* dissent is a dazzling example of judicial exposition. "The Fourteenth Amendment," he insisted, "does not enact Mr. Herbert Spencer's *Social Statics*"—a popular and widely read presentation of the doctrine of laissez-faire. Still, it took thirty years, including a depression and the appointment of a New Deal court before this view was accepted by the Court and substantive due process fell into judicial opprobrium. By the 1950s it seemed that

Peckham and his doctrine were useful to law professors only as an example of what the Supreme Court should not do.

However, in the 1960s and 1970s, scholars and activists looking for a creative way of addressing civil rights problems turned again to *Lochner.* Substantive due process, they reasoned, might be revived as a doctrinal basis for challenging state and federal laws that interfere with fundamental civil and human rights, such as the right to privacy, reproductive rights, and freedom from ethnic or religious discrimination. Reframed in this way, substantive due process continues to live as a credible constitutional doctrine, but the circumstances of the doctrine's birth under the parentage of Rufus Peckham do little to burnish it.

—SCOTT HORTON

BIBLIOGRAPHY

There is no full-scale biography of Peckham, but shorter sketches include Richard Skolnik, "Rufus Peckham" in Friedman and Israel, 3 *Justices* 1685 (the most exhaustive treatment of Peckham's legal career); A. Oakey Hall, "The New Supreme Court Justice" 8 *Green Bag* (1896) (an interesting though somewhat fawning contemporary account of Peckham's career as a lawyer); and *Proceedings of the Thirty-Third Annual Meeting of the New York State Bar Association* (1910), 683–712 (professional reminiscences). A harshly critical dissection of judicial interventionism by the conservative court of the Peckham era is to be found in Louis B. Boudin, *Government by Judiciary* (1932), 2:423–42.

L.B. Proctor, "Rufus W. Peckham" in *Albany Law Journal,* vol. 55 (1897) (contemporary biography up to time of Supreme Court appointment).

MAHLON PITNEY

BORN 5 February 1858, Morristown,
New Jersey

NOMINATED to the Court 19 February 1912
by William Howard Taft

TOOK seat 18 March 1912; resigned
31 December 1922

DIED 9 December 1924 in Washington, D.C.

Scion of a distinguished New Jersey legal family, Mahlon Pitney brought a wealth of political and judicial experience to the Court. From 1895 to 1899, he served in the U.S. House of Representatives, and from 1899 to 1901, was a member of the New Jersey state senate, being its president in 1901. He served on the New Jersey supreme court from 1901 to 1908, when he was appointed chancellor of New Jersey. Four years later President Taft appointed him to the United States Supreme Court.

One of Pitney's principal specialties on the Court was tax cases. His most famous tax opinion, still taught in law schools today, was *Eisner v. Macomber* (1920), in which the Court held that stock dividends were not taxable income within the meaning of the Sixteenth Amendment.

Yet it is for his decisions in labor cases that Pitney is best remembered. Pitney's opinions in a few high-profile cases earned him a reputation in some quarters as an anti-labor reactionary. He wrote the majority opinion in *Coppage v. Kansas* (1915), declaring that a Kansas statute prohibiting an employer from requiring his employees to contract not to join a union impaired the employer's liberty of contract; and his majority opinion in *Hitchman Coal & Coke Co. v. Mitchell* (1917) held that an employer was entitled to an injunction prohibiting union organizers from recruiting employees working under such a contract. Pitney dissented in *Wilson v. New* (1917), which upheld a federal statute regulating the wages and hours of railroad workers; and he voted to strike down an Oregon law prescribing minimum wages for women in *Stettler v. O'Hara* (1917).

Yet for Pitney, the rights of property and contract frequently yielded to the police power of the state. For instance, Pitney voted in *Bunting v. Oregon* (1917) and other cases to uphold maximum hour laws for both men and women; he voted to uphold statutes prohibiting payment of employees in company scrip and requiring at least semimonthly payment of employees in *Keokee Consolidated Coke Co. v. Taylor* (1914) and *Erie R.R. Co. v. Williams* (1914); and he dissented from the majority opinion in *Truax v. Corrigan* (1921), which struck down an Arizona statute prohibiting the issuance of injunctions against labor's peaceful picketing of an employer. Most notably, Pitney authored a trilogy of cases in 1917 upholding various state workmen's compensation statutes. Moreover, he generally displayed a sympathetic attitude toward injured workers in cases arising under the Federal Employers Liability Act and the Safety Appliance Act.

Pitney's reputation as an anti-labor judge was enhanced by his opinions in *Paine Lumber Co. v. Neal* (1917) and *Duplex Printing Co. v. Deering* (1921). Dissenting in the former and writing for the majority in the latter, Pitney opined that an employer whose product was being boycotted by a labor union was entitled to an injunction against the union under the antitrust laws. At the same time, however, he joined the Court's opinion in the first *Coronado Coal* (1922) case, refusing to invoke the Sherman Antitrust Act against the strike of a coal miners' local union. Moreover, throughout his tenure on the Court, Pitney applied the antitrust laws against business with equal zeal. Like many other justices of his period, Pitney brought to the Court the atomistic, competitive world view of nineteenth-century liberalism, which distrusted economic combinations of any kind.

Such liberalism did not yet fully embrace a solicitude for noneconomic civil liberties. Pitney consistently joined in the Court's opinions upholding convictions of wartime dissenters under the Espionage Act, himself writing the majority opinion in *Pierce v. United States* (1920). Moreover, his opinion in *Frank v. Magnum* (1915) upheld against a due process challenge the conviction of a man whose trial had been dominated by a mob.

Yet here again Pitney defies easy categorization. He joined the opinion creating the exclusionary rule for federal criminal cases in *Weeks v. United States* (1914); he voted to strike down a city ordinance mandating segregated housing in *Buchanan v. Warley* (1917); he joined the opinion in *Guinn v. United States* (1915) striking down Oklahoma's racially discriminatory scheme of voter eligibility; and his concurring opinion in *Newberry v. United States* (1921), contending for broad federal power to regulate primary elections for federal officials, anticipated the Court's invalidation of the racially discriminatory primary in the 1940s. Indeed, the complexity of Pitney's record exposes the folly of using vulgar political taxonomy as a means of explaining the judicial behavior of his era.

—BARRY CUSHMAN

BIBLIOGRAPHY

The standard biographical source on Pitney is Alan Ryder Breed, "Mahlon Pitney: His Life and Career—Political and Judicial," (unpublished senior thesis, Princeton University, 1932). David Levitan, "Mahlon Pitney—Labor Judge," 40 *Virginia Law Review* 733 (1954), and Michael R. Belknap, "Mr. Justice Pitney and Progressivism," 16 *Seton Hall Law Review* 381 (1986) offer valuable insights into Pitney's judicial career.

LEWIS FRANKLIN POWELL, JR.

BORN 19 November 1907, Suffolk, Virginia

NOMINATED to the Court 21 October 1971
by Richard M. Nixon

TOOK seat 7 January 1972; retired
26 June 1987

A reluctant nominee who had repeatedly removed himself from consideration earlier, Lewis F. Powell ultimately yielded to the entreaties of Solicitor General Erwin Griswold, Attorney General John N. Mitchell, and Senator Harry F. Byrd, Jr., in October 1971 to accept nomination by President Nixon to succeed the late Justice Hugo L. Black. Given the ABA Committee on Federal Judiciary's highest rating as "the best qualified available," Powell was unanimously and enthusiastically approved by the Senate Judiciary Committee. The full Senate followed suit briskly by confirming him 89–1 on December 7. The sole dissenter was the maverick one-term Democratic senator from Oklahoma, Fred R. Harris, who opposed the nominee as "an elitist who has never shown any deep feeling for little people."

Nothing could have been further from the truth. The then sixty-four-year-old Powell, although to the manner born and destined to reap a very considerable fortune in his long and productive legal career, had dedicated significant aspects of his life to the socioeconomic and political enhancement of his less fortunate brethren; moreover, his record on the bench demonstrated his concerns for "little people" amply and poignantly. His jurisprudence was governed to a considerable degree, indeed a decisive one, by his strivings for fairness, compassion, equity, and an adherence to his perception of genuine societal consensus. Lewis Powell quickly came to be regarded as the conscience of the Court on such emotion-charged issues as race and gender, as well as the omnipresent contentious questions of religion, suffrage, and criminal justice. He prevailed on the side of justice, as he interpreted it, by casting the decisive vote in numerous 5–4 opinions on a host of closely contested cases.

Professor Herman Schwartz, writing in *The Nation*, called him "the most powerful judge of his time," and *U.S. News & World Report* noted that Powell's "courtly manner . . . failed to disguise the immense power he wielded."

Not all new members of the Court pattern themselves consciously on predecessors, although often they evince jurisprudential commitments or practices that trigger comparisons. Justice Powell, however, clearly and consciously endeavored to emulate the second John Marshall Harlan and, to a somewhat lesser degree, Felix Frankfurter. But the second Harlan was his judicial hero. Powell had known him personally, and respected and admired him philosophically and jurisprudentially. In considerable measure, Powell's career on the Court reflected Harlan's approach to adjudication and interpretation—centrist, moderate to conservatively cautious, and historically conscious. But, given Powell's conscience-driven stances on such pressing civil rights and liberties issues as racial and gender discrimination and abortion, it is obvious that he was considerably less consistent jurisprudentially than Harlan. The latter's all but predictable Frankfurterian embrace of judicial restraint, of deference to the political branches of government, of all but commandment-like dedication to the principles of the separation of powers and of federalism, was more than occasionally violated by Powell. His pragmatism, his "conscience" approach to adjudication, his bowing to a perceived need of "balancing of competing constitutional interests," was at least partly un-Harlanesque. Powell's frequent ally, Justice Sandra Day O'Connor, captured that fact well when, in a *Harvard Law Review* tribute to Powell on his retirement, she contended that "at times he may have been willing to sacrifice a little consistency in legal theory in order to reach for justice in a particular case."

On the other hand, the Powell of the realm of economic proprietarian matters; of the suffrage, including reapportionment and redistricting; of criminal justice; of Tenth Amendment issues; of the reach of the federal interstate commerce power; and of access to the courts, especially the excessive utilization of the writ of *habeas corpus*, was vintage Harlan.

Arguably, the opinion for which Justice Powell may well be most remembered is the "affirmative action" case of *Regents of the University of California v. Bakke* (1978), one which he himself viewed as seminal in the universe of racial discrimination. That he was given the assignment of writing the opinion would seem at first blush surprising, for while he had supported the central tenets of the public school desegregation case of *Brown v. Board of Education* (1954), he was no partisan of the all-out approach of activist jurists such as Earl Warren, William O. Douglas, or William J. Brennan, Jr. As a gradualist and as a former state school board president, he consistently opposed mandated busing in order to achieve racial balance. As a lifelong resident of Virginia, he was reluctant to have the judiciary become a (and certainly not *the*) leader in broad-scaled, imposed integration (as opposed to *Brown*-based desegregation). He expressed that view forcefully in such pre-*Bakke* school race cases as *Keyes v. School District #1, Denver* (1973) and *Milliken v. Bradley* (1974), and such post-*Bakke* ones as *Columbus Board of Education v. Penick* (1979) and *Estes v. Dallas NAACP* (1980).

Yet Lewis Powell had had no truck with those in his state who had called for "massive resistance," a program designed to negate the holding in *Brown* and its implementation decision, *Brown II* (1955). Notwithstanding his place in Virginia's conservative establishment, he was opposed to continued segregation, and he publicly characterized the Byrd organization's anti-Supreme Court policy of "massive resistance" and "interposition" as "a lot of rot"—a strong statement for the normally kind and conciliatory Powell. It was he who mounted the opposition to those policies and ultimately succeeded in defeating them. As chairman of the Richmond Public School Board from 1952 to 1961, he provided the indispensable leadership for what proved to be the successful disturbance-free desegregation of the city's public schools. It was not an easy task, but it earned him the support of the NAACP at the time of his appointment to the Court.

Bakke and its two components, known as *Bakke I* and *II*, reached the bench four years after the Court's failure to bite the proverbial bullet of "affirmative action—reverse discrimination" in *DeFunis v. Odegaard* (1974). Then, over Justice Douglas's eloquent dissent, it had mooted the issue because Marco DeFunis, already attending the University of Washington Law School under court order, would soon graduate. At the Court's conference following oral argument in *Bakke*, it became clear that neither Chief Justice Warren E. Burger nor Justice Brennan would be able to harness a majority, or even a plurality, for both aspects of the case. It fell to Powell to construct the two 5–4 opinions, and he accomplished it by creating an intriguing scenario.

First, supported by the chief justice, John Paul Stevens, Potter Stewart, and William H. Rehnquist, he ruled that Alan Bakke—a rejected white applicant, who was admittedly more qualified to enter the University of California's Medical School at Davis than minority students who had been admitted on the basis of a rigid sixteen-out-of-one-hundred racial quota established by the university—would have to be admitted because that rigid racial quota constituted a violation of the Fourteenth Amendment's equal protection clause. Powell's four supporters, however, wanted the issue to be settled on *statutory* grounds—namely, that Title VI of the 1964 Civil Rights Act specifically barred discrimination on the basis of race to any governmentally subsidized institution, such as the University of California. Powell, however, insisted on *constitutional* grounds, for he feared that accepting the statutory basis would too strictly harness affirmative action initiative and experimentation, which he favored and which he expounded on in the second prong of his opinion.

In that part (joined by Brennan, White, Marshall, and Blackmun) Powell upheld on constitutional grounds—the same equal protection clause—the significant concept of utilizing race as a plus. He admonished, however, that it could only be used when a university had a "substantial interest" in a diverse student body "that legitimately may be served by a properly devised admissions program involving the competitive consideration of race and ethnic origin." Thus, over the angry objections of the Stevens group,

Lewis Franklin Powell, Jr.
Photograph by Ken Heinen.
Collection of the Supreme Court of the United States.

the Powell-led majority in *Bakke II* in effect gave a green light to a host of innovative actions on the affirmative action/reverse discrimination front, and this despite his striking down of rigid racial or ethnic quotas.

The future would prove the dissenters' dire prophecies to be generally correct. Indeed, Justice Powell himself would proffer serious objections to the expansive interpretations given to what he had clearly intended to be a narrow holding. He would be particularly disturbed by some of the Court's broad-gauged backing of the use of racial quotas in involuntary school busing—crying out in separate dissenting opinions in two leading cases (decided just one year after his *Bakke* opinions that he was "profoundly disturb[ed]" by this "creation of bad constitutional law." Yet, although he had never intended his *Bakke* holdings to give warrant to what he now decried and although it is, of course, possible to distinguish among and between sundry racial quota cases, there is no doubt that his Solomon-like resolution has resulted demonstrably in an embrace of *Bakke's* permissive, but very little of its restrictive, mandate.

Perhaps that is why, in an un-Harlanesque manifestation, Powell, in evident inconsistency with *Bakke*, supplied the decisive fifth vote in *United States v. Paradise* (1987), narrowly upholding an Alabama federal district judge's orders of 1983 and 1984 requiring Alabama to promote one black state trooper for each white state trooper until the state could develop an acceptable promotion procedure. Brennan's plurality opinion was joined in full by his colleagues Marshall and Blackmun, with Stevens and Powell penning separate concurrences. Justice Powell's vote in favor of promotion quotas represented a clear departure from his contrary stance in *Bakke* nine years earlier, a fact of which he seemed to take note by explaining that a rigid quota was proper in this instance because it was "short in duration" and the "effect of the order on innocent white workers is likely to be relatively diffuse." He pointed to evidence that the state "had engaged in persistent violation of constitutional rights and repeatedly failed to carry out court orders." In effect, Powell's crucial vote meant that strict racial quotas in both promotion

and hiring would likely henceforth be upheld by the United States Supreme Court—as indeed they have generally been to date, with some exceptions.

In no area of constitutional law and interpretation was Lewis Powell more influential than in that of First Amendment issues involving the religion clauses—"Congress shall make no law respecting an establishment of religion, or prohibiting the free exercise thereof." The first of these two phrases provided Powell with almost incredibly predictable triumphs. In the thirty leading cases that the Court decided during his tenure on the issue of the separation of church and state, he was on the winning side in *all thirty*. Nineteen of these found violations of the clause; eleven sanctioned accommodation of sundry forms of governmental aid to religion. No other contemporary justice could boast of such a record. Fearful of the potentials of religiopolitical strife, he unfailingly sensed the apposite stance for the good of society. Toward that end, and unlike several of his colleagues, he firmly embraced Chief Justice Burger's triad requirement articulated in *Lemon v. Kurtzman* (1971) even more consistently and more closely than its own author. That triad, still in existence, albeit somewhat embattled, requires that aid to religion provided by the government: (1) must have a secular legislative purpose; (2) its principal or primary effect must be one that neither advances nor inhibits religion; and (3) it must not foster an excessive entanglement with religion.

Thus, Powell was willing to join the 5–4 majority that sanctioned a Minnesota law providing for an across-the-board tax deduction of up to $500 for parents of *all* elementary, and up to $700 of *all* secondary school children for bona fide educational expenses, identified as "tuition, secular textbooks and instructional materials, and transportation." Distinguishing *Committee for Public Education and Religious Liberty v. Nyquist* (1973), the majority opinion by Justice Rehnquist surprisingly gained Powell's vote, because Rehnquist claimed that the Minnesota law withstood separation of church and state challenges because it was "neutral" in design; it enabled parents of public school children as well as those in parochial and other private schools to avail themselves of the annual deduction (*Mueller v. Allen*, 1983).

On the other hand, Powell was in the 5–4 majority that struck down a Grand Rapids, Michigan, law that authorized state payment for personnel, supplies, and materials furnished to forty religious schools (*Grand Rapids School District v. Ball*, 1985). Although he joined another 5–4 majority in *Lynch v. Donnelly* (1984), upholding the constitutionality of Pawtucket, Rhode Island's, government-sponsored practice of displaying a crèche as part of a Christmas display in a park owned by a nonprofit corporation in the heart of the city's shopping district, he was in full agreement with the 7–2 majority that declared unconstitutional Louisiana's "balanced treatment" statute that required the teaching of "creationism" to balance that of "evolution" in its public school curriculum (*Edwards v. Aguillard*, 1987). There, in a concurring opinion that was vintage Powell, he movingly elucidated Jefferson's and Madison's labors in quest of a full measure of religious freedom and an utter ban on religious establishment.

Justice Powell's prior experience as chairman of the Richmond School Board provided him a well-informed and pragmatically enlightened viewpoint in the many delicate matters the Court faced during his tenure involving public education. His background and many written opinions involving this issue established him as a kind of education authority on the land's highest tribunal. This is true not only in the area of desegregation, where his careful balancing led to the flexible affirmative action compromise in *Bakke*, but in other areas of education law as well. His careful, case-by-case approach, and his distrust of broad, bright-line legal rules in complex subject areas, was as evident in Powell's education jurisprudence generally as it was in *Bakke*. But for all his balancing of competing constitutional interests in those cases, he never lost sight of the central purpose of the schools themselves, namely: education. He was particularly loathe to let abstract principles interfere with the practical pursuit of this purpose.

Perhaps the most important of Justice Powell's many written opinions in cases involving the public schools was that in *San Antonio*

School District v. Rodriguez in 1973. The case was a class action challenging the manner in which the state of Texas supported its local public schools partly through local property taxes. The suit claimed that the state's method violated equal protection by discriminating against children in poorer districts. Justice Powell's opinion for the 5–4 majority proceeded cautiously, with respect for established precedents, the traditional distribution of state and local authority, and the complexity of the subject. He refused to break new constitutional ground by declaring education a "fundamental right," and he declined the opportunity to launch a broad egalitarian legal revolution by declaring wealth a suspect classification. He was not persuaded that in an area as complex as education, levels of educational funding exactly paralleled levels of educational quality. Instead, Powell believed it was reasonable as well as constitutionally permissible for a state to establish a certain minimum funding level for local school districts, and to allow improvements beyond this level for those districts with the resources and the political will to fund them.

In reaching this conclusion, Justice Powell sounded a common theme in his education jurisprudence. He emphasized that the kinds of complex decisions involved in state plans for funding education were precisely the kind that were most appropriate for resolution by those who have the local familiarity and the educational and administrative expertise to decide wisely. For this reason, these kinds of decisions were not appropriate for resolution by the courts, which, as he frequently pointed out, lack such familiarity and expertise.

Beyond obvious constitutional mandates and the manifest requirements of justice, Powell frequently showed a confirmed faith in the manner in which state or local authorities' political traditions had worked out their own modes of operation. He distrusted the ability of the federal courts to improve on these traditions by novel constitutional interpretations requiring broad federally mandated changes. His defense of local control over decisions affecting education was of a piece with his vigorous resistance to the court-ordered elimination of local political patronage and the old system of political parties.

While Powell's jurisprudence in the education area emphasized local control, and while he did not agree that education was a "fundamental right" of constitutional proportions (and thus preserved his flexibility), he nevertheless adhered strongly to the position that an important function of the state is to make public education available to children. In his view, the balance of equal justice required that the state's responsibility for education weigh heavily against competing interests. Thus, he concurred with Justice Brennan's opinion for the Court in the remarkable case of *Plyler v. Doe*, upholding the right of minor children of undocumented alien residents to receive a free public education, like all other children in Texas. Powell's concurrence, however, avoided the implication that education was a "fundamental right," and instead emphasized the balancing of the practical concerns in the case, most especially the potential consequences of denying educational opportunity to thousands of children, many of whom were likely one day to become United States citizens. Justice Powell also objected in principle to a state's penalizing resident children permanently because of their parent's immigration status, and he punctuated the point by indicating that he would take the same position if there were a similar complete denial of any other important state benefit, such as welfare assistance. He distinguished *Rodriguez* on this basis as well, pointing out that there was no question in that case of any child being positively denied an education, as there was in *Plyler*.

In yet another important equal protection case involving education, *Mississippi University for Women v. Hogan*, Powell found himself in dissent. However, his opinion provides an important glance at his particular vision of the equal protection clause. For Justice Powell, that clause was not a constitutional mandate for imposing an ideological uniformity of educational practice across the nation. Instead, the clause embodies a liberating spirit, which a wooden application would stultify. This view required a certain flexibility, and a careful attention to the unique facts of each case, and the potential consequences of a given decision. In *Rodriguez*, this had meant that beyond a basic minimum, the equal protec-

tion clause allows the state the freedom to experiment with educational funding formulae in accord with the will of the local electorate. Similarly, in his dissent in *Hogan*, Justice Powell stated that by:

> applying heightened equal protection analysis to this case, the Court frustrates the liberating spirit of the Equal Protection Clause. It forbids the State from providing women with an opportunity to choose the type of university they prefer.

Instead of reading equal protection as both a protective and liberating aspiration, the Court had, in Justice Powell's view, protected nothing of value by its decision, and had instead simply eliminated one desirable alternative for the women of the state of Mississippi. In effect, the Court's decision violated Powell's jurisprudential principles by ignoring the facts in deference to an unenlightened and unfortunate application of theoretical legal principle.

Finally, as a former school administrator, Powell was always sensitive to intrusion into the affairs of school management by a judiciary ill-equipped to do so competently. Thus, during his very first term, while he wrote the opinion of the Court in *Healy v. James* (1972), and agreed with his fellow justices in finding that a school administration had violated a student's First Amendment rights, Powell trod very carefully. Instead of holding broadly that the school administrators had no authority to deny recognition to a controversial student organization, he proceeded "with special caution, recognizing the mutual interests of students, faculty members, and administrators in an environment free from disruptive interference with the educational process." He asserted that where the necessarily wide latitude for free expression threatens to collide with the equally necessary maintenance of order, the Constitution does not sweep one aside in deference to the other, but "strikes the required balance." Thus, while it would not be unlawful for school administrators to deny recognition to the student group in order to maintain order and discipline, the school would have to make an adequate showing that the proposed organization would likely act beyond mere speech, by disrupting the school's ability to function in an orderly fashion. In the specific case at hand, no such showing had been made, and so the case was remanded for further hearing.

Hence, in *Healy*, a soon-to-be-classic Powellian balance was struck, a balance that looked not only toward the Court's constitutional doctrine, but also to the details of the case, the competing interests that would be affected by the decision, and the purpose of the institution under scrutiny. While *Healy* was not an especially difficult case, Powell showed in his opinion for the Court that he was no ideological warrior. His opinion foreshadowed his continued cautious and balanced jurisprudence, and his view that the most important elements in a given case lay not in any overarching theory, but in the facts and in the practical consequences involved.

Because the facts were paramount, Powell frequently expressed the view that those who were most intimately familiar with them should be allowed the latitude to make the relevant policies. Thus, in his dissent in *Board of Education v. Pico* (1982), he found that the Court's interpretation of the First Amendment to prohibit a local school board from removing certain books from a school library was "a debilitating encroachment upon the institution of a free people." A school library, after all, was part of a school, and the persons responsible for the education of the children should be allowed to decide what was appropriate for that education, and what was not. Far from being government censorship, Powell viewed the book removal as essential a question of educational policy. Therefore, like the selection of textbooks and the design of curriculae, these decisions should be for state and local school administrators to make, not for a federal court.

Similarly, Powell expressed the view that disciplinary regulations are best left to the states and local schools. He evidently did so not for ideological reasons, but because, on balance, he believed that such a disposition of responsibility would allow the schools to function best as educational institutions. He opposed requiring elaborate due process hearings prior to student suspensions, and he refused to extend the Eighth Amendment's cruel and unusual punishment

prohibition to cover "paddling," or corporal punishment, in the public schools. Speaking for a 5–4 majority, as he did so often, Powell observed in *Ingraham v. Wright* (1977) that history, tradition, the common law, and the decisions of most of the states dealing with the question permitted corporal punishment, and prohibited only the use of excessive or unreasonable force. Against this factual background, he was unwilling to find that the mere use of some corporal punishment in the schools was "cruel and unusual." Nor was he persuaded that the Constitution required additional procedural safeguards in administering non-excessive punishment. It was certainly typical of his jurisprudence that in such cases Powell considered not only the rights of the persons who were complaining of harsh disciplinary measures, but also the important interests of other students and the local communities, in an orderly school environment conducive to the school's purpose—providing students with an education.

Justice Powell's commitment to balancing societal and individual privileges and obligations under a written Constitution is appropriately illustrated by his approach to the universe of criminal justice. There, with an eye to the public's very real fear of burgeoning crime, he more often than not chose a "tough" stance on the side of what has often been characterized as the "peace forces" versus the "criminal forces." He frequently evinced sympathy with the difficult tasks confronting law enforcement authorities, perhaps recalling Justice Robert H. Jackson's admonition in a famed dissenting opinion, that there is no obligation "to turn the constitutional Bill of Rights into a suicide pact" (*Terminiello v. Chicago,* 1949).

Profoundly committed to procedural due process and the basic prerogatives of a fair trial, he nonetheless would not embrace a jurisprudence that allowed defendants and their attorneys "to play a game with the courts." Hence, he was willing, for example, to provide his votes to trim excessive, multiple use of *habeas corpus* appeals arising from duly processed state cases such as *Stone v. Powell, Wolff v. Rice*, and *United States v. Janis*, all in 1976. Although not unsympathetic to claims of "unreasonable" searches and seizures (see his early contra-government opinions for the unanimous Court in *United States v. United States District Court,* 1972, and similarly in *Almeida-Sanchez v. United States,* 1973), he had noteworthy limits. He was in the 1984 majorities that recognized a "good faith" limitation on the proscription of the introduction of illegally procured evidence in criminal proceedings, thereby narrowing the reach of the judicially-created exclusionary rule in *United States v. Leon* and *Massachusetts v. Sheppard.* Similarly, he opted for the constitutionality of the composition of state juries that permitted convictions by 9–3, 10–2, and 11–1 verdicts in criminal cases (*Johnson v. Louisiana* and *Apodaca v. Oregon,* both 1972), while rejecting convictions by 5–0 and 5–1 juries in *Ballew v. Georgia* (1978) and *Burch v. Louisiana* (1979).

A personal opponent of capital punishment, he nonetheless remained true to his deferential approach to legislative power, and consistently supported the option of capital punishment, providing due process of law had been followed. He was one of the four dissenters in *Furman v. Georgia* (1972), which seemed to outlaw capital punishment as then constituted, and flayed the majority of five for what Powell viewed as a flagrant disregard of "the root principles" of precedent, judicial restraint, separation of powers, and federalism. His dissent proved to be prolegomenon to the Court's 7–2 reinstatement of the death penalty as a legitimate constitutional punishment, always provided the presence and application of due process of law. "We hold that the death penalty," Powell wrote in *Gregg v. Georgia* (1976) in the controlling opinion jointly authored with Stewart and Stevens, "is not a form of punishment that may never be imposed, regardless of the circumstances of the offense, regardless of the character of the offenders, and regardless of the procedure followed in reaching the decision to impose it." To Powell, the death penalty was an appropriate "expression of society's moral outrage," if that was what the people's representatives determined to write into law. No matter what his personal feelings may have been on the subject, he recognized that retribution is not only permissible, but a fundamental resolve of an orderly societal rejection of "self-help to vindicate wrongs."

Powell, a close student of the purposes of our constitutional scheme, remained acutely aware of its federal basis. He consistently and firmly rejected the notion that the Tenth Amendment ought to be regarded as a "mere truism," and that in the event of conflicts with the national government it should *a fortiorari* be the loser. Indeed, time and again he admonished his colleagues and the polity that the Tenth Amendment was in effect not only part and parcel of the Bill of Rights, but an "essential" one. It was a view that, with but rare exceptions, he customarily shared during his time on the bench, especially with Rehnquist and O'Connor.

That view achieved a surprising victory in *National League of Cities v. Usery* (1976), in which a bare majority led by Justice Rehnquist endeavored to establish a protective states' rights doctrine against federal intrusion. At best, the effort lasted a mere nine years, but it represented a view with which Powell was wholly comfortable. In 1974, Congress had amended the Fair Labor Standards Act of 1938 to extend minimum wage and maximum hours provisions to cover all but a few employees of the fifty states and their sundry political substructures. A battery of cities and states joined the National League of Cities in a suit against the secretary of labor, alleging an unconstitutional application of Congress's power over interstate commerce to the detriment of the states' Tenth Amendment authority. The states had failed to prevail in the federal district court below, but they triumphed in the Supreme Court. Acknowledging the vast range of the congressional interstate commerce power, the majority ruled nonetheless that "there are limits upon the power of Congress to override state sovereignty even when exercising its otherwise plenary powers to tax or to regulate commerce which are conferred by Article I of the Constitution." And, the majority opinion concluded: "We hold that insofar as the challenged amendments operate to directly replace the States' freedom to structure integral operations in areas of traditional governmental functions, they are not within the authority granted Congress by Article I, § 8, cl. 3."

Justice Powell's satisfaction with the gravamen of the *Usery* decision would soon be vitiated, however, largely due to a rather rapid change of mind by Justice Blackmun, who had concurred separately in that case. Now, in two cases that dealt with the imposition of federal rules and procedures over state regulatory powers, one involving the monitoring of a state's gas and electric public utilities (*Federal Energy Regulatory Commission v. Mississippi,* 1982), and the other the question whether a state had a right to impose an age limit of sixty-five on its fish and game wardens (*EEOC v. Wyoming,* 1983), Powell found himself in dissent. He simply could see no constitutional justification for the expansive reading of the interstate commerce powers that drew majority approval in the two cases, without some clearly expressed congressional preemption.

Yet it would be *Garcia v. San Antonio Metropolitan Transit Authority* (1985) that served as the vehicle for Powell's most passionate articulation of what he viewed as constitutionally applicable states' rights under the Tenth Amendment. Because of Blackmun's change of position, *Garcia* in effect now overruled *Usery* 5–4, the slim majority holding that the federal government's minimum wage and overtime requirements for state and local employees was constitutionally justifiable under the commerce clause. Justice Powell was neither amused nor persuaded by this dramatic, speedy overturning of the *Usery* precedent. Dissenting for himself plus the chief justice and Justices Rehnquist and O'Connor, Powell produced a major articulation for the federalist faith, commencing with the statement that he dissented because "I believe this decision substantially alters the federalist system embodied in the Constitution." He pointed out with passion that in our federal system "the States have a major role that cannot be pre-empted by the national government"; that the instant decision, like others of similar concerns, in effect reduced the Tenth Amendment to "meaningless rhetoric"; that it and its kindred rulings "eventually would eliminate the states as viable political entities." With uncharacteristic gloom he wrote a brief concluding separate paragraph that bears quoting:

> Although the Court's opinion purports to recognize that the States retain some sovereign power, it does not identify even

a single aspect of state authority that would remain when the Commerce Clause is invoked to justify federal regulation. . . . As I view the Court's decision today as rejecting the basic precepts of our federal system and limiting the constitutional role of judicial review, I dissent.

Justice Powell's defeat in *Garcia* was one of the few major ones he sustained in his distinguished career. His warm personality, wisdom, gentleness, and determination rendered him a highly successful consensus seeker and Court "marshaller," and he secured more victories in close cases than any of his contemporaries. To a considerable degree that accomplishment materialized because, although instinctively a deferentialist and a true devotee of the Frankfurter-Harlan jurisprudence of judicial self-restraint, he was willing to bend to attain what he viewed as necessities to achieve fairness and justice. Not, to be sure, the "justice at any cost" or "justice *über alles*" of a Douglas, a Brennan, or a Thurgood Marshall, but the kind of justice he viewed as incumbent upon society, notably in such realms as affirmative action, abortion, aspects of privacy (within limits), and separation of church and state. Largely because of his willingness to bend principle in these and related "wrench" issues in order to do "the right thing," even if it had to be on an *ad hoc* basis, he carried the banner for progressive justice without in any sense pursuing a specific agenda, much less a radical one.

His instinct for what the people's conscience would both desire and need rendered him the pivotal justice during his years on the Court. The public, whether professional or lay, grew to understand the central role he played. He became without challenge the most popular and most revered member of the Burger Court. His decisive votes on the pressing issues of the day became *the* key for and of the battle for the identity of his successor when age and ill health dictated his retirement in 1987. No wonder that the ensuing confirmation combat, initially involving United States Court of Appeals judge Robert H. Bork, would turn into one of the ugliest, and one of the most protracted, in two centuries of Supreme Court confirmation proceedings! For the overriding fear of the Powell "swing vote" devotees throughout the land was that his successor would not be a justice like the justice whom sundry retirement commentators labeled as "the best justice." History may very well not accord him that accolade, but it assuredly will view him as a man of splendid acumen, towering influence, absolute integrity, a superb consensus builder, a consistent winner on fundamental issues, and a lovely, compassionate human being.

Withal, he had lived up to his views on "the role of the Court," which he had submitted as a prepared statement to the Senate Judiciary Committee's late 1971 hearings on his confirmation. A sextet, it comprised the following:

1. A belief in the separation of powers; that courts should not encroach on the prerogatives of the legislative and the executive branches.
2. A belief in the federal system of government.
3. An attitude of judicial restraint.
4. A respect for precedent, springing from a belief in the importance of continuity and predictability in the law.
5. The need to decide cases on the basis of law and fact before the court.
6. The responsibility of the Court to uphold the rule of law and to protect the liberties guaranteed by the Bill of Rights and of the Fourteenth Amendment.

Mr. Madison had expressed the fervent hope that the Supreme Court would be peopled by "giants." Lewis F. Powell, Jr., proved to be one.

—HENRY J. ABRAHAM

BIBLIOGRAPHY

There is no biography of Powell as yet, but material on him can be found in numerous law review articles and books. For a fairly accurate prognosis of Powell's behavior on the Court at the time of his appointment, see A.E. Dick Howard, "Mr. Justice Powell and the Emerging Nixon Majority," 70 *Michigan Law Review* 445 (1972). Material on Powell can be found in Henry J. Abraham, *Justices & Presidents* (3d ed., 1992) and *Freedom and the Court* (6th ed., 1994); Jacob W. Landynski, "Justice Lewis F. Powell, Jr., 'Balance Wheel of the Court,'" in Charles M. Lamb and Stephen C. Halpern, eds., *The Burger Court: Political and Judicial Profiles* (1987); and David M. O'Brien, *Storm Center: The Supreme Court in American Politics* (3d ed., 1993).

Among the many articles, see Gerald Gunther, "A Tribute to Lewis F. Powell, Jr.," 101 *Harvard Law Review* 409 (1987); Sandra Day O'Connor, "A Tribute of Lewis F. Powell, Jr.," *ibid.*; Symposium: "Hon. Lewis F. Powell, Jr.," *University of Richmond Law Review* (1977); and Melvin I. Urofsky, "Mr. Justice Powell and Education: The Balancing of Competing Values," 13 *Journal of Law and Education* 581 (1984).

A special and affectionate portrait of Powell can be found in a book written by his first law clerk, J. Harvey Wilkinson, III, *Serving Justice: A Clerk's View* (1974).

STANLEY FORMAN REED

BORN 31 December 1884, Minerva, Kentucky

NOMINATED to the Court 15 January 1938
by Franklin D. Roosevelt

TOOK seat 31 January 1938; retired 25
February 1957

DIED 3 April 1980 in Huntington, New York

Stanley Forman Reed entered this life at the end of December 1884, and did not depart it until after his ninety-fifth birthday, making him the longest-lived of all members of the Supreme Court. Described by those who knew him as a man of courtesy and geniality, he once told Justice Potter Stewart that he would not want to live his life over again, as "it could not possibly be as good the second time." Yet this good-natured Kentuckian was among the least likely members of the mid-century Court to favor rulings broadening the rights of criminal defendants or protecting citizens' constitutional rights against federal governmental encroachment.

Justice Reed's judicial temperament was decisively shaped by his professional life prior to his elevation to the Court in 1938. After earning bachelor's degrees at Kentucky Wesleyan University and Yale, Reed dabbled in state politics, serving a term in the Kentucky legislature as a Wilsonian progressive and helping to manage one of his friend Fred Vinson's congressional campaigns. He also built a thriving law practice in Maysville, Kentucky, based upon a select group of wealthy corporate clients. Yet it was only when he embarked on government service that Reed really made a name for himself. As counsel to the Federal Farm Board from 1929 to 1932, and as head of the Reconstruction Finance Corporation under both Hoover and Roosevelt, Reed was part of a generation of federal administrators who believed passionately in the desire and the capacity of the government to improve American society and American life. When, therefore, after a mixed record as solicitor general, President Roosevelt appointed him to replace the retiring George Sutherland, Reed brought with him to the bench the characteristi-

cally buoyant faith of the New Dealer. It was a sensibility that would color Reed's opinions throughout his nineteen years on the Court.

Thus, in cases involving the scope of Congress's regulatory powers, Reed was usually prepared to defer to the government. The tone was set in one of his very first opinions, *United States v. Rock Royal Cooperative* (1939), in which Reed, writing for a sharply divided Court, found that the commerce clause permitted Congress to fix agricultural prices even where the transaction was complete before any interstate commerce took place. Another representative case was *Gray v. Powell* (1941), in which the petitioner questioned a finding by the Department of the Interior that it was subject to the price stabilization provisions of the Bituminous Coal Act. In rejecting this claim, Reed showed how reluctant he was to interfere with an administrative determination:

> Unless we can say that a set of circumstances deemed by the Commission (sufficient for its findings) is so unrelated to the tasks entrusted by Congress to the Commission as in effect to deny a sensible exercise of judgement, it is the Court's duty to leave the Commission's judgement undisturbed.

The key words here were "tasks entrusted by Congress." Where administrative agencies seemed to fail to live up to their congressional mandates, Reed was quick to uphold legislative intent. In *Power Commission v. Panhandle Eastern Pipeline Co.* (1949), the Court faced the issue of whether the lease of certain land containing natural gas deposits could be voided by the Power Commission under the Natural Gas Act. In ruling against the commission, Reed found that nothing in the statute supported Justice Frankfurter's view that this was a transaction that was subject to Congress's control.

Thus, for Reed, a determination of what Congress meant to do was often dispositive of the issue involved, whether that issue was constitutional or one of identifying administrative prerogatives. Perhaps the best example of this aspect of Reed's jurisprudence is his majority opinion in *United States v. Kahringer* (1953), in which the Court permitted Congress to tax wagering activities that were traditionally the subject of state police powers. For Reed, it was "hard to understand why the power to tax should raise more doubts because of indirect effects than other federal powers." Few justices were as dependable a friend of governmental intervention in the economy as Reed.

Despite this record, Reed is usually considered to have been a conservative. The reason for this lies in that same pro-government temperament that influenced him in favor of progressive legislation. Reed joined the majority in *Korematsu v. United States* (1944), upholding the government's wartime mass internment of Japanese Americans, and wrote the Court's opinion in *United Public Workers v. Mitchell* (1947) upholding the Hatch Act, which barred certain types of political activity on the part of federal employees. The latter case contains a revealing passage which neatly summarizes Reed's notion of the relationship between the Court and the other two branches of the federal government:

> Congress and the President are responsible for an efficient public service. If in their judgement, efficiency may best be obtained by prohibiting active participation by classified employees in politics as party officers or workers, we see no constitutional objection.

When President Harry S Truman issued his order seizing the nation's steel mills, Reed joined Chief Justice Vinson in dissenting from the Court's opinion declaring that order unconstitutional (*Youngstown Sheet & Tube Co. v. Sawyer,* 1952).

For Reed, there seem to have been few limits to what Congress or the president might do, as long as they could articulate a justification based on national security. In writing for the majority that the Justice Department could detain Communist aliens without bail pending a determination of their deportability, Reed saw no need for the government to show any likelihood that the alien would skip bail or engage in espionage before the hearing. "The Attorney

General's exercise of discretion [is] presumptively correct and unassailable except for abuse" (*Carlson v. Landon,* 1957). He also joined Justice Clark's dissent in *Cole v. Young* (1956), to the effect that federal employees ought to be subject to dismissal at any time "in the interests of national security," whether or not they were occupying sensitive positions at the time. And in *Anti-Fascist Committee v. McGrath* (1951), Reed penned an unusually lengthy dissent asserting the power of the Justice Department to designate an organization as "Communist" for the purpose of determining the loyalty of federal employees, without any procedure whereby that organization might contest that designation. In fact, throughout his tenure on the Court, Reed was a consistent supporter of the government and its anti-subversion programs.

These habits of deference to federal authorities do not, however, support characterizing Reed as a believer in judicial restraint. For while Reed showed himself to be the archetypal jaunty New Dealer when a dispute involved the authority of the federal government, displaying the confidence of so many of his mid-century contemporaries in the power and good faith of Congress and president, he was somewhat less likely to uphold state or local regulations in the face of constitutional attack.

Where, for example, the issue involved prior restraints of free speech, Reed's was a dependable voice in favor of broadening First Amendment protections. In a case in which the Court had to decide whether the state of New York could constitutionally bar the sale of sensationalistic "true crime" magazines, *Winters v. New York* (1948), Reed found for the majority that such publications, though "of no possible value to society," were "as much entitled to the protections of Free Speech as the best of literature." The statute was struck down as unconstitutionally vague, provoking a dissent from Justice Frankfurter which called for much the same sort of deference to legislative judgement that Reed customarily displayed when construing federal law.

Similarly, in *Joseph Burstyn, Inc. v. Wilson* (1952), Reed joined Justice Clark's ruling bringing films under the protection of the First Amendment, and wrote a brief concurrence stat-

Stanley Forman Reed
Photograph by Harris and Ewing.
Collection of the Supreme Court of the United States.

ing that he saw no reason for banning from public view the movie in question.

Perhaps most compellingly, Reed dissented from Frankfurter's majority opinion in *Beauharnais v. Illinois* (1952), in which the Court upheld an Illinois statute which prohibited the dissemination of material that portrayed certain classes of people as, among other things, "lacking in virtue." Reed, always a careful reader of statutes, had a field day with the imprecision of such phrasing, asking "are the tests of the Puritan or the Cavalier to be applied, those of the city or the farm, the Christian or the non-Christian, the old or the young?" In view of its rigorous insistence that states should not be in the business of banning the content of speech, however hateful it might be, the *Beauharnais* dissent may take on more significance as time goes on.

Moreover, as befitted a New Dealer, and in keeping with his roots in rural Kentucky, Reed was always a sound friend of the First Amendment rights of organized labor. In *Carpenters Union v. Ritter's Cafe* (1942), the Court upheld a Texas state court injunction against union members picketing in front of a restaurant which was refusing to hire union contractors. Reed could see no reason for such a restraint on picketing, writing that "so long as civil government is able to function normally for the protection of its citizens, such a limitation on Free Speech is unwarranted."

Here was the rub, for where a litigant's free speech rights seemed to bear a distinct menace to the well-being of the public at large, Reed was often willing to uphold state and local enactments burdening that speech. He wrote the majority opinion in *Kovacs v. Cooper* (1949), upholding a local ordinance banning the broadcasts of "loud and raucous" messages via loudspeakers mounted on trucks on the grounds that people in their homes and businesses had a right to be protected from irritating noises. He also joined the majority in *Feiner v. New York* (1951), which held that police had acted constitutionally in arresting a rabble-rousing speaker for disorderly conduct, and in *Breard v. Alexandria* (1951), permitting traveling salesmen to be constitutionally banned from going door to door. As William Francis O'Brien has pointed out, such cases

evince a concern on Reed's part for balancing the rights of the community against First Amendment guarantees to individuals.

O'Brien's view seems to find support in Reed's record on opinions addressing the First Amendment freedom of religion. In this area, Reed was a fairly consistent advocate of the right of communities to impose reasonable restrictions on religious activity for the good of the citizenry as a whole. Thus, in *Jones v. Opelika* (1942), Reed's majority opinion upheld a series of municipal regulations from around the country placing licensing fees on the sale or distribution of all printed matter, including religious tracts passed out door to door by Jehovah's Witnesses. For Reed, the sovereign power of state bodies "to ensure orderly living" justified such ordinances, as long as the transactions regulated were more in the nature of commercial activities than religious rites as such.

While this commercial/religious ritual distinction may have seemed viable to Reed, it suffered a major blow during the very next term, with Justice Douglas's majority opinion in *Murdock v. Pennsylvania* (1943), in which a municipal ordinance obliging fund-raising Jehovah's Witnesses to pay the same licensing fee charged to all other solicitors was struck down as a denial of the plaintiff's First Amendment freedoms. To Douglas, the licensing fee amounted to "a charge for the enjoyment of a right granted by the Federal Constitution." In his dissent, Reed fastened on what he felt to be the injustice of the majority's position removing from religious groups their obligation to help contribute to the maintenance of "the government which provides the opportunity for the exercise of their liberties." No "wall of separation" for Reed; religious bodies had their responsibilities to the general commonwealth, just like everyone else. It was no surprise when Reed was chosen to write the majority opinion in *In re Summers* (1945), which upheld the right of the Illinois bar to refuse membership to a conscientious objector whose scruples would not have permitted him to fulfill his statutory duty to serve in the state militia in time of emergency.

One of the most illuminating of Justice Reed's pronouncements on the subject of religious liberty occurs in *McCullom v. Board of Education* (1948), in which the Court struck down as a violation of the establishment clause a local public school program in which students could voluntarily receive religious instruction on school property and during school hours. Here, the issue was no longer one of obliging religious bodies to bear their fair share of community burdens; rather, the controversy revolved around the extent to which these bodies could be prohibited from taking part in the life of the community's secular institutions. Reed, in the uncomfortable position of lone dissenter, argued eloquently that the long tradition of religious activity in America demanded that all faiths should have the opportunity to participate fully in the community: "Devotion to the great principle of religious liberty should not lead us into a rigid interpretation of the constitutional guarantee that conflicts with the accepted habits of our people." Thus, the important point for Reed remained the avoidance of any rigid wall of separation which would unnecessarily and harmfully prohibit religious groups from either shouldering the burdens or enjoying the benefits of residence in an orderly, democratic society.

Was Reed, then, a communitarian? His First Amendment opinions can certainly be read to suggest as much, and to the extent that a tendency to subsume individual rights or needs to the greater good of the community was a part of the ethos of the New Deal, then Reed can probably be labeled in this way. Yet his principles in this regard were not especially deep. We have already noted his reluctance to admit people to equal standing in the community whom the government for whatever reason had deemed "subversive," and he does not seem to have harbored a sense, so carefully developed by the Warren Court, that a healthy community demanded a zealous attention of law enforcement agencies to the constitutional rights of the accused.

In fact, for example, Reed was less likely than other members of the Court to look favorably on claims that the confessions of criminal defendants had been coerced. His opinion in *Gallejo v. Nebraska* (1951), in which the defendant had been held in solitary conditions without bail for seven days before he finally con-

fessed, is remarkable for the deference it lends to the testimony of the deputy sheriff that no coercion was used. And in *McNabb v. United States* (1943), a case in which federal agents had clearly violated the law by not bringing the defendants into the presence of a magistrate prior to their confessions, Reed authored a dissent which criticized Justice Frankfurter's majority opinion for relying on this "technicality"; for Reed, the jury's determination that the confessions had been voluntary should have been dispositive. Hence, while Reed often had in mind the need to protect the health of the community, his notion of what precisely that "health" consisted of did not always accord with more modern understandings.

Perhaps the best-known of Reed's opinions in the area of constitutional rights was *Adamson v. California* (1947), in which the Court was faced with the issue of whether the Fourteenth Amendment incorporated the Fifth Amendment so as to bind it upon the states. The California statute under review permitted judges and attorneys to comment to the jury on the decisions of defendants not to testify on their own behalf. Reed refused to apply the Fifth Amendment to invalidate this practice, relying both upon the sanctity of the federal system, and upon what he believed to be the reasonableness of permitting the prosecution to bring defendants' failure to take the stand to the jury's attention. *Adamson* represented one of the last instances in which the Court interpreted the Fourteenth Amendment so narrowly, and is a good example of Reed's characteristic lack of sensitivity to the rights of the accused. This might have arisen from his experiences as a practicing lawyer, which were largely limited to various sorts of corporate litigation and government service rather than the less lucrative field of criminal law.

Given this professional background, and keeping in mind his origins in the rural Kentucky of the late nineteenth century, it may be surprising that Reed had one of the best civil rights records on the Stone and Vinson Courts. He wrote the majority opinions in both *Smith v. Allwright* (1944), invalidating the whites-only Texas Democratic primary, and *Murphy v. Virginia* (1946), which struck down a Virginia statute requiring segregated seating on buses passing through the state. Yet these opinions do not evince any deep-seated belief in integration on Reed's part. The result in *Smith* was mandated by the clear fact that the primary was conducted in large part by the state of Texas, and it is doubtful that Reed would have voted as he did had the election been a purely private or informal affair. As for *Murphy*, Reed predicated his ruling squarely on the commerce clause, and the inconvenience consequent on rearranging bus seating every time the vehicle crossed the Virginia line, rather than on equal protection or due process grounds.

That Reed was no principled foe of segregation is demonstrated by his reaction to the momentous case of *Brown v. Board of Education of Topeka* (1954). After many months of studying the question of segregation's effects on both the educational capabilities and job performances of African Americans, Reed could still not bring himself to believe that segregation was equivalent to discrimination, and hence a violation of the equal protection clause. Only after Chief Justice Vinson died, and Reed realized that he would be the lone dissenter in the ruling that recently elevated Chief Justice Warren was planning to hand down, did Reed decide to join the majority in order to bring the important sanction of unanimity to a ruling that was bound to alter forever the fabric of American life. For Justice Frankfurter, this act of selflessness was "the most lasting service" to the country that Reed performed during his tenure on the Court.

Reed retired from the bench in 1957, at the age of seventy-two. He went on to serve President Dwight D. Eisenhower for a brief term as chairman of the Civil Rights Commission, after which he retired to spend the remainder of his days in his beloved Maysville, Kentucky. After Reed's death in 1980, Chief Justice Burger penned a memorial tribute in which he lauded both Reed's judicial temperament and his personal generosity, noting that Reed had sent him a bottle of Kentucky bourbon every Christmas since his accession to the bench in 1969. In the end, Reed may be considered to have been the last of the New Dealers, embodying the goodness of heart and occasional intellectual inconsistency that this appellation implies.

—DANIEL L. BREEN

BIBLIOGRAPHY

There are some Reed papers in the Kentucky Historical Society in Lexington, but there is no full-scale biography. The fullest treatment of his jurisprudence remains William O'Brien, *Justice Reed and the First Amendment: The Religion Clauses* (1958), which views Reed as a pluralist. There is also an unpublished dissertation by Mark J. Fitzgerald, "Justice Reed: A Study of a Center Judge" (University of Chicago, 1950). One of Reed's former law clerks, John D. Fassett, discusses Reed's evolving stance in the *Brown* case in 1986 *Yearbook of the Supreme Court Historical Society* 48. Posthumous tributes to Reed can be found in volume 69 of the *Kentucky Law Journal*. For general works of the Court in this era that examine Reed's role, see Samuel J. Konefsky, *Chief Justice Stone and the Supreme Court* (1946), Herman Pritchett, *Civil Liberties and the Vinson Court* (1954), and Jan Palmer, *The Vinson Court Era: The Supreme Court's Conference Votes* (1990).

WILLIAM HUBBS REHNQUIST

BORN 1 October 1924, Milwaukee, Wisconsin

NOMINATED to Court 12 October 1971 by Richard M. Nixon

TOOK seat 7 January 1972; nominated as chief justice 20 June 1986 by Ronald Reagan; took seat 26 September 1986

William Rehnquist grew up in Milwaukee and was educated at Stanford University, Harvard University, and the Stanford Law School. After graduation, he served as a law clerk to Justice Robert H. Jackson, and then entered into private practice in Phoenix, Arizona. In 1969, through his association with deputy attorney general Richard Kleindienst and his work as a Republican party official in Phoenix, he came to Washington as assistant attorney general for the Office of Legal Counsel. From this position, he was nominated to the Supreme Court where, in 1972, he was sworn in along with Lewis F. Powell. When he was sworn in as chief justice of the United States in 1986, he became only the third sitting justice to be so elevated. Despite widespread disagreement with Rehnquist's views among many legal academics, there is little dispute that he is among the ablest and most learned justices ever to have served on the Court.

Justice Rehnquist's vision of the nation's constitutional structure is firmly rooted in the words and history of that document. It is based on three doctrines: strict construction (of both the Constitution and of statutes), judicial restraint, and federalism. He summarized this vision in a 1976 speech at the University of Texas:

It is almost impossible . . . to conclude that the [Founding Fathers] intended the Constitution itself to suggest answers to the manifold problems that they knew would confront succeeding generations. The Constitution that they drafted was intended to endure indefinitely, but the reason for this well-founded hope was the general language by which national authority was granted to

Congress and the Presidency. These two branches were to furnish the motive power within the federal system, which was in turn to coexist with the state governments; the elements of government having a popular constituency were looked to for the solution of the numerous and varied problems that the future would bring.

In other words, as he stated in dissenting in *Trimble v. Gordon* (1977), neither the original Constitution nor the Civil War amendments made "this Court (or the federal courts generally) into a council of revision, and they did not confer on this Court any authority to nullify state laws which were merely felt to be inimical to the Court's notion of the public interest."

During his early years on the Court, despite the presence of three other Republican appointees, Justice Rehnquist was often in lone dissent, espousing a view of states' rights and limited federal judicial power that many regarded as anachronistic. For example, in *Weber v. Aetna Casualty and Surety Company* (1972), *Sugarman v. Dougall* (1973), and *Frontiero v. Richardson* (1973), he resisted the view of the other eight members of the Court that the equal protection clause of the Fourteenth Amendment applied to, and required heightened scrutiny of, state sponsored discrimination against illegitimate children, resident aliens, and women, respectively. Indeed, he insisted that the Fourteenth Amendment was limited in its application solely to racial discrimination. In the criminal procedure area, he urged that *Mapp v. Ohio* (1961), which applied the exclusionary rule to the states, be overruled, and he seemed hostile to *Miranda v. Arizona* (1966), though never directly arguing that it should be reversed.

Still, even in his initial years on the Court, Rehnquist was less likely to be in dissent than the liberal bloc of William O. Douglas, William Brennan, and Thurgood Marshall, and some of Rehnquist's early dissents, such as in *Memorial Hospital v. Maricopa Co.* (1974), *Cleveland Board of Education v. La Fleur* (1974), and *Fry v. United States* (1975) were to form the basis for majority opinions in the years to come. As Professor Laurence Tribe of Harvard observed, "even in lone dissent, he has helped define a new range of what is possible."

The 1975 term saw Rehnquist come into his own as the leader of the (ever shifting) conservative wing of the Court. In that term he wrote *Paul v. Davis* (1976), holding that reputation, standing alone, was not a constitutionally protected interest subject to vindication under 42 USC §1983; *National League of Cities v. Usery* (1976), in which a majority ruled that the Tenth Amendment limited Congress's power under the commerce clause to regulate the states; and *Rizzo v. Goode* (1976), holding that "principles of federalism" forbade federal courts from ordering a restructuring of state agencies in response to §1983 violations.

National League of Cities used an expansive reading of the Tenth Amendment to strike down a federal statute that regulated the wages and hours of state government employees, despite the fact that such regulation was concededly within Congress's commerce power. It showed that, when faced with a choice between judicial restraint/strict constructionism and state's rights, Justice Rehnquist was prepared to aggressively defend the latter. However, the potential significance of the first decision limiting Congress's commerce power since 1936 was eroded by subsequent Court majorities, first refusing to follow, and then, in 1985, overruling, *National League of Cities* in *Garcia v. San Antonio Metropolitan Transit Authority* (1985). Despite Rehnquist's prediction in dissent that this issue would return to haunt the Court, it seems unlikely that the trend toward national control of virtually any area in which Congress chooses to assert itself will be reversed. Whatever the political leanings of the other justices, a majority generally seems to believe that the strong national/weak state governmental system is the proper direction for the country.

When dissenting, Rehnquist has made his most telling points opposing the majority's efforts to enact "desirable" social policy with little support from the constitutional or statutory provisions that they purport to be interpreting. An example is *United Steel Workers of America v. Weber* (1979). In that case, Kaiser Aluminum Company and the United Steelworkers had devised a "voluntary" affirmative action plan under which half of available positions in an on-the-job training plan would be reserved for blacks. Weber, excluded solely because he was white, filed suit based on Title VII of the Civil Rights Act of 1964. The statute provides that "it shall be unlawful for an employer . . . to fail or refuse to hire . . . any individual . . . because of such individual's race." The statute goes on to say that its provisions are not be interpreted "to require any employer . . . to grant preferential treatment to any individual or to any group because of the race . . . of such individual or group." Moreover, as a unanimous Court had recognized only three years before in *McDonald v. Santa Fe Trail Transportation Co.* (1976), the "uncontradicted legislative history" showed that Title VII "prohibited racial discrimination against the white petitioners . . . upon the same standards as would be applicable were they Negroes." Nevertheless, a 5–2 majority in *Weber* reversed the lower courts and found that discrimination against whites was not within the "spirit" of Title VII and consequently was not prohibited. In a bitter dissent, Justice Rehnquist accused the majority of Orwellian "newspeak" and concluded that "close examination of what the Court proffers as the spirit of the Act reveals it as the spirit of the present majority, not the 88th Congress."

Similarly, in *Roe v. Wade* (1973), where the majority based a woman's right to an abortion on a constitutional "right to privacy" which arose not from the terms but from the "penumbras" of the Bill of Rights, Rehnquist wrote: "To reach its result, the Court necessarily has had to find within the scope of the Fourteenth Amendment a right that was apparently completely unknown to the drafters of the Amendment." Whatever the wisdom of the policies announced in these cases, it is difficult to disagree that Rehnquist's reading of the textual material in question was the more accurate one.

It is ironic that Rehnquist, often condemned as a right-wing ideologue was, in *Weber* and *Roe*, as in many other cases, advocating a view

William Hubbs Rehnquist
Photograph by Joseph Lavenburg, National Geographic Society.
Collection of the Supreme Court of the United States.

of the Court's role that had previously been vigorously advanced by the progressive members of the Court. In *Morehead v. New York ex rel. Tipaldo* (1936), for example, the dissenting opinion of Justice Harlan F. Stone, joined by Louis Brandeis and Benjamin Cardozo, declared:

> It is not for the Court to resolve doubts whether the remedy by regulation is as efficacious as many believe, or better than some other, or is better even than blind operation of uncontrolled economic forces. The legislature must be free to choose unless government is rendered impotent. The Fourteenth Amendment has no more imbedded in the Constitution our preference for some particular set of economic beliefs, than it has adopted in the name of liberty the system of theology which we happen to approve.

In criminal procedure, his views are driven by the same narrow view of the role of courts in a tripartite federal system, and he frankly admits that his goal when he came on the Court was to "call a halt to a number of the sweeping rulings of the Warren Court in this area." In this he generally was joined by the other Nixon appointees and by Justice White. Consequently, the 1970s and 1980s saw a series of decisions aimed at making it easier for the police to investigate crime and harder for defendants to upset their convictions because of police investigatory errors. For example, in *Rakas v. Illinois* (1978), the Court, speaking through Rehnquist, made it more difficult for a defendant to establish standing to litigate search and seizure violations; in *United States v. Robinson* (1973), the scope of police searches incident to arrest was expanded; and in *United States v. Leon* (1984), the Court established a "reasonable good faith" exception to the exclusionary rule in search warrant cases. However, neither Rehnquist nor any of his fellow conservatives sought to undercut the fundamental rights to trial by jury, counsel, and appeal that had been applied to the states by the Warren Court. In a 1985 interview, despite the feeling of most Court watchers that the Burger Court had *not* dismantled the major criminal procedure protections of the Warren Court, including the

Miranda requirements and the exclusionary rule of *Mapp v. Ohio* (1961), Rehnquist pronounced himself satisfied that the law was "more evenhanded now than when I came on the Court."

If Rehnquist has not been successful in exempting states from *congressional* control, he has frequently prevailed in his efforts to exempt state courts from federal *court* interference. To do this, he has taken the 1971 decision in *Younger v. Harris*, which counseled restraint by federal courts in enjoining ongoing state criminal proceedings, and extended it greatly. In *Rizzo v. Goode* (1976) and *Real Estate Association v. McNary* (1981), he held that "principles of federalism" limited a federal court's ability to enjoin not just the judicial branch, but the executive branch of state governments as well, and also that this comity limitation was not confined to criminal proceedings. Nor, as he held in *Doran v. Salem Inn, Inc.* (1975), was it necessary that a state criminal proceeding predate a federal action for the federal action to be barred by principles of comity.

Similarly, in the area of federal *habeas corpus* for state prisoners, Rehnquist and his conservative colleagues have advanced the dual goals of limiting federal court interference with state court adjudications and enhancing the finality of criminal convictions. The most significant holding in this line of cases is the 1977 decision in *Wainwright v. Sykes*. In this case, Rehnquist, writing for a six-justice majority, held that failure to raise an issue at the appropriate stage of a state criminal proceeding barred the federal courts from considering that issue on *habeas corpus*, absent a showing of good cause for the failure and prejudice to his case by the defendant. *Sykes* thus overruled *Fay v. Noia* (1963), which had allowed new issues to be raised on federal *habeas* unless they had been deliberately bypassed by the defendant in state proceedings.

Sykes represented a significant diminution of the power of federal courts to interfere with state convictions. *Sykes* was reaffirmed in 1989 in the significant case of *Teague v. Lane*, authored by Justice O'Connor, where the Court held that "new" rules of criminal procedure generally should not apply retroactively on *habeas corpus* to defendants whose state convictions became final before the new law was established.

Most recently, in *Brecht v. Abrahamson* (1993), a 5–4 majority held, per Rehnquist, that for a prisoner to have his conviction reversed by a federal court on a writ of *habeas corpus*, as opposed to direct appeal, the burden is on the prisoner to show not only that there were constitutional errors at his trial, but that those errors had a "substantial and injurious effect or influence in determining the jury's verdict." As Justice White noted in dissent, the practical impact of this holding in most cases of "trial error" is that "a state court determination that a constitutional error . . . is harmless beyond a reasonable doubt has in effect become unreviewable by lower federal courts by way of *habeas corpus*."

Consistent with his federalism/judicial restraint stance, Rehnquist is the Court's leading advocate of a restrictive interpretation of the establishment clause of the First Amendment, which provides that "Congress shall make no law respecting an establishment of religion." He set forth his view in detail in a dissenting opinion in *Wallace v. Jaffree* (1985), where the majority struck down Alabama's statutorily required "moment of silence" for "meditation or voluntary prayer" in public schools. Rehnquist rejected the "wall of separation between church and state" principle of *Everson v. Board of Education* (1947) that has been the Court's touchstone for forty years, claiming out that history did not support this rigid interpretation of the First Amendment. Rather, as Rehnquist argued, the view of James Madison, the "architect of the Bill of Rights," as to the function of the establishment clause was simply "to prohibit the establishment of a national religion, and perhaps to prevent discrimination among sects. He did not see it as requiring neutrality on the part of the government between religion and irreligion." Consequently, Rehnquist would have found no defect in a state statute that openly endorsed prayer, much less a "moment of silence."

In a similar vein, in *First National Bank v. Bellotti* (1978), Rehnquist, in sole dissent, refused to recognize a First Amendment free speech right for corporations and in *Virginia State Board of Pharmacy v. Virginia Citizens Consumer Council* (1976), he refused to recognize a First Amendment right in consumers to receive commercial information. In short, in the First Amendment area, as in all others, he would generally give the legislative branch, whether state or federal, greater freedom to plot its own course than his colleagues would.

Rehnquist has not gained the support of a majority of the Court for his position that commercial speech is unprotected by the First Amendment. However, in the establishment clause area, he has enjoyed more success, attracting a majority of justices to the proposition that if public funding is provided for certain activities in public schools, it may also be provided for similar activities in private, sectarian schools. Most recently, in *Zobrest v. Catalina Foothills School District* (1993), Rehnquist spoke for a 5–4 majority in holding that where a deaf student would receive a state-funded sign language interpreter in public schools, the establishment clause did not prohibit the provision of such an interpreter in a Catholic school, even though that interpreter would be interpreting religious instruction and services for the student. As the dissent noted, this was the first time the Court had authorized "a public employee to participate directly in religious indoctrination."

By contrast, in the area of school prayer, Rehnquist has consistently been on the losing side. For example, in *Lee v. Weisman* (1992), a 5–4 majority held, through Justice Kennedy, that it was a First Amendment violation for clergymen to be invited to offer prayers at public middle and high school graduation ceremonies. Rehnquist joined Justice Scalia's dissent that accused the majority of "lay[ing] waste a tradition that is as old as public school graduation ceremonies themselves."

When Warren Burger announced his resignation as chief justice in June 1986 and President Reagan nominated Rehnquist as his replacement, there was a firestorm of protest among liberals. Senator Edward Kennedy denounced Rehnquist as having an "appalling record on race" and liberal columnists branded him a right-wing extremist. A concerted effort was undertaken to find something in his past that might provide a basis for defeating the nomination. Assorted allegations were raised concerning contacts with black voters when he was a Republican party official in

Phoenix, the handling of a family trust, a memo he had written to Justice Jackson as a law clerk urging that the "separate but equal" doctrine not be overruled in *Brown v. Board of Education* (1954), and a racially restrictive covenant in the deed to his Phoenix house. The Senate correctly perceived that these allegations were either unproven or, if true, were "ancient history" and irrelevant to his fitness for the post of chief justice. Significantly, no serious charge of misconduct was raised as to Rehnquist's fourteen and a half years as an associate justice on the Supreme Court. In the end, after much sound and fury, he was confirmed by a vote of 65–13.

If the 1975 term had seen Rehnquist "arrive" as a major force on the Court it was the 1987 term, his second year in the center chair, that saw him mature as chief justice. In a speech given in 1976, he had discussed the role of chief justice, citing Charles Evans Hughes as his model:

> Hughes believed that unanimity of decision contributed to public confidence in the Court. . . . Except in cases involving matters of high principle he willingly acquiesced in silence rather than expose his dissenting views. . . . Hughes was also willing to modify his own opinions to hold or increase his majority and if that meant he had to put in disconnected thoughts or sentences, in they went.

Following his own advice, in the 1987 term he achieved a high level of agreement with his fellow justices, ranging from 57.6 percent with Thurgood Marshall to 83.1 percent with Anthony Kennedy. His administrative abilities in the 1987 term won the praise of his colleague, Harry Blackmun, who deemed him a "splendid administrator in conference." For the first time in years the Court concluded its work prior to July 1. During that term, Rehnquist showed that he could be flexible, joining with the more liberal justices to subject the dismissal of a homosexual Central Intelligence Agency employee to judicial review, and to support the First Amendment claims of *Hustler* magazine to direct off-color ridicule at a public figure.

Most significantly, in *Morrison v. Olson* (1988) he wrote for a 7–1 majority upholding the special prosecutor legislation against a challenge by the Reagan administration. In a decision termed an "exercise in folly" by the lone dissenter, Antonin Scalia, Rehnquist held that the appointments clause was not violated by Congress vesting the power to appoint a special prosecutor in a "Special Division" consisting of three United States court of appeals judges. Nor did the act violate separation of powers principles by impermissibly interfering with the functions of the executive branch. While the act can be shown to have theoretical flaws, Rehnquist was surely correct in perceiving that a truly independent prosecutor was a necessary check on the many abuses of executive power, including criminal violations, that were occurring during the latter years of the Reagan administration and in upholding a check on those abuses in an opinion that gained the concurrence of a substantial majority of his colleagues. His performance that term led the *New York Times*, which had vigorously opposed his elevation to chief justice, to praise him with faint damnation: "While he is certainly no liberal, or even a moderate, his positions are not always responsive to the tides of fashionable opinion among his fellow political conservatives."

One of the most interesting features of Rehnquist's tenure as chief justice has been the decline in overall activity of the Court. From the 1980 to the 1988 term, the Court never decided less than 159 cases by written opinion, with the number ranging as high as 216 in the 1981 term. In the 1989 term, this number dropped to 151, in the 1990 term to 129 and in the 1991 term to 127—this despite the fact that the Court's docket steadily increased during this period, from 4,280 cases disposed of in the 1980 term, to 5,825 cases disposed of in the 1991 term.

This trend cannot be attributed to any action or inclination by the chief justice alone, since any time four justices vote to hear a case, certiorari will be granted, whatever the view of the chief. Nor can the trend be fully explained by the overwhelming Republican dominance of the Court (in the 1991 and 1992 terms, Justice White was the only Democratic appointee), since such a partisan Court might be anxious to undo the work of prior Courts.

However, since Republicans generally take a dim view of governmental activism, it does seem likely that the predominantly moderate Republican appointees would be less likely to want to assert their will on the rest of the country, even if it took the form of reversing liberal trends. That is, as the joint opinion of Sandra Day O'Connor, David Souter, and Anthony Kennedy in *Planned Parenthood of Southeastern Pennsylvania v. Casey* (1992) made clear, an allegiance to the principle of *stare decisis* is part of the conservative credo, even if a justice may disagree with an earlier case.

The other likely reason for a diminution of the Court's activity is that, after twelve years of Republican administrations, the *lower* federal courts are also dominated by Republicans. It follows that they are therefore less likely to disagree with each other (creating conflicts in the circuits that the Supreme Court must resolve) and that the Republicans on the Supreme Court are less likely to disagree with their counterparts in the courts below. This supposition is supported by the fact that only about 20 percent of all cases in which certiorari was granted from 1980 to 1992 were affirmed by the Court. Since the purpose of a certiorari grant is thus, overwhelmingly, to vacate or reverse a lower court decision, it follows that general agreement with the lower courts should lead to fewer certiorari grants by the Supreme Court. Finally, even activist conservatives such as Rehnquist, who have shown an inclination toward overruling prior Court decisions, or at least halting what they considered to be dangerous trends, have now, presumably, accomplished their goals to a greater degree than was true a decade ago.

Rehnquist's own level of activity has declined even more than that of the Court itself. In the 1980 through 1982 terms, Rehnquist averaged forty opinions (including dissents and concurrences) per term. By contrast, in the 1989 through 1992 terms, he averaged twenty-one opinions annually. He continues to write his share of majority opinions, but the dissents and concurrences have diminished; for example, in

the 1979 term, he wrote twenty-six dissenting opinions compared to four in the 1990 term. In part, this is because, for the reasons discussed above, he is much less likely to disagree with the majority than in the past. He cast a dissenting vote in nineteen cases in the 1990 term compared to forty-nine in 1981, and compared to forty-two for Justice Stevens in the 1990 term. Also, the marked diminution in his dissenting votes since he became chief justice may reflect his view, noted earlier, that the chief should attempt to exercise a moderating influence and dissent as infrequently as conscience will allow. This view is supported by the fact that his number of dissenting votes dropped off sharply when he became chief. Finally, it is likely that, after twenty years on the Court, he simply feels less need to express his individual views on particular cases, especially given the press of the additional duties that the position of chief justice demands.

While Rehnquist's judicial philosophy is undoubtedly born from a staunch political conservatism, the principles of federalism and strict construction will frequently prevail even when they lead to a "liberal" result. For example, in *Pruneyard Shopping Center v. Robins* (1980), he wrote the opinion upholding state constitutional provisions that allowed political demonstrators to solicit signatures for a submission to the United Nations in a shopping center. He recognized "the authority of the state to exercise its police power or its sovereign right to adopt in its own Constitution individual liberties more expansive than those conferred by the Federal Constitution." Similarly, in *Hughes v. Oklahoma* (1979), he dissented when the Court invalidated a state's attempt to preserve its wildlife. And in *Pennell v. City of San Jose* (1988), he upheld the city's rent control ordinance in the face of a due process challenge by landlords. In numerous criminal cases, such as *United States v. Maze* (1974), and *Ball v. United States* (1985), he voted to reverse criminal convictions on the ground that the government had failed to prove that the defendant's conduct had violated the terms of the (strictly construed) statute.

Though the 1987 term showed that Rehnquist could be flexible as chief justice, that term and the terms that followed also showed him, in most instances, leading the Court in a conservative direction. For example, in a series of close cases decided in the 1987 term ranging across the landscape of the Bill of Rights, the Court denied an equal protection challenge to user fees for school bussing, denied a claim by Indians that a Forest Service logging road through a national forest would interfere with their free exercise of religion, denied food stamps to striking workers, allowed censorship of a school newspaper, upheld federal tort immunity for defense contractors, and allowed illegally discovered evidence to be used against a criminal defendant under the "independent source" exception to the exclusionary rule.

The following term showed that Rehnquist was still prepared to be flexible. For example, in *City of Canton v. Harris* (1988), he joined an opinion by Justice White which held that a city could be liable for damages under 42 USC §1983 for poor training of police officers and that a new trial was not barred, rather than joining Justices O'Connor, Kennedy, and Scalia who, in a concurring and dissenting opinion, would have dismissed the plaintiff's case because she could not have met the "deliberate indifference" standard of proof. However, in this, Justice Kennedy's first full term on the Court, such flexibility was rarely called for, as the conservatives prevailed most of the time. In the leading case of the term, *Webster v. Reproductive Health Services* (1989), Chief Justice Rehnquist, consistent with his views of state's rights and strict construction of the federal Bill of Rights, joined by four others, upheld a Missouri statute that forbade public funding and the use of public hospitals for abortions. Rehnquist observed that "our cases have recognized that the due process clauses generally confer no affirmative right to government aid, even where such aid may be necessary to some life, liberty or property interests of which the government itself may not deprive the individual." Since a state is under no constitutional obligation to provide public hospitals at all, it is free to condition their use however it wishes. This notion, that beneficiaries of public largess must accept the "bitter (restrictions) with the sweet" has been a hallmark

of Rehnquist's jurisprudence since he first expressed it in *Arnett v. Kennedy* in 1974. However, he was unable to convince Justice O'Connor that it was time to abandon the "rigid" framework of *Roe v. Wade* which gave a woman an absolute right to an abortion during the first trimester of pregnancy, despite his drafting of a compromise opinion that continued to recognize a limited constitutional right to abortion.

Subsequently, in *Planned Parenthood v. Casey* (1992), the Court did abandon the rigid trimester framework of *Roe* in favor of a test that considered whether or not a given regulation placed an "undue burden" on a woman's constitutional right to an abortion. However, this reaffirmation of the constitutional right to an abortion of a nonviable fetus left the chief justice largely in dissent, returning to the position that *Roe* should be overruled outright.

But if Rehnquist has not been successful in getting a majority of the Court to overrule *Roe*, substantial inroads have been made into that holding. *Casey*, in which the Court reaffirmed the state's power to prohibit abortions of viable fetuses, is a good example.

In *Casey*, the Court upheld a twenty-four-hour waiting period and an "informed consent" restriction on abortions as well as a parental consent limitation on abortions for minors. The only provision struck down as unduly burdensome was a spousal consent requirement. This relatively tolerant attitude toward many state regulations, as well as the Court's position, stated by Rehnquist in *Rust v. Sullivan* (1991), which upheld the right of government to place restrictions on, or withhold, public funding for abortions, is a far cry from the broad right apparently conferred by *Roe*, as Justice Blackmun's dissenting opinions have consistently emphasized.

Despite the national debate on abortion, it seems unlikely that the country in the foreseeable future will be confronted with a constitutional problem of the magnitude of the legal discrimination against blacks (and the closely related problem of police abuse of the rights of criminal suspects) that faced the Warren Court. Consequently, it is also unlikely that the judicial activism displayed by the Warren Court to deal with these problems will be morally necessary or politically desirable in the future. Thus, while Justice Rehnquist's vision of a vigorous Tenth Amendment checking Congress's power vis-à-vis the states seems unlikely to prevail in the long term, his view of a more limited role for the federal Constitution, and hence for the federal courts, in the politics of the nation will probably be the wave of the future. Having reached its highest point in the 1960s, the "Rights Revolution"—already dying during the Burger Court years—terminated with the appointment of William Rehnquist as chief justice of the United States and probably will not recur after he steps down.

—CRAIG M. BRADLEY

BIBLIOGRAPHY

Rehnquist's views on the Court, the Constitution and the role of the chief justice can be found in his book, *The Supreme Court: How It Was, How It Is* (1987), and in two articles, "Chief Justices I Never Knew," 3 *Hastings Constitutional Law Quarterly* 637 (1976), and "The Notion of a Living Constitution," 54 *Texas Law Review* 693 (1976).

Three books that look at the broad spectrum of Rehnquist's career and jurisprudence are Derek Davis, *Original Intent: Chief Justice Rehnquist and the Course of American Church/ State Relations* (1991); Sue Davis, *Justice Rehnquist and the Constitution* (1989); and David G. Savage, *Turning Right: The Making of the Rehnquist Supreme Court* (1992).

Specialized studies include Craig M. Bradley, "Criminal Procedure in the Rehnquist Court: Has the Rehnquisition Begun?" 62 *Indiana Law Journal* 273 (1987); H. Jefferson Powell, "The Compleat Jeffersonian: Justice Rehnquist and Federalism," 91 *Yale Law Journal* 1317 (1982); and David L. Shapiro, "Mr. Justice Rehnquist: A Preliminary View," 90 *Harvard Law Review* 293 (1976).

Owen Josephus Roberts
Photograph by Harris and Ewing.
Collection of the Supreme Court of the United States.

OWEN JOSEPHUS ROBERTS

BORN 2 May 1875, Germantown,
Pennsylvania

NOMINATED to the Court 9 May 1930
by Herbert Hoover

TOOK seat 20 May 1930; resigned
31 July 1945

DIED 17 May 1955 in Chester Springs,
Pennsylvania

Owen Roberts grew up in Germantown, Pennsylvania, close to Philadelphia, where he passed a quiet, studious childhood. He graduated with honors from the University of Pennsylvania in 1895 following an undergraduate career that included membership in Phi Beta Kappa and an active part in the debate team. Three years later he earned a law degree from the same school, once again with honors.

Roberts achieved immediate success at the bar. He built one of the most successful private practices in Philadelphia by specializing in corporation law, especially railroads and banking, both of which figured prominently in the city's economy. Roberts was a member of the prestigious Philadelphia Law Academy, a leader of the Law Association of Philadelphia, and a part-time law teacher at his alma mater until 1919. As assistant district attorney during World War I, Roberts earned public attention for his successful prosecution of violators of the federal Espionage Act. His impeccable Republican credentials, his strong ties to business, and his great courtroom success caught the attention of President Calvin Coolidge, who in 1924 appointed him as one of two special United States attorneys assigned to investigate the Teapot Dome scandals. Roberts became something of an overnight celebrity with the successful prosecution and then imprisonment of Warren G. Harding's secretary of the interior, Albert Fall. Roberts in 1930 returned to his private practice briefly.

Roberts's notoriety as a federal prosecutor was critical to his appointment to the Supreme Court. President Herbert Hoover in 1930 had nominated Judge John J. Parker to the high court.

The North Carolina judge's nomination, however, stirred powerful resistance from labor and civil rights groups. When the Senate failed to confirm Parker, President Hoover turned to Roberts, the heralded prosecutor of the Teapot Dome scandals, as a nominee above reproach. While both business and labor interests raised questions about Roberts's candidacy, neither group was willing to wade back into another bloody confrontation over a Supreme Court nominee. As a result, Roberts, who had no judicial experience and had not sought the appointment, won Senate confirmation without a dissenting vote.

Roberts probably did not belong on the Court. His experience as a prosecutor and investigator matched his personality; although studious and academically inclined, Roberts was not a scholar. He was, as is true with any good prosecutor, analytical and inquisitive, but he did not posses a philosophical and theoretical turn of mind. By temperament he was not suited to the appellate bench. Moreover, Roberts joined a Depression-era Court identified with entrepreneurial liberty and skepticism about the value of government regulation. Because the Court was deeply divided between warring liberal and conservative factions, Roberts was placed in the unenviable position of being a swing vote, especially in the constitutional struggle over the legitimacy of the New Deal's economic reform measures. Roberts had never been enthusiastic about active government involvement in the economy; he had frequently proclaimed, as did many Republicans of his era, the virtues of states' rights. He took exception to many of the New Deal measures designed to regulate business and promote the rights of labor, believing that the Constitution lacked sufficient authority to sustain either action. His positions, however, were not anchored in any profound understanding of the issues. Roberts was in the unenviable position for an appellate judge of being neither doctrinaire nor theoretically well versed in his positions.

Roberts's rulings in major New Deal cases left Court observers of his era and scholars today puzzled. He had no consistent jurisprudential principles, meaning that his role in conference and in speaking for the majority was unpredictable, some even charged (incorrectly) whimsical.

Much of Roberts's judicial career turned on his reaction to Franklin D. Roosevelt's New Deal economic recovery program. As a swing vote, Roberts's views (and his vote) were especially critical, yet he never developed arguments that clearly delineated them. For example, Roberts delivered the opinion of the Court in *Nebbia v. New York* (1934), where the justices held that a state could regulate business activity in appropriate ways and at appropriate times, including, but not limited to, fixing prices. The issue in *Nebbia* was whether the New York State Milk Board had authority to set the minimum and the maximum prices at which milk could legally be sold. In a strong and detailed opinion, Roberts proclaimed that neither contract nor property rights were absolute; indeed, he held that such rights had to yield to the good of the public. Roberts insisted that if a state's laws had a rational relation to a legitimate state purpose, such as the public welfare, and were neither discriminatory nor arbitrary, those measures had satisfied the requirements of due process of law secured by the Fourteenth Amendment. Roberts ignored the larger economic issues raised by the desirability of preferring free, as opposed to regulated markets. He seemed in one of his first major opinions, therefore, to validate government intervention in the economy. Such was not the case, however.

As conservative opposition to the New Deal hardened, Roberts moved with it, at least initially. He joined with the conservative bloc to form a majority in *Panama Refining Co. v. Ryan* (1935) that struck down Section 9c of the National Industrial Recovery Act (NIRA). The NIRA was the keystone of Franklin Roosevelt's economic recovery plan, but it was hastily drafted and of dubious constitutional authority. Roberts enlisted with a unanimous Court in *Schechter Poultry Corp. v. United States* (1935) that struck down the entire measure. He also voted with the majority in *Louisville Bank v. Radford* (1935) that voided the Federal Farm

Bankruptcy Act of 1934, and wrote the opinion for the Court in *Railroad Retirement Board v. Alton Railroad Co.* (1935). That case involved the Railway Pension Act, which made all persons who had worked for rail carriers within the preceding year eligible for pensions, including those discharged for cause. Roberts agreed with the carriers that no federally imposed pension plan could ever be considered within the powers conferred on Congress by the commerce clause. Finally, Roberts joined with the conservatives in *Carter v. Carter Coal Co.* in 1935 in overturning the Bituminous Coal Act as an invasion by the federal government of powers of economic regulation reserved to the states.

Roberts delivered his most sensational (and controversial) opinion in *United States v. Butler* (1936). The case involved certain provisions of the Agricultural Adjustment Act of 1933 that authorized the federal government to raise farm prices by reducing production. The act was the most important effort by the New Deal to ameliorate the depression in agriculture and raise farm prices by limiting production. Farmers who agreed to reduce crop acreage received benefit payments, the funds coming from a tax levied on the first processor of the commodities. Butler, a processor, refused to pay the tax.

Justice Roberts wrote for a 6–3 majority that overturned the act. Roberts insisted that the only duty a judge had in such cases was "to lay the Article of the Constitution which is invoked beside the statute which is challenged and to decide whether the latter squares with the former." Roberts then proceeded to do just the opposite.

Roberts's decision did, however, settle a long-standing dispute concerning the taxing power of Congress. Article I, Section 8, authorizes Congress to levy taxes "to pay the debts and provide for the common defense and general welfare of the United States." The debate over the meaning of these words ran back to the beginning of the republic, with James Madison and Alexander Hamilton taking different positions. The former insisted that "general welfare" purposes were limited to those already authorized elsewhere in the Constitution; the latter claimed that the language amounted to an independent power to tax and spend, as long as it was done to promote the general welfare. Roberts accepted Hamilton's view and held the processing taxes justified.

Roberts then proceeded, in a quite stunning turn of logic, to find the legislation unconstitutional. His majority opinion concluded that the question of whether or not the Congress could raise and spend money was moot since efforts to regulate and control agricultural production clearly violated the Tenth Amendment's reservation of powers to the states. In essence, Roberts concluded that Congress could do what it wished with its taxing power, but that it could not apply that power in a way that interfered with local control of agriculture. Roberts's logic came under harsh attack from the liberal wing of the Court. In a scathing rebuttal, Justice Harlan Fiske Stone called Roberts's ruling "a tortured construction of the Constitution" and condemned Roberts and the other conservatives for forgetting that "courts are not the only agency of government that must be assumed to have capacity to govern." "The only check," Stone continued, "upon our own exercise of power is our own sense of self-restraint."

Although Roberts was a moderate, centrist justice, his propensity to vote with the conservatives on many critical aspects of the New Deal fueled growing anger in Congress, the White House, and the public toward the Court. Roberts, in fact, had supported certain aspects of the New Deal, and the brunt of criticism directed at him was not altogether justified. For example, in *Ashwander v. Tennessee Valley Authority* (1936), Roberts voted with the majority in upholding the power of Congress to establish the Tennessee Valley Authority (TVA) to develop natural resources, control flooding, stabilize navigation on the Tennessee River, and generate electricity for a severely depressed regional economy.

Faced with growing demands for reform of the Supreme Court, Roberts seems to have softened his attitude toward the New Deal. For example, in 1937, Roberts joined with the liberals to form a majority in *West Coast Hotel v. Parrish* that upheld a Washington state minimum wage law for women. Although scholars have debated the extent to which Roosevelt's proposed Court-packing plan of the same year

figured in Roberts's thinking, it is worth noting that he reached his decision in *West Coast Hotel* before the president announced his plan. In this regard, Roberts's chief shortcoming was not that he succumbed to political pressure, but that he continued to follow an uncertain course in his general approach to the constitutional issues raised by the Depression and the New Deal response to it.

Even though the Court-packing scheme faltered in Congress, Roberts followed a far steadier course toward New Deal measures beginning in 1937. He joined with the Court in sustaining the Farm Mortgage Act of 1935, the National Labor Relations Act of 1935, and the Social Security Act of 1935. Roberts explained his actions by insisting that these New Deal measures were better drafted and constitutionally sounder than earlier legislation. The critics of Roberts, however, concluded that he simply found it easier to go along with the liberals than to endure the increasingly sharp criticism directed against him. In perhaps his most important reversal, he wrote the opinion for the Court in *Mulford v. Smith* (1939) that sustained the constitutionality of the second Agricultural Adjustment Act, finding this time that Congress did have the power, under the commerce clause, to regulate agriculture. Thus, in 1939, Roberts acknowledged what he had refused to recognize in 1936: that the problems confronting agriculture were national in scope and required national legislative attention.

Roberts also played an important role in the Court's emerging civil liberties and civil rights agenda. Once again, Roberts trod an unpredictable path. He wrote the opinion of the Court in *Grovey v. Townsend* (1935) that involved the constitutionality of the all-white primary. R. R. Grovey was a black man who sued Albert Townsend, a state officer in Texas, for denying him the right to vote in the Democratic party's primary election. Roberts rejected Grovey's claim on the grounds that political parties were private organizations to which the equal protection clause of the Fourteenth Amendment did not apply. Roberts's opinion sustained the practice of excluding African Americans from voting in Democratic party primaries. However, in *Smith v. Allwright* (1944), the Court overturned *Grovey* with the only dissent coming from Justice Roberts. This dissent was unexpected because six years earlier, in *Missouri ex rel. Gaines v. Canada* (1938), he had voted with the Court to invalidate the exclusion of African-American students from the state's law school. In doing so, Roberts agreed with the majority that such legislation violated the equal protection clause of the Fourteenth Amendment. Finally, Roberts authored the strongest dissent of his judicial career in *Korematsu v. United States* (1944). This case involved the constitutionality of the forced relocation of Japanese Americans during World War II. Roberts insisted that the orders issued to relocate Japanese Americans on the West Coast were "a case of convicting a citizen as punishment for not submitting to imprisonment in a concentration camp . . . solely because of his ancestry."

In matters of civil liberties, Roberts followed an equally tortured course. In *Herndon v. Lowry* (1937) Roberts delivered the opinion of the Court that set aside the conviction of a black organizer of the Communist party in Georgia for inciting insurrection. By making a distinction in this case between the "clear and present danger" and "bad tendency" tests for freedom of speech, Roberts advanced civil liberties. Three years later, Roberts also delivered the opinion of the Court in *Cantwell v. Connecticut*. Newton Cantwell and his two sons were Jehovah's Witnesses convicted of violating a Connecticut law that proscribed the act of soliciting money for religious, charitable, or philanthropic causes without the approval of the secretary of public welfare. The men's house-to-house solicitation included the loud playing of records that described the books. Roberts took the side of the Witnesses. He held that in balancing the interests of an individual's freedom of religion and the state's interest in preserving order, the Constitution meant to support the former over the latter. Roberts argued that opinions expressed in such a way as to provoke violence and disturb the public order were subject to criminal liability, but that in this case no such threat existed. In the same year, however, Roberts also voted with the majority to uphold in *Minersville School District v. Gobitis* a state-imposed flag salute that the Witnesses refused to obey. Three years later,

the Court reversed its direction and declared flag salute statutes unacceptable, but Roberts held in dissent to his position in *Gobitis*.

Roberts resigned from the Court in 1944. He left angry at the direction taken by the liberal justices President Roosevelt had installed. During his last term on the bench, Roberts found himself almost constantly at odds with the Court's Democratic majority. He dissented fifty-three times, insisting that he was the chief defender of precedent and legal stability. Roberts then returned to his alma mater to become dean of the University of Pennsylvania Law School from 1945 to 1951. He also chaired the security board of the Atomic Energy Commission.

Because Roberts had the temperament and experience of a prosecutor, his years on the Court left little in the way of a substantive constitutional legacy. He was philosophically opposed to the New Deal, but he never developed a sustained jurisprudential position within the Constitution to guide his opposition. The very qualities of independence that made him a brilliant prosecutor weighed against his success as a judge. He refused to allow himself to be classified as either a conservative or a liberal. Such a position, of course, is not unique in the history of the Court. Yet what Roberts considered independence was viewed by many of his critics as unpredictable wavering that actually hindered rather than helped the development of American constitutionalism. There is every reason to believe that Roberts actually enjoyed the role of serving as the Court's swing vote during the turbulent 1930s, but once President Roosevelt began to fill the bench with his appointees, the Republican Roberts found himself increasingly isolated, anachronistic in his views, and far less important than he had been in the 1930s. As his new fellow justices moved on to new constitutional ground, Roberts remained behind, and in so doing Roberts earned his reputation as one of the Supreme Court's lesser lights.

—KERMIT L. HALL

BIBLIOGRAPHY

Henry J. Abraham, *Justices and Presidents: A Political History of Appointments to the Supreme Court*, (2d ed., 1985), provides a thoughtful analysis of the appointment of Roberts to the Court and his difficulties with the justices appointed by Franklin D. Roosevelt. David Burner's sketch in Friedman and Israel, 3 *Justices* 2253, is too generous in attempting to find a pattern to his jurisprudence. Augustus M. Burns's portrait in Kermit L. Hall, ed., *The Oxford Companion to the Supreme Court of the United States* (1992), is a careful overview of Roberts's career that highlights the idiosyncratic nature of his jurisprudence. Paul E. Nelson's unpublished dissertation, "The Constitutional Theory of Mr. Justice Roberts" (University of Chicago, 1960), offers the best argument available that Roberts had a strong theoretical understanding of both the judicial role and the Constitution.

JOHN RUTLEDGE

BORN September 1739, Charleston,
South Carolina

NOMINATED to the Court 24 September 1789
by George Washington; took oath
on circuit court 15 February 1790;
resigned 5 March 1791; given recess
appointment as chief justice 1 July
1795 by George Washington

TOOK seat 12 August 1795; nominated
as chief justice 10 December 1795;
nomination rejected by Senate 15
December 1795

DIED 18 July 1800 in Charleston,
South Carolina

John Rutledge dominated South Carolina politics in the 1770s and 1780s, serving as a delegate to the First and Second Continental Congresses and as the state's chief executive during the Revolutionary War. Rutledge was also elected to the Confederation Congress in 1782, was appointed chief judge of the state court of chancery in 1784, and represented the state at the Constitutional Convention in 1787.

In 1789, President George Washington nominated Rutledge as one of the first six justices of the newly established Supreme Court. Rutledge accepted the commission and rode on circuit, but he did not attend any meetings of the Supreme Court before resigning in March 1791 to become chief justice of the South Carolina court of common pleas. After four years of service as a state judge, Rutledge apparently had second thoughts about the desirability of a seat on the federal Supreme Court. Anticipating Chief Justice John Jay's resignation, Rutledge wrote to President Washington in June 1795, offering to replace him. Washington accepted with alacrity and issued a temporary commission, subject to the acceptance of the nomination by the Senate when it reconvened in December.

Chief Justice Rutledge participated in two cases during the August 1795 term of the Supreme Court, *United States v. Peters* and *Talbot v. Janson*. Both cases involved libels against ships accused of violating the Neutrality Act of 1794, which prohibited the arming of ships in American ports and barred American citizens from serving on foreign privateers. Rutledge announced the opinion in *Peters*, which involved the seizure on the high seas of an American schooner, the *William Lindsey*, by an armed corvette, the *Cassius*, commanded by a United States citizen acting under the authority of a French commission. The *Lindsey*, which had been carrying a cargo of British goods, had been taken before a French prize court in Port de Paix. Because the *Cassius* was the property of the French government, the Court held, only a French tribunal had jurisdiction to decide the dispute.

Talbot v. Janson involved two ships, apparently acting in concert, that had taken as prize a Dutch brigantine. Although the captains of both ships were American by origin, both claimed to have adopted French citizenship. They also claimed that their ships were French, but the owner of the Dutch brigantine alleged that the true owners were Americans. The Court was unanimous in holding that the Dutch shipowner was entitled to restitution and damages, although each justice wrote a separate opinion. Rutledge, in a terse, three-paragraph opinion, eschewed any discussion of the vexed question of whether an American citizen could unilaterally expatriate himself. He based his decision on the grounds that one vessel had been illegally fitted out in the United States and that the other was actually American property. Rutledge did not mention the Neutrality Act, but held that the capture violated the law of nations and the American treaty with Holland.

These two brief opinions are Rutledge's sole legacy as chief justice. Shortly after his nomination for the post (but probably before he had received word of it) he engaged in some intemperate criticism of the then-controversial Jay Treaty of 1794. Opposition to his appointment arose immediately, and when the Senate reconvened in December, it rejected his nomination by a vote of fourteen to ten.

—NATALIE WEXLER

BIBLIOGRAPHY

No reliable full-length biography of John Rutledge exists. The best sources for treatment of his Supreme Court career are Leon Friedman, "John Rutledge," in Friedman and Israel, 1 *Justices* 33, and the volumes of *The Documentary History of the Supreme Court of the United States, 1789–1800*, Maeva Marcus, ed., (1985–).

WILEY BLOUNT RUTLEDGE

BORN 20 July 1894 in Cloverport, Kentucky

NOMINATED to the Court 11 January 1943
    by Franklin Delano Roosevelt

TOOK seat 15 February 1943

DIED 10 September 1949 in York, Maine

Wiley Rutledge was the elder child of a fundamentalist Baptist minister and a mother who died of tuberculosis when Rutledge was nine. Football captain at junior college, he there displayed behavior that at many colleges in today's liberal climate would result in student expulsion and firing a teacher: Rutledge had a romance with his Greek instructor, Annabel Person. Under the repressive, conservative mores of that post-Victorian period, such conduct was permissible, and they married in 1917. Transferring to the University of Wisconsin, he received his B.A. in 1914, but contracted tuberculosis soon after. Recovering, he taught high school in New Mexico for three years. Receiving his law degree from the University of Colorado in 1922, Rutledge taught law there and at Washington University in St. Louis.

Though a southerner, Rutledge displayed liberalism on race matters two decades before *Brown v. Board of Education*. While law dean at Washington University (1931–1935) in segregated Missouri, he solved a "dining imbroglio" at a biracial conference of lawyers by inviting the African-American attorneys to join him at the dean's table. He moved in 1935 to the law deanship at the State University of Iowa. A teacher willing even when dean to give any student an hour of his time, he gained national attention—and notoriety in a conservative state—for supporting Franklin Roosevelt's "Court-packing" plan. He appeared on newspaper rumor-lists for the Court vacancies eventually filled by Douglas and Frankfurter. Roosevelt instead appointed Rutledge to the District of Columbia circuit court, where he took pro–New Deal positions; for example, always siding with labor in cases from the National Labor Relations

Board. In 1943, Rutledge became Roosevelt's last appointee to the Supreme Court.

The brevity of Rutledge's six-year tenure on the Court makes difficult fair assessment of his contribution, although four of its main themes—expanding civil liberties, insisting on fair trials, aiding labor against corporate capital, and sustaining congressional power over the economy—are clear. Not long after his death from cerebral hemorrhage at the age of fifty-five, law review articles evaluating his accomplishments appeared in numbers that would be unusual respecting a justice with a much longer term. This phenomenon was perhaps partly due to his deeply appealing character, noted by commentators as diverse as his law clerks, whom he treated and debated as democratic equals, and a Republican small-Jewish-delicatessen owner whom he befriended and invited to sit among the justices at Harry Truman's inauguration. More of this was likely due to liberal perceptions that his death—two months after the demise of the only justice then more liberal than Rutledge, Frank Murphy—augured a rightward turn from the Court's post-1937 jurisprudential course. The mediocre and conservative Truman appointees proved the perceptions correct.

At the time, Alfred S. Abel equated Rutledge's record with those of two predecessors serving similar short terms, Benjamin R. Curtis (1851–1857) and Benjamin N. Cardozo (1932–1938), while W. Howard Mann called Rutledge "a great judge." However, in a complimentary piece in a symposium which appeared simultaneously in the Indiana and Iowa law reviews, two of Rutledge's former law clerks observed: "Death met him . . . after he had completed his apprenticeship, but before he had proceeded far in a master's work." Fowler Harper's biography fifteen years later, *Justice Rutledge and the Bright Constellation* (1965), asserted, "History is writing Wiley Rutledge into the slender volume of 'Justices in the Great Tradition.'" Almost half a century after Rutledge's premature death, calling him a great justice looks somewhat like calling John Kennedy a great president. It substitutes a wistful "what might have been" for a realistic "what was."

Rutledge's 171 opinions were almost evenly divided among majority, concurring, and dissenting opinions. In cases involving constitutional rights of the accused the four most liberal justices voted for the appellant's claim as follows: Murphy in 98 percent of the cases; Rutledge 91 percent; Douglas 78 percent; and Black 74 percent. In First Amendment cases, Murphy found a violation in 96 percent, while Rutledge, Douglas, and Black each did so in 79 percent. In *Adamson v. California* (1947)—the peak of the "incorporation controversy" over whether the Fourteenth Amendment made applicable to the states all protections of the Bill of Rights—Frankfurter, writing for five justices, said no, while Black urged yes for himself, Douglas, Rutledge, and Murphy. However, where Black argued that the Fourteenth Amendment due process clause embraced exactly the Bill of Rights protections *and no more*, Rutledge joined Murphy's view that the clause embraced at least those protections *and possibly more*.

Some of Rutledge's due process dissents anticipated the positions later taken by the Warren Court, for example, *Mapp v. Ohio* (1961), applying the exclusionary rule to illegally seized evidence in state trials as Rutledge had vainly urged in *Wolf v. Colorado* (1949). Almost certainly what was another of his most important dissents would have picked up more than one supporting Warren Court vote. That was his detailed and passionate forty-page opinion in *Application of Yamashita* (1946). He strenuously objected to the Court's refusal to review the war crimes evidence used, and the short time allowed to prepare the defense, in the military trial of Japan's general in the Philippines. He concluded that never "has any human being heretofore been held to be wholly beyond elementary protection by the Fifth Amendment."

Similarly anticipatory of later constitutional trends were his equal protection dissents in *Kotch v. Board of Pilot Commissioners* (1947) and *Goesart v. Cleary* (1948). In *Kotch*, Rutledge picked up support not only from Murphy and Douglas (expectably) but also from Stanley

Reed (much less so). Rutledge held violative of equal protection the administration of a Louisiana statute that gave unfettered discretion in the licensing of Mississippi River boat pilots to a board of commissioners who for years had nepotistically licensed only relatives and friends. However, Black deserted his usual allies and wrote the majority opinion. Rutledge thus narrowly lost in persuading the Court—then beginning to wrestle with racial segregation—to expand its equal protection scrutiny beyond issues of race. Rutledge's *Goesart* dissent from Frankfurter's majority opinion that Michigan could constitutionally "draw. . . a sharp line between the sexes, certainly" and prohibit all females, other than wives and daughters of male barroom owners, from being bartenders, would surely prevail today. Frankfurter's view seems antediluvian.

Among civil liberties areas, it was with religion cases that Rutledge came closest to persuading his colleagues, providing thus a crucial 1943 vote in reversing the Court's earlier upholding of Jehovah's Witness convictions for distributing religious literature without a license in *Murdock v. Pennsylvania*. He seemingly moved his colleagues somewhat between his dissent in *Everson v. Board of Education* (1947), where the Court upheld paying for bus transportation to parochial schools, and his concurrence the following year in *McCollum v. Board of Education*, where the majority disallowed religious instruction in public schools. In freedom of speech issues Rutledge was not particularly influential. Ironically, his single free speech opinion for the Court is probably his most cited case. *Thomas v. Collins* (1945) held Texas violated the First Amendment by requiring an out-of-state union leader to get an organizer's card from a state official before addressing a union meeting.

Outside the civil liberties area, Rutledge was frequently in the Court majority in areas such as admiralty, taxation, and commerce clause litigation. He penned a commerce clause dissent only once, and spoke eleven times for the Court—notably in *Urie v. Thompson* (1949) where, typically favoring labor, he construed the Federal Employers' Liability Act to extend to liability for job-related silicosis and not only to accident-caused injuries, and in *Bob-Lo Excursion v. Michigan* (1948) where he upheld a Michigan anti-discrimination statute against the objection that, as the offending boat running between Detroit and an amusement park on a nearby Canadian island was engaged in foreign commerce, it was beyond the statute's reach.

Bob-Lo, quite prominent at the time, points to three major reasons why Rutledge's overall contribution, though good, is not likely to go down in history as equivalent to that of Curtis or Cardozo. The first reason is the frequency with which Rutledge's majority decisions were interstitial advances rather than trailblazers or significant solutions to problems puzzling the Court. There is no equivalent to Curtis's Court opinion in *Cooley v. Board of Wardens* (1852) propounding a rule thereafter much used for determining when states may regulate interstate commercial activity. Nor is there one like Cardozo's opinion in *Palko v. Connecticut* (1937) holding that the Fourteenth Amendment due process clause limited states' criminal procedures only insofar as the procedures contravened the "essence of . . . ordered liberty."

The second reason is that Rutledge's dissents often pertained to lesser issues, or to important but rare occurrences (e.g., in Yamashita's case) rather than, as with Curtis's *Dred Scott* dissent (1857), bear on a pivotal point of a major long-term national issue and later come to stand, in the public mind, for the correct position.

The final reason has to do with intellectual creativity and authority, as well as accomplishments in another legal or judicial situation. Cardozo is remembered for his New York court of appeals opinions crucial in developing twentieth-century legal notions of liability. Curtis was rapidly recognized even by colleagues with different political and judicial philosophies as having an extraordinarily crisp and lucid mind. His Court years were followed by activities making him prominent in the public mind of the day— e.g., despite his *Dred Scott* stance, doubting the Emancipation Proclamation, and defending Andrew Johnson when impeached. Rutledge, for all the attractiveness of his moral person and ideals, did not have similar attainments before his Court terms and could not after, as there was no after.

—A. E. KEIR NASH

BIBLIOGRAPHY

Useful biographical sources are the articles written for the 1950 Rutledge symposium that appeared nearly simultaneously in both the *Indiana Law Journal* and the *Iowa Law Review*, particularly Alfred S. Abel, "The Commerce Power: An Instrument of Federalism," Victor Brudney and Richard F. Wolfson, "Mr. Justice Rutledge—Law Clerks' Reflections," and W. Howard Mann, "Rutledge and Civil Liberties" (1950). Landon G. Rockwell, "Justice Rutledge on Civil Liberties," 59 *Yale Law Journal* 27 (1949), whence come this essay's voting statistics, is perhaps the most useful single source. Fowler Harper, *Justice Rutledge and the Bright Constellation* (1965) is more detailed, but decidedly unanalytic and gushing in its approval.

EDWARD TERRY SANFORD

BORN 23 July 1865, Knoxville, Tennessee
NOMINATED to the Court 24 January 1923
    by Warren G. Harding
TOOK seat 19 February 1923
DIED 8 March 1930 in Washington, D.C.

A member of the inaugural staff of the *Harvard Law Review,* Edward Terry Sanford practiced law in Knoxville, Tennessee, for sixteen years before being named special assistant to the attorney general for the fertilizer trust prosecution in 1905. In 1907, he was appointed assistant attorney general, and in 1908, he returned to Tennessee as a federal district court judge. Fifteen years later, President Harding elevated Sanford to the Supreme Court.

Sanford brought to the Supreme Court a quiet moderation, a respect for precedent, and considerable erudition. Chief Justice Taft frequently turned to him to write important cases in such technical areas as bankruptcy and federal jurisdiction. Of the justices of the Taft Court, Sanford was generally among the more hospitable to federal and state exercises of regulatory power. He voted to sustain federal regulation of grain exchanges and stockyards against both substantive due process and Tenth Amendment challenges in *Chicago Board of Trade v. Olsen* (1923) and *Tagg Bros. & Moorhead v. United States* (1930). He voted with the majority in the landmark case of *Euclid v. Ambler* (1926), upholding a zoning ordinance against a substantive due process challenge. He dissented from the Court's holding in *Tyson v. Banton* (1927) that a New York statute regulating theater ticket brokers violated the due process clause; and he specially concurred in *Ribnik v. McBride* (1928), which struck down a statute regulating employment agency fees, only because *Tyson* was controlling authority. Perhaps most notably, he joined Taft's dissent from the Court's opinion striking down the District of Columbia's minimum wage law for women in *Adkins v. Children's Hospital* (1923). Sanford was not a doctrinaire opponent of substantive due process, however. He joined the Court's opinions in

Meyer v. Nebraska (1923) and *Pierce v. Society of Sisters* (1925), which recognized important noneconomic substantive liberties under the due process clause. Moreover, he joined Taft's opinion for a unanimous court holding that a Kansas statute imposing a comprehensive system of labor regulation in certain industries violated the Fourteenth Amendment in *Wolff Packing* (1923).

Sanford's days as an antitrust prosecutor showed through in the trustbusting posture he struck in such cases as *Maple Flooring Manufacturers Assn. v. United States* (1925) and *Cement Manufacturers Protective Assn. v. United States* (1925). His record in antitrust cases brought against labor unions was mixed. He joined Taft's unanimous opinion in the second *Coronado Coal* case (1925), upholding a verdict against the United Mine Workers. On the other hand, he joined the majority opinion in the *United Leather Workers* case (1924) holding that a local strike was beyond the reach of the Sherman Act. In *Bedford Cut Stone* (1927), his respect for precedent was again apparent: he concurred specially in the majority opinion upholding a verdict against the union for boycotting the company's stone only because *Duplex Printing v. Deering* (1921) was controlling authority.

Sanford's positions in cases involving the constitutional rights of African Americans were typical of those of legal thinkers of his day. He joined the majority opinion in *Moore v. Dempsey* (1923), holding that the conviction of black defendants in a trial dominated by a mob deprived them of due process. He also joined the Court's unanimous opinion holding that a Texas statute prohibiting blacks from voting in the Democratic primary violated the equal protection clause in *Nixon v. Herndon* (1927). At the same time, he joined the Court's unanimous decision upholding segregated public education in *Gong Lum v. Rice* (1927), and authored the Court's unanimous opinion in *Corrigan v. Buckley* (1926) holding that private, racially-restrictive real estate covenants were constitutionally permissible.

Sanford is perhaps best known for his contributions to First Amendment jurisprudence. The presumption of constitutionality he indulged with respect to statutes regulating the economy he also extended to measures regulating anti-government speech. Thus Sanford's opinions in *Gitlow v. New York* (1925) and *Whitney v. California* (1927) upheld the prerogative of the states to criminalize advocacy of violent revolutionary action. Yet in both cases he advanced the novel and historically pivotal position that the due process clause of the Fourteenth Amendment applied the protections of the First Amendment against the state governments. In *Fiske v. Kansas* (1927) he overturned the criminal syndicalism conviction of a man whose only offense was membership in the Industrial Workers of the World, which had not been shown to advocate violent overthrow of the government. And in *United States v. Schwimmer* (1929), Sanford dissented from an opinion upholding the denial of American citizenship to a pacifist who would not swear to bear arms in defense of the United States.

Perhaps because of his persistently moderate position on the Court, Sanford occupies a sort of neutral zone in judicial history: neither sanctified nor vilified by historians of the Court.

—BARRY CUSHMAN

BIBLIOGRAPHY

There is no biography of Justice Sanford. Some useful material is contained in James A. Fowler, "Mr. Justice Edward Terry Sanford," 17 *A.B.A. Journal* 229 (1931); John W. Green, "Some Judges of the United States District Court of Tennessee (1878–1939)," 18 *Tennessee Law Review* 227 (1944); and "Proceedings in Memory of Mr. Justice Sanford," 285 U.S. xxxvii (1932). There is a small collection of Sanford's papers at the University of Tennessee Library in Knoxville.

ANTONIN SCALIA

BORN 11 March 1936, Trenton, New Jersey
NOMINATED to the Court 24 June 1986
    by Ronald Reagan
TOOK seat 26 September 1986

The son of an Italian immigrant who taught romance languages, Antonin Scalia studied at the University of Fribourgh in Switzerland and graduated summa cum laude from Georgetown University in 1957, and magna cum laude from Harvard's school of law in 1960, where he served as a note editor on the *Harvard Law Review*.

Scalia worked in private practice in Cleveland, Ohio, until 1967, when he accepted a position on the faculty of University of Virginia's School of Law. In 1971, Scalia entered public service, serving the Nixon and Ford administrations for six years as general counsel for the Office of Telecommunications Policy, chairman of the Administrative Conference of the United States, and assistant attorney general for the Office of Legal Counsel.

In 1977, Scalia returned to academia, accepting a position to teach law at the University of Chicago. He later had visiting appointments at the Georgetown and Stanford law schools. While a visiting professor at Georgetown, he also sat as the resident scholar of the American Enterprise Institute, a conservative Washington think tank.

In 1982, President Ronald Reagan appointed Scalia to the U.S. court of appeals for the District of Columbia, where he served until 1986, when Reagan nominated Scalia to the Supreme Court. On his confirmation by the Senate, Antonin Scalia became the first academic to sit on the Court since Felix Frankfurter.

Justice Scalia is the most colorful and intellectually interesting justice on the contemporary Supreme Court, and one of the most colorful and interesting in the Court's history. His strongly-held conservative views on substantive issues, his fiery temperament, his distinctive approach to interpreting the Constitution, and his brilliant writing ability combine to make him one of the most formidable persons ever to sit on that bench.

Scalia's substantive views of constitutional law are "conservative," as that term is usually used in popular discourse, and by most measures he is indeed the most conservative member of the modern Court. He believes in strict separation of powers among the various branches of the federal government; he favors increasing protection for private property under the takings clause; he does not believe that "affirmative action" should be permitted as a remedy for race discrimination; he favors overruling *Roe v. Wade* and holding squarely that the Constitution does not protect abortion; he does not believe that other "unenumerated rights," such as a right to die with dignity, should be read into the Constitution; he believes that the death penalty is constitutional; he would relax the line of separation between church and state under the free exercise clause and establishment clause of the First Amendment; and he would permit the government to limit the free speech rights of persons who receive government benefits by placing conditions restricting the exercise of those rights on the receipt of those benefits.

Yet to say that Antonin Scalia is a conservative is to say that an eagle is just a bird. For Scalia is not just a conservative, he is a magnificent conservative, often soaring alone above friends and foes with a power and style that are his alone. He is, in short, not just *any* conservative. There is, for example, a libertarian streak to his conservatism that at times places him in alliance with liberals. In the First Amendment area, for example, Scalia has adopted a virtually absolute rule opposing discrimination against speech on the basis of its viewpoint. This caused him to join with liberal justices such as William Brennan and Thurgood Marshall in voting to strike down laws against flag desecration. It also led Scalia to write a far-reaching opinion for the Court in *R.A.V. v. City of St. Paul* (1992) striking down laws targeted at racist "hate speech."

Scalia's distinctive mark, however, is not so much captured by cataloguing his substantive views as it is by examining his judicial personality itself—his zest for intellectual combat, his unique views on constitutional interpretation, and his biting writing style.

Scalia has a gregarious, exuberant personality. He is loquacious in oral argument, loving to put difficult hypothetical and stinging questions to advocates. At times his style in oral argument appears more that of the law professor strutting his stuff before a class than the conventional image of the staid and sober jurist.

In his approach to interpreting the Constitution, and indeed his approach to the task of judging itself, Scalia has adopted three positions that work together to set him apart from most of his colleagues on the Court. These three views of Justice Scalia can for convenience be labeled (1) a skepticism of the value of *stare decisis*; (2) a preference for textualism over the use of legislative history; and, (3) a belief in the primacy of clear-cut rules over amorphous standards.

First, Justice Scalia does not place a high value on the notion of *stare decisis*, adherence to precedent from prior cases. The traditional view of *stare decisis* is that once an important issue has been settled by the Court, it should remain settled unless there are strong reasons for reconsidering the issue and changing the law. The conventional wisdom is that this value of adherence to prior precedent is laudable because it promotes stability in the law, and respect for the Court as an institution. A constitutional system in which the rules are constantly being changed by the Court, the theory goes, is disruptive, weakens the fabric of the law, and creates the appearance that constitutional law is largely a political game, in which the rules change whenever the personnel of the Court changes.

Scalia has largely eschewed these traditional views about *stare decisis*. He believes that as a Supreme Court justice, it is more important that issues be decided correctly than that the Court honor such abstract notions as "stability" and "respect" in order to preserve a legal rule that no longer commands a majority of the Court. While Scalia is often criticized fiercely for his views, often chastised (particularly by liberal critics) as a shrill and strident conservative, his views on *stare decisis* mark one sense in which it should be said that Scalia is the most open-minded of all the justices on the Court. For a

justice who does not believe strongly in honoring precedent, nothing is ever finally decided, and lawyers have the freedom to invite Justice Scalia to take a fresh look at virtually anything. For Scalia, if it has not been decided right, it has not been decided.

His second striking approach to constitutional interpretation is his strong preference for using the language of the text itself in interpreting a provision of the Constitution or a statute, rather than the legislative history of that provision. Once again, this approach sets Scalia apart from most of his colleagues, and from traditional practice.

In the American legal system it is common for lawyers and judges to invoke legislative history to explain the meaning of a law. The traditional justification for this is that the "law" is not the literal words written down on paper, but rather the "intent" or "meaning" of the persons who enacted those words. Because language is inherently ambiguous, and because those who write laws can never cover every conceivable detail or potential application, judges must have the flexibility to "interpret" the language in light of the actual intent of those who wrote it.

For a Supreme Court justice, interpreting the meaning of a statute is often critical, for two quite different reasons. When there is no constitutional issue at stake and the Court is merely interpreting a federal law in order to decide a case brought under that law, it is obviously important to interpret the meaning of the law so that the case can be decided. If an employee sues an employer for discrimination under a particular federal civil rights law, for example, it is important to know whether that civil rights law covers that type of alleged discrimination. Traditionally, the Supreme Court has been willing to examine the legislative history of the law, including such things as reports prepared by congressional committees leading up to the passage of the bill or remarks by members of Congress during floor debates, to shed light on what the law means.

Statutory interpretation is also critical to the task of the Court when the law at issue is challenged as unconstitutional. In many areas of modern constitutional law, the constitutionality

Antonin Scalia
Photograph by the National Geographic Society.
Collection of the Supreme Court of theUnited States.

of the law may in fact turn on the legislature's reasons for enacting it. When a legislature acts with intent to discriminate against religion, for example, it is well-established under current doctrines that the law violates the free exercise clause of the First Amendment. Most members of the Supreme Court are willing to examine the legislative history of a law to determine the legislature's intent in passing it, so that the law may be struck down if that intent proves to be invidious or discriminatory.

Justice Scalia disagrees with both of these uses of legislative history, a disagreement that places him at arresting odds with a majority of his colleagues. To put it bluntly, Scalia believes that legislative history is hokum. Committees prepare elaborate reports and members of Congress make fancy speeches all for the purpose of exerting "spin control" on the meaning of a new law. Congress is a partisan body buffeted by many different ideologies and interest groups, all of whom want to influence how courts will decide the meaning of the law in the future. Liberals want to make the language of a bill seem more liberal, conservatives more conservative. At the same time, all concerned must be careful not to put too much partisan spin on the language of a bill, particularly when compromise is crucial to passage, for fear that votes might be scared away.

Scalia takes the view that in light of all this political reality, it is simply wrong for judges to look into legislative history at all, because it is entirely unreliable. In his view, the only thing that the legislative body actually enacts as a whole is the final language of the law itself, and the Court should confine itself to that language when construing it. Using "objective" tools for discerning the meaning of language and traditional canons of interpretation, the judge should focus on what a law says, not what others claim it meant to say.

Similarly, Scalia is unwilling to look at legislative history to determine the intent behind a law to decide whether it is unconstitutional, except to the extent that such intent is revealed "objectively" through the actual language of the law, or the effects of the law in operation. A good recent example of this was in *Church of the Lukumi Babalu Aye v. City of Hialeah* (1993). At issue was an ordinance passed by the city of Hialeah, Florida, forbidding the ritual sacrifice of animals. A church in the Santeria religion, an ancient religion with roots in Africa and Cuba that includes the ritual sacrifice of animals as part of its religious practice, challenged the ordinance. The Court struck down the ordinance as a violation of the free exercise clause. A majority of the justices, in an opinion written by Anthony Kennedy, explored in detail the legislative history behind the passage of the ordinance, including speeches made by city officials, to reach the conclusion that Hialeah had passed this ordinance largely out of an intent to discriminate against the Santeria religion.

Justice Scalia agreed with the majority of his colleagues that the law was unconstitutional, but he sharply parted company with them on their use of legislative history. "The First Amendment does not refer to the purposes for which legislators enact laws, but to the effects of the laws enacted," Scalia argued. "This does not put us in the business of invalidating laws by reason of the evil motives of their authors." Scalia maintained that if the Hialeah officials had *intended* to discriminate against the Santeria religion, but through "ineptness" had failed to do so, the law would not be unconstitutional. Nor, he claimed, would it matter if "a legislature consists entirely of the pure-hearted, if the law it enacts in fact singles out a religious practice for special burdens."

The third defining characteristic of Antonin Scalia's jurisprudence is his preference for clear-cut legal rules over more amorphous and flexible tests and standards. In many areas of contemporary constitutional law, the Supreme Court has not adopted absolute or clear-cut rules as to what is or is not constitutional, but has instead announced a "standard" or "test," usually requiring the balancing of multiple "prongs" or "factors," that are applied to different situations on a case-by-case basis. These multi-factor balancing tests and standards so permeate existing constitutional doctrine that it is virtually impossible for any member of the Court to avoid using them, and even Scalia at times invokes and applies them. But these flexible balancing tests reflexively rankle Scalia, and he pushes hard, whenever he can, to replace them with more pristine all-or-nothing rules that create much brighter and sharper lines separating the do's and the don'ts of the Constitution.

There are many examples of this proclivity by Scalia for rules over standards. In the separation of powers area, for example, many justices opt for a "functional" approach to such questions as whether Congress may place limits on the power of the president to remove executive officials from office. In *Morrison v. Olson* (1988), for example, a case involving a constitutional challenge to the law that created the office of the "independent counsel," a majority of the Court, lead by Chief Justice Rehnquist, upheld the law. Rehnquist wrote that the critical question was whether the "removal restrictions are of such a nature that they impede the President's ability to perform his constitutional duty." Justice Scalia dissented, with a ballistic attack on the chief justice's invocation of such an uncertain standard. At one point in Scalia's acerbic attack he opined that: "This not the government of laws that the Constitution established; it is not a government of laws at all."

Scalia's penchant for clear rules appears throughout his jurisprudence. He would replace the intricate abortion jurisprudence of *Roe v. Wade* (1973) and the landmark 1992 opinion reaffirming the core of *Roe*, *Planned Parenthood v. Casey*, for example, by a flat-out ruling that the Constitution does not protect abortion at all. Similarly, in the affirmative action area, he would not use the strict scrutiny test followed by a majority of his colleagues, under which racial classifications are examined to determine if they are supported by "compelling government interests" and are "narrowly tailored" to achieve those interests. Scalia would instead adopt an absolute rule of "color-blindness" that abolishes all use of race by government to distribute benefits, and thus all affirmative action. In the free speech area, he favors an absolute rule against viewpoint discrimination.

So too, in the religion field, Scalia supports the proposition that laws of general applicability which do not single out religion for disfavorable treatment should not be struck down merely because they happen to penalize the exercise of a religious belief. In one of his most famous opinions, for example, *Employment Division, Department of Human Services v. Smith*

(1990), the Court was faced with the issue of whether a law that banned the use of the drug "peyote" could be constitutionally applied to the ingestion of small amounts of peyote by Native Americans as part of the sacramental rituals of the Native American Church. Scalia, writing the majority opinion for the Court, upheld the law, ruling that the legislature was not compelled by the First Amendment to make an exception for religious use of the drug. Since the law was "neutral" and of "general applicability," he reasoned, there was no constitutional violation.

Perhaps no multi-factor test used by the modern court draws more ire from Justice Scalia, however, than the three-pronged test of *Lemon v. Kurtzman* (1973), which the Court has used for years to determine whether a law violates the establishment clause. Under the *Lemon* test, a law must have a primarily "secular purpose," must not "advance or inhibit religion," and must not foster "excessive entanglement" with religion. Justice Scalia's bulldog-hatred for *Lemon* is well-illustrated by a colorful passage from *Lamb's Chapel v. Center Moriches School District* (1993), in which he wrote: "Like some ghoul in a late-night horror movie that repeatedly sits up in its grave and shuffles abroad, after being repeatedly killed and buried, *Lemon* stalks our Establishment Clause jurisprudence once again, frightening the little children and school attorneys of Center Moriches Union Free School District." (To this, Justice White's majority opinion wryly responded: "While we are somewhat diverted by Justice Scalia's evening at the cinema, we return to the reality that there is a proper way to inter an established decision and *Lemon*, however frightening it might be to some, has not been overruled.")

A portrait of Justice Scalia would not be complete without discussion of his extraordinary ability as a writer. There simply has not been a writer on the Supreme Court with the poetic imagination, acerbic wit, and argumentative tenacity of Antonin Scalia since Oliver Wendell Holmes. There is, indeed, a stylistic kinship between the two. Scalia, like Holmes, is at his best when writing in dissent. When Scalia can scratch and claw derisively at the perceived backings and filings of the majority, he is at his most venomous—and most eloquent. Scalia, like Holmes, is a master of the sound-bite. There may some-day be books collecting the quips and jabs and aphorisms of Scalia opinions, just as such books abound for Holmes. Wholly aside from the substance of his positions, the freshness and creativity with which he experiments with words and phrases bring a vibrancy to his writing rarely seen in judicial opinions. As part of his attack on legislative history, for example, he once made reference to the futility of parsing the "dimmy past."

In the end, his color and candor may at once define Justice Scalia's strengths and limitations. He does not appear to build coalitions easily among his colleagues. With the possible exception of Clarence Thomas, who often does join with him, Scalia has not formed lasting or consistent alliances with others on the Court who might be thought to share his general inclination toward conservatism, such as William Rehnquist or Anthony Kennedy. His willingness to attack his colleagues in dissenting opinions with bitter derision might, some Court watchers argue, interfere with his ability to work behind the scenes to create solid voting blocs on the Court.

The building of coalitions, however, would not appear to be on his agenda, and indeed, seems basically inimical to his temperament. It is not what he is about. Scalia's role on the Court is rather that of provocateur, gadfly, agitator, and conscience—not a conscience to everyone's liking, to be sure, but a conscience all the same. Antonin Scalia is likely always to remain the aggressive conservative that liberals love to hate—a hatred, one senses, at which he most delights.

—RODNEY A. SMOLLA

BIBLIOGRAPHY

Although Justice Scalia has only been on the Court a few years, his views have elicited a number of law review articles. Among the more useful are: William D. Popkin, "An 'Internal' Critique of Justice Scalia's Theory of Statutory Interpretation," 76 *Minnesota Law Review* 1133 (1992); David Boling, "Comment: The Jurisprudential Approach of Justice Antonin Scalia: Methodology Over Result?" 44 *Arkansas Law Review* 1143 (1991); George Kannar, "Comment: The Constitutional Catechism of Antonin Scalia," 99 *Yale Law Journal* 1297 (1990); and James Edward Wyszynsky, Jr., "Comment: In Praise of Judicial Restraint: The Jurisprudence of Justice Antonin Scalia," 1989 *Detroit Civil Liberties Review* 117 (1989).

GEORGE SHIRAS, JR.

BORN 26 January 1832, Pittsburgh,
Pennsylvania

NOMINATED to the Court 19 July 1892
by Benjamin Harrison

TOOK seat 11 October 1892; retired 23
February 1903

DIED 2 August 1924 in Pittsburgh,
Pennsylvania

His position on the United States Supreme
Court was the only public office George Shiras,
Jr. ever held. Son of a prosperous Pennsylvania
brewer, Shiras received his bachelor's degree
from Yale University in 1853. After studying
briefly at Yale Law School, he read law privately, and won admittance to the bar in 1855.
Quickly building up a lucrative practice, Shiras
represented such illustrious corporate clients as
Carnegie Steel and the Baltimore and Ohio Railroad. His aloofness from factional politics, and
support by powerful men, including Andrew
Carnegie, helped win his 1892 appointment and
confirmation as associate justice.

Shiras joined the Court at a time of economic upheaval in the United States. Reform-
minded Republicans and Democrats, as well as
Populists, Socialists, and Progressives, all pushed
for regulation of big business by both the state
and national governments. Powerful corporate
interests, supported by many lawyers and politicians, fought the new wave of business regulation. On the high bench, Shiras tended to
steer a middle course, often slow to approve
of regulation, but not blindly supporting large
businesses, either.

In the years just before Shiras joined the
Court, justices had been using the due process
clause of the Fourteenth Amendment to insist
that states regulation of business must be "reasonable," and that the courts could determine
what was reasonable, striking down statutes that
did not meet the test. Shiras, however, was
slower to strike down state statutes than were a
number of his colleagues. One of his first important decisions was the majority opinion in

Brass v. North Dakota (1894), dealing with
state regulation of grain elevators. Previously,
the court had upheld such regulation if aimed
at monopolistic situations. In *Brass*, however,
North Dakota was regulating a system of elevators in which healthy competition was present.
Shiras held that because the Court had earlier
ruled that states had the right to regulate grain
elevators, it was not for the judicial branch
to examine myriad individual cases. The legislatures should weigh the different situations in
each state, Shiras concluded. Four justices
dissented angrily.

In other cases of state regulation, Shiras
voted with the majority to uphold Utah's requirement of an eight-hour workday for miners in
Holden v. Hardy (1898). He also wrote the majority opinion in *Knoxville Iron Co. v. Harbison*
(1901), sustaining a Tennessee law that companies paying workers in scrip must be willing to
redeem the scrip in cash.

Shiras was less friendly toward federal economic legislation, such as the Sherman Antitrust
Act, the Interstate Commerce Act, and the federal income tax. The latter provided Shiras with
his one moment of notoriety on the court. In
Pollock v. Farmers' Loan & Trust (1895), the
Court divided 4–4 on some of the most important issues, and the justices decided to rehear the
case when all nine members were present. Shiras
was widely accused of changing his vote, from
upholding the income tax at the first hearing,
to opposing it at the rehearing. Later evidence
seemed to suggest that another justice, not
Shiras, changed his vote. At any rate, Shiras did
vote with the majority in the second *Pollock* case
to strike down the federal income tax. Recent
historians have held that decision contrary to
well-established precedent, revealing a conservative court fighting the new economic trends.

In the civil liberties arena, Shiras was one
of the more liberal justices of his time. It is true
that he voted to uphold state laws separating the
races, or denying rights to blacks, in cases such
as *Plessy v. Ferguson* (1896), and *Williams v.
Mississippi* (1898). But in his majority opinion

in *Swearingen v. United States* (1896), Shiras and four other justices refused to uphold the conviction of a populist editor accused of violating a federal obscenity law in one of his political editorials.

Arguably the most important opinion Justice Shiras wrote while on the bench was in *Wong Wing v. United States* (1896). Congress had passed a series of laws limiting Chinese immigration, and calling for the deportation of Chinese who were illegally in the country. Congress added a provision that United States commissioners (the federal equivalent of justices of the peace) could sentence Chinese aliens to hard labor prior to their deportation. Speaking now for a unanimous court, Shiras held that the Fifth Amendment promise of trial by jury applied to aliens as well as to citizens. Wong Wing had not received a jury trial, and the Court overturned his sentence of a year at hard labor.

Shiras retired in 1903, seventy-one years old and still in good health. In his eleven years on the court, Shiras had avoided extremism; he was a team player who generally sided with the majority, writing only fourteen dissenting opinions during his tenure. He died in 1924 at the age of ninety-two.

—STEPHEN CRESSWELL

BIBLIOGRAPHY

The fullest documentation of Shiras's life is contained in a book written by his son and grandson: George Shiras III and Winfield Shiras, *Justice George Shiras, Jr. of Pittsburgh* (1953). An excellent treatment of the legal culture of Shiras's day is Arnold M. Paul, *Conservative Crisis and the Rule of Law: Attitudes of Bar and Bench, 1887–1895* (1960). See also Paul's solid treatment of Shiras in Friedman and Israel, 2 *Justices* 1577.

DAVID HACKETT SOUTER

BORN 17 September 1939, Melrose,
Massachusetts
NOMINATED to the Court 23 July 1990
by George Bush
TOOK seat 9 October 1990

A Rhodes scholar and graduate of the Harvard Law School, David Souter served New Hampshire for twelve years as a deputy attorney general under Warren B. Rudman. Governor Medrin Thomson, Jr., appointed Souter to succeed Rudman as attorney general in 1976, when the latter won a seat in the U.S. Senate. Two years later, the same governor named Souter to the superior court. Governor John Sununu raised Souter to the state's highest court five years later. George Bush appointed him to the U.S. court of appeals for the first circuit in April of 1990, and then, only seven months later, nominated him to the Supreme Court vacancy created by the retirement of Justice William J. Brennan.

Justice Souter's staid career in the New Hampshire courts offers little from which to discern a personal jurisprudence. He left the court of appeals for the first circuit before he could participate in a decision. Consequently, he came to the Supreme Court a comparative enigma, tentatively labeled a Republican conservative much more for the positions he had assumed as New Hampshire's lawyer and by association with his political mentors and sponsors than by his pronouncements from the New Hampshire bench.

On the whole, his judicial opinions in the high court so far reveal David Souter to be meticulous and exacting, even fussy at times when drafting judicial opinions. His first opinions on behalf of a majority of the Court appeared in cases which involved more technical matters, particularly those relating to the interpretation of federal statutes. In more substantive disputes, he has not fallen in jurisprudential lockstep with the conservative wing of the Rehnquist Court as expected, but has instead emerged as a swing vote. In the 1991–92 term, he appeared more

often than any other justice in the majority in decisions reached 5–4; in the 1992–93 term, he appeared least often in the majority in such cases. In short, he has not proven as ideologically consistent as Justice Scalia or Justice Thomas, but more independent, after the fashion of Justice Stevens (with whom he most often disagrees). In this, he joins the ranks of the vast majority of the Supreme Court's justices, if not the ranks of its most noteworthy.

While Justice Souter has taken his share of conservative positions, particularly respecting the constitutional rights of criminal defendants, he has also voted for expansive interpretations of the Fifth and Eighth Amendments and declined to further restrict the Great Writ. In *Schad v. Arizona* (1992), for example, Souter joined the chief justice and Justices O'Connor, Kennedy, and Scalia in holding that a trial court need not require a jury to adopt unanimously one or the other of alternative legal theories offered by the prosecution in a first-degree murder case before the jury brings in a guilty verdict. In *Payne v. Tennessee* (1991), Souter joined the same clique in reversing *Booth v. Maryland* which had, only four years earlier, found that the admission of victim impact evidence at the sentencing stage in death penalty cases violated the Eighth Amendment.

On the other hand, in *Foucha v. Louisiana* (1992), Souter furnished the swing vote for holding unconstitutional Louisiana's procedures for continuing to confine a prisoner found not guilty by reason of insanity after he had been determined to be no longer mentally ill, and in *Withrow v. Williams* (1991), he wrote for the Court which upheld (5–4) federal *habeas corpus* review of a prisoner's claim of a *Miranda* violation even after the state had given the petitioner a full and fair chance to litigate the constitutional claim.

In other civil rights areas, Souter has proven even less likely to join radical initiatives from the right wing of the bench. In *Planned Parenthood v. Casey* (1992), Souter joined O'Connor and Kennedy in a plurality of the center, refusing to withdraw constitutional recognition of the right to abortion by overruling *Roe v. Wade*

David Hackett Souter
Photograph by the National Geographic Society.
Collection of the Supreme Court of the United States.

(1973), but relaxing constitutional limitations on curtailment of its exercise. In *Lee v. Weisman* (1992), he supplied the fifth vote to invalidate the practice of permitting invited clergy to offer prayers at public school graduation ceremonies, declining to join Justice Scalia's opinion that the long-standing national tradition of baccalaureate prayer, and the absence of any coercion except peer pressure made the practice constitutional. In *Lamb's Chapel v. Center Moriches Union Free School District* (1993), Souter split with Kennedy, Scalia, and Thomas by endorsing the present approach represented by both the three-part test of *Lemon v. Kurtzman* and the notion that, even when it is not coercive, preferential government treatment of religion can violate the establishment clause.

On the other hand, Souter furnished the fifth vote in *Rust v. Sullivan* (1991), upholding a regulation preventing physicians in federally-funded clinics from offering their patients abortion information and referral. That same year he also supplied the key vote in *Barnes v. Glen Theatre, Inc.*, upholding Indiana's law prohibiting nude dancing as entertainment, and joined the chief justice and Kennedy, Scalia, and Thomas in opining in *R.A.V. v. City of St. Paul* (1992) that hate speech, although it amounted to fighting words, was entitled to constitutional protection.

The dockets of his first three terms have presented David Souter with considerably fewer chances to comment on issues of separation of powers and federalism. This comparative paucity of opportunity may otherwise explain his ideological ambivalence in areas other than individual rights. On the one hand, he joined five other justices in *New York v. United States* (1992) in resurrecting a judicially enforceable states' rights limit on the legislative power of Congress under the commerce clause. On the other hand, he supplied the fifth vote in *Quill Corporation v. North Dakota* (1992), reaffirming the power of the federal courts to limit state taxation of interstate direct mail catalog sellers. While he voted to retain judicial power lacking a specific textual foundation in *Quill Corporation*, he supplied the swing vote in *United States v. Williams* (1992), in which the Supreme Court held that a federal court could not dismiss an indictment for a prosecutor's failure to reveal exculpatory information to the grand jury because the grand jury's independence limited federal judicial power.

Attentive to precedent but not enslaved by it, Justice Souter's approach has been conservative both in style and in ideology. This distances him from the more impatient and more blatantly ideological on either end of the ideological spectrum. His presence on the Court will not stop its rightward drift, but it has slowed it more than many Court watchers would have predicted at his confirmation.

—JOHN PAUL JONES

BIBLIOGRAPHY

There has been relatively little written so far about Souter. See, however, David G. Savage, *Turning Right: The Making of the Rehnquist Court* (1992); Christopher E. Smith and Scott P. Johnson, "Newcomer on the High Court: Justice Souter and the Supreme Court's 1990 Term," 37 *South Dakota Law Review* 21 (1992); and the annual "Supreme Court Review" in the *National Law Journal* for 31 Aug. 1992 and 23 Aug. 1993.

John Paul Stevens
Photograph by the National Geographic Society.
Collection of the Supreme Court of the United States.

JOHN PAUL STEVENS

BORN 20 April 1920, Chicago, Illinois

NOMINATED to the Court 28 November 1975
    by Gerald R. Ford

TOOK seat 19 December 1975

After graduating from the University of Chicago in 1941, John Paul Stevens spent four years as a naval officer, then attended the Northwestern University School of Law, graduating first in his class in 1947. After serving as law clerk to Justice Wiley B. Rutledge for the October 1947 term of the Supreme Court, Stevens returned to Chicago to join a prominent law firm where he specialized in antitrust. As he practiced law during the ensuing years, he also taught antitrust law at the law schools of Northwestern and the University of Chicago. In 1970, Richard Nixon appointed Stevens to the United States court of appeals for the seventh circuit, where he served until Gerald Ford appointed him to the Supreme Court.

During his tenure on the court of appeals, Stevens established a reputation as a competent, moderate judge of indisputable integrity. When he was nominated to the Supreme Court, the American Bar Association's Standing Committee on Federal Judiciary reviewed his judicial opinions and characterized them as well-written, highly analytical, closely researched, and meticulously prepared. Many observers expected the appointment of a replacement for the legendary William O. Douglas to be controversial. Douglas's voting behavior had been consistently liberal, while Stevens was an unknown quantity. Some Court watchers speculated that the fifth member of the Court to be appointed after the retirement of Chief Justice Earl Warren would provide the crucial vote for a conservative majority on the Burger Court. Nevertheless, the Senate confirmed Stevens by a unanimous vote.

Stevens quickly established a reputation as a moderate on the polarized Burger Court. His voting behavior demonstrates that this reputation was well deserved. His support for the claimant in civil liberties cases was well below that of Justices Marshall and Brennan, but much higher than all of the other members of that Court. He continued to be characterized as a moderate during the first seven years of the Rehnquist Court in spite of the fact that, as the majority grew increasingly conservative, Stevens began to adopt a liberal position more frequently. Indeed, Stevens supported civil liberties claims in a higher percentage of cases than any of his colleagues during the 1991 term of the Court.

The subtitle that Bradley C. Canon chose for his essay, "The Lone Ranger in a Black Robe," captures the distinguishing characteristic of Stevens's career on the Supreme Court: his independence. Clearly, Stevens has not been a leader on the Court—he has rarely convinced his colleagues to vote with him or to adopt his approaches to constitutional issues. He has dissented in a higher percentage of cases than any of his colleagues except Brennan and Marshall; he has written separate opinions (either dissenting or concurring) at a higher rate than any other justice on either the Burger or Rehnquist Courts. His opinions reflect a propensity to criticize the other justices for misinterpreting constitutional principles. Moreover, he reputedly makes little effort to win over the other members of the Court to his views.

Stevens's tenure on the Court has, nevertheless, been important. First, the independence and creativity of his opinions attest to his ability to transcend traditional doctrine to search for new approaches to complex legal issues. He has made a major contribution to the Court by challenging the other justices to question widely accepted doctrine. A second important contribution lies in the substance of his decision making.

His votes and opinions in the area of civil liberties reveal a commitment to the idea that the Court should take an active role in protecting the rights of those who have traditionally been at a disadvantage in the political process. Stevens accepts the view advanced by Harlan Fiske Stone in the famous *Carolene Products* footnote (1938) that the Court should depart from its usual deference to the elected branches of government when it reviews legislation that interferes with the ability of discrete and insular minorities to be full participants in the political arena. Although the tradition of that doctrine was a constant theme of the Court from the late 1930s through the 1960s, by the time Stevens joined the bench it had come under direct attack. Consequently, his persistent efforts to preserve the Court's role as guardian of the rights of the disadvantaged have been of major significance.

Similarly, in the realm of criminal justice, Stevens has opposed the Burger and Rehnquist Court's efforts to undermine the procedural rules promulgated by the Warren Court regarding the rights of defendants. In the face of growing opposition, for example, he continued to support the retention of the exclusionary rule (*United States v. Leon* and *Segura v. United States*, both 1984) and the series of protections known as the Miranda rights (*Rhode Island v. Innis,* 1980, *Arizona v. Roberson,* 1988, and *Minnick v. Mississippi,* 1990).

Additionally, he has dissented from the Rehnquist Court's decisions that have made it more difficult for state prisoners to obtain federal *habeas corpus* review (*Coleman v. Thompson,* 1991, *Keeney v. Tomayo-Reyes,* 1992, and *Herrera v. Collins,* 1993).

With this in mind, we can now explore Stevens's independence, as well as his commitment to individual rights, by examining his decision making in the areas of equal protection, privacy, and freedom of expression.

During Stevens's tenure on the Court, the justices have grappled with two issues that are central to the interpretation and application of the equal protection clause of the Fourteenth Amendment. He has disagreed with the majority's treatment of both of those issues. First, the Court has determined what criteria will be used in a judicial search for evidence of discriminatory conduct. A public policy that is "facially neutral," in that it does not explicitly provide that members of different groups will be treated differently, may nevertheless have a segregative or discriminatory effect. In order to determine when such a policy is in violation of the equal protection clause, the Supreme Court has adopted the "intent" rule, according to which

plaintiffs must demonstrate that those who made the policy intended for it to have a discriminatory effect. The Court has used the intent rule to decide cases involving school and housing segregation, employment opportunity, and welfare benefits. An alternative, the "effects" rule would make it substantially easier for plaintiffs to prevail, as it would require them to show only that a challenged policy had a discriminatory effect.

In one of his early opinions, *Washington v. Davis* (1976), Stevens identified a major flaw in the intent rule: "the line between discriminatory purpose and discriminatory impact is not nearly as bright, and perhaps not quite as critical" as it appears. He has argued that the rule fails to provide any basis for objective, fair decision making; indeed, in Stevens's view, it precludes the impartial administration of the law. The search for discriminatory intent, he maintains, results in arbitrary decisions upholding policies that clearly disadvantage racial minorities when it cannot be demonstrated that the policymakers intended to discriminate. Conversely, harmless policies are struck down if there is any indication of discriminatory intent. *Rogers v. Lodge* (1982). While Stevens finds the intent rule unworkable he has not advocated the adoption of the effects rule. Instead, he has looked beyond existing choices to search for new methods of determining when public policies are discriminatory.

A second central issue in the jurisprudence of the equal protection clause is the standard of review that the Court applies in different types of cases. The Court has developed a three-tiered analysis to determine the level of scrutiny it will apply to a challenged policy. When ordinary economic regulations are challenged the Court employs an extremely deferential minimum scrutiny, upholding the regulation so long as it is rationally related to a legitimate state interest. In contrast, a policy that distinguishes between people on the basis of race triggers a much tougher standard of review. Maximum, or strict, scrutiny requires that, for a policy to withstand an equal protection challenge, the state must demonstrate that it has a compelling interest and that the policy is necessary to achieve that interest. The third tier of equal protection analysis falls somewhere between the other two. Here the

Court engages in moderate scrutiny, requiring that the challenged policy be substantially related to important governmental objectives. When policies that allegedly discriminate on the basis of sex, alienage, and illegitimacy have been challenged, the Court has applied this intermediate standard of review.

Stevens has rejected that whole framework arguing that the three standards of review cannot adequately explain the Court's decisions. Early in his career on the Court, in *Craig v. Boren* (1976), he admonished:

> There is only one Equal Protection Clause. It requires every state to govern impartially. It does not direct the courts to apply one standard of review in some cases and a different standard in other cases. . . . I am inclined to believe that what has become known as the two-tiered analysis of equal protection claims does not describe a completely logical method of deciding cases, but rather is a method the Court has employed to explain decisions that actually apply a single standard in a reasonably consistent fashion.

In an opinion he wrote in 1985, Stevens offered an alternative approach. In each case, one should ask whether there is a rational basis for the challenged classification. For him, "rational basis" has a specific meaning: "a requirement that an impartial lawmaker could logically believe that the classification would serve a legitimate public purpose that transcends the harm to the members of the disadvantaged class" (*City of Cleburne, Texas v. Cleburne Living Center*). According to Stevens, the answers to several basic questions will reveal whether a policy has a rational basis:

> What class is harmed by the legislation, and has it been subjected to a "tradition of disfavor" by our laws? What is the public purpose that is being served by the law? What is the characteristic of the disadvantaged class that justifies the disparate treatment?

His method, as he has pointed out, would result in the virtual automatic invalidation of racial classifications and the validation of economic regulations. In cases involving classifications based on alienage, gender, and illegitimacy, however, the results would differ, depending on whether the characteristics of these groups are relevant to the purpose the law is designed to serve.

With regard to both the intent-effect rules and the standards of review under the equal protection clause, Justice Stevens has challenged widely accepted assumptions, has rejected traditional modes of analysis, and has reached for new approaches and innovative solutions to tough legal issues. Moreover, Stevens has sought to use those new approaches in a way that is fully consistent with the Court's role in protecting the rights of the disadvantaged.

The legal status of policy making that takes race into account has been one of the most difficult and divisive issues during Stevens's tenure on the Court. Affirmative action programs in education and employment are most often justified as attempts to remedy the effects of America's heritage of racial segregation and discrimination. Several of Stevens's colleagues maintain that racial preferences challenged under the equal protection clause should be judged by the same standard as policies that are intentionally discriminatory. That is, whether a policy is intended to harm or to help, if it is based on a racial classification, it is constitutionally suspect. For example, in *City of Richmond v. J.A. Croson Co.* (1989), a majority composed of Justices O'Connor, Rehnquist, White, Kennedy, and Scalia invalidated a city ordinance that required recipients of city construction grants to subcontract at least 30 percent of their contracts to a minority business. In their view, since the city had not supplied any evidence of specific instances of discrimination against minority businesses, it had failed to establish that there had been injuries and, therefore, could not justify a remedy.

In contrast, several of the other justices have argued that race-conscious classifications that are designed to promote remedial goals should be judged under a more relaxed standard; they should be upheld if they are substantially related to the achievement of important governmental objectives. In *Croson*, Justices Marshall, Brennan, and Blackmun argued that under that standard the set-aside program was constitutional. The city, they noted, had a substantial interest in both eradicating the effects of past racial discrimination and in preventing the city's spending decisions from perpetuating those effects. While the latter group of justices find some forms of affirmative action to be acceptable, the former group maintains that race-based decision making runs counter to the fundamental principle that the Constitution requires equal treatment without regard to race.

Stevens, independent as always, has not joined either group. While he has voted to uphold affirmative action programs more often than not, he has expressed serious reservations about such programs. Most importantly, he has rejected the principle that race should never be taken into account. His opinion in *Croson* attests not only to his independence but to the thoughtful way he has attempted to address a difficult issue. He agreed with the majority that the Richmond set-aside program could not be justified but rejected what he perceived to be the Court's underlying premise that a governmental policy based on a racial classification is never permissible except as a remedy for a past wrong.

He has maintained that some race-based programs may serve other valid public purposes. For example, as he argued in the earlier case of *Wygant v. Jackson Board of Education* (1986), an affirmative action plan for teachers might be justified on the grounds that an integrated faculty could provide educational benefits that an all-white faculty could not. Similarly, he argued, the Richmond plan might have been defended on the grounds that increasing the participation of minority businesses would serve the public interest in the performance of its construction contracts. Additionally, he urged the Court to move away from the debate over which standard of review to apply and to try to identify the characteristics of the classes that might justify their different treatment. Applying that approach, Stevens found the Richmond set-aside program to be a result of generalizations and stereotyped thinking. White contractors, he noted, disadvantaged by the program, would include those who

had discriminated on the basis of race in the past as well as those who had not. Likewise, the class that benefited from the ordinance was not limited to victims of discrimination but included people who had never been in business in Richmond and contractors who may have discriminated against members of other minority groups. Finally, Stevens reiterated a familiar theme in the debate on affirmative action outside the Court when he asserted that the Richmond ordinance stigmatized those it purported to benefit.

Stevens's reluctance to endorse preferential treatment programs appears to be based on a suspicion that decision making based on characteristics that are acquired at birth rather than those that are acquired through individual effort and talent is harmful. It is harmful, as his more conservative colleagues have alleged, insofar as it punishes innocent whites rather than only those who have been guilty of discrimination. But Stevens has also expressed a concern that preferential treatment programs may harm racial minorities by fostering intolerance and antagonism against them and reinforcing a belief in their inferiority. In sum, Stevens's approach to affirmative action includes two principles. First, unlike his more conservative colleagues he believes that race-conscious policies are justified in certain contexts. Second, he maintains that such policies must be used only with the utmost caution, not just because they might harm the white majority, but because they might stigmatize the very people they are intended to benefit.

Stevens has been more willing to accept race-conscious policy making in the context of legislative redistricting. At the end of the 1992 term, the Court ruled on a challenge, under the equal protection clause, to North Carolina's congressional reapportionment plan that was expressly designed to increase minority voting strength by including two districts with a majority of black voters. By a vote of 5–4 the Court held in *Shaw v. Reno* (1993) that whether their purpose is to benefit or harm minorities, racial gerrymandering schemes are racial classifications, subject to the most strict judicial scrutiny. In a dissenting opinion, Stevens contended that when the state creates district boundaries for the purpose of making it more difficult for members of a minority group to win an election it violates the equal protection clause. But he made a crucial distinction: when districts are drawn in order to enhance the power of a weaker group there is no constitutional violation. That distinction between racial classifications that are harmful and those that are beneficial to minorities attests to Stevens's conviction that the Court has a special duty to protect the rights of the disadvantaged.

When Stevens was nominated to the Supreme Court, one commentator concluded that the nominee's decisions on the court of appeals reflected insensitivity, if not hostility, to claims of sex discrimination. His career on the Supreme Court, however, reflects a much different attitude. In fact, in 73 percent of the sex discrimination cases in which he participated, he voted in favor of the claimant. Stevens's decision making here is consistent with his votes and opinions on other issues. While his voting behavior attests to his position as a moderate, his opinions manifest his independence as well as his commitment to protecting individual rights.

In one case, Stevens dissented from the Court's decision to uphold, against an equal protection challenge, a statutory rape law that made it punishable for a man to engage in sexual intercourse with a woman under eighteen years of age (*Michael M. v. Superior Court*, 1981). The majority found that the different treatment accorded to males and females was justified by the fact that women who engaged in sex undertook a risk that men did not: pregnancy. Thus, in order to prevent teen-age pregnancy, as the state sought to do with the statute, it was constitutionally permissible to punish men but not women for engaging in sex. Stevens objected that the law was based on the traditional attitude—possibly reflecting an irrational prejudice—that males were always the aggressors in sexual relationships. The statute authorized punishment of only one of two equally guilty parties and thus contravened the "constitutional requirement that the sovereign must govern impartially."

In a different situation, however, Stevens found that it was appropriate for the state to treat women and men differently. When the majority invalidated a New York law that permitted an unwed mother but not an unwed father to block an adoption simply by withholding consent, Stevens dissented in *Caban v. Mohammed* (1979). Trying to move beyond what he characterized as a merely reflexive rejection of gender-based distinctions, he found that the differences between unmarried fathers and mothers justify differential treatment in adoption proceedings—while it is "virtually inevitable" that the mother, but "much less certain" that the father, will have to make decisions about the care of the child.

In the landmark case of *Roe v. Wade* (1973), the Court held that the Constitution protects a woman's right to choose to terminate a pregnancy during the first six months. As reproducive rights came under increasing attack both on and off the Court during the 1980s and early 1990s, Stevens vigorously supported a woman's right to choice in this matter. He dissented when a five-member majority upheld the constitutionality of the Hyde Amendment, which prohibited the use of federal funds for most abortions, including some that were medically necessary (*Harris v. McRae,* 1980). Stevens castigated the majority for using a sterile equal protection analysis to evade the critical point: to exclude impoverished women from medical benefits that they want and need solely to further the state's interest in potential life was clearly at odds with the rules announced in Roe.

In subsequent cases such as *Thornburgh v. American College of Obstetricians and Gynecologists* (1986) and *Webster v. Reproductive Health Services* (1989), Stevens consistently reiterated his view that the abortion decision should be beyond the reach of the preferences of the majority. The 1992 decision in *Planned Parenthood of Southeastern Pennsylvania v. Casey* by a divided Court indicated that there were three distinctly different views among the justices on the issue of abortion. Four justices (Rehnquist, Scalia, and White, and Thomas) endorsed overruling *Roe v. Wade* and allowing restrictions on abortions so long as the restrictions had a rational basis. Three justices (O'Connor, Kennedy, Souter) affirmed the principle of *Roe* but adopted the "undue burden" standard according to which the Court will uphold regulations so long as they do not present a substantial obstacle to a woman seeking an abortion. Stevens and Blackmun were the only justices who remained fully committed to the principle that a woman has a fundamental right to choose to have an abortion.

While a majority upheld the provisions of the Pennsylvania Abortion Control Act that required a twenty-four-hour waiting period, information about abortion and its alternatives, consent of a parent for a minor seeking an abortion, and reporting requirements on facilities that provide abortion services, Stevens argued such regulations were unconstitutional. He articulated a variation on the undue burden standard that would make it more protective of reproductive rights than the requirement of a substantial obstacle when he asserted that a burden may be undue either because it is too severe or because it lacks a legitimate, rational justification. According to that standard, the twenty-four-hour delay requirement and the counseling provisions would fall.

Although Stevens has been steadfast in his defense of reproductive rights, he has failed to develop any new doctrine that would make a more convincing case than did *Roe* that there is a constitutionally based right to choose to have an abortion. He has instead, challenged the positions of his more conservative colleagues by focusing on the idea that, although a state's interest increases as a pregnancy progresses, life does not begin at conception. Therefore, he points out, the right to choose to terminate a pregnancy prior to viability is just as fundamental as the right to choose not to conceive at all.

Stevens's commitment to a fundamental right to privacy and personal autonomy, so clear in his opinions regarding abortion, was also readily apparent in his opinion in *Bowers v. Hardwick* (1986). In that case, five members of the Court upheld Georgia's sodomy statute against the challenge that it violated fundamental rights of privacy protected by the due process clause. Justice White, writing for the majority, announced that there is no fundamental constitutional right to engage in homosexual sodomy. In his dissent, which was joined by all four members of the minority, Blackmun countered that the case was not at all about a right to prac-

tice sodomy but about the right to be let alone—the right of privacy to make decisions that are for the individual alone to make. Stevens agreed, but wrote a separate dissent focusing on the statute's failure to distinguish either between homosexual and heterosexual sodomy or between married and unmarried couples and the state's selective enforcement of the law to apply only to homosexual conduct. His opinion underlined his commitment to equal treatment as well as to privacy. Equality, Stevens maintained must mean:

> That every free citizen has the same interest in "liberty" that the members of the majority share. From the standpoint of the individual, the homosexual and the heterosexual have the same interest in deciding how he will live his own life, and more narrowly, how he will conduct himself in his personal and voluntary associations with his companions. State intrusion into the private conduct of either is equally burdensome.

Stevens has distinguished himself in the area of freedom of expression, much as he has in other contexts, by refusing to accept doctrine that the other members of the Court rarely question. First, he has rejected the Court's "categorical approach" whereby certain types of expression, such as obscenity and "fighting words" are considered to have so little to do with the exchange of ideas that they are deemed to lie beyond the protection of the First Amendment. He expressed reservations about the categorical approach in an opinion he wrote in 1982, *New York v. Ferber*, but ten years later, he went further to characterize it as "ultimately unsound" and "destined to fail." He admonished that to reduce expression to the two dimensions of protected and unprotected fits poorly with the much more complex reality of communication and fails to take the importance of content and context seriously (*R.A.V. v. St. Paul,* 1992). The decisions of the Supreme Court, Stevens has noted, manifest a much more complex and subtle analysis than the categorical approach would allow. Thus, to analyze previous decisions in terms of the categorical approach does not even accurately portray the Court's decision making.

Second, the Court has often justified invalidating restrictions on expression with a finding that a regulation is content-based—that it punishes expression because of the substance of the message it conveys. Stevens, however, has maintained that a prohibition on content-based regulations is not the real basis of the Court's decision making. Moreover, he has argued that the Court's reliance on the issue of whether a regulation is content-based or content-neutral is neither logically consistent nor useful.

When a majority of five justices held that criminal prosecution for burning the American flag violated the First Amendment, Stevens dissented in both *Texas v. Johnson* (1989) and *United States v. Eichman* (1990). Justice Brennan, speaking for the majority, found that the challenged laws were inconsistent with a principle of the Court's previous decisions: government may not prohibit expression simply because it disagrees with its message. In the Texas case, Brennan noted that the man who burned the flag was prosecuted for his expression of dissatisfaction with the policies of this country. The regulations, in short, were content-based because they restricted political expression based on the substance of the message that a burner of the flag sought to convey. The government's important interest in preserving the flag as a symbol of nationhood and national unity was not sufficient to justify such a restriction on expression.

In contrast, Stevens argued that the intangible value of the flag as a symbol of national commitment to the ideals of liberty, equality, and tolerance, made the case unique. The government, he contended, should have the power to protect the symbolic value of the flag without regard to the substance of the flag burners' message so long as it does not interfere with the speakers' freedom to express the same ideas by other means. The Texas case, he maintained, had nothing to do with the substance of ideas; the prosecution was based on the method of expression rather its content.

In *R.A.V. v. St. Paul* (1992), a majority of the Court found a city ordinance banning the display of symbols that arouse anger in others on the basis of race, color, creed, religion, or gender to be an unconstitutional content-based

regulation of speech. Although he found the ordinance to be unconstitutionally overbroad, Stevens disagreed with the majority's determination that the constitutional flaw in the ordinance lay in its prohibition of expression on the basis of its content. He pointed out that all First Amendment doctrine is based on the content of expressive activity and castigated the majority for using the prohibition on content-based regulations to protect expression—"fighting words"—that the Court previously considered to be unprotected. What the majority did, Stevens remonstrated, was to "turn First Amendment law on its head" by holding that fighting words receive the same sort of protection afforded core political speech. In determining the constitutionality of regulations on speech, Stevens admonished, a number of factors need to be considered, including the content and the context of the expression and the nature and scope of the restriction, not simply whether the regulation is content-based. In short, neither in the flag burning cases nor in *R.A.V.* did Stevens find the issue of content-neutrality useful to a determination of whether a regulation on expression was consistent with the First Amendment.

Although Stevens has explicitly repudiated the categorical approach, his opinions, nevertheless, attest to a conviction that the type of expression has an impact on the level of protection it deserves. Stevens's "continuum of protection" approach is best illustrated in his opinions involving sexually oriented material. In *Young v. American Mini Theaters* (1976), he wrote for a five-member majority upholding zoning ordinances that regulated the location of adult theaters, and asserted that:

it is manifest that society's interest in protecting this type of expression is of a wholly different, and lesser, magnitude than the interest in untrammeled political debate . . . few of us would march our sons and daughters off to war to preserve the citizen's right to see "Specified Sexual Activities" exhibited in the theaters of our choice.

Upholding the authority of the Federal Communications Commission to regulate "patently offensive" broadcasts, Stevens, in *FCC v.*

Pacifica Foundation (1978), reiterated that such expression occupies a very marginal position in the hierarchy of First Amendment values. Moreover, he noted, the protection offered to offensive expression depends on the context in which it is presented. He explained that broadcasting has received the most limited protection from the First Amendment because of its uniquely pervasive presence in the lives of all Americans, including children. Although sexually explicit expression warrants less than full constitutional protection, Stevens has underlined—and this is consistent with his rejection of the categorical approach—that it is entitled to *some* protection (*Fort Wayne Books, Inc. v. Indiana*, 1989).

Stevens's decision making in the area of freedom of expression also evinces his commitment to the tradition of the *Carolene Products* footnote. A concern for enabling the general public to disseminate and receive information and ideas runs through his votes and opinions. Though hostile to the press in the context of defamation (*Philadelphia Newspapers v. Hepps*, 1986), he has emphasized the print media's function in helping citizens to become fully informed regarding matters of public interest. In *Houchins v. KQED* (1978), for example, he based his dissenting argument that the news media should have access to a county jail on the importance of a full and free flow of information about the operation of public institutions to the general public. When the majority upheld a town ordinance that completely banned picketing outside residences, Stevens dissented (*Frisby v. Schultz*, 1988). He concurred when the majority upheld a state statute that restricted corporate spending in state election campaigns, noting the state's interest in preventing political corruption in connection with the enormous corporate wealth accumulated with the help of the state (*Austin v. Michigan Chamber of Commerce*, 1990). When the majority narrowed the definition of a public forum and upheld prohibitions on solicitations on a postal sidewalk (*United States v. Kokinda*, 1990) and at airport terminals (*International Society for Krishna Consciousness v. Lee*, 1992), he dissented. He joined the majority in a decision to invalidate a parade permit ordinance that required applicants to pay a fee to cover potential law enforcement expenses (*Forsyth County*

v. Nationalist Movement, 1992) and dissented when the Court upheld a statute that prohibited campaigning within 100 feet of the entrance to a polling place (*Burson v. Freeman*, 1992).

John Paul Stevens's career on the United States Supreme Court has been distinguished not only by a commitment to the principle that the judiciary should take an active role in protecting those who are at a disadvantage in the majoritarian political process, but also by a persistent refusal to accept firmly established doctrine. It is his independence that has provided the basis for his most important contributions to the Court. If one day the other justices begin to devise new, creative methods for resolving continuing constitutional problems, it will surely be, in some measure, a result of his creative thinking and independence.

—SUE DAVIS

BIBLIOGRAPHY

The fact that relatively little work on Justice Stevens is available is most likely attributable to two factors: he does not stand out as a leader among the other justices, and he is currently serving on the Court. Nevertheless, a number of quite useful examinations of Stevens's judicial career are currently available.

First, an excellent overview of his judicial decision making before his appointment to the high court is provided by Special Project, "The One Hundred and First Justice: An Analysis of the Opinions of Justice John Paul Stevens, Sitting as Judge on the Seventh Circuit Court of Appeals," 29 *Vanderbilt Law Review* 125 (1976).

Second, several commentators in the late 1970s provided insightful analysis of Stevens's first few terms on the Court. See, among others, Comment, "The Emerging Constitutional Jurisprudence of Justice Stevens," 46 *University of Chicago Law Review* 155 (1978); Comment, "Mr. Justice Stevens: An Examination of a Judicial Philosophy," 23 *St. Louis University Law Journal* 126 (1979); and Special Project, "Justice Stevens" The First Three Terms," 32 *Vanderbilt Law Review* 671 (1979).

Third, by the late 1980s Stevens had established a sufficient record for scholars to begin analytical summaries of his approach to judging. For example, Paula C. Arledge, "John Paul

Stevens: A Moderate Justice's Approach to Individual Rights," 10 *Whittier Law Review* 563 (1989), analyzes his decision making in civil liberties cases to demonstrate a commitment to the *Carolene Products* footnote. Bradley C. Canon, "Justice John Paul Stevens: The Lone Ranger in a Black Robe," in Charles M. Lamb and Stephen C. Halpern, eds., *The Burger Court: Political and Judicial Profiles* (1991), offers a useful overview of Stevens's opinions and voting behavior. One commentator has provided a detailed examination of Stevens's approach to the equal protection clause in Note, "Justice Stevens' Equal Protection Jurisprudence," 100 *Harvard Law Review* 1146 (1987). The one book on Justice Stevens, Robert Judd Sickels, *John Paul Stevens and the Constitution: The Search for Balance* (1988), is difficult to find but well worth the effort.

Finally, the justice himself has provided some useful insights into his decision making, especially in the following two pieces: "Address: Construing the Constitution," 19 *U.C. Davis Law Review* 1 (1985), and "Judicial Restraint," 22 *San Diego Law Review* 437 (1985).

Potter Stewart
Photograph by Julianne Baker.
Collection of the Supreme Court of the United States.

POTTER STEWART

BORN 23 January 1915, Jackson, Michigan;
    recess appointment to Court by
    Dwight Eisenhower, 14 October 1958

NOMINATED 17 January 1959; confirmed
    5 May 1959; retired 3 July 1981

DIED 7 December 1985 in Hanover,
    New Hampshire

The life story of Justice Potter Stewart reads like that of many American upper-middle-class white, male, political success stories. Educated at the prestigious Hotchkiss preparatory school, he later earned undergraduate and law degrees from Yale University, studied at Cambridge University, served in the navy during World War II, and went on to work in a leading midwestern law firm. The common adage, "like father, like son," is perhaps more true of Potter Stewart than any other contemporary political figure. Like his father before him, Potter Stewart rose from Republican electoral city politics in Cincinnati to a position of prominence in the judiciary. Perhaps Potter eclipsed his father's success in that he was to serve on the U.S. court of appeals for the sixth circuit (1954–58), and on the U.S. Supreme Court (1958–1981), while his father's judicial service was limited to the Ohio supreme court (1947–59). Also like his father before him, Stewart was generally associated with the moderate forces in the Republican party, and as a Supreme Court justice carved out a unique role as a centrist moderate, exhibiting the characteristics of both lawyer and politician, one not readily identified with an ideological label.

Although he worked within an institution where an ideological "tag" is generally all that the public knows about a justice, Stewart was especially concerned that he not be labeled as either a liberal or a conservative. To Stewart, those labels suggested a judge who acted upon his own economic, political, social, or religious values. In contrast, Stewart asked repeatedly that he be thought of as simply "a good lawyer who did his best." His justice-as-lawyer role model suggested a jurist capable of applying objective legal reasoning to questions before the Court, uninfluenced by his own values. Even at the close of his career on the Court, Stewart had succeeded in eluding the pigeonholers.

The most commonly used terms to describe Stewart—"moderate," "neutral," and "swing voter"—reflected his tendency to vote "liberal" in some cases and "conservative" in others, and his propensity to defy prediction in specific cases. His decisions in cases on such controversial subjects as establishment of religion, pornography, equal protection of the law, and criminal defendants' rights show that he was an independent voice on the Supreme Court. While his colleagues over more than two decades tended to relatively predictably for or against expansive conceptions of individual rights, Justice Stewart appeared to "swing" from the liberal to the conservative position from one case to another, and often staked out a position substantively different from either.

Constitutional scholars, often frustrated in their attempt to pinpoint Stewart's ideology, and most content to discuss the justices as parts of coalitions or voting blocs within the Court, have tended to ignore Stewart's role on the Court, or have assumed that his positions were the result of inconsistent or random decision making. Careful analysis of Stewart's decisions, however, reveals that his unpredictable votes and uniquely fluid voting alignments with other justices with whom he served were not the result of randomness or inconsistency. His patterns in fact reflected the importance of three principles in his "lawyerly" approach to constitutional interpretation. He placed great value on states' rights and he demonstrated an equally strong commitment to narrow, non-anticipatory decision making. Rounding out Stewart's "philosophy" was a exceptionally strong concern about the preservation of judicial autonomy and authority. An appreciation of the significance of these principles for Stewart rationalizes many of his otherwise incomprehensible decisions.

The most significant substantive element in Stewart's jurisprudence was his commitment to states' rights. To most students of constitutional law, states' rights is a relic of our darkest past, a constitutionalism that supported slavery, corporate oligopoly, and the inability of the federal government to deal with twentieth-century problems. The ideology of dual federalism, under which the Tenth Amendment stood as a positive restriction on national authority, was laid to rest in *United States v. Darby* (1941), when Justice Harlan Fiske Stone proclaimed that "the [Tenth] Amendment states but a truism that all is retained [by the states] which has not been surrendered." But Stewart, in contrast with the predominant legal thought of our age and with the Supreme Court on which he served, maintained a commitment to dual federalism, to the belief that states continued to retain substantial constitutional autonomy. Dissenting alone in *Perez v. United States* (1971), he concluded that loan-sharking was only a local business practice, and, therefore, despite its occurrence nationwide, not subject to congressional regulation. His Tenth Amendment reasoning was reminiscent of ideas largely abandoned by the Court during the era of Franklin D. Roosevelt.

Stewart also dissented against incorporating most of the Bill of Rights protections for defendants in state criminal proceedings. He viewed the imposition of these restrictions on the states as an interference with their conduct of their criminal justice systems. Because the operation of a criminal justice system was, for Stewart, an essential function of government, largely definitional of a sovereign state, he was extremely unlikely to favor abridging the autonomy of the states in this area. His votes in *Malloy v. Hogan* (1964), *Benton v. Maryland* (1969), and *Duncan v. Louisiana* (1968) against "incorporation" of, respectively, the privilege against self-incrimination, the ban on double jeopardy, and the right to a trial by jury, as well as his votes in *Escobedo v. Illinois* (1964), *Miranda v. Arizona* (1966), and *Gilbert v. California* (1967), against restrictions on police practices in the states, all spoke to his commitment to the autonomy of state government.

His reluctance to interfere with states' criminal justice systems extended to even those cases in which First Amendment rights were jeopardized. Despite his usual support for the free speech rights of demonstrators and alleged pornographers, in *Cameron v. Johnson* (1965), and *Gunn v. Committee to End the War in Vietnam* (1970), as well as in *Byrne v. Karalexis* (1969), *Perez v. Ledesma* (1971), and *Huffman v. Pursue, Ltd.* (1975), Stewart refused to enjoin states from enforcing their criminal laws against these people without definitive showings of bad faith by the state. He was not unsympathetic to the substantive claims to freedom of speech of the defendants in these cases, but he did not believe that the federal courts ought to enjoin the routine law enforcement processes of the states. In Stewart's view, the First Amendment issues raised in these cases were more appropriately resolved on appeal and not by preventing the constitutionally questionable prosecutions.

His commitment to states' rights also explains his very limited support for voting rights claims which challenged poll taxes, literacy tests, malapportionment, and other state governmental practices which diluted the political strength of black voters. Although he upheld the jurisdiction of the federal courts over such cases and sustained the authority of the attorney general under the 1965 Voting Rights Act, he severely restricted the power of either to reject the state systems they scrutinized. A state's electoral system, like the enforcement of its criminal law, was to Stewart an inherent feature of its sovereignty. He was, therefore, apt to sustain all but the most flagrant abuses and irrational policies.

Stewart was largely alone in his views on federalism through the Warren Court and the early years of the Burger Court. With the appointment of four justices by President Richard Nixon, however, federalism was again in vogue. Stewart had given a speech in 1957 recommending that most civil litigation be "returned" to the state courts. In the mid-1970s, a majority of the Court took significant steps in that direction in several important decisions. In 1976, Stewart and the four Nixon appointees formed a bare majority favoring the autonomy of state and local governments in *National League of Cities v. Usery*. That decision, which immunized state and local government from federal wage and hours legislation applicable to other employers, was the first of its type in nearly forty years. Similar coalitions then proceeded to "return" to the states a modicum of autonomy over their electoral and criminal justice processes.

Only a full appreciation of Stewart's commitment to the principles of states' rights will help one understand his decisions. While other justices were concerned with defining the privilege against self-incrimination or the constitutional principle of one person, one vote, Stewart was more concerned with deciding whether states should be required to respect either.

Perhaps most striking in Stewart's jurisprudence was his commitment to narrow, non-anticipatory opinions. His constitutional decision making was characterized by his narrowing of the issue, the decision, and the remedy. In contrast with contemporary exponents of judicial self-restraint, such as Felix Frankfurter and John Marshall Harlan, who believed in the Court limiting the kinds of cases it took, Justice Stewart's restraint was in the manner of his resolution of the controversial cases of the day. It might be noted in this respect that Stewart, unlike Frankfurter, did not shy away from the high court resolving the legislative malapportionment dispute, and that it was only Stewart, joined in dissent by William O. Douglas, who believed that the Court should decide whether the war in Vietnam was constitutional. It was, rather, his very deliberate, step-by-step process of decision making that best defined his concept of "lawyering." "The law," he told me in our 1976 interview, "is a careful profession." During the same interview Stewart commented on the virtue of this approach. "No one," he said, "is wise enough to see around the next corner." By committing himself no further than was necessary to resolve the case before the Court, he retained considerable freedom in subsequent cases. His voting patterns may, therefore, have been unique and unpredictable, but they were not inconsistent.

The hallmark of a Stewart opinion is that as much attention was paid to clarifying what was not being decided as what was. In *Furman v. Georgia* (1972), Stewart rejected the death penalty, as applied, because of its "freakish" imposition. Unlike William Brennan and Thurgood Marshall, however, he thought it "unnecessary

to reach the ultimate question" of the unconstitutionality of capital punishment *per se*. Similarly, Stewart was seen as a supporter of the media when he voted against enjoining the publication of the Pentagon Papers. What received less attention was that, unlike his more liberal brethren, he specifically left open the possibility of post-publication criminal charges against *The New York Times* and *The Washington Post*. He further allowed for legislation which would permit such injunctions in the future. And in *Virginia State Board of Pharmacists v. Virginia Citizens Consumer Council* (1976), Stewart concurred that commercial speech (advertising) was not "wholly outside" the protections of the First Amendment. He cautioned, nevertheless, that the Court must not be understood to be protecting fraudulent advertisement from state regulation. Because of his limited opinion in *Virginia State Board*, one year later in *Bates v. Arizona State Bar* (1977), Stewart was free to dissent in support of the authority of the state to regulate the advertising of the legal profession.

Stewart's unique ability to narrow decisions and subsequently to distinguish seemingly similar cases made him a critical figure on the Court. His was often the pivotal, tie-breaking fifth vote in controversial decisions. Stewart was able to distinguish pretrial hearings from criminal trials with respect to the access of the press. In *Gannet v. DePasquale* (1979), he wrote for a majority of five that judges may close hearings, but in *Richmond Newspapers v. Virginia* (1980), he concurred with the Court, holding that trials must ordinarily be open. In *Cleveland Board of Education v. LaFleur* (1974), he wrote the Court opinion rejecting a mandatory fifth-month maternity leave policy for elementary school teachers, but shortly thereafter, in *Geduldig v. Aiello* (1974) he upheld discrimination against pregnancy in a state disability plan. On other occasions, Stewart wrote both the *Brewer v. Williams* (1977) and *Rhode Island v. Innis* (1980) decisions, distinguishing squad-car conversations by policy designed to elicit information from the suspect-passenger from those which only result in allegedly voluntary cooperation with the police. Finally, Stewart was the only justice to reject affirmative action programs sponsored by governments in *Regents of the University of California v. Bakke* (1978) and *Fullilove v. Klutznik* (1980), but to uphold a private plan fostered by Kaiser Aluminum Corporation in *United Steelworkers Union v. Weber* (1979).

Stewart also had an almost uncanny ability to seize the middle ground. He was uniquely prone to resolve constitutional controversies with compromises. Such was his disposition of cases on interdistrict school desegregation, capital punishment, and gender discrimination. The conditions under which he would sustain such practices were more moderate than those of either the liberals or the conservatives. Oddly enough, his lone dissent against the proscription of school prayer in *Engel v. Vitale* (1962) reflected his moderate perspective. He viewed voluntary prayer in public schools as a compromise in which the free exercise of those who chose to participate did not burden those who declined to pray. Without evidence of coercion, he saw no need to interfere with this ubiquitous practice. In Stewart's jurisprudence, the skill of precision, characteristic of the lawyer, was, perhaps paradoxically, overlaid with the penchant for moderation and compromise, qualities one associates with the politician.

The third theme in Stewart's decisions which helps to rationalize many of his positions and render them comprehensible is his belief in the importance of our judicial institutions for resolving conflict and his commitment to the integrity and autonomy of judges. These principles have been demonstrated not only by his openness to the use of judicial institutions in areas that others would have preferred to avoid, but also have been manifested in cases challenging the authority of the judiciary. In *Landmark Communications, Inc. v. Virginia* (1978), Stewart concurred with the decision that the state could not punish the press for publishing information about a state judicial fitness proceeding. But in arguing in support of the power of the state to preserve the "quality of its judiciary," Stewart maintained that the state could punish anyone divulging information about such proceedings.

While as a justice, Stewart did not demonstrate any particular reluctance to reverse decisions of lower court judges when he disagreed

with their conclusions, he was especially prone to defend the judiciary from external challenges to their authority. His decision in *Walker v. Birmingham* (1967), upholding the contempt conviction of civil rights protesters who defied a judicial injunction against a march, is an excellent case in point. Despite Stewart's generally strong support for the First Amendment rights of protesters, and despite the clarity of the First Amendment abridgements which occurred in *Walker*, Stewart's concern about the autonomy of the judiciary eclipsed these constitutional considerations. In a clash between First Amendment rights and judicial power, the dictum that one does not disobey a judicial order prevailed.

Stewart's belief in the integrity and autonomy of the judiciary also influenced his positions in cases on criminal procedure. The manifestations of this persuasion were many. He stood foursquare behind the power of judges to hold in criminal contempt those who "misbehaved" in their courtrooms despite the due process questions raised by the summary quality of the procedures employed. He trusted their unilateral fairness. He also opposed expansion of the right to a trial by jury in state criminal cases. This reflected not only his preference for states' rights, but also his trust of the judiciary and belief that a jury was not an essential element of due process of law. Thus, he dissented in *Duncan v. Louisiana* (1968) against the Court's requirement of trial by jury in serious state criminal cases, but also dissented in *Apodaca v. Oregon* (1972) which allowed verdicts in state criminal cases to be reached by non-unanimous juries. A case tried by a judge alone satisfied Stewart's conception of due process but a conviction by a divided jury did not. Similarly, in rejecting an expansion of due process guarantees to minors in such cases as *Kent v. United States* (1966), *In re Gault* (1967), *In re Winship* (1970), and *McKeiver v. Pennsylvania* (1971), Stewart maintained faith in the ability of juvenile court judges to protect the interests of their young charges and to render unnecessary the usual processes of the adversary system. It might also be noted that in the myriad cases brought by indigents who had been denied free transcripts of their trials, Stewart sided with only those convicts who had been refused the requested documents by someone other than a judge. Access to judicial determination of one's right to acquire such materials was all that Stewart was prepared to protect; judges alone remained free to decide whether or not to grant the convict's request.

Finally, with respect to his support for trial judges, Stewart was deferential to their higher sentences after retrials, whereas more severe charges on a retrial by a prosecutor elicited no such presumption of legitimacy from Stewart. He trusted judges to set aside their irritation at having been reversed on appeal, but assumed no similar magnanimity on the part of law enforcement. In sum, many areas of Stewart's jurisprudence are marked by his faith in the ethics and objectivity of the judiciary and his fervent belief in the importance of an autonomous judiciary to which deference and obedience is due.

No retrospective on a late justice would be complete without an assessment of the quality of his constitutional jurisprudence. Stewart rates high on intellect, lucidity, and judicial candor. Opinions written by Stewart are never difficult to decipher; they are short, crisp, and to the point. In this respect, he rivals the craftsmanship of John Marshall Harlan and Robert H. Jackson.

Stewart's justice-as-lawyer role is, however, a problematic concept. It rests on the assumption that each clause of the Constitution has an unambiguous, objective meaning. If this were so, then one might apply the Constitution the way one would apply a commercial code: place the facts of the case alongside the applicable "rules" and automatically reach a "correct" legal conclusion. But this mechanical jurisprudence, so tenaciously embraced by, among others, Owen J. Roberts, is rarely possible. The Constitution's clauses on freedom of speech, due process of law, or equal protection do not admit of lexical definition. Few of its provisions do. The Constitution must be interpreted, and in order to do that a jurist must identify the values underlying the words. Stewart regularly shied away from constitutional theorizing, perhaps out of fear of its being misconstrued as the subversion of the true Constitution in favor of his own image thereof. But a justice must be at least a bit of a political theorist for his or her judgments to be persuasive.

Stewart's commitment to states' rights-oriented federalism significantly influenced his jurisprudence, but it was never clear that this commitment flowed from an appreciation of the values in our system of federalism. Our federal division of power may be understood to: (1) promote democracy by allowing decisions to be made by those who would be affected by them; (2) facilitate good governance by permitting problems to be resolved at the lowest level of government that is equal to the task; (3) encourage the solving of social problems by allowing states to be laboratories for experimentation; and (4) minimize the opportunity for oppressive government through the division of power. That being so, one would have great difficulty understanding why the restriction of individual rights under the Fourteenth Amendment was dictated by federalism. Except in rare instances, broadly defined individual rights are unlikely to interfere with the values that underlie federalism. Yet Stewart tended to begin every Fourteenth Amendment analysis with a presumption of state sovereignty.

The commitment to the narrow, non-anticipatory decision making process, the element of the justice-as-lawyer model most characteristic of Stewart, is similarly problematic. A distinction must be drawn between the Court deciding no more than is before it in the case at bar, on the one hand, and choosing to resolve the case with the narrowest possible reasoning, on the other. The virtue of the former is clear. As Stewart said in an interview, issues not fully litigated in the adversary process should not be disposed of prematurely. When insufficient light is cast on an issue, the Court might well come to the wrong conclusion. But this kind of judicial restraint should not be confused with resolving a constitutional issue with the narrowest possible lawyerly reasoning. To do the latter is to focus on the trees and sometimes miss the forest.

Excessively narrow reasoning breeds unpredictability in the law. One does not know how the Court will resolve the next case. It also provides little guidance for judges faced with similar or related cases in the lower courts; and that, in turn, promotes a lack of uniformity in the decisions made in different jurisdictions. Those are practical problems.

But there is a more serious philosophical problem. Resolving constitutional cases in the narrowest possible manner, like the concept of mechanical jurisprudence, suggests that the Constitution is simply a legal code requiring no theoretical exegesis and/or that the development of constitutional theory is to be avoided whenever possible. This deprives both the people and their political leaders of the opportunity to question and to debate the virtue of our constitutional system and legal values. And the failure to place constitutional questions in a broad context results in inequities in the disposition of cases.

The folly of excessive narrowness is particularly apparent in cases involving gender discrimination and discrimination against pregnant women. Because Stewart favored a nondoctrinal course, he would not define gender as a "suspect classification" when the four comparatively liberal justices voted to do so in 1973. As a result, there was not then a uniform, and there still is not now a reliable, standard for reviewing such cases. The case law on the subject remains largely a patchwork. Similarly, the two constitutional cases on maternity leave (*LaFleur* and *Geduldig*), both written by Stewart, were resolved by entirely different reasoning and reached contrary conclusions. In the broad view, the issue in both was the constitutionality of the states' disfavor of pregnancy vis-à-vis other temporary "disabilities." In an even broader perspective, the issue was gender discrimination.

Given that it was the reluctance of Potter Stewart to view sex discrimination, like race discrimination, as "suspect," that prevented the Court from doing so twenty years ago, it is perhaps a great irony of history that his retirement from the Court paved the way for the first appointment of a woman to the Supreme Court. On Stewart's announcement of his retirement in 1981, then President Reagan announced the nomination of Justice Sandra Day O'Connor. Justice Stewart thereafter dedicated much of his time to family matters and to recording for the blind. He died in New Hampshire on December 7, 1985.

—GAYLE BINION

BIBLIOGRAPHY

There is no biography, but a good brief sketch is by Jerold Israel in Friedman and Israel, 4 *Justices* 2921. One can examine Stewart's decisions in the context of the Court on which he sat in Leonard Levy, ed., *The Supreme Court Under Earl Warren* (1972); David Rohde and Harold Spaeth, *Supreme Court Decision Making* (1976); and Glendon Schubert, *The Judicial Mind Revisited: Psychometric Analysis of Supreme Court Ideology* (1974). Specific analyses of Stewart's jurisprudence include Gayle Binion, "Justice Potter Stewart on Racial Equality: What it Means to be a Moderate," 6 *Hastings Constitutional Law Quarterly* 853 (1979). Two of Stewart's own articles worth looking at are "The Role of the Federal Courts in the Administration of Justice," 30 *Ohio Bar Journal* 480 (June 3, 1957), and "Robert H. Jackson's Influence on Federal State Relationships," 23 *Record of the Association of the Bar of the City of New York* 7 (1968).

HARLAN FISKE STONE

BORN 11 October 1872, Chesterfield,
    New Hampshire
NOMINATED to the Court 5 January 1925
    by Calvin Coolidge
TOOK seat 2 March 1925; nominated chief
    justice by Franklin D. Roosevelt
    12 June 1941; seated as chief justice
    12 October 1941
DIED 22 April 1946 in Washington, D.C.

Harlan Fiske Stone, the son of New England
farming parents, was born on the edge of the
obscure village of Chesterfield, New Hampshire.
During his eventful life he was a New York attorney, dean of the Columbia Law School and
attorney general of the United States. More notably, he served twenty-one years on the Supreme Court. In fact, he was the only jurist in
American history to occupy every seat on the
nation's highest court—from the most junior
associate justice's chair to the center seat of the
chief justiceship. By the time of his death in
1946 he had become one of the best known and
most beloved figures in American legal history.

As a boy, Stone was large for his age and
excelled in sports, especially football. He had a
sharp, methodical mind and developed into a
first-rate student. His close friends called him
"Doc." He was popular and a student leader
at every level of his education. A rare flash of
youthful temper, however, led to his expulsion
from the Massachusetts Agricultural College in
1890. He then enrolled at nearby Amherst College. There Stone made the acquaintance of
the young Calvin Coolidge, the man who would
later nominate him to the nation's highest court.
Prophetically, Stone's Amherst classmates
predicted that "Doc Stone will take warning and
proceed to be the most famous man in [the
class of] '94."

After a brief stint as a high school teacher,
Stone found his way to Columbia Law School.
There his diligence and acute intelligence led to
more academic success and accolades from his
professors. After graduation from law school in
1899, Stone was admitted to the New York bar
and went into practice in New York City with
the firm of Wilmer and Canfield. He also began
part-time teaching at the Columbia Law School.

Stone relinquished his adjunct teaching appointment in 1905 to devote himself to his law
practice, but in 1910, he accepted an appointment as professor and dean of the law school at
Columbia. As a teacher of law, Stone was enamored of the case method which was then becoming the norm at the nation's most prestigious
law schools. By all reports, Stone was a challenging, even inspiring, professor. As a dean he
handled administrative work competently but
without relish. One of the things that troubled
him as a law school administrator was what he
saw as the "the influx to the bar of greater numbers of the unfit." This xenophobia, fully consonant with upper-class thinking of the World
War I period, would be abandoned during
Stone's later years on the Supreme Court.

Dean Stone maintained the trust of the law
faculty at Columbia, but he had great difficulty
working with the autocratic university president,
Nicholas Murray Butler. In 1923, smarting from
a series of skirmishes with Butler and worn
down by "administrivia," Stone resigned from
the deanship and accepted a remunerative position with the esteemed Wall Street firm of
Sullivan and Cromwell.

Stone's private practice of law would be
short-lived. The very next year President
Coolidge chose Stone to be attorney general.
Stone came into the Justice Department with a
mandate to eliminate the corruption permitted by
his predecessor, Harry M. Daugherty. Stone succeeded so well in cleaning up the "Daughteyism"
in the Justice Department that some Democratic
partisans believed his 1925 nomination to the
Supreme Court was sparked by the Republican
party's desire to have him "kicked upstairs."
Stone's most enduring legacy from his Justice
Department tenure may have been his selection
of the twenty-nine-year-old J. Edgar Hoover to
head the recently established Federal Bureau of
Investigation.

Stone was the first nominee to the high court to appear before a Senate confirmation hearing to answer questions. Despite charges that he was "J.P. Morgan's lawyer" (his firm had acted as counsel for the House of Morgan), Stone handled the senators' questions deftly and was confirmed by a vote of 71–6.

The Court that Stone joined in 1925 was headed by the affable William Howard Taft. Taft believed in "massing the Court," i.e., presenting a unified judicial front by discouraging dissenting or concurring opinions. For his first term, Stone dutifully followed the lead of the chief justice and stifled any urges to dissent. To Court watchers of the mid-twenties, Stone looked to be another "safe Republican." Stone's forte as a professor and attorney had been in financial matters, especially tax and patent law. He could be counted on for solid opinions in complex but essentially uninteresting private law cases. In a Court that was increasingly coming to be dominated by constitutional issues, however, most legal experts predicted that Stone would act as a cipher for Taft.

By his second term on the Court, Stone began to slide away from Taft's shadow. More and more often he refused to join the opinions of the chief justice and the Court's "Four Horsemen" (conservative Justices Pierce Butler, James McReynolds, George Sutherland, and Willis Van Devanter). In moving metaphorically to the left of the bench, Stone frequently found himself in league with two of the giants of Supreme Court history, Louis Brandeis and Oliver Wendell Holmes. The phrase "Holmes, Brandeis and Stone dissenting" become a frequent litany at the end of opinions written by Taft and the Four Horsemen. Some of these dissents, particular in civil liberties cases, were among the most eloquently phrased statements in the Court's history. But most of the truly classic dissents from the period—in cases such as *Olmstead v. United States* (1928)—were written by Brandeis or Holmes, not by Stone.

As the silent partner in this triumvirate, Stone was generally overlooked or underestimated. It is true that he did not possess the epigraphical eloquence or the stark philosophical principles of Holmes, nor did he manifest the

crusading zeal or prodigious commitment to factual documentation of Brandeis. Although Stone generally permitted his senior brethren to speak for him, he was a profound thinker with clear principles of his own. His passion for judicial self-restraint in economic regulation cases was every bit the equal of Brandeis or Holmes. If Congress or the state legislatures devised a particular regulatory statute, Stone was loathe to strike it down unless it was totally lacking in a reasonable legislative foundation. On the other hand, if the legislatures came up with a statute which impinged upon the civil liberties of selected Americans, Stone was as quick as his two esteemed brethren to vote against its constitutionality.

Stone would not begin to speak regularly for the liberal dissenters on the Supreme Court until the 1930s. By then, Holmes had retired (to be replaced by Benjamin Cardozo), and a new chief justice, Charles Evans Hughes, had taken Taft's place in the middle. Hughes had previously served on the Court (1910–1916), but had resigned to seek the presidency; now he became the first justice to return to the Court after a resignation. Like the previous chief justice, Hughes was interested in massing the court around single majority opinions. In this regard he was even less successful than Taft. In part, Hughes's failure to mold a unified Court was due to the emergence of Stone as a consistent and strident opponent of judicial conservatism. In addition, unanimity on the Hughes Court was frustrated by the complexities of the Great Depression and the controversial New Deal legislation that demanded judicial review.

Although a lifelong Republican and private critic of the New Deal, Stone was seldom disposed to exalt his own policy preferences over those of the nation's elected representatives. One of Stone's greatest opinions, his dissent in *United States v. Butler* (1936), offers a good illustration of the New England jurist's self-restraining judicial philosophy in full flower. The case involved a judicial test of the Agricultural Adjustment Act (AAA) of 1933, one of the most important pieces of legislation in the early New Deal. In speaking for the six-member Court majority in *Butler*, Justice Owen Roberts held

Harlan Fiske Stone
Engraving by Oskar Stoessel.
Collection of the Supreme Court of the United States.

that the AAA processing tax which furnished revenue to underwrite crop subsidies and soil restrictions was both an unconstitutional infringement on the states' rights to regulate agriculture as protected by the Tenth Amendment to the Constitution and an unreasonably broad reading of the clause in Article I which extends to Congress the right to "provide for the . . . general Welfare."

To Stone, the majority in *Butler* read the U.S. Constitution much too narrowly. In the depths of the Great Depression he maintained that courts should not question the means by which Congress elected to carry into operation its delegated powers. In a classic justification of judicial self-restraint every bit as eloquent as any ever uttered by Holmes or Brandeis, Stone submitted: "The power of courts to declare a statute unconstitutional is subject to two guiding principles of decision which ought never to be absent from judicial consciousness. One is that courts are concerned only with the power to enact statutes, not with their wisdom. The other is that while unconstitutional exercise of power by the executive and legislative branches of the government is subject to judicial restraint, the only check upon our own exercise of power is our own sense of self-restraint. For the removal of unwise laws from the statute books appeal lies not to the courts but to the ballot and to the processes of democratic government. . . ." Later in the opinion he added: "It is a contradiction in terms to say that there is power to spend for the national welfare, while rejecting any power to impose conditions reasonably adapted to the attainment of the end which alone would justify the expenditure."

At the end of the 1935–36 term of the Court, Stone wrote his sister to lament that during that year the Court's majority had been "narrow and obscurantic in its outlook." Referring to the term just completed as "one of the most disastrous in its history," Stone ventured the following: "I suppose no intelligent person likes very well the way the New Deal does things, but that ought not to make us forget that ours is a nation which should have the powers ordinarily possessed by governments, and that the framers of the Constitution intended that it should have."

Throughout the 1930s, Stone privately complained that Chief Justice Hughes kept him on what he termed "short rations," i.e., assigning Stone the mundane financial cases while saving the juicy constitutional and public law cases for other justices. Perhaps Hughes was wary of Stone because he saw him as a rival for the Court's leadership. Stone, after all, had been widely touted as the perfect chief justice after Taft's departure; Hughes, by contrast, was resented by many in the American legal community for resigning from the Supreme Court in 1916 to seek public office.

During the infamous Court-packing controversy of 1937, Stone was active behind the scenes. He told President Roosevelt privately that the bench needed more justices who shared the philosophy of Holmes, Brandeis, and Cardozo, but who were also able to express this philosophy cogently and bear their share of the Court's work. Yet he was definitely opposed to changing the size of the Court. Stone privately fumed when the chief justice wrote a letter to Senator Burton K. Wheeler explaining that the Court was fully abreast of its business and did not need new blood. Stone objected to the propriety of a Court member, even the chief justice, rendering a public advisory opinion. He also was miffed that so few of the members of the Court were consulted prior to the release of the letter. Partly as a result of the letter, the Court-packing bill failed. But, as is well-known, the president ultimately had his way with the Supreme Court because of the defection of Owen Roberts and Chief Justice Hughes himself from the camp of those who feared the exercise of federal governmental power during the Depression.

One problem that Stone had with the "switch in time that saved nine" was that he was skeptical of the authenticity of Hughes's own conversion. Stone privately surmised that the chief justice used the Court-packing issue to grandstand. He also felt that Hughes frequently assigned an opinion to himself when the Court overruled a pre-1937 decision, such as in *West Coast Hotel v. Parrish* (1937). This, Stone believed, made Hughes look good to the liberal law school elite. On the other hand, whenever the chief justice took the conservative position, which he did quite regularly, Stone felt that he silently hid behind the opinion of another justice.

For his part, Hughes learned of the New Englander's hostility to the Wheeler letter and may have even detected Stone's skepticism regarding his own conversion. Obviously there was no love lost between Hughes and Stone. As a result, in the spate of opinions issued in 1937–38 which revivified the New Deal and the "little New Deals" of the states, Stone was only assigned to write for the majority in a single case, *Carmichael v. Southern Coal & Coke Co.* (1937). In upholding the state of Alabama's unemployment compensation law, Stone wrote: "There is no warrant in the Constitution for setting the tax aside because a court thinks that it could have drawn a better statute or could have distributed the burden more wisely. Those are functions reserved for the legislature."

Within the relatively short space of six years following the Court-packing episode and the Hughes/Roberts conversions, a series of retirements and deaths allowed President Roosevelt to name eight men to the Supreme Court whose New Deal credentials were unassailable. When Hughes retired in 1941, Attorney General Robert Jackson was named to the Court and Stone himself moved to the center seat. Hence, by the time of his death in April 1945, Roosevelt had filled every seat on the Court except the one occupied by Owen Roberts. The nation's highest court was now quite properly known as the "Roosevelt Court."

The ironies that would soon confront Stone and the Roosevelt Court were striking. The judicial self-restraint in the face of economic issues that Holmes, Brandeis, and Stone had argued for with varying degrees of passion and logic was now a reality. After 1937, the Court essentially accepted legislative economic regulation through state and federal statutes with only the most perfunctory degree of judicial review. However, unanimity on economic regulation did not mean a successful "massing of the Court" on all issues. Civil liberties questions were becoming more and more pronounced as the Depression merged into another world war. If anything, civil liberties issues would prove to be even more divisive than economic questions. Issues such as freedom of expression, separation of church and state, and racial justice befuddled and divided the Roosevelt Court just as they continue to challenge the Supreme Court in the 1990s.

Moreover, the staunch New Dealers appointed to the Court were bright, accomplished, opinionated, and far from timid. Stone referred to such justices as Black, Douglas, and Frankfurter as "wild horses." Stone's relations with the new justices, both before and after his "promotion" to the chief justiceship, could only be described as strained. For example, he and Black got off on the wrong foot. In his first term, Black dissented far too much for Stone's taste. In addition, Black was openly political and confrontational in his opinions. Stone did not keep his feelings about Black's lack of proper judicial decorum to himself. Stone liked to talk to reporter friends and had a voluminous correspondence with members of the legal community. Apparently, his privately expressed dissatisfaction with Black's performance as a judicial rookie found its way back to the Alabaman. Stone did not possess the personal skills to smooth over the friction, and Black never forgot what he perceived to have been a personal slight. So, sadly, two great jurists who shared so much in terms of philosophy never recovered from a bad initial encounter.

One of Stone's greatest contributions to the Roosevelt Court and to American law generally came in what appeared, at first reading, to be an unimportant case, *United States v. Carolene Products* (1938). The case involved a constitutional challenge to a federal law prohibiting the interstate transportation of "filled milk," i.e., skimmed milk mixed with animal fats. To be expected, given the fact that the case came to the Court after the judicial revolution of 1937 had severely undercut the economic judicial fiat, the Court found the statute constitutionally acceptable.

What made this decision memorable was its fourth footnote, perhaps the most famous footnote in all of Supreme Court history. Here, Stone starkly enunciated what many Court watchers believed had been the case since 1937, that the Supreme Court would henceforth subject statutes dealing with civil liberties and racial issues to a much more searching examination than laws pertaining to economic matters. This was a clear double standard with which the Court in 1938 appeared to be able to live.

Because of its importance, the *Carolene Products* footnote deserves quoting at length: "It is unnecessary to consider now whether legislation which restricts . . . political processes which can ordinarily be expected to bring about repeal of undesirable legislation, is to be subjected to more exacting judicial scrutiny under the general prohibitions of the 14th Amendment than are most other types of legislation. . . . Nor need we inquire whether similar considerations enter into the review of statutes directed at particular religious . . . or national . . . or racial minorities; . . . whether prejudice against discrete and insular minorities may be a special condition, which tends seriously to curtail the operation of those political processes ordinarily to be relied upon to protect minorities, and which may call for a correspondingly more searching judicial inquiry."

In simple terms, this footnote ratified the economic self-restraint so identified with Holmes and Brandeis, while at the same time suggesting that statutes, which on their face restricted civil liberties or the rights of racial minorities, would be subjected to a standard of review more probing than that accorded to economic regulations. This footnote, while technically not part of the holding in *Carolene Products*, has been cited favorably by federal courts hundreds of times in the last half century, specifically in cases involving such "suspect classifications" as race, alienage, and gender.

Most legal historians have identified Chief Justice Hughes's opinion in *West Coast Hotel v. Parrish* (1937) as a watershed in American constitutional law. It was this opinion that announced the new orientation of Roberts and Hughes, which meant that the Court would no longer attempt to act as a super legislature to review economic regulatory statutes. The *West Coast Hotel* decision, however, did not hint at the new judicial activism which would soon infuse the Court on civil rights and civil liberties questions. Stone's *Carolene Products* footnote, by contrast, looked both backward and forward. It also made clear that different standards of

constitutional review would henceforth be exercised in economic regulation and personal rights cases. Thus, an argument can be made that Stone's *Carolene Products* footnote provides a better point of demarcation than *West Coast Hotel* for the shift to the constitutional jurisprudence of the modern era. Two Stone opinions, a dissent in 1940 and a majority opinion in 1941, offer apt illustrations of this new jurisprudence.

The 1941 majority opinion in the case of *United States v. Darby Lumber Company* warrants discussion first. Here, Stone's opinion provided a brilliant and eagerly awaited legal construction of the 1938 Fair Labor Standards Act, arguably the last major piece of New Deal legislation passed by Congress. It is uncertain why Chief Justice Hughes, who generally preferred to keep for himself majority opinions reversing previous laissez-faire decisions, assigned the *Darby* opinion to Stone. In any case, Stone made the most of the opportunity.

Among other things, the Fair Labor Standards Act banned the interstate transportation of merchandise produced by companies that violated federal minimum wage, maximum hours, or child labor precepts. The statute was challenged in federal district court by a Georgia lumber manufacturer who maintained that the law impermissibly intruded into local (intrastate) manufacturing, something he felt was beyond the sweep of federal regulation. The lower court agreed with Darby Lumber, relying on the 1918 Supreme Court opinion of *Hammer v. Dagenhart* in which the Court had been unwilling to construe the commerce clause of Article I ("The Congress shall have Power . . . To regulate Commence . . . among the several states . . .") to permit the regulation of manufacturing. As a result, the *Hammer* Court held unconstitutional the Child Labor Act of 1916.

In reversing the lower court and overruling *Hammer v. Dagenhart*, Justice Stone's majority opinion in *Darby* continued to obliterate the specious distinction between manufacturing and commerce that the Court had set its guns against in *National Labor Relations Board v. Jones & Laughlin Steel Corporation* (1937). The goods produced and marketed by the lumber company, Stone concluded, were part of the stream of commerce and, thus, could be banned under the commerce clause.

Stone's opinion also helped expunge from Constitutional jurisprudence the doctrine of "dual federalism," a nineteenth-century conservative dogma which held that the Tenth Amendment sets an explicit limitation on the powers of Congress. In burying dual federalism, Stone insisted that the Tenth Amendment "states but a truism that all is retained which has not been surrendered. There is nothing in the history of its adoption to suggest that it was more than declaratory of the relationship between the national and state governments as it had been established by the Constitution before the amendment or that its purpose was other than to allay fears that the new national government might seek to exercise powers not granted. . . ." With the 1941 *Darby* opinion, Stone's leading biographer, Alpheus T. Mason, declared that Stone was "now recognized as the intellectual leader of the Court's center."

In the year prior to the *Darby* opinion Stone had hardly seemed at the intellectual center of the Court. With his lone dissent in *Minersville School District v. Gobitis* (1940), Stone appeared to some Court watchers as if he had wandered off the left edge of the political spectrum. Yet, in retrospect, his dissent in *Gobitis* is now seen as one of his finest hours. The case arose when a group of children of the Jehovah's Witnesses religious faith balked at saluting the American flag in their Pennsylvania elementary school. The Witnesses, of course, were not anti-American, but their literal reading of the Old Testament compelled them to refuse to pay homage to a "graven image." They considered and still do consider the stars and stripes to be such an "image" and therefore refuse to salute it.

The Jehovah's Witnesses' principled stand in the late 1930s violated a compulsory Pennsylvania flag salute statute. The Witnesses' children were summarily expelled for violating this law. The Witnesses' attorneys argued that the flag salute statute—a law passed in the midst of patriotic fervor as America prepared for what seemed to be an inevitable world war—was an unconstitutional infringement on the freedom of expression of the Witnesses and, therefore,

should be struck down as a violation of the First Amendment as held applicable to the states by the due process clause of the Fourteenth Amendment.

In an 8–1 decision written by Felix Frankfurter, the Court upheld the Pennsylvania Law. As the Court's only Jewish member in 1940, Frankfurter was particularly sensitive to the rights of religious minorities. But he felt strongly that there were some minimal patriotic expressions that this nation could legitimately ask of its citizens, one of them being the salute of the American flag. Frankfurter, a consistent judicial self-restrainer in civil liberties as well as economic regulation cases, provided a brilliant discourse on the power of a symbol such as the American flag. He argued, however, that while he might not favor flag salute legislation personally, he would not wish to inject his views between the people of state and their elected representatives.

Frankfurter had tried mightily to secure Stone's vote for the majority in *Gobitis*, writing him a five-page letter which even used some of Stone's own language in the *Carolene Products* footnote against his position. Stone would not budge. Shortly before the opinion in *Gobitis* was to be announced in open court, Stone received word that Frankfurter planned to read from the bench his entire lengthy majority opinion. Stone debated whether he should simply announce that he dissented, as was the custom, or whether he should attempt to match Frankfurter's rhetoric by reading his opinion as well. Ironically, Frankfurter elected at the last minute not to read his opinion, merely announcing the result in the case. But Stone was so agitated that he decided to plunge ahead and read his dissent, doing so with a level of emotion rare for him.

In asserting that the Gobitis children were denied their freedom of speech and religion by the Pennsylvania law, Stone declared: "The guaranties of civil liberty are but guaranties of freedom of the human mind and spirit and of reasonable freedom and opportunity to express them. . . . If these guaranties are to have any meaning they must, I think, be deemed to withhold from the state any authority to compel belief or the expression of it where that expression violates religious convictions, whatever may be the legislative view of the desirability of such compulsion."

Stone expressed chagrin later in the day that he was so carried away by emotion that he had read his entire dissent. But he was buoyed by praise from many quarters for expressing such a courageous opinion in the face of the uncritical patriotism of the country in 1940. The chairman of the American Civil Liberties Union, John Haynes Holmes, ventured that Stone's *Gobitis* opinion would "rank as one of the great dissenting opinions in American history." Fully 171 American newspapers editorialized in support of Stone's dissent; only a few joined company with Frankfurter.

Stone's apprehension about the lack of tolerance for religious differences was confirmed by the persecution of the Jehovah's Witnesses in the immediate aftermath of the *Gobitis* decision. In the week of June 12–20, 1940, alone, the Justice Department received reports of "hundreds of attacks on the Witnesses." Among the many incident reports were the following: a Witnesses' Kingdom Hall in Maine was burned; a mob attacked a Witnesses' Bible meeting within a few miles of the nation's capitol; and in Connersville, Indiana, a Witnesses' attorney was beaten and driven from town. The Justice Department attributed this wave of violence directly to the *Gobitis* decision.

The physical attacks against the Witnesses would eventually taper off, but the Witnesses would continue to find their way to the nation's highest court over a variety of issues. In *Jones v. City of Opelika* (1942), a case involving the constitutionality of municipal ordinances levying a license tax on groups selling books and pamphlets door-to-door, the Witnesses took the position that such laws violated their First Amendment rights of freedom of expression and the free exercise of religion made applicable to the states by the due process clause of the Fourteenth Amendment. The Witnesses lost the case by a vote of 5–4. As expected, Stone dissented. However, in another dissent filed by Justices Black, Douglas, and Murphy, something unheard of in Supreme Court history took place. These three justices, all of whom had voted with the

majority in *Gobitis*, confessed that they had changed their minds about the constitutionality of flag salute statutes and now agreed with Justice Stone on this issue.

The about-face of the three liberal justices in *Jones v. Opelika* persuaded the Witnesses to bring another case to federal court on the constitutionality of compulsory flag salute laws. This time the case came from West Virginia. In 1943, along with several other cases involving the Witnesses, the Court handed down the ruling in *West Virginia Board of Education v. Barnette* which explicitly overruled *Gobitis*. The vote was 6–3, with Stone, the three recanting justices, and the recently appointed Wiley Rutledge and Robert Jackson in the majority. Stone, who by this time was the chief justice, graciously allowed Jackson to write the majority opinion. Frankfurter again issued an impassioned dissent. The majority opinion, one of Jackson's best, echoed many of the arguments and even some of the phraseology in Stone's *Gobitis* dissent. Thus, in three short years, Stone as a lone dissenter had turned around the Supreme Court on a major civil liberties issue.

In June 1941, Charles Evans Hughes, citing matters of health and age, wrote President Roosevelt that he wished to retire effective July 1, 1941. Speculation as a successor settled on Attorney General Robert Jackson and Stone. Roosevelt, ever the savvy politician, picked Stone. As the country was poised for war, Roosevelt was mindful of the importance of building consensus. Stone and Jackson both shared FDR's overall philosophy of government, but Stone was a Republican and, of course, possessed extensive judicial experience.

Poet and essayist Archibald MacLeish wrote that the Stone nomination was "so clearly and certainly and surely right it resounded in the world like the perfect word spoken at the perfect moment." When the nomination came up for discussion in the Senate on June 27, 1941, Senator George Norris, the last of the Progressives who had fought Stone's earlier appointment as an associate justice, delivered the only speech. He confessed his error in opposing Stone in 1925 and now strongly endorsed his elevation to the chief justiceship. A few moments later, Stone was confirmed unanimously by a voice vote of the Senate. Jackson would later be appointed to the Court to occupy the seat vacated by Stone.

In the newly confirmed chief justice's obligatory appreciation letter to President Roosevelt, he referred to himself as now having to shoulder "some burdens which John Marshall did not know." He could not have been more prophetic. Marshall, for example, did not even see a single dissent to any opinions of the Court (most of which he wrote himself) in his first three terms as chief justice. By contrast, the pace of dissent on the Stone Court was higher than at any previous time in American history.

The "wild horses"—Black, Douglas, and Frankfurter—now had a similarly rambunctious stablemate in Robert Jackson. Stone basically tried to stay out of the way. Never one to hog the glory, he took pains to assign important majority opinions to each of his brethren. As a result, Stone did not issue any majority opinions during his tenure as chief justice of the significance, for example, of his 1941 opinion in *Darby*.

In many ways, the chief justiceship was a unhappy denouement to an otherwise illustrious public life. Part of Stone's difficulty as chief justice was his tolerance for disagreement. In the minds of some Court colleagues, he let conferences over pending cases and petitions of certiorari continue far too long. The Stone Court did not generally observe the normal Court protocol of allowing the justices to speak in turn in ascending levels of seniority. As a result, the discussions went in many different directions. While Felix Frankfurter, the professor, may have enjoyed the lively exchanges, more efficiency-minded justices chafed at the time seemingly wasted in conferences.

Another problem was that Stone did not have the ability and perhaps the inclination to massage the massive egos of some of his colleagues. As an associate justice, Stone kept to a strict schedule and dispatched routine work with amazing speed. He was troubled that others could not do the same, but he did not have the patience or tact to cajole them into more rapid activity. Justice Jackson believed that Stone's problem as the Court's leader was that he

dreaded conflict. But because he was willing to permit dissension to continue and fester, he unintentionally abetted the already high degree of conflict that was inevitable given the positions and personalities of the "wild horses."

One example of the difficulty that Stone had in massing his own Court can be seen in such a deceptively simple matter as composing a farewell letter to Justice Owen Roberts at the time of retirement in 1945. Roberts was the only member of the Court in 1945 who President Roosevelt did not have a hand in placing in his seat (Stone, of course, had been originally nominated to the Court by Hoover but promoted to the chief justiceship by FDR). At the end of the 1944–45 term Roberts was not a happy justice. He had dissented fifty-three times that year, frequently with bitter and intemperate language. After he announced his plans to retire, Stone drafted a farewell letter couched in cautious, hardly generous language. Some justices signed it, some refused. A second letter, even less flattering to Roberts, was drafted by Hugo Black and made the round of the justices. The negotiations over language continued for weeks. The Black draft eventually received six "votes." Although not satisfied with Black's draft, Stone used it substantially as the basis for his comments about Roberts at the Court's opening session in October 1945. This was a sorry episode that did no credit to the Stone Court.

Assessing the qualities and accomplishments of Harlan Fiske Stone is no easy matter. Published studies of judicial greatness have usually placed Stone in the "great" or "near great" category. Judged against the justices with whom he served, Stone should receive high but not top marks in most categories. For example, although he did not shine as brightly as his compatriots in judicial restraint, Holmes and Brandeis, his was a consistent and solid voice for respect of the legislative prerogative. He did not possess the crusading zeal of a Brandeis, a Black, or a Douglas, but he held strong principles and expressed them cogently at appropriate times: unlike the legal crusaders, he had an impeccable sense of judicial decorum. Judged against other academic lawyers who found their way to the high court, his scholarship was well above average, but not of Frankfurter's caliber. As a legal writer he rose to brilliance on occasion, as in his *Darby* majority opinion or his *Gobitis* dissent, but his prose did not consistently sparkle as did that of Holmes and Cardozo. And, as sensitive as Stone was to civil liberties, he failed to weigh in against the egregious "internment" of Japanese Americans during World War II. Finally, as a chief justice, Stone was honest and solid, but not as effective a builder of consensus as was Taft, or even Hughes.

The end of Stone's long public life came suddenly and with a measure of incongruity. On Easter Monday 1946, Stone was presiding over an opinion day session of the Court. He read a dissent in *Girouard v. United States*, a case addressing the question of whether a conscientious objector was entitled to citizenship. Ironically, Stone was dissenting to a majority view that wrote into law a position that he had himself expressed in a previous dissent. Thus, this eloquent self-restrainer and advocate of judicial consensus was in the anomalous posture of dissenting from one of his own dissents. Stone's reasoning was complicated, but essentially he believed that Congress had acted to interpret the statute at issue, the Naturalization Act of 1940, in a way contrary to his earlier dissent. Thus, ever sensitive to legislative prerogative, he felt bound to express his support for the wishes of elected representatives, even if that meant dissenting and going against a position he had advocated just a few years earlier.

At the end of his opinion in *Girouard*, as almost a fitting epitaph, he stated: "It is not the function of this Court to disregard the will of Congress in the exercise of its constitutional power." Following the disposition of this case, Justice Black announced several opinions. Then it was scheduled for Stone to deliver three decisions. Stone paused for a long moment, then mumbled incoherently. Black, the senior associate justice, sensing that something was wrong, banged the gavel and ended the session. Stone was helped out of the chamber. He then collapsed in a Court washroom and was later taken home by ambulance.

Never regaining consciousness, Harlan Fiske Stone died of a massive cerebral hemorrhage that evening, April 22, 1946. Three days later more than 2,500 people attended his funeral. Of the many stirring eulogies, perhaps Senator Alben Barkley of Kentucky struck the most apt chord: "No Associate Justice or Chief Justice . . . held a more abiding place in the affections of the American people and in the affections of all who knew him intimately and personally."

—JOHN W. JOHNSON

BIBLIOGRAPHY

The Stone papers are in the Library of Congress. Stone's own writings include: *Law and Its Administration* (1915); "The Common Law in the United States," 50 *Harvard Law Review* 4 (1936); "Fifty Years Work of the Supreme Court," 14 *American Bar Association Journal* 428 (1928); and "The Public Influence of the Bar," 48 *Harvard Law Review* 1 (1934). Stone's career has benefited from a masterful biography: Alpheus T. Mason, *Harlan Fiske Stone: Pillar of the Law* (1956), which makes extensive use of Stone's correspondence and other private papers.

Useful on Stone's legal thought are Samuel J. Konefsky, *Chief Justice Stone and the Supreme Court* (1946); G. Edward White, *The American Judicial Tradition: Profiles of Leading American Judges* (1976), 215–29; Allison Dunham, "Mr. Chief Justice Stone," in Allison Dunham and Philip B. Kurland, eds., *Mr. Justice* (1964), 229–49; John P. Frank, "Harlan Fiske Stone: An Estimate," 9 *Stanford Law Review* 621 (1957); Noel T. Dowling, "Mr. Justice Stone and the Constitution," 36 *Columbia Law Review* 351 (1936); Learned Hand, "Chief Justice Stone's Conception of the Judicial Function," 46 *Columbia Law Review* 696 (1946); Herbert Weschsler, "Stone and the Constitution," 46 *Columbia Law Review* 793 (1946); William O. Douglas, "Chief Justice Stone" 46 *Columbia Law Review* 764 (1946); and Noel T. Dowling, "The Methods of Mr. Justice Stone in Constitutional Cases," 41 *Columbia Law Review* 1160 (1941).

JOSEPH STORY

BORN 18 September 1779, Marblehead,
Massachusetts

NOMINATED to the Court 15 November 1832
by James Madison

TOOK seat 3 February 1812

DIED 10 September 1845 in Cambridge,
Massachusetts

Joseph Story was the youngest Supreme Court nominee in history, but he went on to become one of the commanding figures of American legal history. While writing a larger proportion of the Marshall Court's opinions than anyone other than John Marshall himself, Story created an extensive and erudite commercial, insurance, and admiralty jurisprudence in his capacity as circuit justice for the New England states. After 1829, as Dane professor of law, Story was the central figure of the antebellum Harvard Law School; the treatises he wrote in carrying out his professorial duties played a seminal role in the creation of a sophisticated, genuinely American jurisprudence. When one also notes Story's extensive occasional writings, his active (if usually unacknowledged) political activities, and his services as president of a bank and member of the Harvard Corporation, it becomes clear that Story was the busiest justice in the Court's history, as well as one of its best known.

Story's happy marriage, his love of learning and his gregariousness, his liberal attitudes about women, slavery, and the mistreatment of Native Americans, and his basic social conservatism all had their roots in his childhood and his parents. Story's parents came from privileged backgrounds, but his father's medical practice in the declining fishing village of Marblehead inculcated at an early date the lesson that public service is a duty. Dr. Elisha Story, one of the "Indians" at the Boston Tea Party, clearly was the major source of his son's youthful politics and a significant influence on Joseph's lasting ethical and theological beliefs. Joseph's mother, Mehitable Pedrick, was a strong-willed and voluble autodidact; she seems to have played a

decisive role in shaping the future justice's personality. Story attended Harvard College, graduating in 1798 with second honors in his class and a strong taste for belles lettres, an interest that reached its high point with his publication in 1802 of a volume of mediocre poetry entitled *The Power of Solitude*. After overcoming an initial dislike for the "dry and technical principles" of the law, Story became enamored of legal learning; soon after his admission to the bar in July 1801, he wrote to a friend of his "love for my profession. The science claims me as a fixed devotee." Story was to remain a devotee of the law and of legal learning for the rest of his life.

During the first years of the nineteenth century, Story built what was by decade's end a prominent legal practice. At the same time, he was busily engaged in politics. Although in later life he often sought to downplay his early partisanship, the youthful lawyer was an enthusiastic Republican in a state and a profession then dominated by Federalists. Story's involvement in county Republican politics led to his rapid rise in political prominence as the Republicans gained political strength in Massachusetts. He was first elected to the Massachusetts legislature in 1805 and served an unexpired term as a Republican congressman in December 1808–January 1809; he became speaker of the lower house of the state legislature in 1811. Politics and law converged in Story's work as a lobbyist and lawyer in the famous Yazoo affair, which stemmed from the wholesale corruption of the Georgia legislature and its sale of 35 million acres in the state's Yazoo area (now Alabama and Mississippi) at extremely favorable prices. The state's subsequent attempt to rescind the sales sparked a fifteen-year struggle in the courts and Congress over the validity of the rescission and the propriety of reimbursing third-party purchasers of the disputed real estate. Along with the famous Maryland lawyer, Robert Goodloe Harper, Story successfully argued the purchasers' position in the great case of *Fletcher v. Peck* (1810), which held that the original land grants were irrevocable.

With the death of Justice William Cushing in September 1810, it was at last possible for the Republicans, in control of the presidency and Congress since 1801, to secure a majority on the Supreme Court. President James Madison's problem was to identify a suitable replacement for Cushing (a Massachusetts native) from among the small body of Massachusetts Republican lawyers. Madison's first selection declined; the Senate rejected the second; and the third, John Quincy Adams, preferred to remain a diplomat. Story's suitableness for the appointment was suspect to some, particularly to ex-president Thomas Jefferson, who resented Story's role in Congress in terminating the embargo on international trade that Jefferson had employed as retaliation for European attacks on American vessels. However, over Jefferson's private objections—Story, Jefferson wrote, was "unquestionably a tory . . . and too young"—Madison turned to Story. Madison nominated Story and Gabriel Duvall (the latter to succeed Samuel Chase, who had died in mid-1811) simultaneously, and they were confirmed together on November 18, 1811.

With Madison's two appointments, the Court Story joined for the February 1812 term was made up of five Republicans and only two Federalists, but the Court already bore the impress of the views and personality of its Federalist chief justice. Story was in broad agreement with Marshall's nationalism and his preference for public consensus on the Court, and he quickly became Marshall's confidant and ally. Story's original Republicanism had always been more partisan than ideological, and in the 1810s he, like many younger Republicans, found less and less to dislike in Marshall's basic constitutional vision.

The War of 1812 began only a few months after Story took his seat, and much of his early judicial work both on the Court and as presiding judge of the federal circuit court for New England concerned matters arising out of the war and the related federal policies of trade restriction and embargo. The relevant bodies of law—admiralty and prize cases, the law of nations, the historical practice of belligerents—gave ample room for Story's love of recondite legal research, but his frequent disagreements with his colleagues did not arise solely on intellectual grounds. Circuit justice Story was, in a peculiarly personal sense, the representative of the nation and the federal government in a region torn by disagreement over the war and tempted to outright defiance of federal authority. Story's usual response was to assert an expansive view of the nation's rights as a belligerent.

The central doctrinal theme in Story's war-related jurisprudence was the existence and significance of implied federal power to carry out the war. On circuit, in *United States v. Bainbridge* (1816), Story held that Congress's power to create a navy implied the power to permit the enlistment of minors without their parents' permission: "Whenever a general power to do a thing is given, every particular power necessary for doing it is included." In *Brown v. United States* (1814), Story concluded that in the absence of express statutory authorization, the president had the implied power to prosecute the war by seizing enemy property found in the United States, although Chief Justice Marshall for the Supreme Court reversed Story's decision. On the question of confiscation, indeed, Story and Marshall frequently were in public disagreement. Story maintained, and Marshall denied, the power to confiscate the property of American citizens resident in Britain despite their ignorance of the outbreak of war or their good-faith intent to return to the United States in the event of war (*The Venus,* 1814); enemy goods consigned to American buyers prior to the war (*The Merrimack,* 1814); goods purportedly immune under a special license from the British vice-admiral (*The Julia,* 1814; compare Marshall's 1813 circuit decision in *United States v. The Matilda*); and neutral goods carried on a belligerent vessel (*The Nereide,* 1815). In the latter case, indeed, Story prepared and delivered an elaborate 6,000-word dissent from Marshall's opinion in vindication of what he termed "the national rights, suspended upon" the power to confiscate the goods.

Story's solicitude for the "national rights" of the United States at war led him to defend implied judicial power as well. In *Houston v. Moore* (1820), Story dissented from a judgment upholding a state court-martial of a federalized

Joseph Story
Engraving by J. Cheney.
Collection of the Supreme Court of the United States.

militiaman on the ground that the federal courts implicitly had exclusive jurisdiction to try the case. He also repeatedly attempted to establish the existence of a broad, judicially developed federal common law of crimes. In *United States v. Hudson & Goodwin*, decided a few weeks after Story took his seat, the Court endorsed the orthodox Republican view that federalism and separation of powers rendered the exercise of criminal jurisdiction except in pursuance of a statute illegitimate. No justice publicly dissented, but in an 1813 circuit opinion, Story stated that he "considered the point, as one open to discussion, notwithstanding . . . *Hudson*." The opinion argued at length in support of a common law of offenses against the United States, at least within the scope of admiralty jurisdiction, but the government declined to support his views in the Supreme Court, and Story was unable to persuade his colleagues to reopen the issue (*United States v. Coolidge,* 1816). Story was more successful in sustaining judicial power to define criminal offenses under open-ended statutes. In *United States v. Smith* (1820), he carried all but one of his colleagues with him in concluding that a statute criminalizing piracy "as defined by the law of nations" was precise enough to meet what modern lawyers would call the requirements of due process.

Story, like other nationalists of the early republic, saw deep connections between a strong federal government and the growth of commerce and industry. Even as he was defending the existence of broad, implied federal powers, Story spent his first years on the bench laying the groundwork for a law of business and commerce, expounded by the federal courts, that would favor growth and industry. In an early decision on circuit, *De Lovio v. Boit* (1815), Story wrote an elaborate, seventy-page opinion holding that cases involving marine insurance contracts fell within the federal courts' exclusive admiralty jurisdiction. The subject matter of *De Lovio* itself was of great significance in the early nineteenth century, but Story's opinion went beyond insurance to sweep virtually everything afloat—"all maritime contracts, torts, and injuries"—within the federal sphere. Federal courts in admiralty cases sit without juries, and that

aspect of *De Lovio* proved especially popular with New England business because, as Story noted in a letter, merchants "declare that in mercantile cases, they are not fond of juries." The publication of Story's circuit court decisions, which began in 1815, made the justice's pro-business opinions available on a wider basis. On the Supreme Court as well, Story established early on an expertise in maritime, insurance, and commercial cases. In cases such as *Raborg v. Peyton* (1817), which extended the enforceability and thus the utility of bills of exchange, Story consistently rejected older, anti-commercial decisions, "made at a time when the principles respecting mercantile contracts were not generally understood," in favor of legal doctrines favoring the development and expansion of a market economy.

For Story, the nurturance of commerce and the protection of property were two sides of the same coin. In *Fairfax's Devisee v. Hunter's Lessee* (1813), Story for the Supreme Court reversed a Virginia court decision and held that British real property claims—and the interests of the American land speculators who purchased them—were protected from state expropriation laws under the American treaties with Britain. Story's first major constitutional opinion for the Supreme Court, *Terrett v. Taylor* (1815), displayed the centrality of property rights in his legal universe. *Terrett* held that land belonging to the colonial established church in Virginia was vested in the postwar Episcopal Church, even though the Virginia legislature and courts had concluded that recognizing the church's claims violated the Virginia constitution's guarantee of religious freedom. Story's opinion grandly, if rather vaguely, invoked "the principles of natural justice" and "the spirit and letter of the constitution" (without specifying what provision he had in mind); the actual basis of the decision was Congress's legislative jurisdiction over the land in question, which lay within Virginia's contribution to the District of Columbia.

The connection between the protection of vested rights and the encouragement of business became clear in Story's concurring opinion in *Dartmouth College v. Woodward* (1819). Marshall's opinion for the Court held that the college's royal charter was protected against state interference by the Constitution's contracts clause. Story made explicit the applicability of the decision to business corporations, and at the same time reassured state legislators concerned about creating inviolable corporate privileges by admitting the legitimacy of corporate charters reserving certain amending powers to the state.

Story's genuine distaste for the wheeling and dealing of partisan politics did not prevent him from becoming actively involved in the federal political arena almost from the beginning of his tenure on the Court, although his efforts were covert and generally directed toward the improvement and expansion of the federal judiciary. From 1813 on, Story was a confidant of Daniel Webster, then rising toward prominence as an orator in Congress and in oral argument before the Court. Story supplied Webster and other congenial members of Congress with legislative proposals dealing with the courts and later with constitutional arguments to rebut the states' rights views frequently voiced in Congress after 1820. After the conclusion of the War of 1812, Story prodded and cajoled his congressional allies to enact legislation extending the criminal powers of the federal courts, establishing a federal bankruptcy system, and vesting the judiciary with the full range of jurisdiction authorized under Article III. In private, Story commended his proposals to Republican legislators as a means of seizing the "glorious opportunity" the end of the war presented "for the Republican party to place themselves permanently in power."

Publicly, Story read Congress an elaborate lecture on the scope of federal court jurisdiction in his famous 1816 opinion in *Martin v. Hunter's Lessee. Martin* was the aftermath of Story's opinion in the *Fairfax's Devisee* case discussed earlier. Instead of obeying the Supreme Court's mandate, the Virginia court's judges unanimously declared the provision of the Judiciary Act giving the Supreme Court jurisdiction over state decisions unconstitutional. Story's rebuttal, that Supreme Court review of state decisions on federal law issues was consonant with text, history, and practice, was not surprising, but the terms in which he announced it were dramatic. Story vindicated the Court's authority in terms

that unequivocally repudiated traditional Republican rhetoric about states' rights. The Constitution, Story wrote, "was ordained and established, not by the states in their sovereign capacities, but emphatically . . . by 'the people of the United States.' . . . [The Constitution] is crowded with provisions which restrain or annul the sovereignty of the states in some of the highest branches of their prerogatives." He went on to instruct Congress on its obligation to extend federal jurisdiction to the limits of Article III in terms that amounted to a brief in support of the judiciary legislation he was then circulating among members of Congress.

The period from 1812, when Story took his seat on the Court, to 1824 was the most productive in the Marshall Court's history. The Court's membership remained unchanged until Brockholst Livingston's death in 1823, and the justices enjoyed, in the main, a remarkable degree of harmony in their private relations and in their public decisions. In all of this Story was an enthusiastic participant, but one with a distinctive voice. He endorsed the generous view of federal power announced by Marshall's great decisions in *McCulloch v. Maryland* (1819) and *Gibbons v. Ogden* (1824), but Story's own opinions in *Martin* and the war-related cases showed his own nationalism to be less nuanced and more confrontational. Story's colleagues generally shared his pro-business orientation and admired his legal scholarship, but there too, Story sometimes took extreme positions or was too eager to advance his own views of the properly scientific understanding of the law. His most daring decision of the period, however, concerned the international slave trade, which Story on circuit declared an offense against the law of nations (*United States v. La Jeune Eugenie,* 1822). Story's opinion eloquently denounced the trade as "unnecessary, unjust, and inhuman," and "repugnant to the general principles of justice and humanity," but the decision went beyond existing international law and Marshall's notions of judicial prudence. Three years later, a Marshall opinion for the Court (*The Antelope,* 1825) gently but unequivocally repudiated Story's holding.

From his earliest days at the bar, Story was a scholarly lawyer, and as a judge he was able to indulge his interest in exploring what he described in an 1820 letter as an empire of reason. The first volume of Supreme Court reports covering cases decided after Story's appointment contained a separate page of "corrections and additions" to Story's opinions and a note by Story explaining a case that the Court decided by a per curiam order; after Henry Wheaton became the Court reporter in 1816, Story frequently authored unsigned "themes" on legal questions that Wheaton obligingly included in the Court's reports. Story understood his opinions, his extrajudicial writings, and even his political contacts with allies in Congress as part of an effort to make American law into a science in which an independent judiciary discovered and applied an orderly system of legal principles through the exercise of reason. Only if the law could be a science, Story believed, could it play the role he envisaged for it in the disorderly world of a democratic republic.

This vision of scientific law, and scientific lawyers, became increasingly salient as the Marshall Court's institutional and political environment began to deteriorate in the mid-1820s. Story's opinions for the Court in the period expanded on familiar themes. *Martin v. Mott* (1827), for example, broadly interpreted the president's exclusive authority to determine when state militia should be called into federal service, while *Wilkinson v. Leland* (1829) employed extravagant rhetoric about the "sacred" rights of private property on the way to reaching a narrow holding based on the construction of a state statute. *Van Ness v. Pacard* (1829) undermined the property law doctrine of "waste" by interpreting a traditional exception broadly to favor social mobility and investment in the commercial and industrial use of real property. *The Thomas Jefferson* (1825) limited federal admiralty jurisdiction over torts to the ebb and flow of the tide (and thus denied it as to the great body of river commerce), but the decision did not truly contradict Story's usual views. It left maritime contracts in federal court, and was dictated, Story believed, by the very historical materials that he thought a scientific lawyer should consult to answer the question.

The continuity of the Court's decisions, however, was increasingly threatened by forces external to Story's legal science. The election of 1824, in which four Republicans vied for the presidency, shattered the postwar dominance of a nationalist Republican leadership supportive of the Court. Andrew Jackson, the leader in the 1824 popular vote, and the victor in 1828, was in Story's eyes a military chieftain clearly unsuitable for high office. The democratic and states' rights themes associated with Jackson were antithetical to Story's political beliefs, and the justice was not referring solely to the boisterous festivities that accompanied Jackson's inauguration when he described it as "the reign of King Mob triumphant." The posthumous publication of Jefferson's correspondence, with his caustic comments on the Court and on Story personally, lent the dead statesman's prestige to ideological criticism of the Court. Internally, changes in the Court's membership eroded the old practices of consensual decision making and, whenever possible, official unanimity; in 1827, Chief Justice Marshall dissented publicly in a constitutional case for the first time in his tenure (*Ogden v. Saunders*; Story and Duvall joined Marshall's dissent).

In the stormy political waters of the Jackson years, Story strove to preserve the Court's institutional position while defending his political and constitutional values as best he could. He took an active role in pushing the Court toward its decision in *Worcester v. Georgia* (1832) that Georgia's attempt to assert jurisdiction over the Cherokee nation was a violation of the supremacy of federal constitutional and treaty provisions, a decision that was defied by Georgia and at odds with Jackson's popular anti-Indian attitudes.

Story's behind-the-scenes political activity continued unabated. He was, for example, the principal draftsman of the federal crimes act Congress passed in 1825. When the president vetoed a bill to renew the charter of the Bank of the United States in 1832, and in the process denied the finality of the Supreme Court's constitutional decisions, Story was the source of the legal reasoning Webster used to denounce the veto, and the justice probably played a similar role in the genesis of Webster's famous 1830 speech defending the unity and supremacy of the Union against the South Carolinian claim that an individual state could "nullify" federal laws it deemed unconstitutional. The question of nullification, indeed, put Story in the unaccustomed role of supporting Andrew Jackson. When South Carolina threatened to nullify an unpopular federal tariff act, Jackson responded with a proclamation as emphatically nationalist in tone and content as any state paper since Story's *Martin* opinion. Story publicly praised Jackson's proclamation as "among the ablest commentaries ever offered" on the Constitution's meaning; privately, Story noted that he was among Jackson's "warmest supporters . . . just as long as he maintains the principles contained" in the proclamation.

Story's most lasting defense of his vision of constitutional nationalism and legal science came about through the largess of the New England lawyer and senior statesman Nathan Dane. In 1829, Dane offered to endow a chair of law at the Harvard Law School with the express condition that Story be the first incumbent if he were willing, and on August 25, Story was installed as the first Dane professor of law. Under the terms of the endowment, Story was to deliver and revise for publication lectures on a variety of subjects, and over the next sixteen years, Story wrote and published nine treatises. Several of the treatises are classics of legal scholarship. The *Commentaries on the Constitution* (1833) restated the Marshall Court's constitutional legacy for a new generation, and Story ensured for it wide influence by preparing an abridged edition for use as a college and law school text. The treatises on *Equity Jurisprudence* (1836) and *Equity Pleadings* (1838) played a major role in Americanizing English equity, while the *Conflict of Laws* (1834) essentially created that area of law as a systematic area of study. All of the treatises reflected Story's energy, his love of abstruse historical and comparative learning, and his desire to bring order and system to American law. Through them, and through his lectures and personal contact with a law school student body that grew exponentially during his tenure, Story fruitfully pursued the same goal he sought in his opinions. Justice Story's prestige lent authority to Professor Story's legal science, and the professor's scholarship undergirded the justice's opinions and generalized their teaching.

John Marshall's death in July 1835 marked the end of an era for Story, personally and professionally. Marshall's absence from the following term of Court (during which Story presided because the Senate had not yet confirmed Marshall's successor) afflicted Story with grief and loneliness: he wrote a friend that he "missed the Chief Justice at every turn." But Marshall's passing was more than the death of a great and good friend, for Story feared that it marked the end of the Court as he and Marshall had known and revered it. The president chose Roger Brooke Taney to be the new chief justice, even though Taney's Democratic partisanship and Jacksonian ideology had prevented his confirmation when Jackson initially appointed him in early 1835 to be an associate justice.

When the Taney Court convened for the first time in January 1837, all but two of its members were Jackson appointees; when Congress increased the size of the Court to nine justices, Jackson and his handpicked successor, Martin Van Buren, of course filled those positions as well. Many Democrats hailed the changes in the Court as an opportunity to reverse what they say as the aristocratic and anti-democratic jurisprudence of the Marshall era. In an 1835 essay about the late chief justice, Jacksonian editor William Leggett praised Marshall's "spotless purity of life," but wrote pointedly that "we cannot but experience joy" that the Court would no longer be led by a judge who sought always "to strengthen government at the expense of the people." Story anxiously awaited a jurisprudential revolution.

Chief Justice Taney's first term appeared to confirm Story's worst fears, driving him almost to despair and to serious consideration of resignation from the Court, an idea with which he toyed for the rest of his life. In a trilogy of constitutional decisions held over from Marshall's day, the Taney Court distanced itself dramatically from what Story and others believed was correct, Marshallian doctrine.

In *New York v. Miln* (1837), the Court upheld the constitutionality of a state law requiring the masters of ships arriving in the port of New York from outside the state to register all passengers and post bond that none would become wards of the city. The Jacksonian majority insisted that the Marshall Court's precedents on the scope of Congress's commerce power were distinguishable, but deliberately went on to make the provocative assertion that the states' police powers over "safety, happiness and prosperity" were "complete, unqualified, and exclusive." In lone dissent, Story argued that the law interfered with Congress's power to regulate commerce; he concluded with the remark that he had the consolation of knowing that it also had been Marshall's "deliberate opinion" that the law was unconstitutional for the same reason.

Briscoe v. Bank of the Commonwealth involved the validity a state statute establishing a bank and authorizing it to issue notes that would be circulated as legal tender; the defendants maintained that the statute violated the Constitution's prohibition on state issuance of "bills of credit." When the Court first heard the case in 1834, Marshall and Story concluded that under the Court's 1830 decision in *Craig v. Missouri,* the notes were clearly unconstitutional, but in 1837, the Jacksonian justices brushed *Craig* aside and described the states' power to charter banks and define their powers as subject to "no limitation in the federal constitution." Story, once again the sole dissenter, insisted that *Craig* was controlling in an opinion the length of which he justified in part by his "profound reverence and affection for the dead" chief justice.

The Court's third decision in "the revolution of 1837" directly pitted Story against Taney. *Charles River Bridge v. Warren Bridge* stemmed from a state grant to the Charles River Bridge Company of the privilege of collecting tolls for a substantial period as compensation for the expense of building and maintaining the bridge. In 1828, while the privilege was still in effect, the Massachusetts legislature authorized the Warren Bridge Company to build a toll-free bridge a few yards from the old bridge; the old bridge company, the value of its privilege nullified, sued, claiming that the new charter violated the contracts clause. The new chief justice's opinion for the Court refused to construe the Charles River Bridge charter as affording the old company a monopoly on the explicitly instrumental ground that recognizing such an implied monopoly would jeopardize the "millions of property, which have been invested in rail roads and canals. . . . We shall be thrown back to the improvements of the last century."

Story did not disagree, of course, with the desirability of encouraging economic development, but he thought Taney's reasoning bad law and bad economics. In a massive fifty-seven-page dissent joined by the other pre-Jackson holdover and approved in substance by one Jacksonian, Story marshalled case law running back to the Middle Ages to show that the new charter was an unconscioable invasion of a recognized property right; it was Taney, he insisted, who was impeding investment by unsettling the reasonable expectations of the initial investors. Story's friend, the great New York jurist James Kent, wrote him that Taney's opinion "overthrows a great Principle of constitutional Morality" and proved that "we are to be under the reign of little Men." Story agreed; for him, *Charles River Bridge* showed the new Court to be the servant of politics rather than legal science. He was, he wrote a friend soon after the end of the 1837 term, "the last of the old race of Judges."

Story's despair was premature. After the drama of 1837, the Taney Court proved surprisingly moderate. The very next term, in *United States v. Coombs* (1838), Story for a unanimous Court gave an expansive interpretation to Congress's commerce power, and in general, the new justices proved uninterested in rolling back Marshall era precedents on the scope of congressional or federal court authority. The Taney Court, indeed, was if anything more receptive than its predecessor to Story's interest in bringing the law into accord with the needs of business and commerce. In *Louisville Railroad Co. v. Letson* (1844), for example, the Court overruled an 1809 Marshall Court decision in holding that for the purposes of federal diversity of citizenship jurisdiction, a corporation was the citizen of the state that chartered it, not of all the states of which its shareholders were citizens. *Letson,* Story wrote, "gets rid of a great anomaly in our jurisprudence," and he could only be pleased that the decision significantly increased the number of cases involving commercial and industrial development that could be litigated in federal court. Story himself was, as always, busily involved in his discreet lobbying of Congress on behalf of his desired legal reforms. With Webster, Story drafted a bankruptcy bill that was enacted in 1841 during the brief dominance of nationalist Whigs in Congress. On the bench, Story gave the bankruptcy act a sweeping interpretation, holding in *Ex parte Foster* (1842), for example, that the federal courts should enjoin state insolvency proceedings in order to protect the orderly administration of the federal statute. Story's aggressiveness had the unintended consequence of prompting Democratic and states' rights objections to the act, which was repealed in March 1843.

It was with the concurrence of all of his colleagues that Story wrote what was perhaps the most important opinion of his career. *Swift v. Tyson* (1842), which presented a question about the validity of a bill of exchange, was a "diversity" case, in federal court solely because the plaintiffs and defendants were residents of different states. The plaintiffs argued plausibly that the bill was valid under generally accepted commercial law principles, but the defendants cited New York state court decisions under which the bill was invalid. Section 34 of the Judiciary Act required federal courts to treat "the laws of the several states" as rules of decision in common law cases "where they apply" except in situations of conflict with federal law, but Story rejected its applicability in *Swift*. The statute's concern was with local statutes and long established local customs, not with "questions of a more general nature" such as the interpretation of contracts or the resolution of "questions of general commercial law." In cases presenting "general" questions, Story reasoned, "the state tribunals are called upon to perform the like functions as ourselves, that is, to ascertain upon general reasoning and legal analogies" the correct legal answers. *Swift*, in other words, posed a question of legal science, the answer to which was to be ascertained by the reasoned application of the whole body of the law. The federal courts would be acting contrary to legal principle if they blindly followed state decisions that they determined to be erroneous in the light of the law as a whole.

Swift v. Tyson was the mature expression of many long-standing themes in Story's jurisprudence: confidence in legal reasoning as an objective science, the desire to disseminate a progressive and systematic jurisprudence, his belief in the centrality of the federal courts in the creation of a well-ordered market society. The decision was marvellously successful in the short run: both federal and state court judges generally accepted with enthusiasm the concept of a general commercial law supervised by the Supreme Court, and so the doctrine of *Swift* played an important role in the creation of a genuinely national law of business and commerce. In the twentieth century, the case came under mounting criticism: Justice Holmes argued, anachronistically and unfairly, that Story's opinion rested on a fallacious belief in "the common law" as a "brooding omnipresence in the sky" (*Southern Pacific Co. v. Jensen,* 1917), and in 1938, Justice Brandeis for the Court overruled *Swift* as an "unconstitutional" decision in *Erie Railroad Co. v. Tompkins*. In fact, the disagreement between Story and his latter-day critics stemmed not from illogic on Story's part, but from the critics' acceptance of a thoroughgoing legal positivism alien to the mind-set of Story's era.

Story's last years were darkened by the lengthening shadow of slavery. In Marshall's day, the Court generally avoided that potentially explosive topic, but the Taney Court was increasingly unable or unwilling to stay out of the problems human slavery posed for American law and society. Story's personal abhorrence of the institution remained unchanged from his early slave trade opinion, but it was balanced by his concern for the preservation of the Union. In *United States v. The Amistad* (1841), all but one justice joined a Story opinion narrowly construing a treaty and thus insuring freedom for a group of Africans sold into slavery. In *Prigg v. Pennsylvania* (1842), the Court confronted the constitutionality of the federal Fugitive Slave Act and of a state personal liberty law under which Prigg (a professional slave catcher) was indicted for kidnapping. Story's opinion for the Court upheld the federal statute and invalidated the state law and, by implication, all other state legislation interfering with the federal right to reclaim fugitive slaves. Four concurring opinions debated Story's ambiguous suggestions that Congress had exclusive power to enforce the federal right and that Congress could not require state officials to execute the federal legislation. (Story's opinion could be read, probably erroneously, to absolve the free states from anything beyond passive acquiescence.) For Story, *Prigg* was the unavoidable product of the original agreement to protect "the security of this species of property," which he termed "a fundamental article, without the adoption of which the Union could not have been formed." His opinion, therefore, was no more or less than his duty as a judge. For abolitionists, however, the decision revealed the moral bankruptcy of Story's legal science. When Story on circuit carried out *Prigg* by recognizing a slaveowner's rights under the federal act, a critic labelled him "Slave-Catcher-in-Chief for the New England States."

By early 1845, Story's sense of isolation on the Court, and his growing pessimism about the Court's work and the republic's future, finally persuaded him that the time had come to retire to full-time teaching at Harvard. He informed family, friends, and the university that he would resign from the bench in the winter, but after a strenuous summer tour on circuit, Story died on September 10, 1845.

—H. JEFFERSON POWELL

BIBLIOGRAPHY

R. Kent Newmyer, *Supreme Court Justice Joseph Story: Statesman of the Old Republic* (1985), is the definitive biography and a magisterial achievement. There is, unfortunately, no edition of Story's extremely valuable personal papers, but Newmyer's biography lists their scattered locations. Gerald T. Dunne, *Justice Joseph Story and the Rise of the Supreme Court* (1970), an older, very readable narrative of Story's career on the Court, remains useful.

For a brilliant study of the later Marshall Court that is also an important contribution to Story scholarship, see G. Edward White, *The Marshall Court and Cultural Change, 1815–1835* (1988), a volume in the Holmes Devise. Charles Warren, *The Supreme Court in United States History* (rev. ed., 1928), includes extensive discussions of Story's work and remains valuable despite its age.

Specialized studies relating to Story include: Tony A. Freyer, *Forums of Order: The Federal Courts and Business in American History* (1979), an important historical study of a central theme in Story's thought; H. Jefferson Powell, "Joseph Story's Commentaries on the Constitution: A Belated Review," 94 *Yale Law Journal* 1285 (1985), a thematic and rhetorical study of Story's great treatise on the Constitution; and Alan Watson, *Joseph Story and the Comity of Errors* (1992), who argues that a key element of Story's influential theory of the conflict of laws rested on a simple misunderstanding of his continental sources, and that Story's error had dramatic consequences for American law.

For Story's own writings, see especially his *Commentaries on the Constitution of the United States* (1987), a photographic reprint of Story's abridgement of his constitutional treatise, with a valuable introductory essay by Ronald D. Rotunda and John E. Nowak; and William W. Story, *Life and Letters of Joseph Story* (1851), written by Story's son. This two-volume work has all the predictable limitations of genre and bias, but is an important source of the justice's letters and papers.

WILLIAM STRONG

BORN 6 May 1808, Somers, Connecticut

NOMINATED to the Court 7 February 1870
by Ulysses S. Grant

TOOK seat 14 March 1870; retired
14 December 1880

DIED 19 August 1895 in Lake Minnewaska,
New York

William Strong spent ten years on the Supreme Court bench in relative obscurity. As a skilled case writer and expert in patent and business law, he earned the respect of his judicial brethren, but Strong wrote few of the important cases which have shaped constitutional law and has thus stimulated little historical investigation. A product of his times, Strong was a conservative justice more concerned with the rights of private property than the civil rights of black Americans.

The eldest of eleven children of a New England Congregational minister, Strong attended Yale, read law while he taught school, then returned to complete his legal training at Yale. He settled in Reading, Pennsylvania, mastered German, and quickly became a prominent railroad lawyer. He served two Congressional terms as a "Locofoco" Democrat then returned to private practice. In 1857 he was elected to the Pennsylvania supreme court. A staunch unionist, Strong joined the Republican party during his tenure on the state bench and earned a reputation for upholding Republican war measures. Not content with serving the state, he also worked to advance the kingdom of God. He was a devout Presbyterian involved in numerous evangelical reform movements. Concerned that the Founding Fathers had omitted God from the Constitution, Strong headed the national reform movement to amend the preamble to acknowledge "Almighty God as the source of all authority and power in Civil government, the Lord Jesus Christ as the Ruler of all nations, and His revealed will as the supreme law of the land." Strong did not advocate a state church, but believed that law should adhere to Christian prin-

ciples. Strong's background provided the values he would bring to the Supreme Court: strong Christian principles, unionism, a pro-business outlook, and respect for private property.

Strong's appointment to the Supreme Court was surrounded with controversy. Grant appointed Joseph Bradley and Strong on the same day that the Court, in *Hepburn v. Griswold* (1870), declared the legal tender act unconstitutional as it applied to preexisting debts. Strong's support for legal tender on the Pennsylvania bench was well established; consequently Grant was accused of "Court-packing." The timing was unfortunate, but it was to be expected that Grant would appoint justices who would uphold the Republican program. Within months, the Supreme Court dramatically reversed itself on the legal tender issue. Justice Strong was chosen to write the opinion in *Knox v. Lee* (1871), the most important he would write during his tenure on the bench.

Since the authority to make treasury notes legal tender was not an enumerated power, the right, if it existed, was an implied power. Thus Chief Justice Chase and Strong both relied on John Marshall's classic explication of the elastic clause in *McCulloch v. Maryland* (1819) that any legitimate end "consistent with the letter and spirit of the Constitution" was constitutional. Chase admitted that Congress possessed broad implied powers, but ruled in *Hepburn* that the legal tender act violated the "spirit" of the Constitution by impairing the obligation of contracts (constitutionally forbidden to the states rather than the national government), and depriving creditors of their property without due process of law. Overturning *Hepburn*, Strong emphasized in *Knox v. Lee* the broad range of methods available to Congress for carrying out the enumerated powers. Because Congress had power to coin money, it followed, for Strong, that "the power to declare what is money" also belonged to the national government. It was not the prerogative of the Court to judge the "degree of appropriateness" of the means Congress chose to achieve a legitimate end. Strong emphasized the wartime emergency as rationale for the currency law, and made clear his understanding that Congress was not authorized to "make anything which has no value money." Rather the Congress had power to enact laws which made "the government's promises to pay money . . . for the time being, equivalent in value" to that of hard money. Strong probably would not have sanctioned a legal tender act in ordinary times, since he generally voted to support vested property rights.

In Reconstruction matters, Strong was reluctant to follow through with Republican party efforts to effect lasting change in the southern states. Speaking for a unanimous Court, Strong ruled in *Bigelow v. Forrest* (1870) that the Civil War confiscation acts conflicted with the attainder of treason clause of the Constitution. Confiscated property could be held only for the life of the original owner; on his death it reverted back to his heirs. *Bigelow* effectively negated any long-term effects of the confiscation acts, although Strong upheld the validity of the laws in *Miller v. United States* (1871). In *Blyew v. United States* (1872), a test of the 1866 Civil Rights Act, Strong refused to allow removal of a murder trial to federal court even though the only witnesses, who were black, had not been allowed to testify in the Kentucky court. Since the victim was dead, Strong insisted, she had no rights at stake. Thus the federal government lacked jurisdiction. Strong voted with the majority in the *Slaughterhouse Cases* (1873) which, although concerned with white butchers, defined national citizenship so narrowly that the former slaves were left without the protection of the federal government for their basic rights. Overall, Strong appeared relatively unconcerned about federal protection of black citizens.

It was Strong, however, who spoke for the Court on two of the rare occasions when black Americans won legal victories. Three cases involving jury rights for black citizens were handed down on the same day in 1880. In *Ex parte Virginia,* Strong upheld the section of the Civil Rights Act of 1875 which pertained to jury selection—the only part of the statute left standing when the Court declared it unconstitutional in the *Civil Rights Cases* (1883)—and found a

state judge who had routinely excluded blacks from jury duty guilty of violating the act. In *Strauder v. West Virginia,* Strong declared a West Virginia statute which excluded blacks from jury duty invalid as a violation of the equal protection clause of the Fourteenth Amendment. He noted, however, that the issue was not whether some blacks sat on the jury, but whether "all persons of his race or color may be excluded by law, solely because of their race or color." It was the exclusionary statute that proved discrimination for Strong.

Virginia v. Rives, the third jury case, proved less benign and certainly more important over the long run. Although there was no discriminatory state law in Virginia and thus no official state action, blacks were routinely barred from jury duty. Strong refused to acknowledge that the black citizens of Virginia were being denied a jury of their peers. Instead, he argued that juries composed entirely of whites did not indicate discrimination because of race or color. Even an all-white jury could be impartially selected. If there was no state law, there was no discrimination. This decision countenanced a practice which would have been unconstitutional if written into law and presented black citizens the difficult task of proving systematic exclusion from jury duty.

Strong's experience as a railroad lawyer was reflected in his behavior on the Court. He voted with the minority against state regulation in *Munn v. Illinois* (1877), for example, and in the *State Freight Tax Case* (1873), he held a Pennsylvania state tax invalid as a breach of the commerce clause.

In 1877, Strong served on the electoral commission to settle the disputed presidential election of 1876. Like the other members, he voted his party preference, giving Rutherford B. Hayes a majority of one in the commission, and securing the presidency for the Republican party.

Strong retired from the Supreme Court in 1880, still in full possession of his physical and mental faculties. Apparently he meant his resignation to serve as an example to the justices who were no longer up to the task. He spent his remaining years doing Christian benevolent work.

—LOU FALKNER WILLIAMS

BIBLIOGRAPHY

There is, not surprisingly, no published biography of Strong. Stanley I. Kutler's sketch in Friedman and Israel, 2 *Justices* 1153, is the best single source of information on Strong's judicial career. Daniel G. Strong's unpublished dissertation, "Supreme Court Justice William Strong, 1808–1895: Jurisprudence, Christianity and Reform" (Kent State University, 1985), contains excellent information on Strong's early life and career which cannot be located elsewhere, but the chapter on the Supreme Court years is very weak on case analysis. Jon C. Teaford, "Toward a Christian Nation: Religion, Law and Justice Strong," 54 *Journal of Presbyterian History* 422 (1976), is concerned with Strong's religious ideas rather than his judicial career. Charles Fairman's two volumes in the Holmes Devise, *Reconstruction and Reunion* (1971, 1987), are the most exhaustive treatment of the Reconstruction Court. These volumes include analyses of all of Strong's major opinions.

George Sutherland
Photograph by Harris and Ewing.
Collection of the Supreme Court of the United States.

GEORGE SUTHERLAND

BORN 25 March 1862, Buckinghamshire,
England

NOMINATED to the Court 5 September
1922 by Warren G. Harding;
confirmed 6 September 1922;
retired 18 January 1938

DIED 18 July 1942 in Stockbridge,
Massachusetts

George Sutherland, though best known as
one of the conservative "Four Horsemen" (the
others were Pierce Butler, Willis Van Devanter,
and James McReynolds) who opposed Franklin
Roosevelt's New Deal, had a much more complex career on the bench than that nickname
suggests. During his sixteen years as an associate justice, Sutherland penned not only principled
objections to progressive and liberal intrusions
on cherished property and contract rights, but
also impassioned defenses of the rights of the
press and the accused. To his biographer,
Sutherland was consistently "A Man Against the
State," a sobriquet Sutherland earned through a
productive career on the Court. Although many
of the opinions written by Sutherland were overruled and disapproved as the Court drifted away
from its laissez-faire moorings, the clarity and
independence of his judicial contributions serve
even today as examples of well-reasoned decision making.

In 1864, George Sutherland's Scottish father, newly converted to the Church of Jesus
Christ of Latter-day Saints, moved the family
from Buckinghamshire, England, to Utah Territory. His father soon left the new church, so
Sutherland grew up a nonbeliever in Mormon-
dominated Utah. He attended Brigham Young
Academy (later University), leaving after three
years to work as a railroad agent. He then took
his legal education at the University of Michigan, where he studied with two jurists whose
influence can be found in Sutherland's Supreme
Court writings: James Campbell, chief justice of
the Michigan supreme court, and Judge Thomas
Cooley, author of such influential works as the

*Treatise on the Constitutional Limitations Which
Rest upon the Legislative Power of the States of
the American Union* (1868). In 1883, Sutherland
married, moved back to Provo, and began law
practice with his father (the partnership lasted but
three years).

Ten years later Sutherland moved to Salt
Lake City and was elected to the first state legislature in 1896. He moved on to the U.S. House
of Representatives (1901–1903) and the Senate
(1905–1917), where he supported reform measures, including the Pure Food and Drug Act,
held the protectionist line in tariff debates, and
led the fight for federal workers compensation
legislation for employees of interstate carriers.
Sutherland refused to break with the Republican
party in 1912 and carried on the conservative
struggle against Woodrow Wilson's progressive
measures. In 1917, Sutherland, now in private
practice in Washington, D.C., was elected president of the American Bar Association (ABA).
In his presidential address, entitled "Private
Rights and Government Control," Sutherland
stated that, when the choice was between individual freedom and the common good, "doubts
should be resolved in favor of the liberty of the
individual." In September 1922, Warren Harding
tapped his friend and close adviser to fill the
Supreme Court seat vacated when Justice John
C. Clarke resigned.

It would not be long before Sutherland
would be called on to resolve the tension between public needs and private rights. The issue
before the Court in *Adkins v. Children's Hospital* (1923) was the legitimacy of an act of Congress fixing minimum wages for working
women and children in Washington, D.C. There
were two challenges brought to the legislation:
one by a hospital that was paying wages below
the statutory minimum, the other by a female
elevator operator who, it was alleged, would lose
her low-paying job if her employer were forced
to comply with the act.

The statute was attacked as violative of "the
freedom of contract included within the guaranties of the due process clause of the Fifth

Amendment." Sutherland acknowledged that the freedom of contract protected by the Constitution was not absolute, but could not fit this case into any of the exceptions recognized by the Court. Then, in a move that would set the tone for the next dozen years, Sutherland quoted generously and favorably from Justice Rufus Peckham's opinion in *Lochner v. New York* (1905), the *bête noire* for nearly two decades of progressives on and off the Court. Subsequent decisions of the Supreme Court, according to Sutherland, had distinguished but not overruled *Lochner*'s elevation of freedom of contract over the state's police power.

Viewed through the lens of substantive due process, Sutherland could not find the crucial link between ends and means: the statute "extracts from the employer an arbitrary payment for a purpose and upon a basis having no causal connection with his business, or the contract or the work the employee engages to do." In sum, the act was "so clearly the product of a naked, arbitrary exercise of power that it cannot be allowed to stand under the Constitution of the United States."

Reiterating the theme of his ABA address, Sutherland concluded by noting that, far from being harmed, the public good was actually "exalted" by protecting individual liberties, "for surely the good of society as a whole cannot be better served than by the preservation against arbitrary restraint of the liberties of its constituent members." Sutherland's reinvigoration of *Lochner* and the due process clause thus provided the new conservative bloc on the Court— the Four Horsemen were complete when Sutherland took his seat—with the intellectual leadership needed to sustain its crusade against confiscatory, arbitrary, and unreasonable social and economic legislation.

Over the next few years, Sutherland would expand on the ideas introduced in *Adkins*, applying its principles in other regulatory contexts. In *Tyson & Brother v. Banton* (1927), a case concerning the validity of a New York statute forbidding the resale of theater tickets at a higher price, Sutherland refused to recognize that the economic activity at issue was "affected with a public interest" and thereby a legitimate area for

state intrusion. In *Ribnik v. McBride* (1928), a New Jersey regulation of charges by employment agencies was the victim of Sutherland's analysis: "The interest of the public in a matter of employment is not different in quality and character from its interest in the other things enumerated ['the procurement of food and housing and fuel']; but in none of them is the interest that 'public interest' which the law contemplates as the basis for legislative price control."

Sutherland was not an unswerving opponent of the state's police power, however, a point best demonstrated by reference to four cases involving state and local land-use regulation: *Village of Euclid v. Ambler Realty Co.* (1926); *Zahn v. Board of Public Works of City of Los Angeles* (1927); *Gorieb v. Fox* (1927); and *Nectow v. City of Cambridge* (1928). *Euclid* is a landmark decision in the long, intricate history of Anglo-American property law. In his opinion, Sutherland provides a conceptual link between the awkward, common-law, judicially controlled system of private and public nuisance in land management to the modern, comprehensive planning schemes found in a growing number of American central cities and suburbs. At issue was the height, area, and use classification plan designed for a suburb of Cleveland. Ambler Realty asserted successfully in the federal trial court that the local ordinance violated the due process clause and denied equal protection of the laws under the Fourteenth Amendment. Legend has it that, after initially siding with the other three "Horsemen" (who dissented), Sutherland, after considering the positive effects such regulation would have on property rights, joined with the progressives on the Court in reversing the holding below. Other observers of the Court have suggested that the justices were more intrigued by the potential use of zoning to exclude outsiders from protected, single-family residential zones.

Whatever his motivation, Sutherland set a standard of judicial deference accorded state and local officials that allowed for significant public regulation and control of land use for the next several decades. The law of nuisance provided "a fairly helpful clew" for the Court as it sought to determine the point at which to draw "the line which . . . separates the legitimate from the illegitimate assumption of power." Also helpful to the Court were the findings of "commissions and experts" who had thoroughly studied zoning and concluded that there were palpable health and safety benefits to the segregation of incompatible uses. The village of Euclid need not "demonstrate the wisdom or sound policy in all respects of those restrictions" on land use, however, for there was enough to prevent the Court from concluding "that such provisions are clearly arbitrary and unreasonable, having no substantial relation to the public health, safety, morals, or general welfare." This formula, unlike Sutherland's more demanding substantive due process analysis, remains relevant and controlling to this day for the great bulk of cases involving challenges to land use and environmental restrictions.

In *Zahn* and *Gorieb*, both times for a unanimous Court, Sutherland summarily dismissed objections to local zoning and setback schemes. In *Nectow*, however, Sutherland reversed the state court's dismissal of a challenge to a residential zoning classification that left the plaintiff with "no practical use" for his property. Sutherland concluded that there was a "serious and highly injurious . . . invasion of the property of the plaintiff." In other words, the line between the legitimate and illegitimate exercise of the police power, though hard to draw, had been crossed.

Sutherland could be equally protective of other civil liberties when the Court was faced with similar egregious invasions. *Powell v. Alabama* (1932), was the first of two cases to reach the Court involving the prosecution of the "Scottsboro Boys," nine African-American teenagers accused of raping two young white women. Writing for the majority, Sutherland detailed the nightmarish nature of the case: "The defendants, young, ignorant, illiterate, surrounded by hostile sentiment, haled back and forth under guard of soldiers, charged with an atrocious crime regarded with especial horror in the community where they were to be tried, were thus put in peril of their lives within a few moments after counsel for the first time charged with any degree of responsibility began to represent them."

A review of the shoddy performance of the attorneys for the defense convinced Sutherland that "defendants were not accorded the right of counsel in any substantial sense." Sutherland concluded that the defendants were denied their due process rights under the Fourteenth Amendment, as well as their Fifth Amendment-guaranteed right to counsel. Four years later, in *Grosjean v. American Press Co.* (1936), Sutherland cited *Powell* as he spread the protective cloak of the Fourteenth Amendment around the free speech and free press sanctions against federal intrusion found in the First Amendment, in the process invalidating a Louisiana tax on newspapers.

Sutherland's patience with performance of counsel was again tried in *Berger v. United States* (1935), a federal prosecution for uttering counterfeit notes. Here, it was the prosecutor who "overstepped the bounds of . . . propriety and fairness." Mixing the rhetoric of morality with the rules of sport, Sutherland advised the representative of the people that "he may prosecute with earnestness and vigor. . . . But, while he may strike hard blows, he is not at liberty to strike foul ones." In this case, prejudice to the defendant was undeniable, concluded the Court.

One of Sutherland's anti–New Deal cases can be seen as consistent with the sentiments expressed in *Powell* and *Berger*. In *Jones v. Securities and Exchange Commission* (1936), Sutherland compared the SEC's abuse of investigatory powers to the practices of the universally condemned Star Chamber.

In the area of social and economic regulation, as states explored ways to relieve the stresses caused by the severe economic crisis after the stock market disaster of 1929, Sutherland and his fellow conservatives held the line. In *New State Ice Co. v. Liebmann* (1932), the topic of the challenged state regulation was quite mundane, "an ordinary business," according to Sutherland. The Oklahoma legislature, in 1925, had decided to require a license for the manufacture, sale, and distribution of ice, a license New State had not secured. Predictably, the majority found that such unreasonable regulation of a nonpublic business would not be tolerated under the Fourteenth Amendment.

Sutherland offered skepticism about the ability of the state to innovate in crisis times. In a direct challenge to dissenting Justice Louis D. Brandeis's notion of a state laboratory to "try novel social and economic experiments," Sutherland baldly asserted that "it is plain that unreasonable or arbitrary interference or restrictions cannot be saved from the condemnation of that Amendment merely by calling them experimental." This exchange foreshadowed the jurisprudential conflict that would soon burden the Court and the nation.

Two years later, Sutherland found himself speaking for a minority of four, as the Court, led by Chief Justice Charles Evans Hughes, allowed Minnesota's mortgage moratorium legislation to survive their scrutiny. "While emergency does not create power," Hughes wrote, "emergency may furnish the occasion for the exercise of power." The majority found little guidance in the history of the framing of the contract clause, or in case law interpreting that constitutional stricture, turning instead to cases such as *Block v. Hirsh* (1921), in which the Court upheld temporary emergency rent control legislation. The Minnesota debtor relief legislation did not violate the contract clause, the due process clause, or deny creditors equal protection.

Sutherland's response was a masterful blend of history, framers' intent, and judicial precedent. He furnished a riposte for each majority thrust, countering Hughes's assertion that the past furnished no answer with substantive historical footnotes and generous excerpts from relevant case law. This was just the first step down a dangerous hill, warned the four conservative justices: "He simply closes his eyes to the necessary implications of the decision who fails to see in it the potentiality of future gradual but ever-advancing encroachments upon the sanctity of private and public contracts."

Sutherland reached back to the darkest periods of Supreme Court history to amplify the point that the Constitution must "remain unaltered," lest it "become a mere collection of political maxims to be adhered to or disregarded according to the prevailing sentiment or the legislative and judicial opinion in respect of the supposed necessities of the hour." He quoted the

words of Justice David Davis in *Ex parte Milligan* (1866) and Chief Justice Roger Taney in *Dred Scott v. Sandford* (1857)—two of the most widely assailed opinions in the chronicles of the Court—as if to strengthen the image of the conservative bloc as the last defenders of the Constitution in the face of a tyrannical majority.

"The present exigency," Sutherland told the suffering nation, "is nothing new." Then, condescendingly, in terms that suggested the victims were to blame, he instructed his readers that "the vital lesson that expenditure beyond income begets poverty, that public or private extravagance, financed by promises to pay, either must end in complete or partial repudiation or the promises be fulfilled by self-denial and painful effort, though constantly taught by bitter experience, seems never to be learned." The gap between Sutherland's personal and judicial philosophy and the activist agenda of the states and, soon, the federal government was striking. Shortly, matters would come to a head.

Two subsequent Sutherland opinions, the first issued but ten months before the other, best illustrate the shift by the "Nine Old Men" that saved the New Deal and signaled the ascension of a new era of judicial deference to social and economic regulation. In *Carter v. Carter Coal Co.* (1936), Sutherland, for a bare majority of five justices, annulled the Bituminous Coal Conservation Act of 1935 (the Guffey Act), Congress's attempt to replace the regulatory controls wielded by the National Recovery Administration before the Roosevelt administration's defeat in *Schechter v. United States* (1935). The new law created an administrative body (the Bituminous Coal Commission) to formulate regulations and set coal rates, authorized coal taxes, and mandated collective bargaining and other labor reform measures.

Sutherland conceded that the objects of the act were quite worthy, but cautioned that legislative means to accomplish these goals "must be appropriate, plainly adapted to the end, and not prohibited by, but consistent with, the letter and spirit of the Constitution." State sovereignty itself was endangered by the Guffey Act. If the federal government were given such extensive powers, in the future, states might be reduced "to little more than geographical subdivisions of the national domain." Not only was the alleged tax an illegal penalty, but also Congress had no business intruding in the area of labor regulation for "the evils are all local evils over which the federal government has no legislative control. The relation of employer and employee is a local relation." There being no "interstate commercial intercourse" at issue, the labor provisions were invalid under the Constitution. Finally, notwithstanding statutory language to the contrary, Sutherland found that the violations noted in the opinion tainted the whole act, including the price controls.

Though wounded by decisions in cases such as *Schechter* and *Carter Coal*, the New Deal received a substantial boost six months later, in November 1936, when the American electorate reelected Roosevelt in a landslide. In March of the next year, one month after the president introduced his ill-conceived Court-packing plan, the Court announced its opinion in *West Coast Hotel Co. v. Parrish* (1937), overruling Sutherland's holding in *Adkins*. Now that a majority of justices had abandoned substantive due process there was no longer a need to pack the Court.

West Coast Hotel upheld a Washington state statute that authorized the setting of minimum wages for women and children. Chief Justice Hughes deemed *Adkins* "a departure from the true application of the principles governing" state regulation of labor relations. Not surprisingly, Sutherland objected, strongly but respectfully. He invoked the words of Judge Campbell and Judge Cooley, his law school professors, for the notion of the immutability of the Constitution, and the availability of the amendment process as a remedy when change was truly needed. "The judicial function," according to the former senator, "did not include the power of amendment under the guise of interpretation." Sutherland referred his readers to the logic and rationale of his *Adkins* opinion, furnishing a long excerpt, as well.

Justice Van Devanter resigned from the Court two months later and was replaced by Democratic Senator Hugo Black. Sutherland, expressing in his personal correspondence great satisfaction at the defeat of Roosevelt's Court-packing plan, would follow suit shortly thereafter.

If we focus only on substantive due process and the intransigence of the Four Horsemen, Sutherland's legacy seems thin indeed. If we direct our attention instead to the way in which he fashioned and presented his arguments, particularly in his opinions in *Euclid*, *Blaisdell*, *Powell*, and *United States v. Curtiss-Wright Export Corporation* (1936) (outlining the extraconstitutional nature of the conduct of the nation's foreign policy), we cannot help but be struck by Sutherland's mastery of the judicial craft.

—MICHAEL ALLAN WOLF

BIBLIOGRAPHY

Joel Francis Paschal's biography, *Mr. Justice Sutherland: A Man Against the State* (1951) is a fine treatment of the justice's life, work, and philosophy before and during his term on the Court. There are some interesting contributions in Sutherland's Supreme Court memorial, 323 U.S. v (1944), particularly Chief Justice Hughes's essay. Sutherland's papers are included in the manuscript division of the Library of Congress, Washington, D.C. A studious exploration of Sutherland, including insights from his defenders and critics, can be found in William M. Randle's "Professors, Reformers, Bureaucrats, and Cronies: The Players in *Euclid v. Ambler*," Chapter 2 of *Zoning and the American Dream*, Charles M. Haar and Jerold S. Kayden, eds., (1989).

NOAH HAYNES SWAYNE

BORN 2 December 1804, Frederick Country,
	Virginia
NOMINATED to the Court 21 January 1862
TOOK seat 27 January 1862; retired
	25 January 1881
DIED 8 June 1884 in New York City

Although admitted to the Virginia bar in
1823, Swayne soon after moved to Ohio because
his Quaker-inspired opposition to slavery
aroused resentment among his Virginia neighbors. In the 1850s, his uncompromising antislavery position—he frequently defended fugitive
slaves—made him switch from being a
Jacksonian Democrat to the recently created
Republican party. When Supreme Court Justice
John McLean died in Cincinnati on April 4,
1861, Lincoln appointed Swayne as his successor, not only because of the entreaties of Ohio
politicians, but also because Swayne was a
southerner by birth, a dedicated supporter of the
Union, a proven opponent of slavery and a successful corporation lawyer with close ties to the
business community. He served as an associate
justice for nineteen years.

Although Swayne wrote more than 350
majority opinions, only a few had any long-term
constitutional importance. However, the expectations of Lincoln and Republican Reconstruction congressmen were fulfilled because Swayne,
who identified the national interest with the
Republican party, faithfully supported expansion
of federal executive and legislative powers on a
narrowly divided court. He voted with the majority in the *Prize Cases* (1863), which upheld
the constitutionality of Lincoln's blockade of
southern ports before Congress had officially
declared war. In *Ex parte Vallandigham* (1864),
he voted that the civilian courts could not to review a trial by military court. In *Ex parte
Milligan* (1866), Swayne joined in a partial dissent which argued that Congress could determined that the Bill of Rights did not apply in
crisis situations. In *Cummings v. Missouri* (1876)
and *Ex parte Garland* (1867) he supported the

constitutionality of post-Civil War loyalty oaths
for teachers, lawyers, and ministers, and in *Texas
v. White* (1869), he argued in dissent that the
political reality of Texas having left the Union
now made that state's future a question for Congress to decide. He supported the constitutionality of the federal government's issuance of
legal tender on the grounds that Congress's
emergency powers were not restricted to wartime. In *Boudinot v. United States* (1871),
Swayne along with the majority decided that
Congress, not the courts, would have to protect
Native Americans because Congress was not
bound by treaties with the Indians. In all these
cases, Swayne voted to broaden the powers of
the national government.

As was expected from his pre-court history,
Swayne was a consistent champion of the civil
rights of freed African Americans. Even while
on the court, Swayne lobbied for passage of the
Fifteenth Amendment and campaigned for its
ratification by Ohio. His broad interpretation of
the Thirteenth Amendment was especially noteworthy. In *United States v. Rhodes* (1866)
Swayne on circuit contended the amendment not
only abolished slavery but also abolished every
manifestation of bondage. He maintained that the
amendment was closely connected with the civil
rights law, and the two together transformed the
federal system by establishing federal protection
over everyone, at all times and in all places. He
dissented against the Court's decision in *Blyew
v. United States* (1872) which declared that,
since a dead, old, blind, African-American
woman could not profit from any verdict, there
was no harm in Kentucky's exclusion of African-American witnesses from the trial of her
murderer. He voted with the majority in declaring unconstitutional West Virginian and Virginian statutes that excluded African Americans
from jury service in *Strauder v. West Virginia*
and *Ex parte Virginia*, both in 1880.

Civil rights were also utmost in Swayne's
mind when he issued a sharp dissent in the historic *Slaughterhouse Cases*. The majority, he
contended, had distorted the Fourteenth Amend-

ment by taking it out of its historical context and tortuously narrowing its scope. He maintained that, as the first eleven amendments limited the federal government, so the three Civil War amendments directly restricted the power of the states. The federal government was now the protector of the "privileges and immunities" of each and every one of its citizens.

For all his interest in civil rights, Swayne's most important opinions were concerned with economic issues. In *Gelpcke v. Dubuque* (1864), he employed the case of municipal bond default to expand the Court's review power over high state court decisions, thus increasing federal common law jurisdiction. Economics were also involved when Swayne delivered his most famous opinion on his last day on the Supreme Court. In *Springer v. United States* (1881), he upheld the Civil War income tax, arguing that it

was not a direct tax because it fell not on persons, but on profits and income. His position would die when overruled in *Pollock v. Farmers' Loan & Trust Co.* (1895), but would be resurrected during the Progressive Era.

Although chronically sick and mentally deteriorating during the 1870s, Swayne held on tenaciously until President Hayes pressured him to retire. He did this on January 24, 1881, and died in New York City on June 8, 1884.

—WILLIAM BOSCH

BIBLIOGRAPHY

Swayne's life, character, and early court activity are surveyed in David M. Silver's, *Lincoln's Supreme Court* (1956). His later career is related in Robert Fridlington's, *The Reconstruction Court, 1864–1888* (1987).

WILLIAM HOWARD TAFT

BORN 15 September 1857, Cincinnati, Ohio

NOMINATED to the Court 30 June 1921
     by Warren Harding

TOOK seat 3 October 1921; retired
     3 February 1930

DIED 8 March 1930 in Washington D.C.

Unique in the annals of American government, William Howard Taft was both president of the United States and chief justice of the United States Supreme Court. He brought to his role on the Court an unparalleled wealth of administrative experience, which deeply affected both his own personal jurisprudence and the institutional development of the federal judiciary.

Taft was the son of a prominent Ohio lawyer, Alphonse Taft, who was attorney general and secretary of war during President Ulysses S. Grant's administration. Trading on family position and connections, Taft fashioned a meteoric early career. After graduation from the law school of Cincinnati College in 1880, he rapidly became a local prosecutor (1881–82), solicitor for Hamilton County (1885–87), a judge of the superior court of Ohio (1887–90), United States solicitor general (1890–92), a United States circuit judge for the sixth circuit (1892–1900), governor of the Philippines (1900–04); United States secretary of war (1904–09), and finally president (1909–13).

Throughout this rapid ascent, Taft's consummate ambition was to be a justice of the Supreme Court. "I love judges and I love courts," he said in 1911. "They are my ideals, that typify on earth what we shall meet hereafter in heaven under a just God." Ironically, Taft twice declined Roosevelt's offers to appoint him to the Supreme Court, in 1902 and again in 1906, "giving up the hope and ambition of my life" because he believed that the exigencies of duty required that he remain at his administrative post. When as president he appointed Edward Douglass White as the successor to Chief Justice Melville Fuller, Taft ruefully mused that "It seems strange that the one place in the government which I would have liked to fill myself I am forced to give to another."

Taft's turn finally came a decade later when, on White's death, Warren Harding nominated his fellow Ohioan chief justice. To the bafflement of the *The New Republic*, Harding's choice was greeted with "almost universal acclaim." The Senate confirmed Taft on the same day his nomination was submitted. The *New Republic* wondered why "the very Progressivism which President Taft provoked," and which sent him to a humiliating political defeat in 1912, did not "uncompromisingly" oppose his appointment to the Court. Its answer was "the present temporary triumph of reaction." And, no doubt, postwar disillusionment and Harding's sweeping return to "normalcy" marked Taft's natural conservatism as politically ascendant.

But Taft's national rehabilitation was also due to the notable grace and equanimity with which he had accepted the dismal results of the 1912 election, to his patriotic and nonpartisan support of Wilson during the war and the campaign for the League of Nations, and to his joint chairmanship of a National War Labor Board (NWLB) that had supported union organizational rights to a degree unprecedented by any governmental agency. The last was particularly important; in his work as a state and federal judge, Taft had been known as the "father of the labor injunction," a device used by courts to crush union organizing efforts. Taft's stint at the NWLB did much to ameliorate that reputation, and to ensure the remarkable national "outpour of goodwill" that accompanied his entry to the Court.

Taft's predecessor as chief justice was known for his refusal to engage the political branches of government. But Taft, with his wealth of contacts and influence, with his years of executive and lobbying experience, immediately began to put his immense prestige to work to create support for a comprehensive and constructive program of reform. He had long been concerned with the improvement of the judicial branch. In his first State of the Union address, for example, he had firmly declared that "a change of judicial procedure, with a view to reducing its expense to private litigants in civil cases and facilitating the dispatch of business and final decision in both civil and criminal cases, constitutes the greatest need in our American institutions."

Thus accustomed to viewing the judiciary from a presidential perspective, Taft brought to the center chair not merely a new political energy and purpose, but also the firm belief that courts were more than isolated decision makers; they were also and fundamentally an administrative arm of the government whose particular task it was to dispense justice. He longed to instill "the common sense idea of applying to the disposition of business in the courts the same principle that is applied everywhere in the organization of men," which was "the application of . . . energies to a single purpose." For Taft it was evident that courts, like any bureaucratic organization, needed careful and constant supervision, and he was the first practically to apply this insight to the federal judiciary. For this he deserves to be honored as the father of modern judicial management.

The concept of judicial management underlay both the major reforms that Taft was able to achieve during his decade as chief justice. The first was embodied in the Act of September 14, 1922, which established a conference of senior circuit judges composed of the chief justice and the nine circuit senior judges, and which empowered Taft, with certain limitations, geographically to reassign district court judges to meet the needs of judicial business. Taft violated precedent by directly testifying for the bill before the Senate Judiciary Committee, but he viewed the reform as "one of the most important acts in the history of the judiciary."

The conference, which was to be the direct ancestor of the present Judicial Conference, was by law to implement the managerial task of compiling an annual "comprehensive survey of the condition of business in the courts of the United States" and recommending such changes as might be necessary or advisable. Taft's new statutory authority to transfer judges enabled him to oil "the judicial machinery" and "to mass the force of the judiciary where the arrears are greatest." In both respects, the 1922 act recognized federal courts as a single administrative unit and established rudimentary mechanisms through which the achievement of their institutional mission could be monitored and supervised. The result, wrote

Felix Frankfurter and James Landis, was nothing less than "the beginning of a new chapter in the administration of the federal courts."

The second major reform legislation achieved by Taft was the Judges Bill of 1925, which drastically reduced the mandatory appellate jurisdiction of the Supreme Court by allowing it to pick and choose the bulk of its cases through the discretionary writ of *certiorari*. Underlying the act was a reconceptualization of the function of the Supreme Court. Taft had clearly set forth his vision of the Court in his second State of the Union message to Congress: "No man ought to have, as a matter of right, a review of his case by the Supreme Court. He should be satisfied by one hearing before a court of first instance and one review by a court of appeals. The proper and chief usefulness of . . . the Supreme Court of the United States, is, in cases which come before it, so to expound the law, and especially the fundamental law—the Constitution—as to furnish precedents for the inferior courts in future litigation and for the executive officers in the construction of statutes and the performance of their legal duties." The technical jurisdictional provisions of the 1925 act were designed to implement Taft's view that the primary function of the Supreme Court was to supervise and administer the development of federal law, a function that required that the Court be ceded wide managerial discretion. The transformation, well recognized at the time, was "drastic."

Although Taft was unsuccessful in realizing his third major reform project—the effort to achieve congressional authorization for the judicial promulgation of uniform and simple federal rules of civil procedure that merged law and equity—his executive ability and inclinations were everywhere evident in his actions as chief justice. He viewed himself as "the head of the judicial branch of Government," and he made every effort to "come into touch with the Federal Judges of the country, so that we may feel more allegiance to a team and do more teamwork." He actively sought to monitor and guide the selection and appointment of new federal judges, even of Supreme Court justices. He was determined to reduce delays and increase the efficiency of the Supreme Court, in fact achieving a significant reduction in the Court's back-

William Howard Taft, c. 1907
Photograph by George Prince.
Collection of the Supreme Court of the United States.

log. Appalled at the inadequate space and resources available to the Court in its chambers within the Capitol building, Taft lobbied for and obtained congressional authorization and moneys for a new Supreme Court building. The impressive contemporary site of the Court is almost entirely owing to Taft's persistence. Within the Court, Taft continually sought to promote "teamwork," to "mass" the Court so as give "weight and solidarity to its opinions." He was skillful at assigning opinions, reconciling differences, making conferences pleasant and efficient. During the eight full terms of Taft's tenure as chief justice, 84 percent of all decisions decided by written opinions were unanimous. (By contrast, only 20 percent of such decisions were unanimous in the Court's 1991 term.)

Taft's success as an executive chief justice was manifest to all. It is common to rank him with Oliver Ellsworth as one of the primary architects of the federal judicial system. But the success of Taft as an author of judicial opinions is something else again. Brandeis accurately but cruelly observed that Taft was "a first-rate second-rate mind." One might say that Taft had thoroughly mastered and been mastered by the clichés of his time and class. Pitifully few of Taft's more than 250 opinions have survived as living presences in the law. In part this is because, as Taft himself was well aware, he was without auctorial "facility or the graceful literary style." But in part it was also because of Taft's tendency to accept the conventional as the given.

Taft's jurisprudence was dominated by a few major ideas: the importance of nationalism, the defense of property, the necessity for intelligent social management, and the enforcement of law and order.

Taft's idol was John Marshall, "the greatest Judge that America or the World has produced." And, in Taft's eyes, Marshall's great achievement was to set the Court toward a "liberal construction of the Constitution in conferring powers upon the National Government," against "the school of Jefferson" that would have "emphasized unduly the sovereignty of the States." Borrowing from Marshall's opinion in *Gibbons v. Ogden* (1824), Taft wrote Harlan Fiske Stone in 1928 that the "power of Congress" over interstate commerce is "exactly what it would be in a government without states."

In the period before the New Deal, the extent of federal power over interstate commerce was a highly controversial subject, and among Taft's most successful and influential opinions were those that strongly supported the expansion of this federal power. His most important contribution concerned the question of when Congress could regulate intrastate commerce that threatened to obstruct or burden interstate commerce. In such cases as *Stafford v. Wallace* (1922) and *Board of Trade of the City of Chicago v. Olsen* (1923), Taft made clear that "it is primarily for Congress to consider and decide the fact of the danger and meet it. This court will certainly not substitute its judgment for that of Congress in such a matter unless the relation of the subject to interstate commerce and its effect upon it are clearly non-existent." Taft was also highly nationalistic in his interpretation of the dormant commerce clause, which the Court used during the 1920s to strike down state legislation that "directly regulated" or "unduly burdened" interstate commerce. In such decisions as *Hanover Fire Insurance Co. v. Carr* (1926) and *Compania General de Tabacos de Filipinas v. Collector of Internal Revenue* (1927), Taft made clear his determination to use the power of the Court to sustain and protect a national common market. Not surprisingly, Taft also supported a strong doctrine of federal preemption and a robust national federal common law.

Taft's concern to promote a national and uniform market was ultimately rooted in his conception of property rights. As a Yale undergraduate, Taft had been deeply influenced by the social Darwinism of William G. Sumner, and for the remainder of his life Taft accepted without question the principle that human conduct was naturally self-regarding. The challenge was to divert this selfishness into socially productive channels. The primary mechanism for this purpose was the institution of property, "the keystone of our society." To impair property rights was to threaten "our whole social fabric" by undercutting "the motive of enlightened selfishness that to-day is at the basis of all human labor and effort, enterprise and new activity." For Taft, therefore, property rights were to be regarded as uniform and universal, like human nature itself. Such rights were to receive national protection in the constitutional guarantees of the due process clause. Taft believed that "the corner stone of our civilization" lay "in the proper maintenance of the guaranties of the 14th Amendment and the 5th Amendment."

Taft thus supported the general program of the Supreme Court during the 1920s to limit the ability of governments to regulate property. Although Taft dissented in the infamous case of *Adkins v. Children's Hospital of the District of Columbia* (1923), in which the Court struck down a minimum wage law for women in the District of Columbia, he joined the many other similar cases in which the Court used the due process clause of the Fourteenth Amendment to invalidate social legislation. He generally arrayed himself against those, like Brandeis and Holmes, whom he believed were "in favor of breaking down the Constitution, or making it a mere scrap of paper."

In effect, the Court's aggressive reading of the due process clause during the 1920s created national criteria for the acceptability of progressive statutes. Taft was very concerned that access to federal courts be preserved so that these national criteria could be enforced through a centralized judicial system. So, for example, in *Terral v. Burke Construction* (1922) he authored an important opinion using the doctrine of unconstitutional conditions to prohibit states from imposing on foreign corporations the precondition that they waive the right to remove cases to federal courts. He also fought fiercely to preserve federal diversity jurisdiction when it was threatened by progressive senators like George W. Norris and David I. Walsh.

Although Taft was solicitous of property rights, he was also quite aware that the increased "mutual dependence" of modern industrial society required that property be regulated in a manner "appreciative of the change of conditions and the necessity for a liberal construction of the restrictions of the Constitution." He thus joined such important and progressive opinions as *Village of Euclid v. Ambler Realty Co.* (1926), which upheld the constitutionality of city zoning, and *Miller v. Schoene* (1928), which upheld the constitutionality of confiscating infected trees. These opinions are facially inconsistent

with Taft's commitment to preserve property rights; they reflect a deep tension within his jurisprudence between that commitment and his evident appreciation of the necessary prerogatives of managerial expertise in contemporary society, an appreciation no doubt reinforced by his own executive experience.

The primary stratagem Taft employed to ease this tension was his effort in *Wolff Packing Co. v. Court of Industrial Relations* (1923) to articulate a constitutional distinction between ordinary property, which was entitled to full constitutional protection, and property affected with a public interest, which could be subjected to extensive administrative control by the state. Using this distinction, Taft wrote several important opinions upholding the revolutionary efforts of the Transportation Act of 1920 to regulate the income and property of interstate railroads, as in *Dayton-Goose Creek Railroad Co. v. United States* (1924). Taft also used the distinction to uphold regulations of the insurance industry. Although the distinction was conceptually unstable—and therefore did not survive the constitutional revolution of the 1930s—it nevertheless illustrates Taft's sincere effort to reconcile his naturally managerial bent with his equally sincere dedication to rather inflexible notions of property rights.

Taft's managerial propensity is evident in many aspects of his jurisprudence. It is most strikingly visible, for example, in opinions like *United States v. Murray* (1928), *FTC v. Klesner* (1927), *Richmond Screw Anchor Co. v. United States* (1928), or *Girard Trust Co. v. United States* (1926), where he easily and masterfully assimilated the process of statutory interpretation to an intelligent and purposive social pragmatism. It is also apparent in Taft's grasp of the basic principles of administrative law, and his clear understanding that executive agencies needed discretion and authority in order to function effectively. Representative opinions in this regard include *United States v. Stone & Downer Co.* (1927), *FTC v. Curtis Publishing Co.* (1923), *FTC v. Western Meat Co.* (1926), and *J.W. Hampton Jr. & Co. v. United States* (1928). This same understanding underlay Taft's persistent commitment to an expansive interpretation of presidential power. Although some of Taft's opinions in this area, like the notorious *Myers v. United States* (1926), are strident and over-reaching, most, like *McConaughey v. Morrow* (1923) and *Ex parte Grossman* (1925), are entirely convincing in their comprehensive insight into the pragmatic interrelationships among working government agencies.

Taft's view of the law as a purposive social instrument is also evident in his handling of the legal and constitutional dimensions of Prohibition. Taft had initially opposed Prohibition because he believed that it would be unenforceable and hence tend to create a cancerous disrespect for the law. With the enactment of the Eighteenth Amendment, however, Taft dedicated himself to establishing the legal mechanisms necessary for the social control of liquor. His most successful and long-lived opinion, *Carroll v. United States* (1925), completely reinterpreted received Fourth Amendment jurisprudence so as to enable effective supervision of illegal vehicular liquor traffic. The same sustained determination and legal ingenuity is evident in such other important Taft Prohibition opinions as *Olmstead v. United States* (1928), *United States v. Lanza* (1922), *Ford v. United States* (1927), and *Samuels v. McCurdy* (1925).

Throughout his tenure as chief justice, Taft advocated various reforms of the criminal law system so as to render it "more efficient." He thought that the worst danger to the country was the "general spirit of lawlessness" loose in the land. Yet that spirit was not for Taft to be countered merely by more effective mechanisms of social control; equally important was the inculcation of fundamental norms of legality and fair procedure. Thus, writing to the president of the Cincinnati Legal Aid Society, Taft noted that he was strongly in favor of the movement to have public defenders appointed for indigent defendants. "The objection that it would delay matters is exactly the reason why I am in favor of it. Of course I think we ought to speed all prosecutions, but we ought not to speed them at the cost of saving from injustice many who are brought in charged with criminal offenses and not able really to defend themselves."

This commitment to fair procedures and respect for law is one of the foundational pillars of Taft's jurisprudence. In *Cooke v. United States* (1925), for example, Taft pioneered the effort to reconcile norms of due process with the administrative need of trial judges to use criminal contempt to retain control over their courtrooms. In *In re Gilbert* (1928), he delivered a stinging lecture to the bar about the need to scrupulously obey judicial regulation. And, despite his evident commitment to the enforcement of prohibition, he nevertheless struck down the widespread and effective technique of reimbursing the judges in mayoral liquor courts from fines they levied on prohibition offenders. In the important decision of *Tumey v. Ohio* (1927), Taft wrote: "Every procedure which would offer a possible temptation to the average man as a judge to forget the burden of proof required to convict the defendant, or which might lead him not to hold the balance nice, clear and true between the state and the accused denies the latter due process of law."

Taft's concern with societal lawlessness accounted for a good deal of his well-known hostility to prolabor legislation. For Taft "organized labor" was as a class "distinctly arrayed against the Court": "That faction we have to hit every little while, because they are continually violating the law and depending on threat and violence to accomplish their purpose. They are not content to depend only on organization, and the background of lawless trouble is always presented to give them an undue influence." And, to make matters worse, the "undue" influence of labor was for Taft often directed against the maintenance of necessary traditional property rights.

For these reasons Taft had no doubt about the necessity of constitutionally striking down an Arizona law which prevented trial judges from issuing injunctions in labor disputes. As he noted in his notorious opinion in *Truax v. Corrigan* (1921), such injunctions were necessary both to protect property rights in an ongoing business and to prevent violence, since "peaceful picketing was a contradiction in terms." In his labor decisions, Taft tried to walk a narrow line between recognizing labor's right to organize (*American Steel Foundries v. Tri-City Central Trades Council*, 1921), and even encouraging employers to deal honorably with labor unions (*Pennsylvania Railroad Co. v. United States*

Railroad Labor Board, 1923), and scrupulously striking down all organizing tactics that seemed to him lawless and coercive, like picketing and the secondary boycott.

The intrinsic limitations of Taft's jurisprudence are perhaps most strikingly revealed in his labor decisions, for they are manifestly the product of a specific class ideology that identified traditional property rights and social arrangements with individualism and the centrality of personal responsibility and decision making. In his own managerial vision of the judiciary, Taft was able to transcend the notion that courts were merely individual decision makers, and to glimpse the idea of judges as part of a larger and administered system of justice. But Taft never could come to see property and labor as similarly structured systems designed to achieve specific social goals. Property and labor were for him always anchored in the autonomous will of the particular person, from which vantage organized labor appeared as merely a local variant of "socialism," the systemic subordination of the individual. Taft was thus blinded to the directions that the law would shortly take during the New Deal on many of the most significant constitutional issues of his day.

In this sense we can best appreciate Taft as a truly transitional figure. In his own efforts at judicial reform he was able to bring to bear a contemporary and pragmatic understanding of the mechanisms of social relations. He used this understanding to great effect in various aspects of his jurisprudence, most notably in opinions dealing with statutory interpretation, administrative law, and prohibition. But in pervasive and important ways he remained tied to a nineteenth-century naturalized and inflexible image of the person protected by universal and immutable property rights. For this reason, those who charged that the Supreme Court during the 1920s "had reached the zenith of reaction" made no exception for Chief Justice Taft.

—ROBERT C. POST

BIBLIOGRAPHY

The best primary source is the remarkable William Howard Taft papers in the Library of Congress, which include about 750,000 items.

The papers contain a rich trove of documents about Taft's personal philosophy and about the inner workings of Court during Taft's tenure as chief justice. Taft himself published numerous books and articles, the most important being *Popular Government: Its Essence, Its Permanence, and Its Perils* (1913); *Our Chief Magistrate and His Powers* (1916); *Liberty Under Law: An Interpretation of the Principles of Our Constitutional Government* (1922); "The Right of Private Property," 3 *Michigan Law Journal* 215 (1894); and "Three Needed Steps of Progress," 8 *American Bar Association Journal* 24 (1922).

The definitive biography of Taft remains Henry F. Pringle's *The Life and Times of William Howard Taft* (1939), although an interesting modern psychological biography, focusing on the presidential years, is Judith Icke Anderson, *William Howard Taft: An Intimate History* (1981). The best study of Taft's years on the Court is Alpheus Thomas Mason, *William Howard Taft: Chief Justice* (1964). For an excellent contemporary evaluation of Taft's judicial reforms, see Felix Frankfurter and James M. Landis, *The Business of the Supreme Court* (1927).

For good specific studies, see Peter G. Fish, "William Howard Taft and Charles Evans Hughes: Conservative Politicians as Chief Judicial Reformers," 1975 *The Supreme Court Review* 123; Stanley I. Kutler, "Chief Justice Taft and the Delusion of Judicial Exactness—A Study in Jurisprudence," 48 *Virginia Law Review* 1407 (1962), and "Chief Justice Taft, National Regulation, and the Commerce Power," 51 *Journal of American History* 651 (1965); Alpheus T. Mason, "The Labor Decisions of Chief Justice Taft," 78 *University of Pennsylvania Law Review* 585 (1930); Jeffrey B. Morris, "What Heaven Must be Like: William Howard Taft as Chief Justice, 1921–30," 1983 *Supreme Court Yearbook* 80; Walter F. Murphy, "In His Image: Chief Justice Taft and Supreme Court Appointments," *The Supreme Court Review* (1961): 159–63; Walter F. Murphy, "Chief Justice Taft and the Lower Court Bureaucracy: A Study in Judicial Administration," 24 *The Journal of Politics* 453 (1962); and Robert C. Post, "Chief Justice Taft and the Concept of Federalism," 9 *Constitutional Commentary* 199 (1992).

Roger Brooke Taney
Collection of the Supreme Court of the United States.

ROGER BROOKE TANEY

BORN 17 March 1777, Calvert County,
Maryland

NOMINATED to the Court as associate justice
on 15 January 1835 by Andrew
Jackson, but nomination defeated
by indefinite postponement on 3 March
1835; nominated as chief justice on
28 December 1835 by Andrew Jackson

TOOK seat on 15 March 1836

DIED 12 October 1864 in Washington, D.C.

Roger Brooke Taney came from a wealthy
and well-connected Maryland family which
made its fortune in landholding, slaves, and tobacco planting. At age eighteen, Taney graduated from Dickinson College in Pennsylvania,
read law with Maryland judge Jeremiah Chase,
and began practicing in 1799. Initially a Federalist, he served in the state legislature from
1799–1800, but he broke with the party when it
failed to support the War of 1812. In 1816, he
won a five-year term in the Maryland senate. At
the expiration of his senate term in 1821, Taney
moved to Baltimore where his law practice flourished. He also remained politically active and
was elected Maryland's attorney general in 1827.
Taney became a staunch supporter of Andrew
Jackson and in 1828 chaired the Maryland central committee for Jackson's presidential campaign.

In 1831, Jackson appointed Taney attorney
general of the United States, and Taney soon
became one of Jackson's key advisors, helping
shape administration policies on slavery and the
rights of blacks, federal-state relations, and the
Bank of the United States. Like Jackson, Taney
had mixed and often seemingly inconsistent
views on these issues.

During the nullification crisis Taney
strongly supported Jackson's confrontation with
South Carolina. Here Taney was a proponent of
federal power in the tradition of John Marshall.
However, when confronted with questions of
slavery and the rights of free blacks, Taney deferred to state authorities and declined to assert

any federal power. He argued that neither under
the commerce clause nor the treaty power could
the national government regulate slavery and
race relations in the states.

Taney's deference to states' rights on issues
of race and the rights of free blacks anticipated
the views he later articulated in his famous—and
infamous—opinion in *Dred Scott v. Sandford*
(1857). As attorney general, Taney had to comment on the constitutional power of southern
states to prohibit free blacks (from other states
or the British Empire) from entering their jurisdiction. In his official "Opinion of the Attorney
General," Taney asserted that "the African race
in the United States even when free, are everywhere a degraded class, and exercise no political influence. The privileges they are allowed to
enjoy, are accorded to them as a matter of kind-
ness and benevolence rather than right. . . . They
are not looked upon as citizens by the contracting parties who formed the Constitution. They
were evidently not supposed to be included by
the term *citizens*." Taney concluded that the
Declaration of Independence was never meant
to apply to blacks, who were, in the attorney
general's mind, not entitled to the natural rights
of "life, liberty, and pursuit of happiness."

This official opinion of the attorney general
demonstrates that the anti-black, proslavery views
Taney expressed in *Dred Scott* were not an aberration, nor a function of the changing politics of
the 1850s. Rather, these views were part of his
lifelong ideology. This opinion was never published and therefore did not affect public debate,
but it certainly bolstered Jackson's hands-off
policy toward southern regulations of free blacks
from the British Empire and the North.

When examined through the lens of *Dred
Scott*, Taney's views on free blacks become
extraordinarily significant. However, at the time
he entered the Cabinet the most divisive political issue facing the nation was not the status of
blacks, but the Bank of the United States. Taney
wholeheartedly supported Jackson's war against
the bank, and helped the president draft his veto
message which asserted its unconstitutionality.

Jackson's veto was a direct rebuke of Chief Justice John Marshall's opinion in *McCulloch v. Maryland* (1819) that the bank was constitutional. Taney's role in helping to draft Jackson's veto message can be seen as the first step in his gradual dismantling of much of Marshall's jurisprudence.

After the bank veto, Jackson ordered two successive secretaries of the Treasury to begin withdrawing federal deposits from the Bank of the United States. Jackson fired both of them when they refused to do his bidding. Jackson then appointed Taney to the Treasury. Taney immediately began removing deposits from the bank, and the bank's supporters retaliated by blocking his confirmation as secretary of the treasury the following June. Taney then returned to his law practice in Maryland. The following spring, Jackson nominated Taney for the Supreme Court, but in March 1835, the Senate once again refused to confirm him to office.

When Chief Justice Marshall died in July 1835, Jackson nominated Taney to replace him. By the following spring, Jacksonians controlled the Senate, and on March 16, 1836, the Senate confirmed both Taney and Philip P. Barbour, Jackson's nominee to the Court seat made vacant by the retirement of Gabriel Duvall. Although appointed for his political loyalty, Taney also served another purpose. As the Court's first Catholic, his appointment helped solidify Catholic (especially Irish) support for the Democratic party in an age when large numbers of Catholics were beginning to come to the United States.

Taney's confirmation depressed Whigs, who believed the new chief justice would destroy the judicial and economic nationalism created by Marshall. Exacerbating this fear, by the time Taney became chief justice, Jackson had already placed John McLean, Henry Baldwin, and James Wayne on the Court. With the confirmation of Taney and Barbour on the same day, Jackson had a majority of the Court. The addition of John Catron and John McKinley in 1837 created a court with seven Jacksonian Democrats. If Taney wanted to, he apparently had the votes to dismantle the Marshall legacy.

Indeed, for all but the last two years of his tenure Taney had a Democratic, states' rights, proslavery majority on the Court. From 1837 until 1862, only four Whigs served on the Court. Smith Thompson remained on the bench until 1843 and Story, Taney's only rival for intellectual leadership of the court, until 1845. By the mid-1840s, John McLean, who had been appointed by Jackson, had abandoned Jacksonian principles and was on a political trajectory that took him to the Whig, Free Soil, and Republican parties. From 1851 to 1857, Benjamin Curtis, a conservative Whig from Massachusetts, was on the Court. Lincoln placed three Republicans on the Court in 1862 and a fourth in 1863. Thus, in his last two terms, Chief Justice Taney no longer controlled the Court or its jurisprudence.

From 1837 to 1862, the Democratic-Jacksonian majority crafted opinions that were generally supportive of states' rights and slavery and skeptical of national power. In areas of contract and commerce, Taney led a partial retreat from Chief Justice Marshall's nationalist jurisprudence. On the other hand, in some areas, such as procedure, the Taney Court expanded on Marshall's foundation. On slavery, the Taney Court was never jurisprudentially consistent. Until 1861, Taney rejected states' rights when asserted by northerners opposed to slavery, while supporting southern assertions of power over slavery. Similarly, where federal power would protect slavery, Taney was a nationalist; but where the government in Washington might threaten southern bondage, Taney supported a limitation of federal power. The unifying theme of Taney's jurisprudence on slavery, then, was protection of slavery.

The Taney Court's slavery jurisprudence should not be surprising. In addition to the heavy presence of Democrats, until the Civil War the Taney Court always had a proslavery majority. Although Taney freed his own slaves in the 1810s and 1820s, he remained proslavery throughout his public career. From his appointment as chief justice to the outbreak of the Civil War, the Court always had four southerners plus Taney and four northerners. This southern majority was enhanced by the fact that throughout this period at least two and sometimes three of the northerners were Democratic "doughfaces" —northern men with southern principles. Only one justice in this period—John McLean—was openly antislavery, and his opposition to the peculiar institution was relatively mild. On the other hand, the Court had two uncompromisingly proslavery justices, Peter V. Daniel and John A. Campbell, as well other slave-owning southerners whose jurisprudence reflected their sectional and economic interests. By the last antebellum decade, the Supreme Court had become, in the words of David Potter, "the very citadel of American slavery."

Initial Whig fears of Taney eventually proved to be overblown. He was not a radical, but his jurisprudence, especially on economic issues, was clearly different from Marshall's. Marshall generally favored sweeping federal powers over commerce and a strict interpretation of the limitations on the states in such areas as contract and currency. Taney's approach was far more flexible.

Charles River Bridge Co. v. Warren Bridge Co. (1837)—decided during Taney's first term—set the tone for Taney's economic jurisprudence. In 1785, the Charles River Bridge Company had obtained a state charter to operate a toll bridge between Boston and Cambridge. With no other bridge across the Charles River, the company had been enormously profitable, and by the 1830s the bridge was worth a half-million dollars. The single bridge, however, was also no longer adequate for the needs of Boston and its suburbs. In 1828, the Massachusetts legislature chartered the Warren Bridge Company to build a second bridge across the river. Under the charter, the Warren Company could collect tolls to pay back the cost of building the bridge, including a reasonable profit to the company, but after that, the company would turn the bridge over to the state. The Charles River Bridge Company argued that its charter implied it had a monopoly, and that in granting a charter to the Warren company the state effectively violated the contract clause of the Constitution. Speaking for the Court, Taney concluded that "any ambiguity in the terms of the contract, must operate against the adventurers [stockholders] and in favor of the public."

Although Whigs disliked the result (Daniel Webster was the losing attorney and Justice Story dissented), Taney's decision was not a radical departure from the economic jurisprudence of Chief Justice Marshall. Taney simply recognized that the public good required a balance between private interests (the corporation) and the public need, as reflected by the legislature. The Taney Court followed the spirit of *Charles River Bridge* in subsequent cases—allowing states great flexibility in issuing corporate charters, but always reading those charters narrowly in order to protect the public good and the states. Thus, the Taney court had no difficulty in recognizing the right of the state to give companies tax breaks or the power of eminent domain, but in *West River Bridge v. Dix* (1848), the Court also upheld the right of the state to use eminent domain to take property from a corporation.

Taney's decision in *Charles River Bridge* and subsequent cases also reflected his states' rights proclivities. The *Charles River Bridge* opinion deferred to the needs of the states in promoting economic development and also in controlling local industries. Similarly, in *New York v. Miln* (1837) the Court (in an opinion by Justice Barbour) upheld New York City's law requiring ships entering the port to provide detailed information about immigrant passengers. As with the contract clause, the Taney Court reshaped Justice Marshall's nationalist commerce clause jurisprudence to give states more latitude in regulating their economies.

Taney also expanded the power of states in *Briscoe v. Commonwealth Bank of Kentucky* (1837). There he upheld the power of a state chartered bank to issue bank notes. This narrowed the implications of Justice Marshall's opinion in *Craig v. Missouri* (1830), which had prohibited states themselves from issuing paper money. Logically, if the Constitution prohibited a state from issuing currency, then surely a state could not charter a bank to do what the state itself could not do. However, Justice McLean, speaking for the Taney Court, distinguished between a bank issuing notes and a state issuing currency. Carrying on Marshall's nationalist traditions, Justice Story dissented.

The outcome of *Briscoe* dovetailed with Taney's role in dismantling the Bank of the United States three years earlier. In the 1830s, the United States government did not print currency, but only minted a small amount of gold and silver coin, while the Bank of the United States issued bank notes which functioned as a national currency. But with the expiration of the federal charter of the Bank of the United States in 1836, there was no national currency. Had the Taney court ruled differently in *Briscoe* there would have been no currency in the United States, and this might have forced the national government to once again charter a national bank.

Charles River Bridge, *Miln*, and *Briscoe* presaged other cases in which Taney and his colleagues supported state regulation and experimentation in commercial and economic areas. For example, in the *License Cases* (1847) the Taney Court upheld the right of Massachusetts, Rhode Island, and Connecticut to ban the importation of liquor. In the *Passenger Cases* (1849), the Court struck down, on commerce clause grounds, state laws taxing immigrants. Taney, however, dissented, ready to defer to the states. In *Cooley v. Board of Port Wardens of Philadelphia* (1851) the Court upheld a Pennsylvania law requiring that ships entering Philadelphia take on a local pilot. This decision also reflected Taney's general deference to the states, although Justice Benjamin R. Curtis wrote the opinion of the Court.

Despite his general sympathy to the states in economic regulation, Taney did not always limit federal power. Two cases dealing with corporations and interstate commerce suggest the flexibility of Taney on economic matters. In *Warren Manufacturing Co. v. Aetna Insurance Co.* (1837), Taney upheld a Maryland law allowing a Connecticut company doing business in Maryland to be sued in Maryland. Furthermore, Taney held that a judgment against the company in the state court could then be enforced in a federal court. While a victory for state power, this case also helped establish an atmosphere conducive to corporations doing business on a national scale. Under *Warren Manufacturing,* states would have some control over out-of-state companies and could count on the federal courts to help them enforce that control. This decision made it more likely that states would allow out-of-state companies to do business within their jurisdiction. Two years later, in *Bank of Augusta*

v. Earle (1839), Taney further enhanced interstate business while at the same time recognizing the power of the states to regulate their economies. In this case, Taney held that a bank chartered in one state might do business in another unless specifically prohibited from doing so. This ruling did not destroy state power, but it left the states in the position of having to specifically ban out-of-state corporations from doing business within their jurisdictions.

In some commercial cases Taney actually expanded on Marshall's judicial nationalism. In *Swift v. Tyson* (1842), Justice Story, writing for a unanimous Court, held that the federal courts were free to develop their own common law for commercial litigation. This case allowed those engaged in interstate business to rely on general rules of commercial law and consequently limited the power of the states to create unique rules which might burden out-of-state litigants. And in *Genesee Chief v. Fitzhugh* (1852), Taney reversed Marshall's earlier doctrine enunciated in *The Thomas Jefferson* (1825) to actually expand federal jurisdiction. In the 1825 case, Justice Story, writing for the Marshall Court, had allowed the states to regulate traffic on inland waters. By 1852, this made for an impossible set of differing and sometimes contradictory rules in the nation's water commerce. Taney concluded that federal admiralty jurisdiction extended to all navigable rivers and lakes, and not just to those affected by "the ebb and flow of the tide." As Kent Newmyer concluded: "In an explicitly pragmatic response to commercial necessity, Taney reversed Story's earlier ruling, declaring it mistaken law and bad policy, and extended the admiralty jurisdiction of federal courts over the whole system of inland waterways. Marshall, who never liked the *Jefferson* decision, would surely have congratulated his successor."

These decisions, which enhanced federal power, were imperative for the emerging national economy, and did not significantly hamper the ability of the states to control their own economic affairs.

The antebellum court rarely faced questions about politics and fundamental rights in the states. Three cases, *Permoli v. First Municipal-*

ity of New Orleans (1845), *Ex parte Dorr* (1845) and *Luther v. Borden* (1849), illustrate the way in which the Court under Taney's leadership avoided such questions.

Permoli reaffirmed Chief Justice Marshall's holding in *Barron v. The Mayor and City Council of Baltimore* (1833) that the federal bill of rights did not apply to the states. The case questioned the right of the city of New Orleans to prohibit burial masses in certain Catholic churches in the city. Permoli was a Catholic priest who held a mass in his church in violation of a city ordinance. In a unanimous opinion by Justice Catron, the Court dismissed the case for lack of a federal question on the ground that the Bill of Rights did not apply to the new states any more than it applied to the old.

Ex parte Dorr (1845) and *Luther v. Borden* (1849) came out of the Dorr War, an extralegal attempt to bring political reform in Rhode Island. In 1841, Rhode Island was still operating under its colonial charter, and a substantial majority of the adult males could not vote in the state. Malapportionment of the state legislature allowed a small minority of rural farmers to control government in the state and stifle all reform. Led by Thomas Dorr, reformers wrote a new constitution, elected a new government, and for awhile, there were two competing governments in the state. Eventually, Dorr was forced to flee the state, as the governor under the old charter called out the regular militia. Dorr was eventually arrested, convicted of insurrection, and sentenced to life in prison. In *Ex parte Dorr*, the Supreme Court overruled a petition for *habeas corpus* on the grounds that the federal government could not interfere in state criminal proceedings. A year later, the new governor of Rhode Island, who had gained office under a democratic constitution written by the Dorrites, pardoned Dorr.

In *Luther v. Borden* a Dorrite, Martin Luther, sued a state militiaman, Luther Borden, for trespass for searching his home and arresting him during the rebellion. Luther argued that Rhode Island had not had a republican form of government and under that clause of Article IV of the Constitution the Supreme Court had jurisdiction. Taney, writing for the Court, rejected Luther's arguments, concluding that the legitimacy of the old charter government was a "political question to be settled by the political power" of the people within the state.

In these cases, Taney declined to assert federal power over questions of politics and rights in the nation. This was consistent with Taney's beliefs about states' rights and limitations on the national government. However, the subtext to these decisions, and to most of the Taney court's decisions on interstate commerce, was slavery.

In their study of antebellum constitutionalism, *Equal Justice Under Law*, Harold M. Hyman and William M. Wiecek refer to slavery as the "Nemesis of the Constitution." The characterization is apt. In terms of his historical reputation no one suffered more from this nemesis than Taney. Had Taney died or left the bench in 1850, or even 1856, before his opinion in *Dred Scott v. Sandford* (1857), he would be remembered as a great chief justice, well-liked by his colleagues and admired by the citizenry. But, in his last fourteen years on the Court, Taney faced cases on slavery and the Civil War that left his reputation permanently flawed.

As an adult Taney personally divorced himself from slavery. This is to his credit, and on that level made him distinct from most all southern presidents from George Washington to Andrew Johnson—none of whom ever freed their slaves in their lifetime. Nevertheless, Taney never divorced himself from his southern roots, his ideological support of slavery as an institution and his beliefs in the racial inferiority of blacks. Throughout his career, Taney's jurisprudence was overwhelmingly proslavery and anti-black.

As chief justice, Taney's first major encounter with slavery came in 1841 in two cases, *The United States v. Amistad*, and *Groves v. Slaughter*. The case of the *Amistad* was the first great slavery-related *cause célèbre* to reach the Supreme Court. The *Amistad* was a Spanish schooner filled with slaves recently (and illegally) imported to Cuba from Africa. While being transported from one part of Cuba to another, the slaves revolted, killing some of the crew and demanding that they be taken back to Africa. The remaining crew members sailed east during the day, but at night reversed course, heading north and west, in hopes of reaching a southern state in the United States. Instead, the craft was eventually boarded by the Coast Guard in Long Island Sound. Various suits arose over the status of the vessel and the slaves on it. Ultimately, the Supreme Court ruled that the blacks had been illegally taken from Africa, could not be held as slaves under Spanish or American law, and were to be returned to Africa. Justice Story wrote for the Court, with Taney remaining silent. By 1841, even many proslavery advocates found the African trade to be immoral and a violation of natural law, as well as most public law (although not international law). Thus Taney's acquiescence in freeing the *Amistad's* slaves cannot be seen as antislavery.

On its face, *Groves v. Slaughter* (1841) also did not raise pro- or antislavery issues. Rather, it was essentially a commerce clause case—the only major slavery case to come before the Supreme Court that directly raised commerce clause issues. Mississippi's 1832 constitution prohibited the importation of slaves for sale. This was not an antislavery provision, but an attempt to reduce the flow of capital out of the state. Slaughter, a professional slave dealer, had sold slaves in Mississippi and received notes signed by Groves and others. Groves and his codefendants later defaulted on the notes, arguing that the sales of slaves in Mississippi were void. Thus the suit was between slave sellers and slave buyers.

Speaking for the Court, Justice Smith Thompson, a New York Whig, held that the notes were not void because Mississippi's constitutional clause prohibiting the importation of slaves was not self-executing. Thompson held that absent legislation implementing the prohibition, the Mississippi constitutional clause was inoperative. This was a reasonable result based on commercial rules, and was consistent with the outcome in *Bank of Augusta v. Earle* (1839). In that case, Earle and other Alabamians had refused to honor bills of exchange they had issued on the grounds that they had been bought by an out-of-state bank, and out-of-state banks could not operate in Alabama. Taney had ruled that out-of-state banks could operate in any state in the absence of an explicit act of the legislature to the contrary.

Similarly, in *Groves,* the Court held that the Mississippi purchasers could not hide behind a clause of the state constitution and refuse to pay the notes they had signed for the slaves they had purchased without an explicit statute in Mississippi banning slave sales. This result was "neutral" with regard to slavery.

Indicative of what would be his highly partisan approach to slavery throughout the rest of his career, Taney wrote a separate concurrence, insisting that the federal government had no power over slavery. This issue was, of course, not directly before the Court, but Taney did not want to leave any implication that under the commerce clause Congress might regulate slavery. He declared that "the power of this subject [slavery] is exclusively with the several States, and each of them has a right to decide for itself whether it will or will not allow persons of this description to be brought within its limits from another State, either for sale or for any other purpose . . . and the action of the several States upon this subject cannot be controlled by Congress, either by virtue of its power to regulate commerce, or by virtue of any other power conferred by the Constitution of the United States."

On the other side of the question, Justice McLean asserted in a concurrence that the free states could prevent the importation of slaves if they wished and that Congress could not interfere. Sounding much like Taney, McLean declared that "the power over slavery belongs to the States respectively. It is local in its character, and in its effects" and that "each state has a right to protect itself against the avarice and intrusion of the slave dealer; to guard its citizens against the inconveniences and dangers of a slave population." He argued that "The right to exercise this power by a State is higher and deeper than the Constitution." In essence, both Taney and McLean agreed that a state might legally ban the importation of slaves. This principle supported northerners interested in keeping slaves out of their states and the southern desire to make sure that the federal courts could not interfere with slavery on the local level.

In 1841, then, both supporters and opponents of slavery on the Court were anxious to see the issue remain solely in the hands of the states. By 1842, however, Taney would no longer be content with that interpretation of slavery, unless it was a slave state making the determination.

In 1842, the Supreme Court heard *Prigg v. Pennsylvania*, its first case involving the fugitive slave clause of the Constitution. *Prigg* involved the constitutionality of a Pennsylvania personal liberty law requiring that slave catchers receive a proper writ from a state judge before removing any blacks from the state. Edward Prigg had seized a woman and her children without any state process and was subsequently convicted of kidnapping in Pennsylvania. In a sweeping victory for slavery, which shook to the core his antislavery reputation, Justice Story struck down the Pennsylvania law, upheld the federal fugitive slave law of 1793, and further declared that slave owners had a constitutional right to seize their slaves anywhere they found them, without resort to any sort of legal process, as long as the seizure could be done without a breach of the peace. In reaching these conclusions, Story swept aside the facts of the case, which showed that at least one of the people Prigg seized had been born in Pennsylvania, and therefore free under that state's laws.

In his opinion, Story asserted that the federal government could not require state officials to enforce the federal fugitive slave law of 1793, although he urged them to do so as a matter of patriotism, moral obligation, and (unenforceable) constitutional duty. This holding was consistent with prevailing notions of federalism and states' rights, and Taney should have applauded it. Indeed, later in his career, in *Kentucky v. Dennison* (1861), Taney would argue that the federal courts could not order state governors to enforce the criminal extradition clauses of the same 1793 law. But Taney did not endorse this view in *Prigg*. In a partial concurrence, Taney argued that state officials ought to be required to enforce the fugitive slave clause. This was the beginning of Taney's assertion of Marshallian-like federalism in order to protect slavery.

In *Strader v. Graham* (1850), Taney once again spoke out on slavery. Strader was the owner of a steamboat that had transported Graham's three slaves to Ohio, where they disappeared. Under Kentucky law, a steamboat operator was liable for the value of any slaves who escaped by boarding the boat without written permission of the owner. Strader, however, argued that the blacks were free because Graham had previously allowed them to go to Indiana and Ohio. Speaking for a unanimous Court, Taney ruled against Strader, arguing that the status of the blacks could only be decided by Kentucky, which had ruled they were slaves. Kentucky was free to ignore the laws of Ohio and Indiana on this question. Taney declared that "every State has an undoubted right to determined the *status* or domestic condition of the persons domiciled within its territory" except as "restrained" by the Constitution. This wording certainly applied to fugitive slaves, which the northern states could not declare free, but it also held open the possibility that slave owners had other federal rights to carry their slaves into the North or the federal territories. Part of this implication became explicit in *Dred Scott v. Sandford* (1857).

Dred Scott was the slave of Dr. John Emerson, a military physician who had taken Scott to Fort Snelling, in present-day Minnesota. At the time, this part of the Louisiana Purchase was free territory under the Missouri Compromise. After Emerson's death, Scott sued for his freedom on the grounds that he had become free in Minnesota, and once free, always free. After nearly eleven years of litigation in state and federal courts, the Supreme Court finally decided the case in 1857. Although every one of the justices wrote an opinion, Taney's was the "Opinion of the Court." In his sweeping fifty-five-page opinion, Taney sought to settle the divisive political questions of slavery and race in favor of the South.

Three aspects of Taney's opinion made it infamous. First, in a tortured interpretation of the Constitution's clause on territorial jurisdiction in Article IV, Taney ruled the Missouri Compromise unconstitutional. Thus, on a totally unpersuasive textual analysis, Taney struck down a major piece of congressional legislation that had been the keystone of sectional compromise for more than a generation.

Second, Taney ruled that under the Fifth Amendment's due process clause slaves could not be freed by federal law. In essence, Taney held that slavery was a protected species of property, and that under the Constitution the Congress could not deprive any citizen of this kind of property. This interpretation of the Constitution pleased the South while angering the North, but it flew in the face of national law predating the Constitution, in which Congress had banned slavery from some federal territories. Moreover, the use of the Fifth Amendment seemed, to many northerners at least, cynical and ironic. It was that amendment, after all, that asserted that no person could be denied life, liberty, or property without due process of law. Taney stressed the "property" in slaves, and protected it, but ignored the obvious possibility that the amendment might ban slavery in all federal jurisdictions because slavery denied people liberty without due process.

Even more egregious than these two assertions was Taney's assertion that blacks—even if free and allowed to vote in the states where they lived—could never be citizens of the United States and have standing to sue in federal courts. In a thoroughly inaccurate history of the founding period, Taney argued that at the adoption of the Constitution blacks were not "included, and were not intended to be included, under the word 'citizens' in the Constitution, and can therefore claim none of the rights and privileges which the instrument provides and secures to citizens of the United States. On the contrary, they were at that time [1787] considered as a subordinate and inferior class of beings who had been subjugated by the dominant race, and, whether emancipated or not, yet remained subject to their authority, and had no rights or privileges but such as those who held the power and Government might chose to grant them." Taney concluded blacks were "so far inferior, that they had not rights which the white man was bound to respect."

Taney had hoped to end all controversy over slavery in the territories with this opinion, but he severely miscalculated. Northern anger over the opinion fueled the Republican party and helped put Lincoln in the White House. Rather than acknowledge the complexity of slavery, Taney simply tried to sweep away the opposition to the institution, and he failed miserably.

Two decisions following *Dred Scott* showed the proslavery cynicism of Taney's jurisprudence. In *Ableman v. Booth* (1859), Taney rejected Wisconsin's attempts to remove from federal custody the abolitionist Sherman Booth, who had helped a fugitive slave escape. Taney refused to even consider the constitutionality of the new Fugitive Slave Law of 1850, even though it was substantially different from the law upheld in *Prigg* in 1842. Taney dismissed Wisconsin's states' rights arguments as though he had never heard of the idea, and in his *Ableman* opinion endorsed a sweeping federal power to support slavery.

In *Kentucky v. Dennison* (1861), however, Taney changed his tune once again. This was a suit by the state of Kentucky to force Governor William Dennison of Ohio to extradite a free black named Willis Lago who had helped a slave woman escape from Kentucky. The obvious proslavery result would have been to side with Kentucky. This would have also been consistent with Taney's opinions in *Prigg*, *Dred Scott*, and *Ableman*, where he rejected states' rights in favor of federal protections of slavery. But in the spring of 1861, when the case was decided, seven slave states had already left the Union. Sympathetic to the southern cause, Taney avoided writing an opinion which would have given the federal government the power to force state governors to act. Thus, in an opinion reminiscent of Marshall's tactics in *Marbury v. Madison*, Taney castigated Dennison, but refused to order him to act.

Taney remained on the court until his death in 1864. During his last few years as chief justice he did everything in his power to thwart Abraham Lincoln's policies. In *Ex parte Merryman* (1861), Taney denounced Lincoln for the military arrest of a Marylander who was organizing Confederate troops, destroying bridges, and in other ways making war against the United States. Lincoln ignored Taney's fulminations, and kept Merryman in Fort McHenry. Failing to recognize the nature of the Civil War, Taney dissented in the *Prize Cases* (1863) and opposed the taxation of judges' salaries to help pay for the war. He secretly drafted an opinion declaring conscription unconstitutional, but no case ever reached the court in which he could use the opinion.

By the time he died, Taney was a minority justice, ignored by the president and Congress, held in contempt by the vast majority of his countrymen, and only respected in those places that proclaimed themselves no longer in the Union. Taney's obvious tilt toward the Confederacy showed that he had traveled far from the days when he had advised Andrew Jackson on how to suppress nullificationists. Indeed, he had become one himself in all but name.

Taney's reputation as a judge is mixed. At his death few had anything good to say about him. Congress refused to appropriate money to put his bust in the Supreme Court chambers. Yet it is clear that his impact on the law was great. For the first twenty years of his tenure he successfully guided the Court and helped develop important constitutional doctrines. He is most remembered for *Dred Scott*, which is the most infamous decision in American constitutional history. *Dred Scott*, however, should be seen as only part of a series of decisions designed to strengthen slavery, protect the South, and in the end, to undermine the cause of the Union after 1861. While Taney was creative in finding legal solutions to questions about banking, commerce, and transportation, he ultimately failed in creating a jurisprudence that could defend fundamental liberty and human rights. That failure will always overshadow his successes.

—Paul Finkelman

BIBLIOGRAPHY

The best biography of Taney remains Carl B. Swisher's classic *Roger B. Taney* (1935), but see also Frank Otto Gatell, "Roger B. Taney," in Friedman and Israel, 2 *Justices* 635, which provides a good short biographical sketch of Taney along with some of his opinions.

Harold M. Hyman and William M. Wiecek's *Equal Justice Under Law* (1982) is the best book available on the constitutional history of antebellum America. For the Court under Taney, see the comprehensive and classic Carl B. Swisher, *The Taney Period* (1974), the fifth volume in the Holmes Devise. R. Kent Newmyer's *The Supreme Court Under Marshall and Taney* (1974) provides a good short history of the court during Taney's service.

David Potter's *The Impending Crisis, 1848–1861* (1976) is a history of the years leading up to the Civil War, which puts many of Taney's opinions on slavery into historical context. On slavery and the legal system, see Paul Finkelman, *An Imperfect Union: Slavery, Comity, and Federalism* (1981), a study of the interstate movement of slaves, which includes detailed analyses of many Taney opinions, and *Slavery in the Courtroom* (1985). For the most infamous of Taney's opinions, see the prize-winning study by Don Fehrenbacher, *The Dred Scott Case: Its Significance in Law and Politics* (1978).

Clarence Thomas
Photograph by the National Geographic Society.
Collection of the Supreme Court of the United States.

CLARENCE THOMAS

BORN 23 June 1948, Pinpoint, Georgia
NOMINATED to the Court 1 July 1991
   by George H. W. Bush
TOOK seat 23 October 1991

Clarence Thomas, the 106th justice of the United States Supreme Court, is the second African American ever to serve on the Court. Thomas replaced the first African American justice, Thurgood Marshall, who had come to the bench as a civil rights litigator appointed by a Democratic president. Thomas, a conservative Republican, was appointed by a Republican president following a career as a political appointee.

President Ronald Reagan appointed Thomas, who had come to Washington as an aide to Republican senator John Danforth, to Assistant Secretary for Civil Rights at the Department of Education in 1981, and the following year appointed him chair of the Equal Employment Opportunity Commission. In both of those positions, Thomas endorsed increasingly conservative approaches to issues concerning discrimination. He opposed most forms of affirmative action, including quotas and timetables, and in his frequent speeches and writings, offered his own career as an example of self-reliance overcoming racial discrimination.

Thomas was nominated to the United States court of appeals for the D.C. circuit in 1989, and after serving a little over a year on that Court, was nominated to the Supreme Court. At the initial confirmation hearings held by the Senate, a well-coached Thomas presented himself as an American success story, stressing his humble beginnings in Pinpoint, Georgia. He also portrayed himself as open-minded, declaring that the conservative positions he had taken as a political appointee would not necessarily follow him to the bench, and that he had not even considered his views on some controversial issues, such as the validity of the Court's opinion on abortion in *Roe v. Wade* (1973). Articles and speeches in which Thomas had seemed to endorse a natural law philosophy drew questioning, but again, Thomas disassociated himself

from all of his earlier positions. The Judiciary Committee split, seven to seven, on whether to endorse Thomas. Then the controversy that was to make Thomas's name the object of national scorn, derision, passionate defense and pity, broke when the public learned of the allegations of Anita Hill.

A former employee of Thomas's who had subsequently become a law professor at the University of Oklahoma, Hill submitted affidavits to the Judiciary Committee alleging that Thomas had subjected her to repeated sexual harassment during the time that she worked for him. The Judiciary Committee had decided not to call Hill as a witness at their hearings but, after Hill's affidavit was leaked to the press, angry responses from constituents led the Senate to order the Judiciary Committee to hold additional hearings concerning Hill's charges. Thomas categorically denied that any of the events Hill described had ever occurred. Because the hearings were televised, the entire nation joined the Judiciary Committee in trying to decide who was telling the truth, Hill or Thomas. Both were compelling witnesses, Hill with her prim and forthright demeanor, supported by witnesses who testified that she had complained of sexual harassment at the time; Thomas, with his outraged charge that he was being subjected to a "high-tech lynching for uppity blacks," backed by women who had worked for him who testified that Hill's charges were incredible. With the testimony so balanced, it may have been the chair of the Judiciary Committee Joseph Biden's declaration that Thomas was entitled to the benefit of the doubt that led to the Senate's decision to confirm Thomas—by a vote of 52–48, the narrowest margin of votes received by any justice in more than a century.

Because of the prolonged confirmation hearings, Thomas was not sworn in until October 23, after the term had already begun. During his first years on the bench, Thomas became known for his identification with the radically conservative judicial philosophy of Antonin Scalia. Thomas and Scalia voted together in substantially more than 80 percent of all cases. Like

Scalia, Thomas believed in principle more than in precedent. In case after case, he declared his willingness to jettison decades or even centuries of judicial interpretations of the Constitution in favor of what he found to be the original intent of the framers of the Constitution. In his first term, Thomas wrote opinions advocating radical restructuring of the Court's approach to constitutional provisions, including the Sixth Amendment's right to confront witnesses, which Thomas argued should apply only in very limited circumstances (*White v. Illinois,* 1992); the Eighth Amendment's prohibition of cruel and unusual punishment, which he would have found irrelevant to contentions about inhumane prison conditions or brutality toward prisoners (*Hudson v. McMillian,* 1992); the speedy trial clause (*Doggett v. United States,* 1992); and the First Amendment right of association (*Dawson v. Delaware,* 1992).

Thomas usually voted against claims raised by criminal defendants, except in a pair of cases where he voted to uphold allegations of prosecutorial overreaching (*Williams v. United States,* 1992, dissenting opinion), and *Jacobson v. United States* (1992), where Thomas contributed the deciding vote in defendant's favor. He valued federalism over individual rights, voting to limit the federal *habeas corpus* remedy, see *Wright v. West* (1992), and, perhaps surprisingly for the former head of a federal agency, often voted to curtail federal agency power.

In several opinions, Thomas manifested a special interest in cases involving race. In *Georgia v. McCollum* (1992), for example, Thomas questioned whether the Court's decisions promoting jurors' rights would undermine the ability of minority defendants to ensure that they be judged by an unbiased jury; in *United States v. Fordice* (1992), Thomas expressed his concern about the future of historically significant black colleges in the face of integrationist policies.

In the last opinion of his first term, Thomas had the opportunity to answer the question he had evaded at his confirmation hearings, voting with a four-justice dissent in *Planned Parenthood of Southeastern Pennsylvania v. Casey* (1992), to overrule *Roe v. Wade.* His second term showed no significant change of direction, either in his philosophy of constitutional interpretation or in his voting companions. Thomas had taken his place, with Scalia, on the conservative wing of the Court.

—SUSAN N. HERMAN

BIBLIOGRAPHY

The following articles by Thomas, published before he was nominated to the Court, provide insight into his views on affirmative action and natural law: "Affirmative Action Goals and Timetables: Too Tough? Not Tough Enough!" 5 *Yale Law & Policy Review* 402 (1987); "The Higher Law Background of the Privileges or Immunities Clause of the Fourteenth Amendment," 12 *Harvard Law & Public Policy Journal* 63 (1989); "Toward a 'Plain Reading' of the Constitution: The Declaration of Independence in Constitutional Interpretation," 30 *Howard Law Journal* 983 (1987).

Biographical material on Clarence Thomas and a discussion of his views and of the explosive confirmation hearings may be found in Timothy M. Phelps and Helen Winternitz, *Capitol Games* (1992), and L. Gordon Crovitz, ed., *Clarence Thomas: Confronting the Future, Selections from the Senate Confirmation Hearings and Prior Speeches* (1992). Additional analysis of the Thomas confirmation hearings and their implications for the confirmation hearing process generally may be found in Paul Simon, "Advice & Consent: Clarence Thomas, Robert Bork and the Intriguing History of the Supreme Court's Nomination Battles" in a symposium in 65 *Southern California Law Review* (1992) and in Toni Morrison, ed., *Race-ing Justice, Engendering Power: Essays on Anita Hill, Clarence Thomas, and the Construction of Social Reality* (1992).

SMITH THOMPSON

BORN 17 January 1768, Dutchess County,
New York

NOMINATED to the Court 8 December 1823
by James Monroe

TOOK seat 10 February 1824

DIED 18 December 1843 in New York City

Smith Thompson served on the United States Supreme Court for twenty years. During that long tenure, he authored more than eighty-five opinions, and states' rights served as the most significant theme of his judicial writing. Thompson consistently opposed the centralizing federalism of Chief Justice John Marshall.

Thompson came to the Court as a successful New York politician. After practicing law for several years, he became part of the Livingston faction. A string of political offices culminated in his appointment as state chief justice, replacing James Kent. His states' rights beliefs became clear in a decision upholding a state monopoly grant to steamboat promotor Robert Livingston that was later undercut by Chief Justice John Marshall in *Gibbons v. Ogden* (1824), which held the monopoly violated federal commerce powers. President Monroe appointed Thompson secretary of the navy in 1818, and, while Thompson maneuvered for a possible presidential campaign, Monroe named him to the Supreme Court to fill the seat vacated by fellow New Yorker Brockholst Livingston. Thompson continued to be an active politician on the bench and even launched an unsuccessful campaign for governor of New York against Martin Van Buren in 1828.

Thompson's devotion to states' rights played a role in his appointment, and once on the bench, he opposed John Marshall's centralizing tendencies. This can be seen in *Ogden v. Saunders* (1827), in which Thompson joined the majority to uphold the constitutionality of state insolvency statutes limiting debt liability contracted prior to the passage of the acts, and thus overruling the chief justice's holding in *Sturges v. Crowinsheld* (1819). Thompson defended the acts as legitimate exercises of state bankruptcy authority held concurrently with federal bankruptcy power.

These commitments are also evident in his two most important decisions. In 1831, he dissented from Marshall's opinion in *Cherokee Nation v. Georgia*, which denied jurisdiction to hear the tribe's complaints against their forced removal. Along with Joseph Story, Thompson disagreed with Marshall's assertion of federal control over the tribe and argued that the Cherokee should be considered a foreign nation with a right to be heard in the Supreme Court. Seven years later, in *Kendall v. United States*, Thompson authored the majority opinion upholding the power of a District of Columbia circuit court to order an officer of the executive branch to perform a ministerial duty. The case involved a suit for payment against the postmaster, and Thompson's opinion served to limit the autonomous authority of the president.

Thompson served on the Court and continued to dabble in politics until his death in 1843.

—MICHAEL GROSSBERG

BIBLIOGRAPHY

There has been little written of Thompson; see, however, Gerald T. Dunne's sketch in Friedman and Israel, 1 *Justices* 473.

Thomas Todd

BORN 23 January 1765, King and Queen
County, Virginia

NOMINATED to the Court 3 March 1807
by Thomas Jefferson

TOOK seat 4 May 1807

DIED 7 February 1826 in Frankfort, Kentucky

The youngest son of Richard and Elizabeth
Richards Todd, Thomas Todd exemplified the
American revolutionary ideals of civic virtue,
independence of mind, and entrepreneurial zeal.
As the author of a Supreme Court memorial
explained in 1839, Todd's early experience with
hardship—extreme poverty, the loss of both
parents, a bankrupt guardian—fostered "that
energy and enterprise which afterwards signal-
ized his character."

These qualities emerged well before Todd's
nomination to the Court. After a stint in the Virginia line late in the Revolution, he graduated
from Liberty Hall (now Washington and Lee
University) and accepted a post as tutor in the
household of up-and-coming attorney Harry
Innes, a cousin. When Innes moved to Kentucky
(then Virginia's westernmost county) in 1783 to
become judge of the supreme court of judicature
for the Kentucky district, Todd accompanied the
family as tutor and law clerk. No doubt in response to ripe opportunities presented by chaotic
land titling in "Kentucke," Todd mastered surveying (a lucrative sideline in emerging states)
and land law—perhaps the most exacting (some
would say arcane) legal specialization available
to a nineteenth-century practitioner.

Within a few years, Todd had gained a reputation as a gifted businessman, lawyer, and pen-
man; he also found his new state's Jeffersonian
political culture entirely congenial. His countrymen chose Todd to serve as clerk of the Kentucky house of representatives from 1792 to
1801, as well as clerk of several conventions
organized to negotiate the terms of statehood
with Virginia (culminating in adoption of the
1792 separation agreement, by which Virginia
granted statehood to Kentucky), and draft a state

constitution. Between 1801 and 1807, he served
ably as associate justice, and then chief justice,
of the Kentucky court of appeals. Todd had
crossed the Appalachians with little more than
ambition in his pocket; by 1807, when Jefferson
tapped him for the federal bench (and, with it,
the seventh or western circuit court), he had established a respected law practice (first in
Danville as a circuit-riding frontier lawyer, then
in the capitol city of Frankfort), and a reputation
for honesty and precision. He also had amassed
a fortune, much of it through land agency and
speculation.

Todd has yet to attract a biographer, partly
because his written legacy seems thin. He produced only twelve opinions for the Court, mainly
in land cases (including a *per curiam* opinion in
McKim v. Voorhies [1812], which one authority wrongly terms a "statement" rather than an
"opinion"); one narrowly procedural concurrence
in an 1812 chancery case (*Wallen v. Williams*);
and a little-known 1810 opinion, dissenting in
part, in *Finley v. Lynn*. None of these rulings
contributed directly to American constitutional
law—the main avenue to judicial 'greatness.' In
addition, because historians rarely consult the
manuscript minute books of Todd's busy circuit
court (shared with Judge Robert Trimble of
Kentucky), where many learned opinions appear
in politically explosive contract, taxation, and
land cases, much of his legal writing escapes
notice. To make matters worse, Todd missed five
out of nineteen terms for illness or misadventure,
eschewed publicity, and left few private papers.
Hence, scholars wryly conclude, with G. Edward
White, that Todd's "most conspicuous act" as a
jurist was perhaps to "marry Dolley Madison's
sister" in 1812.

These impressions are mistaken. First, as
White also notes, Todd's colleagues viewed him
as an invaluable "strategic member" of the bench
and the quintessential team player. Despite a
Jeffersonian cast of mind, he staunchly supported
Marshall's judicial federalism when it mattered
most—in rulings to which devotees of states'
rights objected most strenuously; in the process,

he antagonized friends and family in Kentucky. In 1819, for example, he toed the Marshallian line on the controversial question of state taxation of the Second Bank of the United States in *McCulloch v. Maryland* and, five years later, in *Osborn v. Bank of the United States* (an Ohio case appealed from his own seventh circuit when Ohio refused to comply with *McCulloch*). Todd had been a charter bank stockholder; he apparently thought that the institution would benefit the capital-poor republic, so long as stockholders elected Jeffersonian directors. Kentuckians disagreed. Between 1819 and 1825, Kentucky's new, aggressively anti-Federal Relief party loudly denounced *McCulloch*, *Osborn*, and the "traitorous" Todd as sellouts to an aristocratic "Monied Hydra"; similar remarks filled newspaper columns in Tennessee, Ohio, and Missouri.

At the least, then, Todd was a disciplined, thick-skinned judge: although "bred in a different political school from that of the Chief Justice," wrote Joseph Story, Todd "never failed to sustain those great principles of constitutional law on which the security of the Union depends. He never gave up to party, what he thought belonged to the country."

Yet he also was a hardworking, substantial scholar and a savvy politician content to remain in the wings. As Story and Marshall said repeatedly, Todd was a fount of specialized legal information, and (as rebellion and anti-judicial sentiment advanced in the West and South after 1819) a reliable source of political advice, notably about the objectives of seemingly lawless, contract-smashing state assemblies.

A few examples make the point: Todd quietly labored to shore up the Marshall Court's claim of jurisdiction under Section 24 of the Judiciary Act of 1789; defend the sanctity of agreements (including treaties and interstate compacts, both of which mightily concerned John Marshall) in several cases involving pacts between states or with Indian nations; and generally advance Marshall's campaign for economic union and judicial control of capitalist development. In a little-read 1818 decision in *Robinson v. Campbell*, for instance, Todd refused to allow Tennessee legislators to question,

merely on the ground of shifting boundaries or inconvenience to settlers, the validity of titles originating in Virginia law and secured by an 1802 compact between Tennessee and Virginia.

To encourage stability in landholding and what he termed in *Robinson* "the purposes of justice," and perhaps to lend support (with Joseph Story) to the notion that virtuous republicans kept their promises, Todd leaned hard upon traditional English rules in land and contract cases and resisted legislative innovation whenever it seemed to limit the courts' ability to defend old, lawful claims of right against junior, merely equitable, or doubtful claims. In 1814, Todd insisted in *Vowles v. Craig*, a land case appealed from Kentucky, that a seller could not reclaim part of a tract once the land had been conveyed lawfully, even when the original survey was erroneous and the buyer received a windfall of 700 acres. Buyers should be able to *rely* on the terms of lawful agreements. In *Preston v. Browder* (1816), North Carolina land claimants pegged their hopes to a survey rendered illegal by a 1777 statute that expressly placed off limits Cherokee lands not yet ceded by treaty. Todd praised state legislators for insisting on cession in advance of surveys and refused to legitimize the specious claim. How, asked Todd in *Preston*, could Americans "parcel out vacant lands to industrious people" or provide an "easy subsistence for families" if they ignored sound laws, "provoking hostilities with . . . tribes" and "diminishing the strength of the country"? In an extensive republic, stability and prosperity depended on close attention to law and to collective as well as individual honor.

At the same time, Todd contributed heroically to the Story-Marshall campaign to stem corruptions of legal science in his native trans-Appalachian West, often by doing the spadework for subsequent constitutional interpretations. When the Panic of 1819 triggered a rash of emergency banking and contract measures (alongside Bank of the United States taxation bills) throughout the West and South, Todd and Trimble labored long and hard at circuit court sessions in Frankfort, Chillicothe, and Nashville to unhinge state debtor relief measures—among them, "three-quarters" execution laws (postponing forced sales until buyers could offer at least three-fourths of the property's pre-panic value), replevy statutes (authorizing debtors, once creditors refused to accept emergency paper money in debt settlement, to offer a state-supported bond promising future settlement), and state-funded debtor banks in Tennessee, Missouri, and Kentucky.

Time and again, the two increasingly unpopular judges blasted relief laws as unconstitutional abrogations of the contracts clause and denounced currency issued by unstable "debtor banks"; their incendiary 1819 and 1820 circuit court opinions in well-publicized actions of debt like *Bank of the United States v. Joshua Norvell* and *Bank of the United States v. James Morrison*, for instance, elicited extraordinary rage in public prints, as did pro-Bank rulings in hundreds of additional debt cases docketed after 1819. Other decisions (such as *Wayman v. Southard* and *Briscoe v. Commonwealth Bank of Kentucky*) eventually worked their way to the Supreme Court as tests of the constitutionality of emergency economic legislation and debtor bank-generated bills of credit; in the resulting "Kentucky Cases," Marshall reworked but did not fundamentally alter the research and arguments deposited in seventh circuit opinions.

Finally, Todd laid foundations for the Court's notorious opinions (Story's in 1821, Bushrod Washington's in 1823) in another Kentucky land case, *Green v. Biddle*, which pronounced the state's compensatory occupant laws an abrogation of the 1792 Separation Agreement with Virginia and thus a violation of the contract clause. In case after case on circuit, including dozens of suits brought by heirs of John Green (the plaintiff in *Green v. Biddle*), Todd beat back adverse, equitable claims of settlers and speculators in order to defend the legal right of out-of-state claimants. In an unpublished circuit court opinion in the 1819 case of *John Green's Heirs v. Bernard Gittner* involving many of the parties named in Biddle's case, Todd took dead aim at allegedly unprincipled occupant laws and aggressive deployment of the rules of equity to defeat lawful claims, laying out many of the precedents to which Story and Washington later referred. So reliant were they on Todd's work

that Story, in a letter to Todd, referred to *Green v. Biddle* as "our opinion." Todd did not mindlessly oppose local control over land titling; rather, he abhorred what he took to be a rising tide of immoral disregard for the terms of promises, whether made by states or individuals.

Todd's contributions to American jurisprudence, in short, far exceed his reputation. Few judges were so fluent in the particulars of the common law, relevant treatises, and conflicts of law jurisprudence; Story said for good reason that Todd enjoyed "the legal confidence of all who knew him." Many of the memorable constitutional statements fielded by the Marshall Court before 1825–26, when members began to soften legal purism and economic nationalism, commenced as land or contract disputes in the seventh circuit; Todd stood at the ready with copious research and well-crafted opinions in hand. Todd entered public life as a foot soldier and perhaps died a foot soldier (albeit a wealthy one, with an estate exceeding $70,000). But this unassuming closet Jeffersonian was an indispensable member of Marshall's federalizing cavalry, devoted simultaneously to his chief justice and to the moral fabric of the republic. Small wonder that his colleagues held him, to borrow the Supreme Court memorializer's elegant phrase, in "sacred regard."

—SANDRA F. VANBURKLEO

BIBLIOGRAPHY

There are no full biographies of Todd; for short sketches, see Fred Israel, "Thomas Todd," in Friedman and Israel, 1 *Justices* 407; Charles Lee, Jr., "Thomas Todd," in John Kleber, ed., *The Kentucky Encyclopedia* (1992), 888; and "The Honorable Thomas Todd, Formerly Chief Justice of the State of Kentucky . . . ," in 13 Peters (1839), iii-viii, the best contemporary sketch and the official Court memorial.

On the seventh circuit, see Thomas Speed, *History of the United States Courts in Kentucky* (1896), a still-solid descriptive account of an evolving federal judicial presence in nineteenth-century Kentucky; Mary K. Bonsteel Tachau, *Federal Courts in the Early Republic: Kentucky, 1789–1816* (1978), a pathbreaking study of personnel and practice of the earliest Kentucky bench; and Sandra F. VanBurkleo, "'The Paws of Banks': The Origins and Significance of Kentucky's Decision to Tax Federal Bankers," 9 *Journal of the Early Republic* 457 (1989), a revisionist study of the milieu giving rise to relief parties, bank taxes, and controversial seventh circuit court rulings.

For the Supreme Court during this period and Todd's contributions, see George Haskins and Herbert Johnson, *Foundations of Power: John Marshall, 1801–1815* (1981), and G. Edward White, *The Marshall Court and Cultural Change, 1815–1835* (1988), volumes 2 and 3 of the Holmes Devise.

ROBERT TRIMBLE

BORN 17 November 1776, Berkeley County,
Virginia (now part of West Virginia)

NOMINATED to the Court 11 April 1826
by John Quincy Adams

TOOK seat 9 May 1826

DIED 25 August 1828 in Paris, Kentucky

Robert Trimble had a tragically short tenure on the United States Supreme Court. Sudden illness and death cut short what many of his contemporaries thought would be a very distinguished judicial career.

Appointment to the Court capped Trimble's successful career as a Kentucky lawyer and jurist. Like many other judges, he repeatedly left the state bench to earn a higher income as a practicing attorney. Nevertheless, a flourishing and lucrative practice did not deter Trimble from accepting appointment by James Madison as the federal district judge for Kentucky in 1817. Amid bitter battles over state-federal jurisdictional questions, Trimble supported the supremacy of the federal government. His staunch advocacy of federal supremacy led John Quincy Adams to nominate Trimble to the high court on the death of Kentuckian Thomas Todd. Five senators voted against the nomination because of Trimble's belief in federal supremacy. On confirmation, he became Adams's first and only appointment to the Court.

During his brief two terms, Trimble agreed with Chief Justice John Marshall in the vast majority of cases. Of the 103 opinions delivered during those two sessions, he spoke for the Court sixteen times. Most of the cases given to Trimble dealt with technical litigation and procedural matters. His most important opinion came in *Ogden v. Saunders* (1827), when he departed from his faith in federal supremacy. Speaking for the majority, he upheld the constitutionality of a New York bankruptcy law against claims that by authorizing the discharge of the person of the debtor and the debtor's future property the act violated the contract clause of the Constitution. Marshall, along with Joseph Story and Gabriel Duvall, dissented and claimed the act impaired the obligation of contract.

Trimble's other major decision came in *The Antelope* (1827). In this case, the Court had to confront the legality of the slave trade under international law. The case involved a foreign ship seized by an American revenue cutter and the fate of its cargo of slaves. Two years before the Court had ruled in the same case that no matter how reprehensible, the slave trade had not been outlawed and thus slave ships could not be seized. Trimble reinforced this decision by upholding the return of the slaves to their owners.

Trimble caught a "malignant bilious fever" and died shortly after his second term on the Court. Eulogies spoke of the great promise he had shown as a justice and his colleagues mourned what had been the start of an illustrious career on the bench.

—MICHAEL GROSSBERG

BIBLIOGRAPHY

The only biographical sketch of Trimble is by Fred L. Israel, in Friedman and Israel, 1 *Justices* 511.

WILLIS VAN DEVANTER

BORN 17 April 1859, Marion, Indiana
NOMINATED to the Court 12 December 1910
    by William Howard Taft
TOOK seat 3 January 1911; retired 1 June 1937
DIED 8 February 1941 in New York City

Willis Van Devanter was born in Marion, Indiana, but migrated to Wyoming territory as a young man soon after completing his education at the University of Cincinnati Law School. He became involved in Wyoming politics as a member of a political machine run by Francis E. Warren. His law practice represented a series of railroads, including the Burlington and the Union Pacific, experience which later contributed to his being labeled a tool of railroad interests. Through service as chief justice of the Wyoming territorial supreme court (1889–90) and as assistant U.S. attorney general in the Department of the Interior (1897–1903), he gained knowledge in the areas of Indian rights and land claims that he also put to use during his service on the Supreme Court. Van Devanter preceded his service on the high court with seven years on the eighth United States circuit court of appeals, to which he was appointed in 1903 by Theodore Roosevelt. Van Devanter was appointed to the Court in 1910 as a result of heavy-handed lobbying by then Senator Francis E. Warren, although the appointment was opposed by William Jennings Bryan, who criticized Van Devanter's links with railroad interests.

As a member of the Court, Van Devanter lived a quiet existence, seldom making public appearances and writing few controversial opinions. His colleagues were glad to hand over to him cases in his areas of expertise, the unglamourous fields of public land law, admiralty, water rights, Indian claims, and corporation law. Van Devanter was regarded as skilled in handling procedural and jurisdictional disputes. He was one of the least productive of the justices on the Court during his twenty-six years of service, authoring only 346 opinions, one concurring opinion, and four dissents. His lack

of output is generally attributed to a severe writer's block, but others point out that Van Devanter, while apparently skilled in discussing cases in conference, lacked any strong judicial philosophy that might have prompted him to take a leading role in writing opinions.

In Van Devanter's first decade on the Court, he wrote opinions in several of his areas of expertise, including land disputes stemming from the Homestead Act, Indian claims, and cases concerning railroads. Several early rulings, including his best-known opinion in the *Second Employers' Liability Cases* (1912), indicated some progressive leanings, but these disappeared during his career on the Court.

Van Devanter's knowledge of Indian life and customs was reflected in his opinion in *United States v. Sandoval* (1913), which some commentators have suggested has a Brandeisian flavor, albeit one patronizing in tone. The case concerned the prohibition on bringing alcoholic beverages into an Indian community, in this case two pueblos held in fee simple. Van Devanter upheld the prohibition, citing studies of primitive Indian culture that ascribed to them an inferior intellect.

In the much better known *Second Employers' Liability Cases* (1912), Van Devanter's ruling reflected the progressive attitude that the exercise of broad government power was justified when the interests of the working public benefited. Congress had passed a law in 1906 making railroads liable for employees injured on the job. The Supreme Court had overturned this law in 1908, and Congress had responded with the Second Employers' Liability Law, designed to correct the provisions of the first law to which the Court had objected. Railroads responded to this second effort with more than 600 test cases, and Van Devanter's opinion was the result. He had first upheld the law in *Kieran v. Portland* (1911), which applied to injured railroad workers employed in interstate commerce.

The second opinion concerned congressional power to make a railroad liable for an employee injured in interstate commerce through the actions of a fellow employee not working in interstate commerce. Van Devanter upheld the law, arguing that Congress could do whatever was necessary "to save the act of interstate commerce from prevention or intervention, or to make that act more secure, more reliable, or more efficient." He wrote that the purpose of the statute was to prevent negligence on the part of the railroad by imposing greater liability, and that was well within the powers of Congress in regulating interstate commerce. The result of the opinion was to assign greater responsibility to the railroads, do away with the fellow servant rule, and limit the use of the doctrines of contributory negligence, all goals of various groups within the progressive movement.

Despite this opinion, however, Van Devanter remained loyal to the railroads, as was evidenced by numerous other rulings. For example, in *St. Louis, Iron Mountain and Southern Railway v. Wynne* (1912), he rejected an Arkansas law designed to impose heavy penalties on railroads whose trains killed wandering livestock. Van Devanter wrote that the statute, instead of providing an incentive for settling just claims, antagonized the railroads by depriving them of just recourse in cases of excessive fines. In *Burke v. Southern Pacific Railroad* (1914), Van Devanter's opinion strictly limited the power of the U.S. Land Office to divest railroads of land grants that had subsequently been found to have valuable mineral deposits. And, despite some assessments of his ruling in the *Second Employers' Liability Cases* as liberal, the justice showed that his support for liability legislation was not unqualified. In his opinion in *New York Central v. Winfield* (1917), he rejected the application of state liability statutes to railroads, arguing that the federal law was designed to be uniform, consistent, and to supersede state laws.

Under the leadership of the man who had appointed him, and who now joined the Court as chief justice in 1921, Van Devanter continued to be largely unproductive as a writer of opinions but served the Court in other ways. He became a good friend and confidante of Taft, and one author has suggested that perhaps the chief justice was content to have Van Devanter remain mute, so long as he voted with the conservative side and sup-

ported the more scholarly opinions penned by George Sutherland. Van Devanter is remembered during this period for his strong support of Taft's conservative leanings, for his work on Court reform in 1925, and for his authorship of one significant opinion handed down in 1927.

One of Chief Justice Taft's goals for the Court was to streamline it and give it more control over its own jurisdiction. Several pieces of legislation to that end were introduced in Congress, culminating with the Jurisdictional Act of 1925. This law reduced the number of cases heard by the Court on appeal by broadening the justices' discretion in granting writs of *certiorari*. The statute also made judgments in the courts of claims and certain decisions in the courts of appeals final and allowed constitutional questions to continue to rise from state courts on writs of error. Justice Van Devanter was the chief author of this portion of the reform legislation, and put his reputed political expertise to use as the Court's representative before congressional committees holding hearings on the bill.

Recognized by some as strongest among the small number of opinions Van Devanter wrote in the 1920s was that in *McGrain v. Daugherty* (1927). This ruling, reflecting Van Devanter's expertise in procedural matters, upheld the right of the Senate to arrest a person who had refused to honor a subpoena commanding his testimony in an investigation of the Justice Department. Van Devanter concluded that the Senate had acted properly because the investigation served a legitimate legislative purpose.

By the beginning of the 1930s, any judicial philosophy that Van Devanter had formulated could be described as strongly conservative, if not reactionary. He was described by colleague Harlan Fiske Stone as the "Commander in Chief of Judicial Reaction." He was not a supporter of civil liberties, and he opposed New Deal economic programs almost without exception. While he wrote none of the important opinions, he could be counted among the majority in every ruling overturning Roosevelt's major programs until his retirement in 1937. It has been suggested that he probably delayed his retirement simply to remain on the Court as an opponent of Roosevelt.

Van Devanter's concern about infringements on economic liberties did not carry over to protection of individual rights. A few examples will suffice. In *Near v. Minnesota* (1931), a case testing the reach of freedom of the press, Van Devanter agreed with the minority's contention that a state "press gag" law should be upheld. A year later, he dissented from the Court's invalidation of the Texas white primary law in *Nixon v. Condon* (1932). He did, however, vote to extend the Sixth Amendment right to counsel in the infamous "Scottsboro Boys" case (*Powell v. Alabama*, 1932).

Van Devanter achieved his greatest fame on the Court as one of the "Four Horsemen" who consistently opposed the economic programs of Franklin D. Roosevelt. He supported Justice Sutherland's dissent in *Home Building and Loan Association v. Blaisdell* (1934), a mortgage moratorium case in which Chief Justice Charles Evans Hughes tentatively indicated that the Court might show some sympathy for emergency legislation designed to cope with the Depression. Van Devanter went on to vote against the National Recovery Act, the Agricultural Adjustment Act, the Wagner Act, the first Frazier-Lemke Act, the Guffey law, and the gold clauses. He wrote none of these majority opinions but was a strong supporter of the conservative viewpoint. In the spring of 1937, he worked with Chief Justice Hughes to thwart Roosevelt's proposed Court-packing plan, advising his chief to respond in writing, rather than send the justices to testify to, and to be questioned by, a congressional investigating committee.

Van Devanter retired in May 1937, soon after the Court issued its first opinions in support of the New Deal philosophy. He became the first justice to take advantage of a new law permitting members of the Court to retire at full pay. Some said he also timed his retirement to create the maximum embarrassment for the president, since it now became clear that a little patience would have enabled Roosevelt to avoid the political fiasco engendered by his Court-packing

proposal. After resigning from the Supreme Court in 1937, he moved to New York where he presided in the United States district court until his death in 1941.

Historians have billed Van Devanter as an "unimaginative conservative" with strengths largely in negotiation and knowledge of judicial procedure. Louis Brandeis considered Van Devanter one of the most skillful members of the conference and compared him (favorably) to a Jesuit cardinal in his abilities. One study lists him as one of the eight "failures" in Court history because of the small number of opinions he produced and his failure to emerge as an identifiable leader among his colleagues. Others have suggested that Van Devanter has fared poorly with evaluators because he is best known as a reactionary conservative in a period dominated by liberal writers.

—REBECCA SHEPHERD SHOEMAKER

BIBLIOGRAPHY

There exists no published biography of Willis Van Devanter. The best primary source for his judicial career are his professional papers, located in the Library of Congress. Most of the detailed studies of Van Devanter's career remain unpublished dissertations. They include Lewis H. Gould, "Willis Van Devanter in Wyoming Politics, 1884–1897" (Yale, 1966); James O'Brien Howard, "Constitutional Doctrines of Mr. Justice Van Devanter" (University of Iowa, 1937); and Ronald F. Howell, "Conservative Influence on Constitutional Development, 1932–37: The Judicial Theory of Justices Van Devanter, McReynolds, Sutherland, and Butler" (Johns Hopkins, 1952).

Paul M. Hollinger has published two brief articles on aspects of Van Devanter's career: "The Appointment of Supreme Court Justice Van Devanter: A Study in Political Preferment," 12 *American Journal of Legal History* 324 (1968); and "Mr. Justice Van Devanter and the New Deal: A Note," 31 *History* 57 (1968).

Frederick Moore Vinson
Photograph by Harris and Ewing.
Collection of the Supreme Court of the United States.

FREDERICK MOORE VINSON

BORN 22 January 1890, Louisa, Kentucky

NOMINATED to the Court 6 June 1946
   by Harry S Truman

TOOK seat 24 June 1946

DIED 8 September 1953 in Washington, D.C.

Fred Vinson was educated at Kentucky Normal School, obtained a law degree in 1911 from the law department of Centre College, and subsequently practiced law in Louisa and Ashland, Kentucky, including brief service as Ashland's city attorney and commonwealth attorney. In 1924, he was elected to the House of Representative in the Kentucky ninth congressional district. Although defeated in the 1928 congressional elections, he was reelected in 1930 and ensuing elections and became a powerful member of the House Ways and Means Committee and chairman of its tax subcommittee. Vinson's judicial career began in May 1938, when President Roosevelt named him to the court of appeals for the District of Columbia. In 1942, Chief Justice Hughes appointed him chief judge of the wartime emergency court of appeals.

Vinson resigned from the bench in May 1943 to become director of the Economic Stabilization Board. He then held a series of increasingly responsible executive positions. In March 1945, he was the federal loan administrator, from April to July the director of war mobilization and reconversion, and then secretary of the treasury. Thus, before becoming chief justice, federal legislative, judicial and executive powers had been exercised by the kind and affable Fred Vinson.

Legal acumen and jurisprudential scholarship played no role in Truman's nomination and appointment of Vinson as the thirteenth chief justice. Rather, political philosophy and Vinson's personality—friendly, sociable, humorous, patient, relaxed, and respectful of others' views— were the motivating factors. Truman hoped that the latter attributes in particular would unite the increasingly fractious Supreme Court. Given the personalities and intellectual strengths of asso-ciate justices such as Felix Frankfurter, Hugo Black, William O. Douglas and Robert Jackson, even reducing that tension and dissension would have been a formidable task. Vinson, then fifty-six years old, did not succeed.

Evaluation of Vinson's seven-year Supreme Court tenure must, therefore, rest on his judicial opinions, which were nourished by an intellect that eschewed theoretical grandeur. Instead, he thought in terms of specific problems and formulated responses designed to meet present contingencies, not unforseen and unpredictable future events. His mind, ideas, and jurisprudence were, in this sense, pragmatic. Whether a longer tenure would have changed that judicial posture is doubtful. Vinson's opinions are devoid of any trace of John Marshall's statesmanship or Oliver Wendell Holmes's rhetoric. Of course, their sheer paucity may render any such comparison grossly unfair. Nevertheless, although not the most insignificant chief justice (that title might be accorded to Rutledge or Ellsworth), Vinson's opinions have virtually disappeared.

In the realm of federal legislative powers that is not surprising, since Vinson was aligned with the victors. Following the 1937 Court-packing plan, the Supreme Court conceded virtually unlimited scope to the congressional commerce power. Sustaining the validity of economic legislation did not, therefore, require or permit memorable or original judicial opinions. It did, however, enable Vinson to unremittingly endorse the concept and promote the possibility of national, rather than fragmented, power and policies. Expansion, not contraction, of the commerce clause was a constant refrain of Vinson's opinions. That is particularly evident even where Congress remained silent. On this aspect of the commerce clause's federalist dimensions, Vinson was hostile toward any state burdens on interstate or foreign commerce. Between 1937 and 1946, the Supreme Court had allowed some state regulation and taxation to operate on such commerce. Reflecting an antipathy to state encroachments on federal government domains, Vinson was very unwilling to concede their constitutionality. Only after elaborate scrutiny of national needs and interests balanced against local benefits was there a possibility that state regulations and taxes might not be invalidated. Cases such as *Independent Warehouses v. Scheele* (1947), *Bob-lo Excursion Co. v. Michigan* (1948), and *Breard v. Alexandria* (1951) exemplify this Vinson approach.

Similarly, presidential and federal executive power received Vinson's constitutional imprimatur, as exemplified in his dissent in *Youngstown Sheet & Tube Co. v. Sawyer* (1952). By a 6–3 majority, the Supreme Court held that President Truman possessed no power derived from the Constitution, either as chief executive or as commander in chief, to seize and operate privately owned steel mills. Without congressional authorization, the president's actions were unconstitutional. Even before that seizure occurred, but while Vinson was chief justice, he had privately advised Truman that, in his opinion, the Constitution permitted such a seizure, and Vinson restated that view in his dissent.

The chief justice attributed to the framers an awareness "that there is real danger in Executive weakness." Crises and emergencies clearly exposed not only this peril but also the corresponding need for almost executive omnipotence. On Vinson's assessment, these factors coalesced when Truman directed the secretary of commerce to take possession and operate the plants and facilities of specified steel companies. Given American military commitments in Korea, this presidential action to avert a steelworkers' strike came at a time when "vigor and initiative," not "inertia," were necessary. At least to Vinson, the reasons were obvious: a serious emergency existed and the nation's vital interests included the continuing production of steel. Vinson's response to critics, including those justices who perceived unbridled executive power resulting in executive tyranny and autocracy, was emphatic: "Those who suggest that this is a case involving extraordinary powers should be mindful that these are extraordinary times." For President Truman, this "hit the nail right on the head." Others, however, merely saw this dissent as but another example illustrating that Vinson, despite being elevated to the pinnacle of the Supreme

Court, remained in spirit and deed ensconced in the other branches of the federal government.

Vinson's Bill of Rights and Fourteenth Amendment opinions reinforced this perception. The evidence here is indisputable: individuals and their constitutional rights were, for the chief justice, subordinate to federal and state powers. Of course, within the context of a larger perspective—the previous history of Supreme Court decisions on such rights—this may conform with rather than deviate from the predominant trend of constitutional law. Only a quantitatively small number of civil rights cases decided during the Vinson years—*Shelley v. Kraemer* (1948), *Hurd v. Hodge* (1948), *Sipuel v. Board of Regents of the University of Oklahoma* (1948), *McLaurin v. Oklahoma State Regents* (1950) and *Sweatt v. Painter* (1950)—may represent an aberration. For others, particularly leftists ensnared in the Cold War and McCarthyism hysteria, Vinson's Supreme Court tenure offered no protection against repressive congressional laws and committees, executive investigations or criminal prosecutions.

The most notorious and, in terms of practical consequences, the most important Vinson opinion sustained, against First Amendment free speech challenges, the convictions of twelve U.S. Communist party leaders. Their indictment under the 1940 Smith Act alleged a conspiracy to teach or advocate the forceful overthrow of the United States government and membership in an organization advocating such an overthrow. In his plurality opinion, Vinson transformed the Holmes/Brandeis formulation and application of the clear and present danger test. The constitutionally protected realm of free speech could be legislatively invaded to the extent necessary to obviate dangers provided its gravity and probability of occurring had been assessed.

Two immediate results ensued from *Dennis v. United States* (1951). First, the constitutionality of the Smith Act was upheld. Second, other federal prosecutions could and did successfully proceed against what government officials considered to be potentially subversive doctrines. Noncriminal sanctions and deprivations applied to Communists and others suspected of disloyalty were also constitutionally vindicated by

Vinson's refutation of counterarguments premised on the Bill of Rights in such cases as *American Communications Association v. Douds* (1950); *Bailey v. Richardson* (1951), and *Joint Anti-Fascist Refugee Committee v. McGrath* (1951).

To what extent did these opinions rest on Vinson's view of the necessity to sustain and defer to exercises of national and federal authority? Some relative indication can be gleaned from his First Amendment free speech decisions involving, via the Fourteenth Amendment, state laws and regulations. At least on some occasions he was prepared to invalidate local ordinances to vindicate assertions of individual rights. This civil libertarian posture is revealed in *Saia v. New York* (1948), *Niemotko v. Maryland* (1951) and *Kunz v. New York* (1951). However, counter examples such as *Kovacs v. Cooper* (1949) and *Feiner v. New York* (1951) return Vinson's image to that of an authoritarian advocate.

Similarly, within the criminal law context, despite some ambivalence, governmental interests in law enforcement, not individual rights and immunities, prevailed. This general stance pervaded the plethora of procedural and substantive criminal law issues in state and federal courts, where Vinson usually rejected Fourth Amendment claims. However, this trend was not completely devoid of exceptions. Indeed, a 1940 Fourth Amendment Vinson opinion in the court of appeals (*Nueslein v. District of Columbia*) clearly indicated the possibility of such occurrences. Successful invocation of defendants' rights during the Vinson era are few, but do include *Niemotko v. Maryland* (1951), *Fowler v. Rhode Island* (1953), *Jennings v. Illinois* (1951), and *Brock v. North Carolina* (1953).

Even more tentative was Vinson's approach to cases under the First Amendment's establishment clause, which *Everson v. Board of Education* (1947) extended to the states via incorporation through the Fourteenth Amendment. Two obvious conclusions emerge. First, Vinson was prepared to apply the Bill of Rights, at least to some extent, to the states with the consequential diminution of state authority and federalism implications. Second, this was only the commencement, not the end, of Supreme Court explorations among the religion clauses. Necessarily, Vinson's votes to allow school districts to reimburse parents for transporting their children to parochial schools in *Everson*, to invalidate a released time program where ministers taught religion in schools during schooltime (*Illinois ex rel. McCollum v. Board of Education,* 1948), and to uphold such a program where students had such instruction outside school premises (*Zorach v. Clauson,* 1952) are, therefore, not reliable guides as to how his views concerning federal and state authority, individual rights, and the judicial function might eventually have coalesced to mould his posture in this aspect of First Amendment jurisprudence.

In stark contrast, it is usually suggested that no such equivocation surrounded Vinson's utilization of constitutional law to eliminate racial discrimination. Three categories of cases involving the equal protection clause are involved. First is the invalidation of racial restrictions on Japanese pertaining to landholding and fishing rights in *Oyama v. California* (1948) and *Takahashi v. Fish and Game Commission* (1948). Second, there are the cases involving restrictive covenants that prevented African Americans from buying houses in white neighborhoods. In *Shelley v. Kraemer* (1948), Vinson spoke for the Court in holding that the equitable state court enforcement of such private racial covenants constituted state action forbidden by the Fourteenth Amendment's equal protection clause. That decision was also applied by the chief justice, in *Hurd v. Hodge* (1948), to the District of Columbia.

Doctrinally, these cases are among Vinson's most interesting, complex, and adventurous opinions. Even so, it is doubtful whether they reveal any significant new dimension to his decisions or decision-making process. Indeed, there is a conspicuous effort to locate *Shelley* within the parameters of previous state action cases, and to continue to see that concept as a rigid limitation on, rather than a malleable entrance to, Fourteenth Amendment rights. Significantly, Vinson subsequently dissented in *Barrows v. Jackson* (1953) when all the other justices held that a state court's award of damages for breach of a racial covenant infringed the equal protection clause.

State segregated graduate education constituted the third category of racial discrimination cases in which Vinson participated. State action in *Sipuel* (1948), *McLaurin* (1950) and *Sweatt* (1950) unconstitutionally denied African American university students equal protection of the laws. In one respect, these decisions simultaneously pointed in antithetical directions: the separate but equal doctrine was not rejected or abandoned, but the application of a rigorous equal facilities test eliminated, as a practical matter, the maintenance of racial segregation in state graduate and professional schools. Ultimately, that tension would be broken in *Brown v. Board of Education* (1954). By then, however, Vinson was no longer on the Court.

Compared to other justices, including chief justices, Vinson wrote comparatively few opinions. Even so, it has been suggested "that Vinson did all his 'writing' with his hands in his pockets, outlining the general approach to his clerk[s] and then suggesting but few revisions in the draft." Therefore, how and why he cast his vote in deciding cases may well have been more influential and may be more revealing than his written opinions. A further impediment is the unevenness of quality, in prose and legal analysis, among those opinions. At best, they were succinct and precise. As a result, their clarity was bereft of irrelevant erudition and relentlessly drove toward a seemingly inevitable result. The worst were vacuous. Fine distinctions and silent avoidance of precedents are their dominant characteristics.

All of Vinson's perspectives, however, gained sustenance from a single premise: authority, not freedom, ought to prevail when a choice had to be made. If, almost without exception, that dictated the constitutional validity of federal and state exercises of legislative, executive, and judicial powers, the result was to be celebrated as a victory for patriotism, not decreed as a defeat of liberty. Whether or not Vinson's sentiments are endorsed, their promulgation has one virtue: the inevitable juxtaposition of the opposing view that mandates sacrificing the common good to individual rights and freedoms. That, of course, especially for the Supreme Court, is the enduring American dilemma: when, where, and how majoritarianism or constitutionalism should be triumphant.

—JAMES A. THOMSON

BIBLIOGRAPHY

The Vinson papers are in the Margaret I. King Library at the University of Kentucky in Lexington. General studies on Vinson include Francis A. Allen, "Chief Justice Vinson and the Theory of Constitutional Government: A Tentative Appraisal," 49 *Northwestern University Law Review* 3 (1954) and John P. Frank, "Fred Vinson and the Chief Justiceship," 21 *University of Chicago Law Review* 212 (1954). The most critical view of Vinson is in Fred Rodell, *Nine Men: A Political History of the Supreme Court from 1790 to 1955* (1955).

For analyses of the "Vinson Court" see C. Herman Pritchett, *Civil Liberties and the Vinson Court* (1954); Jan Palmer, *The Vinson Court Era: The Supreme Court's Conference Votes: Data and Analysis* (1990); and Francis H. Rudko, *Truman's Court: A Study in Judicial Restraint* (1988).

For particular cases and issues, see Michael R. Belknap, *Cold War Political Justice: The Smith Act, the Communist Party, and American Civil Liberties* (1977); Maeva Marcus, *Truman and The Steel Seizure Case: The Limits of Presidential Power* (1977); and Clement E. Vose, *Caucasians Only: The Supreme Court, the NAACP, and the Restrictive Covenant Cases* (1967).

MORRISON REMICK WAITE

BORN 29 November 1816, Lyme, Connecticut

NOMINATED to the Court 19 January 1874 by
    Ulysses S. Grant

TOOK seat 21 January 1874

DIED 23 March 1888 in Washington, D.C.

Morrison Waite's appointment as the seventh chief justice of the Supreme Court was hardly auspicious. For one thing, Waite was nominated by President Ulysses S. Grant, renowned for heading one of the most corrupt administrations in American history. Moreover, Waite was not even Grant's first choice. Following unsuccessful attempts to place Roscoe Conkling, Caleb Cushing, and George H. Williams on the high court, and after consideration of at least two others, Grant submitted Waite's name to replace Chief Justice Samuel Chase on Jan. 21, 1874. Two days later an exhausted Congress confirmed the nomination. As Rockwood Hoar observed, Waite had been "that luckiest of all individuals known to the law, an innocent third party without notice."

That Waite had been "without notice" prior to his appointment was fairly certain. He was born in Lyme, Connecticut, on November 29, 1816 to an old New England family that produced a number of lawyers, including his father, Henry, who served as chief justice of the state supreme court. Like his father and grandfather before him, Morrison attended Bacon Academy and Yale College. After graduation, he studied law in his father's office, but in 1838, moved to Maumee City, Ohio, where he was admitted to the bar and began a law practice largely devoted to commercial and corporate transactions. In 1840, he returned briefly to Connecticut to marry Amelia C. Warner, a second cousin. Ten years later, he moved to Toledo and set up practice with his younger brother Richard.

Waite's political involvement during his years building a successful law practice was minimal. He served briefly on the Toledo city council, sat for one term in the state legislature, and made an unsuccessful run for Congress in 1862. Thanks in large part to geographic circumstances, Waite was appointed by President Grant in 1871 to serve as counsel for the United States during the arbitration negotiations in Geneva over the *Alabama* claims from the Civil War. Following his return from Switzerland, he served as delegate and president of the Ohio state constitutional convention, the position he held when nominated in January 1874 to the Supreme Court.

The membership of the Court that Waite was chosen to lead reflected a variety of abilities, personalities, and beliefs. There was one Democratic holdover from the pre–Civil War period, Nathan Clifford, whose age and increasing senility proved a constant challenge to Waite's patience and good nature. Lincoln's former political manager, David Davis, harbored an ongoing desire for the presidency, as perhaps did Stephen J. Field of California. Intellectually, the two dominant forces on the Court were Samuel Miller and Joseph P. Bradley, the latter becoming Waite's most consistent ally, while the former would always resent the fact that he had not been elevated to the chief justiceship by Grant. The rest of the Court consisted of Republican appointees of lesser talents: Noah H. Swayne, Ward Hunt, and William Strong. While never a dominant intellectual force on the Court, Waite was an "adept" social and managerial leader, using his inherent graciousness and good cheer, along with his power as chief justice to assign opinions, to mold an unusually harmonious Court.

Over the course of Waite's fourteen-year tenure as chief justice, the Supreme Court decided some 3,470 cases with opinions, of which 967 were authored by Waite himself. His tendency to go along with the Court's majority was evidenced by the fact that he dissented in only fifty-four cases, less than 2 percent of the total number of decisions. The large number of cases, as well as the variety of issues confronted, was less a testament to the Court's interests and work ethic than to the simple lack of discretion the Supreme Court exercised during this period in hearing appeals.

Among the public and private law issues that Waite and the Supreme Court encountered between 1874 and 1888, two were of paramount importance. One centered around the scope and meaning of the Reconstruction amendments, particularly as they affected the lives and future of the 3.5 million former slaves. The other, and to some extent related, issue was the role of government with regard to the growth of industrialism and the emergence of big business in late nineteenth-century America. Waite's contributions to the resolution of both these concerns are therefore key to understanding his judicial philosophy and his role in American constitutional development.

Following the Civil War, Republicans in Congress had passed a series of measures intended to protect the economic, social and political rights of African Americans in the South who had recently been emancipated under the Thirteenth Amendment. As a further guarantee, Congress also enacted the Fourteenth Amendment, which forbade states to deprive any citizen of their "life, liberty or property . . . without due process of law" and which required states to grant to all citizens the "equal protection of the laws," as well as the "privileges and immunities" of all citizens. When this still proved insufficient to ensure the full participation of the freedmen in the political process of Reconstruction in the South, Republicans added the Fifteenth Amendment to the Constitution in 1868. Under this amendment, the right to vote could "not be denied or abridged by the United States or by any state on account of race, color, or previous condition of servitude." Sections in both the Fourteenth and Fifteenth Amendments gave Congress authority to enforce the amendments' provisions "by appropriate legislation."

Following reports of ongoing terrorism directed against blacks attempting to vote or participate in political activities, Congress passed a series of three measures in 1870–71 known as the enforcement acts. These measures set out a wide variety of possible crimes directed against potential voters, and provided the machinery for federal enforcement through the Department of Justice. On March 27, 1876, the Supreme Court announced two decisions dealing with convictions under these statutes: Chief Justice Waite

authored the majority opinion in both. In *United States v. Cruikshank,* the Court reviewed the convictions of three men accused of massacring at least 105 blacks and three whites outside the Grant Parish courthouse in Colfax, Louisiana, on Easter Sunday, 1873. In overturning the convictions, Waite admitted that the right to assemble peacefully was constitutionally protected, and that under the Fifteenth Amendment Congress could protect this right from infringement on account of race. Indeed, they had done so in the enforcement acts. The problem was whether or not the indictments under which the defendants had been tried were sufficient in law, and Waite argued they were not, since they had failed to allege that the murders had been committed because of the victims' race. "We may suspect that race was the cause of the hostility," Waite concluded, "but it is not so averred."

In *United States v. Reese,* Waite went further and declared two sections of the May 1870 enforcement act unconstitutional. In overturning the convictions of two Kentucky election inspectors for refusing to allow one William Garner, a citizen "of African descent," to vote, Waite held that the Fifteenth Amendment did not "confer the right of suffrage upon anyone." It did prohibit states from discriminating or "giving preference" in exercising voting rights on account of race, but the statutes under review did not specifically require this; hence, they were invalid.

Waite's opinions in *Reese* and *Cruikshank* were part of a series of Supreme Court rulings after 1873 that seemingly left the Reconstruction amendments and the various federal laws enforcing them "almost wholly ineffective" in protecting the rights of blacks in the South. In *Virginia v. Rives* (1880), the Court ruled that the absence of blacks on juries was not proof of racial discrimination. And most prominently, in the *Civil Rights Cases* (1883), the Court struck down the Civil Rights Act of 1875, which forbade racial discrimination in places of public accommodation. Yet a careful review of Waite's, and the Court's, opinions in other cases during these years suggests something other than outright hostility to the interests of African Americans. In *Strauder v. West Virginia* (1880), a state law requiring all-white juries was struck down as a violation of the equal protection clause of the

Morrison Remick Waite
Photograph by C. M. Bell.
Collection of the Supreme Court of the United States.

Fourteenth Amendment. And that same year, in *Neal v. Delaware,* the Court held that state judges could not exclude blacks from jury duty.

Moreover, Waite supported strong congressional powers, particularly when it came to protecting voting rights. In three cases, *Ex parte Siebold* (1880), *Ex parte Clark* (1880), and most importantly *Ex parte Yarbrough* in 1884, the Supreme Court, with Waite's concurrence, upheld federal authority to protect voters from racially motivated infringement of their rights in state and local elections and under any circumstances in federal elections. This commitment to "preserving federalism," as one scholar has put it, entailed a willingness to accept broad national authority while recognizing the limits of that authority in light of state actions and prerogatives.

To that extent, Waite was neither ahead of nor behind the views of most moderate white northerners, or of southern leaders such as South Carolina's Wade Hampton, who accepted black social inferiority, but retained a concern for the protection of the "free ballot and a fair count." Like many other white Americans of the time, Waite believed the key to the future for African Americans in the South was education. He actively supported the Slater and Peabody Funds, two northern philanthropies set up to provide money for schools and colleges in the South for blacks, and he unsuccessfully lobbied Congress to provide federal funds for such efforts.

Waite's willingness to abandon blacks in the South to the mercy of their state governments despite the due process and equal protection guarantees of the Fourteenth Amendment reflected an increasing attention after 1874 to similar claims made by businessmen in defense of their property interests. The late nineteenth century witnessed the tremendous growth of industry and business in America, a growth fueled by massive immigration, technological innovations, and government support on all levels. Changes resulting from this expansion were not entirely welcome, and various groups in American society, particularly farmers and workers, responded through organization and political action. At the same time, businessmen and their attorneys discovered a federal judiciary increasingly willing to consider claims that economic regulation was unreasonable and, more important, unconstitutional.

Railroads were emblematic of late nineteenth-century industrialism, and in the eyes of American farmers were the root cause of most of their troubles. During the late 1860s, farmer protest groups sprang up around the country, and in the Midwest were particularly successful in capturing control of state legislatures. These states enacted a series of laws, known as the Granger laws, which regulated railroads and related businesses. In the landmark ruling *Munn v. Illinois* (1876), Waite, speaking for a 7–2 majority of the Court, upheld an 1871 Illinois statute regulating grain storage warehouses. Waite rejected the argument that the state regulations had deprived the warehouse owners of their property without due process of law and sustained the laws as a valid use of state police power. Under this power, according to Waite, "the government regulates the conduct of citizens one towards another, and the manner in which each shall use his own property, when such regulation becomes necessary for the public good."

If government can regulate private property, under what circumstances could it do so? For Waite, those circumstances existed when "one devotes his property to a use in which the public has an interest." The Chicago grain storage elevators of Ira Munn were an important part of a vast national commercial network, and were therefore affected with a "public interest." Finally, Waite rejected the notion that the laws denied owners "reasonable compensation," and that in any case, what was or was not reasonable was a "judicial" matter to be decided in the courts. The power to fix maximum rates is implied in the power to regulate, he asserted. "We know that this is a power which may be abused; but that is no argument against its existence. For protection against abuses by legislatures the people must resort to the polls, not to the courts."

Scholars still debate the extent to which Waite's opinion in *Munn* was his own and not Justice Bradley's and the degree to which he misused the concept of public interest as enunciated two hundred years earlier by the English jurist Lord Hale. Nonetheless, his decision in this case clearly reflects a number of themes that appear throughout his career on the bench. Support for state regulation of business was certainly a principal theme. As a successful railroad and corporation attorney before he came to the Supreme Court, Waite was not unsympathetic to the interests and concerns of businessmen. Moreover, as a Republican, Waite had little patience with the states' rights arguments of the pre–Civil War era. Yet he also recognized that changing times and economic circumstances required some limitations on corporate activity, and along with a democratic faith in popular sovereignty, believed that state legislatures should be the source of such limitations. In his view of state police powers, corporations, and the contract clause of the Constitution, Waite harkened back to Taney's ruling in the *Charles River Bridge* case (1836). For example, in *Wright v. Nagle* (1879), Waite allowed the state of Georgia authority to authorize new bridges for its rivers on the grounds that there was no "exclusive right to public franchises." And in *Stone v. Mississippi* (1880), Waite upheld a state ban on a previously granted lottery charter, arguing that "the legislature cannot bargain away the police power of the State," a power that "extends to all matters affecting the public health or the public morals."

As he had in *Munn*, Waite found little merit in businessmen's contention that economic regulation was a deprivation of their property rights under the due process clause of the Fourteenth Amendment or a violation of the contract clause of the Constitution. In *Railroad Company v. Richmond* (1878), he warned that "appropriate regulation of the use of property is not 'taking' property within the meaning of the constitutional prohibition." And in a series of decisions after 1878, the Waite Court upheld state regulation of railroad rates, culminating in 1886 with its ruling in *Stone v. Farmers' Loan & Trust Company*. In that case, the state of Mississippi had specifically granted the Mobile and Ohio Railroad Company the power to fix rates. Subsequently, the state had created a special commission with the power to determine reasonable rates and charges for railroads operating within the state. The railroad contended that this was a direct violation of its charter rights and a deprivation of its property without due process of law.

In rejecting the railroad's arguments, Waite noted that the "great purpose" of the statute was to "regulate in some matters of a police nature the use of railroads in the State." Citing *Munn* and the other railroad cases he upheld both the states' power to regulate rates and their use of a commission in doing so. Even though the railroads were given authority to fix rates, such a grant was not a "renunciation of the right of legislative control so as to secure reasonable rates." Remarkably, Waite did make an important concession to the railroads in the case. The chief justice admitted that "it is not to be inferred that this power of limitation or regulation is itself without limit. . . . Under pretense of regulating fares and freights, the State cannot require a railroad corporation to carry persons or property without reward; neither cannot it do that which in law amounts to a taking of private property for public use, without just compensation, or without due process of law." Although not completely appreciated at the time, this statement would provide an opening wedge in the 1890s for the Court to begin striking down the very kinds of economic regulation now being upheld. With Waite gone, and the addition of the "new conservative" justices such as Gray and Brewer, the dissents of Justice Field in the Granger and railroad rate cases would become the basis of a new line of majority opinions striking down state economic and social regulations.

Waite's support for state regulatory authority also encompassed financial and debt obligations. Again, the issue involved railroads. To encourage and assist the construction of railroads, many states and localities had authorized large bond issues as a means of financing public improvements. When the economic benefits did not appear and those issuing the bonds were forced to assume an unwelcome debt, some states stepped in and attempted to repudiate or reduce the debt. In a series of cases Waite and the Supreme Court upheld these state actions. In *Louisiana v. Lumel* (1882), for example, Waite cited the Eleventh Amendment's prohibition on suits by citizens of one state against another state in blocking a suit by an outside bondholder when Louisiana attempted such a repudiation in 1879. According to Waite, "The officers owe duty to the state, and have no contractual relations with the bond-holders. They can act only as the State directs them to act, and hold as the State allows them to hold."

As was true with respect to civil rights, Waite supported broad national regulatory authority over commercial matters, believing that the commerce power must "keep pace with the progress of the country." In 1866, Congress gave the Western Union Telegraph Company the "right to construct, maintain, and operate lines of telegraph through and over any portion of the public domain of the United States." Shortly thereafter, the Florida legislature granted the Pensacola Telegraph Company the right to construct and run telegraph lines in several northern counties that connected to other states. In *Pensacola Telegraph Company v. Western Union Company* (1878), Waite rejected an attempt by the Pensacola Company to prevent the Western Union franchise from operating in those areas covered by its service. He declared that the authority of the government of the United States "operates upon every foot of territory under its jurisdiction. It legislates for the whole nation, and is not embarrassed by State lines. Its peculiar duty is to protect one part of the country from encroachment by another upon the national rights which belong to all." The state chartered corporation, therefore, had to give way to a federally supported one.

Similarly, in the *Sinking Fund Cases* (1879), the chief justice supported significant national control over federally chartered corporations. Waite upheld congressional statutes requiring the Union Pacific and Central Pacific railroads to set up special funds explicitly reserved for the repayment of the debt on bonds issued by the federal government to enable the original construction of the railroads. In doing so, he cited the critical role railroads had come to play in national commerce, as well as the fact that as national corporations they were subject to federal restrictions. Going back to *Munn,* Waite stated that both railroads were private corporations whose property is "to a large extent devoted to public uses." As such, these businesses were subject to regulation, including "regulations by which suitable provision will be secured in advance for the payment of existing debts when they fall due." Requiring the railroads to create these sinking funds was a kind of "deposit of security" intended to protect the public and insure the "solvency" of the railroads themselves.

Morrison Waite's commitment to "preserving federalism" in the area of civil rights can therefore be seen as of a piece with his economic views. Although it would be Justice Field's dissents that would provide the basis for the Supreme Court's rejection of economic and social legislation in the 1890s and after, Waite's view of state and national regulatory powers was never totally repudiated, even during the Progressive Era and the zenith of judicial activism in protecting corporate property rights from government interference in the 1920s. To that extent, his constitutional philosophy could be seen as part of the liberal tradition of American politics. At the same time, his faith in a legislative rather than judicial approach to solving the problems of an increasingly complex industrialized society would seem to place him in the "judicial restraint" tradition of modern-day conservatives.

According to Felix Frankfurter, Waite's opinions on the Supreme Court were generally "humdrum, matter of fact, dry lawyer's English." It was a characterization Waite himself would probably not have disputed. His strengths were his character and leadership, and an ability to recognize his own limitations. A moderation that provoked disparaging evaluations of his abilities and beliefs during his tenure now seem more like the work of a judicial statesman in the tradition of other great chief justices like John Marshall and Earl Warren. He most certainly helped restore the prestige of the Supreme Court as an institution to at least its stature before the "self-inflicted wound" of the *Dred Scott* decision in 1857. That he was devoted to his Court service is undeniable. In 1885, he suffered a breakdown, probably from overwork, but refused to retire. Three years later, he was still drafting opinions and leading the Court—almost literally up to the moment of his death on March 23, 1888, of pneumonia.

—ROBERT M. GOLDMAN

BIBLIOGRAPHY

The main body of primary source material is located in the Waite collection at the Library of Congress. Materials relating to the Supreme Court during Waite's chief justiceship are located in the Supreme Court records at the National Archives. Waite has not gone unnoticed by historians. There are two full-length biographies, the more recent and balanced is C. Peter Magrath, *Morrison Waite: The Triumph of Character* (1963). The most comprehensive account of the Supreme Court during Waite's tenure can be found in Charles Fairman's contribution to the Holmes Devise, *Reconstruction and Reunion, 1864–88*, part two, (1987). For an appraisal of Waite as chief justice, see D. Grier Stephenson, "The Chief Justice as Leader: The Case of Morrison R. Waite," 14 *William & Mary Law Review* 899 (1973). A persuasive reevaluation of Waite's civil rights decisions is Michael Les Benedict, "Preserving Federalism: Reconstruction and the Waite Court," 1978 *Supreme Court Review* 39. Two older studies still worthwhile are Felix Frankfurter, *The Commerce Clause Under Marshall, Taney and Waite* (1937), and the chapter on Waite in Kenneth Umbreit, *Our Eleven Chief Justices* (1937).

Earl Warren
Photograph by Harris and Ewing.
Collection of the Supreme Court of the United States.

EARL WARREN

Born 19 March 1891, Los Angeles,
    California
Nominated as chief justice 30 Sep. 1953
    on recess appointment by Dwight D.
    Eisenhower
Took seat 1 March 1954; retired 23 June 1969
Died 9 July 1974 in Washington, D.C.

The constitutional mark left at the end of Earl Warren's fifteen-year term as the fourteenth chief justice of the Supreme Court of the United States reflected the tremendous changes in American society during the 1950s and 1960s. These changes involved a significant expansion in the rights and liberties of individuals in the name of securing the goals of social and political equality. Warren's judicial legacy is striking in two important respects: First, the decisions of the Court he led for fifteen years contributed substantially to the expansion of the constitutional rights of Americans and to the expansion of the role of the federal government in enforcing and protecting those rights. Second, his willingness to adapt and create legal doctrines to fit his ideological beliefs and commitments represented an enhanced role for the Supreme Court in superintending governmental decision making on an order of magnitude not seen since the New Deal.

Especially significant during the time of Warren's stewardship was the Supreme Court's role in eradicating vestiges of public and private discrimination, in expanding the scope of protections for individuals accused of committing crimes, in ensuring the rights of free expression and religious freedom, and in improving the processes of representation and democracy in order to ensure a more responsive and effective government. To his critics, Warren is held responsible for expanding precipitously the powers of the judiciary. The Warren Court, it is charged, replaced the will of the elective branches of government with the will of unelected judges and limited the discretion of local officials to establish procedures and policies free of second-guessing by the national judiciary.

Whether supportive or hostile to the outcomes and strategies of Earl Warren and the Court over which he presided for nearly twenty years, all agree that Warren played an enormously influential role as leader of a fractured institution during a critical period in recent American history. The revolution in American law wrought by the Warren Court was, as Anthony Lewis put it, a "revolution made by judges." And, like any revolution, this one had its leader—Earl Warren.

The bulk of Earl Warren's pre-Court years were spent serving his home state of California. Warren grew up in the central California city of Bakersfield; he received an undergraduate degree from the University of California, Berkeley, and a law degree from Berkeley's Boalt Hall School of Law. Following service during World War I, Warren began his legal career as deputy city attorney with the city of Oakland, and next served as deputy district attorney for Alameda County. He served for fourteen years as the county's district attorney and, in 1939, was elected as California's attorney general. In 1942, he was elected governor of the state, a position he held until his appointment to the Court.

There is an incongruity between Earl Warren's service in the cause of expanding the civil rights and liberties enjoyed by American citizens in his role as chief justice and his participation in important episodes in California history in which rights and liberties were curtailed. As attorney general, Earl Warren publicly, and rather hyperbolically, opposed the nomination of Berkeley law professor Max Radin to the California supreme court. In doing so, Warren engaged in the sort of red-baiting that he would come to despise, asserting, without credible evidence, "that Radin constantly gives aid and comfort to Communists and other radicals. . . ."

Warren's service as attorney general and governor will forever be remembered for his decision to order the evacuation of Japanese Americans from their homes and to intern them in various camps throughout California. While Warren would come to express regret for this decision decades later, at the time he defended the decision vigorously. In a 1943 speech, Warren warned that "if the Japs are released, no one will be able to tell a saboteur from any other Jap." Accordingly, he urged, "we don't propose to have the Japs back in California during this war if there is any lawful means of preventing it." By his actions, Warren "engineered one of the most conspicuously racist and repressive governmental acts in American history." Although his role in the evacuation of Japanese Americans stands in sharp contrast to his later role, as chief justice, in securing the civil rights and liberties of American citizens, his contributions over the course of his public life to the cause of social justice must include a significant caveat.

In his role as the chief law enforcement officer for the state of California, Warren was a vigorous crime fighter and effective administrator. He fought organized crime by prosecuting the fruits of organized criminal activities, including gambling, bootlegging, and graft. He ran for governor on a platform of good government and independence from special interests. Although a lifelong Republican, he received the Democratic nomination as well. While it has become a commonplace to view Warren's pre-Court career as a Republican prosecutor as inconsistent with his commitment on the bench to the rights of accused, Warren was known to be fair, in his law enforcement career, to the rights of defendants as well as victims. He was, in the words of Professor Arthur Sherry, "keenly conscious of the risk of convicting an innocent person" and scrupulously monitored his staff's law enforcement conduct. On balance, Warren's reputation after nearly two decades of service to California's citizens was as a solid, well-meaning, and rather nonpartisan public servant.

Earl Warren was well known to President Dwight Eisenhower as an important figure in national politics. He had run for vice-president on the losing ticket in 1948 and had been a prominent candidate for the Republican party's presidential nomination in 1952. Eisenhower made and then kept his promise to appoint Warren to the Court early in his presidential term, and named him to replace Chief Justice Fred Vinson after the latter's death in the autumn of 1953.

Historians' judgment that Earl Warren ranks with John Marshall as one of the two greatest chief justices in the Supreme Court's history is based on Warren's performance as a leader of the Court during a time of tremendous social and political controversy. While scholars have struggled to carve out from Warren's decisions a discernible judicial philosophy and jurisprudential compass, Warren has never been regarded a great jurist, as a judge who has shaped the course of the law through his written opinions. One of Warren's biographers, G. Edward White, has argued that there is indeed a coherent jurisprudential line in Warren's judicial writings. Warren, White claims, "equated judicial lawmaking with neither the dictates of reason . . . nor the demands imposed by an institutional theory of the judge's role, nor the alleged 'command' of the constitutional text, but rather with his own reconstruction of the ethical structure of the Constitution."

While this "ethicist" approach to judging pointed to particular judicial results—quite liberal results—it is less clear that such a description captures fully the structure of reasoning in Warren's decisions. Quite often, Warren's opinions are stolid and doctrinally underdeveloped. In other instances, notably *Brown v. Board of Education* (1954) and *Miranda v. Arizona* (1966), Warren relied on a body of empirical data and social science without explaining adequately the bases of this approach and the link between the empirical evidence and the stated doctrine. Nevertheless, Earl Warren stands out as a great chief justice, one whom Justice William J. Brennan described as the "Superchief," because of his performance as leader of the Court. Rather than exercising influence through an outpouring of carefully crafted judicial decisions, Warren was content to affect the course of the law chiefly through the powers of the office of chief justice and especially through his considerable interpersonal skills and political savvy. His most notable victories, namely *Brown*, *Baker v. Carr* (1962), and *Miranda*, reflect the work of a skillful judicial leader, one with a keen sense for politics as "the art of the possible."

The Supreme Court that Warren joined in 1954 was fractured by conflicts among strong judicial personalities. Warren's predecessor, Fred Vinson, had failed miserably at the task of contending with the justices of the Court. Intimidated by the Court's most forceful members and intellectually underequipped, Vinson had died frustrated with his inability to shepherd these nine men through the minefield of cases that the Court had before it during the postwar decade. By contrast, Warren proved remarkably able to deal with conflicts among his colleagues in his first years on the Court. His most challenging task was in bringing together the alliances formed among the intellectual leaders of the Court. This group included Felix Frankfurter, Robert Jackson, Hugo Black, William O. Douglas, and later in Warren's term, John Marshall Harlan and William J. Brennan. While Black, Douglas, and Brennan represented, across a range of cases, one faction and Jackson, Frankfurter, and later Harlan, represented another, each of these justices were individualistic and even obstinate in ways that made the Supreme Court a difficult institution to manage in the first decade of Warren's leadership.

The mercurial Frankfurter, a former Harvard Law School professor and a judicial conservative, posed a special challenge to Warren. Warren successfully placated Frankfurter in his first couple of years on the Court. Faced with the desegregation decisions immediately on taking the oath of chief justice, these first years were critical in shaping the direction of the Warren Court. Frankfurter initially admired Warren for his shrewd political instincts and his apparent willingness to learn the ropes from the more senior justice. By Frankfurter's final term on the Court in 1962, however, the relationship between the two men had soured, as Warren solidified his grip over the increasingly liberal Court majority.

Not surprisingly, Warren's relationship with the justices who were more sympathetic to his ideological instincts posed less of a challenge. While Black and Douglas were no less powerful personalities than Frankfurter and Jackson, their energies could be more easily turned by Warren to furthering their jurisprudential agendas through written decisions. The two liberals remained rather cantankerous, however, notwithstanding the fact that they had a strong ideological ally in Warren. For instance, Black's persistent squabbles with Jackson and Frankfurter were beyond Warren's ability to control. Douglas was frequently incorrigible as well. Ever the skilled politician, Warren remained wisely patient, waiting until Jackson and Frankfurter retired and taking advantage of both the considerable experience and intellect of Black and Douglas and of the qualities of the new justices to move the Court past internecine conflicts and in a more pronounced liberal direction.

By far the most important ally in this quest would be William J. Brennan, who served with Warren for nearly the entire fifteen years. Brennan is widely regarded as the intellectual catalyst of the Warren Court's doctrinal revolution. Warren soon found that he could count on Brennan to draft intellectually rigorous opinions defending results that jibed with Warren's preferences and philosophies. In cases such as *New York Times v. Sullivan* (1964), a key libel case, and *Baker v. Carr* (1962), the reapportionment decision, Brennan fashioned creative rationales for expanding the scope of individual rights under the Constitution. The Warren-Brennan alliance represented the key to the success of the Court's expansion of individual rights and of the role of the judiciary. Where Black and Douglas were idiosyncratic and often divisive in their temperament and in their jurisprudence, Warren and Brennan proved the perfect combination of political and intellectual skills mobilized in the pursuit of a doctrinal agenda.

Earl Warren's ability as a leader was tested immediately on his appointment to the Court. By the time of his arrival, the Court had heard arguments in a consolidated series of cases challenging the constitutionality of segregated public schools. The most ambitious of the claims raised by the appellants was the call for an overruling of *Plessy v. Ferguson* (1896), in which the Court had enunciated the doctrine of "separate but equal" and had upheld the constitutionality of segregated public facilities. At conference following the oral argument in the first case to reach the Court in the spring of 1953, the Court was divided. On taking office, Warren presided over reargument in the case and then set out to manufacture a unanimous court for the proposition that segregated public schools constituted an unconstitutional deprivation of the equal protection of the laws.

Scholars who have examined closely the decision-making process in the segregation cases agree that Warren played a pivotal role in securing assent by each justice to the ruling in *Brown*. This road to unanimity began with Warren's expressed view in the conference held after reargument in the first segregation cases that *Plessy* should be overruled. He worked on securing a unanimous result through conversations with the fence-sitting justices and through circulation of the drafts of an opinion in the case. Warren's decision for the unanimous Court in *Brown* concentrated on taking the doctrinal legs out from under *Plessy*, relying on sociological data and on a forceful explication of the view, eloquently presented to the Court by NAACP lawyer Thurgood Marshall, that "separate is inherently unequal."

When the time came to fashioning a decision in the remedial portion of the segregation disputes, Warren turned to Felix Frankfurter and borrowed the famous phrase "all deliberate speed" to describe the time period in which local decision makers were obliged to desegregate the schools. Warren was also determined to ensure that there was unanimous support for the remedial element of the Court's desegregation rulings. The result was its unanimous decision in *Brown II* (1955). Ironically, while the cautious language of *Brown II* was intended to cabin the role of the federal judiciary in superintending local decisions, the result of the "all deliberate speed" standard has been to thrust the federal courts continuously into disputes over the pace and scope of desegregation in various areas.

By contrast to the relatively ameliorative tone of *Brown II*, Warren proved willing to lay down an unmistakably direct instruction to governmental officials to obey the mandate of the segregation rulings. In *Cooper v. Aaron* (1958), the Supreme Court was faced with defiance by a state official who believed that the Court's *Brown* decision was not the law of the land. In response to the state official's argument that the people of his state have a "right to have a doubt" concerning the legal effect of the Court's desegregation decisions, Chief Justice Warren declared that he had "never heard a lawyer say that the statement of a Governor as to what was legal or illegal should control the action of any court." The chief justice secured unanimous agreement on the principle "that the federal judiciary is supreme in the exposition of the law of the Constitution . . ." The Court's statement in *Cooper* proved a watershed in the effort of the federal government to confront local officials' unwillingness to carry out their desegregation responsibilities.

In his influential monograph on judicial review and constitutional theory, Professor John Hart Ely explains much of the Warren Court's constitutional jurisprudence as a coherent effort to respond through creative judicial intervention to failures in the political process, failures which have had the effect of disenfranchising political minorities and impeding democratic processes. Professor Ely's reconceptualization of the Warren Court's rights revolution trains attention away from what has often been seen as Warren's and his allies tendencies to substitute their own views of what the Constitution means; instead, Ely grounds the jurisprudence of the Warren Court majority in democracy and fair representation, regarding the Court in this era as not antidemocratic but, on the contrary, facilitative of democracy in its proper form. The strongest support for the thesis that the Supreme Court was, under Warren's strong leadership, democracy-enhancing and process-perfecting are the Court's opinions in the constitutional cases concerning representation and the political process.

Legislative apportionment in many ways represents the quintessential dispute over the proper role of the judiciary in ensuring fair representation. The Supreme Court revisited the constitutionality of various malapportioned legislative districts in the early 1960s against the backdrop of precedents holding apportionment to be a non-justiciable political question. The lodestar decision was *Baker v. Carr* in 1962, in which the Court declared that the apportionment issue was justiciable and therefore within the discretion of the federal courts to consider and resolve. The contrary position, spelled out earlier by Frankfurter in his opinion for the Court in *Colegrove v. Green* (1946), and in his dissent in *Baker*, was that reapportionment disputes represent a political thicket into which the Court should not enter. Such questions are, Frankfurter wrote, properly political and therefore outside the appropriate range of judicial scrutiny. The decision in *Baker* was a decisive rejection of this "political question" theory. While the Court majority declined to reach the merits of the constitutional argument in *Baker*, leaving this issue open for another two terms, what it *did* decide was that questions of fair representation raised by disputes concerning reapportionment and similar controversies were within the scope of the judicial function.

In 1964, the Supreme Court reached the merits of an apportionment scheme in the case of *Reynolds v. Sims*. *Reynolds* concerned an apportionment scheme in the state of Alabama in which the votes of residents of rural areas were accorded vastly more significance, because of their relative numerical weight, than voters in urban areas. This predicament was common in the South, where black voters tended to be concentrated in the urban regions of the state and where white citizens had a vested interest in ensuring that the current political structure continue. *Reynolds*, and related cases that the Court had before it at the same time, triggered Warren's instincts for political fairness and equality. "How long should we have to wait?" Warren asked Alabama's attorney who attempted to reassure the justices that Alabama would correct its representational flaws in time. Warren authored the opinion for the Court in this case, declaring that "legislators represent people, not trees or acres" and announcing the "one man, one vote" rule mandating that state legislative districts represent an equal number of constituents.

The desideratum of the Court's apportionment decisions was to provide both a precedent for judicial intervention into the political arrangements of states and a bright-line rule for the construction of all legislative districts except the United States Senate. Friends and foes of the Warren Court's apportionment decisions shared the view that they were significant in their effects on the relationship between federal constitutional doctrine and local political decision making or, more simply, on the relationship between law and politics. What remains controversial to this day, however, is whether the enunciation of the "one man, one vote" rule as the strict criterion of fair apportionment rep-

resents the best way of correcting flaws in the political processes of states. The persistence of the *Reynolds* rule has restricted the state's abilities to experiment with alternative representational schemes that may improve the political process, while maintaining fair, if not numerically equal, representation. To Warren, however, the effects of the reapportionment decisions were transformative in just the right way. The decisions represented the critical link in the Court's efforts to limit the effects of race discrimination and the efforts to shut out minorities from effective participation in state political systems. Indeed, Warren opined that had the Court decided *Baker v. Carr* early on, the desegregation decisions would have proved unnecessary.

Judicial intervention in the name of securing fair representation represented a key theme in Warren's jurisprudence throughout his tenure. Two important cases decided in Warren's final term illustrate the scope of this philosophy. In *Powell v. McCormack* (1969), the Court considered whether the decision by the House of Representatives to unseat Representative Adam Clayton Powell violated the Constitution. In his opinion for the Court, Chief Justice Warren explained the limited power of the House to discipline its members, stressing the right of the people to elect their representatives. *Powell* represented a rare case in which the Court invalidated an internal decision of the legislature on what amounted to democratic "fairness" grounds.

In *Allen v. State Board of Elections* that same term, the Court considered what scope to accord to Section 5 of the Voting Rights Act of 1965. Section 5 provided that changes in state voting schemes be subjected to review by the Department of Justice prior to taking effect. The Court, in an opinion written by Warren, rejected the view that the statute was limited to only those state enactments which prescribe who may register to vote. Warren wrote that the act "was aimed at the subtle, as well as the obvious, state regulations which have the effect of denying citizens their right to vote because of their race." Accordingly, he interpreted the act to subject to federal review any state voting enactment "which altered the election law of a covered State in even a minor way."

Both *Powell* and *Allen* reflect the extent of Warren's commitment to enforcing a vision of the Constitution in which fair representation is ensured through strict constitutional and statutory review. While the basic underpinnings of these rulings, particularly *Baker* and *Reynolds,* have survived more or less intact, the Burger and Rehnquist courts have proved far less willing to implement this vision of democratic fairness in the manner of Earl Warren and his allies. Scholars writing at the time of the key Warren Court decisions of the 1960s confidently predicted that the Court would act to police the democratic process for unfairness and inequalities. The phrase "due process of lawmaking" was coined to capture the spirit of the Court's decisions to scrutinize closely the processes of governmental decision making and to strike down on occasion decisions that failed to measure up to a standard of fair representation. This spirit proved short-lived though. Efforts to revive a sustained process-perfecting approach to judicial review are often grounded in a nostalgic appreciation of the Warren Court's commitments to procedural fairness in government. There is relatively little basis in contemporary constitutional jurisprudence, though, for confidence that this commitment will be fulfilled.

The Warren Court is widely regarded to have made its greatest mark in the area of individual rights and liberties. It is associated with a jurisprudence of robust personal freedom and searching scrutiny of governmental conduct that arguably infringes on this freedom. The most controversial area in which the Warren Court changed the distribution of authority and prerogative between the individual and the state was in the area of criminal law and the rights of the accused. Reflecting his pre-Court commitment to fairness in law enforcement, Warren proved willing to look closely at police conduct and to consider whether the accused had been treated fairly. In such cases, observes Professor White, "Warren saw himself as vindicating an innate right of citizens to be presumptively free from the coercive mechanisms of government." In *Watkins v. United States* (1957), for example, Warren wrote an opinion for the Court in which he held that Congress, acting

through the House Un-American Activities Committee, had improperly held Watkins in contempt of Congress for failing to disclose certain information. Congress had failed, wrote Warren, to provide the defendant with "a fair opportunity to determine whether he was within his rights in refusing to answer." Judicial redress for the failure of the government to provide a criminal defendant with due process would represent a common theme through Warren's constitutional jurisprudence.

The most famous of these criminal procedure decisions was *Miranda v. Arizona* (1966). Miranda had been arrested and questioned without being advised as to his constitutional rights, including the right to have an attorney present for questioning. In an opinion another justice described as "entirely" Warren's, the chief justice relied on an elaborate description of historical and contemporary police practices, all with an eye toward persuading the reader that the requirements the Court imposed in this case, namely, what are commonly described as the *Miranda* requirements, would not unjustifiably burden law enforcement officials. By all rights, *Miranda* was the quintessential Warren opinion: It was far-flung, relying on a patched together history and impassioned plea for fairness rather than a closely reasoned doctrinal story. And it unhesitatingly imposed substantial restrictions on governmental conduct. While *Miranda* generated a storm of controversy at the time of the decision and for years afterward, Warren's approach to constructing a code of police conduct in the arrest and interrogation situation has largely been vindicated; most regard the criminal process as substantially fairer as a result of *Miranda.*

A far less generous reading is accorded Chief Justice Warren's work in the area of obscenity and the First Amendment. Warren's jurisprudence in the First Amendment area was of a piece with his thinking across the range of the Constitution's guarantees of individual rights. Often following the carefully constructed doctrinal rationales of his ally, William Brennan, Warren predictably voted to strike down a variety of government restrictions on freedom of expression and of religion. Where the issue was, however, government restrictions on allegedly obscene speech, Warren fell out of step with the standard liberal tradition. Warren believed steadfastly in what he called "a right of the government to maintain a decent society." Accordingly, he gave the government much latitude to prohibit the trafficking of allegedly pornographic materials. The concern in such cases, argued Warren, was with the conduct of the individual, not with the content of the material. In this way, Warren attempted to steer away from coaxing the Court into the position of *ad hoc* censor. He emphasized in his obscenity opinions that it was to the local communities that the Court should delegate the principal role in combating obscenity and its effects. In the final analysis, Warren's struggle to carve out a special jurisprudence in the obscenity area was widely regarded as a failure. Simply, it became impossible to reconcile the Warren Court's studied commitment to freedom of expression and reluctance to play the role of censor through content-based restrictions on speech with his unguarded hostility to pornography.

Warren placed his stamp on the Court's expansive rights jurisprudence during the decade and half in which he served as chief justice. In the constitutional rights area, perhaps more than any other, the Warren Court was committed to a capacious jurisprudence of rights and liberties under the Constitution. As a court, this approach reached its apotheosis in cases such as *Griswold v. Connecticut* (1965), in which the majority found a right to privacy in the penumbra of the Bill of Rights. While the Warren Court's expanding approach to construing the Constitution largely jibed with the public's view of the proper role of the Court and of the relationship between governmental conduct and individual rights, many commentators felt uneasy with the Court's broad interpretations of the Bill of Rights. Indeed, the Court was continuously faced, in the later years of the Warren Court and beyond, with disputes that posed questions concerning how far the results and rationales of Warren could be pushed. Nonetheless, the Warren Court's constitutional jurisprudence proved resilient even after Warren left. Indeed, not a one of the Warren Court's key civil liberties cases—not *Brown*,

Baker, *Miranda*, or *Griswold*—has been overturned by judicial decision or constitutional amendment.

Where the Warren Court had perhaps its most lasting impact was with respect to the role of the judiciary in reviewing governmental decisions. Earl Warren rarely explained in any detail his views concerning the appropriate role of the judiciary in the democratic system. Truly, his actions in creating an activist Supreme Court spoke louder than his words on the subject. His actions included a plethora of decisions in which the court subjected governmental decisions taken by institutions at all levels to searching scrutiny. Warren was untroubled with the expanding judicial role portended by the liberal direction of the Court's constitutional jurisprudence. He eschewed the cautious role commended by notable liberals such as Benjamin Cardozo and Oliver Wendell Holmes. Where there was a wrong to be corrected and a right to be vindicated, Warren was content to have the Court provide redress through the means available to it. Warren's jurisprudence, as Professor Martin Shapiro has labeled it, was decidedly a "jurisprudence of values" in which the right result took precedence over doctrinal clarity and consistency.

The Warren Court played a crucial, if overlooked, role in reshaping the distribution of powers among governmental decision makers in all levels of the federal system. Within the national government, this impact was felt through a changing scope of the Constitution's separation of powers. And with respect to the relationship among the national government and the state and local government, the impact of Warren Court decisions was felt in the area of federalism. As it happens, there were relatively few cases before the Supreme Court during the Warren years that directly concerned an issue of separation of powers or of federalism as labeled in arguments made to the Court. Certainly, scholars regard the key disputes involving the nature and scope of separation of powers and federalism as being more prominent in the eras before (especially during Reconstruction and the New Deal) and after (especially in the 1980s) Earl Warren took office. In the Warren years, the disputes among institutions in the federal government and among the federal government, the states, and local governments, ordinarily arose indirectly, that is, under the rubric of the Bill of Rights. Nevertheless, the effect of the Warren Court's jurisprudence in the constitutional area was to change dramatically the relationship among governmental institutions, in particular, expanding the scope of the federal government's power to establish federal regulation under the Constitution's grants of authority.

The decisions in several civil rights cases decided in the 1960s contributed to this expanded federal role. Following Congress's burst of civil rights legislation enacted in the mid and late sixties, the Court was faced with challenges to the legislature's constitutional power to pass laws directed at private and state governmental conduct. In every case, the Warren Court upheld Congress's constitutional powers. In the process, the Court created a jurisprudence in which legislative attempts to ameliorate the effects of segregation and discrimination were given the most capacious interpretations.

The difficulty with the Warren Court's approach was that in the rush to make emphatic the Court's commitment to furthering the cause of federal civil rights legislation and enforcement, it failed to establish doctrines of federalism that would clarify the limits of federal, state, and local power. In short, the Warren Court created a jurisprudence of civil rights without creating or maintaining a workable jurisprudence of federalism that would remain in place once state-federal disputes over civil rights were settled.

In a sense, this outcome was another consequence of the dilemma created by the Warren Court, and Chief Justice Earl Warren's approach to judging in particular: the commitment to a set of particular results without the doctrinal underpinnings sufficient to resolve difficult problems that would arise later. In the area of individual rights and liberties, this dilemma was considerably less onerous; after all, the signal sent by the Warren Court was to stand committed to individual freedoms and to err on the side of protecting such freedoms even when the doctrinal pegs proved slippery. However, with respect to disputes concerning the proper allocation of power among governmental institutions, the fail-

ure to establish coherent and persuasive doctrinal frameworks invited unique and difficult problems. Indeed, the controversies over separation of powers and federalism that loomed large in the Burger and Rehnquist courts were partly a product of the questions left unanswered and the doctrinal anomalies left unresolved by the Warren Court.

The Court that Warren left in 1969 was a Court dominated by an liberal, activist approach to judging in which a solid majority was committed to expanding the scope of individual freedoms even where the Constitution's text was less than clear and the Constitution's history indeterminate. Students of the Warren Court have provided rationales of the Court's decisions, as well as of Warren's individual decisions, that suggest that the Court's approaches during this era were neither intellectually rudderless nor democratically illegitimate, but instead were grounded in creative yet doctrinally respectable interpretations of the Constitution's commands and the expressed views of Congress through its statutes. Critics have challenged the Warren Court's legacy both on the grounds that its jurisprudence, however ideologically appealing, is without adequate doctrinal anchors, and also because it represents a dramatic expansion in the powers of the unelected federal judiciary at the expense of the more democratic institutions, namely Congress, the president, and state and local governments.

In an essay written at the end of Earl Warren's tenure, Professor Philip Kurland observed with respect to the Warren Court's legacy that "history has a nasty way of measuring greatness in terms of success rather than in terms of goodness." While Professor Kurland was suggesting that the future would regard the Warren Court's judicial revolution as a failure, however good were its intentions, history has been rather kind to the Warren Court. Public opinion was remarkably supportive of the Warren Court's decisions over the course of the 1950s and 1960s. Indeed, the triumph of the Court was its success in leading the way toward a reconstructed constitutional system, a system in which egalitarian goals and the goals of fair representation were expanded and protected against governmental encroachments. There had been other periods of judicial activism; it is not at all clear that the Warren Court's activist legacy was different in kind than the Court of John Marshall in the early nineteenth century or the New Deal Court of the 1930s. In fact, scholars have noted a different kind of activism—a conservative activism—in the decisions of the Supreme Court under William H. Rehnquist. The Warren Court stands out primarily for the goals it expounded and enshrined into constitutional law through its decisions and for its success in grounding these efforts in the evolving public opinion of American society. As the public and legislative debate concerning the nomination of Robert Bork to the Supreme Court recently taught, the jurisprudence of the Warren Court has insinuated itself into the sensibilities of a substantial majority of Americans. If, as Professor Kurland suggests, history measures greatness by success, then the legacy of the Warren Court has remained quite secure indeed.

As for Earl Warren's particular role in constructing this legacy, it seems clear in retrospect that this judicial revolution required the sort of judicial leader he represented. While his individual contributions to legal doctrine remain limited, his ability to formulate judicial strategies, illustrated most famously in *Brown* and *Baker*, was impressive. It was largely to due to his uncanny abilities to lead the Court in a liberal direction during a turbulent fifteen years that he enjoys the reputation as one of the Supreme Court's greatest chief justices.

—DANIEL B. RODRIGUEZ

BIBLIOGRAPHY

The Memoirs of Chief Justice Earl Warren (1977) are rather disappointing in their treatment of his judicial career. His papers, in the Library of Congress, offer a somewhat more illuminating account of his tenure on the Court. The most important biography is G. Edward White's *Earl Warren: A Public Life* (1982). Its treatment of Warren's career is definitive; however, White's thesis concerning the conceptual underpinnings of Warren's jurisprudence is somewhat idiosyncratic. The other important book on Warren's career is Bernard Schwartz's *Superchief* (1983). This is less a biography of Warren and more a chronological examination of the Warren Court through a close look at its decisions. Other biographies on Warren are rather unilluminating accounts of his political and/or judicial career. A useful collection of essays examining the decisions of the Warren Court is *The Supreme Court under Earl Warren* (1972), which includes an interview with Warren on the role of the Court and insightful essays by two of the Court's most prominent academic critics, Alexander M. Bickel and Philip B. Kurland. More sympathetic accounts of Warren's jurisprudence include Archibald Cox, *The Warren Court* (1968), and Anthony Lewis, "Earl Warren," in Friedman and Israel, 4 *Justices* 2721. John Ely's *Democracy and Distrust* (1980) is the most important effort to construct a comprehensive theoretical defense of the Warren Court's constitutional jurisprudence against charges that the Court was merely political and theoretically ungrounded. A competing view of the Warren Court's philosophy is described by Martin Shapiro in *Law and Politics in the Supreme Court* (1964) and "Fathers and Sons: The Court, The Commentators, and the Search for Values," in Vincent Blasi, ed., *The Burger Court: The Counter-Revolution that Wasn't* (1983).

There are a slew of books and articles on specific Warren Court decisions. On the desegregation cases, the most notable treatment is Richard Kluger's *Simple Justice* (1975). A recent account that makes use of Earl Warren's papers is Mark Tushnet, "What Really Happened in *Brown v. Board of Education*," 91 *Columbia Law Review* 1867 (1991). The *Supreme Court Review* is an annual anthology of articles that examine important recent decisions of the Court. The issues published during Warren's tenure as chief justice contain many interesting discussion of key Warren Court cases.

BUSHROD WASHINGTON

BORN 5 June 1762, Westmoreland County,
Virginia

NOMINATED to the Court 29 September 1798
by John Adams

TOOK seat 4 February 1799

DIED 26 November 1829 in Philadelphia,
Pennsylvania

A favorite nephew of George Washington
and the heir to Mount Vernon at the death of
Martha Washington, Bushrod Washington studied at the College of William and Mary, apparently from 1775 to 1778, and again in 1780, on
the latter occasion as a law student of George
Wythe. After military service in the Virginia
campaign and the siege of Yorktown in 1781,
he continued his legal education in Philadelphia
from 1782 to 1784 under statesman and jurist
James Wilson.

Admitted to the Virginia bar, he began the
practice of law in his home county and also
served in the state legislature and as a Federalist delegate to the Virginia convention for the
ratification of the federal Constitution. After an
unsatisfactory effort to relocate his practice in
Alexandria, he then moved to Richmond, where
he became much more successful. Washington
and John Marshall frequently appeared as opposing counsel in cases before the Virginia court of
appeals; and during 1797, he worked on an edition of his notes on cases heard by the Court
between 1790 and 1796.

By the time the two volumes of his notes
were published in 1798 and 1799, President John
Adams had offered him an appointment as associate justice of the Supreme Court to fill the
vacancy created by the death of his law teacher,
James Wilson. Washington withdrew his announced candidacy for a seat in the Congress and
accepted, becoming at age thirty-six the youngest appointee yet to serve on the Court.

On receipt of his commission, Washington
departed immediately for service on the circuit
court that sat for the Carolinas and Georgia and
then took his seat on the Supreme Court for the

first time in February 1799. He was virtually the
only sitting justice of any intellectual vigor when
Marshall accepted an appointment as chief jus-
tice in 1801 and began the transformation of the
Court into the powerful body that it became.
Washington served on the bench thirty-one years
in all, twenty-eight of them in the heyday of the
Marshall Court.

Given their existing friendship and agreement
on many political and legal matters, the collaboration between the two Virginians was long and
close. Indeed, in an often quoted letter to Thomas
Jefferson (who had appointed him), Justice William Johnson observed that Marshall and Washington "are commonly estimated as one judge."
Johnson's implication, too readily accepted by
many later historians, that Washington was a cipher, without influence of his own on the Court,
is assuredly an exaggeration. It is true that Washington over his long tenure disagreed with the
chief justice only eight times. He wrote relatively
few decisions, some eighty-one in all, of which
only three were dissents. He was also the author
of two concurrences and seven *seriatim* opinions,
most of the latter before Marshall joined the Court
or when he was absent.

This record, however, has to be set in the
context of the Marshall Court, for which the
chief justice wrote many of the decisions and
always sought as much unanimity as possible.
Washington's activity was, even so, greater than
that of most of the justices apart from Joseph
Story and Johnson. Too, he generally agreed
with Marshall and remained particularly committed to the principle that the justices should, where
at all possible, resolve their disagreements before announcing a decision. He was respected,
moreover, by his fellow justices for the learning
and patience he brought to the discussions that
preceded final decisions, as well as for his integrity and willingness to work vary hard on the
business of the Court.

Washington proved a particularly active
judge on circuit, serving continuously after the
Judiciary Act of 1802 on the third circuit, which
included Pennsylvania and New Jersey. He was

among the Federalist judges who vigorously enforced the Alien and Sedition Laws of 1798, although less vindictively than some of his colleagues. In the circuit court case of *United States v. Bright* (1809), he strongly upheld the right of federal courts to overrule the actions of a state by convicting a Pennsylvania militia general for obeying an order of the governor to defy a recent decision of the Supreme Court (*United States v. Peters*). In his last years, Washington published, with the assistance of Richard Peters, Jr., the district judge who sat with him on the third circuit, four volumes of reports of cases decided in the court.

Of Washington's Supreme Court opinions, three—a concurrence, a majority opinion on a rehearing of a case, and a *seriatim* opinion—have particular significance for the history of the Marshall Court. They also effectively illustrate Washington's general agreement with the Court's efforts to strengthen the authority of the national government and of its courts, and also to guarantee the force of private contracts and encourage the free flow of commerce. Yet, they also show Washington as providing at times a moderating influence on those trends in an effort to accommodate to political reality and to permit some reasonable sphere of activity for the states.

Thus, in the famous case of the *Trustees of Dartmouth College v. Woodward* (1819), Washington accepted the general conclusion of Marshall's majority opinion that an effort of the state of New Hampshire to alter the colonial charter of the college by introducing public control through the appointment of its trustees by the governor violated the protection guaranteed by the contract clause of the Constitution. Washington was, however, unhappy with the chief justice's opinion, which was written on broad principles and without any effort to find precedents for his decision. As a consequence, he wrote his own concurring opinion, reaching the conclusion that the charter was indeed a valid contract, but by a much more specific argument. Washington then went on to raise a second question, whether the charter of a corporation was protected by the contract clause, concluding in this instance that the charter of a charitable institution such as Dartmouth College was so pro-

tected, but that non-charitable corporations were not. Washington was here contesting another concurring opinion written by Joseph Story, which explicitly included business corporations under the contract clause. Had Washington's view prevailed, the Dartmouth College decision might not have achieved its full significance as a guarantor of such private incorporations.

In *Green v. Biddle* (1823), Washington managed, successfully this time, to moderate a decision of the Court without altering its substance. The case tested the force of the compact concluded between Virginia and Kentucky in 1792 by which Virginia consented to the formation of the new state from its territory, but required that all its previously issued private land titles remain valid. In 1797, Kentucky attempted to provide by a so-called occupying claimant law that if others had subsequently settled on lands without a legal title, but had improved them, the original owners would be required to forego rents and to pay reimbursement to such illegal occupants before they could recover possession.

In the original hearing in 1821, Justice Story wrote a sweeping opinion, based on broad principles of natural law, that overturned the Kentucky legislation and aroused a storm of political protest. The Court agreed to a rehearing at the instigation of Henry Clay. On this occasion, Washington wrote an opinion that still upheld the validity of Virginia titles and the sanctity of private property, but on more legalistic grounds and by reference to the Court's authority under the contract clause. He also assured Kentuckians that they could still take lands for public use or resale, provided just compensation was paid the original owners. The opinion perhaps rested on somewhat shaky ground in trying to apply the contract clause to the interstate Kentucky-Virginia agreement, and it did not in the least assuage Kentucky interests. But it accorded with both Washington's bent to provide maximum protection for property rights and inclination to limit state sovereignty.

Washington was, within limits, more sympathetic to state authority in his *seriatim* opinion in *Ogden v. Saunders* (1827), a decision involving the constitutionality of a state bankruptcy law. The Court had wrestled with this thorny question for some years, torn between a belief that under the Constitution, bankruptcy statutes were the sole preserve of Congress, and a recognition that the persistent failure of Congress to pass a such an act created an undesirable void. The justices were also divided as to whether bankruptcy laws were an impairment of the contract clause. In 1814, Washington had taken an extreme view in a circuit court decision in which he argued that the states lacked any constitutional power whatsoever to enact bankruptcy laws. Then, in 1819, a badly split Supreme Court achieved an outward show of unanimity by ruling in *Sturges v. Crowninshield* that state bankruptcy laws were permissible in the absence of action by Congress, but that the law under review was unconstitutional because it extended to debts contracted prior to the enactment of the legislation and hence impaired the obligation of contract. Washington had accepted the decision, perhaps out of his desire for unanimity, but also because he may have changed his mind about state legislation in some circumstances.

Now, in *Ogden v. Saunders,* the Court with somewhat different membership again disagreed on a state bankruptcy law that applied only to obligations incurred after its passage. Marshall, in the only minority constitutional opinion that he ever wrote, insisted all contracts, past or future, were protected by the Constitution; and two justices voted with him in the minority. The four justices in the majority wrote separate and differing opinions, but upheld the validity of the law under review, and in one degree or another, the constitutionality of state bankruptcy laws generally. Washington's was the most restrictive, essentially following the precedent of *Sturges;* that

is, allowing such laws in the absence of an act of Congress and approving the present law because it applied only to future debts. As with many of his decisions, he had demonstrated his concern for attention to past precedent in legal decisions.

Through much of the decade of the 1820s, Washington had suffered periods of illness that at times prevented his sitting both on circuit and in the Supreme Court. On other occasions he rallied and was as active as ever. At his final session of the Supreme Court in early 1829, he wrote an unusually large number of opinions— six in all. Then, in late November, he died in Philadelphia where he had been attempting until almost the end to carry out his circuit court duties. In his obituary in the reports of the Supreme Court, John Marshall wrote, "No man knew his worth better or deplores his death more than myself."

—THAD W. TATE

BIBLIOGRAPHY

David Leslie Annis's dissertation, "Mr. Bushrod Washington, Supreme Court Justice on the Marshall Court" (Notre Dame, 1974), provides a full account of Washington's life and service on the Court; Albert Blaustein and Roy Mersky, "Bushrod Washington," in Friedman and Israel, 1 *Justices* 243, is a good sketch; G. Edward White, *The Marshall Court and Cultural Change, 1815–35* (1988), volume 3 of the Holmes Devise, provides a perceptive account of Washington at 344–54, and deals fully with his post-1815 decisions; in the same series, George Lee Haskins and Herbert A. Johnson, *Foundations of Power, John Marshall, 1801–15* (1981), cover Washington's early years on the Court.

JAMES MOORE WAYNE

BORN ca. 1790, Savannah, Georgia

NOMINATED to the Court 7 January 1835 by
    Andrew Jackson; confirmed 9 January
    1835

DIED 5 July 1867 in Washington, D.C.

James Moore Wayne was born about 1790
in Savannah, Georgia, the twelfth of thirteen
children of Richard Wayne and Elizabeth
Clifford. Raised on his family's rice plantation,
Wayne enrolled at the College of New Jersey
(now Princeton University) in 1804 at age fourteen and received his degree in 1808. He then
studied law under the tutelage of several lawyers
in Georgia and Connecticut, and in 1810, entered
law practice in Savannah.

Throughout the following two decades,
Wayne gradually gained national prominence
through his work in Georgia state politics and
in the judiciary. From 1815 to 1817, Wayne
served in the Georgia legislature and as a member of the Savannah board of aldermen. From
1817 to 1819, he held the office of mayor of
Savannah. From 1819 to 1828, he served first as
judge on the Savannah court of common pleas
and then as judge on the local superior court. In
1828, Wayne was elected to the United States
House of Representatives, where he served for
three terms and garnered recognition as a leading Democrat and supporter of President Andrew
Jackson, who nominated him to fill the seat vacated by the death of William Johnson.

As associate justice, Wayne developed a
particular interest and expertise in admiralty
cases, and many of his most distinctive opinions
in his first two decades on the Court propounded
his view of the expansive power enjoyed by
Congress in its regulation of waterways. For
example, in *Waring v. Clarke* (1847), Wayne
wrote on behalf of the Court in according broad
federal admiralty jurisdiction in a case involving a ship collision nearly 100 miles up the
Mississippi River, reasoning that such power
should extend to sea waters flowing by tide or
otherwise into rivers and ports. In the *Passen-*

ger Cases (1849), the Court struck down two
state laws levying taxes on ship captains for each
immigrant carried on the ground that the laws
constituted improper incursions into congressional power over foreign commerce; in a separate concurring opinion, Wayne asserted that the
laws were invalid because the commerce power
was vested exclusively in Congress. Similarly,
in *Cooley v. Board of Wardens* (1852), in which
the Court announced the so-called "Cooley doctrine" of "selective exclusiveness" in balancing
federal and state powers with regard to foreign
and interstate commerce, Wayne dissented on
the ground that the commerce clause demanded
exclusive federal regulation of foreign and interstate commerce.

Wayne's tenure was also marked by his
personal conflict and ambivalence regarding his
position as a southern justice and slave owner
who supported the Union cause during the Civil
War, yet who regularly favored slave interests
in his rulings on the Court. In the momentous
decision of *Dred Scott v. Sandford* (1857),
Wayne agreed with Chief Justice Roger Taney's
opinion holding that Congress had the authority
neither to prohibit the introduction of slavery into
the territories, nor to recognize as free those individuals such as Scott who had been brought
into the territories. Nevertheless, Wayne refused
to join the Confederacy or to leave the Court
during the Civil War; as a result, the Confederacy labeled him a traitor, charged him in a
Confederate court with being an enemy alien,
and confiscated his property in Georgia. In the
Prize Cases (1863), Wayne joined the Court in
upholding the constitutionality of President
Abraham Lincoln's proclamation of a Union
naval blockade of Confederate ports during the
war; yet, by war's end, he voted to strike down
Reconstruction measures such as the test oath
laws in *Cummings v. Missouri* (1867) and *Ex
parte Garland* (1867), and refused to sit as circuit court judge in states under military Reconstruction rule.

Wayne died of typhoid on July 5, 1867, in
Washington, D.C. Despite his repudiation of and

by the Confederacy during the Civil War, he was buried in Savannah, Georgia.

—Margaret M. Russell

Bibliography

The most comprehensive study to date of Wayne's life and work is Alexander A. Lawrence's *James Moore Wayne, Southern Unionist* (1943). Also of note are the following brief sketches: Alexander A. Lawrence, "Justice Wayne and the *Dred Scott* Case," *Proceedings of the Fifty-Seventh Annual Session of the Georgia Bar Association* 196 (1940); George G. Battle, "James Moore Wayne: Southern Unionist," 14 *Fordham Urban Law Journal* 42 (1964); and Warren Grice, "James M. Wayne," *Georgia Bar Association Proceedings* 179 (1938).

BYRON RAYMOND WHITE

BORN 8 June 1917, Fort Collins, Colorado

NOMINATED to the Court 3 April 1962
by John F. Kennedy

TOOK seat 16 April 1962; retired 28 June 1993

"Conventional wisdom," as chronicled by a sympathetic former law clerk, "suggests that Justice White has been a disappointment because he did not turn out to be the 'liberal' that many expected of President John F. Kennedy's first appointee." Contrary to this received wisdom, I want to argue that Byron R. White was appointed to the Supreme Court because he was a Kennedy liberal and that, although the justice grew marginally more conservative during his three decades on the bench, on the whole he adhered faithfully to the liberal values that led to his appointment. The considerable divergence that existed between White's voting record and the voting patterns of other liberal justices emerged almost entirely during the first decade of White's judicial tenure—his decade on the Warren Court. That divergence, I suggest, resulted less from changes in the views of Byron White than from a transformation in the content of liberalism in the mid to late 1960s.

One must start by delineating the contours of what is labeled "Kennedy liberalism"—the ideology that produced Byron White's appointment to the Supreme Court. Using a three-fold analysis, we can then understand how Justice White approached the three values for which history will remember the Supreme Court during his period of tenure: pragmatism, egalitarianism, and individualism. Far from betraying the liberalism embodied by the Kennedy administration and epitomized by the Warren Court, White consistently advocated and adhered to Kennedy liberalism with its emphasis on pragmatic social reform and an unshakable, if not impassioned, devotion to equality. The one area where the justice departed from liberals such as his close personal friend, William J. Brennan, who sat on the Court with White for all but three of the latter's terms, was individual rights. This,

however, neither surprised Court observers nor represented an ideological shift for John F. Kennedy's first appointment to the high court.

Byron White served as deputy attorney general from 1961 to 1962, and was very much a part of the Kennedy team in the Department of Justice; in fact, he as much as anyone put the team together. Thus, even in the absence of direct evidence, there is every reason to believe that White shared the Kennedy administration's liberal values.

These values included an unapologetic and undying belief in rationalism. The Kennedy team possessed enormous faith in the ability of people to resolve problems through reason. Members of the administration had "an abiding faith in man as a rational being committing rational acts," and those working in the Justice Department "cared deeply and professionally about the law" as the rational means to achieving social change. As is shown by Robert Kennedy's two weeks of telephone conversations with Governor Ross Barnett of Mississippi concerning the registration of James Meredith at the University of Mississippi, Kennedy and his cohorts assumed that confrontation should be avoided, that mediation was preferable to coercion, and that reasonable people could always work things out. They understood that law, administered in a practical and sympathetic fashion by evenhanded officials, was essential to producing such compromises.

As an attorney in private practice in Colorado during the 1950s, Byron White had seemed to his partners to be a pragmatic problem solver, and he adhered to this pragmatism on joining the Kennedy administration. His pragmatism in the Justice Department is evidenced by a key episode in the Kennedy years: the appointment of Burke Marshall as assistant attorney general for civil rights. White, who played an active role in the appointment, "thought that the Administration ought to locate the primary leadership in the civil rights fight outside the Department of Justice . . . so that initiative, aggressive action, education, persuasion should emanate from a different source than the Department." He viewed the department solely as "a law enforcement agency" and "when you mix law enforcement with other things . . . the two together . . . [become] less effective." Robert Kennedy agreed. For that reason, he "didn't want to have someone in the Civil Rights Division who was dealing not from fact but was dealing from emotion . . . [or] in the interest of a Negro or a group of Negroes or a group of those who were interested in civil rights." White expressed the same idea when he commented that "it would be more interesting to get a first-class lawyer who would do the job in a technically proficient way that would be defensible in court—that Southerners would not think of as a vendetta, but as an even-handed application of the law." As an aide to Kennedy added, "As Bob and White looked ahead to the role the Justice Department would play in the gathering struggle over civil rights . . . they felt the only proper course for the Department would be to proceed in strict accordance with the law, avoiding any appearance of pitting one social point of view against another." Such an approach might not lead to a triumphant victory for any theoretical principle of equality, but it would produce practical advances toward equal civil rights.

All of this is not to claim that Robert Kennedy and Byron White did not favor the cause of civil rights; they clearly did. As Robert Kennedy understood it, one of his main duties in life was to "be kind to others that are less fortunate than we," and therefore he and White searched for someone "sensitive . . . to the cause of equal rights," even though "not identified with it." But, while Kennedy and White believed in equality, they understood the success of the civil rights movement to depend upon the political process, not the law.

Robert Kennedy decided early on that the best way he and the Justice Department could help the civil rights cause was to enforce the federally guaranteed right of blacks to vote. As he explained, he "felt strongly that this was where the most good could be accomplished. . . . From the vote, from participation in the elections, flow all other rights far, far more easily. A great deal could be accomplished internally within a state if the Negroes participated in elec-

tions and voted." For this reason, the attorney general encouraged civil rights leaders to focus their drive on voting rights and assisted them by a six-fold increase in the number of voter-registration suits which the Justice Department filed.

Promoting the right of blacks to vote was consistent with a broader faith in the right to vote and the democratic process in general. The Kennedy team was quite sympathetic, for example, with the one man, one vote line of cases growing out of the 1962 precedent of *Baker v. Carr.* The most hesitant member of the team was Solicitor General Archibald Cox, but the rest of the Department of Justice team pushed him hard in the direction of urging judicial enforcement of equal voting rights. Byron White supported this effort, arguing with Cox that the government had to take an *amicus* posture in favor of the result to which the Court ultimately came in *Baker.*

When Charles E. Whittaker resigned from the Supreme Court in the spring of 1962, President Kennedy appointed Byron R. White to replace him because everyone who participated in the nomination process perceived White as a loyal member of the liberal Kennedy team. There were two other serious candidates for the position—William H. Hastie and Paul Freund—but Chief Justice Earl Warren and Justice William O. Douglas found both of them too conservative and hence objectionable. As Warren said of Hastie, "He's not a liberal, and he'll be opposed to all the measures that we are interested in." The opposition of Warren and Douglas killed consideration of Hastie and Freund, and when Senator Richard Russell threatened to bring a delegation to the White House to seek the appointment of a conservative, President Kennedy moved quickly to appoint to the Court his liberal deputy attorney general.

On ascending the bench, Byron White continued to make judgments about the substance of the law not on grounds of abstract philosophical theory or technical legal doctrine, but on the basis of "a pragmatic estimate as to how effective" his choice "would be." As he wrote in his 1965 dissent in *Miranda v. Arizona* (1966), constitutional decisions "cannot rest alone on syllogism, metaphysics or some ill-defined notions of natural justice"; the Supreme Court and each of

Byron Raymond White
Photograph by Harris and Ewing.
Collection of the Supreme Court of the United States.

its justices had a continuing duty "to inquire into the advisability of its end product in terms of the long-range interest of the country." Or, as he maintained a decade later in *Gertz v. Robert Welch, Inc.* (1974) with a quotation from the writings of Benjamin N. Cardozo, "The juristic philosophy of the common law is at bottom the philosophy of pragmatism. . . .The rule that functions well produces a title deed to recognition."

White's concern with the actual functioning of the law rather than with theory and technicality is so clear and so widely accepted that just a few examples will suffice. One example from the Warren Court era was his concurring opinion in *Griswold v. Connecticut* (1965), where the justice refused to join in the opinions proclaiming a constitutional right to privacy and debating its source; instead, he decided the case on the wholly practical ground that he could not "see how the ban on the use of contraceptives by married couples in any way reinforce[d] the State's ban on illicit sexual relationships." Similarly, in *Batson v. Kentucky* (1986), White explained that he had written his majority opinion in *Swain v. Alabama* (1965) not because he felt compelled by precedent, but because he wanted to give a practical warning to "prosecutors that using peremptories to exclude blacks [from juries] on the assumption that no black juror could fairly judge a black defendant would violate the Equal Protection Clause," and when he learned that *Swain* was not giving that warning, he did not feel that precedent or legal theory precluded him from joining in overruling it in *Batson*. Finally, in *Furman v. Georgia* (1972), White relied on "common sense and experience" to hold the death penalty unconstitutional, since "its imposition" had become a "pointless and needless extinction of life with only marginal contributions to any discernible social or public purpose."

In short, White was part of a generation trained in legal realism and sociological jurisprudence, and, as such, he was far more interested in the practical ramifications of the Supreme Court's decisions than the theoretical soundness of its opinions. White thereby fit into a long line of liberals, beginning with Louis D. Brandeis, who were willing to ignore precedent and alter doctrine in the interest of progressive social change.

Justice White quickly demonstrated his commitment to an active involvement by the federal courts in the protection of civil rights. In leading cases like *Goss v. Board of Education of Knoxville* (1963), *Griffin v. County School Board of Prince Edward County* (1964), and *Green v. County School Board of New Kent County* (1968), he joined a unanimous Court in its efforts to begin making the promise of school desegregation real, and in two important cases in which state and local governments adopted legislation making housing integration more difficult, *Reitman v. Mulkey* (1967) and *Hunter v. Erickson* (1969), he authored important 5–4 and 8–1 opinions striking down discriminatory legislation. When the Court began to divide during the early years of the Burger Court, White remained on the side of the pro-integration forces in all the main constitutional cases—*Swann v. Charlotte-Mecklenburg Board of Education* (1971), *Palmer v. Thompson* (1971), *Milliken v. Bradley* (1974), and *Arlington Heights v. Metropolitan Housing Corp.* (1977)—although now sometimes in dissent.

In *University of California Regents v. Bakke* (1978), White authored a joint opinion that upheld the constitutionality of affirmative action and explicitly noted that "Government may take race into account when it acts not to demean or insult any racial group, but to remedy disadvantages cast on minorities by past racial prejudice." Two years later, in *Fullilove v. Klutznick* (1980), and then again, three years prior to his retirement, in *Metro Broadcasting, Inc. v. FCC* (1990), the justice joined opinions that upheld the power of Congress to adopt race-conscious policies designed to increase minority participation in federally funded public works projects and minority ownership of radio and television broadcasting stations, respectively. However, in *City of Richmond v. J. A. Croson Co.* (1989), White joined the Court in striking down a city-sponsored affirmative action program modeled on the federal program upheld in *Fullilove*. He was less tolerant of local governments attempting to implement affirmative action programs, particularly in light of the Fourteenth Amendment's "distrust of state legislative enactments based on race."

White remained strongly committed on the Court to the position he had held earlier at the Justice Department in respect to voting rights. In *Gray v. Sanders* (1963), in *Wesberry v. Sanders* (1964), and ultimately in *Reynolds v. Sims* (1964), he joined a series of majority opinions that produced the one person, one vote rule in legislative apportionment cases. In his plurality opinion in *United Jewish Organizations v. Carey* (1977), and in his dissent in *Shaw v. Reno* (1993), which was decided on his last day on the Court, White expressed his view that state efforts to draw legislative districts so as to ensure minority political representation in compliance with the Voting Rights Act represented an attempt "to provide minority voters with an effective voice in the political process" and, therefore, did not violate the Constitution.

White's limited departures in statutory construction cases—such as *Jones v. Alfred H. Mayer Co.* (1968), *Runyon v. McCrary* (1976), and *Patterson v. McLean Credit Union* (1989)—from the egalitarian agenda of progressives are trivial in comparison with the vast areas of the law—school desegregation, affirmative action, voting rights, and reapportionment—where he consistently supported the principle of equality.

There was one side to the Warren Court's liberalism that Justice White never shared: a commitment to individual rights. Byron White's hostility to judicial protection of individual rights did not signal an ideological change from when he first entered government and initially came to the Court. In fact, White's deference to the legislative process reflected the training he received as a young student at Yale Law School in the late 1940s, the heyday of legal realism. The legal realists taught that since all legal reasoning ultimately reflects the judge's policy preferences, the judiciary should therefore defer to the policy choices made by the legislative and executive branches as the democratically elected branches of government accountable to the people.

Despite his concurrence in *Griswold*, White took a hostile attitude toward judicial enforcement of fundamental yet unenumerated rights. Dissenting in *Roe v. Wade* (1973), he found "nothing in the language or history of the Con-

stitution to support the Court's judgment," and, therefore, thought that the abortion controversy "should be left with the people and to the political processes the people have devised to govern their affairs." He expressed similar views, this time for the majority of the Court, in *Bowers v. Hardwick* (1986), in which the Court refused to extend the right of privacy to include a right to engage in homosexual sodomy. He noted that "the Court is most vulnerable and comes nearest to illegitimacy when it deals with judge-made constitutional law having little or no cognizable roots in the language or design of the Constitution." White continued to disagree with the course upon which the Court had embarked in *Roe*, and, one year prior to his retirement, in *Planned Parenthood v. Casey* (1992), joined opinions that expressed a willingness to overturn the landmark case.

In addition to the narrow scope he accorded the right to privacy, White also disfavored an expansive view of individual rights in two other key areas: the rights of criminal defendants and the rights of protesters. This was not surprising, since the Kennedy Justice Department, of which Byron White was so central a part, also had an unfavorable record toward individual rights in these two areas, particularly toward the rights of the accused. Indeed, Robert Kennedy himself had built his early reputation as counsel to the Senate's Select Committee on Improper Labor Activities, where he had vigorously pursued the likes of Dave Beck and Jimmy Hoffa and had "attack[ed] organized criminals with weapons and techniques as effective as their own." Even Arthur Schlesinger, Kennedy's sympathetic biographer, agreed that Kennedy "had displayed an excess of zeal" and "was a man driven by a conviction of righteousness, a fanaticism of virtue, [and] a certitude about guilt that vaulted over gaps in evidence." This tough attitude toward racketeering and other crime, and a corresponding tendency to construe the law of criminal constitutional procedure narrowly, continued after Kennedy became attorney general, when he proposed that the administration support legislation to permit wiretapping when authorized by a federal judge, a proposal that Byron White as deputy attorney general strongly supported.

The Kennedy Justice Department's faith in the prevailing power structure also demonstrated itself in its attitude toward the rights of protesters. The department did not understand the function of protest or how to deal with it, and accordingly, did a terrible job providing protection for civil rights demonstrators in the South. Death and mayhem resulted among civil rights workers on many occasions from the absence of federal protection, and the "unbelievable position of confidence" which the Kennedy Justice Department had maintained "in the minds of the oppressed" rapidly eroded. When several black leaders, including Jerome Smith, a CORE official who had been bludgeoned by southern police, met in 1963 with Robert Kennedy and Burke Marshall, they reported that begging for federal protection while fighting for the American dream of equal rights made them "nauseous," while Smith acknowledged he would "never" serve in a war on behalf of the United States. When Kennedy reported his shock at these statements, the black leaders, in turn, "were shocked that he was shocked." In his years as attorney general, Robert Kennedy simply could not understand this fear and distrust of government.

Once elevated to the Supreme Court, White continued to adhere to the attitudes on criminal procedure and radical protest that had been prevalent in the Justice Department during his time as deputy attorney general. As a result, those who had hoped that White, as Kennedy's first appointee to the Supreme Court, would regularly side with Chief Justice Earl Warren in important cases were quickly disillusioned. A mere two months after his appointment, he wrote his first major dissent in *Robinson v. California* (1962), in which the Court held that the states could not make narcotics addiction a crime. Justice White's string of dissents from some of the major criminal procedure opinions of the Warren Court continued thereafter. He dissented in *Escobedo v. Illinois* (1964), which invalidated a confession obtained at a police station from a defendant who had asked to see his lawyer, and in *Miranda v. Arizona* (1966), which prohibited all custodial interrogation in the absence of an attorney.

In his dissents, White expressed a pragmatic concern similar to that held by Robert Kennedy

and the Kennedy Justice Department about the effectiveness of law enforcement. In *Miranda*, for instance, he wrote that the majority's rule would "slow down the investigation and apprehension of confederates" and "return a killer, a rapist or other criminal to the streets . . . to repeat his crime." In *Berger v. New York* (1967), which invalidated state legislation authorizing wiretapping upon the issuance of a judicial warrant, the justice argued that official eavesdropping and wiretapping are "irreplaceable investigative tools which are needed for the enforcement of criminal laws." Similarly, "practical considerations" led the justice in *Minnesota v. Dickerson* (1993) to uphold the right of the police to seize, without a warrant, concealed contraband detected while frisking a suspect.

Nevertheless, White proved not to be a complete conservative. He joined the Court's opinion in *Gideon v. Wainwright* (1963) requiring appointment of counsel for all indigents accused of felonies. In 1967, he authored two leading decisions, *Camara v. Municipal Court* (1967) and *See v. City of Seattle* (1967), that applied the Fourth Amendment to administrative searches, and shortly after Earl Warren's retirement as chief justice, he joined the majority in *Furman v. Georgia* (1972), which temporarily suspended use of the death penalty. In the past decade, he even dissented on occasion from majority opinions upholding warrantless searches in criminal cases, and in *James v. Illinois* (1990), provided the critical fifth vote in a 5–4 decision refusing to enlarge an exception to the exclusionary rule. In one of the last Court opinions he wrote, *Helling v. McKinney* (1993), White held that the Eighth Amendment's prohibition against cruel and unusual punishment prevented prison authorities from exposing prisoners to unreasonable health risks by placing them in cells with smokers.

Similarly, a mixed but ultimately anti-individualist pattern emerges from White's votes and opinions in cases involving freedom of expression. During his first few years on the Court, the justice often voted to protect the right of free expression for protesters. In *Edwards v. South Carolina* (1963) and in *Brown v. Louisiana* (1966), he joined decisions of the Court reversing convictions of young blacks who had marched along the grounds of the state capitol to protest against racial discrimination and who had refused to leave a segregated reading room of a public library. He also concurred in *Tinker v. Des Moines School District* (1969), which permitted high school students to wear black armbands in protest against the Vietnam War.

But White soon pulled back from a broad reading of the First Amendment. In *Cox v. Louisiana* (1965), he would have affirmed the conviction of a minister who had led a march on a local courthouse to protest the arrest of students who had picketed stores maintaining segregated lunch counters. The next year, he became part of a 5–4 majority in *Adderley v. Florida* (1966) affirming the convictions of black students who had demonstrated on the premises of a jail, and two years after that case, he joined another majority in *United States v. O'Brien* (1968) that affirmed a conviction of an anti-war protester who had burned his draft card. Arguably, demonstrations in a jail yard and public burnings of draft cards somehow threatened the ability of government agencies—the prison system and the Selective Service System—to carry out their functions, but a year after *O'Brien*, the justice made clear that he would permit the prosecution of protesters even when their protests did not threaten the power structure. In his dissent in *Street v. New York* (1969) and in his later refusal to join the majority in *Cohen v. California* (1971), he signaled his view that offensive protest, such as burning the flag or including four-letter expletives in political speeches, was not constitutionally protected. In *Texas v. Johnson* (1989) and *United States v. Eichman* (1990), in which the Court reaffirmed that burning the American flag was protected expression under the First Amendment, Justice White joined the dissents, which compared flag burning to "an inarticulate grunt or roar that . . . is most likely to be indulged in not to express any particular idea, but to antagonize others."

White's views about the inappropriateness of threatening and offensive protest were probably shared by most liberal Americans in the early 1960s. His views were certainly shared by his colleagues in the Kennedy Justice Department. By the late 1960s, however, many liberals had changed their views: Robert Kennedy himself, after attending a June 1968 meeting with black militants in Oakland, California, where he was abused with statements such as, we "don't want to hear none of your shit. What the goddamned hell are you going to do, boy," told an aide that he was "glad" he had gone to the meeting, since the militants "need to know someone who'll listen." He knew that many blacks have "got a lot of hostility and lots of reasons for it" and that, "when they get somebody like me, they're going to take it out on me." He also knew that, "after all the abuse the blacks have taken through the centuries, whites are just going to have to let them get some of these feelings out." As Kennedy biographer Arthur Schlesinger commented, Robert Kennedy had taken a "long journey" from his first meeting with black militants nearly five years earlier. Byron White, having gone to the Court, never took that journey and so remained in a world where rational discourse rather than emotion was the essence of political expression in a free society.

The late 1960s wrought a fundamental change in the goals of many American liberals. In the early 1960s, the goal of liberals—and the primary goal of the Warren Court—was the use of national power, including the judiciary's power, to facilitate pragmatic social change, especially in the areas of racial equality and legislative apportionment. For this purpose, the government was to be trusted and its power enhanced, not impaired. When he was appointed to the Court in 1962, Byron White agreed with this liberal agenda of democracy, equality, and pragmatic social reform.

But the Warren Court also had a second goal—the enhancement of individual rights and the consequent restriction of governmental authority. Justice White never signed on to this anti-statist program. When he came to the Court in the early 1960s, it was a subsidiary part of the Warren agenda. But, as first the racial protests, then the Vietnam War and the anti-war protests, and finally the misfeasance of the Nixon years convinced many Americans that government often cannot be trusted, the goal of creating individual rights to restrict governmental power assumed increasing centrality for the liberal wing on the Court, coming to fruition in cases like *Roe*. Byron White disagreed. As he suggested in *Bowers*, the judiciary's recognition of anti-statist individual rights would not create a better world for the weak and powerless any more than anti-statist property-rights jurisprudence did in the 1930s. Only the power of government could, in White's view, improve the world.

—WILLIAM E. NELSON

BIBLIOGRAPHY

For the account of the inner workings of the Department of Justice during the Kennedy Administration, I relied on Victor S. Navasky's *Kennedy Justice* (1971), Arthur Schlesinger, Jr.'s *Robert Kennedy and His Times* (1978), and *Robert Kennedy: In His Own Words*, edited by Edwin O. Guthman and Jeffrey Shulman (1988).

On the twenty-fifth anniversary of Justice White's appointment to the Supreme Court, 58 *University of Colorado Law Review* (1987) published an issue dedicated solely to the justice. It includes a variety of articles, several of which I consulted: William E. Nelson, "Deference and the Limits to Deference in the Constitutional Jurisprudence of Justice Byron R. White"; Donald W. Hoagland, "Byron White as a Practicing Lawyer"; Jonathan D. Varat, "Justice White and the Breadth and Allocation of Federal Authority"; Pierce O'Donnell, "Common Sense and the Constitution: Justice White and the Egalitarian Ideal"; and Lance Liebman, "Justice White and Affirmative Action."

EDWARD DOUGLASS WHITE

BORN 3 November 1845, near Thibodaux,
Louisiana

NOMINATED to the Court 19 February 1894,
by Grover Cleveland

TOOK seat 12 March 1894; nominated
as chief justice 12 December 1910
by William Howard Taft; took seat
19 December 1910

DIED 19 May 1921 in Washington, D.C.

Edward Douglass White, the ninth chief
justice of the United States, was a southern
gentleman, a Jesuit-trained Roman Catholic, and
a man early acquainted with defeat. The son of
a plantation owner, he attended Georgetown
University until the Civil War ended his formal
education. He joined the Confederate army, was
promptly captured, and was imprisoned for several months. Far from becoming the stereotypi-
cal embittered southerner, White apparently
gained some perspective on the defeat with
maturity. "Young man," he once told a law clerk,
"you'll be lucky when you're my age if you've
only been a damned fool once."

After the war, White read law in a New
Orleans office, opened his own practice there,
and became active in Louisiana's Democratic
party. By 1874, when he was elected to the state
senate, he had established one of the city's largest law practices. White's support of the successful candidate for governor two years later won
him an appointment to the state supreme court,
but he served for only a year; the state constitution of 1879 established a minimum age of
thirty-five for supreme court justices. White, then
thirty-four, had to resign, start another law practice, and resume his political activity. He was
elected to the United States Senate in 1888, but
a partisan dispute over the state lottery kept him
in Louisiana until 1891.

The tensions of White's early career may
have contributed to his developing a nervous
habit which made writing arduous in an era when
nearly all professional work was done in long-
hand. For the rest of his life, White could not

write unless he pressed the first finger of his right
hand against his nose and held the pen between
his thumb and second finger. There is no evidence, however, that this difficulty affected either the quantity or quality of his work.

When Justice Samuel Blatchford retired,
Senator White had characteristics which commended him to President Cleveland as a good
choice for the Court. First, White was a senator;
second, he was a Democrat; and third, his opposition to a tariff bill gave Cleveland reason to
want him out of Congress. After the Senate had
rejected two of his nominees, Cleveland tried the
familiar ploy of nominating one of the Senate's
own. It succeeded, and White took his seat in
March 1894. A few months later, the forty-eight-
year-old bachelor married Leita Montgomery
Kent, the widow of a Washington lawyer. The
marriage, like White's service on the Court, was
by all accounts a happy association, and lasted
until his death.

White's appointment as chief justice in 1910
was a departure from custom in two ways. Except for John Rutledge, who was confirmed as
chief justice in 1795 but never served, White was
the first associate justice to be promoted. White
was also a Democrat appointed by a Republican
president, William Howard Taft. But Chief Justice Melville Fuller's death coincided with so
many Court vacancies that Taft may have felt it
necessary to elevate a sitting justice to insure continuity; and the fact that three of Taft's six appointees to the Court were Democrats suggests that
partisan loyalty mattered little to the president.
White's fellow justices thought highly enough of
him to petition Taft to promote him. White's biographer, Robert Highsaw, suggests that the
justice's high productivity may have impressed
Taft, and that their views on most issues were
compatible. A biographer of Taft has suggested
that White's age (sixty-five) made him an attractive choice. Taft's greatest ambition was to be
chief justice, not president; twelve years White's
junior, he may have acted in the hope that the
position would be vacant after he left the White
House and was young enough to fill it. The fact

that any such strategy on Taft's part was success-ful—President Warren Harding appointed him to succeed White—makes this conclusion tempting without much evidence to support it.

Two chief justices later, Robert H. Jackson wrote: "Never in its entire history can the Su-preme Court be said to have for a single hour been representative of anything except the rela-tively conservative forces of the day." The Court on which Edward White served from 1894 to 1921 provides ample support for this generali-zation, whether we take "conservative" in its lit-eral meaning or in its informal association with wealth, advantage, and privilege. White was at home in this intellectual environment, and at-tuned to the prevailing ideology of the day. Some cases from this period which strike us as infa-mous examples of this conservatism, like the endorsement of racial segregation in *Plessy v. Ferguson* (1896), may seem more important in retrospect than they did at the time. White con-curred without opinion in *Plessy*. Although a single, unverifiable report states that he had been a member of the Ku Klux Klan, little informa-tion survives about his racial views.

The primary challenge which faced White and his colleagues was fashioning a judicial re-sponse to legislation aimed at controlling the ef-fects of the concentration of wealth, and the sub-sequent, if not consequent, abuse of power which the industrial revolution had brought to this coun-try. These laws fell into two general categories: efforts to retard the concentration of wealth, and efforts to benefit workers facing employers far more powerful than they. Year after year, the Court confronted both kinds of laws.

The prevailing sentiment in the legal pro-fession in the 1890s was adverse to this kind of legislation. At colleges and law schools, which were replacing the kind of apprenticeship White had served as the source of legal training, law-yers were exposed to the social Darwinist views of professors like Christopher Tiedemann, who urged generations of students to resist "the im-pulse of a generous nature . . . to call loudly for the intervention of the law to protect the poor wage-earner from the grasping cupidity of the employer [who] has acquired this superior posi-tion . . . through the exertion of his powers; he

is above, and can to some extent dictate terms to, his employees, because his natural powers are greater." The justices were not immune from the socialization going on within their profession.

By the time White took his seat, the Court had developed an approach to these laws that was hostile without being suicidal. This hostil-ity persisted, with some ups and downs, until 1937, when Franklin Roosevelt's threat to en-large the Court induced a judicial retreat from activism in economics which may or may not have been permanent.

However conservative White's general ide-ology was, it is not clear how fully he shared the social Darwinist ideology of his profession. His papers were destroyed after his death, and he was silent in many landmark cases. For example, he dissented without opinion in both *Lochner v. New York* (1905), which struck down a maxi-mum working hours law, and *Bunting v. Oregon* (1917), which appeared to overrule *Lochner*; he concurred without opinion in both *Muller v. Oregon* (1908), which upheld a maximum hours law for women, and in *Hammer v. Dagenhart* (1918), which invalidated Congress's attempt to discourage child labor. The opinions White did write—and his productivity was high—show that he took an active part in erecting and main-taining judicial barriers to progressive legislation. As chief justice, he took an equally active part in preventing judicial activism from becoming suicidal.

The "rule of reason," which severely lim-ited the government's power to control monopo-lies, was White's primary contribution to con-stitutional law. The Sherman Antitrust Act of 1890 forbade all combinations "in restraint of trade or commerce among the several States, or with foreign nations." White concurred without opinion in *United States v. E.C. Knight Co.* (1895), which effectively derailed antitrust pros-ecutions for the rest of the nineteenth century by declaring that commerce did not include manu-facture. Two years later, White was willing to go even further than the Court majority in weak-ening the Sherman Act. His dissent in *United States v. Trans-Missouri Freight Association* (1897) won three other votes, thus coming a single justice short of a majority.

White insisted that the Sherman Act could not be read literally. Any contract restrained trade. "To define, then, the words 'in restraint of trade' as embracing every contract which to some degree produced that effect would be violative of reason, because it would include all those contracts which are of the very essence of trade." The common law, therefore, had evolved the "rule of reason" which ordained that "reasonable contracts cannot be embraced within the provisions of the statute." The Court's ruling, therefore, meant that "a law in favor of freedom of contract . . . is so interpreted as to gravely impair that freedom." White's doctrine still remained one vote short in 1904 in the famous *Northern Securities* case.

White's opportunity to write his doctrine into dogma—without precipitating a showdown with a trustbusting administration—came during his first term as chief justice. In *Standard Oil Company v. United States* (1911), the Court, by an 8–1 vote, ordered the dissolution of the Standard Oil trust. White again endorsed "the standard of reason which had been applied at the common law and in this country." He declared, "the criterion to be resorted to in any given case . . . is the rule of reason guided by the established law." Justice Holmes later remarked, "The moment I saw that in the circulated draft, I knew he had us. How could you be against that without being for a rule of unreason?"

As an exercise in judicial power, *Standard Oil* was an accomplishment worthy of John Marshall. By conceding a battle to the legislative and executive branches, White won both a campaign and a war. The impact of *E.C. Knight* and *Standard Oil* after 1911 defeated virtually all trust prosecutions. "Reasonableness," of course, is in the eye of the adjudicator, and the rule of reason greatly expanded the Court's power, making it the arbiter of reasonableness.

As an exercise in constitutional interpretation, however, the rule of reason suffers from the defects of *Lochner* and its line of substantive due process cases. The *Standard Oil* doctrine edits both the statute and the Constitution by adding words not included in either, almost as blatantly as the opinion White joined in *Hammer v. Dagenhart* which edited the Tenth Amendment by adding the word "expressly." Such free translation of text is neither unknown nor uniformly unwelcome in the late twentieth century; but the typical defense of it, familiar after the *Carolene Products* footnote (1938), is not applicable in antitrust cases; the interest being protected is neither a specified constitutional right nor an excluded minority group. Instead, the White Court expanded judicial power to serve the interest of the privileged few, a group which, moreover, had lost a fair fight in the political arena.

Another judicial barrier to progressive legislation which White helped to fashion came from the Court's reading of the federal commerce power. In *Northern Securities*, while Holmes's dissent promulgated the rule of reason, White based his dissent on the doctrine of dual federalism: the proposition that national and state governments are each sovereign within their own spheres; the non-exercise by one government of its own power does not permit the other government to exercise the power, however innocuously; and the states retain all power not delegated to the national government. The power to regulate combinations like the Northern Securities Company, White insisted, was "entirely distinct from the power to regulate the acquisition and control of such instrumentalities." Congress could do the latter, but the former power belonged to the states. White's dual federalism never commanded a Court majority as his rule of reason did, but he and it did have some successes. He wrote for the Court in the *Employers' Liability Cases* (1908), for example, holding that the commerce clause does not include the power to regulate employer-employee relations. *Hammer v. Dagenhart*, in which Chief Justice White did not even write, was perhaps the greatest victory for his dual federalism.

Edward Corwin credited White with resurrecting dual federalism, which had prevailed since the Taney Court, but by 1904 seemed "about to pass into eclipse beneath the waxing orb of the commerce power." Perhaps, Corwin suggested, White's Jesuit education made him sympathetic to the doctrine by teaching him "its medieval counterpart, the dual jurisdiction over common territory of Church and State." It is also possible that the time and place of White's young manhood favorably disposed him toward state sovereignty. But the difficulty with these explanations is that White was not uniformly hostile to national usurpations of state power; he voted to limit national power when Congress attempted to bar articles from interstate commerce that were not inherently dangerous, but rather because they were associated with some practice Congress wanted to control.

If the possibility occurred to White that the corporations that Congress tried to restrict might have been considerably more powerful than the states in which he situated the power to restrict them, the justice never indicated such awareness. At any rate, White was fighting a rearguard action. Dual federalism did not survive the New Deal; *United States v. Darby Lumber Co.* (1941) repudiated *Hammer v. Dagenhart*.

White's contributions to doctrine outside the area of economic regulation show that his jurisprudence was motivated no more by distrust of the national government than by deference to the states. The first, chronologically, of the two instances in which White succeeded in writing erstwhile minority opinions into law broadly interpreted Congress's power over acquired territories; the resulting rule has proved more nearly permanent than either the rule of reason or dual federalism. The events of 1898, the year in which the Hawaiian Islands were annexed, the Spanish-American War ended, and the resulting Treaty of Paris ceded Puerto Rico, Guam, and the Philippine Islands to the United States, made future judicial involvement with these questions a virtual certainty, and the Court's docket between 1901 and 1905 was thick with them.

Article IV of the Constitution left no doubt that Congress had the power to govern territories and to make states out of them, and the Louisiana Purchase of 1803 had effectively settled any doubts about Congress's power to acquire territory. The questions presented to the Fuller Court concerned an issue which had not yet been decided: the applicability of constitutional guarantees to territories. *Downes v. Bidwell* (1901) involved a statute which established a civil government for Puerto Rico and levied a tax on goods imported thence to the United States. An importer insisted that the territory was a part of the United States; the tax, therefore, violated the provision in Article I, Section 8 that all duties be uniform throughout the country. The Court upheld the law, but without a majority opinion. Justice White was part of the 5–4 majority, but he refused to join Justice Henry Brown's opinion which hinted that some constitutional guarantees might apply to territories without restriction. White's concurring opinion propounded the "Insular Doctrine," the theory that constitutional limitations on congressional powers applied to territories only after they were incorporated into and become an integral part of the United States. Four years later, White's doctrine claimed a majority in *Rasmussen v. United States* (1905), and in 1914, a unanimous Court accepted it in *Ocampo v. United States*.

White's Insular Doctrine has been called a new *jus gentium*; it is similar to the Roman doctrine whereby usages common to different peoples were incorporated into the "law of nations" and applied to conquered territories, while the *jus civile* applied only to Roman citizens. White invoked "the general rule of the law of nations" by which "the acquiring government fixes the status of the acquired territory." The majority decision in *Downes*, he wrote, therefore "rests on the erroneous assumption that the United States under the Constitution is stripped of those powers which are absolutely inherent and essential to the national existence." Puerto Rico "was not a foreign country because it was subject to the sovereignty of and was owned by the United States;" however, it "was foreign . . . in a domestic sense, because the island had not been incorporated into the United States, but was merely appurtenant thereto as a possession. Until Puerto Rico was incorporated—that is, when Congress said it had been—the uniform duty provision of Article I "was not applicable to Congress in legislating for Puerto Rico."

Unincorporated territories were thus in a kind of limbo where Congress's Article IV power to govern applied, but the limitations on Congress's power, including the Bill of Rights, did not. White's customary solicitude for business may have influenced his opinions in the

Puerto Rico tax cases; he recognized that the imperialists wanted to retain their gains and yet, at the same time, domestic interests wanted protection against an influx of duty-free sugar and tobacco from the islands. Here, as with the rule of reason, judgments of the quality of White's intellectual contribution to constitutional law and of the effectiveness of his leadership on the Court should be separated from any judgments about the wisdom or justice of his doctrines.

The protracted political controversy which culminated in *Virginia v. West Virginia* (1907) showed White as the arbiter of divisions of power among states and between the states and the national government. When Virginia seceded in 1861, the western part of the state refused to leave the Union. West Virginia became a separate state two years later; it agreed to assume a fair share of the prewar Virginia state debt, and Congress ratified the compact. West Virginia did not make good on its promise, however, and in 1907, Virginia brought suit. The Supreme Court ordered West Virginia to pay in 1915; no money was forthcoming and Virginia reinstated the suit. The Court faced the possibility that West Virginia might continue to defy direct orders. A state's obligation to obey the Court was already beyond dispute, but it was not clear how the Court could make West Virginia pay. The fact that the state's defiance of an order would embarrass the Court was clear, however.

White's opinion carefully avoided the dangers that the case presented. The chief justice reaffirmed the principle "that judicial power essentially involves the right to enforce the results of its exertion," and went on to suggest that the remedies for defiance included not only judicial enforcement but congressional legislation. Neither Congress nor the Court had to act further. West Virginia paid its share of the debt.

A general evaluation of White's jurisprudence can easily describe what it is not. White was no Felix Frankfurter, with his concern for judicial self-restraint, nor a Hugo Black, with his literal reading of the constitutional text, nor an Edwin Meese, with his "jurisprudence of original intention." While White may have practiced judicial restraint in the pragmatic sense of keeping the Court out of confrontations, he had no

hesitation about holding the other branches of government to notions of fundamental principles of justice or "inherent" rights, concepts which come close to a "natural law" doctrine. This attitude was not unusual in the nineteenth century, when few were embarrassed to suggest that positive law incorporated higher law principles; the abolitionists, for example, had made similar arguments in opposing slavery. One difficulty with natural law arguments was that a consensus that fundamental principles existed was not accompanied by consensus on what constituted those principles; these arguments, therefore, can be and have been advanced to defend contradictory positions.

As both justice and chief justice, White was an unambiguous success in his own time. His major opinions show impressive knowledge of law and a facility for creative reasoning, and Court votes show his skill at promoting consensus and at keeping the Court out of trouble. But the fact that two of his doctrines, the rule of reason and dual federalism, did not survive his tenure even by a generation indicates that his ability to persuade his colleagues may have been greater than his ability to adapt doctrine to changing conditions. And assessment of the rightness or wrongness of his opinions, and of the directions in which he influenced the Court, will probably depend on the views of the observer.

Some commentators found roots of White's Jesuit education in these decisions. The rule of reason and the Insular Doctrine reveal that, far from limiting himself to any minimalist doctrine of constitutional interpretation, White freely drew on common law and Roman law to graft concepts onto the Constitution. White may well have been one of the last American judges to merit the description "natural law" jurist; he might even have welcomed the label.

Since White's success with the Insular Doctrine antedated his promotion, these cases show that his leadership on the Court did not depend solely on his position as chief justice. Neither did the intellectual manipulation in *Standard Oil* on which Holmes remarked; any justice can do that sort of thing, and many have. But the chief justiceship enhanced White's opportunities to lead, since the formal powers of the position gave him ample occasion to exert informal influence. The chief's presiding role allows him to set both agenda and tone; his skill in performing these tasks influences the collegiality and productivity of the Court, for good or for ill. As David Danelski has written: "In terms of influence, then, the ideal chief justice is a persuasive, esteemed, able, and well-liked judge who perceives, fulfills, and even expands his role on the Court." Until White's last few years, when he stayed too long on the Court, his performance came close to this ideal.

Danelski borrows from small group studies to posit two types of leadership within the Court. The *task leader* "makes more suggestions, gives more opinions, and successfully defends his ideas more often than the others." The *social leader* "attends to the emotional needs of his associates," and typically "is the best-liked member of the conference." One individual can fulfill both these roles—Danelski argues that Charles Evans Hughes did—but the positions are to some extent mutually contradictory; people who win arguments are not always liked.

There is no doubt that White acted as social leader. Even those who do not describe his abilities in superlatives attest to his personal charm. This consensus, and the fact that the White Court included such luminaries as Holmes, Hughes, and Louis Brandeis might lead to the expectation that White would not have been task leader as well. But all the evidence suggests that he was. The high productivity, low dissension, and warm collegiality revealed in volumes of *United States Reports* and in individual memoirs attest to White's ability both to set tasks and stroke the egos of his colleagues.

Dissent was less common in the late nineteenth and early twentieth centuries than it is now, and unanimity remained the norm until Hughes's tenure as chief justice. Even the relatively contentious Fuller Court reached unanimous decisions in 70 to 75 percent of its cases in most terms. White had much more success than Fuller in achieving unanimity; his figures compare favorably with Taft's. In 1912, for instance, only 9 percent of the cases had dissents. Productivity also rose under White by roughly

40 percent. This pattern began to change in 1916; productivity decreased slightly from then on, and the dissent rate climbed as high as 25 percent. The presence on the Court of such notorious combatants as Brandeis, James McReynolds, and John Clarke probably combined with White's failing health to weaken his leadership. Soon after Taft took over, Brandeis remarked that "the judges go home [from conference] less tired emotionally and less weary physically than in White's day."

White was always well-liked, on and off the Court, but opinion about his performance is divided. Several years after his death, Justice Holmes wrote, "If [Associate Justice Charles Evans] Hughes had been appointed then, . . . I think the history of the Court would have been better than it is." In 1970, a poll of legal scholars rated White among the "near great" Supreme Court justices, while rating Hughes among the "great" judges. White's biographer, Robert Highsaw, rates him lower than the panel did, attributing his subject's success to "the fact that, though he was far from a mediocrity, he was not such an outstanding man that he aroused any considerable opposition."

In one sense, White accomplished in *Standard Oil*, *Rasmussen*, and to a lesser degree in *Virginia v. West Virginia* exactly what Hughes did in the "switch in time which saved nine" of 1937. Less dramatically—and perhaps, therefore, more successfully—than Hughes, White withdrew from disputes which the Court, lacking both the purse and the sword, was doomed to lose. Yet the observation White's biographer makes of his dual federalism, that it constituted a brilliant rearguard action, seems true in general of White's contribution to public law. At least those values he defended most, corporate power and imperialism, while far from obsolescent, seem not to have needed much judicial help. A Brandeis—or even a Holmes, who, we now know, had little more sympathy than White had for progressive legislation—might have acted on the need to interpret constitutional principles in the light of the immense socioeconomic changes that occurred in their time, and which had rendered obsolescent such verities as the harmony of worker-employer relations assumed in Hamilton's *Federalist* 35 and uncritically endorsed in several White Court rulings. But White used his talents, jurisprudential and political, in the defense of values which seem less admirable now than they did in his time.

—JUDITH A. BAER

BIBLIOGRAPHY

The only biography of White is Robert B. Highsaw, *Edward Douglass White: Defender of the Conservative Faith* (1981), and while biased toward its subject, is valuable for its clear presentation of constitutional doctrine. David J. Danelski, "The Influence of the Chief Justice in the Decisional Process," in Sheldon Goldman and Austin Sarat, eds., *American Court Systems: Readings in Judicial Process and Behavior* (2d ed., 1989), 486–99, is the definitive study of the distinguishing features of the chief justice's position.

Other works that are useful for understanding White and his Court include Dean Acheson, *Morning and Noon* (1965), Chapters 4 and 5, in which the former secretary of state, who clerked for Louis Brandeis from 1919 to 1921, presents a revealing picture of "our Court" under White; Edward S. Corwin, *The Twilight of the Supreme Court* (1934), a valuable analysis of the important constitutional issues of White's day; Mark De Wolfe Howe, ed., *The Holmes-Laski Letters* (2 vols., 1953), a valuable source of Holmes's trenchant opinions about his colleagues; and Stephen B. Wood, *Constitutional Politics in the Progressive Era* (1968), an explanation of the events, judicial and political, culminating in *Hammer v. Dagenhart.*

CHARLES EVANS WHITTAKER

BORN 22 February 1901, near Troy, Kansas

NOMINATED to the Court 2 March 1957
   by Dwight D. Eisenhower

TOOK seat 27 March 1957; retired 31 March
   1962

DIED 26 November 1973 in Kansas City,
   Missouri

Charles Evans Whittaker was no child of privilege, no great public servant, no brilliant legal scholar. His beginnings, his background, indeed his legal career all suggest a man of modest ambition, inauspicious achievement, and unremarkable intellect. Unfortunately, Whittaker's appointment to the Court did nothing to alter the character of his life; indeed, all the literature on this justice concludes that Whittaker was in every way unsuited for his exalted position. His indecision and intellectual torment drove him to retire after only five years on the bench.

Whittaker's early life retells the quintessential American rags-to-riches story. Born in rural Kansas, he dropped out of high school at sixteen and completed law school without ever finishing high school or college. He practiced law for nearly thirty years, advising primarily Kansas City's major corporations. Whittaker's service as a federal trial and appellate judge positioned him well when President Eisenhower, looking for nominees with judicial experience, sought a replacement for Justice Stanley Reed.

Whittaker came to the Court too late to participate in the Warren Court's first activist phase, marked by its 1957 decisions providing constitutional protections to suspected Communist party members, and he left before the liberal Warren Court came into its own in the mid-1960s. In a sense, Whittaker reflected the Court's uneasy transition from the conservatism that had long characterized the institution; his inconsistency and confusion mirrored the larger struggle taking place between proponents of judicial restraint such as Justices Frankfurter and Harlan and ardent civil libertarians such as Chief Justice Warren and Justices Black, Douglas, and Brennan.

Except in cases dealing with outrageous police or prosecutorial conduct towards a particularly helpless defendant, Whittaker took a conservative position on most civil liberties issues. He was a legal technocrat rather than a judge; he narrowed the scope of constitutional questions to avoid framing great, enduring principles. His most impressive votes for broad constitutional rights came in two cases overturning provisions of the Naturalization Act, which stripped native-born Americans of their citizenship if they deserted the military during wartime (*Trop v. Dulles,* 1958) or if they voted in foreign elections (*Perez v. Brownell,* 1958). He was less certain of himself in cases dealing with the military's authority to court-martial civilians, taking a middle ground between the majority's decisions for the civilians and Justice Frankfurter's arguments on behalf of the military. Whittaker said that the military ought to be able to prosecute *employees* but not *dependents,* a distinction he did not (or could not) justify in *Kinsella v. Singleton* (1960), *McElroy v. Guagliardo* (1960), and *Grisham v. Hagan* (1960).

More typical of Whittaker's voting pattern were his plainly inconsistent votes in cases challenging the constitutionality of coerced confessions in murder cases. He sided with an uneducated black defendant in *Moore v. Michigan* (1957), but the next year, in *Thomas v. Arizona* (1958), he voted for the state after the police put a noose around the neck of a black man in the course of a twenty-hour interrogation. In cases involving civil liberties, Whittaker had the most conservative voting record of anyone on the Court during his tenure.

After three years on the Court, Whittaker was already paralyzed by the conflict between his conservative instincts, his occasional liberal leanings, and the pressure levied by the crush of Court work. Whittaker's inability to produce an intellectually coherent rationale for his own decisions made him a "prize target" for Justice Frankfurter's relentless lobbying. His distress infiltrated even the most mundane cases. When Whittaker was unable to compose his majority opinion in a case involving the application of the Internal Revenue Code to the disbursement of a life insurance claim, Justice Douglas, who had already penned a dissent in the case, wrote it for him (*Meyer v. United States,* 1960).

After leaving the Court, Whittaker returned to his roots in corporate law by becoming counsel to General Motors. He also became an outspoken critic of the social protest movements waged by civil rights demonstrators and anti-war protesters during the late 1960s. His choice as a forum for his beliefs, the *F.B.I. Law Enforcement Bulletin*, testifies as much as anything else to his law-and-order instincts.

—VICTORIA SAKER WOESTE

BIBLIOGRAPHY

No biography has been written of Whittaker, and only a few law review articles specifically analyze his jurisprudence. For brief sketches, see Leon Friedman, "Charles Whittaker," in Friedman and Israel, 4 *Justices* 2893 (probably the most complete existing account of Whittaker's record) and Michael Parrish's piece in Levy, Karst, and Mahoney, 4 *Encyclopedia of the American Constitution* 2060 (1986). See also D.M. Berman, "Mr. Justice Whittaker: A Preliminary Appraisal," 24 *Missouri Law Review* 1 (1959).

William O. Douglas, *The Court Years: 1939–1975* (1981), contains some useful information about Whittaker. Although Justice Douglas objected to Whittaker's unreflected conservatism, he respected Whittaker personally, and the few Whittaker anecdotes here are told with warmth and charity. Bernard Schwartz, on the other hand, in *Super Chief: Earl Warren and His Supreme Court—A Judicial Biography* (1983), provides an adoring portrait of Warren that describes Whittaker with contempt.

JAMES WILSON

BORN 14 September 1742, Carskerdo,
Fifeshire, Scotland

NOMINATED to the Court 24 September 1789
by George Washington

TOOK seat 2 February 1790

DIED 21 August 1798 in Edenton,
North Carolina

Born on a farm in Scotland, but educated at the University of St. Andrews where he studied Latin, Greek, mathematics, logic, moral philosophy, ethics, natural and political philosophy, and became acquainted with the literature of the Scottish and English enlightenment, Wilson was well prepared to take an active part in revolutionary activities when he arrived in America in 1765. Wilson determined, after a short time as a tutor at the College of Philadelphia, that studying law would more likely lead to his advancement and arranged to read law with John Dickinson. Less than a year later, Wilson was ready to practice on his own, and established himself in Reading; in 1770, he moved to Carlisle, and then in 1778 to Philadelphia, all the while expanding his clientele.

During these same years Wilson became highly involved in patriot politics. In 1774, he revised and published a pamphlet that he had written six years earlier, *Considerations on the Nature and Extent of the Legislative Authority of the British Parliament*. His radical view that Parliament had no legislative authority over the colonies contributed effectively to the patriot cause, and publication of it enlarged his reputation in America and England. Wilson attended the first and second Pennsylvania provincial conventions as a delegate, as well as the Second Continental Congress, where he was not an early supporter of independence. Yet Wilson was one of three (out of seven) Pennsylvania delegates who signed the Declaration of Independence.

Wilson's private activities, in addition to his service in the Continental Congress, contributed to his belief that a more powerful central government was needed. As an attorney, he had an extensive admiralty practice and became convinced of the necessity to create a federal court supreme over state courts. His business dealings led him to take an active part in the establishment of the first national bank, the Bank of North America. When the bank was attacked in 1785, Wilson wrote a defense of it, *Considerations on the Power to Incorporate the Bank of North America*, in which he formulated arguments favoring the implied powers of the Confederation Congress to charter a bank. Wilson also found time to pursue his own scholarly studies in political theory, history, and philosophy, and his preeminence in these fields was recognized by the American Philosophical Society, which elected him a member in 1786.

It was hardly surprising, therefore, that the Pennsylvania legislature appointed Wilson a delegate to the federal convention in 1787. By that time his views on government had become clear. In the convention he advocated popular election of both houses of Congress as well as of the executive, no property qualifications for voting, no restrictions on the admission of new states to the union, the supremacy of the national government for the purposes of the new union, the creation of a supreme court with judges appointed by the president and with the power of judicial review, and congressional authority to establish inferior federal courts. Wilson was a member of the committee of detail that prepared a draft of the Constitution. Although not every measure that Wilson supported was adopted by the federal convention, he did all in his power as a member of the Pennsylvania convention to aid the successful outcome of the ratification contest. George Washington rewarded Wilson's efforts by nominating him to the Supreme Court.

Wilson's moment of glory as a Supreme Court justice came, oddly enough, while sitting as a circuit judge (a duty required by the Judiciary Act of 1789) in Pennsylvania in April 1792. There the court, by refusing to hear the petition of William Hayburn, a veteran of the Revolutionary War seeking a pension under the Invalid Pensions Act of 1792, exercised judicial review for the first time. Although the court wrote no opinion, it did send a letter to President Washington explaining its actions. The court could not proceed, the judges declared, "because the business directed by this act is not of a judicial nature" and "because, if, upon that business, the court had proceeded, its *judgments . . .* might, under the same act, have been revised and controuled by the legislature, and by an officer in the executive department. Such revision and controul we deemed radically inconsistent with the independence of that judicial power which is vested in the courts; and, consequently, with that important principle which is so strictly observed by the Constitution of the United States."

Known for giving long and learned grand jury charges while on circuit—Attorney General Edmund Randolph referred to him as "the professor"—Wilson's few Supreme Court opinions, with the exception of *Chisholm v. Georgia* (1793), are short and unremarkable except for their inherent interest as rulings of a justice who had helped to frame the Constitution. In each case he upheld the power of the national government: in *Hylton v. United States* (1796) Wilson, who had affirmed the constitutionality of the federal Carriage Tax Act while on circuit, merely reiterated his belief that the tax was valid; in *Ware v. Hylton* (1796) he enforced the supremacy clause of the Constitution by declaring that a federal treaty was superior to a state law.

Wilson wrote an extensive, learned dissertation in *Chisholm* that led him to the same conclusion as a majority of the Court, sustaining the right of a citizen of one state to sue a different state in the federal Supreme Court. After defining the concepts of sovereignty and statehood and describing the practice of other states and kingdoms, Wilson determined that nothing stood in the way of the Supreme Court's jurisdiction over the state of Georgia. The "general texture" of the Constitution also contributed to Wilson's view that the people of the United States formed a nation and instituted a national government with complete power to achieve the purposes of the union, and that "with Regard to such Purposes," it would be incongruous for "any Man or Body of Men—any Person natural or artificial, . . . to claim successfully, an entire Exemp-

tion from the Jurisdiction of the national Government." But it was the language of the Constitution itself that in the last analysis convinced Wilson of the accuracy of his belief: "The judicial Power of the United States shall extend to Controversies between two States." "Can the most consummate Degree of professional Ingenuity," Wilson asked, "devise a Mode by which this 'Controversy between two States' can be brought before a Court of law; and yet neither of those States be a Defendant?"

James Wilson's exceptional intellectual promise, so evident throughout his career, should have made him a natural leader of the fledgling Supreme Court. But Wilson's preoccupation with financial affairs during the later years of his brief tenure on the bench—he even spent a short time in jail for debt in 1797—robbed him of the time and the stature to put his imprimatur on the Court's jurisprudence. Desirous of becoming the first chief justice in 1789—he actually wrote to President Washington on April 21, 1789 requesting the position—Wilson masked his disappointment at receiving a commission only as associate justice. When a vacancy occurred in the chief justiceship in 1795, and then again in 1796, Wilson hoped that he would be appointed. He was passed over both times, most probably because his speculation in western land had hurt his reputation. Wilson's frustration, coupled with constant worry about money, seriously affected his health, forced him to neglect his Supreme Court duties, and ultimately led to his death.

—MAEVA MARCUS

BIBLIOGRAPHY

While more has been written about James Wilson than any other of the first six justices, little of it concerns his tenure on the Supreme Court. Grand jury charges given by Wilson while on circuit, as well as letters relevant to his Supreme Court service, can be found in the volumes of *The Documentary History of the Supreme Court of the United States, 1789–1800*, Maeva Marcus, ed., (1985–). A useful, complete biography is Charles Page Smith, *James Wilson: Founding Father, 1742–1798* (1956). A concise, instructive, and authoritative essay about Wilson, written by Robert G. McCloskey, appears in Friedman and Israel, 1 *Justices* 79.

LEVI WOODBURY

BORN 2 December 1789, Francestown,
New Hampshire

NOMINATED to the Court 20 September 1845
by James K. Polk

TOOK seat immediately as a recess
appointment; confirmed by the Senate
on 3 January 1846

DIED 4 September 1851 in Portsmouth,
New Hampshire

Woodbury graduated from Dartmouth College in 1809, studied law under Judge Jeremiah Smith and at Litchfield Law School, and began a law practice in 1812. During the War of 1812, Woodbury defended Madison's unpopular policies in his native New Hampshire. He then served as a New Hampshire supreme court justice (1817–1823), governor (1823–24), state legislator (1825), United States senator (1825–31; 1841–45); secretary of the navy (1831–34) and secretary of the treasury (1834–41). In his political career, Woodbury was a loyal Democrat, a stalwart defender of Jackson's policies against the bank of the United States, and a proponent of Manifest Destiny and Texas annexation. In September 1845, President James K. Polk appointed Woodbury to the Court, rewarding him for his service to the Democratic party. Woodbury was never, however, terribly interested in the Court, and remained an active presidential hopeful while on the Court. He was seriously considered for the presidency in 1848, and had he lived longer it seems likely Woodbury, and not Franklin Pierce (New Hampshire's other great Jacksonian politician), would have been the Democratic nominee in 1852. His judicial opinions reflect his Jacksonian ideology and his presidential aspirations.

Woodbury was one of the lesser lights to serve on the Supreme Court. Polk appointed Woodbury to replace the late Joseph Story in the New England seat on the Court. Never a legal scholar—and thus not substantively a replacement for Story—Woodbury was pedantic, competent, and hardworking. In his six terms,

Woodbury wrote more than 17 percent of all majority opinions (forty-three opinions in 244 cases) as well as fourteen concurrences and dissents. However, his hard work led to little of lasting value; his Court career was one of virtually unblemished mediocrity.

As a senator, Woodbury had criticized the Court for its "sleepless opposition . . . to the strict construction of the Constitution" and its support for "a diseased enlargement of the powers of the General Government and throwing chains over States-Rights." As a justice, Woodbury tried to reverse these trends. Thus he wrote a separate opinion in the *License Cases* (1847) upholding state power to prohibit the sale of liquor that traveled in interstate commerce. Here Woodbury clearly articulated his overriding judicial philosophy: "I carry with me, as a controlling principle, the proposition, that State powers, State rights, and State decisions are to be upheld when the objection to them is not clear," and obviously not in conflict with the Constitution. Woodbury rejected the idea that state laws could be declared unconstitutional by "some remote or indirect repugnance to acts of Congress." A "potential inconvenience" was not enough "to annul the laws of sovereign States, and overturn the deliberate decisions of State tribunals." For Woodbury to reach that conclusion there had to be "an actual collision, a direct inconsistency" and a "clashing of sovereignties."

Consistent with this ideology, he dissented in the *Passenger Cases* (1849), arguing that states could constitutionally regulate the entrance of immigrants into their jurisdictions. Woodbury wrote a fifty-five page dissent (enormous at the time), arguing that since colonial times Massachusetts (and other states) had regulated immigration, and this was fully constitutional. Similarly, in *Waring v. Clarke* (1847), he argued in dissent that states had jurisdiction over navigable rivers within their boundaries.

A rare break from his states' rights views was Woodbury's majority opinion in *Planters' Bank v. Sharp* (1848). Here Woodbury wrote to strike down a Mississippi statute and state court decision under the contract clause. Woodbury noted that such a decision had to be reached with "no peculiar liberality of construction in favor of a corporation." He reiterated that a state "under its general legislative powers" could regulate or prohibit sales of certain kinds of property "or sales by certain classes of persons or corporations." However, in this case, Mississippi had chartered the bank, and thus Mississippi's subsequent statutory prohibition on the bank's normal business activities constituted an impairment of contract in violation of the Constitution.

Ironically, Woodbury's most famous and important opinion of the Court, in *Jones v. Van Zandt* (1847), expanded federal power at the expense of the states. But this case involved slavery, and like other Jacksonian Democrats, Woodbury supported southern interests on slavery, even when they clashed with other ideological interests. In 1843, Wharton Jones, a Kentucky slave owner acting under the Fugitive Slave Law of 1793, sued John Van Zandt, an Ohio farmer, for helping his slaves escape. Van Zandt argued that he had found the group of blacks walking on a road in Ohio, and he had presumed they were free because slavery was illegal in Ohio. Thus, when he gave them a ride in his wagon he had not aided in their escape, and that offering them a ride could not be considered concealment of a fugitive slave within the meaning of the federal law. Van Zandt claimed he had no "notice" that the blacks he offered a ride to were, in fact, slaves.

Woodbury rejected these defenses, asserting that "the Constitution itself" in the fugitive slave clause "flung its shield, for security" over slavery "and the right to pursue and reclaim" slaves and "within the limits of another State." This conclusion nationalized southern legal presumptions that all blacks were slaves, and destroyed the legal presumptions of the free states that all people were presumptively free. While enhanc-

ing the federal government's power to protect slavery, at the expense of northern states' rights, Woodbury reiterated the principles of Jacksonian-southern states' rights advocates that "the supposed inexpediency and invalidity of all laws recognizing slavery or any right of property in man" was "a political question, settled by each State for itself; and the federal power over it is limited and regulated by the people of the States in the Constitution itself, as one of its sacred compromises. . . ." This extraordinarily proslavery decision enhanced Woodbury's prospects as presidential candidate. It also accurately reflects his jurisprudence, which combined Jacksonian, proslavery, and states' rights principles with a overall goal of leaving the bench for the White House.

—PAUL FINKELMAN

BIBLIOGRAPHY

There is no biography of Woodbury. Frank Otto Gatell, "Levi Woodbury," in Friedman and Israel, 2 *Justices* 843, provides a good short biographical sketch of the justice along with some of his opinions. Donald B. Cole, *Jacksonian Democracy in New Hampshire, 1800–1851* (1970) places Woodbury in the context of New Hampshire politics. Harold M. Hyman and William M. Wiecek, *Equal Justice Under Law* (1982), is the best book available on the constitutional history of antebellum America, while R. Kent Newmyer, *The Supreme Court Under Marshall and Taney* (1974), is the best short history of the court during Woodbury's service.

Carl B. Swisher, *The Oliver Wendell Holmes Devise History of the Supreme Court of the United States* 5 *The Taney Period* (Macmillan, 1974), is a classic history of the Taney court.

Levi Woodbury, *The Writings of Levi Woodbury*, 3 vols. (1852), provides access to some of Woodbury's writings, most of which are political.

WILLIAM BURNHAM WOODS

BORN 3 August 1824, Newark, Ohio

NOMINATED to the Court 15 December 1880
by Rutherford B. Hayes

TOOK seat 5 January 1881

DIED 14 May 1887 in Washington, D.C.

William B. Woods is remembered more for his role as a United States judge of the fifth circuit court than for his six years of active service on the United States Supreme Court. A native of Ohio and a Union veteran, Woods settled in Alabama after the Civil War, and was active in Republican politics there. After his appointment to the fifth circuit court (encompassing states of the deep South), Woods was the first circuit judge to consider the newly passed enforcement acts, designed to enforce blacks' political and civil rights. In considering these laws, Woods was also called on to consider the meaning of the Fourteenth Amendment. Did the amendment's privileges and immunities clause protect citizens from hurtful actions of private citizens, or only from hurtful legislation? In collaboration with Supreme Court Justice Joseph P. Bradley, who was assigned to the fifth circuit, Woods developed a sweeping view of the Fourteenth Amendment in several early cases during Reconstruction.

In 1880, President Hayes tapped Woods for the high bench; Hayes was attracted by the idea of appointing a southerner, yet was reassured by Woods's status as a Union veteran. Ironically, while on the Supreme Court, Woods joined the majority in reversing his earlier broad interpretation of the Fourteenth Amendment. Undoubtedly Woods's most noted case is *United States v. Harris* (1883). This case involved a prosecution under the Ku Klux Act of 1871; the defendants allegedly had used violence to curtail blacks' civil rights. In this case, however, Woods held that Congress had overreached its powers in passing the Ku Klux Act. Laws of Congress could not punish mob action in this kind of case; only state law could do that. The duty of the national government was simply to work against state laws that discriminated against certain classes of citizens. In the *Civil Rights Cases* (1883), Woods joined the majority in holding that the Fourteenth Amendment could not prevent private acts of discrimination, such as the refusal of a theater owner to sell first-class tickets to blacks.

In *Presser v. Illinois* (1886), Woods's majority opinion reinforced his new limited view of the Fourteenth Amendment. A citizen had been arrested for carrying arms in a private militia contrary to Illinois law. He sought to have his conviction overturned on grounds that the Second Amendment granted the right to bear arms, and the Fourteenth promised to protect this right for all United States citizens. Woods's opinion, however, made it clear that the Second Amendment only prevented Congress from interfering with the right to bear arms; state governments traditionally controlled militias and there was nothing in the Fourteenth Amendment that warranted interference with state laws in this sort of case.

Justice Woods was a workhorse while a member of the court; he wrote some 160 majority opinions during his relatively short tenure, most of them dealing with real estate, mortgages, patents, and taxation. Only eight times in his six years on the court did Woods dissent. Illness struck suddenly in the spring of 1886, and one year later Woods died. Woods's status as a forgotten justice is probably related to his short tenure and his tendency to side quietly with the majority. He may also have failed to win respect over the years because of his status as a "carpetbagger." His shifting interpretation of the Fourteenth Amendment gave him the appearance of having a muddled judicial philosophy.

—STEPHEN CRESSWELL

BIBLIOGRAPHY

On political matters and his appointment, see Thomas E. Baynes, Jr., "Yankee from Georgia: A Search for Justice Woods," 1978 *Supreme Court Historical Society Yearbook* 31, which also provides analysis of Woods's voting on the high court. A good overall treatment of Woods's career is Louis Filler, "William B. Woods," in Friedman and Israel, 2 *Justices* 1327.

SUBJECT INDEX

INDEX OF CASES